Safeguarding Traditional Cultures:
A Global Assessment

Edited by Peter Seitel

Center for Folklife and Cultural Heritage
Smithsonian Institution
Washington, D.C.

© 2001 by the Center for Folklife and Cultural Heritage
Smithsonian Institution
Washington, D.C.
ISBN 0-9665520-1-6
Library of Congress Control Number: 2001012345

Manufactured in the United States of America

Designed and typeset in Berkeley and Berkeley Black typefaces by Peter Seitel
Cover design by Kristen Fernekes

Preface

This volume grows from a conference entitled "A Global Assessment of the 1989 *Recommendation on the Safeguarding of Traditional Culture and Folklore*: Local Empowerment and International Cooperation" held at the Smithsonian Institution in Washington, D.C., from June 27–30, 1999. The conference and this publication were produced through the cooperation of UNESCO, Division of Cultural Heritage, and the Smithsonian Institution, Center for Folklife and Cultural Heritage.

Though the United States is not a member of UNESCO and the Smithsonian not officially charged with representing official policy, long standing concern and involvement with the issues of traditional culture and folklore brought the two institutions together to organize the conference.

The *Recommendation* referred to is an international normative instrument adopted by the General Conference of UNESCO at its 25th session in Paris in 1989. The purpose of the 1999 conference was to assess the implementation of the *Recommendation*, bring together points of view and perspectives on the *Recommendation* from around the world, and suggest ways in which the *Recommendation* might develop in the future so that its purpose, the safeguarding of traditional culture and folklore, might be achieved.

The conference was supported by financial contributions from the Smithsonian Institution, the Japanese Ministry of Foreign Affairs (UNESCO/Japan Funds in Trust), the U.S. Department of State, the Rockefeller Foundation, and the National Endowment for the Arts.

Some 37 participants from 27 nations participated directly in the conference, with scores of additional observers. The participants were practitioners, community cultural advocates, government officials, scholars, and others. Prior to the conference, regional committee reports, questionnaires, and analyses were produced for discussion. Conference participants gathered in a wonderful spirit of intellectual and cultural fellowship. They discussed, debated, and deliberated upon both similarities and differences in the ways to go about safeguarding traditional culture and folklore. That the conference took place during the annual Smithsonian Folklife Festival was an added, though planned, bonus. The Festival provided an excellent frame of reference for considering the issues of cultural conservation, preservation, and advocacy.

Publishing the Proceedings

Proceedings are often a somewhat rough as a publication, but nonetheless allow for the inclusion of the voices of those who participated and the various documents and analyses produced before, during, and after the conference . The text offered in this publication is taken from a mixture of prepared and revised documents, speeches, and taped remarks generally re-edited. It attempts overall to accurately reflect the findings, ideas, tensions, and debates expressed through the conference.

Interesting, insightful, wonderful ideas emerged. The proceedings attest to the ability of people of goodwill from around the world to gather together and share their ideas about safeguarding the legacy of humankind.

The Smithsonian and UNESCO are now proud to distribute this report to cultural institutions around the world in order to share those ideas and that goodwill even further.

Mounir Bouchenaki
Assistant Director-General for Culture
UNESCO

Richard Kurin
Director,
Center for Folklife and Cultural Heritage
Smithsonian Institution

Acknowledgements

Many people deserve praise for the fruition of the 1999 conference and the present book. The contributors and other conference participants are of course crucial, and their contributions are documented in at least some measure in this volume. Many volunteers made the meeting work, taking notes, seeing to participants' needs — in general, helping to create the infrastructure of an international meeting. Translators, financial administrators, transportation specialists, and many other professionals also performed crucial tasks. Thanked here by name are those who came together specifically for the project, oversaw a portion of its development, and contributed by their work to the articulation of its central themes. Among them are people who: defined the subject matter of the conference, suggested participants, communicated with them, developed formats for meetings and book, and directly oversaw or adivsed about the production of the conference event and the publishing of this volume. Many deserve recognition and gratitude for more than one category of contribution. The names of these crucial people appear in the order of the alphabet.

Noriko Aikawa, Linda Benner, Carla Borden, Caroline Brownell, Andy Buckman, Olivia Cadaval, Maria Elena Cepeda, Brenna Dailey, Shelton Davis, James Early, Dawn Elvis, Kristen Fernekes, John W. Franklin, Amy Horowitz, Peter Jaszi, Richard Kurin, Enrique Lamadrid, Lisa Maiorino, Anthony McCann, Jonathan McCollum, Sherylle Mills, Leslie Prosterman, Chad Redwing, Pam Rogers, Mara Schlimm, Anthony Seeger, Peter Seitel, Kenn Shrader, Brad Simon, Kate Stinson, Barbara Strickland

Grateful acknowledgement is also made to the financial sponsors of the conference and publication, the Smithsonian Institution, the Japanese Ministry of Foreign Affairs (UNESCO/Japan Funds in Trust), the U.S. Department of State, the Rockefeller Foundation, and the National Endowment for the Arts.

Contributors

Andy P. Abeita, an American Indian stone and bronze sculptor, is President of the Council for Indigenous Arts and Culture in Peralta, New Mexico, U.S.A. He is also President of Laboraex Consulting, an international commercial trade consulting firm.

Noriko Aikawa is Director of the Intangible Cultural Heritage Unit in the Division of Cultural Heritage at UNESCO in Paris, France.

Robyne Bancroft is an Aboriginal Australian (Goori) affiliated with the Australian National University in Canberra, Australia.

Tressa Berman teaches in the Social and Behavioral Sciences Department at Arizona State University West in Phoenix, Arizona, U.S.A.

Janet Blake is a Visiting Research Fellow in the School of Law, University of Glasgow, Scotland.

Stepanida Borisova is affiliated with the Ministry of Culture of the Sakha Republic (Yakutiya), in Yakutsk, Russia.

Mounir Bouchenaki is the Director of the Division of Cultural Heritage and World Heritage Centre at UNESCO in Paris, France.

Manuela Carneiro da Cunha is Professor of Anthropology at the University of Chicago.

Russell Collier is a member of the Strategic Watershed Analysis Team in Hazelton, British Columbia, Canada. He is a functioning member of the Canadian Gitxsan Nation.

Rachid El Houda is an architect DPLG with many years' experience in the preservation of historical monuments. A member of the College of Moroccan Architects, he has worked for the last three years on the major project for the preservation of the Medina of Fez.

Mahaman Garba is an ethnomusicologist at the Centre de Formation et de Promotion Musicale (CFPM) in Niamey, Niger.

Mihály Hoppál is Director of the European Folklore Institute (the former European Centre for Traditional Culture) in Budapest, Hungary.

Florentino H. Hornedo is Professor in the College of Arts and Sciences, Ateneo de Manila University in Manila, the Philippines.

Pualani Kanaka'ole Kanahele is an officer of the Edith Kanaka'ole Foundation in Hilo, Hawai'i.

Junzo Kawada is Professor of Cultural Anthropology on the Faculty of International Studies at Hiroshima City University in Hiroshima, Japan. His work, *La Voix,* has been translated from Japanese by Sylvie Jeanne, Editions Ecole des Hautes Etudes en Sciences Sociales, Paris, 1998.

Heikki Kirkinen is Vice-President of the European Academy of Arts, Sciences and Humanities at the University of Joensuu in Finland.

Grace Koch is the Archives Manager, Archives and Production Program, at the Australian Institute of Aboriginal and Torres Strait Islander Studies (AIATSIS) in Canberra, Australia. She has recently published "Songs, Land Rights, and Archives in Australia" in *Cultural Survival Quarterly* 20(4): 38-41.

Namankoumba Kouyaté is Chargé d'Affaires a.i. and Counselor for Political, Economic and Cultural affairs at the Embassy of the Republic of Guinea in Bonn, Germany.

Richard Kurin is Director of the Center for Folklore and Cultural Heritage at the Smithsonian Institution in Washington, D.C., U.S.A.

Kurshida Mambetova is Head of the Culture Department, National Commission of the Republic of Uzbekistan for UNESCO, in Tashkent, Uzbekistan.

Renato Matusse is Secretary General of the SADC Sector for Culture, Information and Sport, in the Southern African Development Community, Maputo, Mozambique.

Anthony McCann, one of the project coordinators for the Smithsonian-UNESCO Conference, is a PhD. Candidate in ethnomusicology at the University of Limerick in Ireland.

J. H. Kwabena Nketia is Director of the International Centre for African Music and Dance at the University of Ghana School of Performing Arts in Accra, Ghana.

Lyndel V. Prott is Chief of the International Standards Section, Division of Cultural Heritage at UNESCO in Paris, France.

Kamal Puri is Professor of Law at the University of Queensland in Brisbane, Australia and President of the Australian Folklore Association, Inc. His recent publications include "Legal Protection of Expressions of Folklore" (1998) XXXII UNESCO's *Copyright Bulletin* 5, and "Cultural Ownership and Intellectual Property Rights Post Mabo: Putting Ideas into Action" (1995) 9 *Intellectual Property Journal* 293 (Canada).

Miguel Puwainchir is Mayor of the Huamboya Municipality, Province of Morona Santiago, Ecuador.

Gail Saunders is Director of Archives in the Department of Archives in Nassau, The Bahamas.

Anthony Seeger, former Director of the Smithsonian Folkways Recordings, is Professor of Ethnomusicology at the University of California at Los Angeles, U.S.A.

Rajeev Sethi is Principal of Rajeev Sethi Scenographers Pvt. Ltd. in New Delhi, India.

Mohsen Shaalan is General Director of traditional handcraft centers in the Fine Arts Sector of the Ministry of Culture in Cairo, Egypt.

Samantha Sherkin, Ph.D, is a consultant in the Intangible Cultural Heritage Unit of the Division of Cultural Heritage of UNESCO in Paris, France.

Bradford S. Simon received degrees in anthropology from Brown University and University College London and in law from the School of Law at the University of California at Berkeley.

Preston Thomas is Commissioner of the Aboriginal and Torres Strait Islander Commission in Phillip, Australia.

Sivia Tora is Director of Culture and Heritage in the Ministry of Culture and Heritage in Fiji.

Yamaguti Osamu is Professor of Musicology at Osaka University Graduate School of Letters in Osaka, Japan and Visiting Professor at the University of the Air in Tiba, Japan. His recent publications include *Applicative Musicology* (in Japanese), Tokyo: University of the Air Publishers, 2000.

Zulma Yugar is Director General for Cultural Promotion in the Vice Ministry of Culture, La Paz, Bolivia.

Table of Contents

I. Preliminaries

II. Strategic Perspectives on Local Culture

Foundational Perspectives: Affirmations of the Indigenous in an Age of Globalization

Legal Perspectives and Local Traditions: Toward Legislative and Judicial Remedies

Practical Perspectives: Local Traditions and Methods of Preservation

Regional Perspectives: Reports of UNESCO Regional Seminars

III. A Call for Action

Final Report of the Conference

Part I

Preliminaries

Message from Mr. Federico Mayor
Director-General of UNESCO
June 27, 1999

It is with pleasure that UNESCO is co-operating with the prestigious Smithsonian Institution in the organization of this meeting on the global assessment of the application of the UNESCO 1989 *Recommendation on the Safeguarding of Traditional Culture and Folklore*. I am also pleased that the Organization is able to participate in the 34th annual Smithsonian Folklife Festival, a Festival that celebrates cultural diversity. This Conference aims to evaluate the manner in which the *Recommendation* has been implemented and thus assess the present situation of intangible cultural heritage in the world; to analyze the role that intangible cultural heritage can play in resolving local and national problems relating to major contemporary concerns; and to draw up a new strategy for the coming years.

I would like here to highlight the important role that the Smithsonian Center for Folklife and Cultural Heritage has played in the preparation of this meeting, a co-operative effort with UNESCO that is itself of great significance. As some of you may recall, the founder of the Center for Folklife and Cultural Heritage, Ralph Rinzler, was also an active member of the United States' National Commission for UNESCO. I take this opportunity to pay tribute to his memory. Ralph Rinzler was a tireless supporter of the promotion of local expressive systems and of their continuity within host communities. In his eyes, living culture, a form of democracy, was as important as any other type of democracy.

Following the Second World War and thanks to the initiatives of governments and prominent personalities, UNESCO was created for the purpose of promoting international peace and common welfare through intellectual and moral collaboration among nations. To quote the inspiring words of the American poet Archibald MacLeish, inscribed in the Constitution of UNESCO:

> Since wars begin in the minds of men, it is in the minds of men that the defences of peace must be constructed.

Throughout the twelve years that I have been Director-General of UNESCO, I have consistently worked to place this fundamental idea of the Organization's founders at the core of all UNESCO programmes, and to promote a culture of peace and democracy. I am quite aware of the difficulties inherent in such a difficult undertaking, yet it is imperative that we persevere with determination.

It is UNESCO's duty, as an intergovernmental organization, to listen to governments in order to trace out the main lines of educational, scientific and cultural programmes. However, UNESCO is also attentive to the aspirations and needs of various communities and civil society, with the aim of assisting people in discovering, and implementing, the most appropriate solutions according to circumstances. To quote a celebrated poem by Walt Whitman, entitled "To You":

Stranger, if you passing meet me and desire to speak to me, why should you not speak to
   me?
And why should I not speak to You?

This is our goal - to encourage people of different origins to speak together and share their particular cultural values as equal partners.

The UNESCO 1989 *Recommendation*, whose implementation you will be examining, was a first attempt to provide a common international basis for policies for safeguarding traditional culture and folklore. The assessment now being made should take account of the sum of political, economic and social changes of the past ten years. As we enter the third millennium, we should be commemorating the natural and cultural heritage that we have inherited from past generations; indeed, in our search for economic growth and technological progress, we have often overlooked our roots. For a long time many people thought that "heritage" meant "tangible heritage"; in other words natural or cultural sites, monuments, and so forth. However, in recent years, with all the turmoil of globalization and the rapid growth of the market economy, the spiritual and symbolic value of the intangible cultural heritage - that is to say, of traditional and popular cultural expression - has been revealed and recognized. Tangible and intangible heritage relate to human creativity in everyday life. On the one hand, human beings have changed the natural environment through their ancestral activities while, on the other hand, they have accumulated a sizeable store of knowledge, rituals, languages and oral traditions, including tales, epics, theatre and music.

I am particularly pleased that this important event is taking place at the Smithsonian Institution, which has long been a partner of UNESCO. I should like to refer here to the Smithsonian's Man and the Biosphere Biodiversity Program (SIMAB), a programme that commenced in 1986 as a joint effort between the two organizations.

Exactly one century separates the creation of the Smithsonian Institution and that of UNESCO. It has been a century of rich experience dedicated to the spread of knowledge in different parts of the world. The work of the Smithsonian complements the global activities of UNESCO. Considering our past achievements, I am confident that today's event will constitute a milestone for future co-operation.

Finally, I should like to express my sincere gratitude to the Japanese Ministry of Foreign Affairs, the United States Department of State, the Rockefeller Foundation, the National Endowment for the Arts, and the Smithsonian Institution Office for International Relations for their generous financial contributions that have made this gathering possible.

I wish you every success in your deliberations.

Opening Address

Mounir Bouchenaki
Director
Division of Cultural Heritage, UNESCO

Mr. Chairman, Vice Chairman, Ladies and Gentlemen, Dear Colleagues:

Allow me first of all to tell you how pleased I am to be among you today, representing the Director-General of UNESCO, Mr. Federico Mayor, at the opening of this important conference in Washington. I also wish to pay my respects and appreciation to Mr. Michael Heyman, Secretary of the Smithsonian Institution, for the kind words that he has just addressed to us all here today. I would also like to express my gratitude to Dr. Richard Kurin, Director, and Dr. Anthony Seeger, Curator, Center for Folklife and Cultural Heritage, and their colleagues, for having worked closely with UNESCO in organizing this conference, and for having welcomed it on the premises of the prestigious Smithsonian Institution. Finally, I would like to express my gratitude to the Japanese Ministry of Foreign Affairs, the U.S. Department of State, the Rockefeller Foundation, the National Endowment for the Arts, and the Smithsonian Institution Office of International Relations (OIR) for their generous financial contributions to making this gathering possible.

UNESCO has been happy to cooperate with the Smithsonian Center for Folklife and Cultural Heritage, a Center whose basic tenets are dedicated to "the increase and diffusion of knowledge," and more particularly to "promote the understanding and continuity of contemporary grassroots cultures." These principles correspond to those expressed in the Constitution of UNESCO, signed in London on 16 November 1945 by thirty-seven countries. "That since wars begin in the minds of men, it is in the minds of men that the defenses of peace must be constructed. That ignorance of each other's ways and lives has been a common cause, throughout the history of mankind, of that suspicion and mistrust between the peoples of the world through which their differences have all too often broken into war." One of the purposes and functions of UNESCO is to maintain, increase, and diffuse knowledge through international intellectual cooperation in the fields of education, science, and culture.

Ladies and Gentlemen, UNESCO is very pleased to be able to partake in the thirty-fourth annual Smithsonian Folklife Festival, an exhibition of living cultural heritage from across the United States and around the world, celebrating the vitality and diversity of traditional and popular cultural expression. This Festival, an event organized to raise consciousness and disseminate knowledge about diverse cultures, is itself an extension of the Smithsonian Institution outdoors, dispersed along the National Mall of the United States, where it embraces the same goal but with a somewhat different approach. In demonstrating culture as dynamic, alive in various settings, this Festival provides a direct opportunity for intercultural dialogue, where tradition-bearers, including storytellers, elders, balladeers, artists, healers, and builders, as well as academics and a broad public, are able to share and exchange their knowledge. Such activity offers an excellent occasion not only to under-

5

stand, appreciate, and respect different aspects of "other cultures" but also to identify common features among different cultures.

Ladies and Gentlemen, today, as we enter a new millennium, many countries have begun to adopt a broader and more inclusive definition of the word "heritage"; i.e. the heritage of ideas, the scientific heritage, and the genetic heritage are all part of the ancient heritage that we must safeguard. In addition, we must ensure the preservation of the ethical heritage, a heritage in which diversity is embraced in its infinite forms as a means to establishing unity, a oneness that represents our strength and our hope for the future.

UNESCO is most famous for the "World Heritage List," established on the basis of the Convention for the Protection of the World Cultural and Natural Heritage adopted by the UNESCO General Conference in 1972 and managed by the World Heritage Centre, which I am honored to lead. The primary objective of this action was to provide a legal mechanism that could ensure the safeguarding of tangible heritage for future generations. The term "tangible heritage" was here extended to include cultural monuments, cultural and natural sites, and cultural landscapes. However, despite its great significance, none of the provisions of this Convention apply to the intangible cultural heritage, namely the entire treasure house of popular arts and customs, such as languages, dances, songs, rites, ceremonies, and crafts that have been handed down over centuries. Yet, the intangible, like the physical and natural heritage, is itself vulnerable and, as such, is at risk of being swept away by the global trend towards homogenization and the pressures of a market economy that continually applies commercial standards to aspects of life which cannot be reduced to economic profit and loss. Nonetheless, technological development, including cinema, radio, television, and electronic telecommunications, has provided us with mediums to preserve and diffuse the world's cultural heritage, a service which has greatly contributed to the security and enhancement of our daily life together.

As Director of the World Heritage Centre and the Division of Cultural Heritage and as an archaeologist myself, I feel that all forms of cultural heritage, including tangible and intangible heritage and natural heritage, must be respected and recognized as being closely affiliated. For instance, intangible heritage provides an understanding of spiritual values, historical signification, and symbolic interpretation to both cultural monuments and cultural and natural sites, a fact that must be recognized and respected in present and future generations.

UNESCO wishes to draw your special attention to the subtitle of the conference: *local empowerment and international cooperation*. These principles are in conformity with wishes recently expressed by the two governing bodies of UNESCO, namely the General Conference and the Executive Board. Throughout the last few years, these bodies have been underlining the need for the Organization to strengthen activities relating to the reinforcement of indigenous capacity-building. Moreover, for the activities in the field of cultural heritage, both for its preservation and its management, the governing bodies constantly stress that active participation by local communities and their young people in implementing activities should be reinforced. I am happy to note that each one of you present here today has deeply committed yourself to some concrete actions for empowering local communities in the task of preserving and revitalizing intangible cultural heritage in various parts of the world.

I am also happy to see here today a number of young persons, including those from nearby institutions and those who came from abroad, participating in this conference. It is important that young people take active part in reviewing the results of the forthcoming conference since it is they who will ensure the safeguarding and transmission of intangible cultural heritage to future generations. In the words of Wordsworth, "The child is father of the man." That is to say, it is the young who hold the future in their hands, it is they who will carry humanity through to a new era.

Ladies and gentlemen, at all times and in all places, each and every human being is unique. Each person's uniqueness, embodied and multiplied in diverse cultures, is the most outstanding characteristic of the human species. This quality forms the basis for the establishment of cultural freedom, a collective freedom in which a group, or individuals, may be free to develop a way of life of its own choice.

In order to achieve such freedom, it would be necessary to promote cultural diversity throughout the world. Promoting diversity would certainly slow down the process of global uniformity, which seems, paradoxically, to lead to global anonymity. As Claude Lévi-Strauss states, if cultural diversity is "behind us, around us and before us," then we must learn how to let it lead, not to the clash of cultures, but to their fruitful coexistence and to intercultural harmony.

I would like here to talk about a group of people who have recently, and peacefully, attained their political autonomy, a group who have consciously retained three traditional ancestral principles as a means of ensuring their cultural specificity and peaceful cohabitation with other ethnic and cultural groups. I am referring to the people of Nunavut, living in the north of Canada. These principles are "patience," "sense of sharing," and "art of adaptation." Mr. John Amagoalik, President of the Commission for the establishment of Nunavut, recounts the following:

> *Patience* I discovered as a child when I saw my father waiting for hours in an ice hole until the seal came up to take a breath. This patience we needed for negotiation for the establishment of Nunavut. *Sense of sharing* — This is another foundation of our culture. We will continue to apply this principle in our political responsibilities. *Art of adaptation* — This principle has been put into practice by our ancestors for 4,000 years. Without adaptation, there is no survival!

Ladies and gentlemen, this conference can make an enormous contribution to the future direction of the safeguarding of the world's intangible cultural heritage. In so doing, the recommendations of this conference will also affect the future of the world's tangible and natural heritage, as all forms of cultural heritage are intricately intertwined. As Miguel de Unamuno states, "The ultimate purpose of culture will perhaps be to achieve the spiritual unity of humanity."

Recommendation on the Safeguarding of Traditional Culture and Folklore
Adopted by the General Conference
at its Twenty-fifth session, Paris, 15 November 1989

The General Conference of the United Nations Educational, Scientific and Cultural Organization, meeting in Paris from 17 October to 16 November at its twenty-fifth session,

Considering that folklore forms part of the universal heritage of humanity and that it is a powerful means of bringing together different peoples and social groups and of asserting their cultural identity,

Noting its social, economic, cultural and political importance, its role in the history of the people, and its place in contemporary culture,

Underlining the specific nature and importance of folklore as an integral part of cultural heritage and living culture,

Recognizing the extreme fragility of the traditional forms of folklore, particularly those aspects relating to oral tradition and the risk that they might be lost,

Stressing the need in all countries for recognition of the role of folklore and the danger it faces from multiple factors,

Judging that the governments should play a decisive role in the safeguarding of folklore and that they should act as quickly as possible,

Having decided, at its twenty-fourth session, that the safeguarding of folklore should be the subject of a recommendation to Member States within the meaning of Article IV, paragraph 4, of the Constitution,

Adopts the present Recommendation this fifteenth day of November 1989:

The General Conference recommends that Member States should apply the following provisions concerning the safeguarding of folklore by taking whatever legislative measures or other steps may be required in conformity with the constitutional practice of each State to give effect within their territories to the principles and measures defined in this Recommendation.

The General Conference recommends that Member States bring this Recommendation to the attention of the authorities, departments or bodies responsible for matters relating to the safeguarding of folklore and to the attention of the various organizations or institutions concerned with folklore, and encourage their contacts with appropriate international organizations dealing with the safeguarding of folklore.

The General Conference recommends that Member States should, at such times and in such manner as it shall determine, submit to the Organization reports on the action they have taken to give effect to this Recommendation.

A. Definition of Folklore

For purposes of this Recommendation:

Folklore (or traditional and popular culture) is the totality of tradition-based creations of a cultural community, expressed by a group or individuals and recognized as reflecting the expectations of a community in so far as they reflect its cultural and social identity; its standards and values are transmitted orally, by imitation or by other means. Its forms are, among others, language, literature, music, dance, games, mythology, rituals, customs, handicrafts, architecture and other arts.

B. Identification of Folklore

Folklore, as a form of cultural expression, must be safeguarded by and for the group (familial, occupational, national, regional, religious, ethnic, etc.) whose identity it expresses. To this end, Member States should encourage appropriate survey research on national, regional and international levels with the aim to:

a) develop a national inventory of institutions concerned with folklore with a view to its inclusion in regional and global registers of folklore institutions;

b) create identification and recording systems (collection, cataloguing, transcription) or develop those that already exist by handbooks, collecting guides, model catalogues, etc., in view of the need to coordinate the classification systems used by different institutions;

c) stimulate the creation of a standard typology of folklore by way of: i) a general outline of folklore for global use; ii) a comprehensive register of folklore; and iii) regional classifications of folklore, especially field-work pilot projects.

C. Conservation of Folklore

Conservation is concerned with documentation regarding folk traditions and its object is, in the event of the non-utilization or evolution of such traditions, to give researchers and tradition-bearers access to data enabling them to understand the process through which traditions change. While living folklore, owing to its evolving character, cannot always be directly protected, folklore that has to be fixed in a tangible form should be effectively protected.

To this end, Member States should:

a) establish national archives where collected folklore can be properly stored and made available;

b) establish a central national archive function for service purposes (central cataloguing, dissemination of information on folklore materials and standards of folklore work including the aspect of safeguarding);

c) create museums or folklore sections at existing museums where traditional and popular culture can be exhibited;

d) give precedence to ways of presenting traditional and popular cultures that emphasize the living or past aspects of those cultures (showing their surroundings, ways of life and the works, skills and techniques they have produced);

e) harmonize collecting and archiving methods;

f) train collectors, archivists, documentalists and other specialists in the conservation of folklore, from physical conservation to analytic work;

g) provide means for making security and working copies of all folklore materials, and copies for regional institutions, thus securing the cultural community and access to the materials.

D. Preservation of Folklore

Preservation is concerned with protection of folk traditions and those who are the transmitters, having regard to the fact that each people has a right to its own culture and that its adherence to that culture is often eroded by the impact of the industrialized culture purveyed by the mass media. Measures must be taken to guarantee the status of and economic support for folk traditions both in the communities which produce them and beyond. To this end, Member States should:

a) design and introduce into both formal and out-of-school curricula the teaching and study of folklore in an appropriate manner, laying particular emphasis on respect for folklore in the widest sense of the term, taking into account not only village and other rural cultures but also those created in urban areas by diverse social groups, professions, institutions, etc., and thus promoting a better understanding of cultural diversity and different world views, especially those not reflected in dominant cultures;

b) guarantee the right of access of various cultural communities to their own folklore by supporting their work in the fields of documentation, archiving, research, etc., as well as in the practice of traditions;

c) set up on an interdisciplinary basis a National Folklore Council or similar coordination body in which various interest groups will also be represented;

d) provide moral and economic support for individuals and institutions studying, making known, cultivating or holding items of folklore;

e) promote scientific research relevant to the presentation of folklore.

E. Dissemination of Folklore

The attention of people should be drawn to the importance of folklore as an ingredient of cultural identity. It is essential for the items that make up this cultural heritage to be widely disseminated so that the value of folklore and the need to preserve it can be recognized. However, distortion during dissemination should be avoided so that the integrity of the traditions can be safeguarded. To promote a fair dissemination, Member States should:

a) encourage the organization of national, regional and international events such as fairs, festivals, films, exhibitions, seminars, symposia, workshops, training courses, congresses, etc., and support the dissemination and publication of their materials, papers and other results;

b) encourage a broader coverage of folklore material in national and regional press, publishing, television, radio and other media, for instance through grants, by creating jobs for folklorists in these units, by ensuring the proper archiving and dissemination of these folklore materials collected by the mass media, and by the establishment of departments of folklore within those organizations;

c) encourage regions, municipalities, associations and other groups working in folklore to establish full-time jobs for folklorists to stimulate and coordinate folklore activities in the region;

d) support existing units and the creation of new units for the production of educational materials, as for example video films based on recent field-work, and encourage their use in schools, folklore museums, national and international folklore festivals and exhibitions;

e) ensure the availability of adequate information on folklore through documentation centers, libraries, museums, archives, as well as through special folklore bulletins and periodicals;

f) facilitate meetings on exchanges between individuals, groups and institutions concerned with folklore, both nationally and internationally, taking into account bilateral cultural agreements;

g) encourage the international scientific community to adopt a code of ethics ensuring a proper approach to and respect for traditional cultures.

F. Protection of Folklore

In so far as folklore constitutes manifestations of intellectual creativity whether it be individual or collective, it deserves to be protected in a manner inspired by the protection provided for intellectual productions. Such protection of folklore has become indispensable as a means of promoting further development, maintenance and dissemination of those expressions, both within and outside the country, without prejudice to related legitimate interests.

Leaving aside the "intellectual property" aspects of the protection of expressions of folklore, there are various categories of right which are already protected and should continue to enjoy protection in the future in folklore documentation centers and archives. To this end, Member States should:

a) regarding the "intellectual property" aspects:

Call the attention of relevant authorities to the important work of UNESCO and WIPO in relation to intellectual property, while recognizing that this work relates to only one aspect of folklore protection and that the need for separate action in a range of areas to safeguard folklore is urgent;

b) regarding the other rights involved:

i) protect the informant as the transmitter of tradition (protection of privacy and confidentiality);
ii) protect the interest of the collector by ensuring that the materials gathered are conserved in archives in good condition and in a methodical manner;
iii) adopt the necessary measures to safeguard the materials gathered against misuse, whether intentional or otherwise;
iv) recognize the responsibility of archives to monitor the use made of the materials gathered.

G. International Cooperation

In view of the need to intensify cultural cooperation and exchanges, in particular through the pooling of human and material resources, in order to carry out folklore development and revitalization programs as well as research made by specialists who are the nationals of one Member State on the territory of another Member State, Member States should:

a) cooperate with international and regional associations, institutions and organizations concerned with folklore;
b) cooperate in the field of knowledge, dissemination and protection of folklore, in particular through:

i) exchanges of information of every kind, exchanges of scientific and technical publications;

ii) training of specialists, awarding of travel grants, sending of scientific and technical personnel and equipment;

iii) the promotion of bilateral or multilateral projects in the field of the documentation of contemporary folklore;

iv) the organization of meetings between specialists, of study courses and of the working groups on particular subjects, especially on the classifying and cataloguing of folklore data and expression and on modern methods and techniques in research;

c) cooperate closely so as to ensure internationally that the various interested parties (communities or natural or legal persons) enjoy the economic, moral and so-called neighboring rights resulting from the investigation, creation, composition, performance, recording and/or dissemination of folklore;

d) guarantee the Member State on whose territory research has been carried out the right to obtain from the Member State concerned, copies of all documents, recording, video-films, films and other material;

e) refrain from acts likely to damage folklore materials or to diminish their value or impede their dissemination or use, whether these materials are to be found on their own territory or on the territory of another State;

f) take necessary measures to safeguard folklore against all human and natural dangers to which it is exposed, including the risks deriving from armed conflicts, occupation of territories or public disorders of other kinds.

The UNESCO *Recommendation on the Safeguarding of Traditional Culture and Folklore* (1989): Actions Undertaken by UNESCO for Its Implementation

Noriko Aikawa
Director
Intangible Heritage Unit, UNESCO

This paper concerns actions undertaken by UNESCO for the implementation of the 1989 *Recommendation*. It covers: (i) the development of UNESCO's programs for traditional and popular cultures since the adoption of the *Recommendation* in 1989; (ii) the increased interest of Member States in the Intangible Cultural Heritage Program; and (iii) activities undertaken by UNESCO to assist efforts to apply the different parts of the *Recommendation*.

After sixteen years of a long, arduous, and costly process, the UNESCO General Conference established the first international standard-setting instrument for the protection of traditional culture and folklore. A description of this lengthy process is given in the document entitled "A Historical Study on the Preparation of the UNESCO 1989 *Recommendation on the Safeguarding of Traditional Culture and Folklore*."[1] It is interesting to note here that once this instrument was established, UNESCO Member States showed little interest in its application, in spite of the requirements addressed to Member States on the first page of the *Recommendation* to apply its provisions, to put its principles and measures into effect, to bring it to the attention of authorities, bodies, and institutions concerned with folklore, and to submit reports to UNESCO on the action they have taken in regard to the *Recommendation*.

In February 1990, the Director-General of UNESCO sent a letter to Member States inviting them to take all necessary steps to implement the *Recommendation* and to report to him all actions taken. In spite of a reminder letter sent in April 1991, only six countries submitted reports, and those reports merely reflected measures taken to familiarize the concerned national authorities with the *Recommendation*. Due to such a small number of reports received from Member States, the Director-General decided not to submit the report to the General Conference in spite of Article 17 of the Rules of Procedure concerning recommendations to Member States and international conventions.

This passive reaction by Member States was prefigured by an expert cited in Canadian attorney Marc Denhez's 1997 pre-evaluation report[2] on the 1989 *Recommendation*; the expert warned in 1992 that difficulties might arise because the *Recommendation* gives neither specific mandate to UNESCO nor any explanation of how it should be implemented. Since the *Recommendation* is addressed entirely to Member States, UNESCO's role is limited to promoting it and encouraging the implementation of its provisions.

The International Council of Organizations for Folklore Festivals and Folk Art (CIOFF), an NGO having a formal consultative relation with UNESCO, made a valuable contribution to UNESCO's efforts to promote the *Recommendation*. Its activities included seminars organized by CIOFF Switzerland (1990), CIOFF Italy (1991), and CIOFF Spain (1992), aimed at increasing awareness of the *Recommendation* within both the public and private sectors and at encouraging its implementation.

UNESCO, for its part, whilst pursuing activities for the promotion of the *Recommendation* among Member States, was facing a new reality at the onset of the 1990s. Following the end of the Cold War, former Communist countries experienced drastic political and economic mutations. A number of ethnic groups who attained their independence sought their cultural identity in their traditional local cultures. In Latin America, the 1992 commemoration of the 500-year encounter with Europe celebrated a new identity based on hybrid cultures and multilingualism. The rapid expansion of the market economy throughout the world and the tremendous progress of information and communication technology began to transform the world into a uniform economic and cultural space. Under these circumstances, many UNESCO Member States began taking an interest in their traditional popular cultures. They rediscovered their spiritual values and their role as symbolic reference to an identity rooted in the memory of local communities, after the manner of great historical monuments such as the Borobudur Temple, which, as is well known, was restored by UNESCO.

It was felt necessary, therefore, for the Organization to review and reorient its program regarding traditional popular cultures. In 1991, the General Conference decided that the program entitled the "Non-Physical Heritage" be placed between the programs "Enhancement of Cultural Identities" and "Physical Cultural Heritage" in order to "highlight the dual role played by the program of the non-physical heritage."[3]

In 1992, UNESCO conducted a scientific evaluation of all activities carried out over the two preceding decades in the field of traditional popular cultures.[4] After the evaluation, the title of the program "Non-Physical Cultural Heritage" was modified to "Intangible Cultural Heritage." In June 1993, UNESCO organized an international conference[5] at its Headquarters to draw up new guidelines for the Intangible Cultural Heritage Program, thanks to the generous sponsorship of the Japanese Ministry of Foreign Affairs. The UNESCO/Japan Funds-In-Trust for the Safeguarding and Promotion of the Intangible Cultural Heritage was established in the same year, providing a yearly financial contribution that has given a significant impetus to the program.

To begin with, and as a matter of urgency, the 1993 guidelines urge that the guardians and creators of intangible cultural heritage, as well as policy makers, administrators, and the public, should pay greater respect to their traditional and popular culture and should recognize the need for its preservation and transmission. Secondly, the crucial role of the populations and communities who produce or reproduce cultural forms and creative expressions at the local level is to be stressed. The third issue concerns the priority of revitalizing these cultures by adapting them to the contemporary world. In this respect, the selection of the aspects of culture to be revitalized should be made by people of the local community concerned. Also urgent is the safeguarding of heritages threatened by extinction, particularly those of Indigenous and minority peoples. The guidelines also include the following precautions to be taken in conceiving and implementing the program:

- not to crystallize the intangible cultural heritage, whose fundamental characteristic is to be permanently evolving;
- not to take this heritage out of its original context, as, for example, "folklorization" does;
- to be aware of the obstacles that threaten the survival of the intangible cultural heritage;
- to give greater emphasis to the intangible heritage of hybrid cultures, which develop in urban areas; and

- to employ a different methodology for intangible cultural heritage than for tangible cultural heritage.

Not only its priorities but also UNESCO's role and methods of work should match the needs of contemporary realities; that is, UNESCO should play instigating and catalyzing roles. As an instigator, it encourages Member States or specialized institutions to launch projects given priority by UNESCO's General Conference. As a catalyst, it creates partnerships and networks and seeks financial support from foundations and other partners. UNESCO is called upon to continue the following methods: (i) create networks of institutions and specialists; (ii) help Member States to define their strategic options; (iii) support the organization of training courses and festivals; and (iv) encourage the mass media to disseminate the intangible cultural heritage.

It should be noted that the above guidelines suggest new policies complementary to the principles and measures defined in the 1989 *Recommendation*. Together with the 1989 *Recommendation*, they laid the foundations for the UNESCO Medium-Term Strategies for 1996–2001[6] in the field of Intangible Cultural Heritage. A number of international and regional projects — particularly pilot projects for Vietnam, Hungary, Mexico, and Niger endorsed by the International Consultation of 1993 — were implemented. A new project entitled "Red Book of Endangered Languages" was also launched.

In October 1993, the UNESCO Executive Board adopted the decision[7] presented by the Republic of Korea inviting Member States to take necessary steps concerning "living cultural property" ("Living Human Treasures") as an effective means to implement the *Recommendation* of 1989. The Republic of Korea proposed that UNESCO Member States establish a system to give official recognition to persons possessing exceptional artistry and traditional skills in order to encourage the development and transmission of such talent and know-how and safeguard the traditional cultural heritage. UNESCO made a survey of this system, which has been successfully practiced by some countries of East Asia, such as the Republic of Korea, Japan, Thailand, and the Philippines, since the 1950s and drew up guidelines[8] explaining how to establish the system and how it is to function. UNESCO hopes that this project will compensate for a lack in the *Recommendation* regarding the recognition and protection of these practitioners of traditional cultures. UNESCO's role is to provide assistance, often in the form of consultants, to help the authorities of Member States accomplish the following: (i) establish legislation to protect the intangible heritage; (ii) identify the possessors of relevant know-how; (iii) formulate a national register of types of intangible heritage to be protected; and lastly (iv) prepare a roster of potential candidates for inclusion on the list of National Living Human Treasures. UNESCO is also organizing training workshops twice a year to show the successful experience of some countries and has recently invited all Member States to apply to attend these workshops. Nearly fifty Member States have expressed interest in establishing a program of Living Human Treasures.

In November 1993, the UNESCO General Conference adopted a Draft Resolution presented by Hungary that initiates a pilot project to create in Budapest an interregional network of research institutions specializing in traditional cultures of Eastern and Central Europe. The project was proposed by the Hungarian authorities as a follow-up action to the recommendation endorsed by the international expert meeting in June 1993. The European Centre for Traditional Culture (ECTC) was thus created with the support of UNESCO. The Centre has contributed to the wide dissemination of the 1989 *Recommendation* in Eastern and Central Europe and has compiled a substantial database on institutions specializing in European traditional popular cultures.

In 1995, the Czech Republic took an initiative which paved the way for a series of assessments of the application of the *Recommendation*. It organized, in collaboration with UNESCO, the first seminar on the application of the 1989 *Recommendation* for countries of Eastern and Central Europe. The UNESCO Secretariat and the Institute of Folklore in Strá nice, led by Professor Josef Jancar, drew up a questionnaire to survey the state of the identification, conservation, preservation, dissemination, and protection of and international cooperation regarding traditional and popular cultures in the countries concerned. The replies to the questionnaire sent to all the National Commissions concerned were assembled and analyzed by the Strá nice Institute and presented to the seminar. Professor Jancar should be commended for agreeing to update the report in April 1999 by means of a second questionnaire. On the basis of recommendations put forward by the seminar, the authorities of the Czech Republic presented a Draft Resolution to the UNESCO General Conference in 1995, which thereupon decided that a worldwide appraisal of the safeguarding of traditional and folk heritage should be carried out, taking as its reference point the 1989 *Recommendation*.[9]

A series of surveys was then carried out through a detailed questionnaire addressed to Member States, and a total of eight seminars were organized in different parts of the world. The present conference is the culmination of these regional seminars — Czech Republic (1995),[10] Mexico (1997),[11] Japan (1998),[12] Finland (1998),[13] Uzbekistan (1998),[14] Ghana (1999),[15] New Caledonia (1999),[16] and Lebanon (1999).[17] These surveys and seminars contributed significantly to drawing the attention of Member States to the *Recommendation*.

Since 1995, increased interest in the concept of "intangible cultural heritage" has been expressed by Member States through UNESCO's two governing bodies, the General Conference and the Executive Board. For example, in October 1996, the Executive Board recommended that, in preparing the 1998–1999 Program, special attention should be given to formulating and implementing strategies for the safeguarding, revitalizing, and disseminating of intangible heritage.[18] In June 1997, the Executive Board again recommended that emphasis be placed on the preservation of oral traditions, endangered languages, and forms of cultural expression, particularly those of minorities and Indigenous peoples.[19] The debate of the General Conference in October 1997 confirmed the strong interest of Member States in the intangible cultural heritage and revealed that the Intangible Cultural Heritage Program should be given one of the highest priorities in the cultural field.[20]

Member States' commitment to intangible cultural heritage was strengthened by a Draft Resolution presented by Morocco and supported by many countries including Saudi Arabia, Cape Verde, United Arab Emirates, Spain, Lebanon, Mali, and Venezuela. Taking the 1989 *Recommendation* as its reference point, the Resolution urged the General Conference to highlight the importance of the intangible cultural heritage for peoples and nations by proclaiming cultural spaces or forms of cultural expression part of the "Oral Heritage of Humanity." After an extensive debate, the General Conference adopted this Resolution unanimously.[21]

The purpose of this project is to pay tribute to outstanding masterpieces of the oral and intangible heritage of humanity. This program will enable UNESCO to proclaim biennially several masterpieces of oral and intangible cultural heritage. An international jury, composed of nine members, will select and recommend to the Director-General a list of candidates to be submitted for this award. This project was initially proposed as one means to fill a gap in the World Heritage List, which does not apply to the intangible cultural heritage. The proposal, submitted by the Director-General to two 1998 sessions of UNESCO's

Executive Board, generated a lively discussion, in which it was decided to extend the scope of the project, henceforth called "Proclamation of Masterpieces of Oral and Intangible Cultural Heritage of Humanity."[22]

It is interesting to observe that throughout these numerous debates, wishes were expressed to broaden the concept of intangible heritage, which was already a vast area in the 1989 *Recommendation*. Discussions also placed emphasis on the important role of possessors of knowledge, techniques, and artistry of intangible heritage, as well as on the indispensable role of the local community. More specifically, Member States stressed intangible heritage as a means of affirming cultural identity and its contemporary socio-cultural role in communities. The Director-General of UNESCO was also requested to study means of disseminating, preserving, and protecting intangible heritage for the benefit of its communities of origin.[23]

Amongst its efforts to promote the 1989 *Recommendation*, UNESCO has undertaken various activities in addition to the three major projects already described. In the field of *identification of folklore*, a handbook for collecting musical heritage[24] was published, and a handbook for collecting know-how of traditional architecture is now under preparation. *A Guide for the Preparation of Primary School African Music Teaching Manuals* was also published.[25]

Regarding *conservation*, a network of folklore archives of Balkan countries was created by UNESCO in Sofia in 1995. With respect to *preservation*, UNESCO organized an intergovernmental conference on "African language policies."[26] It also helped the governments of Vietnam and the Lao People's Democratic Republic draft plans for safeguarding, revitalizing, and disseminating intangible heritage of minority and Indigenous groups.[27] Two books on the intangible heritage of Indigenous peoples of these respective countries will be published soon.

For the *dissemination of folklore*, UNESCO has supported a number of festivals including the Market of African Performing Arts (MASA) (Abidjan, Côte d'Ivoire, 1997, 1999), the Fez Sacred Music Festival (Morocco, 1996, 1997), and the Samarkand Eastern Music Festival (Samarkand, Uzbekistan, 1997, 1999). The Organization published an *Atlas of the World's Languages in Danger of Disappearing*[28] in English, French, and Spanish. It continued its long-standing collaboration with the International Council for Traditional Music (ICTM) and the International Music Council (IMC) in producing the prestigious UNESCO *Collection of Traditional Music of the World*. Initially launched in 1960, this collection is the oldest of its kind and has grown to over one hundred titles. UNESCO is proud to have played a significant role in enabling the world's peoples to discover one another's music.

In the *protection of folklore*, UNESCO assisted the Strá nice Institute with the preparation and publication of *Principles of Traditional Culture and Folklore Protection Against Inappropriate Commercialization*[29] and *Ethics and Traditional Folk Culture*.[30] UNESCO and WIPO organized a World Forum on the protection of Folklore in Phuket in 1997.[31] As a follow-up to this Forum, the two organizations held four regional seminars about legal measures that might be recommended regarding traditional knowledge and artistic expressions: for Africa (Pretoria, March 1999),[32] for the Asia-Pacific region (Hanoi, April 1999),[33] for the Arab States (Tunis, May 1999),[34] and for Latin America and the Caribbean (Quito, June 1999).[35] All of these meetings reached the conclusion that intellectual property law does not give appropriate protection to expressions of folklore or traditional knowledge, and a *sui generis* regime specific to this purpose needs to be developed.

Finally, in the furthering of *international cooperation*, UNESCO's priorities have been networking and training. Efforts have been made to create a network of traditional-music institutions for Africa and for Arab countries. As mentioned earlier, a network of folklore institutions in Europe has been developed, based on the European Centre for Traditional Culture (ECTC) in Budapest. A network of bamboo-work specialists is being created in cooperation with the International Network of Bamboo and Rattan (INBAR). In training, several regional courses have been organized in the field of traditional music and handicraft.

During the last decade the 1989 *Recommendation* has served as a principal reference document for all of the aforesaid activities. The time has come today to reflect upon the *Recommendation* as an instrument of policy in contemporary and future contexts for both UNESCO and its Member States.

Notes

1. This volume, 42–56.
2. Marc Denhez, Pre-evaluation of the 1989 UNESCO *Recommendation* on the Safeguarding of Traditional Culture and Folklore, 1997.
3. 26 C/5 Approved.
4. Protection of the Intangible Cultural Heritage: Survey and New Prospects. Serge Gruzinski. UNESCO document CLT/ACL/IH-18.3.93.
5. UNESCO Final Report: International Consultation on New Perspectives for UNESCO Programme: The Intangible Cultural Heritage, June 1993.
6. 28 C/4 Approved.
7. 142 Ex/Decisions, 10 December 1993.
8. Guidelines: "Living Human Treasures" System.
9. 28 C/5 Approved.
10. Regional seminar on the application of the UNESCO *Recommendation on the Safeguarding of Traditional Culture and Folklore* in Central European countries. Strá nice, 19–23 June 1995.
11. Regional seminar on the application of the UNESCO *Recommendation on the Safeguarding of Traditional Culture and Folklore* of Latin America and the Caribbean, Mexico, 22–24 September 1997.
12. Preservation and promotion of the intangible cultural heritage, Tokyo, 24 Feb.–2 March 1998.
13. Regional seminar on the application of the UNESCO *Recommendation on the Safeguarding of Traditional Culture and Folklore* in Western European countries, Joensuu, 4–6 September 1998.
14. Regional seminar on the application of the UNESCO *Recommendation on the Safeguarding of Traditional Culture and Folklore* in the countries of Central Asia and the Caucasus, Tashkent, 6–8 October 1998.
15. Regional seminar on the application of the UNESCO *Recommendation on the Safeguarding of Traditional Culture and Folklore* in African countries, Accra, 26–28 January 1999.
16. Regional seminar on the application of the UNESCO *Recommendation on the Safeguarding of Traditional Culture and Folklore* in the countries of the Pacific, Noumea, 11–12 February 1999.
17. Regional seminar on the application of the UNESCO *Recommendation on the Safeguarding of Traditional Culture and Folklore* in the Arab States, Beirut, 10–12 May 1999.
18. Preliminary proposals concerning the Draft Programme and Budget for 1998–99 (29 C/5) — (150 Ex/5, Part I and Add. and Parts II and III and 150 Ex/INF. 7, 150 Ex/INF.8 and 150 Ex/INF.9, para. 49).
19. 29 C/6 Recommendations by the Executive Board on the Draft Programme and Budget for 1998–99, Paris, 1997.
20. General Conference, 29th Session, Reply by the ADG/CLT to Commission IV-Debate I.
21. Records of the General Conference, Paris, 21 October–12 November 1997, Vol. I Resolutions, No. 23.
22. 154 Ex/13, 19 March 1998, 155 Ex/15, 25 August 1998, 155 Ex/15 Add. & Corr. 155 Ex/Decisions.
23. "Further invites the Director-General to study means of disseminating, preserving and protecting these immaterial or intangible cultural spaces for the benefit of the communities of origin," para. 12, 3.5.1, 154 EX/Decisions.
24. Geneviève Dournon, *Guide pour la collecte des musiques et instruments traditionnels* (Paris: UNESCO, 1981).

25. J.H. Kwabena Nketia, ed., *A Guide for the Preparation of Primary School African Music Teaching Manuals* (Ghana: Afram Publications Limited, 1999).

26. Intergovernmental Conference on Language Policies in Africa, Harare, 17–21 March 1997.

27. International expert meeting for the safeguarding and promotion of the intangible cultural heritage of minority groups in Vietnam, Hanoi, 15–18 March 1994; International expert meeting for the safeguarding and promotion of the intangible cultural heritage of the minority groups of the Lao People's Democratic Republic, Vientiane, 7–11 October 1996.

28. Stephen A. Wurm, *Atlas of the World's Languages in Danger of Disappearing* (Paris: UNESCO Press, 1996).

29. *Principles of Traditional Culture and Folklore Protection Against Inappropriate Commercialization* (Strá nice: Institute of Folk Culture, 1997).

30. *Ethics and Traditional Folk Culture: Study on Moral Consciousness and Conduct in Manifestations of Traditional Folk Culture* (Strá nice: Ustave Lidové Kultury, 1999).

31. *UNESCO-WIPO World Forum on the Protection of Folklore*, Phuket, Thailand, April 8–10, 1997 (Paris/Canberra: Pacific Linguistics, 1996).

32. UNESCO-WIPO African Regional Consultation on the Protection of Expressions of Folklore, Pretoria, 23–25 March 1999.

33. UNESCO-WIPO Regional Consultation on the Protection of Expressions of Folklore for Countries of Asia and the Pacific, Hanoi, 21–23 April 1999.

34. UNESCO-WIPO Regional Consultation on the Protection of Expressions of Folklore for Arab Countries, Tunis, 25–27 May 1999.

35. UNESCO-WIPO Regional Consultation on the Protection of Expressions of Folklore for Latin America and the Caribbean, Quito, 14–16 June 1999.

The UNESCO Questionnaire on the Application of the 1989 *Recommendation on the Safeguarding of Traditional Culture and Folklore*: Preliminary Results

Richard Kurin
Director
Center for Folklife and Cultural Heritage, Smithsonian Institution
Washington, D.C.

Introduction

The *Recommendation on the Safeguarding of Traditional Culture and Folklore* was adopted by the General Conference of UNESCO at its twenty-fifth session on November 15, 1989, in Paris. It is the only existing international standard instrument specifically directed to traditional and popular culture. The *Recommendation* grew out of a series of seminars and meetings following the request of the Government of Bolivia in April 1973 that a protocol be added to the Universal Copyright Convention, one that would protect the popular arts and cultural patrimony of all nations. After sixteen years of analysis conducted through a series of expert meetings, the 1989 UNESCO General Conference finally adopted the *Recommendation*. Unlike a convention or declaration, a recommendation is a flexible instrument — a statement of principles — which may be applied by governments though legal and other measures.

The 1989 *Recommendation* defined "folklore, or traditional and popular culture" as "the totality of tradition-based creations of a cultural community, expressed by a group or individuals and recognized as reflecting the expectations of a community in so far as they reflect its cultural and social identity; its standards and values are transmitted orally, by imitation or by other means. Its forms are, among others, language, literature, music, dance, games, mythology, rituals, customs, handicrafts, architecture and other arts." The *Recommendation* elaborated a number of goals for policies and practices concerned with the safeguarding of traditional culture and folklore. Following the adoption of a recommendation, UNESCO Member States are supposed to submit a report to the Secretariat indicating the actions taken toward its realization. The UNESCO Director-General issued a letter in 1990 requesting such a report. Only six nations responded. In 1994, UNESCO issued a "Questionnaire on the Application of the *Recommendation*"(see the Appendix to this article for the English version) to Member States in order to ascertain the impact of the *Recommendation* and gather information about the policies and practices in those nations. This report offers a summary of the responses to that questionnaire.

Responses to the questionnaires also formed, in part, the basis of UNESCO-sponsored regional seminars on the topic. Those discussions offered a rich, interpretive view of the circumstances and issues of policies and practices regarding traditional and popular culture. Results of those discussions are included in final reports approved by regional seminars and submitted to UNESCO. (See Section III in this volume.)

Respondents

The questionnaire was sent to National Commissions for UNESCO of Member States. Usable responses were received from 103 nations. Other nations participated in the various regional seminars and in some cases produced narrative reports that, while on the topic of the questionnaire, did not follow its structure and, thus, did not constitute a specific, technical response. Nations responding to the questionnaire with a formally filed response included:

Andorra, Argentina, Armenia, Australia, Austria, Azerbaijan, Bangladesh, Belarus, Bhutan, Bolivia, Brazil, Bulgaria, Burkina Faso, Burundi, Cambodia, Cameroon, Central African Rep., Chile, China, Congo (Kinshasa), Cook Islands, Costa Rica, Croatia, Cuba, Czech Republic, Denmark, Ecuador, El Salvador, Eritrea, Estonia, Fiji, Finland, Gambia, Georgia, Germany, Ghana, Greece, Guinea, Hungary, Iceland, Indonesia, Iran, Israel, Japan, Kazakhstan, Kenya, Kiribati, Korea (South), Kyrgyzstan, Laos, Latvia, Lesotho, Lithuania, Madagascar, Malaysia, Maldives, Mali, Mauritius, Mexico, Moldova, Monaco, Mongolia, Nauru, Nepal, New Zealand, Niger, Nigeria, Niue, Norway, Pakistan, Panama, Papau New Guinea, Paraguay, Peru, Philippines, Poland, Portugal, Romania, Russia, Rwanda, Samoa, Seychelles, Slovenia, Spain, Sri Lanka, Swaziland, Sweden, Switzerland, Tajikistan, Tanzania, Thailand, Togo, Tonga, Turkmenistan, Uganda, Ukraine, Uruguay, Uzbekistan, Vanuatu, Venezuela, Vietnam, Zambia, Zimbawe

Where it could be determined, almost two-thirds of respondents were members of National Commissions for UNESCO. Others were officials with government ministries of education or culture, or with folklore/cultural institutions.

By and large, respondents were knowledgeable and informed about the situation of folklore in their nations. But in several cases, respondents indicated that they were not so well-informed. In fact, some respondents reported inaccuracies that were obvious to the author. For example, one respondent reported there were no trained folklorists or archivists in a nation that had many such persons. Yet, to be consistent, the respondent's answers were recorded as given. Other responses gave clear evidence of consultation with specialists or members of folklore organizations. Indeed, many of the questionnaires were filled out by specialists, then forwarded to a UNESCO National commission for submission to UNESCO headquarters in Paris. The degree of elaboration in filing the questionnaires varied greatly — some included long and detailed explanations, while others were more perfunctory. Ten nations submitted a first report and then a revised one, in four cases several years later. For another nation, two reports came in, one from the CIOFF representative, another from the UNESCO National Commission. While almost all the national submissions followed the questionnaire, two nations submitted responses only loosely related to it, presenting a challenge to analytic coding. Responses were received in several languages: English (72), Spanish (14), French (15), Russian (1 and updated in English), and Portuguese (1, and another in Portuguese with English translation).

Though not standardized by reporting year, the responses are roughly synchronic, filed over several years, from 1995 to 1999. This is fairly standard in large global efforts, especially in a survey that is the first of its kind.

The Questionnaire

The questionnaire is subdivided into sections including: a) Introduction, b) Application of the *Recommendation* As a Whole, and c) Application of the Principal Provisions of the *Recommendation*. The latter is further subdivided into subsections on Identification of Folklore, Conservation of Folklore, Preservation of Folklore, Dissemination of Folklore, Protection of Folklore, and International Cooperation. This is followed by a final section on the Eventual Improvement of the *Recommendation*. Introductions to each substantive section review the UNESCO *Recommendation* and provide a description of the subject activity, e.g., "preservation," "conservation," "dissemination." Overall, the questionnaires provide a substantial wealth of information on how different nations deal with folklore and traditional culture at the level of institutional practice and policy formulation at the end of the twentieth century.

The questionnaire itself is complicated, with a combination of closed- and open-ended questions. In some cases, single questions actually embed more than one query, making answers ambiguous (e.g., "Does this policy reflect the ongoing transformations in your country and region, and if so, in what way?" If the transformations are underway regionally but not nationally, is the answer yes or no?). The questionnaire assumes, and indeed in prefatory sections promulgates, a commonality of terminology (e.g., "conservation," "preservation," "transmission"). This terminology is used in a technical way, but is also highly subject to individual interpretation given the varied, everyday uses of those terms. Even in a technical sense, some terms, e.g., "folklore" and "traditional popular culture," taken to be synonymous by some, are thought to refer to quite different phenomena by others. For example, one African respondent noted that "oral tradition" is taken to be a broader, more appropriate term in his nation. A European respondent noted that "folklore" in his country was not "popular traditional culture," while in Latin America, it was. With some terminology, there are repeated misunderstandings (e.g., "regional" sometimes refers to a subnational region, other times to a supranational region). These problems may be exacerbated by translation.

Various regional adaptations were made to the standard questionnaire. African respondents elaborated upon the section of the questionnaire dealing with conservation, adding several subquestions on various types of archives. Eastern European respondents added a question on the effect of current events on cultural rights.

Though the questionnaire itself imposed a standardized response, it allowed ample room for explanation and commentary. Responses differed considerably in the degree to which all closed-ended questions were completed. Some respondents left long sections of the questionnaire blank. Others wrote paragraph after paragraph of lengthy description and explanation. Instructions could have been clearer as to expectations. Objective definitions meant to guide respondents were somewhat ambiguous.

The questions and answers varied in their domain of reference. Questions tended to refer to the nation as a unitary whole, yet many answers seemed very particularistic — oriented to the specific organization or agency responding. Again, the questionnaire lacked clarity here.

Descriptive Statistical Analysis

Responses from the questionnaires were examined and coded. Several questions of a difficult, ambiguous nature and embedded questions are not included. The more discursive responses were coded in terms of specified content analyses.

Responses from the questionnaires are renumbered below for clarity in discussion. The original number in the UNESCO questionnaire is given in brackets. The results are based upon 103 submitted responses to the questionnaire. The data includes non-responses. In most cases, a non-response to a question usually indicates a negative response more strongly than an affirmative one (unless the question is asked as a negative). The grouping of responses to questions displayed below tries to reflect this pattern to allow easy discernment of combined results.

Application of the Recommendation *As a Whole*

1. [B.3.a.]   Are the bodies, organizations, and institutions concerned in your country aware of the *Recommendation*?

    58%   Yes (60)
    33%   No (34)
    9%   No response (9)

2. [B.3.b.]   Has the *Recommendation* been published in the official language of your country?

    43%   Yes (44)
    50%   No (52)
    7%   No response (7)

3. [B.3.c.]   Has your country submitted a report to UNESCO?

    13%   Yes (13)
    69%   No (71)
    18%   No response (19)

Application of the Principal Provisions of the Recommendation

4. [C.4.a.1] How are matters of traditional culture/folklore handled in your country?, e.g., as part of national cultural policy? as a subject of separate policy?

    55%   National only (57)
    17%   National and separate or institutional (18)
    12%   Separate or institutional only (12)
    3%   No policy (3)
    13%   No response (13)

5. [C.4.a.2] In both cases, indicate priorities of this policy. Percent of respondents naming each element (given multiple item responses)

    49%   Safeguarding (50)
    49%   Dissemination (50)
    38%   Transmission (39)
    34%   Revitalization (35)

        32%   Protection (33)
        26%   Research (27)
        22%   Preservation (23)
        17%   Normative Action (17)
        8%   Conservation (8)
        2%   International Cooperation (2)

6. [C.4.b.1] Does this policy reflect the ongoing transformations in your country and region, and if so, in what way?

        67%   Yes (69)
        16%   No (16)
        2%   Yes and No (2)
        6%   No response (16)

7. [C.4.b.2] What transformations are affecting policy? Percent of respondents naming each element (given multiple item responses)
        39%   Taking new realities into account (40)
        24%   Elaboration of further legal measures (25)
        17%   Elaboration of a new policy (18)
        11%   Preparatory measures (11)
        8%   Other (8)

8. [C.4.c.] What measures, in your opinion, are needed to elaborate a new policy or prepare a new one concerning traditional culture and folklore? [indicate level] Percent of respondents naming each element (given multiple item responses)

        77%   National level (79)
        66%   UNESCO cooperation (68)
        47%   Regional level (49)
        37%   NGO cooperation (38)

Identification of Folklore

9. [C.5.a.] Are there lists and inventories of folklore institutions in your country?

        68%   Yes (70)
        28%   No (29)
        4%   No response (4)

10. [C.5.a.2] Are they regionally standardized?

        12%   Yes (12)
        61%   No (63)
        27%   No response (28)

11. [C.5.a.3] Are they computerized?
        21%   Yes (22)
        58%   No (60)
        20%   No response (21)

12. [C.5.b.] Does your country have databanks of institutions dealing with the intangible cultural heritage?

    30%   Yes (31)
    61%   No (63)
    9%   No response (9)

13. [C.5.c.] Are classification systems used by your institutions coordinated (a) nationally and (b) regionally?

    43%   Yes (44 — 16 national, 1 both, 27 unspecified)
    49%   No (50)
    9%   No response (9)

14. [C.5.d.] Is your country encouraging the creation of a standard typology of folklore? (a) nationally and (b) regionally?

    58%   Yes (60 — 33 national, 1 regional, 14 both, 12 unspecified)
    35%   No (36)
    1%   Not desirable to do so (1)
    6%   No response (6)

Conservation of Folklore

15. [C.6.a.] Please describe the existing infrastructure for the conservation of folklore. Does it meet your country's needs?

    30%   Yes (31)
    53%   No (55)
    17%   No response (17)

The pattern of responses for the description of infrastructure was so spotty and inconsistent as to preclude useful analysis.

16. [C.6.a.2] If not adequate, indicate the required measures (for improvement). Percent of respondents suggesting a category of measure (given multiple item responses)

    22%   Improvement of institutions (23)
    18%   Development of regional/local organizations (19)
    11%   Coordination of activities (11)

17. [C.6.b.] Are these organizations coordinated by a central body?

    31%   Yes (32)
    44%   No (45)
    25%   No response (26)

18. [C.6.c.] Are collecting and archiving methods harmonized in your country?

    22%   Yes (23)
    64%   No (65)
    15%   No response (15)

19. [C.6.d.] What system of training professional collectors, archivists, documentalists, and other folklore conservation specialists exists in your country?

    48%   Some system (49)

With components indicated as a percent of all respondents (given combination responses)

31% On the job/non-school training (32)
24% Undergraduate courses (25)
11% Graduate courses/degree (11)
 8% Outside-the-country training (8)
27% No system (28)
25% No response (26)

20. [C.6.d.2]   Is [this system] adequate to your country's needs?

18% Yes (19)
46% No (47)
36% No response (37)

21. [C.6.d.3] If not [adequate], indicate the measures taken to improve it. With components indicated as a percent of all respondents (given combination responses)

14% Improvement of institutions (14)
13% Improvement of training opportunities (13)

22. [C.6.e.] Does a system of training voluntary (non-professional) collectors and archivists exist in your country?

20% Yes (21)
71% No (73)
 9% No response (9)

23. [C.6.f.] To what extent do the people concerned have access to the materials conserved?

61% Accessible (63 — 12 unqualified, 51 restriction/condition mentioned)
 4% No accessibility (4)
35% No response (36)

Preservation of Folklore

24. [C.7.a.] Does your country run courses on folklore in school or out-of-school curricula? Describe the courses.

52% Yes (54)

With types indicated as a percent of all respondents (given combination responses)

19% Primary school (20)
33% Secondary school (34)
30% College (31)
26% Extracurricular/specialized training (27)
48% No response (49)

25. [C.7.b.] Does the national legislation of your country ensure the right of access for the communities concerned with their own culture?

> 80%   Yes (82)
> 11%   No (11)
> 10%   No response (10)

26. [C.7.c.] Is there a National Folklore Council or similar coordinating body for the preservation of folklore in your country?

> 40%   Yes (41)
> 54%   No (56)
>   6%   No response (6)

27. [C.7.d.] What kind of moral and economic support is provided in your country to the individuals and institutions promoting folklore? With types indicated as a percent of all respondents (given combination responses)

> 78%   State support/subventions (80)
> 51%   Mass media (53)
> 43%   Private funding (44)
> 37%   Legislative measures (38)
> 17%   Other means (18)

28. [C.7.e.] Has research work contributed to the preservation of folklore in your country? If yes, indicate the type of improvement.

> 80%   Yes (82)

With types indicated as a percent of all respondents (given combination responses)

> 46%   Research documentation itself (47)
> 39%   Dissemination of information (40)
> 18%   Awareness generated (19)
> 13%   Integration into society (13)
> 14%   No (14)
>   7%   No response (7)

Dissemination of Folklore

29. [C.8.a.] Describe major folklore events held in your country after 1989 (fairs, festivals, films, exhibitions, seminars, training courses, etc.).

> 87%   Some response (89)

With types indicated as a percent of all respondents (given combination responses)

> 80%   Festival or fair (82)
> 44%   Seminar, conference, workshop (45)
> 43%   Exhibition (44)
> 22%   Other, e.g., film/television series (23)
> 13%   No response (13)

30. [C.8.b.] Is there any infrastructure to promote broader coverage of folklore material in mass media?

40%   Yes (41)
52%   No (54)
 8%   No response (8)

31. [C.8.c.] Is there an extended coordinated system for the dissemination of folklore in your country?

33%   Yes (34)
59%   No (61)
 8%   No response (8)

32. [C.8.d.] What are the education materials available in your country to disseminate traditional and popular culture?

68%   Extant materials (70)

With types indicated as a percent of all respondents (given combination responses)

47%   Publications, textbooks, booklets (48)
33%   Videos, films (34)
18%   Cassettes, CDs, recordings (19)
17%   Other materials (incl. Web) (18)
32%   No response (33)

33. [C.8.e.] What are the institutions which are able to disseminate information on folklore?

83%   Institutions disseminating information (86)

With types indicated as a percent of all respondents (given combination responses)

66%   Cultural, educational organizations (68)
35%   Governmental organizations (36)
32%   Media organizations (33)
30%   Associations, NGOs, others (31)
17%   No response (17)

34. [C.8.g.] Is there any body which is in a position to check whether a proper approach is applied for the dissemination of traditional and popular cultural expression?

35%   Yes (36)
38%   No (39)
28%   No response (29)

Protection of Folklore

35. [C.9.a.] Does the national legislation of your country contain provisions on the "intellectual property aspects" of traditional culture and folklore?

50%   Yes (52)
31%   No (32)
18%   No response (19)

36. [C.9.b.] What kind of support do folklore artists in your country enjoy (e.g., economic, social, and legal status)?

> 61%   Support for artists (63)

> With types indicated as a percent of all respondents (given combination responses)

>> 27%   State support (unspecified/fiscal/in-kind) (28)
>> 14%   State honor or status (14)
>> 5%   State job (5)
>> 10%   No such support (10)
>> 29%   No response (30)

37. [C.9.e.] What measures, in your opinion, are needed to enhance the legal protection of traditional culture and folklore or to adapt to new circumstances?

> 63%   Specific measures suggested (65)

> With types indicated as a percent of all respondents (given combination responses)

>> 35%   National laws or legislation (36)
>> 17%   Advice from UNESCO et al. (18)
>> 14%   National plans or policies (14)
>> 13%   Consciousness-raising (13)
>> 10%   Enforcement of laws (10)
>> 3%   International convention (3)
>> 37%   No specific measures suggested (38)

International Co-Operation

38. [C.10.a.] Can you provide information on bi/multilateral projects and actions carried out in the field of traditional and popular culture by your country?

>> 48%   Yes (49)
>> 14%   No (14)
>> 39%   No response (40)

39. [C.10.b.] What kind of activities in the field of folklore has your country implemented in cooperation with UNESCO and other international or regional organizations since 1989?

> 65%   Any activity (67)

> With types indicated as a percent of all respondents (given combination responses)

>> 25%   Cooperation with UNESCO (26)
>> 9%   Cooperation with CIOFF (9)
>> 10%   No activity (10)
>> 25%   No response (26)

40. [C.10.c.] In what concrete fields and activities of traditional culture does your country cooperate with other countries of your region (e.g., research, festivals)?

65%   Any cooperation (67)

With types indicated as a percent of all respondents (given combination responses)

54%   Festivals, performances, craft programs (56)
22%   Research and publication (23)
20%   Seminars, experts, training (21)
35%   No response (36)

Interpretations

Given the responses to questions about the application of the *Recommendation* as a whole, it would not appear that the *Recommendation* is high on the agenda of the international community. Only a small majority of responding nations were aware of the *Recommendation*. It might be assumed that many more unresponsive nations are unaware of the *Recommendation*. Even of those who were aware of it, only a minority of respondents had published the *Recommendation* in their own language. Only a handful submitted a report to UNESCO.

One of the reasons for a lack of awareness may be the lack of articulation between the *Recommendation* and other human rights and cultural accords. A quick perusal of other UNESCO documents and reports of various international conferences dedicated to cultural issues reveals few references to the *Recommendation on the Safeguarding of Traditional Culture and Folklore*. Better dissemination of the *Recommendation* and coordination of its findings with other international instruments may rectify the problem.

In examining the application of the principal provisions of the *Recommendation*, correlations in the pattern of responses were investigated. Nations were grouped in continental clusters to determine whether there was a tendency for some nations to see cultural policy as a part of larger national policy or separate from it. There was no such pattern.

Other patterns in the responses to the questionnaire can be sought by using two competing hypotheses suggested by social science literature. The first of these, here called "the modernization hypothesis," would predict that more modernized nations have less folklore and traditional culture. Folklore and traditional culture, associated with a pre-modern era, would exist on the margins of society, in unmodernized, isolated pockets of the society. This form of culture would be devalued and discarded. Its knowledge would be replaced by a formal education system, its means of social communication replaced by the mass media. In such societies, folklore and traditional culture would not be seen as valuable; there would be little in the way of societal protections and no or few policies for their enhancement. By way of contrast, folklore and traditional culture would be stronger in less modernized nations. This form of culture would be more central than marginal, a force in people's lives, a fact of everyday existence. It would be recognized in custom and law, valued, and protected. Thus, according to this hypothesis, more modernized nations would indicate less elaboration in institutions, laws, training, programs, and public awareness of traditional culture and folklore in their questionnaire responses, while less modernized nations would be much more positive.

The competing hypothesis, called here "the post-modern," would reverse this expectation. Less modernized nations would have a "take-it-for-granted" view of traditional culture and folklore, finding this form of culture an aspect of continuing and daily experience not requiring much elaboration, government attention, or activity. Folklore, as the culture of the people, would not be threatened nor would it require governments or scholars to somehow discover, interpret, or protect it. More modernized nations, on the other hand, would see the need to elaborate, invent, mythologize, and construct their folklore as part of a modern, nationalizing project. Traditional culture and folklore would be seen as an essentializing ideology for articulating a national identity and mobilizing a national (or sub- or supranational) consciousness. Folklore would have to be recovered, studied, interpreted, institutionalized, and then disseminated back to the general population by government and educational organizations. In this view, more modernized nations would have more positive responses to questionnaire items indicating greater investment in and elaboration of formal institutions, training programs, legislative remedies, and the like.

In order to test correlations in national policies, circumstances, and strategies in terms of these competing hypotheses, nations were clustered according to a modernization index constructed by the researcher from data available in the *United Nations World Statistics Pocketbook*, published by the Department of Economic and Social Affairs in 1998, and based upon statistics available as of August 1997. The index was constructed from the following often-used variables:

Tourist arrivals as a percent of the population ($r = .65$)
Gross domestic product per capita ($r = .81$)
Motor vehicles per 1,000 inhabitants ($r = .91$)
Telephone lines per 100 inhabitants ($r = .95$)
Urban population percentage ($r = .77$)
Foreign-born percentage of the population ($r = .52$)
Tertiary-level female students per 100,000 inhabitants ($r = .80$)
Newspaper circulation per 1,000 inhabitants ($r = .73$)
Television receivers per 1,000 inhabitants ($r = .87$)
Energy consumption per capita in kilograms coal equivalent ($r = .88$)

Operationally, greater modernization was indicated by more tourist arrivals, larger per capita domestic product, more motor vehicles, more telephones, a higher percentage of urban population, more foreign-born inhabitants, more females in tertiary education, more newspapers and televisions, and a high per capita energy consumption. These attributes of the selected variables could indicate a more highly industrial and post-industrial society, composed of large percentages of city residents and large influxes of newer residents, educating its population in non-traditional ways, influenced by mass media, and communicating in ways not dependent upon oral, face-to-face transmission. That is, taken at face value, these attributes could indicate a conventional description of modernization. Lower measures would indicate the attributes of less modernization — more rural, more native born, fewer females in tertiary education, lower energy consumption, lower GDP, fewer telephones, motor vehicles, and newspapers.

The variables were statistically standardized and equally weighted, so as to allow the adding of scores to form an index. All the variables registered moderate to very strong correlations with the overall index as indicated by the coefficients given in the list above ($r = .95$ for telephones, the strongest correlate of a high modernization index, to $r = .52$ for the presence of foreign-born inhabitants). The scores of each of 102 nations were then computed (and adjusted in cases where a statistic was unavailable). The mean score was 20, the highest 127, the lowest 1. The 39 nations above the mean were assigned the category "more modernized," the 63 nations scoring below the mean were categorized as "less modernized."

Modernization scores were then correlated to answers on the questionnaire to ascertain patterns. Few emerged. There were only slight correlations between modernization and policy priorities. For example, there was a slight tendency (gamma = +.36) for less modernized nations to name "protection" of traditional culture and folklore as a priority. There was very slight (gamma = +.10) tendency for the same nations to favor "revitalization." These low correlations belie any real significance.

As might be expected, there was a tendency for the more modernized nations to computerize their folklore databanks, but not overwhelmingly so. Nations were asked to describe the adequacy of their existing infrastructure for conserving folklore. Overall, most nations reported that the infrastructure was inadequate. There was only a very slight (gamma = +.20) correlation of more modernized nations with the reportage of adequacy in conserving folklore. The same weak pattern held for training. Overall, the great majority of nations thought training opportunities inadequate to the need. Modernization scores weakly correlated (gamma = +.35) to perceived adequacy of training opportunities in-country, with more modern nations more likely to indicate adequacy than others. With regard to legislative protection for the intellectual property aspects of traditional culture, the correlation was also very weak, but ran the other way. There was a slightly greater chance (gamma = +.17) that less modernized nations had placed protective provisions into law. Indeed, the same pattern existed with regard to the support of folk artists by the government, with a somewhat greater chance (gamma = +.26) that folk artists received government support for their work in less modernized nations.

Generally, there was no significant pattern of response that varied with the measure of modernization. And no responses had high correlations with any single measure of modernization — above the +.80 generally used as evidence of relationships among variables. Thus, there is no simple pattern of variability explaining the responses. This might be due to the difficulty of operationalizing a definition of high and low modernization. For example, it could be argued that the very same attributes indicative of modernization could also advance traditional culture. Tourists could be attracted by the continued existence of traditional cultures, communities, marketplaces, and performances. Television programs and newspapers could heighten public consciousness of folklore. Tertiary education could include emphasis on traditional and folk sciences. Telephones could enhance, not detract from, oral culture. Folk culture might thrive in city neighborhoods and the occupational traditions of an industrial work force.

Conclusion

There is no basis offered by the results of the UNESCO survey for accepting either the modern or post-modern hypothesis about the relationship between society and national policy with regard to traditional culture and folklore. In fact, simple statistical analysis of the responses indicates a vast under-institutionalization and under-elaboration of the field. That a correlational analysis reveals only weak associations suggests that the formation of national policy is quite open to broad and varied action, not determined by GDP or usual measures of socio-economic development. While better measures of national policy goals and activities can be designed for a future survey, and while more elaborate types of correlation analyses can be applied with newly collected UNESCO data, the result of this survey is cause for optimism. There is a perceived need for much to do in the traditional culture and folklore field. There is a basis for moving ahead with national and international policies. And, perhaps most importantly, there is a wide range of possibilities for effective action, so that the policy options available to some nations are available to most, if not all. National policies are not pre-determined, nor does "one size fit all." Nations can decide on a particular constellation of policies — presumably within the ethical and conceptual framework of the United Nations Declaration of Human Rights, the 1989 *Recommendation*, and other international accords — that meet the needs of their citizens and fit the circumstances of their societies.

Appendix

Excerpt from the UNESCO Questionnaire on the Application of the
Recommendation on the Safeguarding of Traditional Culture and Folklore

B. Application of the *Recommendation* As a Whole
3. In the preamble to the *Recommendation*, the major guiding principles for its application are defined as follows:

"The General Conference recommends that Member States should apply the following provisions concerning the safeguarding of folklore by taking whatever legislative measures or other steps may be required in conformity with the constitutional practice of each State to give effect within their territories to the principles and measures defined in this *Recommendation*.

"The General Conference recommends that Member States bring this *Recommendation* to the attention of the authorities, departments or bodies responsible for matters relating to the safeguarding of folklore and to the attention of the various organizations or institutions concerned with folklore and encourage their contacts with appropriate international organizations dealing with the safeguarding of folklore.

"The General Conference recommends that Member States should, at such times and such manner as it shall determine, submit to the Organization reports on the action they have taken to give effect to this *Recommendation*."

a. Are the bodies, organizations and institutions concerned in your country aware of the *Recommendation*?
[ ] Yes [ ] No

If yes, indicate their names and how and when they were informed:

b. Has the *Recommendation* been published in the offical language of your country?
[ ] Yes [ ] No

Replying to the UNESCO Secretariat's circular letter of 1990 on the application of the Recommendation, seven (7) Member States only sent in their respective reports. They contain information mainly on how the Recommendation has been made public and brought to the attention of the authorities and bodies directly concerned. Some reports stress that the national legislation applied in their country adequately reflects the provisions of the Recommendation and state that there is no need for additional modifications.

c. Has your country submitted a report to UNESCO?
[ ] Yes [ ] No

If no, give reasons:

C. Application of the Principal Provisions of the *Recommendation*
4a. How are matters of traditional culture/folklore handled in your country?, e.g., as part of national cultural policy? as a subject of separate policy?
In both cases, indicate priorites of this policy.
b. Does this policy reflect the ongoing transformations in your country and region, and if so, in what way?

c. What measures, in your opinion, are needed to elaborate a new policy or prepare a new one concerning traditional culture and folklore?

> at the national level
> at the regional level
> in cooperation with UNESCO
> in cooperation with specialized NGOs

D. Identification of Folklore

5a. Are there lists and inventories of folklore institutions in your country?

If yes, are they regionally standardized?

Are they computerized?

b. Does your country have databanks of institutions dealing with the intangible cultural heritage? If yes, indicate lists of menus covered by databanks.

c. Are classification systems used by your Institutions co-ordinated (a) nationally and (b) regionally?

d. Is your country encouraging the creation of a standard typology of folklore?

If yes, at what level?

Summary Report on the Regional Seminars

Anthony Seeger
Smithsonian Institution

Introduction

Prior to the Global Conference in Washington D.C., UNESCO convened eight regional seminars to discuss the 1989 *Recommendation on the Safeguarding of Traditional Culture and Folklore*. They met over a period of four years: in June 1995 in Strá nice (Czech Republic) for Central and Eastern European countries; in September 1997 in Mexico City (Mexico) for Latin America and the Caribbean; in February/March 1998 in Tokyo (Japan) for Asian countries; in September 1998 in Joensuu (Finland) for Western European countries; in October 1998 in Tashkent (Republic of Uzbekistan) for Central Asia and the Caucasus; in January 1999 in Accra (Ghana) for the African region; in February 1999 in Noumea (New Caledonia) for the Pacific countries; and in May 1999 in Beirut (Lebanon) for the Arab states. Delegates to the regional seminars were selected by the National Commission for UNESCO of each Member State.

A local official opened each regional seminar. Then a UNESCO representative introduced the history of the 1989 *Recommendation* and outlined the issues to be addressed. A summary of the synoptic reports on the application of the *Recommendation on the Safeguarding of Traditional Culture and Folklore* in the region (the questionnaires filled out by a person appointed by each country's UNESCO National Commission) was presented to begin the discussions. Each country delegate then presented a short report on his or her own country. The specific agenda of issues to be discussed in the plenary meeting varied to some extent in accordance with the region and the interests of the countries in it. In each regional seminar, three working groups were formed to address three issues, which remained constant for most seminars: (1) national policy in the field of intangible heritage, (2) legal protection, and (3) documentation and dissemination. Rapporteurs prepared summaries of the discussions and recommendations of each of the working groups. At the end of each Seminar, the reports and recommendations of each working group were discussed in plenary. A final report and recommendations addressed to governments of Member States and to UNESCO were presented, discussed, amended, and approved by the plenary.

This Summary Report has been prepared from the Final Reports of the eight regional seminars. Their reports revealed that each region has a somewhat different perspective on the issues raised in the *Recommendation*, deriving in part from the history and particularities of the region, the background and interests of the participants, and the dynamics of the seminars themselves. There were clearly some common areas of concern, some regional differences in emphasis, and some common recommendations.

Common Areas of Concern

1. All of the seminars welcomed UNESCO's initiative in holding seminars on the application of the 1989 *Recommendation on the Safeguarding of Traditional Culture and Folklore* in different regions of the world. They called upon UNESCO National Commissions to increase the dissemination and application of the *Recommendation* in their respective countries.

2. All the Final Reports stressed the importance of traditional culture and folklore and expressed the participants' concern about the marginalization of traditional culture and folklore in their countries — using expressions like "fragile," "disappearing," and "neglected" to characterize the state of affairs. Several regions also specifically singled out local languages as being seriously threatened (Africa, Latin America).

3. Implicitly or explicitly, members of every seminar expressed their concern that the younger generation was not being exposed to traditional culture in a way that would enable them to secure its transmission and make use of it in creative ways.

4. Virtually all the regional seminars recognized the evolving nature of traditional culture and folklore and urged that nations also give attention to new and creative use of traditions.

5. Every seminar recommended calling the attention of national cultural policy makers to the importance of traditional culture and folklore for the entire nation, as the basis of cultural identity, a factor for the consolidation of cultural pluralism and sustainable human development, and a source of contemporary creativity.

6. Every seminar, except those in Europe, expressed concern about the lack of training of those working in the areas of traditional culture and folklore and at the lack of opportunities for people working in those fields to obtain adequate training.

7. Every seminar expressed concern at the lack of adequate legal protection for the producers of traditional culture and folklore and for the products of their knowledge, and recommended the development of legal instruments and other means to protect them.

8. Several seminars considered it necessary to control the excessive commercialization of traditional culture and folklore prevalent in some countries (Central and Eastern Europe, Asia, Africa, Arab states).

9. Many seminars expressed concern about tourism, which, most felt, brought both advantages and disadvantages to carriers of traditional culture and folklore and to the intangible heritage as a whole.

10. Several seminars expressed concern over the lack of regional collaboration and the insufficient standardization of databases and training in their regions (Central and Eastern Europe, Central Asia and the Caucasus).

11. Several seminars endorsed the programs "Living Human Treasures" (Asia/Pacific, Latin America) and "The Proclamation of Masterpieces of the Oral and Intangible Heritage of Humanity" (Western Europe), both of which are actively promoted by UNESCO.

Some Regional Variations

Some regional seminars had distinctive perspectives on the issues of traditional culture and folklore that appeared repeatedly in their recommendations. While these may reflect some regional differences, these regional perspectives can add considerably to the understanding of traditional culture and folklore.

1. Members of the Latin America Regional Seminar recognized the importance of multi-culturalism and stressed the significance of hybrid culture — cultures that combined aspects of two or more contributing cultures — a recognition of the effect of their own historical experience on traditional culture and folklore. They also underlined the essential role that folklore creators, actors, bearers, and transmitters play as agents of democratic development and integration.

2. Members of the Pacific States Regional Seminar stressed that intangible, tangible, and natural heritage cannot easily be distinguished by Pacific peoples — because natural and cultural, tangible and intangible are inextricably bound together in their cultures. They underlined the considerable significance of customary law, traditional knowledge as well as its confidentiality, and participation of the people of the community concerned in any action regarding the heritage. They also recommended that the bearers of traditional culture and folklore should be part of discussions and policy-making on the subject.

3. The members of the Asia Regional Seminar stressed the importance of considering traditional "high" (or court) culture in addition to traditional culture and folklore, partly because court cultures are found with a greater frequency in this region than in most others. They deplored the lack of policy documents and appropriate guidelines for documentation as well as for tourism development. They also regretted the lack of trained personnel in general. They expressed their concern over the problem of distortion when traditional cultural expressions are presented at "Folklore Festivals" as attractions.

4. The Central Asia and Caucasus Regional Seminar analyzed extensively the significance of traditional culture and folklore for national identity — reflecting their own recent history. They found traditional culture and folklore to be an extremely important facet of the formation of national identities of newly independent States. They also discussed the necessity to pay attention to the identities of minority ethnic groups often displaced for political reasons. They strongly deplored the weakened infrastructure of research institutions and archives which, under the Soviet regime, were financed by the states.

5. The African region recognized that the concept of identity has evolved extensively over the last decade. During the period of nation-building, a national cultural identity based on traditional cultural values was stressed, but today multiple identities — family, clan, ethnic, national, and regional — are emphasized. The value and role of the mother tongue and traditional cultural knowledge were also strongly highlighted. The seminar expressed widespread concern about the misuse of traditional culture and folklore by commercial entities, and stressed the need for surveying and cataloguing all forms of expression in order to protect them.

6. As was the case for Central Asian countries, Central and Eastern Europe expressed concern about the poor financial situation of the existing state-owned structure for the preservation of traditional culture and folklore following the introduction of a liberal capitalist economy. They also underlined the need to establish a close link between theoretical and practical activities.

7. The seminar for Western European countries emphasized the necessity to preserve cultural diversity endangered by the concentration of material and intellectual resources at the global level. In light of this concern, special effort needs to be made to promote the protection of traditional culture and folklore of minority groups, whose cultures are vulnerable but intrinsically invaluable to humanity.

8. The Arab states stressed the challenges presented by globalization and the transformations of their own societies to the maintenance of traditional culture and folklore and distinctive identity.

Traditional Culture and Contemporary Issues

The opinion was expressed in several seminar reports that traditional knowledge and expression can aid nations and their populations in dealing with the serious challenges confronting all nations today: sustained human development, peaceful coexistence, globalization, and the alienation and education of youth.

1. Several regions stressed the importance of traditional culture and folklore — and other accumulated knowledge and practice developed locally over long periods of time — for sustained social and economic development.

2. Globalization was recognized as a powerful influence in all regions, one that has both positive and negative potential. Some new technologies can be harnessed for better preservation and protection of some forms of traditional culture and folklore; other technologies further marginalize them and their creators.

3. Peaceful coexistence may be encouraged by the understanding of shared culture and the appreciation of differences, and by using traditional means of dispute settlement.

4. Several regions stressed that one of the problems faced by youth today is that they do not understand or appreciate the significance of their own culture, which should therefore be included to a greater degree in educational curricula.

Comments on the *Recommendation* Itself

All of the Regional Seminar Final Reports mentioned the importance of the 1989 *Recommendation on the Safeguarding of Traditional Culture and Folklore* as a reference document. Many of them complimented UNESCO on having prepared it and expressed the hope that Member States would do more to disseminate it and to implement its provisions.

Some of the seminars observed that the term "folklore" has a pejorative connotation in their region and recommended that it be replaced by other words (Africa, Pacific, Latin America). In some places the term "traditional and popular culture" was substituted (Africa), while in others "traditional and popular culture (folklore)," was proposed. Some terminological change was recommended in any event.

Several of the seminars recommended that the 1989 *Recommendation* be modified or a new instrument be developed that would include specific additional features. Others indicated that changes were probably desirable without explicitly naming them. The changes that were specifically recommended included:

- The inclusion of a code of ethics (Central Asia, Asia, Central Europe, Arab states) that would declare principles of respect for traditional culture and folklore of all nations and ethnic groups and protect the knowledge bearer, the collector, and the form itself
- The creation of an international legal framework to improve the protection of traditional culture and folklore (Final Reports often recommended that UNESCO and WIPO develop this together)
- The practice of including customary owners of traditional cultural knowledge as principal participants in and beneficiaries of the process of documenting and disseminating their knowledge (Latin America, Pacific)
- The recognition of the collaborative role of non-governmental organizations and institutions of various kinds that can be of assistance in the preservation of traditional culture and folklore (Latin America)

- The widening of the scope of the *Recommendation* to include the evolving nature of traditional culture and folklore (Latin America)

Recurring Recommendations

Final Reports of the regional seminars contained recurring recommendations to the governments of Member States and to UNESCO. These recommendations provide valuable indicators for future directions and are outlined as follows.

Recommendations to Government

- Incorporate programs relating to traditional culture and folklore in educational curricula at all levels and include traditional culture and folklore within the framework of national educational policies.
- Develop legislative protection for traditional culture and folklore. In countries where such protections already exist, further assess and improve the effective application of this legislation.
- Develop copyright laws and other legal tools protecting individual and collective creators, practitioners, and collectors of traditional culture and folklore.
- Support the development and coordination of regional organizations working in cultural fields. For example, support the establishment of information systems linking institutions, inter-organizational exchanges, improved archival structures, and greater access to cultural resources.
- Actively disseminate and implement the 1989 *Recommendation*, and integrate the safeguarding and revitalization of traditional culture and folklore in national cultural policies with regard to the 1989 *Recommendation*.
- Develop practices to assure that traditional communities benefit from commercial uses of their folklore when they agree to its use.
- Include members of traditional communities in decision-making bodies that consider issues affecting them.
- Include innovations, hybrid forms, and new ideas when defining traditional culture and folklore.
- Work with local communities to devise means of avoiding the destructive aspects of excessive commercialism and tourism.

Recommendations to UNESCO

- Initiate and coordinate regional meetings relating to traditional culture and folklore that encourage cooperation between experts, researchers, and practitioners in areas relating to traditional culture and folklore.
- Designate and support Regional Intangible Cultural Heritage Centers with networks that coordinate the activities of different cultural institutions in Member States and foster expertise and technology in relevant fields.
- Formulate standard policies and procedures for traditional culture and folklore management through the proposed regional Centers, which would, for example,

develop systematized approaches to the collection, documentation, conservation, and dissemination of traditional culture and folklore.

- Provide training in the use of new technologies for documentation, preservation, and diffusion.
- Encourage governments to develop national legislation protecting traditional culture and folklore. In countries where such legislation exists, encourage reassessment of the legislation and its adaptation to current concerns and future objectives relating to the protection of traditional culture and folklore.
- Organize regional meetings of experts in legal aspects of traditional culture and folklore to examine various possibilities of legislative protections and their applications to ensure they reflect the needs of respective countries.
- Develop a code of ethics that declares principles of respect for traditional culture and its practitioners.
- Avoid using the word "folklore" because of its pejorative connotations.
- Develop working partnerships with institutions of civil society — including grassroots organizations, non-governmental organizations and private funding agencies.
- Revise the 1989 *Recommendation on the Safeguarding Traditional Culture and Folklore* or create a new international instrument.

Conclusion

The Global Conference, to be held in Washington D.C. in June 1999, will build upon the years of work and preparation that have gone into the regional seminars. We have an opportunity to turn the recommendations of these eight regions into a final set of recommendations to propose to UNESCO and its Member States. A great deal of work has already been done, and we must be grateful to all those who participated in the regional seminars and worked so hard to produce the final reports and recommendations that we can work from. We can take inspiration from what they have already accomplished.

A Historical Study on the Preparation of the 1989 Recommendation on the Safeguarding of Traditional Culture and Folklore

Samantha Sherkin
Consultant
Intangible Cultural Heritage Unit
Division of Cultural Heritage, UNESCO

Introduction

The General Conference of UNESCO adopted at its twenty-fifth session (1989) the *Recommendation on the Safeguarding of Traditional Culture and Folklore*. This act was the culmination of over fifteen years of observations, examinations, and analyses undertaken by UNESCO into the possibility of establishing an international instrument designed to protect the intangible cultural heritage, or folklore.[1] Despite its great significance, this endeavor was laborious, costly, and dilatory because it was affected by many events within and outside of UNESCO. The effort may also have been impeded procedurally because it was at once closely affiliated with, yet distinguished from, efforts to provide copyright protection for intellectual property. Specifically, a distinction developed between the overall question of folklore and the intellectual property aspect of folklore,[2] creating a conceptual dilemma that has continually confronted both UNESCO and the World Intellectual Property Organization (WIPO). Yet, impediments aside, this memorable action was welcomed by Member States, particularly countries of Africa, Latin America, Asia, and the Pacific, who have long been concerned for their intangible cultural heritage. Such preoccupation has manifested itself in a variety of acts, including the adoption of national legislation and the organization and promotion of local and regional art and music festivals.

This report, based on a study of the files available at UNESCO Headquarters, will review the historical events including conceptual trends, tendencies, and impasses that led to the eventual adoption of the 1989 *Recommendation*. As will be illustrated, theoretical preferences played a profound role in shaping the direction of events.

Phase One: 1952–1971

The creation and eventual adoption of the UNESCO *Recommendation on the Safeguarding of Traditional Culture and Folklore* was the result of a multiyear process that aimed to establish legal protection for the world's intangible cultural heritage. Throughout these years of intense examination and deliberation, interest in cultural heritage, both tangible and intangible, increased within UNESCO and many of its Member States, a fact confirmed by the organization of regional festivals and conferences and by UNESCO's adoption of related legislation, such as the *Recommendation on the Means of Prohibiting and Preventing the Illicit Export, Import, and Transfer of Ownership of Cultural Property*[3] adopted by the General Conference of UNESCO at its thirteenth session (November 1964). The latter Recommendation aimed to protect national material cultural heritage from illicit operations that threaten it. Shortly thereafter, the General Conference at its fourteenth session, November 1966, adopted a *Declaration of Principles for International Cultural Cooperation*, which was aimed at providing individuals with equal access to knowledge and enjoyment of the arts. Concurrently, in a regional context, the National African Radio and Television Union (URTNA) organized a meeting in Tunis (1964), which focused on the itemization and preservation of folklore, while a World Festival of Black African Art convened shortly thereafter in Dakar (1966).

However, in the initial years of UNESCO investigations into the safeguarding of intangible cultural heritage, a theoretical dilemma was born, one that continues today: namely, whether to protect folklore within or outside of the law of copyright.

The intimate, international relationship between copyright and folklore began in UNESCO in 1952 with the adoption of the Universal Copyright Convention. This Convention, along with the International Union for the Protection of Literary and Artistic Works (Berne Convention), established standards of copyright protection which each country agreed to observe in its national legislation.[4] This national legislation would be extended to protect works from any other signatory country. In short, these Conventions aimed to curb the international exploitation of literary and other works by implementing laws that would enable judges to apply penalties for infringements of copyright.

An affiliation between copyright and folklore was also codified at national and regional levels.[5] For example, in 1956, the Government of Mexico adopted a Copyright Statute, a mixed revenue-based approach, in which works deriving from the pubic domain (like folklore) were to become registered with a Copyright Directorate.[6] In 1967, Papua New Guinea passed the National Cultural Preservation Ordinance, a mixture of preservation and custom approaches, which, prior to independence (1975), aimed at preserving and protecting authentic cultural material from cultural loss and invasion. Shortly thereafter, in 1968, Bolivia passed Supreme Decree No. 08396, a sole copyright approach, whereby ownership and control of certain works become vested in the State.[7] UNESCO and BIRPI[8] jointly organized a Regional Meeting on the Study of Copyright in Brazzaville in 1963; here, for the first time, a recommendation relating to folklore was adopted.[9]

The relationship between folklore and copyright was further explored in 1967 at the Stockholm Conference of the Berne Convention, where a specific attempt was made to protect expressions of folklore at the international level by means of copyright law. Moreover, it was suggested that the concept of folklore become the subject of a worldwide Convention. But after much negotiation, it was concluded that the conceptual and definitional complexity of folklore prevented the immediate development of such a Convention. It was deemed preferable to add a provision to the Berne Convention, one founded on general rather than specific principles. As a result, a new provision was adopted, yet it only provided vague guidelines for the protection of folklore. In fact, the word "folklore" did not appear in the provision itself. The provision is quoted below:

Article 15

4(a) In the case of unpublished works where the identity of the author is unknown, but where there is every ground to presume that he is a national of a country of the Union, it shall be a matter for legislation in that country to designate the competent authority which shall represent the author and shall be entitled to protect and enforce his rights in the countries of the Union.

Article 15, 4(a) is the only legislative history that attests to the international intention to establish a means to protect folklore.

International interest in providing comprehensive protection for intangible cultural heritage continued into the following decade. In 1971, UNESCO prepared a document entitled "Possibility of Establishing an International Instrument for the Protection of Folklore" [Document B/EC/IX/11-IGC/XR.1/15]. This study did not arrive at a specific solution but recommended that a progressively deteriorating situation made further work on the protection of folklore urgent. As will be explained below, this document came to play a constructive role at the outset of what became years of analysis and deliberation.

Phase Two: 1972–1979

The years between 1972 and 1979 were formative in the project to protect intangible cultural heritage both within and outside of UNESCO. In this period attitudes towards traditional culture were changing worldwide, as many pre- and post-independence developing countries engaged in the process of nation-building. They reinvented and revived local traditions, constructing national sentiment and identity, and also increasing the commercial utilization of folklore. This enthusiasm resulted in regional art festivals, including the first National Cultural Festival (Libreville, 1974) and the World Festival of Black African Art (Lagos, 1977), and in academic analyses, such as the 1975 investigation by the Nordic Institute of Folklore into the relation between copyright and folklore.

UNESCO, responding to the growing interest among its Member States, began convening meetings and intergovernmental conferences on matters relating to tangible and intangible heritage. Between 1972 and 1979, UNESCO convened three Intergovernmental Conferences on Cultural Policies: Yogyakarta (1973), Accra (1975), and Bogota (1978). All three conferences requested UNESCO assistance in preserving cultural heritage and popular traditions.[10] At its nineteenth session, November 1976, the UNESCO General Conference officially launched the UNESCO Comprehensive Program on the Intangible (non-physical) Cultural Heritage, the aim of which was to promote appreciation and respect for cultural identity, including different traditions, ways of life, languages, cultural values, and aspirations.[11] Shortly thereafter, in conjunction with this program, UNESCO convened two meetings on the study of oral tradition, the first in Manila (1978), the second in Katmandu (1979).

The beginning of this era of cultural policy formation can be placed in November 1972, when the General Conference of UNESCO at its seventeenth session adopted the Convention concerning the Protection of the World Cultural and Natural Heritage. This Convention protects tangible material items which are considered to possess outstanding value to human history, art, science, or aesthetics. Despite its great importance, this Convention neither applies nor extends to intangible cultural heritage. To address this need, the Government of Bolivia put forward a request[12] in April 1973 that a Protocol be added to the Universal Copyright Convention that would protect the popular arts and cultural patrimony of all nations.[13] In December 1973, the question was submitted to the Intergovernmental Copyright Committee,[14] which decided to entrust it to UNESCO. The organization was requested to determine the extent to which the protection of folklore might involve copyright[15] and to report to both the Intergovernmental Copyright Committee and to the Executive Committee of the Berne Union at their forthcoming meeting (December 1975). It is significant that the subject of folklore was here explicitly divided between the overall question of folklore and the intellectual property aspect of folklore. This duality, as will be repeatedly illustrated, has persisted.

In 1975, at the request of the Intergovernmental Copyright Committee, UNESCO submitted a document it had prepared in 1971 entitled "Possibility of Establishing an International Instrument for the Protection of Folklore" [Document BIEC/Ixil 1-IGC/XR.1/15]. After much deliberation, the Intergovernmental Copyright Committee and the Executive Committee of the Berne Union concluded that although folklore was in need of protection, a solution at the international level was unrealistic. Moreover, they felt that the problem was of a cultural nature and, as such, was beyond the bounds of copyright. The Committees referred the problem to the Cultural Sector of UNESCO for further study.

As years passed, the schism between the overall question and the intellectual property aspect widened, shaping the development of methods and means for the protection of folklore. For example, in 1976, UNESCO and WIPO, citing the "intellectual property aspect of folklore," undertook a joint effort for its protection by preparing the Tunis Model Copyright Law for Developing Countries. This Model aimed to provide a reference that countries could employ when drafting their national copyright law; Section 1, paragraph 3, protects folklore (as intellectual property) within the framework of copyright.[16] The conceptual division widened in July 1977 following the Expert Committee on the Legal Protection of Folklore convened in Tunis.[17] This Committee,[18] comprising both folklorists and lawyers, determined that problems in the protection of folklore (overall) were essentially cultural, involving issues such as definition, identification, conservation, and preservation. As such, the problems required an interdisciplinary examination, one that should be conducted under the sole auspices of UNESCO. The intellectual property issue, in contrast, was deemed relevant only in matters where folklore was utilized to promote a national cultural identity, and as such, should be pursued jointly by UNESCO and WIPO. In short, it was concluded here, as it was at the 1975 meeting of the Intergovernmental Copyright Committee and the Executive Committee of the Berne Union, that copyright law was an ineffective and non-adaptable means for the (overall) protection of folklore. These findings were further endorsed in the succeeding meeting of the Intergovernmental Copyright Committee and the Executive Committee of the Berne Union, which convened in November/December 1977 in Paris.

In May 1978, the Secretariats of UNESCO and WIPO formally agreed that UNESCO would examine the question of safeguarding folklore on an interdisciplinary basis and within the framework of a global approach, while WIPO would participate only in circumstances involving aspects of copyright and intellectual property. The two organizations agreed to reconvene in 1979 in order to conduct a further joint study on these matters. This was the authoritative agreement that demarcated, both conceptually and practically, "folklore" from "intellectual property." Subsequently, the General Conference of UNESCO adopted at its twentieth session, October/November 1978, Resolution 5/9.2/1 in order to "identify ways of providing for folklore at the international level."

In accordance with their agreement of 1978, the Secretariats of UNESCO and WIPO reconvened on 27 February 1979 for further deliberations. In March 1979, the Third Session of the Permanent Committee of the WIPO Permanent Program for Development Cooperation Related to Copyright and Neighboring Rights met in Dakar. One of the studies examined at this session was conducted by WIPO and the Executive Committee of the Berne Union[19] in February 1979. It focused on the possibility of establishing draft provisions for the national protection of works of folklore, and recommended that a joint WIPO-UNESCO Working Group be organized, as soon as possible, to consider both domestic and international aspects of the issues.

In August 1979, pursuant to Resolution 5/9.2/1, and in conjunction with the overall approach to folklore assumed by UNESCO Secretariat, the Director-General of UNESCO addressed a letter to Member States accompanied by a "Questionnaire on the Protection of Folklore." This interdisciplinary questionnaire covered the definition of folklore and its identification, conservation, preservation, utilization, and protection against exploitation. The purpose of this survey was to evaluate the present situation of intangible cultural heritage in Member States and to seek ways to develop additional measures to ensure the authenticity of folklore and protect it against distortion. In line with the agreement of 1978, WIPO would be involved only in matters concerning copyright and intellectual property. The division of labor on folklore had so solidified by this time that it seemed to create an impasse in theoretical and practical developments throughout the following decade.

Phase Three: 1980–1989

Numerous projects between 1980 and 1989, national and international in scope, strove to promote and protect tangible and intangible cultural heritage. National activities included festivals such as the eighteenth International Folkloric Festival (Portugal 1982) and conferences such as the twelfth session of the International Center of Bantu Civilizations (CICIBA, Libreville, 1982). On an international scale, UNESCO continued to convene intergovernmental conferences such as the World Conference on Cultural Policies (MONDIACULT, Mexico, 1982). UNESCO expanded its activities in the field of intangible heritage, establishing a special Section on Non-Physical Heritage (1982) and developing by 1984 a new program entitled "Study and Collection of Non-Physical Heritage." UNESCO worked with WIPO to establish a legal mechanism to protect folklore, convening many international and regional meetings whose conceptual organization confirmed the dichotomy between the overall question of folklore and its intellectual property aspect. The latter received much attention between the years 1980 and 1984, when UNESCO and WIPO organized four meetings of Expert Committees (1980, 1981, 1982, 1984) and four Regional Meetings (1981, January/February 1983, February 1983, 1984). The overall question of folklore received much attention in later years through the sole efforts of UNESCO.

In January 1980 in Geneva,[20] following deliberations of the Executive Committee of the Berne Union and the Intergovernmental Copyright Committee (February 1979) and the decisions of UNESCO and WIPO Governing Bodies, UNESCO and WIPO jointly convened the first meeting of the Working Group on the Intellectual Property Aspects of Folklore Protection. The primary objectives of this meeting were to study a Draft Model Provision for National Laws on the Protection of Creations of Folklore, and to examine international measures for the protection of works of folklore. This meeting, the first of its kind, reflected a growing international concern for the protection of intangible cultural heritage, particularly those aspects relating to intellectual property.[21] With respect to the Model Provisions, the Working Group recommended that the Secretariats should prepare a revised draft and commentary thereon and present it for further consideration to a subsequent meeting. It was also suggested that the Secretariats should continue to study the intellectual property aspects of folklore at the international level and should also identify and pursue regional possibilities for the protection of folklore.

UNESCO initiatives continued to expand in 1980 with the approval and adoption by the General Conference at its twenty-first session of various programs and resolutions. These included approval of a triennial working period (1981–83) involving the convocation of two Committees of Governmental Experts in protecting folklore. In accordance with the UNESCO-WIPO agreement of 1978, the first Committee would meet under the sole auspices of UNESCO with a view to defining measures to safeguard the existence, development, and authenticity of folklore and to protect it against distortion. The second Committee would meet under the joint auspices of UNESCO and WIPO with a view to drawing up proposals for regulating the intellectual property aspects of folklore protection. In addition, the General Conference approved the joint convening of three regional Working Groups by the Secretariats of UNESCO and WIPO[22] to search for ways to apply these regulations at regional levels. The General Conference also adopted Resolution 5.03, which declared that folklore was of considerable importance and deserved international regulations to ensure its protection, preservation, and development. Subsequently, the Secretariat was invited to conduct further studies regarding technical and legal aspects of this question and to present its findings to the General Conference at its twenty-second session.

In February 1981, UNESCO and WIPO convened the second meeting of the Working Group on the Intellectual Property Aspects of Folklore Protection (Paris).[23] The Group concluded that the Model Provisions and related commentary thereon should be presented for further consideration at a meeting of governmental experts jointly convened by UNESCO and WIPO in 1982.[24]

In October 1981 in Bogota, UNESCO and WIPO jointly convened the first Regional Meeting of the Expert Committee. The Committee recommended that, in addition to the adoption of a model national law, immediate attention should be given to the establishment of international measures for the protection of folklore.

Thus, by the onset of 1982, much international attention had been directed towards the intellectual property aspect of folklore and ways to ensure its protection through copyright law. The two Working Groups on the Intellectual Property Aspects of Folklore Protection (Geneva, Paris) and the Regional Meeting of the Expert Committee (Bogota) substantiate this point. However, in February 1982, a shift in focus occurred when UNESCO, addressing the overall question of folklore, organized a Committee of Governmental Experts on the Safeguarding of Folklore (Paris).[25] The aim of this meeting was to analyze various aspects of folklore with a view to defining measures aimed at safeguarding its continued existence, development, and authenticity and protecting it from distortion. The results of this meeting are memorable, for it was here that for the first time a definition of folklore was firmly established. In short, the Committee adopted a series of recommendations,[26] most of which focused on the importance of institutional infrastructure. The recommendations placed a strong emphasis on the need for UNESCO to establish a task force of experts in documentation, archiving, and classification of material relating to traditional culture. They also suggested that UNESCO should continue its efforts to formulate an international recommendation on the preservation and safeguarding of folklore and should proceed with WIPO in the examination of the intellectual property aspect of folklore. Yet it was recommended that this aspect not be immediately considered.[27]

In June/July 1982, UNESCO and WIPO jointly organized a meeting of a Committee of Governmental Experts on the Intellectual Property Aspects of the Protection of Expressions of Folklore (Geneva). The primary purpose of this meeting was to draw up model provisions for national laws to protect expressions of folklore using principles similar to those of intellectual property law and taking into account the results of previous meetings. Such provisions would make utilization of folklore subject to authorization and allow the imposition of prohibitions or restrictions on cultural distortions and economic exploitation of folklore materials. Authorization implies a fee, a fixed amount collected either by the community concerned, which corresponds to the author in copyright law, or by a competent authority usually nominated by the state. Collected fees would be used to promote or safeguard national culture, folklore, or a combination of the two.[28] At this fruitful meeting the Committee adopted the Model Provisions for National Laws on the Protection of Expressions of Folklore Against Illicit Exploitation and Other Prejudicial Actions.[29] Many hoped that these provisions would serve as a basis for a subsequent international regulation.

This focus on an international legal instrument continued throughout 1983, when UNESCO and WIPO jointly convened the second and third Regional Meetings of Expert Committees in New Delhi (January/February) and Dakar (February). These meetings, like the preceding one (Bogota), recommended the elaboration of a specific international regulation of the intellectual property aspects of folklore, an action, it was argued, that could be implemented more quickly than an interdisciplinary operation. In addition, these Committees reiterated that emergency action be taken towards the preservation of popular traditions.

However, in addition to UNESCO-WIPO efforts, UNESCO also began to assume a more active role independent of WIPO in the protection of folklore. This was evident at the 116th session of the UNESCO Executive Board (May/June 1983), where a report entitled "Preliminary Study on the Technical and Legal Aspects of the Safeguarding of Folklore" (Document 116 EX/26)[30] was submitted for examination.[31] The Board was invited to decide whether it would submit to the General Conference at its twenty-second session a proposal concerning an international regulation for the safeguarding of folklore.[32] The Executive Board adopted Decision 5.6.2, in which it decided to follow up this matter inviting the Director-General to pursue the technical, legal, and administrative aspects of general regulations concerning the preservation of folklore. It recommended that during the 1984–1985 biennium a Committee of Experts carry out a thorough study of the possible scope of such regulations. Lastly, in accordance with the findings of Document 11 6/FX 26, the Executive Board decided to propose to the General Conference that UNESCO and WIPO continue their efforts towards the formulation of international regulations for the preservation of folklore as intellectual property.

Pursuant to the recommendations of the Executive Board, the General Conference, at its twenty-second session (October/November 1983), approved an interdisciplinary study of ways and means of safeguarding folklore.[33] To this end, the General Conference endorsed the creation of another Committee of Governmental Experts to perform the analyses. The Executive Board would review these findings at its 121st session, spring 1985, following which the General Conference would deliberate the matter at its twenty-third session (October/November 1985).

The binary approaches to folklore — one addressing its overall nature, the other its existence as intellectual property — persisted in 1984. Throughout this year, UNESCO and WIPO continued their joint efforts by organizing the fourth Regional Meeting of the Expert Committee (October, Doha), and a Committee of Experts on the International Protection of Expressions of Folklore by Intellectual Property (December, Paris).[34] Both meetings addressed the need for specific international regulations to protect expressions of folklore through intellectual property law. The Paris meeting concluded that the Secretariats of UNESCO and WIPO should continue to explore a treaty for intellectual property type of protection for expressions of folklore and prepare a document which would consider alternative means of implementing this protection. All findings were to be submitted to the Executive Committee of the Berne Union and the Universal Copyright Committee.[35] However, this joint meeting in Paris was the last of its kind. UNESCO and WIPO convened no further conferences on this matter for the remainder of the decade.

Following Decision 5.6.2, adopted by the UNESCO Executive Board at its 116th session and noted by the General Conference at its twenty-second session, the Second Committee of Governmental Experts on the Preservation of Folklore was convened 14–18 January 1985 in Paris.[36] The aim of this meeting was an interdisciplinary study of possible regulations that could safeguard folklore as a whole. Little attention was paid to the intellectual property aspects of folkiore.[37] For this reason, WIPO felt that its contribution to the work of the Committee would be marginal and, thus, declined to participate.[38] This reasoning was transmitted in a letter of 11 January 1985 by the Director of the Public Information Division of WIPO to the Director of the Copyright Division of UNESCO. An excerpt of this letter is cited below:

> The preparatory document . . . quotes from the decision of Unesco's Executive Board . . . concerning the separation of Unesco's work on general regulations concerning the preservation of folklore and Unesco's work, jointly with WIPO, on specific regulations regarding the 'intellectual property' aspects of such preservation . . . . [T]his separation is clearly necessary in order to ensure rational and coordinated methods of work without duplication. Particularly in view of the fact that WIPO will not be represented at the second session of the Committee, we would be grateful if you could, if necessary, remind the participants that this separation has already been agreed and should be maintained.

The Committee concluded that international regulations be established in the form of a Recommendation rather than Convention to Member States. A Recommendation, unlike a Convention or declaration, is a flexible instrument whereby the General Conference formulates principles and invites Member States to adopt any means, legislative or otherwise, in order to apply them. The Committee also suggested that an interdisciplinary approach to folklore be embraced, one that would address its definition, identification, conservation, preservation, and utilization. The Committee also recommended that the General Conference examine the development of infrastructure possibilities, including the establishment of an international register, network, and standard typology of folklore and cultural property.

Shortly thereafter, the General Conference at its twenty-third session, October/November 1985, adopted Draft Resolution 15.3, in which it decided that the question of safeguarding folklore could be the subject of an international instrument in the form of a Recommendation to Member States. Subsequently, the Director-General was invited to convene a special Committee of Governmental Experts to examine the question and report on this matter at the twenty-fourth session of the General Conference.

Pursuant to Draft Resolution 15.3 and in accordance with the Governing Bodies of WIPO, UNESCO and WIPO agreed to organize a Committee of Governmental Experts in 1987. The aim of this Committee was to continue the examination of measures to be taken to ensure both the preservation of folklore within a global and interdisciplinary framework and the international protection of intellectual property aspects of folklore. To this effect, the Copyright Division of UNESCO assembled a Special Committee of Technical and Legal Experts on the Safeguarding of Folklore to convene in June 1987. The working document for this Committee was that elaborated by the Second Committee of Governmental Experts on the Preservation of Folklore (January 1985). However, WIPO later decided that it did not wish to be included in the organization of this meeting. The Organization felt that the intellectual property aspects of the international protection of folklore expressions, of concern to both UNESCO and WIPO, could only be addressed after the question of the preservation of folklore, of concern to UNESCO alone, had been clarified.[39] Despite its withdrawal, a representative of WIPO from the Copyright Law Division attended the meeting. The Special Committee[40] deliberated over the general question of folklore, particularly the means to create appropriate infrastructures for its protection, including the establishment of a universal typology and the promotion of international cooperation. The committee suggested that such efforts could be achieved through the provision of intellectual and technical assistance to Member States, particularly the developing countries, for the establishment of centers and the training of specialized personnel. The legal protection of folklore was not widely considered, as it was identified as problematic in nature. Some delegations felt that the intellectual property aspect of the issue belonged in the hands of other bodies, while others maintained that the intellectual property aspect covered only part of the legal protection of folklore.[41] The Committee desired that the General Conference would embrace its conclusions and decide on the preparation of an international instrument, preferably a Recommendation to Member States, in conjunction with Draft Resolution 15.3 and the findings of the Second Committee of Governmental Experts on the Safeguarding of Folklore (Paris, 1985).

Subsequently, the General Conference at its twenty-fourth session, October/November 1987, adopted Resolution 15.3 in which it expressed a desire that an international instrument on the safeguarding of folklore be prepared in the form of a Recommendation to Member States. For this purpose, the General Conference approved the organization of a Special Committee for the preparation of a final draft of a Recommendation to be submitted to the General Conference at its forthcoming session.

On 1 June 1988, the first draft of a Recommendation (Document CC/MD/4) prepared by the Special Committee of Governmental Experts (1987) was distributed to UNESCO Member States for their opinions and observations.[42] On the basis of comments transmitted, a revised document (Document CCI/MD/8)[43] was submitted to the Special Committee of Governmental Experts who convened from 24 to 28 April 1989.[44] This Committee was responsible for preparing a draft Recommendation to Member States on the safeguarding of folklore. It is significant that WIPO was not represented at this meeting. Following its deliberations, the Committee unanimously approved the draft Recommendation on the Safeguarding of Folklore and submitted it to the General Conference for adoption, as provided for in Article IV, paragraph 4, of the UNESCO Constitution and Article 11 of the Rules of Procedure concerning Recommendations to Member States. Subsequently, the General Conference at its twenty-fifth session adopted the *Recommendation on the Safeguarding of Traditional Culture and Folklore*.

Conclusion

The process of adopting an international instrument for the protection of folklore was laborious and costly and took more than fifteen years. Yet the adoption of the 1989 *Recommendation* occurred despite many obstacles because the document appealed to a large majority of UNESCO Member States. It was of particular interest to the countries of Central and Eastern Europe, which had ideological reasons at the time to preserve and accentuate the importance of popular ethnic culture, as well as to the countries of Africa, Latin America, Asia, and the Pacific, which have long been concerned about the erosion and exploitation of their intangible cultural heritage. The latter concern is illustrated in the following declaration transmitted by a representative of Tunisia:

[T]he Ministry of Cultural Affairs considers that Tunisia has much to gain from adopting Unesco's Recommendation on the safeguarding of folklore, in view of its rich artistic heritage which is in danger of being exploited or even distorted by our own people and by foreigners for commercial purposes.

However, the entire process of adopting the *Recommendation* became enmeshed in a divisive debate based in the perceived opposition between the overall question of folklore and its intellectual property aspect. The positions of UNESCO, WIPO, and UNESCO Member States became dominated by this issue. The text of the *Recommendation* itself tries to satisfy both theoretical camps. As Professor Lauri Honko, Director of the Nordic Institute of Folklore (Turku, Finland) states:

The Recommendation wisely emphasizes positive aspects of folklore protection such as proper ways for the preservation and dissemination of folklore. The negative aspects such as the problematic application of the "intellectual property right" (chapter F:a) are relegated aside.[45]

It may be questioned whether this division was correct or even useful. At any rate, the attempt to avoid the dilemma posed by the apparent opposition between two views may well have contributed to the *Recommendation*'s shortcomings. For this reason, it might be worthwhile to change the method of approach in future action aimed at altering the existing *Recommendation* or preparing a new instrument, by developing a coherent theoretical basis and clear ideas of the practical results desired.

Table 1. Chronological list of organizations and events relating to the preparation of the 1989 *Recommendation on the Safeguarding of Traditional Culture and Folklore*

6 September 1952	Adoption of the Universal Copyright Convention (Geneva); revised in 1971 (Paris)
14 July 1967	The Executive Committee of the Berne Union: Stockholm Conference of the Berne Convention
1971	UNESCO Secretariat: Preparation of Document B/EC/IX/11 1-IGC/XR.1115 "Possibility of Establishing an International Instrument for the Protection of Folklore"
16 November 1972	UNESCO General Conference (seventeenth session): Adoption of the Convention Concerning the Protection of the World Cultural and Natural Heritage
24 April 1973	Government of Bolivia: Official request from the Government of Bolivia that a Protocol be added to the Universal Copyright Convention for the protection of folklore
1976	UNESCO-WIPO: Preparation of the Tunis Model Copyright Law for Developing Countries

11–15 July 1977	UNESCO: Expert Committee on the Legal Protection of Folklore (Tunis)
24 May 1978	UNESCO-WIPO: Agreement reached between the Secretariats of UNESCO and WIPO regarding the safeguarding of folklore
Oct./Nov. 1978	UNESCO General Conference (twentieth session): Adoption of Resolution 5l9/2.1, in order to "identify ways of providing for folklore at the international level"
27 February 1979	UNESCO-WIPO: Joint inter-Secretariat meeting with UNESCO and WIPO
31 August 1979	UNESCO Secretariat: Circulation to UNESCO Member States of the "Questionnaire on the Protection of Folklore"
7–9 January 1980	UNESCO-WIPO: First Meeting of the Working Group on the Intellectual Property Aspects of Folklore Protection (Geneva)
Sept./Oct. 1980	UNESCO General Conference (twenty-first session): Approval of a triennial working period (1981–1983) in the domain of protecting folklore; adoption of Resolution 5.03, confirming the importance of folklore and the possibility of establishing international regulations towards its protection
9–13 February 1981	UNESCO-WIPO: Second Meeting of the Working Group on the Intellectual Property Aspects of Folklore Protection (Paris)
14–16 October 1981	UNESCO-WIPO: First Regional Meeting of the Expert Committee (Bogota)
22–26 February 1982	UNESCO: Committee of Governmental Experts on the Safeguarding of Folklore (Paris)
28 June–2 July 1982	UNESCO-WIPO: Committee of Governmental Experts on the Intellectual Property Aspects of the Protection of Expressions of Folklore (Geneva)
31 Jan.–2 Feb. 1983	UNESCO-WIPO: Second Regional Meeting of the Expert Committee (New Delhi)
23–25 February 1983	UNESCO-WIPO: Third Regional Meeting of the Expert Committee (Dakar)
May/June 1983	UNESCO: 116th session of the UNESCO Executive Board; adoption of Decision 5.6.2, endorsing the continuation of efforts towards the protection of folklore
Oct./Nov. 1983	UNESCO General Conference (twenty-second session): Endorsement of a further Committee of Governmental Experts to carry out analyses towards the protection of folklore
8–10 October 1984	UNESCO-WIPO: Fourth Regional Meeting of the Expert Committee (Doha)
10–14 December 1984	UNESCO-WIPO: Committee of Experts on the Protection of the Intellectual Property Aspects of Folklore (Paris)

14–18 January 1985	UNESCO: Second Committee of Governmental Experts on the Safeguarding of Folklore (Paris)
Oct./Nov. 1985	UNESCO General Conference (twenty-third session): Adoption of Draft Resolution 15.3, in which the question of safeguarding folklore could be made the subject of an international instrument in the form of a Recommendation
1–5 June 1987	UNESCO: Special Committee of Technical and Legal Experts on the Safeguarding of Folklore (Paris)
Oct./Nov. 1987	UNESCO General Conference (twenty-fourth session): Adoption of Resolution 15.3, endorsing the preparation of an international instrument, in the form of a Recommendation, on the safeguarding of folklore
1 June 1988	UNESCO Secretariat: Circulation of the first draft of a Recommendation (Document CC/MD/4), prepared by the Special Committee of Technical and Legal Experts on the Safeguarding of Folklore (1987)
24–28 April 1989	UNESCO: Special Committee of Governmental Experts to prepare a draft Recommendation to Member States on the safeguarding of folklore (Paris)
15 November 1989	UNESCO General Conference (twenty-fifth session): Adoption of the *Recommendation on the Safeguarding of Traditional Culture and Folklore*

Notes

1. The *Recommendation* (para. A) provides a definition to the term "traditional and popular culture," which may also be applied to the term "intangible cultural heritage" as follows: "Folklore (or traditional and popular culture) is the totality of tradition-based creations of a cultural community in so far as they reflect its cultural and social identity; its standards and values are transmitted orally, by imitation or by other means. Its forms are, among others, language, literature, music, dance, games, mythology, rituals, customs, handicrafts, architecture and other arts."
2. "Study of the Possible Range and Scope of General Regulations Concerning the Safeguarding of Folklore (1)." Document UNESCO/PRS/CLT/TPC/II/3.
3. The General Conference at its 16th session, November 1970, adopted an international convention for this purpose.
4. The Universal Copyright Convention was first adopted by the Intergovernmental Copyright Conference in 1952 (Geneva), and was later revised in 1971 (Paris). The Berne Convention has been in force since 1886 but has been repeatedly modified. It too was amended in 1971 (Paris).
5. The following states began adopting copyright legislation as a means for dealing with national folklore: Tunisia (1967), Chile (1970), Morocco (1970), Algeria (1973), Senegal (1973), Kenya (1975), Mali (1977), Burundi (1978), Côte d'Ivoire (1978), Guinea (1980), and Burkina Faso (1983).
6. Protection under this Statute does not extend to originating or "basic" work.
7. In this way, traditional works including popular art, traditional music, and literature fell within the private domain of the State.
8. [Bureaux internationaux réunis pour la protection de la propriété intellectuelle (Geneva, Switzerland)].
9. It was decided that the best means to safeguard the integrity of African heritage, or folklore, and to protect it from exploitation would be the adoption by local governments of appropriate legislation.
10. Recommendations from the Intergovernmental Conference on Cultural Policies in Accra led to the

launching by the UNESCO General Conference of a "Ten Year Plan for the Preservation and Promotion of the Performing Arts and Music in Africa and Asia" (19 C/5, Approved, para. 4121). A colloquium for this plan convened at UNESCO Headquarters in June 1977.

11. This program was launched in conjunction with Program Resolution 4.111.

12. The request of the Government of Bolivia was expressed by the Minister of External Relations and Religious Affairs to the Director-General of UNESCO in a written communication dated 24 April 1973 (Ref. No. DG 01/1006-79).

13. It has been suggested that an initial impetus leading to the onset of sixteen years of international debates for the protection of intangible cultural heritage may have occurred in the early 1970s when Western musicians utilized an Andean folk song entitled "El Condor Pasa" without copyright protection. This song later became a remunerative success. (Cited from a draft pre-evaluation on the Recommendation on the Safeguarding of Traditional Culture and Folklore [1989], prepared by Mr. Marc Denhez, 26 March 1997, for UNESCO).

14. The Intergovernmental Copyright Committee, a body established under Article 11 of the Universal Copyright Convention, is responsible for dealing with matters concerning the application, operation, and revision of the Copyright Convention.

15. These two Committees convene biennially.

16. Two basic features of this Model Law are the following: (i) it is compatible with the Universal Copyright and Berne Conventions, and (ii) its provisions allow for different legal approaches of the countries for which it is intended. In addition, the Model Law provides legislation for the author's economic and moral rights, as well as for the protection of traditional cultural heritage. In short, it established a *domaine public payant* whereby the users of works of folklore pay a percentage of the receipts from the use of the work or its adaptation to a competent authority. The Model Law was itself progressive, as many countries that employed *domaine public payant* did not often accord either copyright or moral rights to the protection of folklore.

17. This Committee was convened pursuant to Resolution 6.121, adopted by the General Conference at its nineteenth session, Nairobi, November 1976.

18. The Committee included participants from the following nine Member States: France, Ghana, India, Italy, Mexico, Democratic Republic of Germany, Senegal, Tunisia, and USSR. A representative from WIPO attended in an observer capacity.

19. These Committees convened from 5 to 9 February 1979.

20. Experts from 16 countries were participants, while representatives of two Intergovernmental and seven international Non-Governmental Organizations attended as observers. The meeting was opened by the Director-General of WIPO and, on behalf of the Director-General of UNESCO, the Director of the Copyright Division.

21. In the words of the Director of the Folklife Center (USA), "The auspices under which the meeting was held reveal a rise in the level of seriousness with which the nations of the world are beginning to regard the issue of protecting their folk cultural traditions" (Director's Column, *Folklife Center News* vol. 3, no. 2 [January 1980]: 2).

22. The General Conference specified that these Working Groups become classified in Category VI (i.e., Expert Committees); the number of participants in each meeting is limited to between six and eight.

23. Experts who participated were the same as those who convened for the First Meeting (1980). Representatives of two intergovernmental and ten international non-governmental organizations attended as observers. On behalf of the Director-Generals of UNESCO and WIPO, the meeting was opened by the Director of the Copyright Division and the Director of the Public Information and Copyright Department, respectively.

24. By September 1981, UNESCO had received ninety-two replies from seventy Member States to the "Questionnaire on the Protection of Folklore," circulated in August 1979. On the basis of comments transmitted, a document entitled "Study of the Measures for Preserving Folklore and Traditional Popular Culture" was drafted. This report later became the Working Document at the meeting of Governmental Experts on the Safeguarding of Folklore (Paris, February 1982).

25. This meeting conformed to the decision of the Executive Board (1 l2EX/Decisions 4.6.1), and was sponsored by the Programme Support Unit, Copyright Division. A total of 123 persons were present, including eighty participants, five representatives of UN and Special Agencies, thirty-five observers from non-governmental organizations, and three members of the UNESCO Secretariat.

26. A letter dated 1 March 1982 from the Permanent Delegate of the United Kingdom to the Director

of the Copyright Division, UNESCO, stated that "while the British Government fully sympathized with the intentions behind these recommendations, they would have administrative difficulties in implementing all of them."

27. Professor L. Honko, Director of the Nordic Institute of Folklore (Turku, Finland), describes this meeting as the one that created a "positive" concept of folklore protection. He defines the approach undertaken as comprehensive — scholarly, informative, and ideological; the final recommendations produced a wealth of ideas and methods for the safeguarding of folklore. (These comments were taken from his report, "A Working Document for the Second Committee of Governmental Experts on the Safeguarding of Folklore 1985.")

28. Professor Honko describes the approach adopted at this second meeting as representing a "restric-tive" concept of the safeguarding of folklore. According to Professor Honko, "It is between these two concepts of safeguarding, the comprehensive and the specific one, that the philosophy of work initiated and carried out by UNESCO alone or by UNESCO and WIPO has oscillated during the past decade. . . . Although these two concepts of safeguarding folklore are interrelated, they do not seem to be very well integrated in the work carried out jointly by UNESCO and WIPO. One reason for this may be that the comprehensive approach is relatively new and in need of precision, whereas the specific approach is already nearing its logical end" (ibid).

29. None of UNESCO Member States have yet applied these provisions.

30. This study was based not only on the findings of the Intergovernmental and Regional Committees of Governmental Experts convened between 1980 and 1983 but also on the responses received from the UNESCO "Questionnaire on the Protection of Folklore" circulated in August 1979.

31. This act was Agenda Item 5.6.2. (22/04/83) at the Executive Board's 116th session. In light of the findings of the 1981 and 1982 Committees of Governmental Experts, and pursuant to Resolution 5/03, adopted by the General Conference at its twenty-first session, the Director-General submitted this Document to the Executive Board.

32. Section 5, paragraph 149, of Document 116 EX/26 states, "The various reports etc. reflected in the present study converge towards the conclusion that it is not only desirable but urgent that measures be adopted at the international level to preserve folklore."

33. This interdisciplinary examination was to be pursued in conjunction with the activities envisaged under Programme XI.2 (Culture and the Future).

34. The meeting of the Expert Committee followed the decision of the UNESCO Executive Board (16 EX/5.6.2) adopted at its 116th session and the decision of the Governing Bodies of WIPO at their fourteenth series of meetings (October 1983).

35. The Executive Committee of the Berne Union and the Intergovernmental Copyright Committee reconvened in December 1983 (Geneva).

36. Representatives from forty-one Member States participated in the proceedings of this Committee.

37. Focus was limited to the ways in which local communities could obtain remuneration and to the means by which folklore could be protected against illicit exploitation.

38. It is important to here note that a similar shift occurred within UNESCO. Until 1985, although the Culture Sector and the Division of Copyright had jointly conducted a global study on the question of the safeguarding of folklore, Copyright assumed the majority of responsibility. However, following the recommendations of the 1985 Expert Committee, Copyright decided to limit its involvement solely to matters involving utilization of folklore, leaving remaining efforts to the Culture Sector.

39. Such views were expressed in two pieces of correspondence. The first letter dated 15 August 1986 from the Director, Copyright Law Division, WIPO, to the Director, Copyright Division, UNESCO, stated that WIPO wished that the examination of international protection of the expressions of folk-lore by intellectual property be postponed to a later date. The second letter dated 29 September 1986 from the Director, Copyright Law Division, WIPO, to the Director, Copyright Division, UNESCO, elaborated the reasons for requesting postponement. Specifically, WIPO felt that one of the basic obstacles to the adoption of an international instrument on the protection of the expres-sions of folklore by intellectual property is the lack in many countries of appropriate and reliable sources for the identification of expressions of folklore to be protected. For this reason, WIPO main-tained that only when progress is made in the field of identification of national folklore could there be any chance for success in developing international protection for the expressions of folklore by intellectual property laws. Moreover, identification is part of a bigger task, namely the preservation of folklore, an aspect that falls under the sole auspices of UNESCO. It was thus felt that only when

the question of the preservation of folklore is clarified could UNESCO and WIPO continue their joint efforts in the protection of the intellectual property aspect.

40. The meeting of the Special Committee of Technical and Legal Experts on the Safeguarding of Folklore was convened at UNESCO Headquarters (Paris). It was a Category II Meeting, organized by the Copyright Division and Programme Support. A total of 200 persons present included 150 participants, four observers of Member States, ten representatives of UN and Special Agencies, twenty-six observers from non-governmental organizations, five observers from intergovernmental organizations, and five members of UNESCO Secretariat. It is significant that the number of Member States sending delegates to this meeting was thirty-four, fewer than those sent to the meetings of 1985 (forty-four) and 1987 (forty-one).

41. At the twenty-third session of the UNESCO General Conference, several representatives of Member States expressed the view that the protection of folklore should not be considered from the point of view of copyright, as works of folklore fall within the public domain and, as such, deserve protection from national legislation. A subsequent letter from the Ambassador of Mexico to the Director-General of UNESCO expressed the following view: "The safeguarding, preservation, promotion, dissemination of folklore obviously cannot be dealt with in the context of intellectual property, which has to do more with commercial considerations."

42. All comments received from Member States welcomed the initiative undertaken by UNESCO towards the adoption of a Recommendation on the Safeguarding of Folklore by its General Conference.

43. Twenty-six written draft amendments to the first draft of the Recommendation were submitted to the Committee for consideration.

44. The Sponsoring Unit for this meeting was the UNESCO Copyright Division. A total of 164 persons present included 120 participants, ten representatives of UN and Special Agencies, thirty observers from non-governmental organizations, and four members of the UNESCO Secretariat.

45. This comment is taken from a report written by Professor Honko following the examination of the draft Recommendation (Document CC/MD/4).

The 1989 *Recommendation* Ten Years On: Towards a Critical Analysis

Anthony McCann
with James Early, Amy Horowitz, Richard Kurin,
Leslie Prosterman, Anthony Seeger, and Peter Seitel
Center for Folklife and Cultural Heritage
Smithsonian Institution
Washington, D.C.

Introduction

The 1989 *UNESCO Recommendation on the Safeguarding of Traditional Culture and Folklore* represents an historic step in the formulation of cultural heritage policy, one that moves the global family of nations significantly closer to a convention on the important topic it addresses. Folklore and traditional culture play an important role in shaping the consciousness of a majority of the world's population. They contribute immeasurably to the quality of life on our planet. Yet they often seem inimical to — and often suffer great injury from — the culture of the economy and technology that dominates the globe. The 1989 UNESCO *Recommendation on the Safeguarding of Traditional Culture and Folklore* addresses this universal problem and makes progress toward some remedies. The present commentary shares the intent of that document.

This critique is based on reports from regional conferences and on additional readings and consultations. It offers some criticisms of the 1989 document, proposes some revisions, and suggests actions that will move UNESCO closer the goals shared by the 1989 document and this one. At the most general level, it addresses these questions: Are the perspectives and methods articulated in the 1989 document still valid after ten years? How may they be improved for the work over the next decade in a way that will lead to an international Convention on Folklore and Traditional Culture?

The Need to Expand the 1989 *Recommendation*

The principal critique of the 1989 document to be made is that it is too limited — not in its field of focus, which, as noted, this document shares, but in the way it defines the elements which compose that field of focus. In the interest of better informed, more effective governmental action, the present document proposes expanding the enumeration and description of groups that have a stake in creating, preserving, studying, and disseminating folklore and traditional culture. It also urges a more inclusive definition of folklore and traditional culture itself, one that includes not only artistic products like tales, songs, decorative designs, and traditional medicines but also the knowledge and values that enable their production, the living act that brings these products into existence, and the modes of interaction with which the products are appropriately received and appreciatively acknowledged. Finally, the critique will raise questions about particular points of terminology and interpretation in the 1989 document.

Specifying the Role of Folklore and Traditional Culture
(In the Preamble to the *Recommendation*)

With sharpening of focus, the important role that folklore and traditional culture play in the contemporary world can be better understood and addressed with public policy. But even more importantly, this keener perspective will help the family of nations to appreciate that the beauty and wisdom of folklore and traditional culture are produced by particular people, and without them would not exist. The policy to be developed and shaped into an international convention must be systematically informed by this fact: there can be no folklore without the folk, no traditional culture without living participants in a tradition. The well-being of these agents of creation — whose strength and numbers are threatened daily by well-known forces such as ethnic cleansing, economic marginalization, a global entertainment industry, and religious fundamentalism — must be placed at the center of international cultural policy.

The important role that folklore and traditional culture play in contemporary society needs to be specified in policy. They do nothing less than validate the social identities of citizens and empower them for creative problem-solving. Public recognition of these aesthetic achievements, philosophical visions, and ethical understandings helps mobilize the creative energies of individuals to engage in a dialogue about the present and future.

Folklore and traditional culture have positive roles to play in a wide range of social contexts, from fostering intergenerational communication and continuity to creating culturally resonant sounds and images adaptable for use in commerce and entertainment. Not to address the social worth of folklore and traditional culture and their creators, to leave them to be distorted or banished by political or economic forces, leads to a myriad of woes: from individual identities of youth shaped by transnational market forces rather than by locally relevant, community-based ideas; to local communities who are only cultural consumers, not producers — the detritus of history, rather than its makers. Not to address the social worth of folklore and its creators is to abandon the discourse of cultural heritage to its debasement by fomenters of ethnic conflict.

Expanding the Groups Addressed by the *Recommendation*
(In all of its parts)

The groups whose institutional activities are addressed by the 1989 document are primarily research scholars and government cultural workers. These must be expanded to include local groups of producers, non-governmental organizations, and various private-sector institutions in the culture industry whose business interests from research to marketing intersect with the activities of folklore and traditional culture.

The work of scholars and government cultural workers is addressed principally in the sections of the *Recommendation* that pertain to the study of folklore: identification of folklore (Section B), conservation of folklore (Section C). and international cooperation (Section G) among state and scholarly organizations. The *Recommendation* should be expanded in this area to include the kinds of ethical protocols followed by members of many scholarly societies, such as those governing the giving of informed consent to be studied, maintaining secrecy of traditions and of particular sources of information where necessary, compensation for participation in research, and proper attribution of contributions to research. This re-situates and expands the call for an international code of ethics for dealing with folk groups articulated in the 1989 *Recommendation* under Dissemination of Folklore, Section E(g).

The creators and sustainers of folk and traditional cultures are clearly the most important constituency to be considered in formulating policy, for without them there is no living folklore and the crucial role it plays at many points in society. Ways must be found of actively involving these local producers of folklore and traditional culture — whether organized into corporate enterprises or as individual practitioners — in the process of researching, framing, and implementing any UNESCO Recommendation that may become binding on member nations. They bring perspectives and have vested interests that are central to the issues involved.

The same can be said of the many NGOs whose practices regularly address the traditional cultures and folklore of local groups, usually for the purpose of devising and implementing plans for sustainable economic development. Many NGOs have extensive knowledge about the important role that traditional culture can play in education and development and about the intersection between local groups and global economic and cultural industries.

Many businesses today create wealth using the forms and materials of traditional cultures — local cooperatives that produce and market handmade crafts, industrial textile manufacturers that employ traditional designs, producers of audio recordings of traditional music, pharmaceutical manufacturers that use indigenous knowledge of healing plants, promoters of tourism, and entertainment conglomerates that employ various forms of ethnic representations for motion pictures, amusement theme parks, and children's toys. This large commercial sector has developed ways of dealing with folklore and traditional culture that affect their production, dissemination, and preservation. These institutions must also, therefore, be brought into the process of devising and implementing policy in this area.

In general, the *Recommendation* needs to address the market as an important factor in the evolution of folklore and traditional culture. Regulation of market forces — already instituted in a great many other areas — may be needed to assure the continued health of folklore and traditional culture. The creators and perpetuators of folklore and traditional culture may need protection from market forces and/or support for alternate forms of exchange if that is their desire; or they may need help in devising ways to participate in the market, if that is their desire. The choice of protection or participation is perhaps nowhere as problematic as in the area of tourism, which can bring benefits to local communities if they can participate with some degree of control and share in income generated, but which can also have negative, culturally destructive side effects.

Expanding and Sharpening the Definition of folklore
(In Section A of the *Recommendation*)

Another point of expansion needed to fully address the important role of folklore and traditional culture is their definition. Among academic folklorists, this definition has undergone a paradigmatic shift from one based on the individual items of folklore (tales, songs, decorative designs, and traditional beliefs and medicines) to a more inclusive one based on the event of creation or recreation as a social act. The current academic definition of folklore is based on that act, on the knowledge and values that enable it, and on the modes of social exchange in which it is embedded. Folklore is not only the song, but also the stylistic, compositional, and symbolic knowledge that practitioners exercise in its creation and the event it is performed at, which affects its selection, style, and significance. This expanded operational definition has proved to be most productive in research into the many dimensions of meaning expressed in a particular instance of folklore performance and in critical understanding of the relationship between folklore and other social sciences such as linguistics, anthropology, and history. Understanding folklore as social activity rather than as items also articulates the connection between the preservation of folklore and the cultural dimensions of human rights concerns.

To the other social groups who also have a stake in folklore and traditional culture, a definition based on the act of creation or re-creation, its antecedent knowledge and value, and its historical context of performance is also more productive of meaningful insight and action. The information specified by this definition is necessary to understand the connection, for example, between folklore, on the one hand, and, on the other, shared cultural identity, philosophical vision, ethical understanding, and aesthetic achievement. These aspects of shared knowledge are bases for social value and collective action. Seen in the perspective of this broader definition, the problem of preserving folklore for its important social role is clearly situated within the historical context of local communities. Recommendations and policies about folklore and traditional culture must address the realities of that context and the institutional practices of all the groups that affect its condition and existence.

It is felt that some terms are used in the 1989 *Recommendation* to name aspects of folklore and traditional culture in ways that embed them in practices prejudicial to their continued existence. Principal among the questioned terms is "intangible cultural heritage" itself. To be sure, the term makes sense within the administrative logic of UNESCO, where it is theoretically equal and opposite to "tangible cultural heritage." But it is strongly felt that describing folklore and traditional culture as "intangible" weakens its assessed worth. The term does not define folklore in a way that implicates the significance of its social role. The phrase "community-based culture" applied to folklore, for example, implies shared values and resources for collective action. The term "intangible" also encourages the use of models for understanding and action drawn from policies that address "tangible" heritage, thus reinforcing the notion of folklore as items rather than as social activity.

It is also felt that "intangible" weakens the status of folklore and traditional culture in legal practice and, hence, lessens the possibility of protecting it with tools such as copyright. In a similar mode, an objection was also made to calling folklore part of the "universal heritage" of humankind. While the intent of this terminology may be to valorize folklore, its effect could be construed as placing folklore within "public domain" and hence not subject to protection by copyright.

The use of the metaphorical adjective "fragile" to describe folklore and traditional culture was also felt to obscure the referent and place it in a misleading field of understanding. The intention of using this descriptor is clearly to indicate the existence of a problem in need of solution. But fragility is the internal quality of an independent object or thing, and, as we have seen, folklore is a kind of knowledge and social action embedded in an historical context. It was strongly felt that words like "marginalized" and "disempowered" were better descriptors of the plight facing traditions and their practitioners, because they envision folklore and the danger to it as parts of the wider world of relationships that engender its plight.

In the same conceptual vein, the use of the subordinating conjunction that begins Section F, Protection of Folklore, was questioned. In this passage, "In so far as folklore constitutes manifestations of intellectual creativity whether it be individual or collective, it deserves to be protected in a manner inspired by the protection provided for intellectual productions." "In so far as" means "to the extent that" (not "because"), and its use implies that there is some folklore and traditional culture that is not the result of individual or collective creativity, and, thus, not subject to legal protection. All folklore can be attributed to individual and/or collective creativity, so that the "in so far as" should be changed to "because."

Expanding and Sharpening the Definition of Folk Group
(In all parts of the *Recommendation*)

Another point of expansion of the 1989 document is the definition of the folk group itself, the social entity that creates and sustains folklore. While it is nowhere specified in that document, one could assume from reading the *Recommendation* that it envisions a dangerous nineteenth-century idealization of "one nation, one ethnicity." The overwhelming majority of nations contain many ethnicities, a cultural diversity that assumes even greater complexity because of transnational relationships between ethnicities located in different nations. This cultural complexity, and the way folklore and traditional culture are embedded within it, needs to be addressed by UNESCO policy.

Further, ethnicities are only one of the kinds of groups that create and perpetuate folklore. Others include, but are not limited to, Indigenous (or tribal) peoples, religious groups, and occupational groups. The folklore and traditional culture of each of these groups plays important roles both within the group and for the nation within which the group is located. But the varying structure of the groups makes their problems and the possible remedies for them quite different from one another. These and other kinds of folk groups need to be recognized in the UNESCO *Recommendation* so that their cultural needs can be assessed and appropriate policies developed.

Democratic Expansion of Roles
(In all parts of the *Recommendation*)

A final point of expansion is in the roles that are to be played by the different parties to the policy. Access to those roles needs to be democratically expanded. The roles of educator and disseminator, for example, should not be assumed to be reserved for scholars. The creators and perpetuators of folklore and traditional culture must have access to those roles as well. Devising policy about the dissemination of folklore should also address the need for greater access for the creators and perpetuators of folklore to the technical and institutional means of dissemination. In education, creators and perpetuators of folklore should be included in all aspects of curriculum development and teaching, not merely relegated to the role of providers of cultural materials to be structured, presented, and interpreted by others.

Under the auspices of UNESCO, and using all the methods and channels of communication open to the member nations, the parties to the policy recommendations — practitioners, scholars, government cultural workers, cultural entrepreneurs, and NGOs — should form a network for the exchange of information and opinion. Such a consultative body could address the subtleties of and offer solutions for local, national, and international issues in the field of folklore and traditional culture. It could also develop the agenda for a UNESCO convention on folklore and traditional culture.

Part II

Strategic Perspectives on Local Culture

Foundational Perspectives: Affirmations of the Indigenous in an Era of Globalization

The Globalization of Interculturality

Miguel Puwainchir
Mayor
Huamboya Municipality, Morona Santiago Province
Ecuador

In this paper, I would like to discuss the idea of interculturality and its importance to one of the themes of this conference, the coexistence of cultures. Every person is born with his or her own culture. We all occupy a distinct space, where we create our lives — often in the midst of a struggle between cultural complexes — and where we also create new human beings who inherit our culture. We want these children, and others like them, to live at peace with nature. And based on this cultural value — which flows from Indigenous thinking, for I myself am a Shuar — I would like to state the following.

The manner in which national republics were built was irresponsible, for it has led to the development of national cultures that disregard the diversity of cultures existing within these modern states. Part of this state formation has been the adoption of unrealistic laws, a situation that has given rise to constant struggle.

A clear example of this is in my own country, Ecuador, in which recognition of intercultural relations, or plurinationalism, has been achieved only through the joint action of all Indigenous groups in the country. We have been able to establish a respected space for ourselves both socially and politically. And consequently, our laws have changed because we Indigenous people contributed to changing them. We have participated in democratic elections, and through this, we have managed to carve out a respectable space for ourselves. Currently, there is an Indigenous woman, a Quechua, who is a representative in our National Congress and the Vice President of the Republic of Ecuador. So now an Indigenous woman has also been able to carve out a space for herself, not only men.

I must say with courage and pride that we value our identity. We value our culture. We have maintained our identities as members of our cultures, and we have resisted being assimilated by other cultural groups. Where we are treated with contempt and called "Indios" — not members of humanity in the full sense of the word — we have struggled to defend ourselves. We work toward good intercultural relations.

When countries develop social pathologies, it is not only because there are economic problems but also because social and cultural differences are marked by difficulties. And consequently, we believe that those of us who have our own culture must remain hopeful and engaged in the struggle to secure a space in this world of modern technology, in which minorities are often invited to disappear. In the future, states should have no single state culture. Local cultures should not be turned into objects of folklore, of marketing, and of commerce, nor should the only places for old cultures be repositories in museums or descriptions in books. And we must avoid being represented only in monuments. No, we are a culture that is alive. We are a culture that generates and regenerates itself, and we shall struggle to continue living despite the great threats we face.

I am a Shuar. I am proud to be one that nature made so. This is why I walk and I work as a Shuar does. I come from a family of warriors that shrank human heads. Today we want to shrink human egos so they will accept a globalization of cultures that does not merge the many into one. And we want state and national governments to support changes in laws so that they promote, defend, and foster different cultures and include cultural matters in their national educational curricula. Then this form of knowledge will not be seen as relegated only to Indians, anthropologists, artisans, and musicians, but be part of mankind's legacy.

That is what we mean by intercultural relations. We ourselves would like to learn about other cultures. We would like to know them, however, without losing what we are, our own identities. And this is why we ought to establish and defend a global policy of a two-way street for cultures. And so on this occasion, I believe that UNESCO and we the participants at this gathering, be we here as official delegates or as observers, should think of ways to further the existence and the development of these many cultures with the tools available to us in our work. The globalization of interculturality will help our culture and our people continue to exist.

And consequently, I recommend to the leadership of UNESCO and other organizations such as the Smithsonian that we submit as our only resolution the idea that the entire year 2000 should be the World Year of Cultures. This would be a time for state and national governments in the world to change their way of thinking about the diversity of cultures within their borders and to promote and celebrate the richness of our cultures in both small communities and large cities. Let us promote and celebrate them, even as technology is trying to destroy us and file us in some old museum.

Let me finish by saying that we still have time. In this world there are people who have hope — people like us, who are hoping to change conditions and promote interculturality. That is what will save us from the destruction done to the world under a pretext of "modern development." We must defend the way we think. We must defend our human geography and must struggle to continue living in this world despite a multitude of adversities and threats. We must require that governments respect the cultures of the world. And this means they must respect mankind's right to continue living through these many cultures. I thank you very much.

The Role of Education: Acculturation Back into the Future

Pualani Kanaka'ole Kanahele
The Edith Kanaka'ole Foundation
Hilo, Hawai'i

Aloha. Hello to all of us. I am very happy at this time to talk to us about my *kupuna*, or the Native Hawaiians. I am honored first of all to participate in this process for identifying and bringing clarity to Native life and culture, which are the sources for the stories, music, and dances that hold clues to ancestral thoughts, actions, and values. I admire and am in awe of all of you so passionate about the traditions you grew up with that you have taken on the continuation of these traditions as your responsibility. I would like to talk about "acculturation back into the future," because that is a large part of who we Native Hawaiians are. We have acculturated, and we have been able to go back in order to go into the future.

I come from the Pacific, and so I know exactly what the Fijian woman Sivia Tora was talking about today when she said that natural and cultural, tangible and intangible heritages are one. My cultural identity is that of a Native Hawaiian, someone who comes from the oceans. We are ocean people. We are island people. And if we identify ourselves with our environment, then what will our cultural identity be twenty years from now, when there is little or no environment left?

One of our most important genealogical chants begins with the birth of the coral polyp. And then everything else evolves from the coral polyp, because it becomes the food source for everything around it. The coral also becomes the source of material for the making of an island. And so when I talk about cultural identity, I am talking about myself as a Native and my association with that coral and with the island and with the sea. And with that particular chant. And when I talk about environmental deterioration, I'm talking about hotels being built on our coral polyp. And the fact is, we cannot fight it as well as we can fight for our clothing or making certain kinds of jewelry or dyeing certain kinds of costumes for dancing. We cannot fight the disappearance of our environment and of my identity connected with it

Of course, there will always be people traveling in and out of Hawai'i because we live in the middle of the Pacific, and in this world one can go almost anywhere one wants. We need to learn how to get along with them. They also, on the other hand, when they're coming in, need to learn who is living here, what the people are like, and what one can learn from them. I think that it's all been a one-way street of "I'm going there, and I'm going to enjoy myself. And I'm taking who-I-am with me," instead of learning what and who were there first.

Our official history also negates our Hawaiian culture and those who have practiced it. First, of course, is the coming of the English explorers, Captain Cook and others, and then the Americans, who were missionaries, educators, business people, and plantation owners. Whalers also came, a different sort of people. So that's what we acculturated into.

What is not in the history books is our genealogy. And the genealogy clearly tells us that we are related to the elements. So if your name is something like Kauilanuimaki'aikalaniokauila, you are related to the lightning form that is in the sky, the fire of the sky. Therefore, you are also related to the fire of the earth and the fire of the ocean. And so all of these fires are related, and the three elements are related through the fire. So our names give us a lot of history about who we are. They tell us we are related to the environment, the natural elements. They may also tell us what our ancestors did, through occupational names. Some names are Kalaiwa'a, which means our ancestors were canoe carvers. Some names tell us that we are Kalaimoku, which means our ancestors were related to the chief. Some names tell us that we are Ka'ana'ana, which means our ancestors were related to that part of the culture that prayed people to death. And so our names tell us a lot about who we are and what our ancestors did. Nothing is completely lost if we look hard enough for it. This is not in our history books.

We finally learned how to write in the mid-nineteenth century, when young Hawaiians were taken under the wing of the missionaries and taught to write Hawaiian, people like [David] Malo, [Samuel] Kamakau, and many others. These were the young men who went out and collected the oral history of our people, knowing at the time that our history was slipping away from us very, very quickly. The latter part of the nineteenth century was when the history that was collected was then gathered and translated by people like [Ralph] Kuykendall. Eventually, with the translation help of Hawaiians, our history books were compiled by writers like Gavan Daws and Ruth Tabrah. People like Kuykendall and [Nathaniel] Emerson were the writers of our cultural books.

At the turn of the century, we lost our country to the United States. They saw Hawaiian culture as a form of entertainment. And we became deeply lost in our acculturation into Western society. As far as Western society was concerned, we knew nothing and had to start from scratch. We found out in the 1940s, 1950s, and 1960s — our parents did anyway — that education was a very necessary part of our existence. So they sent us to be educated. We all had to go to college — to learn to be a teacher, an archaeologist, a historian, and the like. A whole bunch of us Native Hawaiians went to college.

During this time some people still held on very stubbornly to their cultural traditions. And the cultural traditions meant specialization — you didn't do everything, as our occupational names indicate. If you were Kalaiwa'a, you only did canoes, which means you knew something about the forest, something about the birds in the forest, etc. If your specialty was chanting the history of our people, you knew something about dancing, something about the birds, something about the forest. And so some of us kept our traditions and kept them underground. We maintained our traditions, and we are now very grateful to our ancestors who were so stubborn about maintaining them.

Today there are many educated Hawaiians who do not know their culture. Only a few educated Hawaiians do. And what we are coming to realize today is that, while education is power, culture is passion and soul. We have recently learned to take cultural practices into the school and college curriculums. We are teaching our Hawaiian children, our Hawaiian students in college, who they are. And to do this, we've gone back to the idea of what one's name is and what it can tell you about where you are from. We are beginning like that and, I think, are learning to acculturate back into our culture.

Being educated has also helped us fight our battles. Being smart in our culture has taught us how to find our souls — and how to fight our battles with an even larger rod. And so, we don't allow the archaeologist to translate our culture for us, or to interpret our culture for us. He can tell us what he knows as far as archaeology is concerned but cannot interpret our culture for us.

At present we occupy a very good place. There is a lot of interest in our culture, and even though we're still fighting battles, we know how to fight them. We know what kinds of things to call on.

We are returning to cultural ceremonies because of the repatriation of bones from the

Smithsonian, which was our first move to reclaim our ancestors. As soon as the laws were signed, we came to get all of our ancestors. We took them home and replanted them in the ground. This created new ceremonies, because we never before had ceremonies for reburying our ancestors. New ceremonies began, based on the old ones. And so I think we are in a good place, moving ahead by moving back into the past. The future seems close and bright.

Everything Relates, or a Holistic Approach to Aboriginal Indigenous Cultural Heritage

Robyne Bancroft
Australian National University

As a Goori (Aboriginal) Australian woman, from a strong matrilineal line, I begin according to the protocol in my communities and in my country. Firstly, I introduce the Indigenous people to whom I am related. I am Gumbaingerri born of Bundjalung/Thungutti descent. My people come from the northeast coast of New South Wales, a state in Australia. Secondly, I wish to acknowledge the Lenape/Delaware, the original Indian owners of the land on which this conference is being held. As a cultural heritage practitioner, I am honored to be invited to participate in this very important conference. I wish to thank Mr. Mounir Bouchenaki, Madam Noriko Aikawa, and UNESCO staff as well as Dr. Anthony Seeger and Smithsonian staff for the opportunity to participate in this conference on Indigenous cultural heritage.

Before I commence my paper, I should also explain its title, "Everything Relates," by noting where we are coming from, where we are now, and where we are going. I have given much thought to the presentation of my paper, finally deciding to approach it as Indigenous oral transmission, by talking to you from the heart, with passion and feeling for things that are a part of my being, my cultural identity.

Introduction

Australian Indigenous peoples (Aboriginal and Torres Strait Island) number less than a quarter of a million. We live side by side with approximately eighteen million non-Aboriginal people in a country the size of the United States of America. Information dissemination may sometimes be slow in so large a country. Under the auspices of the Aboriginal and Torres Strait Island Commission, one government body speaks for many Aboriginal people. Other government organizations, non-governmental organizations, and independent Indigenous heritage practitioners specialize in particular issues while maintaining a holistic approach.

At colonization, Australia had over 250 Indigenous languages. This great diversity of peoples is still active today. The first attempts at genocide were massacres, poisonings, and introduced diseases which all but decimated Aboriginal peoples. Even today, much of this history is hidden. Our history of over 60,000 years makes us the oldest living culture on this planet. All peoples of the world should be proud of this. Sadly, this feat of survival and adaptation has been largely ignored and unappreciated. Today as we approach the new millennium, we Aboriginal people continue to struggle to survive. Our life expectancy is approximately twenty years less than that of non-Aboriginal people, which increases the pressure and stress on a few Elders to maintain our cultural heritage. Also, many of our people live in cities and urban situations, a circumstance that may isolate them from taking part in revitalizing our cultural heritage.

Indigenous Australia is both historically and culturally diverse. The growing effects of dispossession have created another level of diversity within Aboriginal Australia. Successive Australian governments continue to develop and apply policies with minimum consultation with Aboriginal people, resulting in ineffective and inappropriate programs that hinder rather than support cultural maintenance and revival. Aboriginal people seek international support through the development of appropriate instruments or conventions that provide guidance for the Australian government in developing culturally appropriate policies. Inclusion of Aboriginal people with cultural knowledge and experience would result in a more holistic approach to the development of policy with greater benefit to Aboriginal Australians.

Background: A Brief Overview on Land

Land is the overriding issue to Aboriginal people. The importance of land and all that is involved with the land should never be underestimated. Most Indigenous people know intimately the flora and fauna of the landscape within their boundaries and those that border them. Custodians of their ancestral lands, most Indigenous groups take their responsibilities seriously. In this decade, we have seen the historic Torres Strait court decision that non-Indigenous Australia's continual reference to the country as *terra nullius* is not valid. It is ironic that after we have occupied the continent for more than 60,000 years, it took clarification under English law, the laws of the colonizers, to confirm that the land actually was occupied by our ancestors.

Now we have what is called Native Title. If we can prove the accuracy of our genealogies back to the arrival of the first White settlers in our area, and prove we know and are still continuing our cultural heritage, then we may get to become official "custodians" of our lands. The socio-economic contribution of and advantage to groups of land custodians needs much more consultation and discussion. My question is, who really benefits? I believe, at this stage, the Act continues to create confusion and mistrust and threatens further to divide Aboriginal groups.

Royal Commission of Inquiry into Aboriginal Deaths in Custody

This Commission was established as a result of many public demonstrations and much political lobbying by Aboriginal people. It investigated the high proportion (a ratio of thirty to one) of Aboriginal deaths in police and prison custody over many years. For Aboriginal people, only two percent of the Australian population, this situation was and is clearly unacceptable. The Commission made 330 recommendations for change to take into "serious" account the basic human rights of prisoners. Monitoring officers were employed to assist states and territories in the implementation of these recommendations. However, I believe, many of the recommendations are yet to be fully addressed. It was obvious to readers of the report and to Indigenous people involved with deaths in custody that the Commission had little or no understanding of Aboriginal cultural identity and heritage. The Commission's last recommendation called for a national reconciliation program.

Reconciliation

A Reconciliation Council was established with Aboriginal and non-Aboriginal members and coordinators in every state and territory. The Council's vision — "a united Australia which respects this land of ours, values the Aboriginal and Torres Strait Islander heritage and provides justice and equity for all" — has met with mixed reactions from the general population. In order to address its vision, the Council produced a brochure that included issues such as (1) understanding our country, (2) sharing histories, (3) working together. Many people of good will in Australian communities are working hard at promoting and understanding reconciliation.

Another report concerned the "Stolen Generations" — babies and children taken from their parents under government policy. Most of the time there was nowhere to run or hide when the police and welfare officers came for the children. At puberty, the boys and girls were sent to work, generally as an unpaid work force for settlers, squatters, and others who required free labor. The country was built on the "backs of the Blacks," and many non-Indigenous Australians established pastoral dynasties by appropriating and controlling Aboriginal people and their lands.

I will note in passing two issues that cause much concern and distress to Aboriginal people: (1) amendments to the Commonwealth Heritage Act, and (2) government cuts of bilingual programs. These are very important issues and need much more consultation and negotiation with Indigenous people.

I would like to discuss at greater length two issues of interest to me personally with which I am involved: (1) women's business, and (2) repatriation of Indigenous ancestral human remains.

Women's Business

Many years ago, anthropologists, White men, came to collect information about us. They spoke to the men, and the men gave them information on their stories. We waited for them to come to us, but they never returned. We want our stories recorded so the young women will be able to continue and keep our information alive — not let it die. We want this for our *jarjums* (young children) to come. We have already lost so much of our language, we do not want our stories to go (disappear).

So in the 1960s spoke my grandmother, who was fluent in three dialects. She was born in 1905.

Now, they come to ask us our stories — now, when most of us have forgotten so much. We have been so caught up in living day to day, and now there are very few of us left. Look who's here — only three or four of us left. It's time for you to come home my girl, keep our stories going, and take over doing what I do — talking to everyone about Goori people and our heritage.

So spoke my mother, born in the third decade of this century, who remembers her mother's tongue but has no one to speak it to.

I am in the fourth generation of women on my matrilineal side since colonization who continue our genealogies and oral traditions. I continue to practice cultural heritage maintenance through revitalization of stories and language. From the day they were born, my children have been told of stories about our community and its use of our language, and now my daughter continues this tradition to her children. I am on several cultural heritage committees, and I am the Aboriginal Representative on the International Council of Monuments and Sites (ICOMOS). ICOMOS members in Australia actively lobby the government on unfair legislation and other practices regarding Indigenous heritage issues.

It saddens me to hear of Indigenous women's struggle to maintain their cultural identity. In this decade, Aboriginal women from South Australia went through many judicial proceedings known collectively as the Hindmarsh Bridge case, trying to stop development on a sacred site for women only. The behavior of government in this case was unbelievable.

Repatriation

Repatriation of ancestral human remains is a great concern. Some overseas countries have repatriated remains only because of a concerted campaign by Aboriginal people. Many institutions have yet to comply with requests for repatriation. I believe this can be done through negotiation and consultation, without acrimony among those involved. I have worked in the sensitive area of classifying and reorganizing ancestral remains after they have been repatriated. This work has been undertaken with community support. The geographical origin of many repatriated ancestral remains has not been identified. Some Aboriginal groups have offered to rebury these unprovinced ancestral remains, but other groups do not agree because they feel, "What if these are our ancestors' remains? Then they should be reburied in our country, not in someone else's country."

In Australia, many Aboriginal groups do not have land for reburial. Thus, ancestral remains are left, by agreement of both parties, in museums and other institutions while Aboriginal people come to terms with the issues involved. One solution would be for the government to acquire land especially for such reburial. For the last five years I have been asking, "What do we do with unprovinced ancestral remains? Are they to remain in museums and other institutions, or do we have other options? Should we plan something similar to the Tomb of the Unknown Soldier, and where would the resources for it come from?"

An interesting related point is that Aboriginal people are now asking for more physical information about their ancestral remains before reburial takes place. How old was the person? Was the person male or female, child or adult? What can be known about his or her lifestyle? In other words, ancestral remains can speak to us about many things. The date of 60,000 years that we Aboriginal people use has come from scientific investigations. Some communities agree to further information-gathering, and some communities do not.

A few years ago, human remains were found protruding from a farm riverbank after a period of heavy rains. The farmer who owned the property contacted the police, who in turn contacted government archaeologists. The local Aboriginal groups wished to know more about the remains and agreed that investigations should be carried out. What emerged was a history of an older woman and a younger man who died some 7,000 years ago, and were buried with grave goods. A beautiful double-strand necklace made from hundreds of kangaroo teeth has been reassembled. This necklace, along with some stone tools, is kept by the Aboriginal people, who use them as teaching tools for Aboriginal and non-Aboriginal children and adults. In a gesture of reconciliation, the non-Indigenous farmer offered a site on his property for reburial, and this was accepted by the people.

In conclusion, I have attempted to inform you very briefly about where we have come from, where we are now, and where we hope to go. Recommendations for a holistic approach include: a code of ethics; biological diversity; printed as well as interactive media for information storage and dissemination; resources for other agencies besides government; gender issues; repatriation of human remains; intellectual property rights; spirituality; terminology and language used. Our values, beliefs, and cosmologies retold through diverse oral traditions relate to our identity. I am aware of many other related issues and hope to take part in forums where these will be discussed in more detail.

Let me reiterate what I said at the beginning of this paper: what Aboriginal people seek is international support through the development of appropriate instruments or conventions that will provide guidance for the Australian government in developing culturally appropriate policies. Inclusion of Aboriginal people with cultural knowledge and experience would result in a more holistic approach to the development of policy, with greater benefit to Aboriginal Australians.

Appendix: Aspects of Australian Heritage Policy

The Aboriginal and Torres Strait Heritage Protection Act, 1984 was subject to a review in 1996 by the Hon. Elizabeth Evatt AC. The Evatt Report recommended that intellectual property and other intangible aspects of Indigenous heritage be considered in legislative and policy reforms. It also recommended that the protection of cultural heritage should continue to recognize the changing nature of culture and should strive to include living culture/tradition as Aboriginal people now see it.

An Inquiry into Aboriginal and Torres Strait Island (ATSI) Culture and Heritage was begun by the House of Representatives Standing Committee on ATSI affairs following a change in government in 1996. Its purpose was to inquire into and report on the maintenance and promotion of Australia's Indigenous arts, cultures, and cultural identity — encompassing the full range of artistic and cultural activities, both traditional and contemporary, including visual art, craft, language, design, dance, music, drama, storytelling, folklore, writing, sound, films, heritage, traditional cultural practices, and beliefs.

The 1997 report by the Australian Heritage Commission, "Australia's National Heritage: Options for Identifying Heritage Places of National Significance," reminds us all of the importance of knowledge. It points out that Indigenous people have a strong sense that heritage includes intangible aspects such as language, song, stories, and art, and that they can be critical of a notion of heritage based too narrowly on "place."

A working party was established on the "Protection of Aboriginal Folklore," and its report was released in 1981. The report recommended a draft law called the "Aboriginal Folklore Bill."

As the above indicates, Australia has contributed to Indigenous heritage policy through many reports and inquiries. It is critically important that these reports and inquiries be implemented. They should not to be ignored or thrown in the "too-hard" or "impractical" basket.

Taking Stock: The Gitxsan Experience in Cultural Survival

Russell Collier
Strategic Watershed Analysis Team
Hazelton, British Columbia

Introduction

It's astonishing to me, but where I live in mid-northern British Columbia, a province in western Canada, there is a prevailing attitude that anything "cultural," especially anything that can be called aboriginal culture, is somehow irrelevant to mainstream society, or, at best, is quaint and amusing. This is true in most of the non-Gitxsan communities who share the same living space we do in our traditional territories. To us, however, Gitxsan culture is central, necessary to our survival as a people, and though we have a strong streak of sometimes ribald humor in our cultural makeup, there is nothing quaint and amusing to us about our culture. We're not dead or assimilated yet. And one of the lessons we have learned over the past 100–120 years is that, far from being a "culture under glass," as in a museum diorama, our culture not only is alive and well but also is becoming central to mainstream society in ways unimagined by our conquerors. Expression of our cultural identity in a modern context is having a profound effect on the larger society we live in.

I would also venture to say that, given that UNESCO has sponsored this conference, and, moreover, is following up on recommendations made over ten years ago at an earlier UNESCO conference, there are many people around the world who would agree that "safeguarding traditional culture and folklore" is far from irrelevant, quaint, or amusing. Properly focused, traditional culture can be a very powerful force.

In this introductory part of my paper, it is appropriate for me to greet you all formally, in my own terms, as a functioning member of the Gitxsan Nation. First of all, I would like to recognize and thank our hosts, the UNESCO sponsors, for this opportunity to speak and to meet with you all.'*Toyi xsi nissim, 'toyi xsi'm*. I see you and I recognize you and your right to speak, your authority to represent your own people, and I thank you for recognizing the same for me and my people. Second, I would like to recognize and thank all of you here today. *'Toyi xsi nissim, 'toyi xsi'm nun*. I see all of you here and I recognize you and your right to speak on behalf of your own nations, and I thank you for the recognition to do the same for my own people. My English-Canadian name is Russell Collier, and on my father's side, I am descended from a long line of ancestors from Cornwall, England. On my mother's side, my Gitxsan name is Hli Gyet Hl Spagayt Sagat, which means "the man who comes from the sharp pointed mountain" in our language. I am descended on her side from a lineage that originates in our territory from before the last major ice age, around 10,000 years ago.

I do not do this lightly, nor without the knowledge that many governments around the world might not look favorably upon an aboriginal person, especially a Canadian Gitxsan, speaking so freely before you. In many places around the world, there are many dangers inherent in speaking out as an aboriginal person who comes from a group claiming a relatively large portion of a provincial land base. In some places around the world, what I represent is so threatening to some established governments, the powers that be would rather exterminate than negotiate. And yet, I believe a part of the answer of how we are all going to survive in the next century without killing each other over cultural differences lies in our ability to tolerate and sometimes accommodate these cultural differences.

Background

We Gitxsan have occupied our traditional territories, in our terms, "since time immemorial." When we launched our land-claims court case in 1984, this phrase was not considered useful in legal terms, so we dated our oral histories using the geological evidence contained in them and found we'd been here on our land since sometime before the last major ice age, that is, more than 10,000 years before the present. We have oral histories containing enough detail to positively connect our claims back at least that far.

In our province, the government has never rightfully concluded land-claims settlements with our people. Nor have they done so with the majority of First Nations in our province. For over 120 years, our people have been protesting the lack of proper negotiations to settle our outstanding land claims with the province of British Columbia. As far back as the mid-1800s, Gitxsan chiefs were trying to formally initiate land-claims negotiations to resolve this issue. We were refused and rebuked. The provincial government simply assumed the right to extinguish unilaterally all aboriginal title and rights. They went so far as to outlaw and make punishable under law expressions of our culture such as our feasts and our art forms and even the ability to launch land-claims actions.

In 1977, the Gitxsan gave to the Government of Canada a declaration, which outlined title to our territories as sanctioned in our oral histories, totem poles, our songs, and our dances. Then we established the Gitxsan-Carrier Tribal Council, an organization dedicated to confirming our title to our lands. Within this organization, we began gathering information from our elders, especially the oral histories, or *adaawk* as we call them, that detail our use and occupancy and our lineages for very specific geographic areas. In all, there are around 300 audio cassette tapes of information from our elders, irreplaceable knowledge of a time not so long ago in our history. We also began a genealogical research program covering around forty of our *Wilps* — Houses or extended families — developing complete genealogies for all our people. It is possible to locate the familial position of any member of our nation within their lineage with great accuracy now as a result of this research.

In 1984, the Gitxsan submitted to court our statement of claim for the longest running land-claims court case in Canadian history. It pertains to some 30,000 square kilometers of territory, with an additional 28,000 square kilometers claimed by our close neighbors and allies, the Wet'suwet'ens.

Ripples and Waves

Every action we have taken has generated new information and material. I cannot overemphasize this. Once we began our court case, we were committed to proving our existence by exhaustively researching our oral histories. We have around 10,000 items in our library, about 8,000 of which we used as exhibits in our 1987 legal action. The legal collection, comprising everything that went to court, occupies over 300 boxes in two archive rooms. It's an astonishing amount of information about two tribal peoples, the Gitxsan and the Wet' suwet'en. Together, this represents a unique collection of indigenous cultural identity. Few other First Nations in Canada have been as thoroughly researched as we have.

We've had to learn sophisticated methods of storing, annotating, and delivering our entire store of legal information. We've had to become adept at translating the legal and political outcomes of our court case challenge into local realities.

One very large wave has grown from our submitting our folklore, our traditional oral histories, for consideration as evidence in our land-claims court case. This was a landmark legal decision, on December 11, 1997, that confirms oral histories as admissible evidence in establishing aboriginal title to large tracts of land in our country. Understandably, our country is concerned about the impact of this decision, and understandably, most of the First Nations in Canada see this as a huge victory along the way to validating our existence in a society that prefers the Hollywood version of history — "The only good Indian is a dead Indian."

Some smaller, but by no means insignificant, ripples spreading outward from this decision, popularly called the *Delgamuukw* decision, have been noted around the world by aboriginal peoples hoping that they too can use its legal framework to establish their own title to their own homelands. Australian, New Zealand, U.S.A., Canadian, Thai, Indonesian, Central and South American, and African tribes have sought to use this decision to bolster their own claims to territory with varying degrees of success. Recently, tribes in Papua New Guinea have begun using techniques for mapping oral histories originating in Gitxsan territory to demarcate their own exterior boundaries to establish protection of their tribal territories under their own federal laws. The ripples and waves are spreading far and wide.

Where Are We Today?

Today, we have a collection of information unequaled by anyone else. We have detailed information not only about our own legends and folklore, but also about long-term changes in weather, geology, and wildlife. We have over 300,000 pages of information largely ignored by the original trial judge, Alan McEachem, with around 40,000 mappable bits of information that describe an entire culture from the Ice Ae to European contact and the present. The collection is stored in a variety of media. The oldest part is on paper and audio cassette, with some on video cassette. All are deteriorating with age. The library we use to house our irreplaceable culture is relatively ancient technology — eighteenth or nineteenth century, with a few twentieth-century features added.

We stand on the edge of influencing changes in Canadian politics and lands-and-resources decisions to a major degree. And for the first time in Canadian history, we have established that oral histories are admissible as evidence for claiming aboriginal title. We are still adding to our base research and documentation and expect to become a major influence within ten years, possibly five years. It all started with deciding we could not accept assimilation or loss of our culture.

American Indian Arts and Crafts:
A Study on Handcrafts and the Industry

Andy P. Abeita
President
Council for Indigenous Arts and Culture
New Mexico

I am a Native American Indian artist and the first American Indian president of the Indian Arts and Crafts Association (IACA), created in 1974, a national trade association recognized as a 501 (c)(6) trade organization under the U.S. Internal Revenue Service codes. Our membership, national and international, totals over 700. The IACA is the only trade association in the United States specifically founded to promote, protect, and preserve the Native American Indian arts-and-crafts industry.

I have spent the last ten years working under the aegis of the IACA preserving aboriginal arts and crafts and seeking legal protections for them. Recently, I have created an educational resource organization with a not-for-profit 501 (c)(3) status in order to adequately address a variety of concerns — government and public-sector, art-and culture-related, legal and educational. The recently created Council for Indigenous Arts and Culture received its federally designated 501 (c)(3) status in 1998 and is the brain child of the research discussed below.

I speak four Indian languages and have worked professionally as an artist for the last fifteen years. I come from a small American Indian community called Isleta Pueblo, located thirteen miles south of Albuquerque, New Mexico.

For centuries, art and handcrafts have played an important role in the religious and social lives of Indigenous peoples all over the world. Throughout our Native American history it has been no different. The images you see in almost all designs used in Native American arts and crafts are religious. Even the hand processes used in creating such works reflect an individual artisan's relationship with the tools that begin with a beating heart, mind, and spirit. Our ties to this earth and to our Creator are evident in almost all images in the cultural arts of the Native American artisan.

History: Case Description

In Isleta Pueblo over the last fifty years, we have seen our artist population decline from three hundred to thirty full-time craftsmen and women. The most significant losses were in the late 1970s and 1980s. Until recently we had been famous for our fine-coiled red-clay pottery. It is fast becoming a dying art. Unfair competition from imported fakes and mechanically cast pottery often sold to an unsuspecting consumer as Indian and handmade has made it almost impossible to compete in the commercial marketplace. This forces many potters and silversmiths to discontinue their trade, denying the next generation a chance to continue the tradition.

Currently, I am actively networking with many American Indian tribes and Canadian aboriginal peoples. The primary objective is to help these indigenous tribes develop protective mechanisms to ensure the future preservation of our cultural and traditional properties. In discussions of the use of ancestral images or of arts-and-crafts copyright issues, a movement organized at the local level is the most promising way I have found to connect with the source of the problem.

In 1996, I started laying the groundwork for tribes to consider developing a collective-certification trademark that each tribe could register with the U.S. Patent and Trademark Office. The trademark would be indelibly marked into the handmade products of each artisan of each respective sovereign tribe, thus authenticating the work as a genuine original deriving from the Indian Nation as a whole and from an individual member within that constituency.

I have been personally involved in the development of the trademark project in American Indian communities. Currently, we are creating policies for protecting a trademark's use by artisans, as well as policies and regulations for its use in commercial trade within and outside of tribal jurisdictions.

American Indian tribes involved in this project are trying to facilitate this new arts-and-crafts initiative. But until recently they did not realize the magnitude of the problem, and finding funding sources within a limited, government-appropriated budget is almost impossible.

History: Statistical Data

In 1979, the U.S. Bureau of Indian Affairs conducted a nationwide census survey of 500 American Indian tribes in the United States. The purpose of the survey was to establish statistical data on native populations and to make economic development projections regarding those populations. Included in this survey were the Indian tribal nations of Zuni (with a population of 10,000), Hopi (13,000), Navajo (245,000), and many river-pueblo tribes of New Mexico with an average population of 3,000 to 5,000 each. These few Indian tribes are notable for being the nation's leading producers of handmade Indian arts and crafts, both ethnic and contemporary, in the current commercial market.

The census survey found a 30–40% unemployment rate in these communities in 1979. In these same communities up to 85% of the families surveyed reported that arts and crafts was either a primary or secondary form of income. Industry experts with the Indian Arts and Crafts Association point out that the Indian arts-and-crafts industry was at an all-time peak at around that time.

In another U.S. Bureau of Indian Affairs census taken in 1995, the same tribes reported an unemployment rate of between 50% and 65%.

In 1985, a survey by the U.S. Department of Commerce indicated that the Indian arts-and-crafts industry was estimated to be generating between $700 and $800 million annually in gross revenue.

In 1997, at the meeting sanctioned by the Indian Arts and Crafts Association in Albuquerque, New Mexico, the U.S. Indian Arts and Crafts Board reported to a multi-tribal delegation that the industry was generating well over one billion dollars annually and growing.

	1979	1985	1995	1997
Unemployment Rate	35 %		57.5 %	
Industry Annual Gross Revenue		$750 million		$1.2 billion

Statistics clearly indicate that the industry is growing. The Indian Arts and Crafts Association reports that more businesses than ever are carrying American Indian-style handcrafts and jewelry. The association has a mailing list of over 20,000 businesses. But the rising rates of both unemployment and gross revenue expose a perplexing question: if the supply is growing, who is making the product?

The promotion and commercial success of American Indian goods have also created an onslaught of commercial imitations. These have found their way into the marketplace locally in Indian country as well as nationally. Imitations have also begun to take over a substantial portion of the international market.

Investigative reports from cities around the world, such as Santa Fe, Los Angeles, New York, Paris, Milan, Tokyo, and Frankfurt, indicate that large quantities of fake arts and crafts are being represented as authentic and original American Indian art works. The statistical data found in the surveys by the Bureau of Indian Affairs are yet to be analyzed by either tribal entities or U.S. governmental agencies. But the surveys have led the Indian Arts and Crafts Association and the Council for Indigenous Arts and Culture to use the data as best we can.

The U.S. Customs Service reports that since 1990, the Philippines, Mexico, Thailand, Pakistan, and China combined have been importing into the United States an average of $30 million annually in American Indian-style arts and crafts. Although the U.S. Customs Service stated that the dollar amount was only an estimate, the numbers are significant nonetheless.

The U.S. Customs law, *1989 Omnibus Fair Trade Bill reg.19 CFR sec. E 134.43*, requires that any and all Indian-style jewelry or crafts imported into the United States must have a country-of-origin stamp "indelibly" marked into each individual piece of jewelry or craft. The down side of the law is a loophole in its language. The intent of the law is to force importers and manufacturers to mark their goods indelibly with the country of origin, by die-stamping or otherwise permanently marking them. But many manufacturers have found that attaching a small soldered wire to jewelry with a tag indicating the country of origin enables the products to pass U.S. Customs inspection. (There are over 330 ports of entry into the United States.) After the goods have passed through the customs port, many unscrupulous importers and unethical arts-and-crafts dealers simply snip off the wire tags and begin to sell the goods as authentic American Indian art works. The cost of products created in many foreign countries can be as low as one fourth the cost of U.S.-produced goods because of the low wages paid to workers in those countries.

The information from the U.S. Customs Service indicates that manufacturing copies of American Indian ethnic and contemporary arts and handcrafts has enhanced the incomes of many individuals, companies, and countries outside of the United States and Canada. Living in a free society, American Indians are not against free enterprise or the jobs created by a successful industry. But the key to successful and ethical marketing of any ethnic or commercially produced good, regardless of the country you live in, is to properly identify the individual producer and/or the country the good was produced in. As the old saying goes, "Give credit where credit is due."

In 1997, I was appointed by the United Nations International Trade Center to represent the United States as delegate to a UNESCO/ITC world conference held in Manila, the Philippines. The conference's title was "International Symposium on Crafts and the International Market: Trade and Codification." Its focus included three basic elements: (1) the promotion and marketing of artisanal handmade goods, (2) the protection of handmade artisanal goods, and (3) the codification of artisanal goods through the World Customs Organization (WCO).

Currently, I hold a position on an ad hoc committee created under the auspices of the United Nations, the International Trade Commission, and the World Customs Organization. The committee has thirty-seven members, each representing a different country. The purpose is to provide the logistical trade information needed to amend the International Harmonized Tariff Schedule (IHTS) to better protect and further develop the handcraft trade worldwide. If successful, this united effort will provide recommendations to the World Customs Organization for the protection of handcrafts under international trade law. If they become law, these recommendations will modify current provisions of the IHTS system. Currently, international trade law does not provide a way for the system to differentiate commercial, mechanically produced jewelry or handcrafts from authentic, handmade arts and crafts.

A few of the underlying concerns that many countries are facing today in the world handcraft sector are the following:

- The production of authentic, handmade products and their distribution in national and international markets has crucial economic importance because of the thousands of jobs created by this sector of commerce.
- Promoting ethnic and contemporary handcrafts provides a way for artisans and their respective countries to express their identities and provide the world with the beauty and historical meaning of cultural arts that originate authentically among particular peoples and nations. Many handmade products currently produced for the commercial market are recognized as being centuries old in both design and handcraft technique. Nearly every country in the world produces handcrafts that embody its cultural heritage, often with religious or other symbolism that has deep social and historical significance.
- Currently there are no data available from international trade experts to help countries ascertain whether and to what extent their handcraft industries are subject to trade competition from others, especially those who use mainstream mechanized production methods.

Most delegates to the Manila symposium from eighty-seven countries agreed, in both committee and plenary discussions, with regard to folklore and traditional culture, that if authentic traditional handcrafts are not protected they will soon die. Today many singular cultures are assimilating into a multicultural society. In order to preserve the continuity of traditional Indigenous cultures, we must find the means to recognize common concerns and develop legal strategies to engage international issues when we find those common concerns.

References

Cirillo, Dexter. 1992. *Southwestern Indian Jewelry*. New York: Abbeville Press.

Indian Arts and Crafts Association (IACA) and the Council for Indigenous Arts and Culture. 1999. *Collecting Authentic Indian Arts and Crafts: Traditional Work of the Southwest*. Summertown, Tenn.: Book Publishing Company.

Jacka, Lois and Jerry. 1988. *Beyond Tradition: Contemporary Indian Art and Its Evolution*. Flagstaff, Ariz.: Northland Publishing.

Morris, Walter F. Jr. 1996. *Handmade Money: Latin American Artisans in the Market Place.* Washington, D.C.: Organization of American States.

Schrader, Robert Fay. 1983. *The Indian Arts and Crafts Board.* Albuquerque: University of New Mexico Press.

A Seed Is Not Shy of Germination

Rajeev Sethi
Principal
Rajeev Sethi Scenographers Pvt. Ltd.
New Delhi, India

The idea of culture made Field Marshal Goering reach for his gun. Chairman Mao conceived of his great revolution as cultural. Gandhiji preferred to use the word *subhayata*, which is "civilization." And a Sufi poet is said to have described culture as the fragrance that is left behind after the incense stick of life has burnt.

There are no barriers to fragrance. Boundaries created fifty years ago by colonial history in South Asia fractured my subcontinent. But they cannot change the essence of shared experiences, history, and geography which permeate South Asia, as much a part of its wilderness as of its villages or cities.

And this leads to my first recommendation. On culture and political boundaries: Although UNESCO is limited to representing countries, I think we now need a different platform for our cultural paradigm, one that will lead to more holistic understandings and policies. Because culture has permeated the political boundaries of countries, it requires a new *zonal* game plan to document, to administer, and to disseminate. In culture, we are not just looking at representative nations. We are looking at something quite different from what the UN can handle. As I was listening to many of my South Pacific colleagues and to people from Arab and European nations, it struck me that their concerns did not stop at the borders of the countries whose names appear on their conference ID tags. They had to do with a larger zone. So that is one recommendation.

Unfortunately, since culture defies definition, it has no single face for the common man, and therefore has no ballot value. It has no official program or policy, no appropriate budgets. And no one knows this better than UNESCO. On the one hand, the practical son-of-the-soil types dismiss culture as merely leisure-time activities, a song-and-dance routine. And on the other hand, culture is confined to hothouses under the guise of documentation, preservation, and silk-lined museum shelves. Yet others view it as life itself.

Now, many Philistines talk of poverty and expect culture to take a back seat. To say that a country is poor and that culture must be treated as a luxury is like requesting someone to stop breathing because the air is polluted. Conventional economic indices may rate most of us as poor, but our wealth of heritage could make us forerunners in an alternative developmental paradigm. I believe sustainable economic growth is itself a cultural process, and this has already been recognized by UNESCO. I see red whenever I hear dilettantes whisper, "Let culture be. The people will decide." Sure, but look which people. Look around at the greed and the chaos around you, and see who's winning and at what cost.

The mandarins in the finance planning departments may have to first understand what promotes productivity and what leads to intolerance and contempt, breeding new insecurities and uncontrolled pollution. What my country spends on the entire Department of Culture is a tiny fraction of what it spends on VIP security — could there be a connection here?

In this age of liberalization, I'm all for the middle path: liberalization with defined measures of control and a social contract with the money tigers that can check the abuse of culture in the name of so-called development. What we now require is parliamentary intervention and appropriate legislation that will give more teeth to the Department of Culture. I feel UNESCO must alter time-honored perceptions of culture and set up interministerial task forces to make culture less cosmetic. I'm asking them to give themselves much more teeth. I think it's about time they asked UNIDO, WTO, and WHO how their practices affect culture.

In my own country, of course, there are so many issues. In agriculture there is the shift to greater automation of production. This also involves the whole system of terminator seeds, which further marginalizes people and drastically alters their lifestyles. The Ministry of Health needs to know that our indigenous medicines are receiving more attention outside the country at the same time that thousands of untranslated manuscripts gather dust in forgotten libraries all over India. And some are rotting under the various state Departments of Culture.

When a steel factory is built in a tribal belt, does someone in the Tribal Welfare Department have a greater say in the matter? Does the industrialist give thought to its impact on tribal aspirations and culture, on their traditions, and ultimately on the quality of their lives? Hundreds of thousands of tribals have been displaced involuntarily from their ancestral occupation through arbitrary deforestation, false promises, and intimidation. Has this provoked the Department of Culture to sponsor even one study to examine these charges or the altered social conditions?

Who protests when pesticides poison our foods? Or preservatives debase our cooking and eating styles? And who has studied how fertilizers and hybrids have changed our perception of season and the ecological and agricultural cycles? When a river is poisoned, all the culture that it supports also dies. Shouldn't the Department of Culture think about all this as being a cultural as well as an environmental concern?

There is urban development done without building codes, allowing cities and towns to disregard local climate, aesthetics, materials, and skills — what we call tangible culture. Does cultural identity not suffer when the built environment envelops us in a homogenized, spiritless landscape? and when the education system teaches us to abandon what is our own? Rampant consumption breeds its own insecurities. It thrives on them.

In this age, consumer is king and culture is its handmaiden. Indian television sought heavy public investment on the ground that it would serve rural needs. A lot of public investment was sought on this basis. In fact, in all your countries in the developing part of the world, we argue for television in front of the people by saying it is going to serve rural development. Today instead it is mostly subservient to gross urban demands manipulated through advertising by a growing, articulate, and very resourceful breed of white-collar communicators. Using public resources, they profoundly convert culture into an entertainment activity with programs that take away even the little leisure time in which we entertain ourselves. Television today caters to a plethora of urban neuroses. More than other media, it intimidates people in rural areas and affects the way they have begun to perceive and express themselves through gross imitation and identification. But my answer to television is not to shy away from it. We must take it by the horns, by an alternative channel. This is why we want culture to have more teeth and its finger in every pie.

Now I want to speak directly to some of my colleagues who have been expressing their concern for some form of culture that they have had for hundreds of years and are afraid to see change. Perhaps they feel, "When you slip, you don't know where you fall." Here tradition is one form of stability.

But the loss of a particular custom or ritual from memory or practice has not been an enduring concern of mine. The potter has stopped making, for instance, some very beautiful votive offerings? Well, too bad, but so what? It may be that there is no longer a felt need to propitiate certain deities linked to fatal diseases now extinct. These potters may have to learn to make rural refrigerators and architectural elements, as they have done in our part of the world. A man driving a tractor does not need the same footwear and plow as his forebears. The village shoemaker and carpenter therefore cannot expect the customary exchange of grains for their work.

Let me give one final, evocative example. For millennia in India, women have gone to the well, and they have invented many songs to lessen the drudgery of carrying a water pot. In singing the songs, women share many secrets with their daughters and with their colleagues. It's a very good time for them. But basically these songs are used to lessen drudgery. Now, there's a tap in the back yard. Good. I think that is definitely a civilizing process. So the songs will die. And the pot will change because it doesn't have to be carried on the head or on the hip. Well, these things have always been dying. They've always been changing. What should concern us is how the expressive need and energy so delicately enshrined in the women's songs can now find a new vehicle for communication. What kind of environment can we build that will enable creativity to flower? What is replacing that which must go? What do we want to preserve, and how and for whom would we preserve it?

Our concern must be to ask constantly and persistently: From here to where? Can people participate and relate their actions *creatively* — that's the key word — to the pace of the development, and can they absorb its consequences with any sense of quality?

There is, of course, a critical lack of comprehensive schemes for the welfare of artists and artisans. I don't know if it is featured in the *Recommendation*, but the artistic tradition will live only as long as the artists will. There are many artists who have nowhere to go when they become old. There is nobody looking into these issues. And obviously, when the young see their own parents have not gotten anywhere in their profession, then they are not interested. The issue of the artist as a person must be addressed in our planning, and why are we asking for special considerations for this person must be carefully specified.

No one can have a final say in these questions of culture. As breathing is to life, they will always be a crucial part of our existence. Culture is the fragrance of any civilization. Today the air we breathe is polluted because we have not invented new systems to check the decay: How to restore to a society its self-purifying mechanism? How to prevent our senses from shrinking further? How to celebrate innovation and decry the mediocrity of imitation? There are many questions. And answers will come from those who don't take freedom for granted.

You know, yesterday I heard so many papers I felt surely my soul would find no more words. Today I've used a lot. It's like being in a labyrinth with no outlets. I can therefore only use pain as a metaphor for what I feel every time I come to such a meeting, pain that I have not found an appropriate medium to represent our different experiences.

All of us I feel are politicians here in a good measure. We, like all our constituents, are the basket makers of the world. But even as we weave our baskets here, most of our children out there are really more interested in basketball. And only a few of us really know how to play. And so we get hit again and again with careening balls that go through or bounce off. Our bottomless baskets can contain little. My culture has taught me not to be impatient or to hold onto or crave accumulative results. It has taught me that my *raison d'être* is to do my allotted task when action is vastly superior to inaction. And that who wins or loses, no matter what happens, is not the concern of mortals.

I see here a lot of foot soldiers, most of us winning a battle here or losing one there — yet painfully conscious that we are actually losing the war. What concerns me is that even as we win or lose our little battles, we are nowhere near evolving a game plan for the war. Is there a general in our army? An SOS number to call?

We cannot just rely upon UNESCO. I don't mean that it is a "white elephant." But it is not an unencumbered fire-fighting force that can reinforce our separate struggles. UNESCO is a representative body. It is a tool of governments, and the governments will listen to some of you and will not listen to some of you — nothing like the World Wildlife Fund or even Amnesty International, which, if they were to call, the governments might listen to. At least they have begun to listen now.

I think the formation of an unencumbered body for cultural policy cannot happen without UNESCO taking a study on it: What would be the agenda for such a body? What would be its composition? So just as I recommended a conference between UNESCO and WTO and other international agencies to work out the contradictions and complementarities of their respective approaches, I think UNESCO should also convene a conference to conceive of an NGO that is not encumbered by governments, one that can spearhead the movement we are all very connected with. Thank you.

Legal Perspectives and Local Traditions: Toward Legislative and Judicial Remedies

The 1989 UNESCO *Recommendation* and Aboriginal and Torres Strait Islander Peoples' Intellectual Property Rights

Submitted by Commissioner Preston Thomas
representing The Aboriginal and Torres Strait Islander Commission
Prepared by the Indigenous Cultural and Intellectual Property Task Force
Australia

Introduction

The 1989 UNESCO *Recommendation* is a document with high aspirations, one that presents an important opportunity to consider elaborating an international instrument to protect intangible cultural heritage. Depending on the way it is developed, and the eventual form it assumes, this type of instrument could also provide a basis for the development of national laws recognizing the rights of Indigenous peoples to control their cultural heritage. As yet these rights find relatively little expression in most jurisdictions.

This paper considers the 1989 *Recommendation* from the perspective of Australia's Aboriginal and Torres Strait Islander peoples. It explores the potential of the current *Recommendation* to provide for the kinds of legislative reform that will be necessary for effective recognition and protection of the cultural and intellectual property rights of Indigenous Australians. A recent review of Indigenous cultural and intellectual property rights in Australia (in a comprehensive report-in-progress called *Our Culture, Our Future: Report on Australian Indigenous Cultural and Intellectual Property Rights*) indicates a need to consider wide-ranging reforms, including the introduction of *sui generis* laws.

The Aboriginal and Torres Strait Islander Commission (ATSIC) presented a paper to the Symposium on Traditional Knowledge held in Noumea, 15–19 February 1999, that outlined the work in progress — mostly drawing on the above-mentioned report *Our Culture, Our Future* — to consider what reforms are necessary to provide better protection for Indigenous cultural and intellectual property rights.

The report *Our Culture, Our Future* and the summary presented to the Noumea symposium detailed some of the developments in Australia to protect Indigenous intellectual property rights. These include the development of an Authenticity Label to identify the community of origin for Indigenous artworks, and the consideration of reforms to copyright and other intellectual property laws. ATSIC is working closely with government interdepartmental committees to pursue these developments.

The present paper seeks to complement the one we presented to the Noumea symposium. It also builds on that paper to explore ways, based on the Australian experience, in which the 1989 *Recommendation* might be elaborated to accommodate some of the elements that are necessary to provide effective protection for Indigenous cultural and intellectual property rights.

In particular, ATSIC is keen to explore ways to develop a system that enables Aboriginal and Torres Strait Islander peoples to control decision-making in regard to the protection and uses of their cultural heritage, including its intangible components.

The discussion in this paper also seeks to reinforce the Indigenous views presented to the UNESCO-WIPO World Forum on the Protection of Folklore in Phuket, Thailand, 8–10 April 1997, and the UNESCO Symposium on the Protection of Traditional Knowledge and Expressions of Indigenous Cultures in the Pacific Islands held in Noumea, New Caledonia, 15–19 February 1999.

The Relationship between the 1989 *Recommendation* and Other International Developments

The 1989 *Recommendation* is not an instrument specifically for Indigenous peoples. However, given that it offers the elements of an instrument that is focused on the protection of intangible cultural heritage and expressions (defined in the *Recommendation* as "folklore") of peoples in general, Indigenous peoples clearly look to this development as an opportunity to produce an international instrument that can also protect their distinct rights in cultural heritage.

International instruments that provide for the protection of intangible cultural heritage are few. Rarer still are instruments that provide specifically for Indigenous peoples" heritage in the fullest sense. To consider how the UNESCO *Recommendation* might achieve this, the need to ensure consistency between the *Recommendation* and other developing international instruments and standards must be addressed. These instruments and standards include:

- the Draft Declaration on the Rights of Indigenous Peoples
- the UN Study on Indigenous Cultural Heritage
- the current program by the World Intellectual Property Organization (WIPO) to explore the interests of "new beneficiaries" in intellectual property
- developments by the Conference of Parties to the Convention on Biological Diversity (CBD), particularly in relation to the implementation of Articles 8(j) and 10(c)
- the relationship between the CBD and the Trade Related Intellectual Property Rights Agreement (TRIPS)

The further development of the UNESCO *Recommendation* should also have regard to the growing body of Indigenous statements such as the *Mataatua Declaration*.

Before providing comments on the *Recommendation*, it is useful to briefly review some of the characteristics of the cultural heritage of Aboriginal and Torres Strait Islander peoples.

Australian Indigenous Peoples' Traditional Culture

Indigenous culture is expressed in different ways. Australian Indigenous peoples have many and diverse cultures. These cultures comprise a living heritage, an evolving, adapting, and dynamic tradition, and they are expressed through a diverse array of forms. These include not only song, dance, story, and artistic expressions; they also include medicinal, therapeutic, and healing practices, food procurement and preparation, and the use of plants and animals for everyday life as well as for ceremonial and ritual purposes.

Indigenous culture is holistic: it does not separate tangible from intangible. To Australian Indigenous peoples, the distinction between tangible and intangible is a false one. Intangible heritage cannot exist without tangible heritage and vice versa. Both are integral parts of cultural heritage. Although the focus of the 1989 *Recommendation* is on the intangible component, it is critical to ensure that there is sufficient regard given to the interrelationships between intangible and tangible expressions.

What Is to Be Protected: "Intellectual Property," "Traditional Culture," "Folklore," or "Heritage"?

An important consideration in the *Recommendation* is the definition of the subject matter said to constitute "folklore," especially the terminology used to do this.

Australian Indigenous peoples emphasize the interrelationships between their artistic expressions and their cultural knowledge relevant to the conservation and sustainable use of biological diversity. Some arguments support the use of the term "Indigenous intellectual property" to refer to all these elements of culture. According to a United Nations paper, Indigenous intellectual property comprises "(a) folklore and crafts, (b) biodiversity, and (c) Indigenous knowledge."[1] Alternatively, as Erica-Irene Daes suggests, the term "cultural heritage" may be more appropriate.[2]

Is "Folklore" an Appropriate Term?

The term "folklore" derives from a European context and has also been adopted by some anthropologists who have applied it to developing nations such as those in Africa. The term has been used to refer to customs and traditions of village "folk." The term as used in the UNESCO and WIPO discussions gives primacy to "artistic" expressions based in oral traditions and performances.

The use of this term is not appropriate to describe the living heritage of Indigenous peoples. It trivializes the significance that Indigenous peoples place on their intangible heritage as an integral part of their cosmology. It also places an unwarranted emphasis on artistic expressions to the detriment of the other elements of culture such as ecological knowledge and does not sufficiently emphasize the holistic nature of this heritage.[3] This paper will use the terms "cultural and intellectual property," "cultural heritage," and "cultural expressions" instead of "folklore."

Also to be considered in elaborating standards to protect Indigenous intangible heritage is the importance of customary law. Indigenous customary law may be defined "both as a body of rules backed by sanctions and as a set of dispute resolution mechanisms."[4] A comprehensive report by the Australian Law Reform Commission in 1986 considered the extent to which the legal system might contemplate recognition of Aboriginal and Torres Strait Islander customary law. That report included a proposal for an Aboriginal Customary Laws (Recognition) Bill.

Since Indigenous cultural and intellectual property is defined, managed, and controlled in accordance with customary law, it may be argued that the development of effective standards should focus on recognizing and protecting customary laws in the first instance — on the assumption that recognition and protection of intangible heritage can flow from that as a consequence.

Aboriginal and Torres Strait Islander Peoples' Cultural Expressions

Based in oral transmission and sanctioned by customary codes, the control and management of Indigenous peoples" cultural expressions are determined by complex systems of group rights and interests that derive their authority from ancestral traditions rooted in an ancient cosmology known as the Dreaming. Flowing from the Dreaming, intricate knowledge systems link designs and images with cultural, ceremonial, and ritual performances. Knowledge of the locations, properties, and uses of flora and fauna, and the secret and sacred knowledge of sites, places, and objects vital to the maintenance and renewal of cosmology also form elements of these systems.

Exploitation of Indigenous Cultural and Intellectual Property

Maintaining the integrity of their cultural heritage is vital to Indigenous peoples" identity and self-determination. However, when the many and diverse expressions of cultural heritage are documented, recorded, or fixed in sound, film, or video recordings, art works, and published materials, they fall prey to misuse and exploitation. This presents a dilemma: the "fixation" of cultural expressions offers a means of preserving and creating awareness about them, but at the same time, it unfortunately creates opportunities for exploitation and unauthorized uses. There are increasing incidences of exploitation of all forms of Indigenous cultural heritage, including ecological and biological knowledge.

Among the ways and means of safeguarding cultural heritage, an instrument would need to provide effective measures to prevent misuse and exploitation. It is not sufficient, however, to prevent exploitation; there should also be effective measures to provide for compensation in cases where there has been exploitation and misuse, and appropriate mechanisms to enforce criminal or other sanctions where exploitation has occurred. Perhaps most important is the need for Indigenous peoples' control over their own cultural heritage.

Beyond Intellectual Property Laws: Towards a *Sui Generis* Approach

In the Australian legal context, much discussion about Indigenous intellectual property rights is conducted within a framework of existing intellectual property laws — particularly copyright. However, it is now commonly accepted that intellectual property laws do not offer a sufficient basis for the effective protection of *full* Indigenous rights in cultural heritage, including intangible components and traditional knowledge. Intellectual property laws do not protect the communal rights of Indigenous peoples, nor do they allow for protection in perpetuity. Intellectual property laws are based on individual rights and emphasize economic over cultural rights. These laws focus on a single, identifiable creator or author, whereas in Indigenous communities, rights and interests in intellectual creations are more diffuse. They are distributed and managed throughout the community in complex ways according to ritual, socio-political, familial, and affinal relationships.

Appropriate reforms to copyright, patent, trademark, and design laws must, of course, be vigorously pursued. Test cases pursued through the courts also provide an important avenue for extending the capacity for existing laws to protect Indigenous cultural and intellectual property rights. Possible reforms should be pursued through native title, land, heritage, and other laws as well as within copyright laws. However, the basis for an approach to protecting Indigenous cultural heritage in its fullest expression may best be pursued through the development of a *sui generis* system that empowers local communities and appropriate traditional groups to control decision-making about protection and use of their cultural and intellectual property.[5]

A *sui generis* system should provide for protection and for appropriately sanctioned uses of Indigenous cultural heritage. If elements of cultural heritage are authorized by the owners of this heritage for use by the wider community, there will need to be measures to provide for the equitable return of benefits to the group or community. This in turn will require an appropriate body to be identified or established that determines group rights in ownership and control over cultural heritage, and which decides the types and levels of benefit-sharing (or compensation) and how these are to be distributed within the group or community. A *sui generis* system will, therefore, need to establish administrative processes that can achieve these objectives. A possible structure might involve a series of cascading local and regional tribunals managed by a central administrative body. This notion is discussed further below.

Attempts at Recognition and Reform

There have been some attempts in Australia to address the problem of misuse and exploitation of Indigenous cultural heritage. A growing body of cases illustrates some of the ways in which the Australian legal system has sought to deal with notions of Indigenous rights in land, heritage, and culture. These are summarized in the Appendix.[6]

In addition, as noted earlier, the government is currently considering a report commissioned by ATSIC called *Our Culture, Our Future: Report on Australian Indigenous Cultural and Intellectual Property Rights*. ATSIC is working with the government through an interdepartmental committee to explore ways in which the many recommendations of that report might be implemented. Among the many areas being pursued to achieve better protection for Indigenous intellectual property is the development of a Label of Authenticity that will identify the community of origin for Indigenous works of art.

Although there is a growing body of court cases, decisions, reports, and inquiries, much of the discussion is contained within the framework of existing intellectual property laws. While many of these reports, inquiries, and court cases have — either implicitly or explicitly — drawn attention to the need to contemplate a new, *sui generis* approach, there have been very few attempts to design such an alternative system. In 1981, a Working Party established to explore this subject presented its report to the government. The 1981 *Report of the Working Party on the Protection of Aboriginal Folklore* proposed a new legislative system based on what it presented as an "Aboriginal Folklore Act." The report acknowledged the problems in the use of the term "folklore," but nonetheless proposed a model that offers some potential for use within the current debate.

The "Aboriginal Folklore Act" would establish a system for determining the control and use of "folklore." This system would provide for an Aboriginal Folklore Board representative of Indigenous communities to advise the Minister and for a Commissioner for Aboriginal Folklore who would have responsibility for administering the system.[7] The report has not yet been implemented.[8]

The model proposed in that 1981 report remains, in our estimation, a useful basis for the design of an alternative to intellectual property rights systems. In the present-day context, however, such a centralized system may not be appropriate. The 1981 model could be adapted to provide for decentralized community decision-making based on local group autonomy. It may be possible to conceive of a system of cascading tribunals at local and regional levels with a national administrative body. Existing structures and processes for administering land-rights and native-title laws could be explored for their capacity to provide the kind of control over decision-making for intellectual property advocated here. Copyright-type collecting societies could also be considered as possible structures for administering group rights in Indigenous cultural and intellectual property.

Concluding Suggestions: The 1989 *Recommendation* and Australian Indigenous Peoples' Cultural and Intellectual Property Rights

ATSIC recognizes that the 1989 UNESCO *Recommendation* is a document with high aspirations, and that, as such, any development of an enforceable instrument is likely to be a long way off. Notwithstanding this, and given both the complexities of establishing an effective system for recognition and protection of Indigenous intellectual property rights and the relatively slow pace of reform, it is important to grasp any opportunity that might arise to develop a global, *sui generis* approach to protect traditional culture. The *Recommendation* could be elaborated to grow from a predominantly copyright-based concept towards a model law for empowering communities to control their group rights in cultural and intellectual property, and a concept of "cultural heritage" as a holistic, complete system of intangible and tangible heritage.[9]

To achieve the kinds of protection and recognition of Indigenous rights outlined in this paper, the following revisions to the *Recommendation* are suggested.

1. Elaborate and develop the *Recommendation* further as a Convention or other enforceable instrument.
2. Include in that Convention or instrument obligations on signatory countries to implement it effectively.
3. Replace the term "folklore" with a more appropriate term such as "cultural and intellectual property" or "cultural heritage."
4. Expand the definition of "folklore" to include traditional scientific and ecological knowledge relevant to natural and cultural resources and to traditional territory.

Suggestions for elaborating and strengthening copyright-related elements of the present text:

1. Ensure that folklore is protected in perpetuity.
2. Ensure that the protection of folklore does not require folklore to be in fixed form.
3. Ensure that measures are incorporated to (a) prevent the intentional destruction or distortion of folklore, (b) prohibit wrongful attribution of the source of folklore material, and (c) provide protection for sacred and secret materials.
4. Consider incorporating criminal sanctions for unlawful use of folklore and appropriate mechanisms to enforce such sanctions.
5. Ensure consistency with existing copyright and other intellectual property laws.

Suggestions for potential development of the *Recommendation* as a *sui generis* model law for empowering community rights in intellectual and cultural property and traditional knowledge:

1. Include provisions to establish an administrative structure.
2. Include provisions to establish a competent authority to administer the instrument.
3. Include provisions to monitor and report on progress in implementing the instrument.
4. Provide a means to ensure an appropriate and equitable return of benefits to the owners of folklore resulting from its commercial use.
5. Ensure that the protection of folklore does not in any way restrict its continued development — through customary or traditional uses and innovations — within the communities from which it originates.

Appendix

Some Australian Cases Concerning Indigenous Land, Heritage and Culture

Foster v. Mountford 1976.
This decision upheld the rights of a community to prevent the publication of a book that included photographs and descriptions of secret ceremonies. The information in the book had been divulged in confidence to the author, and the book's publication constituted a breach of that confidence.

Milirrpum v. Nabalco 1971.
This landmark case failed to uphold Aboriginal peoples' connections to land as proprietary rights, but it did accept Aboriginal customary law as a "system of law."

Bulun Bulun 1988, Yumbulul v. Reserve Bank 1991, Milpurrurru v. Indofurn 1995, Bulun Bulun v. R & T Textiles, 3 Sept. 1998.
These cases have generally extended the capacity for the *Copyright Act 1968* to protect the interests of Indigenous artists. In the most recent of these, *Bulun Bulun 1998*, the decision linked intellectual property rights in art works to the rights of a group (such as a clan group) to claim copyright.

Mabo v. State of Queensland (No. 2), 1992.
Known as the *Mabo* decision, this landmark decision recognized, within the common law of Australia, the existence of a system of Indigenous customary land tenure known as native title. It overturned the notion that Australia at the time of European occupation was a *terra nullius,* or unoccupied land. The precise nature of the content of native title — including whether this includes cultural and intellectual property rights — has yet to be tested (but see below regarding *Ben Ward*).

Ben Ward & Ors v. State of Western Australia, 24 Nov 1998.
This determination regarding native title upheld a number of rights, including, significantly, the right of the claimant group to control cultural knowledge. This case establishes a precedent for intellectual property related rights which flow from native title, or which are elements of the enjoyment of native-title rights.[10]

Notes

1. United Nations Economic and Social Council, "Intellectual Property of Indigenous Peoples: Concise Report of the Secretary-General," E/CN.4/Sub.2/1992/30, 6 July 1992.

2. United Nations Economic and Social Council, "Study on the Protection of the Cultural and Intellectual Property of Indigenous Peoples," by Erica-Irene Daes, Special Rapporteur to the Sub-Commission on Prevention of Discrimination and Protection of Minorities and Chairperson of the Working Group on Indigenous Populations, E/CN.4/Sub.2/1993/28, 28 July 1993, esp. p. 9.

3. See, for example, Michael Davis, "Competing Knowledges: Indigenous Knowledge Systems and Western Scientific Discourses." Paper presented at Science and Other Knowledge Traditions Conference, 2327 August 1996, at James Cook University, Cairns.

4. The Law Reform Commission, *The Recognition of Aboriginal Customary Laws*, Report No. 31 (Canberra: Australian Government Publishing Service, 1986) 32, citing Diane Bell.

5. There is an extensive and growing body of works that explore this subject, but see, for example, Darrell Posey and Graham Dutfield, *Beyond Intellectual Property: Toward Traditional Resource Rights for Indigenous Peoples and Local Communities* (Ottawa: International Development Research Centre, 1996).

6. For a summary of most of these see for example Ian MacDonald, *Protecting Indigenous Intellectual Property Rights: A Copyright Perspective* (Sydney: Australian Copyright Council, March 1997). For a discussion of *Bulun Bulun 1998* see Martin Hardie, "The Bulun Bulun Case," *Indigenous Law Bulletin* (November 1998):24–26.

7. Commonwealth of Australia, *Report of the Working Party on the Protection of Aboriginal Folklore*, Department of Home Affairs and Environment, Canberra, December 1981.

8. Robin Bell, "Protection of Aboriginal Folklore: Or, Do They Dust Reports?" *Aboriginal Law Bulletin*, December 1985 (reproduced from UNESCO Review 10 (1985):17–19.

9. This section draws on Terri Janke, "UNESCO-WIPO World Forum on the Protection of Folklore," *Art, Antiquity and Law*, vol. 2, issue 4 (December 1997):405–17.

10. For a brief summary of this case see Greg McIntyre, "Brief Summary of Mirriuwung-Gajerrong Decision," *Native Title News* 3 (12):194–96.

References

Bell, Robin. 1985. Protection of Aboriginal Folklore: Or, Do They Dust Reports? *Aboriginal Law Bulletin* 17, reproduced from *UNESCO Review* 10:17–19.

Commonwealth of Australia. 1981. *Report of the Working Party on the Protection of Aboriginal Folklore*. Canberra: Department of Home Affairs and Environment.

Davis, Michael. 1996. Competing Knowledges: Indigenous Knowledge Systems and Western Scientific Discourses. Paper presented to Science and Other Knowledge Traditions Conference, 23–27 August, at James Cook University, Cairns, Australia.

Hardie, Martin. 1998. The Bulun Bulun Case. *Indigenous Law Bulletin* (November):24–26.

Janke, Terri. 1997. UNESCO-WIPO World Forum on the Protection of Folklore. *Art, Antiquity and Law* 2(4):405–17.

MacDonald, Ian. 1997. *Protecting Indigenous Intellectual Property Rights: A Copyright Perspective*. Sydney: Australian Copyright Council (Discusses Bulun Bulun 1988).

McIntyre, Greg. Brief Summary of Mirriuwung-Gajerrong Decision. *Native Title News* 3(12):194–96.

Posey, Darrell, and Graham Dutfield. 1996. *Beyond Intellectual Property: Toward Traditional Resource Rights for Indigenous Peoples and Local Communities*. Ottawa: International Development Research Centre.

United Nations Economic and Social Council. 1992. Intellectual Property of Indigenous Peoples: Concise Report of the Secretary-General. E/CN.4/Sub.2/1992/30 (6 July 1992).

_____. 1993. Study on the Protection of the Cultural and Intellectual Property of Indigenous Peoples. By Erica-Irene Daes, Special Rapporteur to the Sub-Commission on Prevention of Discrimination and Protection of Minorities and Chairperson of the Working Group on Indigenous Populations, E/CN.4/Sub.2/1993/28 (28 July 1993).

Weiner, Janice. 1987. Protection of Folklore: A Political and Legal Challenge. *International Review of Industrial Property and Copyright Law* 18 (1–6):57–92.

Protection of Traditional Culture and Folklore

Kamal Puri
Professor of Law
University of Queensland
Brisbane, Australia

> From our point of view, we say — you have come as invaders, you have tried to destroy our culture, you have built your fortunes upon the lands and bodies of our people, and now . . . want a share in picking out the bones of what you regard as a dead past. We say it is our past, our culture and heritage and forms part of our present life. As such it is ours to share on our terms.
>
> — Ros Langford[1]

Introduction

Copyright law is believed to offer important protection for the rights of Indigenous peoples. Yet as this short paper will demonstrate, a significant amount of Indigenous cultural material and folklore does not meet the criteria for Australia's intellectual property laws.

Protection of folklore is necessary to ensure the lasting survival of Indigenous people. Folklore helps Indigenous communities to preserve their cultural identity and pride. Folklore also functions as social cement to help maintain cultural identity and cohesion.

Folklore embraces conceptual and creative aspects: customs, songs, pageantry, traditional visual designs and crafts, myths, legends, languages, body painting, rock painting, ground painting, music, drama, dance, religious ceremonies, rituals, technical skill, architecture, and herbal and medicinal knowledge.

Meaning of Folklore

Folklore is tradition-based and reflects Indigenous communities' cultural and social identity. It manifests the collective wisdom and culture of Indigenous peoples. It is usually imparted orally, visually, by imitation, or in performance. Another notable feature of folklore is that it is living heritage and it evolves continuously. "Folk" refers to a group of people unified by a linking factor such as common occupation, language, or religion, who possess their own unique traditions. "Lore" refers to a body of traditional facts or beliefs; it includes doctrines, precepts, and ordinances.

Issues

Authentication

There is a wide-scale reproduction and imitation of Aboriginal designs by non-Aboriginal commercial interests. This raises serious concerns among Aboriginal people regarding the potential loss of authenticity and homogeneity of their works.

Ownership

Non-exclusive rights are a peculiar feature of Aboriginal customary law that is not read-ily compatible with the Western notion of exclusive rights under the copyright system. Copyright law is founded on the underlying premise of individual property rights and indi-vidual creativity. Western culture extols the value of the individual above and beyond that of the benefit derived from the collective good. In contrast, a clan or group framework operates in Aboriginal society to govern social and legal relationships.

Expropriation

Aboriginal people fear that unfettered and prolonged appropriation of their unique artis-tic styles and customary traits will eventually lead to destruction and/or debasement of their culture.

Protection of Economic Interests

Use of Aboriginal designs by non-Aboriginal entrepreneurs is widely prevalent in art and the tourist industry. Domestic and foreign tourists crave to acquire Aboriginal paintings, artifacts, music, etc. Naturally, Aboriginal communities from whom these works emanate expect prior authorization and compensation.

Appropriate Protection

Three factors seem to limit the efficacy of the current copyright system to provide ade-quate protection to Aboriginal cultural and intellectual property rights. First, there is the requirement of originality — the work must originate from the author and not be copied from another work. However, in the case of Aboriginal art, the work's value lies not in its originality or individuality but in its conformity to tradition.[2] Second, under the copyright law, a work must exist in writing or some other material form in order to be protected by copyright. However, many Aboriginal works exist in the oral tradition, and hence it is not possible to give them a fixed form. Finally, the term of copyright protection poses a prob-lem because most Aboriginal works are very old and are therefore considered to have fallen in the free-for-all basket, i.e., the public domain.

Current Legal Protection

The *Copyright Act 1968* (Australia) confers exclusive proprietary rights. Basically, it upholds individual ownership. The Act confers purely economic rights. As yet, the law confers no moral-rights protection. While the Act does not discriminate against Aboriginal works, the latter fall outside the parameters of copyright as currently defined. For exam-ple, the Act does not protect cultural material such as rock art and works that are not in material form, e.g., body or sand painting.

Judicial Recognition of Aboriginal Customary Laws

Foster v. Mountford[3]

This case involved sale of a book written by anthropologist Dr. Mountford. The book contained an Aboriginal group's sacred knowledge divulged to the anthropologist thirty-five years ago by tribal leaders. The court banned the book because the publication was considered to have been in breach of confidence.

Bulun Bulun v. Nejlam Investments and Others[4]

This was the first high-profile copyright action involving reproduction of an Aboriginal artist's painting on T-shirts. The case was settled out of court for $150,000, thus sending warning signals to the commercial world that Indigenous works in traditional styles may qualify for protection under the Australian copyright law.

Yumbulul v. Aboriginal Artists Agency Ltd.[5]

This case involved alleged reproduction of an Aboriginal art work, *Morning Star Pole*, on $10 currency notes by the Reserve Bank of Australia. The action against the Reserve Bank was settled by agreement. However, the action against the agent who had acted for the Aboriginal artist was unsuccessful because the judge refused to accept that the artist had misunderstood the nature of the document he had signed giving permission for the reproduction of his design. Be that as it may, this decision marked an important judicial milestone in the application of the *Copyright Act 1968* to Indigenous artistic works. The court accepted that the *Pole* was an original artistic work in which copyright subsisted, and that the Aboriginal artist was the owner of the copyright in it. The Federal Court's dicta also pointed to the need to recognize Aboriginal customary law dealing with ancestral designs, especially notions of communal ownership. As noted by one commentator, the proceedings did much to stimulate the debate about appropriate protection for Aboriginal art, especially the inadequacies that exist in the law.[6]

Bancroft v. Dolina Fashion Group Pty. Ltd.[7]

This case involved dresses with an "Aboriginal look." The print supplied by the fabric maker was allegedly a direct copy of an Aboriginal painting. The case was settled out of court. The defendant destroyed the remaining stock of the fabric.

Mabo v. State of Queensland (No. 2)[8]

In this path-breaking decision, the High Court of Australia recognized that, under Australian common law, Indigenous rights in land survived European occupation unless the Crown had made an express appropriation of those rights. This decision can be interpreted and extended to encompass intellectual property rights on the same footing as land rights.[9] Arguably, this recognition of customary law has added much impetus to the concept of a separate body of copyright law that recognizes the unique position of Australia's Aboriginal people within a different construct. As one commentator points out:

> If the interests of Aboriginal artists are recognised on the terms of Aboriginal law, rather than only when they fit within the alien legal categories of the Anglo-Australian legal system, then an important step will have been taken towards a reconciliation between the "enlightenment" and the "dreaming" traditions which co-exist on the Australian continent.[10]

Milpurrurru v. Indofurn Pty. Ltd. and Others[11]

This decision has been referred to as the "Mini-Mabo" for intellectual property rights. The case involved reproduction of artistic works on carpets. The court held that the unauthorized reproduction caused a breach of copyright. More importantly, customary Aboriginal laws were taken into account in quantifying the damages which had been suffered. This decision demonstrated a sensitive and flexible approach of the court:

- Exemplary damages were awarded for culturally based harm, the court acknowledging cultural sensitivity.
- The Aboriginal custom of not using the names of deceased artists was respected.
- Lump-sum damages were awarded to enable Aboriginal clans to take account of collective ownership of the designs.
- Additional damages were also awarded for humiliation or insulting behavior to a particular cultural group.

The court recognized the difficulty in applying the Western copyright regime to Indigenous peoples. This litigation brought to the fore the fact that the Western legal system and the Aboriginal customary laws are two conflicting legal systems. The latter emphasize group ownership and community involvement in decision-making, whereas the Anglo-Saxon legal system focuses on individual ownership and personal rights.

Bulun Bulun and Another v. R & T Textiles Pty. Ltd.[12]

In this case, the elders of the Ganalbingu people from Arnhem Land in the Northern Territory tried unsuccessfully to have communal title in their ritual knowledge and art work recognized and protected by the Australian law. The Federal Court held that the copyright law did not confer group ownership or communal title in an artistic work. However, the judge stated that there was a fiduciary relationship between the artist (Bulun Bulun) and his people, which gave rise to fiduciary obligations on the part of the artist. This finding was based on the obligations of the artist under the laws and customs of the Ganalbingu people. But this did not mean that the Aboriginal laws and customs were part of the Australian law. What it meant was that the Australian legal system treated Aboriginal laws and customs as part of the "factual matrix" which characterized the relationship as one of mutual trust and confidence.

Viability of Copyright Protection

A prerequisite for copyright is that a work must be original. Yet many Indigenous artists draw upon their cultural heritage by painting pre-existing clan designs, which have been handed down for generations. Again, for copyright to vest under the *Copyright Act*, there must be an identifiable author. Yet because of the nature of Indigenous cultural expressions, such a person is not easily identified and, therefore, cannot be protected. These requirements of authorship and ownership under the copyright system are thus incompatible with group or collective ownership.

The "originality" requirement is another barrier. Folklore draws upon pre-existing tradition: sacred restricted ancestral designs must be replicated precisely. By the copyright yardstick, the condition of originality is not met. However, note that in *Yumbulul*,[13] originality was acknowledged explicitly: "there is no doubt that the pole was an original artistic work."

To obtain copyright protection, the work must be recorded or written in a permanent or tangible form; non-permanent forms of cultural expression, such as dance, song, and the performance of a story do not meet the requirement. Consequently, oral tradition is not protected, and the Indigenous community can only seek protection against the reproduction of that oral tradition through the breach of confidence action. Furthermore, once the oral tradition has been formulated into a material form, the author then gains exclusive rights under the *Copyright Act 1968* regardless of whether or not the author is an Indigenous person or comes from the Indigenous community. What's more, copyright law does not recognize the Indigenous customary rules which restrain reproduction of Indigenous arts and cultural materials. Since folklore exists practically in collective and individual memories, it does not have any material form. Copyright protects the form and not the substance, so traditional themes and artistic styles and techniques may not get protection.

Duration of protection under the copyright system is grossly inadequate. Ancestral designs are intrinsically perpetual in nature.

The Designs Act 1906 also offers only limited protection for Indigenous cultural and intellectual property rights because (i) traditional rights to Indigenous designs are perpetual; (ii) design protection is for commercial interests; (iii) Indigenous law is concerned with communal rights rather than individual ownership, and (iv) the costs of protecting all designs belonging to an Indigenous community would be too great.

Indigenous knowledge regarding scientific, pharmaceutical, and agricultural processes and products is generally unpatentable because under the *Patent Act 1990,* there are stringent requirements regarding novelty and inventive ingenuity that have to be met. Furthermore, the invention would not be considered novel due to the need for a prior art base; the invention must involve an inventive step when compared with the art base; and the high cost of patenting, around A\$14,000, would often exclude Indigenous communities.

Indigenous peoples are able to register their Indigenous words, symbols, and motifs under the *Trade Marks Act 1995*. Yet many Indigenous communities would be loath to do so because the trademark applies to the registered owner, who has monopoly control, not the collective group.

In addition, the *Cultural Heritage Act* is generally inadequate because it does not recognize many rights Indigenous people consider important in maintaining their culture. This is firstly because the focus of cultural heritage laws is on tangible material, such as objects, sites, and areas. Intangible materials, such as stories, dreaming tracks, and songs, are not protected. Secondly, the focus is on historical and scientific value rather than cultural and spiritual value. Thirdly, past heritage is considered more important to protect than living heritage. Lastly, the Indigenous participation in the decision-making process is usually limited; a government minister usually decides when to act to protect. However, there has recently been a turnaround concerning the focus of Indigenous cultural heritage legislation, with the development of cultural heritage agreements and the restoration of fishing, hunting, and gathering rights in some states and territories.

While the Australian Constitution allows the Commonwealth to make special laws with respect to people of race, the copyright law is not always appropriate to protecting Indigenous rights because of its focus on economic and individual rights rather than on communal and personal rights. The Australian legal system appears not to recognize communal ownership and instead focuses on individual ownership. Most countries throughout the world also focus on individual rather than communal ownership, resulting in an unequal representation of Indigenous peoples with regards to copyright laws.

Currently, a few measures directed at Indigenous cultural and intellectual property rights protection are being formulated on an administrative and management level. These include setting up a collecting society for collecting royalties for Indigenous artists and creators, funding a national label of authenticity for Indigenous art, and developing material transfer agreements and bio-prospecting licenses. Other protocols and guidelines recently adopted by the Commonwealth include self-determination for the return of Indigenous ancestral remains and sacred objects. Likewise, museums have implemented guidelines and protocols for the digitization of Indigenous objects.

Protection of Intangible Cultural Heritage

UNESCO's *Convention Concerning the Protection of the World Cultural and Natural Heritage of 1972* divided cultural heritage into monuments, protected buildings, and protected cultural sites, with the overall criterion for protection being "outstanding universal value." However, this preoccupation with the protection of physical things has meant that no thought is being given to the protection of intangible cultural heritage. It is therefore heartening to note that the recent report of the *Australian Copyright Law Review Committee on the Simplification of the Copyright Act 1968* has recommended abolition the requirement of "material form" in copyrightable subject matter.

Proposal for Reform

The Australian Working Party of 1981 recommended a special legislation, Aboriginal Folklore Act, which should provide for the following:

- a prohibition on non-traditional uses of sacred/secret material
- prohibitions on debasing, mutilating, or destructive use
- payment to traditional owners of items being used for commercial purposes
- a system of clearances for prospective users of items of folklore
- an Aboriginal Folklore Board to advise the Minister on policy matters
- a Commissioner for Aboriginal Folklore to issue clearances and negotiate payments

The report suggested a mechanism for the examination by the Aboriginal Folklore Board of proposed uses of items of folklore by non-customary users on a case-by-case basis. These recommendations have been collecting dust.

Conclusion

In most parts of the world, there are no specific laws to protect traditional knowledge and expressions of Indigenous culture. Consequently, almost all Indigenous communities have been forced to become secretive and, where possible, to turn to traditional customary laws to safeguard their culture and knowledge from indiscriminate exploitation and subjugation by the dominant Western culture. It is strongly recommended that UNESCO should rally behind Indigenous peoples of the world by adopting a common approach so that their special needs could be represented at domestic, regional, and international levels.

As this brief paper indicates, appropriation of traditional knowledge and expressions of Indigenous cultures is rapidly reaching pandemic proportions. There is a wide dissemination of Indigenous cultural expressions without authorization and recompense to the traditional owners. Also, with the gradual establishment of museums and cultural centers and increased public awareness, there are serious issues emerging which involve repatriation of cultural objects. While on the one hand, easy access to modern technology (e.g., television, computers) has made Indigenous communities more aware of their cultural heritage and traditional knowledge, on the other, the same technology has accelerated the means by which non-Indigenous users can appropriate cultural items and traditional knowledge for commercial exploitation (e.g., digitization of traditional images). Another area of great concern is Indigenous knowledge of plants and medical treatments. Examples abound of cases where plants from the Indigenous societies are being patented by multinational enterprises and marketed as pharmaceuticals. Many of these plants have enormous emotional and economic importance for Indigenous peoples including use for ceremonies, healing, and traditional farming.

In sum, the current intellectual-property regime is unsuited to give adequate protection to traditional knowledge and expressions of Indigenous culture because it focuses on individual rather than communal rights. Moreover, the primary, if not the sole, objective of the Western intellectual property system is to protect economic rather than cultural interests. As one commentator has put it succinctly: "European law is based on the individual."[14]

Furthermore, the copyright mould does not fit the traditional works well because of their antiquity. In any case, until recently, there was a tendency to trivialize the expressions of Indigenous culture (e.g., Aboriginal art, music, dance, and myths), perhaps a carry-over of the colonization era. The culture of denigrating Indigenous customs and traditions presumably on the ground that they did not match with the modern "civilized" societies' values and standards meant that no thought was given to accommodating the needs and aspirations of Indigenous creativity. I believe that this notion is reflected in the TRIPS Agreement, which is completely oblivious to protection of Indigenous cultural knowledge and resources.

Notes

1. Ros Langford, "Our Heritage — Your Playground" (1983) 16 *Australian Archaeology* 1 at 6.
2. See C. O'Brien, "Protecting Secret Sacred Designs — Indigenous Culture and Intellectual Property Law" (1997) 2 *Media and Arts Law Review* 57 at 65.
3. (1976) 29 FLR 233.
4. Unreported, Federal Court of Australia, Darwin (NTG 3 of 1989).
5. (1991) 21 IPR 481.
6. C. Golvan, "Aboriginal Art and the Protection of Indigenous Cultural Rights" (1992) 56 *Aboriginal Law Bulletin* 5 at 7.
7. (Unreported, Federal Court of Australia, 12 December 1991).
8. (1992) 66 ALJR 408.
9. See further, K. Puri, "Copyright Protection for Australian Aborigines in the Light of Mabo" in Stephenson and Ratnapala (eds.), *Mabo: A Judicial Revolution* (University of Queensland Press, 1993) at 132.
10. S. Gray, "Enlightenment or Dreaming? Attempting to reconcile Aboriginal Art and European Law" [1992] *Law Institute Journal* 47.
11. (1994) 30 IPR 209.
12. (1998) 41 IPR 513.
13. *Yumbulul v. Aboriginal Artists Agency Ltd.*, note 6, above.
14. A. Seeger, in *Borrowed Power: Essays on Cultural Appropriation* (eds. B. Ziff and P. Rao (Rutgers University Press, New Jersey, 1997) at 55.

Some Considerations on the Protection of the Intangible Heritage: Claims and Remedies

Lyndel V. Prott
Chief
International Standards Section
Division of Cultural Heritage, UNESCO

Introduction

Much discussion on the protection of "intangible cultural heritage" proceeds as though this concept were uniform and the objectives of those seeking to protect it were in all cases the same. Before any serious work can be done on protection, these assumptions should be analyzed, and the needs and objectives for each category of cultural heritage should be examined. This would help answer questions such as whether legal protection is required and would be sufficient; what, if any, the appropriate analogies in existing law are; and whether a *sui generis* scheme should be developed.

To note the need to analyze the components of "intangible cultural heritage," to distinguish the different objectives of protection, and to explore the varied threats and the diverse means that might be used against them is not to disregard the holistic approach traditional communities take to their heritage. That holistic approach is to be taken into account in achieving an adequate level of protection. But it is clear that the threat to particular aspects of heritage is more serious, if only because in those cases the would-be users are much more powerful.

Such an analysis would start by listing what is regarded as intangible cultural heritage by the individuals and communities seeking protection. Even when they agree that protection is necessary, they all may not see the same needs in protecting a particular kind of traditional knowledge or share the same objectives for what they call "protection." The *Recommendation on the Safeguarding of Traditional Culture and Folklore* lists "among others" the cultural forms to be protected as "language, literature, music, dance, games, mythology, rituals, customs, handicrafts, architecture and other arts" that reflect the cultural and social identity of a community.

As an experiment, I have attempted to look at certain aspects of the intangible heritage and at the various elements that would be concerned in their protection. This paper is not intended to define this concept, even less to offer an authoritative or even tentative list. It simply illustrates the range of intangible heritage to be protected, the threats posed now or likely to be posed in the near future and the means — economic, social, or legal — which might be available to counter those threats and meet the objectives of protection.

Current anthropological studies emphasize that it is social process that needs to be preserved, rather than merely the items produced, to ensure the continued creation of these valued products. This social process is currently interfered with by other social processes now very evident: globalization, tourism, commodification. But cultural items are produced by diverse social processes; and rather than trying first to categorize those processes, it seems easier to gain an initial perspective by looking at the kinds of traditional culture that have been cited as needing protection and then to consider the social processes which created them.

What Kinds of Intangible Heritage?

Below, to begin this quest for perspective, are fifteen items, in no particular order. Some of course overlap (language and oral history; music and dance, etc.); others are dependent on the availability of material elements (handcrafts, on availability of materials husbanded by traditional ecological skills) or on outside factors (maintenance of a viable ecological unit, for example). The list is only intended to illustrate the problematic of adequately protecting intangible heritage. The objectives, needs, and means cited may not be accurate or complete and may be subject to disagreement. The list is intended as a starting point for assessing the objectives to be pursued, the needs to be met, and the kinds of means to be used, legal and non-legal.

Language

Objective: to preserve threatened languages.

Needs: to maintain a viable language community, a minimum number of mother-tongue speakers.

Means: endangered-language programs; mother-tongue or bilingual education programs; recording of elderly speakers; "living cultural treasures" program for epic and poetry reciters; prize for "oral cultural heritage."

Oral History

Objective: to maintain living oral tradition by addition of modern historical items and repetition of existing histories.

Needs: to support traditional oral historians and encourage imitation by the young.

Means: to encourage participation in education; to record; to encourage respect for, e.g., by prize.

Traditional Religion and Ritual

Objective: to retain existing religious beliefs and practices.

Needs: to ensure survival of a group, i.e., by ensuring adequate economic support and cultural continuity; to ensure continued access to religious sites; to ensure maintenance of ceremonial objects in the community or their return from outside the community where necessary; to ensure continuity of the skills used to create ritual objects.

Means: ensuring of social and economic support sufficient for group survival; legal protection of religious property; return programs where necessary; legal guarantees of access to sites; legal guarantees of freedom of religious practice (provided not contrary to human rights); preservation of craft skills for ritual objects.

Sacred Images and Themes

Objective: to ensure respect.

Needs: to prevent use by non-entitled; continued induction of young, authorized artists to this tradition.

Means: legal regulation to prevent non-authorized use; support for traditional training and induction methods; support for social unit to whom tradition belongs and for unit within it that decides on entitlement.

Non-Sacred Designs, Artistic Themes, and Handicrafts

Objective: to ensure continuity and survival of handicraft traditions; to convert into source of income.

Needs: to ensure supply of raw materials (species of woods, cane, etc., in threatened areas); development of markets; training; legal protection requiring authorization for use by someone other than the artist (if the cultural product is regarded as individual property) or the community (if it is regarded as community property).

Means: protection of materials needed (especially where production is dependent on a continued local supply); commercial advice and training; legal regulation to prevent imitation by non-authorized persons; training programs; "living cultural treasures" program; income support; encouragement of sponsorship, e.g., by tax deductions; development of markets (commoditization); active museum collecting programs; artists-in-residence programs; prizes; handicraft fairs.

"Handicrafts" probably needs to be broken down into separate areas such as wood and stone sculpture, pottery, and wickerwork so as to cover the particular needs of each. As an example, the case of textiles can be examined:

Traditional Textile Skills
(e.g., embroidery, weaving, tapestry, quilting, knitting, lace-making, and carpet-making)

Objective: to preserve and ensure continuation of skills.

Needs: preservation of equipment (e.g., looms, shuttles); cultivation and maintenance of raw materials (e.g., wool, flax, silk, and vegetable dyes); appropriate working places.

Means: active museum programs on history, with examples of different patterns from various groups; recording work songs, etc.; recording work methods for later reintroduction if necessary; commoditization to ensure economic return; replacing disappearing clients (e.g., churches) by others; recording methods of handing down.

Traditional Skills Related to Tangible Cultural Heritage
(e.g., all the skills associated with vernacular architecture)

Objective: to maintain stock of skills for restoration, maintenance, and replacement of tangible heritage created by traditional skills.

Needs: to ensure the handing on of skills and the survival of tools and raw materials.

Means: support of senior craftsmen to ensure survival; training schemes to ensure passing on; "living cultural treasures" program; mandatory use in government-owned properties; education programs to enhance appreciation.

Traditional Music

Objective: to ensure continuation of traditional forms of music; to ensure consent for use.

Needs: training; traditional instruments.

Means: support of instrument-making and repair through workshops; encouragment and income support for itinerant performers; recording of music; establishing or maintaining of legal right to recompense for use by persons outside the community.

Traditional Dance

Objective: to ensure traditional dance forms continue.

Needs: training; maintenance of associated skills (costume; choreography; traditional music).

Means: support for specialist schools; "living cultural treasures" program; festivals; teaching appreciation in education programs; recording of choreography; quality control; encouragement of quality cultural tourism.

Cuisine

Objective: to maintain distinctive culinary habits; to maintain sustainable lifestyle; to encourage healthy diet.

Needs: to maintain availability of traditional ingredients (e.g., in viable fishing, hunting, and cropping areas); to maintain traditional cooking implements and know-how.

Means: recording recipes; "living cultural treasures"; establishment of eco-reserves; quality cultural tourism.

Tracking and Hunting Skills
(e.g., recognition of animal spoor, imitation of animal calls, fishing, and navigating)

Objective: to retain traditional knowledge for the community; to ensure traditional food supply.

Needs: a viable social unit; an adequate ecological reserve.

Means: allowing sufficient time from education for children to learn the skills within a community; reconsideration of educational programs; encouraging traditional festivals related to seasonal activities; exemption of traditional lifestyle from imposed regulation or prohibition.

Traditional Practices of Husbanding Nature

Objective: to preserve ecological practices; to disseminate knowledge of good ecological practice.

Needs: preservation of an ecologically viable unit; preservation of traditional seed stocks and animal species.

Means: national protected areas for continuance of traditional lifestyles; education in the value of ecologically based lifestyles.

Traditional Medical Knowledge

Objective: to ensure survival of traditional knowledge; to ensure commercial return for its bearers.

Needs: to ensure continued supply of plant and other material; to ensure maintenance of an ecologically viable unit; to ensure consent of and/or recompense to community for advice.

Means: legal requirement of consent of community for commercial exploitation of knowledge or of recompense for its use.

Traditional Methods of Conflict Resolution
(e.g., the Polynesian way and the methods in some African communities)

Objective: to maintain successful conflict resolution practices; to study and disseminate them for use elsewhere.

Needs: respect for traditional methods in addition to imported ones.

Means: supporting analysis and comparative studies by institutes of conflict resolution; supporting practice of these skills at the community level; inserting them in educational programs; fostering their use in appropriate circumstances inside and outside their community of origin.

Traditional Relationships between Different Ages in the Community

Objective: to maintain traditional respect for age.

Need: counter the globalization of "youth culture."

Means: review of educational programs; support of traditional political and judicial systems (e.g., chieftaincy); support for apprenticeship systems.

These examples may or may not accurately reflect the wishes of traditional communities. They are intended simply to show the variety of aims, threats, and possible remedies that may exist and need to be considered before embarking on any program of protection. Such considerations are particularly important when developing legal protections, and even more so when such protection is envisioned on the international level.

Other Considerations

Many other considerations must be borne in mind in developing protections for folklore and traditional lifestyles.

First, folklore is not static; it develops. The principles of sustainable cultural development require that the members of a culture are themselves empowered to preserve and develop it. It is also clear that some aspects of traditional cultures such as child marriage, female genital mutilation, and acts contrary to human rights can hardly be maintained in the face of general international agreement on human rights standards.

Secondly, for community-based systems, the intrusion of individualism from an encroaching culture may make decisions about preservation and development of traditional cultures particularly acute and prone to gender or age conflicts.

Thirdly, some of the solutions being sought may already be the subject of discussion in other fora such as the *Draft United Nations Declaration on the Rights of Indigenous Peoples*, discussions of cultural rights, and the *Convention on Biological Diversity 1992*. It should be noted, however, that none of these has yet successfully established the full range of protection being sought.

Fourthly, some of the proposals, like the *Draft Declaration on the Rights of Indigenous Peoples*, may run into conflict with other strongly held politico/legal views such as rights of property, which are in some legal systems guaranteed by a constitution and in others so strongly represented in a civil code or political tradition as to be deeply entrenched.

Fifthly, in many indigenous communities, traditional knowledge and skills are seen holistically: there is something artificial in separating out traditional knowledge of medicine, of husbanding nature, of religion, and so on, since they are interdependent and part of a whole conception of life and natural cycles.

Finally, the commodification of traditionally created goods may be acceptable in some cultures but unacceptable in others, especially where a religious element is present. On the other hand, the recognition of the right of a community, akin to a moral right, to stop unauthorized use or distortion may assist the preservation of traditions.

Conclusion

Preserving the social processes which have produced folklore and traditional knowledge is much more difficult than just recording them or preserving the results in a museum. For example, where traditional skills are handed down from elderly persons with a lifetime of expertise, with decades of experience in increasing cultural knowledge, and with primary responsibility for their transmission to the next generation, respect for the aged is a very important aspect of that transmission. In a society where youth is elevated as equally or more important, that transmission may well be interrupted and the traditions less respected than the radical, the new, the exotic. Similarly, the sharp division in some cultures between the social processes undertaken by women and those by men may be radically changed by new ideas of gender equality which interfere with the traditional attribution of roles and skills.

These changes therefore may make it extremely difficult to preserve folklore and its creative processes in isolation from society-wide processes that involve many value judgments about empowerment of local communities, of women, of the young. Some of these problems can be dealt with: an example is the use of a "living cultural treasures" program, which shows social approbation, including at the international level, of supreme exponents of traditional cultural skills.

However, the revolution created by global television and Internet communication provides powerful images and values that counter those inherited in many societies. These images are driven by commercial incentives, and any effort to oppose them by programming dominated by other motivations runs into theoretical ("censorship") and economic ("freedom of trade") arguments.

In this dynamic there is a place for legal regulation, but too much should not be expected of it. Law which runs counter to the most powerful social processes currently at work is unlikely to be successful in the long term without a degree of compulsion not acceptable in most societies today. Therefore it should be used as one of a number of social controls, such as education, while using incentive schemes (prizes, tax incentives, sponsorship arrangements) to work with existing elements of the social processes of the communities concerned. Above all, it should seek to empower those persons who are bearers of traditional culture to continue to provide alternative models of behavior and different criteria of "success" than those portrayed by other means from outside the community.

The 1989 UNESCO *Recommendation on the Safeguarding of Traditional Culture and Folklore* has been in place for ten years, and it is time to assess its future role within UNESCO Member States in order to ensure the safeguarding and revitalization of the world's intangible cultural heritage. One option suggested has been an amendment of the *Recommendation* or its replacement by another Recommendation.

While some UNESCO Member States consider that the time has come for UNESCO to create an International Convention for the safeguarding of intangible cultural heritage after the manner of the *World Heritage Convention of 1972*, presently applicable only to tangible (cultural and natural) heritage, it is premature to decide what form such a convention might take: preservation of the intangible is more likely to need a different *sui generis* regime developed for the specificities of this particular type of heritage.

Another suggestion has been to amend the World Heritage Convention, but amendment of the Convention has so far been decided against and, for many reasons, a listing system is unlikely to produce all the kinds of protection being sought. Other analogies have been proposed such as those with intellectual property regimes: these need to be examined closely, but four regional meetings held in 1998–1999 by UNESCO and the World Intellectual Property Organization (WIPO) all came to the view that intellectual property law did not give appropriate protection to expressions of folklore or traditional knowledge. Experience with the 1989 *Recommendation* also needs to be taken into account in preparing a draft Convention.

Any legal instrument or amendment of an existing instrument prepared by UNESCO must, according to its internal regulations, start with a feasibility study. In such a study all these aspects would need to be examined.

Global Steps to Local Empowerment in the Next Millennium: An Assessment of UNESCO's 1989 *Recommendation on the Safeguarding of Traditional Culture and Folklore*

Bradford S. Simon

Introduction

Since 1989, when the 1989 *Recommendation on the Safeguarding of Traditional Culture and Folklore* ("the 1989 *Recommendation*") was unanimously adopted at a UNESCO General Conference,[1] the 1989 *Recommendation* has stood, in the words of one commentator, as "the highest profile declaration on the importance of intangible heritage in the World."[2] Nonetheless, in the years after its adoption, the 1989 *Recommendation* has lost momentum, due in part to internal UNESCO matters, a lack of international response,[3] and the difficulty of protecting a living heritage that is constantly evolving.[4]

The ten years since the 1989 *Recommendation* was adopted have witnessed several trends that confirm the importance of protecting folklore on a global scale. These same trends, however, call into question some assumptions of the 1989 *Recommendation*.

The first trend is the growing role of information as a driving force in the global economy, powered by the ability to reproduce and distribute it ever more quickly and cheaply by new technology. The laws that control the flow of information, namely intellectual property laws, have acquired increasing prominence.[5] The intellectual property laws developed in Western countries over hundreds of years have now been made global through international legal mechanisms such as GATT (General Agreement on Tariffs and Trade) and TRIPS (Trade Related Aspects of Intellectual Property Rights).[6] TRIPS codifies the internationalization of culturally contingent and historically derived forms of intellectual property protection.[7] Over 115 nations are signatories to this treaty, which grants the World Trade Organization enforcement powers.

As will be discussed later (Section III), these laws reflect particular values and rationales, which necessarily exclude defined types of cultural practices from the protected ambit of "innovations" and "works of authorship." When these practices are excluded, therefore placing them in the public domain, it is reasonable to expect certain consequences. As one commentator notes, "In an economic era defined by global information technologies, a monopoly right in the fruits of information is indispensable for the generation of new capital and invaluable for maintaining a global competitive edge."[8] The fear is that information derived from Indigenous groups will become part of the global flow of information at the same time that it is excluded from controlling mechanisms and disassociated from its origins. This exclusion will first be felt economically by groups[9] that are unable to profit from their own information. These same groups are denied access to protected information and innovations that they are unable to afford. This disparity is likely to have a permanent and profound effect: the devaluation and loss of important knowledge and of its association with those who traditionally maintained it.

The second trend in the years since 1989 is the growing international recognition of the relationship between biological and cultural diversity and the growing concern with the depletion of both, which is manifest in the UNCED Convention on Biological Diversity. Recognition of the loss of cultural diversity is one of the motivations of the conference for which this assessment has been prepared. Whether that loss is called "a creeping mono-culture,"[10] "Coca-Colonization," or "McWorld,"[11] the fear, and increasingly the reality, is of a world dominated by one species, one economic system, a homogenized commodity marketplace, one view of innovation, and one form of relationship to the natural environment. The loss of cultural diversity arises not only from physical extinction but also, in daily increments, from cultural assimilation.[12] One author claims that "the traditions of the Maori in New Zealand, the native Hawaiians and native Americans in the United States, and certain Indigenous cultures of Latin America have become commercialized to such an extent that their cultural and religious significance has been virtually erased from public memory."[13] The staggering historical loss of cultural diversity continues and increases its pace.[14] For example, an estimated 300 million Indigenous people belonging to around 5,000 groups live in over seventy countries.[15] In Brazil alone, it is estimated that one Indian tribe has disappeared in each year since 1900.[16] Further, one expert estimates that ninety percent of the roughly 6,000 languages being spoken today will die out within around 100 years.[17]

A central premise of the Convention on Biological Diversity is that today Indigenous communities preserve much of the world's remaining biodiversity.[18] The loss of cultural diversity is certain to increase the loss of biological diversity. Species and varieties are becoming extinct at an unprecedented rate due to cultural extinction, destruction of habitat,[19] and the use of fewer, high-yield commercial varieties in agriculture. Losses in cultural diversity and biological diversity are historically and ecologically intertwined. This relationship is especially clear when one considers, for example, that traditional agriculture maintains myriad genetic varieties (many of which increase yield of other varieties) and that the store of Indigenous peoples' knowledge about their surrounding biological diversity is estimated to increase pharmaceutical screening efficiency sixfold.[20]

The third trend, and one this author believes to be of major importance, is the fact that over the past ten years, tribal, Indigenous, and other groups have produced increasingly sophisticated arguments laying claims to their intellectual resources, phrased in the language of Western intellectual property laws. Examples include the *Mataatua* and *Bellagio Declarations*.[21] The 1989 *Recommendation* does not adequately deal with many of the central concerns expressed in these discussions. This point will be demonstrated throughout this assessment.

This paper has several goals. The first section attempts to capture several key concerns espoused not only by academics and organizations (such as UNESCO and the WIPO) but also by tradition-bearers and their communities. It will suggest issues that the 1989 *Recommendation* and other such documents must take into account. Section II assesses UNESCO's 1989 *Recommendation* in light of these concerns and points out possible changes to better take them into account. Section III considers UNESCO efforts in this area apart from the 1989 *Recommendation* and presents a number of possible legal options in an attempt to foster further dialogue.

Given the inherent complexity of regulating and protecting local culture and the rapidity with which cultural diversity and its bearers are disappearing, this assessment will argue for an immediate multifaceted legal response. Namely, it urges action that is:

- international in scope, to recognize the global nature of the problem;

- local in immediate effect, to support and empower those who have produced, transmitted, and preserved folklore;
- feasible in implementation, acknowledging that no single legal mechanism can effectively address all the concerns implicated; and
- cognizant that there is great need for and value in ongoing local, national, and regional experimentation with different options in addition to a unified international effort.

Accordingly, Section IV proposes that an international instrument, with minimum rights and national treatment, could effectively empower local communities within a global framework. By drawing on some of the options discussed in the preceding section, it suggests the sort of minimum rights that could be included in such an instrument.

I. Areas of Concern in Folklore Protection

The following concerns are central to discussions about the protection of folklore. They are drawn from the *Mataatua Declaration*, the 1989 *Recommendation*, the *Model Provisions*,[22] and academic discussions. These concerns are not described in an overall order of importance, because the relevance of any single concern varies throughout the range of cultural practices encompassed by any definition of "folklore." These concerns are intended to be descriptive of concerns (and are characterizations of more complex and varied ideologies) raised in public tribal and Indigenous group discourses, but not comprehensive or universally applicable. The concerns include: (1) authorization, (2) informed consent, (3) maintaining secrecy, (4) compensation, (5) attribution, (6) preventing distortion, (7) continuing folkloric traditions, and (8) education. In Section II the author will use these concerns to assess the efficacy of the 1989 *Recommendation*.

Authorization

A central issue in the discussions on the protection of folklore is the demand by Indigenous people and other groups that they be able to authorize use of expressions of their folklore by others. A necessary correlate is recognition that Indigenous peoples are the exclusive owners in some sense of their cultural and intellectual property.[23] One frequently cited lawsuit, *Milpurrurru v. Indofurn Pty. Ltd.*, involves the sale of rugs made in Vietnam containing sacred Australian Aboriginal designs that depict stories of the Dreamtime.[24] These images are the Aboriginals' main historical method of value transmission, and only certain individuals are allowed to reproduce them, and even then only after extensive training. Further, within Aboriginal tradition only those who have been initiated can view them.[25] Thus, as one commentator notes, the commercial sale of the rugs meant that sacred symbols (1) were being copied and seen by unauthorized people, (2) were being presented outside the context from which they derive their meanings, and (3) were being misrepresented — buyers might believe they had bought "authentic" art. Many variations on this story could be told in domains of music, dance, ceremonies, and clothing. Although a tag on the rugs claimed that money was going to the Aboriginal artist, this was not true. Even if compensation had been paid, this would not address more central concerns as to the propriety of the use. Often the use of folklore expressions in non-traditional contexts implicates moral interests, not only, or even primarily, economic ones.

Informed Consent

Informed consent is primarily a concern when research by outsiders involves direct inter-action with Indigenous peoples and their ecological surroundings. This research includes academic fieldwork, such as that conducted by anthropologists. Although the academic work may be beneficial, the "subjects" deserve — and they have been demanding — more say about how it is conducted and used. A recent example is the Human Genome Diversity Project, which seeks to record genetic information from so-called isolates of historic inter-est.[26] Indigenous groups have reacted strongly against this project of Western academia, and the *Mataatua Declaration* calls for an immediate halt to it "until its moral, ethical, socioeconomic, physical and political implications have been thoroughly discussed, under-stood and approved by Indigenous Peoples."[27]

Secrecy

Maintaining secrecy, which may also be thought of as the right to determine whether and how information is divulged and commercialized, is increasingly viewed as a vital concern by Indigenous peoples. It is significant to note, in a legal perspective, that Indigenous pro-posals emphasize control more than compensation, namely the right to prevent the disclo-sure and/or commodification of knowledge, plants, animals, and objects.[28]

Compensation

The ability to seek compensation is associated with the ability to define the conditions of use. Until the mid-1980s there was little, if any, discussion of compensating people in developing countries for use of biological resources, and the discussion of intellectual prop-erty emerged even later.[29] The *Model Provisions* provide for compensation for "artistic" expressions of folklore, and the *Suva Declaration* seeks compensation for Indigenous intel-lectual property,[30] although the former does not seek to assure that compensation benefits the community from which the folklore originates. For example, assuming the above use of Aboriginal sacred symbols was by law required to have been appropriately authorized, the stewards of that information could seek compensation for its use. Similarly, Indigenous communities that provide plant resource information subsequently commercialized by pharmaceutical or agro-industry companies argue they are entitled to receive compensa-tion. In fact, approximately three-quarters of the plant-derived drugs now in use were dis-covered through research involving Indigenous groups, and in the United States alone the sale of plant-derived drugs reached an estimated fifteen billion dollars in 1990.[31] The active ingredient in the neem plant, used for thousands of years by Indigenous farmers in India as a natural insecticide and to treat skin disorders, is now the subject of a patent granted in the United States to W.R. Grace, which has allegedly indicated it has no plans to compensate anyone in India who provided the enabling knowledge.[32] [See Puri in this vol-ume pp.97–103.]

Another example that has attracted media attention illustrates how copyright law grants rights to users of folklore without any benefits to its stewards and performers.[33] Sherylle Mills, an intellectual property attorney, describes how in 1992, two Frenchmen created an album *Deep Forest*, which combined samples of music from Ghana, the Solomon Islands, and African pygmies with "techno-house" rhythms.[34] The album sold over two million copies and received a Grammy nomination.[35] The music from the album has been used by, and presumably licensed to, such companies as Sony, Porsche, and Coca-Cola.[36] Besides distorting sacred music and failing to attribute its source, the record producers likely paid no benefits to the sources of the music samples. In fact, United States copyright law would not protect the tradition-bearers unless they had fixed their rendition in a tangible form,[37] and even then, protection would not extend to melodies or words that are in the public domain through years of use.

Correct Attribution

Attribution is the right to require that commercial expressions of folklore accurately identify their sources. In the *Deep Forest* example, the album's liner notes make no mention that the Solomon Islands was the source of music sampled in one hit song. Similarly, Enigma's 1995 hit, *Return to Innocence*, used a recording of Amis tribesmen in Taiwan with no attribution or compensation.[38] Correct attribution helps protect consumers from false associations, while building accurate associations between "consumers" and the community where the folklore originates. Correct attribution thus serves an educational as well as an economic function.

Preventing Distortion

Preventing distortion, simply stated, means that appropriate groups have the ability to control how folklore is used. In the previously mentioned Australian example, the use of sacred symbols on carpets is argued to be harmful to the interests of the Aboriginal people and should be prevented as a violation of their moral rights (*droit moral*). These rights have long been recognized as an integral part of intellectual property laws in France but not the United States. Moral rights in artistic property are separate from economic rights and generally remain with an artist even after he or she has transferred the economic rights. The implications of moral rights on the protection of folklore will be discussed in Section III.

Continuing Folklore Traditions

Protecting folklore is not the same as protecting historical monuments. It directly implicates the living communities engaged in producing and transmitting knowledge on a daily basis. Therefore, it is imperative for those who seek its protection to be ever vigilant against the threat of laws that would reify folklore and place it in the control of external bodies. In fact, currently the term "folklore" itself is thought to suggest ossification and public domain and, therefore, to be inappropriate. The *Mataatua Declaration* recognizes this and proclaims that in their policies and practices, states and national and international agencies must "[r]ecognise that Indigenous Peoples also have the right to create new knowledge based on cultural traditions."[39]

Education

Finally, many parties, including UNESCO and many Indigenous groups, acknowledge a common, international interest in sharing and promoting folklore in a manner consistent with the above concerns. The *Mataatua Declaration* summarizes this succinctly, stating in its preamble "that the knowledge of the Indigenous Peoples of the world is of benefit to all humanity" and that they are "willing to offer it to all humanity provided their fundamental rights to define and control this knowledge are protected by the international community."[40]

II. The 1989 *Recommendation*[41]

The preamble to the 1989 *Recommendation* states that "folklore forms part of the universal heritage of humanity and that it is a powerful means of bringing together different peoples and social groups and of asserting their cultural identity."[42] The 1989 *Recommendation* continues by recognizing the "extreme fragility of the traditional forms of folklore," and the "need in all countries for recognition of the role of folklore and the danger it faces from multiple factors." It concludes that "the governments should play a decisive role in the safeguarding of folklore and that they should act as quickly as possible" by taking "whatever legislative measures or other steps" are necessary to give effect to the principles and measures contained in the 1989 *Recommendation*.

At a general level, it is difficult to fault the 1989 *Recommendation*'s systematic call for Member States to identify, conserve, preserve, disseminate, and protect folklore.[43] However, the 1989 *Recommendation* has come under criticism by experts because, while it attempts to impose requirements on Member States, it provides insufficient explanation of how to implement them, such as could be expressed through model provisions.[44] This may be why, in 1991, when UNESCO sought follow-up comments from Member States, only six eventually replied.[45] The replies were so general that one commentator stated, "It is impossible to deduce concrete conclusions."[46] One expert advised that the 1989 *Recommendation* be allowed to "hibernate." In 1992, further assessments were made of the 1989 *Recommendation*, "questioning the overall validity of the initiative and of the procedure that led to [its] development."[47]

Policy Implications of Word Choice

Whenever an international instrument is drafted, particularly by an organization as prominent as UNESCO, it will be closely scrutinized by Member States, non-governmental organizations, and concerned individuals and groups throughout the world. These groups look to an international instrument for diverse purposes: from ensuring compliance by Member States to justifying individual and state actions. Thus, it is crucial to ensure that actions enjoined by the instrument's terminology are in harmony with the instrument's intent. Throughout the 1989 *Recommendation* language and emphasis both help and hinder the document's stated goal of protecting folklore.

The 1989 *Recommendation*'s Definition of "Folklore"

The 1989 *Recommendation* defines "folklore" broadly as "the totality of tradition-based creations of a cultural community, expressed by a group or individuals and recognized as reflecting the expectations of a community in so far as they reflect its cultural and social identity; its standards and values are transmitted orally, by imitation or by other means."[48] Further, "[i]ts forms are, among others, language, literature, music, dance, games, mythology, rituals, customs, handicrafts, architecture and other arts."[49] In the 1989 *Recommendation*, folklore is no less than what some anthropologists define as "culture."[50]

A history of UNESCO's struggle to define this term may be found elsewhere,[51] but one document notes that by 1995 "complete unanimity (had) not been reached. On the contrary, it begins to seem that the definition must not be made a matter for dispute if the work is to progress."[52] The same report concludes, "Logically, this does not appear very satisfactory, for how can it be possible to safeguard something that cannot even be defined?"[53] One assessor of the 1989 *Recommendation* concludes with the following:

> After this many years of discussion, this may simply be an area in which there is little alternative but to return to still another elephant parable — as unsatisfactory as it is — namely that this animal is difficult to define, but relatively easy to recognize. Barring a major investment in further philosophical discussions, that *may be the best that this subject matter can expect in the way of definitions at this time* (emphasis in original).[54]

The author sees little harm in an over-broad definition as a potential motivator in a general policy statement, but any actual legal mechanism will require a more limited definition. This is consistent with the author's view that no single mechanism is likely to meet all, or even many, of the concerns described above in protecting folklore (especially so broadly defined); but many different mechanisms, each with an appropriately limited definition, could work together to meet many of these interests.

Perhaps more fundamental is the dissonance between the language used in the 1989 *Recommendation* and that used in discussions by Indigenous peoples. No Indigenous declaration uses the word "folklore." The *Mataatua Declaration* refers to "Indigenous intellectual and cultural property" and "cultural heritage,"[55] and the *Suva Declaration* calls for "the United Nations Development Program (UNDP) and regional donor to continue to support discussions on Indigenous Peoples' knowledge and intellectual property rights."[56]

A second problem in language use is that the 1989 *Recommendation*, recognizing the difficulty of protecting "living folklore," primarily addresses folklore that has been removed from its original context. Thus, Section C states, "While living folklore, owing to its evolving character, cannot always be directly protected, folklore that has been fixed in a tangible form should be effectively protected." Its main emphasis falls on archiving, typologies, museums, publications, etc. This may explain why Member States seem unclear about the steps that should be taken to preserve and promote living folklore.

The Designation of Folklore as "Universal Heritage"

In its preamble, the 1989 *Recommendation* sets forth several justifications for the protection of folklore, including a statement that folklore "forms part of the universal heritage of humanity."[57] Certainly, it is important to identify a common goal that will motivate and unite concerted international action in support of the 1989 *Recommendation*'s principles. However, the phrase "universal heritage of humanity" has been historically used to justify appropriation and therefore should be used, if at all, with some qualification.

It may make sense to describe ancient monuments that need protection as "universal heritage" — although the debates over the "Elgin Marbles" suggests that this usage also may be challenged. But when the "objects" of regulation are ongoing practices of living communities, declaring those practices part of "universal heritage" encourages, and may even justify, a way of thinking neither shared by the communities involved nor beneficial to their long-term interests. The *Mataatua Declaration*, *Suva Declaration*, and the *Convention on Biological Diversity* make the point quite clearly. At best, the phrase shows a misunderstanding of how folklore is created and perpetuated, and at worst, its claim is yet another act of appropriation and colonization, especially in the minds of many local and Indigenous people. One author notes critically how the "fruits of Indigenous and local knowledge are tagged 'common heritage of humanity,' rather than the evolving product of defined living communities."[58] If all folklore is logically the common heritage of all people, then on what basis can a local individual or group lay paramount claims over its use, dissemination, or protection?

Even if the intent is not to appropriate, declaring folklore part of "universal heritage" may place it in the "public domain," where it may be used without consent, compensation, or attribution. Many originators and stewards of folklore would surely take issue with this fundamental tenet espoused in the preamble to the 1989 *Recommendation*.

There is, however, a "universal" incentive to protect folklore behind which all Member States can unite. Every nation, region, and tribe, etc., has its own folklore and traditional culture that its members wish to protect. Therefore, the protection of folklore is of *universal interest*. As the growing eradication of cultural and biological diversity is increasingly becoming a global concern, each Member State should agree to protect and respect the folklore of others in order that their own be respected and protected in turn.

Accordingly, the author submits that in this area, where there is a vital concern that groups work together, any further work by UNESCO should be especially sensitive to universalistic claims to particular folklore, which are likely to be offensive to many of those the 1989 *Recommendation* is aiming to assist. Rather than choose a fundamentally divisive premise, UNESCO could proclaim that it is in the universal interest to protect the folklore of all peoples and nations. This would allow the Member States and constituents in them to align behind a common interest, while preventing the 1989 *Recommendation* or other instrument from being used to justify appropriation of folklore by any taker.

Assessment in Light of the Key Concerns in Section I

Authorization

Control of folklore — by the individual or group that serves as its steward and is responsible for its perpetuation — is central to its protection. And central to control is the ability to grant authorization or withhold it for particular uses. Nowhere does the 1989 *Recommendation* call for giving control to the tradition-bearers or their communities. Section F provides some indirect support for control by stating that "in so far as folklore constitutes manifestations of intellectual creativity, . . . it deserves to be protected in a manner inspired by the protection provided for intellectual productions."[59] This statement, however, is problematic. First, the use of "in so far as" might imply an assumption that a significant portion of folklore is neither creative nor intellectual and hence is relegated to the public domain.

Second, for that folklore which is deemed creative, the 1989 *Recommendation* states that it should be protected in a manner "inspired by" the protection provided to "intellectual productions." Although this latter term is left undefined, the implication is that folklore expressions and intellectual productions are two separate, mutually exclusive categories. Separating folklore from other intellectually creative works may imply that even folklore judged "creative" merits less protection — protection "inspired by" but not necessarily "equal to" the protection afforded to "intellectual" works.

UNESCO's policy on the protection of folklore should be especially attuned to the use of language and its implications. UNESCO should clearly recognize that many folkloric expressions are already protected under existing copyright laws and also that, although these protections are often insufficient to meet the interests outlined earlier in this assessment, such laws can still be of benefit. At the same time, and while balancing other interests, UNESCO should develop and recommend other forms of protection to Member States to give relevant groups specific, additional tools to assure appropriate control.

Informed Consent

Section F(b)(i) states, specifically referencing privacy and confidentiality, that "the informant as the transmitter of traditions" should be protected. There is also a call for the international scientific community to adopt a code of ethics to ensure a proper approach to and respect for traditional cultures.[60] There is, however, no specific call for obtaining informed consent, or for including tradition-bearers in the adoption of an ethical code.

Secrecy

The 1989 *Recommendation* assumes that all folklore should be disseminated as long as it is not distorted. The dissemination of all folklore is readily encouraged throughout the 1989 *Recommendation* (e.g., Section B(c)(i), seeks a typology of folklore by way of "a general outline of folklore for global use"; Section C(g), seeks the creation of "security and working copies of all folklore"; and Section E is premised on the need to widely disseminate all folklore). Of course, it can be crucial to disseminate folklore outside of its traditional context in order to create international awareness and respect for diversity. However, nowhere does the 1989 *Recommendation* acknowledge that in some cases no dissemination is proper, even of the non-distorting kind. In contrast, this point receives emphasis in Indigenous and local community discussions. The *Mataatua Declaration* specifically calls for an appropriate body to monitor the commercialization of Indigenous cultural properties and for national and international agencies to recognize that Indigenous people have the right to protect and control dissemination of customary knowledge.[61] The *Suva Declaration* "urges Pacific Governments who have not signed GATT to refuse to do so and encourages those Governments who have already signed to protect against provisions which facilitate the expropriation of Indigenous peoples' knowledge."[62] The Charter of the Indigenous-Tribal Peoples of the Tropical Forests states, "Since we highly value our traditional knowledge and believe that our biotechnologies can make an important contribution to humanity, including 'developed' countries, we demand guaranteed rights to our intellectual property, and control over the development and manipulation of this knowledge."[63]

Further work by UNESCO should expand the 1989 *Recommendation*'s call to protect the privacy and confidentiality of informants by seeking the protection of confidential or sacred folklore from inappropriate use. As the author will propose below, the right of a community to prevent the misappropriation of historically restricted folklore should be facilitated in the law.

Compensation

While Section G(c) seeks to insure that various "interested parties" enjoy the economic, moral, and neighboring rights in folklore, it remains completely neutral as *to which* interested parties, such as the originating communities, are entitled to control the moral and economic rights.

Correct Attribution

The 1989 *Recommendation* has an entire section on the identification of folklore, and a separate section on dissemination. In many ways, the 1989 *Recommendation* supports the interest of correct attribution through archiving, publishing, and education. Despite urging its identification by outsiders, Section B states that folklore should be safeguarded "by and for the group . . . whose identity it expresses." Even so, nowhere does the 1989 *Recommendation* explicitly call for the correct attribution of folklore that is to be disseminated.

Preventing Distortion

Section G of the 1989 *Recommendation* states that distortion "should be avoided." This seems to imply that distortion is a relatively minor matter. However, as already described in the *Milpurrurru* case, such distortion can offend central community tenets and practices. Since this issue is of primary concern to Indigenous groups and tradition-bearers, UNESCO should study further what distortion is, what kinds of distortion are acceptable to the tradition-bearers and the originating community, and how certain distortions can be prevented. A balance must be struck, however, lest anti-distortion efforts unduly promote claims of ethnic and cultural purity by those seeking an absolute form of ownership of their cultural patrimony.[64]

Continuing Folklore Traditions

In marked contrast to documents produced by Indigenous peoples, the 1989 *Recommendation* places emphasis throughout on the role outsiders (researchers, archivists, institutions, and governments) play in the identification, dissemination, and conservation of folklore. Section C(g) states that the cultural community should be assured of access to its folklore but on the whole, the role of tradition-bearers is seldom discussed in the 1989 *Recommendation*.

For example, Section C urges the conservation of folklore through national archives and museums and the training of "collectors, archivists, documentalists, and other specialists in the conservation of folklore," but it does not discuss the support, training, or participation of tradition-bearers and other interested community members in such conservation efforts. In contrast, the *Suva Declaration* urges steps to strengthen the "capacities of Indigenous peoples to maintain their oral traditions, and [to] encourage initiatives by Indigenous peoples to record their knowledge in a permanent form according to their customary practices."[65]

Another example of this imbalance is Section D, which urges that folk traditions be economically supported, but presents an action plan to support academics, not tradition-bearers, by creating educational curricula and National Folklore Councils. Similarly, subsection (a) of Section E encourages events where folklore can be performed and shared but emphasizes its dissemination through the media, museums, archives, the scientific community, and institutions. Instead of requesting funding of tradition-bearers, the UNESCO document seeks "full-time jobs for folklorists."

By emphasizing the interests and contributions of outsiders and de-emphasizing the crucial roles tradition-bearers play in the protection and dissemination of folklore, the 1989 *Recommendation* implies that originating communities do not have a significant interest in the folklore they create and pass on. This view reflects and bolsters the notion that folklore is part of the "universal heritage" of humankind. If the originating communities do not have a controlling interest in their own folklore, this errant logic would run, they do not need to be consulted over its use and preservation, which can be managed for them.

Education

The 1989 *Recommendation* proclaims, "It is essential for the items that make up this cultural heritage to be widely disseminated so that the value of folklore and the need to preserve it can be recognized."[66] Though a laudable concern, the emphasis is on creating typologies, training folklorists, establishing new museums, and arranging festivals. The 1989 *Recommendation* does not make a point to encourage community education by its own members.

Conclusion

When considered in its entirety, the 1989 *Recommendation* does touch upon all eight key areas of concern outlined in Section I, but its approach is inadequate. When it addresses central concerns, it often does so with a clear bias toward the researcher, the global public (humankind), and fixed expressions of folklore removed from their cultural contexts. In some cases its language and intent are incompatible with the tenor of Indigenous discussions cited.

III. Other Options

In the words of one commentator, "[I]t would be in the interests of Member States to learn *what all their options are* . . . [so that they] may then feel more *comfortable* in selecting a strategy suited to their own purposes"[67] (emphasis in original). To this end, a discussion of various options follows, including (1) extant UNESCO efforts, (2) modifications to existing intellectual property laws as implemented by GATT TRIPS, and finally, (3) an international contracting framework proposed by the author in an attempt to open dialogue. Several of the options in (2) have already been touched upon in many publications, so the author will provide relatively brief discussions of the underlying legal concepts before focusing on how they may be used to advance some of the interests already identified.

UNESCO Efforts

Model Provisions

This brief assessment of the *Model Provisions* concludes that their potential has been unrealized partly because they fail to adequately resolve issues of authorization and compensation and could even serve to disempower local groups. The *Model Provisions* were approved by a Committee of Governmental Experts, convened by WIPO and UNESCO in 1982.[68] It was anticipated that they would be a model for national and international protection. In broad strokes, the *Model Provisions* protect "artistic expressions" of folklore from unauthorized use by a "competent authority" outside of their traditional or usual context for gainful intent.[69] The *Model Provisions* require attribution for certain uses of "identifiable" folklore expressions and provide penalties for harmful distortions.

The *Model Provisions* appear to address concerns of authorization, compensation, prevention of distortion, education, and continuation of folkloric traditions. Despite this, after more than ten years, not a single state has adopted the *Model Provisions*.[70] In 1984, WIPO and UNESCO convened a Group of Experts, the majority of whom concluded that, despite the increasing and uncontrolled use of folklore, an international treaty was premature.[71] The main issues they identified were (1) the lack of appropriate sources for identifying expressions of folklore and (2) the lack of mechanisms for dealing with folklore that can be found in more than one country.[72]

One commentator believes the *Model Provisions* to be flawed because "it [*sic*] offers protection against *verbatim* reproduction and *modest* distortion . . . assuming that the original has been accurately recorded, and assuming that the original has been withdrawn from the 'public domain' and duly registered as such . . . [but] [t]his model is more awkward to apply in case of *massive* distortion" (emphasis in original).[73] In addition to reproduction and distortion, two other concerns may be raised: authorization and compensation.

By leaving authorization to a "competent authority," the *Model Provisions* beg the question that is central to most Indigenous discussions on this topic: namely, who *is* the competent authority? Worse, the fact that the *Berne Convention* uses the same phrase suggests that copyright offices are the appropriate authority. It seems possible that the easy and likely designate in most cases would be the state, in the form of a copyright office. But in many cases this would not be desirable. For example, in the United States, the inappropriateness of granting the Copyright Office the authority to authorize uses of Hopi folklore is obvious. In the United States, Native Americans would presumably have the political power to prevent adoption of this provision, but in some other countries, where Indigenous groups are not as powerful, a state agency might be able to control such authorizations. What recourse would an Indigenous community have, if it were to object to a use authorized by its national government?

The second issue is compensation. Under the *Model Provisions* the competent authority, although not required to, may assess license fees. These revenues are meant to go towards promoting "national" culture, and there is no assurance or requirement that any of the fees will benefit the originating community.

In short, the *Model Provisions* fail to recognize and confront the complexity of the political relationships between states and Indigenous groups within them. This is the reality that Indigenous groups currently express in such documents as the *Mataatua Declaration* and the *Suva Declaration*.

Masterpieces of the Oral and Intangible Heritage of Humanity

UNESCO adopted regulations in 1998 to implement a program to "pay tribute to outstanding masterpieces of the oral and intangible heritage of humanity." Under the program, every two years the Director-General will proclaim no more than ten awards. Between six and ten recommendations will be made to the Director-General by a jury of "creative workers" and "experts" in appropriate disciplines and from different geographic regions. Governments and certain intergovernmental and non-governmental organizations may submit candidates, with no more than one being submitted every two years from each Member State.[74]

The program could provide a visible, feasible, and effective role for UNESCO to draw attention to the importance of folklore without the need to wait for international agreements. It has clear potential to serve the interests of education, compensation, attribution, prevention of distortion, and continuation of folkloric traditions through generations. In addition to the monetary grants that are to be paid (although exactly to whom is unclear), the concomitant licensing of a UNESCO certification mark could also give the tradition-bearers increased visibility. This in turn could lead to increased compensation and respect for the tradition-bearer. However, just like intellectual property law discussed herein, such incentive programs cannot address all concerns in protecting folklore.

There are several potential limitations within the program as currently proposed. First, its narrow focus on the more "romantic" conception of authorship characteristic of copyright laws and "high art" is indicative of a shift away from the broad definition of folklore contained in the 1989 *Recommendation*. This particular focus may lead to recognition of Western-style artists at the expense of others. Second, implicating no more than ten examples of intangible heritage every two years, the program will have only a limited impact in the daily preservation of folklore. It may be hoped, however, that Member States will choose to adopt their own similar programs on a national level, which would increase the number of beneficiaries.[75] Third, the system currently depends on the value judgments and beneficence of Member States for selecting the examples of oral and intangible heritage to be submitted, since the tradition-bearers or their communities cannot submit examples directly. Again, in states where tensions exist between Indigenous groups and the state government, there is no reason to believe this program will benefit these groups in any way. Years of history suggest the opposite: The groups that are most in need due to state neglect are the very ones likely to be left out of the nomination process.

Intellectual Property

Appropriateness of Intellectual Property Laws

Before turning to a discussion of particular intellectual property concepts as embodied in Western intellectual property law regimes, specifically in the United States, a justification and appropriate caveats must be made. Many commentators have claimed that the globalization of intellectual property laws is one of the problems facing the protection of traditional culture, rather than a possible solution. One commentator calls GATT TRIPS "a form of passive coercion,"[76] while another concludes that these laws "exacerbate . . . de-culturization by promoting 'McWorld' over native traditions and customs."[77] Another states that "applying the customary tools of intellectual property (patents, copyrights, trademarks, trade secrets, and plant variety protection) to Indigenous knowledge is likely to do more harm than good, both to Indigenous groups and to others."[78] Surendra J. Patel concludes an article on intellectual property rights for Indigenous knowledge with a recommendation that "we should make a 180-degree about-face on empty debates on using and modifying the intellectual property rights system" because "[t]he course followed so far is a dead end."[79] The 1989 *Recommendation* itself refers to intellectual property, but pointedly declares that this "relates only to one aspect of folklore protection."[80] A further criticism is that concepts such as "tangible," "intangible," "artistic," "sacred," etc., cannot be used in those Indigenous societies where such distinctions are not made.

All laws embody and inculcate values; intellectual property laws are no different. It has been pointed out many times that the individualistic values embodied throughout all intellectual property laws are premised on culturally bound and historically derived concepts of "authorship" and "innovation."[81] For example, the *Bellagio Declaration* states, "Contemporary intellectual property law is constructed around a notion of the author as an individual, solitary and original creator, and it is for this figure that its protections are reserved."[82] The *Mataatua Declaration* seeks a different intellectual property-rights regime which incorporates: (1) collective and individual ownership, (2) protection against debasement of culturally significant items, (3) a cooperative framework, and (4) a multigenerational coverage span, with the first beneficiaries to be the direct descendants of the guardians of traditional knowledge.[83]

Another fundamental problem with trying to harness historically Western intellectual property laws in the protection of folklore is the incentive structure that provides their rationale.[84] Their economic rationale is that a limited, government-granted monopoly on material that could otherwise be readily copied by others allows the author or inventor to capitalize on his or her work for a limited time and simultaneously makes the inventive or creative elements embodied in the work or invention available to the public at large; eventually, the work or invention enters the public domain. Thus, in copyright, the author obtains the exclusive right to sell copies of the work for a limited time; during this time, others are free to copy the ideas, but not the expressions. After a period of time, the expression itself enters the public domain. This calculus aims at balancing incentives to produce with the public benefit of making the expression available to others. Too much protection for the author is thought to create a net inhibition on creativity in the broader society by preventing the ability of one author to draw on the work of another; whereas too little, it is feared, will stunt individual creativity.[85] One wonders how this simplistic economic incentive structure (e.g., the author gets a royalty for each copy sold) maps onto complex social relationships involved in artistic creation and innovation different from those recognized in the West.[86]

Moreover, the rationale relied on by the United States may even be based on an inaccurate understanding of Western reality.[87] Many Continental European countries emphasize natural rights, which grant both economic and moral rights to authors, yet have substantively similar intellectual property laws. The point here is that, as Western intellectual property laws — and any laws pertaining to folklore — become more common around the globe, careful attention must be directed to how these laws interact with the complex and varying social relations of those engaged in the ongoing practices of folklore.

The following subsections discuss copyright, trademark, patent, and trade secret law, focusing on areas where they may be put in the service of several of the central concerns.[88] I argue that one avenue worth further exploration is expanding the newly internationalized trade-secret concept and linking it to an international contractual framework.

Copyright Implications for Folklore[89]

Indigenous people and academics have focused on copyright as having the most potential of all the Western intellectual property laws.[90] Copyright superficially appears appropriate because two of the concerns — control over images and other artistic works and compensation for authorized use — are typically dealt with by copyright. If a copyright, or a right similar to copyright, is recognized in a given expression of folklore, then the owner, be it an individual or group, can authorize use, seek compensation, impose use restrictions to prevent distortion, and assure correct attribution. This is the body of law that was successfully used by the Aboriginal artist in the *Milpurrurru* case discussed above in Section I. But even though copyright has been the first choice of many, there has also been a recognition that copyright law presents several problems in this context.[91]

These problems include the limited duration of copyright, the emphasis on individual authorship/ownership, the fair-use exception (which typically extends to parody) and, perhaps, most fundamentally, the fact that copyright does not extend to "ideas." Thus, a painter of sacred images copied from a prior public domain work (e.g., no longer protected by copyright due to the passage of time) would, under current copyright law, own rights in the work only if enough "original" expression is added (assuming that threshold could be met, let alone whether it is an appropriate standard to apply). Even these rights would be insufficient to prevent use of the images, where all that is copied is already in the "public domain" (e.g., the incremental "original" expression is not copied). Nor would any copyrights prevent anyone from copying the sacred "ideas" embodied by the images. Further, the copyright ownership would be placed in the hands of the individual artist who created the work, even if this would be inappropriate in the particular society. Many societies do not define ownership in an individualistic way, and to give all rights to an individual could negatively impact on long-standing relations between such individuals and clan elders, for example, who provide the initial training and authorization. Whether under an economic incentive theory, as in the United States, or under a natural rights authorship theory, as in France, it is the individual that is meant to be rewarded.

Of course, since the majority of copyrights in the United States are in fact owned by corporations due to the "work made for hire" doctrine, there is precedent for assuring joint ownership. One method, which already exists and provides for the most flexibility, is the right to license or assign[92] all or parts of a work to others. This licensing and/or assignment could become complex, given that multiple parties would be involved. The objectification of relationships in license and assignment agreements could also affect those relationships in unexpected ways. On the other hand, with minimal education, standard forms of licensing and assignments could be devised and used. Because copyrights are infinitely divisible, with careful thought, a group could approximate, within the dominant copyright law context, that group's desired legal relationships, both within the group and with respect to those "outside" it.

Another option is to expand the joint authorship concept. Currently, under United States law, where two or more individuals collaborate with the intent that their expressions be merged into a single work, each will be considered a joint author, so long as each contributed copyrightable expression. They would each have the right to exploit the work, subject only to an accounting for profits to the other. Under existing law, it would not be a huge stretch to proclaim those directly involved in the collaborative effort joint authors, so long as the combined result is a copyrightable work. Whether this would sufficiently recognize the authority of all the appropriate people is a different story. All that can be said here is that these are options that could be pursued, and the results analyzed.

It is also possible to recognize traditional forms of ownership. This could be done through a mechanism (contractually between the group members, or statutorily) which delegates to tribal authorities and other officially recognized groups the right to determine who is an "author," or at least who is an owner and can exercise control. It may also be possible to incorporate a group's traditional customary law concepts within the dominant legal framework of the state.

Among the exclusive rights granted to the copyright owner is the right to create derivative works, which could be used to prevent some distortions.[93] Derivative works are new works that are based on existing works. In the United States, this concept initially arose because courts held that translations did not constitute "copies." The concept has been extended to cover new versions of software, the creation of movies based on books, etc. When a new work incorporates too much of a pre-existing work without authorization, it is an infringing derivative work (unless it is a "fair use"). If the derivative work contains only a small or substantively unimportant amount of the pre-existing work, no infringement will be found. The exclusive right to create derivative works serves the interest of preventing distortion, if the distorted work contains sufficient amounts of the pre-existing work to constitute an infringement.

In short, copyright law may have some use in serving the interests of compensation, authorization, attribution, and preventing distortion, but it will not be effective in many situations.

Moral Rights Implications for Folklore

Moral rights (*droit moral*) are typically treated as non-economic rights provided under copyright laws. They include the rights to attribution and integrity contained in the *Berne Convention*, which provides, "[i]ndependently of the author's economic rights, and even after the transfer of the said rights, the author shall have the right to claim authorship of the work, and to object to any distortion, mutilation or other modification of, or any other derogatory action in relation to, the said work, which would be prejudicial to his honor or reputation. . . ."[94]

Although moral rights have been traditionally recognized in Continental European countries, it was only when the United States joined Berne that limited moral rights were specifically created in the United States through the *Visual Artists Rights Act* (VARA). In addition to VARA, courts in the United States have used the *Lanham Act* to forbid false authorship attributions, but the latter is not effective in preventing distortions.[95]

VARA covers only single-copy or limited-edition visual or sculptural works and photographs produced for exhibition purposes only.[96] Authors of these works have the rights of attribution and integrity, separate from their economic rights. The attribution right allows the author to disclaim association from works he or she did not create or works that are distorted in a manner prejudicial to his or her reputation, as well as claim authorship over works he or she did create. The integrity right prohibits intentional distortion or mutilation that would be prejudicial to the author's honor or reputation and any grossly negligent destruction of a work of "recognized stature."[97]

Moral rights appear to readily lend themselves to protecting the folklore concerns of attribution and preventing distortion and are utilized in the *Model Provisions*. However, once again issues arise about who should be vested with the power to claim and enforce moral rights. In fact, the theory of authorship underlying moral rights is an even more romantic conception than that in the economic-incentive rationale for copyright in the United States.

Trademark Implications for Folklore[98]

The author believes trademark and related areas of law could be of some assistance in the areas of attribution, compensation, education, and preventing distortion. However, because trademarks relate to the sale of goods or services, they are by definition commercial. Therefore, any trademark approach could be expected to increase commodification. Further, it would not protect against the disclosure of secrets.

In addition to registering trade or service marks for specific goods or services and preventing others from using confusingly similar marks, groups could register certification marks. The group could then license use of a certification mark under conditions it specifies. As long as a mark chosen is not generic, the certification mark could be used, for example, to identify only those artists who manufacture particular crafts in a traditional manner. The registrations owned by the Council of the Cowichan Indian Band for both word and design marks ("Genuine Cowichan" and "Cowichan") do just this. They are "to be used by persons authorized by the certifier, [who] will certify that the goods, namely clothing, blankets and rugs, have been manufactured by members of the Coast Salish Nation in accordance with traditional tribal methods and that the wool and yarn used therein have been made in accordance with traditional tribal methods."[99] However, a search of the United States Patent and Trademark Office database showed no other certification mark registration by Indigenous groups.

Under the Indian Arts and Crafts Act of 1935, discussed further below, the Indian Arts and Crafts Board, a government agency, certifies that a given artist is an "Indian."[100] This is viewed by at least some individuals and tribes as effectively granting citizenship to certain tribes on the one hand, and preventing members of non-federally recognized tribes from claiming their art is "native-made," on the other.

As an alternate to this certification, groups could register collective marks. In this context, any member of the group — and only a member of the group — could use the mark to identify goods or services. Collective marks can be used not only to identify goods or services but also to denote membership in an organization.[101] For example, the Inter-Tribal Indian Ceremonial Association, Inc., has applied for a collective (membership) design mark for denoting membership in an organized collective association which "promotes the preservation of the Native American or American Indian culture, traditions, art and related activities."[102] A collective organization would hold title for the entire group.

Of course, there are major limitations in trademark law with respect to the protection of folklore. First, trademark law generally is only implicated when consumers are likely to be confused as to the source of the goods or services, or where there is a false attribution of origin. It is not effective where material distortions in the mark (whether the mark is a symbol, pottery shape, scent, color, or words) are such that consumer confusion would not result. The latter is often the case with parodies. However, in the United States and some other countries, trademark law will provide a remedy even where there is no consumer confusion for "famous" marks.[103] Second, and more fundamentally, trademark law is premised on and supports commodification. While it may be highly effective for groups with distinct and commercially viable folklore, for many other groups it will either be offensive in its commercial nature or of limited benefit.

UNESCO may be an appropriate body to establish a certification mark program on an international scale. It could be used, for example, in conjunction with its *Masterpieces of the Oral and Intangible Heritage of Humanity* program, discussed above.[104] Use of the mark(s) could be restricted, for example, to situations in which compensation returns to the originating community in a manner approved by the community, and in which appropriate steps are being taken to preserve the particular folklore in its living context. The synergy of a global UNESCO "brand recognition" along with the necessary involvement of local tradition-bearers and their communities would be one way of promoting the sale of appropriate folkloric works, within the greater context of preservation.

In addition to the above uses of trademarks, it is also possible for individuals or groups to seek cancellation of federally registered marks that are immoral or scandalous, or which falsely suggest an association with or disparage particular groups or institutions. The Trademark Trial and Appeal Board recently held that the registered mark "Redskins" (referring to Native Americans and featuring a stereotype image of a Native American) used by a professional football team disparages Native Americans and will be cancelled.[105] This cancellation does not mean the former owner of the trademark must cease using it, but it does mean the mark owner cannot rely on federal protection and associated benefits.

The inability to obtain or maintain federal registration, along with the educational impact from the publicity surrounding a cancellation action, could be an effective deterrent to the inappropriate adoption of marks incorporating sacred symbols or referring to groups in an offensive manner. To make this weapon effective, multiple Indigenous groups within a Member State could work together, perhaps through a non-profit organization, to police registrations, seek cancellation in proper circumstances, and educate the public on the harm which results from the use of such marks. Under recent judicial precedent, a party has standing to oppose registration of a mark simply because it offends the party's religious values.[106] A prior decision already established that individual Native Americans have standing to seek cancellation of a mark that disparages them as Native Americans.[107]

It may also be feasible to lobby for a change in the law so that the relevant group considered in deciding whether or not a mark is scandalous would not be the population at large, as is the current United States law, but the group to which the mark refers, or from which it originates. This would further the interests of authorization, preventing distortion, and education. The United States Patent and Trademark Office has recently sought comments, as part of a statutorily required study, on how official insignia of federally or state-recognized Native American tribes might be better protected under trademark law. The study is due to go to Congress no later than September 30, 1999, and must address issues such as the definition of "official insignia," the impact of legislation on international legal obligations, and the administrative feasibility.[108] This study may provide an important opportunity to deter harmful uses of sacred symbols and to strengthen control over them by the group that holds them sacred. It may be more practical and beneficial to empower governmental or non-governmental agencies to monitor and prosecute infringements on behalf of the originating communities with the latter's authorization.

Truth in Labeling Requirements

As discussed above, trademark law may be a powerful way to protect folklore, albeit indirectly, but it may depend upon enforcement through expensive and complex procedures. For this reason, laws that prohibit the false designation of goods as "folklore" or "traditional art" enforceable by the state may be beneficial. Established laws in the United States that prohibit the false designation of "Indian" arts and crafts may be examined to assess the benefits and limitations of such labeling requirements.

Section 305(c) of Title 25 of the United States Code makes it unlawful for a person to display for sale or sell a good "in a manner that falsely suggests it is Indian produced, an Indian product, or the product of a particular Indian or Indian tribe or Indian arts and crafts organization." It also provides a mechanism for the Indian Arts and Crafts Board to assist Native Americans and their tribes and associations to register their own certification marks.[109] Under this law, both members of Indian tribes and the United States government may prosecute violators, so that Indian tribes with limited resources are not left with the expensive and time-consuming task of enforcing labeling requirements.

New Mexico has embraced this principle and expanded it. In New Mexico, not only is it unlawful to misidentify a good as "Indian," but it is also the affirmative duty of anyone selling an Indian product "to make due inquiry of his suppliers concerning the true nature of the materials, product design and process of manufacture to determine whether the product may be lawfully represented as authentic Indian craft."[110] In New Mexico, violations of the labeling requirements result in both civil and criminal penalties.

Labeling laws appear to offer many benefits. First, they are relatively simple to draft and police, since they do not require complex registration schemes. Further, the statute could enable both government enforcement and a private right of action. Finally, the proscribed behavior may be defined with enough clarity that it is easily understandable and avoidable by merchants. Labeling laws protect the interest of attribution by prohibiting the sale of falsely labeled imitations. Compensation will be furthered where merchants turn to those folklore products that can accurately be labeled authentic. Finally, distortion may be lessened in the mind of consumers when labeling creates a more informed marketplace. Consumers will learn to distinguish the authentic from the inauthentic items, and demand for the latter can be expected to decrease.

Labeling requirements have limitations. Labeling requirements do not control the use or misuse of folklore once purchased. Nor can labeling requirements assure that the originating group provided informed consent for the initial sale or that they obtained fair compensation. Finally, labeling laws do not prevent distortions, so long as the goods at issue are not falsely passed off as authentic or Indian.

Patent Implications for Folklore[111]

The criteria of novelty and non-obviousness, the unpatentability of products of "nature," the concept of "inventor," and the limited duration of protection all present substantial obstacles to the patenting of non-Western forms of innovation.[112] "Novelty" means that the claimed invention differs from the prior art in that no single invention or descriptions of it contain all elements of a claim.[113] Even where an invention is novel, it may not be patentable because it is "obvious." [114] An invention is obvious if a person with ordinary skill in the relevant art could reasonably believe, at the time of the invention's conception, that it was to be expected. As one commentator notes, "Patents reward the kind of individual, secretive effort epitomized by the lone scientist in his basement laboratory."[115]

The ideology of the sole inventor may be descriptively suspect in industrialized nations, but it meshes with romantic conceptions of inventorship. In non-Western and Indigenous societies, individual inventorship is likely to be more suspect even as an ideology. In the latter case, knowledge is often descriptively and conceptually seen as collective and built upon prior knowledge. Singling out an individual as an inventor entitled to monopoly rights would be problematic. Although similar concerns arise with respect to copyright laws, the impact in that context would be less, since patent rights are so "strong." That said, the internal division and conception of ownership within a group is separable from the issue of ownership with respect to those outside the group.

The non-obvious criterion effectively requires some "inventive step," such as through purification of naturally occurring substances. The application of this requirement to folklore is problematic. First, rarely would a shaman have an incentive (other than to get a patent) to take this step. Second, these steps favor those who possess sophisticated laboratory techniques. For example, Naomi Roht-Arriaza describes how the neem seed has been used in India for hundreds of years as a pesticide, yet the only patent protection obtainable is for the laboratory-purified derivatives, which is held by the company that made the purification. No compensation or recognition is due, under the patent laws, to the people who discovered the beneficial uses and ensured the perpetuation of the seeds.[116] Patent law as currently conceived raises other issues, given its emphasis on "reproducibility" and maintaining knowledge in secret prior to obtaining a patent.

One author, Michael J. Huft, considers closely the concept of co-inventorship.[117] After discussing United States case law on joint-inventorship, Huft argues that in many situations the collaboration of an Indigenous healer with a Western drug developer should result in each being a joint-inventor.[118] The difficult issue is exactly what contribution, under existing law, is required for the Indigenous knowledge to be deemed an element essential to the "conception" of the invention as described in the patent claims. Legislative modifications may be possible to specifically define the circumstances in which parties are considered joint-inventors. Such recognition would serve the concerns for compensation, attribution, and to a lesser degree authorization (any joint-inventor can exploit the patent without the permission of any other joint-inventor). However, it would do so only for the individual involved, absent agreements within the community as to the division of ownership interests. Another proposal would require — as part of any patent application in which the invention is derived from Indigenous knowledge — a declaration that informed consent has been obtained.[119] A patent issued with a false statement of informed consent could be subject to revocation.

Trade Secret Implications for Folklore

Trade secrets have received scant attention in the literature on folklore protection.[120] Yet of all the standard intellectual property law regimes, trade secrets may be most fruitful in advancing the concerns of secrecy, compensation, authorization, informed consent, and preventing distortion, especially when used in conjunction with the contractual framework described in the following section. Perhaps the lack of discussion is due partly to the fact that only with TRIPS have trade-secret laws become an increasingly international requirement.[121]

In the United States, trade-secret law developed through the courts rather than the legislature. Thus, it is conceptually flexible and expansive: information of any kind which has potential commercial value and which has been the subject of reasonable steps to maintain its confidentiality will be protected.[122] The owner will be able to get judicial relief against those who have stolen or revealed it in violation of a duty of trust. Misappropriation includes both the disclosure or use of the trade secret of another without express or implied consent and the acquisition of a trade secret by a person who knows or had reason to know the trade secret was acquired by improper means (e.g., theft, bribery, misrepresentation, breach or inducement of a breach of a duty to maintain secrecy).[123] A trade secret is not lost, for example, where an employee reveals the information, if there is an express or implied duty to maintain the secrecy of the information. Remedy may be had against the employee and against the third party if he or she knew or had reason to know of the misappropriation.

A trade secret can consist of any kind of information (formulas, processes, inventions, etc.) so long as it has the potential (even if unrealized) to provide a commercial advantage. In determining what makes particular information a trade secret, courts typically consider numerous factors: the extent to which the information is known outside the owning entity, the extent to which it is known by members inside the entity, the extent to which measures have been taken to protect the secrecy, and the value of the information to the owning entity.[124]

Once a trade secret is established, it may be sold or licensed to others. If a court finds theft or misappropriation has occurred, it may issue an injunction preventing use of the information, and it may award compensatory damages. Trade secrets are generally owned by collective entities, such as corporations. Because absolute secrecy is not required, but only "reasonable precautionary measures," courts typically look to the type of secrecy employed in the industry involved. Courts have been guided in this area by close contextual analysis and not ideological conceptions of "authors" and "inventors," creating a flexible area of law that is fruitful to explore.

For example, it would be fully consistent with existing concepts of trade-secret law to protect knowledge from disclosure outside of a group if that group (or appropriate people in it) can show the information was subject to disclosure restrictions, written or implied, which are part of the cultural practices of that group. Thus, trade-secret law readily lends itself to incorporating concepts and practices of the applicable groups themselves. Within a given group, some information will not be subject to restrictions while other information will be. Where the customs and practices show that the party disclosing or using the information knew or should have known of these restrictions, use of the information would be a misappropriation.

Contractual Framework

Legally recognizing misappropriation in certain kinds of traditional or Indigenous knowledge in itself not only promotes the interests of authorization, secrecy, compensation, informed consent, and preventing distortion but also provides a "property" hook on which a contractual framework can be hung. In the biodiversity literature, there has been much emphasis on contractual arrangements.[125] One frequently cited example is a contract between Merck Pharmaceuticals and INBio, a private non-profit biodiversity institute created by the Costa Rican government.[126] The agreement is said to provide Merck with a certain number of natural extracts in exchange for up-front money and royalties on any commercialized products. INBio is required to provide some of the funds to natural conservation, and Merck is to provide technical training to Costa Ricans.[127] In this particular contract, however, it is unclear whether and how Indigenous individuals and communities will benefit, since the contract does not directly implicate INBio's relationship with the suppliers of the information and samples.

The potential of private contracts nonetheless provides, as noted by Naomi Roht-Arriaza, the benefits of allowing Indigenous and local communities to bypass the state and negotiate on their own behalf.[128] Further, contracting provides parties with the potential to ensure that the use of information and resources is acceptable to the community and that benefits go back to the community.[129] One patent scholar notes that "the low frequency of these transactions, coupled with high policing and enforcement costs, make such private contracts preferable to a worldwide system of intellectual property rights in Indigenous plant and animal species."[130]

On the other hand, oft-noted problems with private contracts include disparities between the parties in information, bargaining power, and enforcement capacity. Perhaps more problematically, when the information is available from several groups within a state or in different states, the party seeking the information will go to the group or state that has it at the lowest cost (meaning at no cost where no property right is recognized). Thus, although private contracts may benefit groups that adopt the practice, those who do not or cannot require contracts (in effect, giving away its information and resources) will be the target of increased exploitation. The groups seeking contracts may ultimately find they have priced themselves out of the market simply by refusing to give away the information.

Despite these problems, the *Mataatua Declaration*, for example, specifically calls for the consent of the appropriate Indigenous people prior to any commercialization of biogenetic resources obtained from the community,[131] which presumably would be embodied in some form of binding arrangement. Given that authorization, informed consent, and compensation are key issues, it is hardly surprising that Indigenous groups and local communities want to maintain control and not delegate it to states or other entities, as would be done under the *Model Provisions*.

What is proposed here, in necessarily broad form, is a kind of overarching contractual framework, such as that provided by the Uniform Commercial Code in the United States. This framework, which applies to the sales of goods, aims at ameliorating disparities in information and bargaining power by implying terms (such as warranties) and requiring certain agreements to be in writing.

For example, drawing on the discussion of trade secrets above, a "uniform folklore code" could be applicable to any information which:

1. constitutes folklore which has potential commercial value; and
2. is subject to restrictions on disclosure, as shown by past and present cultural practices.

Once the subject of the uniform folklore code is defined, the parties would be required to negotiate a contract for the information, or the law would presume an illegal misappropriation where the information is obtained in violation of the restrictions in (2) or from any-one who the obtainer knew or should have known obtained the information in violation of (2). Violations could be enforceable by the group itself or, with its consent, a governmental agency or NGO, and violators could be subject to penalties.

Once the party that desires the information is forced to deal with the authority that traditionally controls the information, the law should require that all contracts involve the informed consent of the relevant group or community. A court could consider whether informed consent was obtained by determining whether the group or individual traditionally vested with control over the information was consulted and consented. Obviously, many other factors could be added to create presumptions as to whether there is informed consent.

Additionally courts could imply certain terms where the contract is silent. Some examples could be implying:

i.   minimum royalties set by the state;
ii.   a provision providing for attribution of the community as creator and steward of the information in appropriate places, such as publications, patent applications, and copyright registrations;
iii. a provision that grants the community control over distorting uses; and
iv.   a provision designating an NGO as a third-party beneficiary to enforce the contract where it has authorization from the group.

Additionally, other terms could be filled in where the contract is silent.

A framework such as the above provides both the flexibility to empower local groups to contract for highly specific terms and protection from overreaching. Importantly, this sort of framework, if done on an international scale, can minimize the potential for increased exploitation which may otherwise arise when only some groups (or groups in some states) are able to protect their knowledge through contracts. Such a framework would extend protection by uniformly defining what material must be obtained through contract (without use of it being presumed an unlawful misappropriation), thus mandating at least face-to-face interaction to determine those contractual terms.

IV. Towards an International Approach

Although some hold it impossible to define and, therefore, regulate folklore, since 1989 more and more people have recognized the need to protect folklore as a part of preserving cultural and biological diversity. If any universal goal unites us now, this is surely one. But we must avoid another ten years of waiting for the formulation of a single all-encompassing and effective solution. Instead, Member States should be provided with many options. These options should have the potential to function within an international framework we hope to develop. I have brought together several options that could advance some key concerns by modifying existing intellectual property laws. I have also suggested that a contractual framework could empower local communities.

An international instrument could be drafted which provides both clear direction and room for experimentation. Such an instrument would specify minimum rights and provide for national (non-discriminatory) treatment, such as in the *Berne Convention*. Any minimum right adopted should balance being specific enough to provide clear guidance with being broad enough to allow each Member State to experiment with different means of fulfilling its obligations. The following ways of asserting some substantive minimum rights are culled from the above discussion and could be incorporated in such an instrument:

1. recognizing traditional communal forms of authorship and ownership in copyright (including moral rights as well as economic rights), such as by incorporating concepts of a group's customary law within the definition of copyright "authorship" and "ownership";
2. preventing the registration of sacred symbols and words as trademarks, except where authorized by the group itself;
3. requiring all patent applicants who used information derived from a group's folk knowledge of plants or other resources during the process of invention to sign a sworn declaration that the information was provided with the informed consent of the relevant individual and/or group, and making negligent and intentionally false statements punishable and issued patents subject to revocation (possibly with royalties disgorged);
4. expressly expanding trade-secret law to recognize a group's restrictions on the disclosure of potentially commercially valuable information, as such restrictions are shown through the past and present cultural practices of the group;
5. adopting a contractual framework applicable to potentially commercially valuable and traditionally restricted folklore, requiring informed consent for its use, and implying terms such as attribution rights and minimum royalties, as well as setting presumptions as to whether such consent has been obtained from the relevant group.

The above are a small sampling of the kind of minimum rights which could be included. UNESCO should take a leading role in the development of such an instrument. Prior to the adoption of a new instrument, UNESCO should also work to educate Member States and groups within them on the tools that could be created on a national basis.

Conclusion

International work with attention to local relations must be the goal, because although folklore is "local," its loss is surely a global phenomenon. Legal options should aim to empower those who are stewards and innovators of the folklore being protected, taking cognizance of the varied and complex social relations in and through which folklore is embodied and changes. Effective solutions will consist of both international cooperation and local empowerment.

Notes

The author wishes to thank the law firm of Thelen Reid & Priest LLP, Dean A. Morehous, and Rauer Meyer for encouraging the work on this essay and providing the resources to complete it. The author wishes to acknowledge the capable and astute editorial and intellectual assistance of Esther Eidenow, along with the opportunity, support, and critical feedback from Anthony McCann and Sherylle Mills at the Smithsonian Institution. Although the author claims few original thoughts, he takes sole responsibility for any expressions which are.

1. UNESCO, 1989 *Recommendation on the Safeguarding of Traditional Culture and Folklore*, adopted by the General Conference at its twenty-fifth session, Paris, 15 November 1989.

2. Marc Denhez, "International Protection of Expressions of Folklore: UNESCO Follow-Up to the 1989 *Recommendation on the Safeguarding of Traditional Culture and Folklore*," p. 2 (UNESCO-WIPO/FOLK/PKT/97/17).

3. *Id.*, p. 7.

4. Marc Denhez, draft "Pre-Evaluation on the Activities Related to the Preparation, Adoption and Implementation of the 1989 *Recommendation on the Safeguarding of Traditional Culture and Folklore* (1989)," p. 25.

5. Carl Shapiro and Hal Varian, *Information Rules: A Strategic Guide to the Network Econom.* (Harvard Business School Press, 1999).

6. *TRIPS Agreement*, 33 I.L.M. 81 (1994). See Ruth L. Gana, "Has Creativity Died in the Third World? Some Implications of the Internationalization of Intellectual Property," 24 *Denv. J. Int'l L. & Pol'y* 109 (1995).

7. *Id.*, p. 119.

8. *Id.*, p. 119.

9. Although this assessment uses the terms "group," "insider," and "outsider," it must be recognized that such lines are often very difficult to draw, and in fact are often drawn by outsiders with the power to make and enforce such distinctions on others.

10. In Curtis M. Horton, "Protecting Biodiversity and Cultural Diversity Under Intellectual Property Law: Toward a New International System," 10 *J. Envtl. L. & Litig.* 1 (1995), p. 5.

11. Doris Estelle Long, "The Impact of Foreign Investment on Indigenous Culture: An Intellectual Property Perspective," 23 *N. C. J. Int'l Law & Com. Reg* 229 (1998), p. 240.

12. Assimilation is defined as "one of the outcomes of the acculturation process, in which the subordinate or smaller group is absorbed into the larger or dominant one and becomes indistinguishable from it in cultural terms." The author goes on to note that "the concept of assimilation has been widely questioned in modern anthropology, and most writers now argue for a more careful examination of the different dimensions of cultural interchange and social dominance in situations of contact between different sociocultural systems." In Charlotte Seymour-Smith, *Macmillan Dictionary of Anthropology* (Macmillan Press Ltd., 1986).

13. 23 *N. C. J. Int'l Law & Com. Reg.* 229 (1998), p. 242. The author comments, "Thus, tourists in New Zealand watch performers clad in bastardized versions of 'traditional' Maori dress perform a welcoming ceremony although the performers have no concept of, or appreciation for, the cultural significance of the rituals."

14. See 10 *J. Envtl. L. & Litig.* 1.

15. *Id.*, p. 4.

16. *Id.*

17. *Id.*

18. Naomi Roht-Arriaza, "Of Seeds and Shamans: The Appropriation of the Scientific and Technical Knowledge of Indigenous and Local Communities," 17 *Mich. J. Int'l L.* 919 (1996), p. 927.

19. *Id.*, p. 926. The author notes that 97% of the vegetable varieties sold by commercial seed houses in the United States at the start of the century are now extinct; half of Europe's domesticated animal species have become extinct in this century; most of the remaining biodiversity is concentrated in "gene-rich" Southern countries where most Indigenous and traditional communities are located. The West's focus on a few varieties which maximize yield, while perhaps economically efficient from a short-term perspective, may reveal itself to be all too short term, as environmental conditions change.

20. In 10 *J. Envtl. L. & Litig.* 1, p. 5. For a listing of several examples of Western drugs which are derived from Indigenous and local communities see 17 *Mich. J. Int'l Law* 919, p. 920.

21. The Bellagio Declaration, reprinted in *Shamans, Software, & Spleens: Law and the Construction of the Information Society*, by James Boyle (Harvard University Press, 1996). The *Mataatua Declaration* was adopted by over 150 delegates from 14 countries at the First International Conference on the Cultural and Intellectual Property Rights of Indigenous Peoples (2–18 June 1993, Whakatane).

22. *Model Provisions for National Laws on the Protection of Expressions of Folklore Against Illicit Exploitation and Other Prejudicial Actions.*

23. *Mataatua Declaration*, Preamble.

24. This story is summarized from Christine Haight Farley, "Protecting Folklore of Indigenous Peoples: Is Intellectual Property the Answer?," 30 *Conn. L. Rev. 1* (1997), p. 4.

25. *Id.*, p. 5.

26. 17 *Mich. J. Int'l L.* 919, p. 947.

27. *Mataatua Declaration*, Section 3.5.

28. 17 *Mich. J. Int'l L.* 919, p. 954.

29. Michael J. Huft, "Indigenous Peoples and Drug Discovery Research: A Question of Intellectual Property Rights," 89 *Nw. U.L. Rev.* 1678 (1995), p. 1685.

30. The *Suva Declaration* resulted from a UNDP Consultation on Indigenous Peoples' Knowledge and Intellectual Property Rights, Suva, Fiji (April 1995). It calls on governments and corporate bodies responsible for the destruction of Pacific biodiversity to stop their destructive practices, compensate the affected communities, and rehabilitate the affected environment.

31. In 10 *J. Envtl. L. & Litig.* 1, pp. 6–7.

32. See 17 *Mich. J. Int'l Law* 919, p. 922.

33. For more information on the topic of copyright and Indigenous music, see Sherylle Mills, "Indigenous Music and the Law: An Analysis of National and International Interests," in *1996 Yearbook for Traditional Music* 58.

34. *Id.*, p. 59.

35. *Id.*

36. *Id.*

37. Although GATT TRIPS requires protection of live musical performances from unauthorized distribution.

38. "Taiwanese Pop Going Aboriginal," *Toronto Star,* 30 January 1999.

39. *Mataatua Declaration*, Section 2.2.

40. *Mataatua Declaration*, Preamble.

41. See Marc Denhez, "International Protection of Expressions of Folklore: UNESCO Follow-Up to the 1989 *Recommendation on the Safeguarding of Traditional Culture and Folklore*" for a summary of UNESCO's drafting and adoption of the 1989 *Recommendation*.

42. Of course, asserting cultural identity by no means automatically leads to bringing people together, as history, including recent history, too painfully teaches.

43. The following describes the separate elements of the 1989 *Recommendation*, which calls for the identification, conservation, preservation, dissemination, and protection of folklore.

    Identification: Member states are encouraged to identify folklore through surveys, to be incorporated in regional and global registers. States are to create identification and recording systems and work towards a standard typology, by way of a general outline of folklore, a comprehensive register, and regional classifications.

    Conservation: In order to conserve that folklore which is fixed in a tangible form, Member States should establish archives, including a centralized archive. States should establish museums and emphasize the living or past aspects of those cultures by showing their context. Archivists and collectors should be trained. Finally, copies should be made for regional institutions to assure access to the culture community from which the folklore derives.

    Preservation: Recognizing that each people has a right to its own culture and that its adherence to that culture is often eroded by industrialized culture, each state should implement curricula emphasizing respect for folklore and promoting a better understanding of cultural diversity. Each state is asked to guarantee the right of access of cultural communities to its own folklore, and to provide moral and economic support for individuals and institutions studying, promoting, cultivating, or holding items of folklore. States are also to promote scientific research.

    Dissemination: Dissemination should be effected to show the value of folklore and the need to preserve it, and its importance as an ingredient of cultural identity. Distortion should be avoided, "so that the integrity of the traditions can be safeguarded." International, national, and regional events should be organized to disseminate and publish folklore. Various media industries should be encouraged to incorporate folklore material in national and regional press, television, radio, etc., through the hiring of folklorists in these entities. The international scientific community should be encouraged to adopt a code of ethics ensuring "a proper approach to and respect for traditional cultures." Regions, municipalities, and other groups should be encouraged to establish full-time jobs for folklorists and to stimulate and coordinate folklore activities.

Protection: "In so far as folklore constitutes manifestations of intellectual creativity whether it be individual or collective, it deserves to be protected in a manner inspired by the protection provided for intellectual productions." The 1989 *Recommendation* states that "[s]uch protection of folklore has become indispensable as a means of promoting further development, maintenance and dissemination of those expressions, both within and outside the country, without prejudice to related legitimate interests." In addition to publicizing the UNESCO and WIPO efforts in relation to intellectual property, states are asked to protect the privacy and confidentiality of the informant as the transmitter of tradition; protect the interests of the collector by ensuring proper conservation; safeguard the materials themselves so that they are not misused; and place responsibility on archives for monitoring the use made of the materials they contain.

International Cooperation: Finally, the 1989 *Recommendation* urges increased cultural cooperation and exchanges. These exchanges should include cooperation between states, international and regional associations and institutions, in order to exchange information, train specialists, promote bilateral or multilateral projects to document folklore, and organize meetings on specified topics. States should work in concert to insure that economic, moral, and neighboring rights which result from the investigation, creation, composition, and performance of folklore are enjoyed internationally. Finally, states are to take necessary steps to safeguard folklore against all human and natural dangers, and to refrain from acts likely to damage folklore materials or diminish their value.

44. Prof. Eisemann, Chair of the Legal Committee of the General Conference, quoted in draft "Pre-Evaluation on the Activities Related to the Preparation, Adoption and Implementation of the 1989 *Recommendation on the Safeguarding of Traditional Culture and Folklore* (1989)," p. 8.

45. See draft "Pre-Evaluation on the Activities Related to the Preparation, Adoption and Implementation of the 1989 *Recommendation on the Safeguarding of Traditional Culture and Folklore* (1989)," p. 26.

46. *Id.*

47. Quoted in draft "Pre-Evaluation on the Activities Related to the Preparation, Adoption and Implementation of the 1989 *Recommendation on the Safeguarding of Traditional Culture and Folklore* (1989)," p. 27.

48. 1989 *Recommendation*, Section A.

49. *Id.*

50. Indeed, Tylor, who is considered a founder of modern anthropology, wrote that culture "is that complex whole which includes knowledge, belief, art, morals, law, custom, and any other capabilities and habits acquired by man as a member of society." In more recent times this descriptive definition has been eschewed in favor of an analytical one, focusing on patterns abstracted from observed behavior. In *Macmillan Dictionary of Anthropology.*

51. See draft "Pre-Evaluation on the Activities Related to the Preparation, Adoption and Implementation of the 1989 *Recommendation on the Safeguarding of Traditional Culture and Folklore* (1989)," pp. 8–12.

52. "Study of the Possible Range and Scope of General Regulations Concerning the Safeguarding of Folklore," p. 8, quoted in draft "Pre-Evaluation on the Activities Related to the Preparation, Adoption and Implementation of the 1989 *Recommendation on the Safeguarding of Traditional Culture and Folklore* (1989)," p. 10.

53. *Id.*

54. Draft "Pre-Evaluation on the Activities Related to the Preparation, Adoption and Implementation of the 1989 *Recommendation on the Safeguarding of Traditional Culture and Folklore* (1989)," pp. 11–12.

55. *Mataatua Declaration,* Sections 1.1 and 1.8.

56. *Suva Declaration.*

57. 1989 *Recommendation.*

58. 17 *Mich. J. Int'l Law* 919, pp. 929–30.

59. 1989 *Recommendation*, Section F.

60. 1989 *Recommendation*, Section G(g).

61. *Mataatua Declaration,* Sections 1.8, 2.1

62. *Suva Declaration.*

63. Charter of Indigenous-Tribal Peoples of the Tropical Forests: Statement of the International Alliance of the Indigenous-Tribal Peoples of the Tropical Forest, Penang, Malaysia, 15 February 1992, quoted in Darrell A. Posey, "International Agreements and Intellectual Property Right Protection for

Indigenous Peoples," in *Intellectual Property Rights for Indigenous Peoples*, Tom Greaves, ed. (SFAA 1994) p. 234.

64.   For a discussion of the potential harm of "absolutist" claims to ideas and the resulting "border controls" on the flow of information, namely reification of ethnic and nationalist claims of "purity" see Michael F. Brown, "Can Culture be Copyrighted?" *Current Anthropology*, volume 39, number 2 (April 1998).

65.   *Suva Declaration.*

66.   1989 *Recommendation*, Section E.

67.   Draft "Pre-Evaluation on the Activities Related to the Preparation, Adoption and Implementation of the 1989 *Recommendation on the Safeguarding of Traditional Culture and Folklore* (1989)," p. 69.

68.   See "1967, 1982, 1984: Attempts to Provide International Protection for Folklore By Intellectual Property" prepared by the International Bureau of WIPO for the UNESCO-WIPO World Forum on the Protection of Folklore for a discussion of this process.

69.   More specifically, the *Model Provisions* cover only "artistic" expressions of folklore, regardless of whether they are fixed in tangible form. These explicitly include verbal expressions such as folk tales, folk poetry, and riddles; musical expressions such as folk songs; and expressions by action, such as folk dances. Also included are material expressions such as drawings, paintings, carvings, musical instruments, and architecture.

      Any use of an expression of folklore through publication, reproduction, distribution, public recitation or performance outside of its "traditional or usual context" with gainful intent is subject to authorization. In order to balance between protection against abuses, on the one hand, and the encouragement of ongoing development, on the other, the authorization requirement does not apply where the expression of folklore is used for educational purposes. Nor does it apply where elements are "borrowed" to create an "original work," providing such utilization is compatible with fair practice.

      Each nation is to designate one or more "competent authorities" to whom an application for authorization is to be made. Where the competent authority grants authorization, it may fix and collect fees, to be used in promoting national culture or folklore. Use of folklore without required authorization is prohibited, and the user may be subject to fees and a fine.

      Separate from the authorization requirement, the origin of an expression of folklore must be indicated in any printed publication and in connection with any communication to the public, where such expression is "identifiable." Failure to acknowledge the source results in a fine. Purposeful deceit as to the origin of objects or performances, as expressions of folklore of a certain community, where in fact they do not originate, is punishable by a fine and imprisonment. Finally, any person who makes, distributes, or offers for sale objects, or publicly performs or organizes public performances or broadcasts of expressions of folklore in a way that purposefully "denatures" them in a manner "prejudicial to the cultural interests of the community concerned" is punishable by a fine or imprisonment.

70.   In 1997, at a joint UNESCO and WIPO World Forum, a Plan of Action noted that there is no international standard for protection and that copyright is inadequate. UNESCO and WIPO were asked, as part of the Plan of Action, to set up a Committee of Experts to undertake regional consultations and to complete the drafting of an international agreement on the *sui generis* (unique) protection of folklore by the second quarter of 1998.

71.   "1967, 1982, 1984: Attempts to Provide International Protection for Folklore by Intellectual Property" prepared by the International Bureau of WIPO for the UNESCO-WIPO World Forum on the Protection of Folklore, p. 12.

72.   *Id.*, p. 13.

73.   Draft "Pre-Evaluation on the Activities Related to the Preparation, Adoption and Implementation of the 1989 *Recommendation on the Safeguarding of Traditional Culture and Folklore* (1989), pp. 53–55.

74.   155 EX/Decisions (Paris, 3 December 1998). The regulations define several criteria. These include both cultural criteria and protection criteria. Examples of cultural criteria include the submission's outstanding value as "a masterpiece of human creative genius," its "roots in the cultural tradition or cultural history of the community concerned," its role as a means of "affirming the cultural identity of the peoples and cultural communities concerned," its excellence in the application of the skill and technical qualities displayed, and its risk of disappearing. In addition to cultural criteria, a plan of action must be submitted showing how the folklore expression will be preserved, protected, sup-

ported, and promoted over the next decade. It must provide details of its compatibility with the 1989 *Recommendation*. Importantly, details of the measures taken to involve the communities concerned in preserving and promoting their own oral and intangible heritage also must be provided.

75. Such as exist in Japan, for example.

76. 24 *Denv. J. Int'l L. & Pol'y* 109, p. 112.

77. 23 *N. C. J. Int'l Law & Com.* Reg 229, p. 244.

78. Stephen B. Brush, "A Non-Market Approach to Protecting Biological Resources," in *Intellectual Property Rights for Indigenous Peoples*, Tom Greaves, ed. (SFAA 1994) p. 133.

79. Surendra J. Patel, "Can the IPR System Serve the Interests of Indigenous Knowledge?" in *Valuing Local Knowledge,* Steven B. Brush and Doreen Stabinsky, eds. (Island Press 1996), p. 319.

80. 1989 *Recommendation* Section F(a).

81. See Peter Jaszi and Martha Woodmansee, "The Ethical Reaches of Authorship," *South Atlantic Quarterly,* 95:4 (Fall 1996), which argues that "author" in the modern sense of a "sole creator of unique literary and artistic works" is a relatively recent invention, and calls for a re-envisioning of intellectual property to address such issues as joint ownership. See also James Boyle, *Shamans, Software, & Spleens: Law and the Construction of the Information Society* (Harvard University Press, 1996) and 23 *N. C. J. Int'l Law & Com.* Reg 229, p. 246.

82. *Bellagio Declaration.*

83. *Mataatua Declaration,* Section 2.5.

84. Even within the West, the underlying rationale varies. The United States emphasizes the economic incentives over moral rights inhering by nature in the author, whereas Continental Europe emphasizes a more "romantic" conception of authorship and concomitant moral rights over economic incentives.

85. The author ultimately views this calculus as, at best, different for different types of work (software with a market life of 2 years, as compared with a novel which may have a market life of 100 years) and, at worst, entirely indeterminate.

86. Consider, for example, twin carvings (*ere ibeji*) of the Yoruba, in Nigeria. The Yoruba have one of the world's highest twinning rates, and they attach special significance to twins. If twins are treated properly, they can bring great rewards to their family, but those who mistreat twins may bring grave misfortune upon themselves. Twins are believed to share one soul, and therefore, if one dies, there is fear that the remaining twin will follow his or her sibling back into the woods, from which twins are thought to come.

    The family that has twins traditionally purchases a wooden figure from a carver who sculpts the figure, more or less as he pleases. When a twin dies, the figure undergoes ceremonies with a priestess. It is then delivered to the family. The family dresses it, adorns it with jewelry of spiritual significance, feeds it, and brings it to the marketplace and festivals. In many ways it is treated as a living member of the family. Over time, the dressing, feeding, and cleaning of the figure alter the original sculpture. To the carver it is perhaps simply a material object or work of "art," but to the family it is surely much more.

    What is the "work" in this instance? Is it the original figure purchased by the family? Is it the figure as it undergoes physical changes? Are multiple works involved? Who is the author? Is it the original carver, or the family, or both? More importantly, who should be given the incentive to encourage the protection of this tradition? What should this incentive be? Art production, and all intellectual endeavor, is ultimately a product of complex social relationships. The economic incentive given by copyright law, which grants the carver copyrights in the sculpture, is likely to be impotent in assuring the ongoing vitality of this tradition. The unthinking application of Continental European "moral rights," which act to prevent distortion, could actually end the practice, by allowing one such carver to prevent a family from violating the integrity of the original work. Consider that in some instances the traditional wooden figures are being replaced with imported Western plastic dolls; clearly granting monopoly rights to the sculpture will do little to alter this fact. See Brad Simon, "The Envisioning of Envisioning Africa," *Journal of Museum Anthropology* 16(2):55.

87. For example, many have noted that the weakness of copyright protection and the perceived lack of patent protection did little to slow the growth of the software industry in the United States.

88. The following discussion is presented with the recognition that: (1) intellectual property laws as currently conceived can only provide a limited means of meeting some of the interests identified above in Section I; (2) GATT TRIPS is a reality, along with the culturally specific forms of intellec-

tual property laws perpetuated by it; (3) any implementation of any law regulating folklore requires a coherent, on-the-ground assessment of its impact; and (4) there is a great need to consider non-Western mechanisms of protecting intellectual property to expand the limited discourse.

89.   See the Copyright Act of 1976, as amended, at 17 United States Code, Sections 101-810; 1001-1010. Copyright law protects "works of authorship" and grants the owner a bundle of exclusive rights, typically the rights to make copies or authorize others to do so, make derivative works, sell, display, or perform the work. The laws of most countries grant these rights to the owner of an original work. The owner is typically the "author" unless the author assigns or licenses one or more of the exclusive rights to another. Copyright covers literary works, audiovisual works, computer software, graphic works, musical arrangements, and sound recordings.

   Copyright typically exists in the United States for the life of the author plus 70 years. After this time, the work enters the public domain. Corporate entities, not individuals, are deemed the author and owner of the majority of works. This is due, in large measure, to the "work for hire" doctrine, which provides that an employee who creates a copyrightable work within the scope of his or her employment does so for the employer, who is considered not only the owner, but also the "author."

   Copyright is often said to be weak because it does not protect ideas, but only their unique expression. That is, a copyright in a poem, which contains information about medicinal uses of plants, does not extend to the information, but only prevents someone from copying the expression contained in the poem itself. Because a copyright lasts relatively long, compared with a patent, the monopoly impact would be substantial were it to cover the idea itself. In fact, where there are few ways of expressing a given idea, the courts have developed the "merger" doctrine to deny copyright protection.

   Not all copies of copyrightable expression are infringements. For example, copyright law recognizes a "fair use" exception. Courts will consider the nature of the work copied (fictional works obtain more protection than factual), the amount copied, the use for which the copying was made (educational versus commercial), and whether the copying harmed the market for the copied material. Unlike a patent, copyright does not protect against independent creation. Thus, two authors can own copyrights in substantially the same work, so long as neither copied the work of the other.

   The United States used to require that the copyright owner place a specified notice on each copy, otherwise the work would enter the public domain, although this is no longer the case since United States acceded to Berne. In the United States, a copyright must be "fixed in a tangible medium," but this is not a requirement under TRIPS.

90.   See 30 *Conn. L. Rev.* 1, p. 16, which notes the first attempts at granting legal protection for folklore were through copyright laws in such countries as Kenya, Tunisia, and Chile.

91.   In "1967, 1982, 1984: Attempts to Provide International Protection for Folklore By Intellectual Property" prepared by the International Bureau of WIPO for the UNESCO-WIPO World Forum on the Protection of Folklore (UNESCO-WIPO/FOLK/PKT/97/19), p. 5, the author states, "It seems copyright law is not the right means for protecting expressions of folklore. This is because, whereas an expression of folklore is the result of an impersonal, continuous and slow process of creative activity exercised in a given community by consecutive imitation, works protected by copyright must, traditionally, bear a mark of individual originality. . . . Copyright is author-centric and, in the case of folklore, the author — or at least in the way in which the notion of 'author' is conceived in the field of copyright — is practically missing."

92.   A license is a transfer of less than all of the rights held by the owner, whereas an assignment is a transfer of all rights held by the owner.

93.   17 USC Section 106.

94.   *Berne Convention for the Protection of Literary Works* (Paris Text, 1971).

95.   See *Dodd v. Fort Smith Special School District No. 100*, 666 F. Supp. 1278 (W.D. Ark, 1987).

96.   17 USC Section 101.

97.   17 USC Section 106A(3).

98.   See the Lanham Act, 15 United States Codes, Sections 1051-1127. Trademark law protects the images, symbols, names, or even the overall "look and feel" that distinguishes a particular product or service. A trademark can include distinctive shapes, scents, color, as well as the more typical word or design. Marks which are arbitrary or fanciful with respect to the goods or services may be registered, whereas a mark which merely describes the goods or services may only be registered if the mark has acquired meaning as a source identifier. Words which are "generic" in that they sim-

ply name the genus of products or services ("Filter Company" for a company selling or making filters) can never function as a mark.

Once a trademark is established, only the trademark owner may use the name or symbol in connection with similar commercial products. The use of marks which are likely to cause consumer confusion can be enjoined by court order, and damages may be obtained. By restricting use of trademarks, the law protects both the goodwill that businesses build through the sale of their products, and the consumers' expectations that the product he or she purchases is authentic and of predictable quality based on past purchases. Unlike copyright, the protection lasts indefinitely, so long as the mark has not been abandoned. Although in the United States, trademark rights arise through use in commerce, trademarks may also be registered at the federal level. Federal registration results in several benefits, namely the presumption of nationwide use rights, constructive notice to third parties, and the ability for a mark to become "incontestable" after five years of use.

In addition to trademarks, several countries also recognize "collective marks" and "certification marks." A collective mark, like a trademark, may consist of a design, symbol, word, product shape, etc., that is used by members of a group or organization to identify goods members produce or simply the fact that individuals are members. Collective marks are entitled to registration and the same protection as other types of marks. The primary function is to identify goods or services which emanate from the group members, and hence only members can use the mark. The organization itself must use a different mark to identify its goods or services.

A certification mark authorizes organizations to "certify" characteristics or qualities of products and services manufactured or provided by others. Certification marks may include regions of origin (e.g., "Stilton" cheese); product quality ("Good Housekeeping Seal of Approval"); service quality ("AAA"); or method of manufacture (e.g., "method champenoise"). Certification marks, unlike other trademarks, may not be licensed or assigned, on the theory that doing so eradicates the meanings the mark may have developed.

One additional noteworthy aspect of federal trademark law is that certain types of marks may be refused registration. These include "immoral," "deceptive," or "scandalous" marks, as well as marks which "disparage or falsely suggest a connection with persons, living or dead, institutions, beliefs, or national symbols, or bring them into contempt, or disrepute." Although few United States cases have decided what constitutes "immoral" matter, a mark's scandalous character is to be determined (1) in the context of the marketplace as applied to the goods or service described in the application, and (2) from the standpoint of a substantial composite of the general public, which is not necessarily the majority.

99. USPTO Reg. Nos. 2221870, 2222979, and 2219102.
100. See 30 *Conn. L. Rev* 1, pp. 49–51 for a discussion of this law.
101. A search of the trademark register shows that the National Board of the Young Men's Christian Associations owns a collective (membership) mark for "Indian Guides Father and Son Pals Forever YMCA" (USPTO Reg. No. 0780752). Perhaps more interesting, there is a collective (membership) registration for the mark "Fagowees" (which is said to come from the Nomacadicindian Tribe, and which features a design of a tomahawk-wielding "Indian" cartoon) for indicating membership in a social club (USPTO Reg. No. 1128077).
102. USPTO Serial No. 73/767992.
103. Federal Anti-Dilution Act, 15 USC 1125(c). Dilution laws, recently federalized, allow the owner of a "famous" trademark to seek an injunction to prevent the use of marks that, although not confusingly similar, are likely to dilute the strength of the mark, either through blurring or tarnishing the consumer associations. For example, the use of "Enjoy Cocaine" in the same type style as "Enjoy Coke" could tarnish consumer associations, and thus be stopped.
104. See Decisions Adopted by the Executive Board at its 155th Session (Paris, 19 October–5 November 1998; Tashkent, 6 November 1998), (155 EX/Decisions).
105. *Suzan Shown Harjo et al. v. Pro-Football, Inc.*, Cancellation No. 21,069 (TTAB 1999). The TTAB noted that the mark was not scandalous; however, because of its continuous renown and acceptance, the word for the football services is inconsistent with "the sense of outrage by a substantial composite of the general population that would be necessary to find the word scandalous."
106. *William B. Ritchie v. Orenthal James Simpson* (3/15/1999, No. 97-1371) holds an individual had a "real interest" and "reasonable" belief of damage and could therefore seek cancellation of "O.J. Simpson," "O.J.," and "The Juice" where the individual alleged he believes "in the sanctity of mar-

riage" and that the marks are synonymous with "wife-beater," and submitted petitions of many people claiming the marks are scandalous and encourage spousal abuse.

107. *Harjo v. Pro Football Inc.*, 30 USPQ2d 1828 (TTAB 1994).
108. Public Law 105-330 (1998).
109. Although this law has apparently never been enforced, enforcement may be more likely if the Interior Department enacts regulations, which it has never done since the law was first passed in 1935.
110. New Mexico Statutes, Sec. 30-33-6.
111. See the Patent Act, 36 United States Code, Section 1-376. A patent is a monopoly right granted by a government that allows an "inventor" to prevent others from manufacturing, selling, or using the invention, as specifically described in the claims of the patent, for a limited time. An invention must be new, non-obvious, and useful. Unlike every other country in the world, the United States has a "first to invent" system, meaning that rights accrue to the first inventor, not the first to file for a patent. Any invention that is published anywhere, put in public use, or placed on sale in the United States more than one year prior to the filing of a patent application is considered to be in the public domain, and hence freely available. Patents do not extend to naturally occurring matter, although they may be obtained for purified or genetically altered versions of naturally occurring substances.
112. See 17 *Mich. J. Int'l Law* 919, for an insightful discussion of this situation.
113. 35 USC Section 102.
114. 35 USC Section 103.
115. 17 *Mich. J. Int'l Law* 919, p. 936.
116. 17 *Mich J. Int'l Law* 919, p. 938.
117. 89 *Nw U.L. Rev.* 1678.
118. 89 *Nw U.L. Rev.* 1678, p. 1730.
119. 10 *J. Envtl. L. & Litig.* 1, p. 36.
120. 30 *Conn. L Rev.* 1., p. 53, concluding that trade secret protection will be available in only a limited number of cases.
121. See 23 *N. C. J. Intl Law & Com.* Reg. 229, p. 441.
117. The Uniform Trade Secrets Act of 1979 (The National Conference of Comissioners on Uniform State Law, 1979).
123. The Uniform Trade Secrets Act, Section 1.
124. See James Pooley, *Trade Secrets: How to Protect Your Ideas and Assets* (Osborne/McGraw-Hill, 1982), pp. 19–23.
125. See for example, the following chapters in *Intellectual Property Rights for Indigenous People* (supra, note 58): Janet Mc. Gowan and Iroka Udeinya, "Collecting Traditional Medicines in Nigeria: A Proposal for IPR Compensation," Stephen R. King, "Establishing Reciprocity: Biodiversity, Conservation and New Models for Cooperation Between Forest-Dwelling Peoples and the Pharmaceutical Industry," and "Policies for International Collaboration and Compensation in Drug Discovery and Development at the United States National Cancer Institute: The NCI Letter of Collection."
126. See 17 *Mich. J. Int'l L.* 919, p. 958.
127. *Id.*, p. 958.
128. *Id.*, pp. 959–60.
129. *Id.*
130. Robert Merges, "Contracting into Liability Rules: Intellectual Property Rights and Collective Rights Organizations," 84 *Calif. L. Rev.* 1293 (1996), p. 1362.
131. *Mataatua Declaration,* Section 2.9.

The Role of UNESCO in the Defense of Traditional Knowledge

Manuela Carneiro da Cunha
Professor of Anthropology, University of Chicago

At this historical juncture, UNESCO can play a central role in the protection of intellectual rights in traditional culture. A widespread shift in legal thinking toward a generalized privatization of knowledge suggests the extension of intellectual property rights (IPRs) to cover traditional knowledge. But in this paper, I argue that such a measure, while attending to a matter of equity, would endanger the continued production of this knowledge. To pursue both equity and preservation, I argue that traditional knowledge should be put in the public domain, but only under two conditions: if the public domain itself is protected from misappropriation and if there is a fair retribution whenever such knowledge leads to commercial ventures. Just as TRIPS (Trade-Related International Property Agreements) has ensured that the private domain as expressed by Intellectual property rights is protected worldwide, the public domain needs to be similarly protected from piracy. Each country can enforce such regulation of the public domain within its own boundaries. Yet one country's public domain might be privatized in another country. Thus, UNESCO and WIPO are in a unique, instrumental position to carry out this project, which is clearly within their mandate.

The Public and the Private Domain

A double standard prevailed until a few years ago for seeds, drugs, and other such products in contrast to genetic resources and associated knowledge. The latter, on the premise that they could potentially benefit all of humankind, were deemed to be its common heritage and hence freely accessible. Seeds and drugs, on the other hand, while equally potentially beneficial to mankind as a whole, were protected by intellectual property rights (Cunningham 1993). Two alternative responses to this inequity came initially to mind (we will later see that there are more than just two options). One's choice seemed to be either to pursue a privatization of genetic resources and traditional knowledge or to advocate a suspension of intellectual property rights on products derived from them, putting these products into the public domain. In the seventies and the eighties, and in connection with seeds, this latter option seemed to gain some ground, particularly through the FAO (Food and Agriculture Organization), which acknowledged the contribution of generations of farmers. The version of UPOV (Union for the Protection of Plant Varieties) that was accepted in 1975, for instance, exempted farmers from the regulations imposed on everyone else regarding the exchange of seeds or their reutilization from one year to the next.

In the early nineties, privatization gained momentum. UPOV was amended in 1991 and toughened, affording protection to plant breeders that comes very close to patenting. In 1992, the Convention for Biological Diversity (CBD) established that genetic resources

143

should fall under the sovereignty of national states. Furthermore, many states translated sovereignty into property, though the two concepts are by no means equivalent. But the most drastic of all these instruments, because of the commercial sanctions attached to it, was TRIPS, which came out of the Uruguay Round of the GATT Negotiations in 1994. TRIPS provisions are mandatory for every member of the World Trade Organization. Under TRIPS, intellectual rights were granted protection irrespective of the country where the right had originated. States must internalize legislation accordingly, although at different paces; developing nations were given until 2000 to comply, whereas the least developed countries were granted another five years.

Although I lumped them together for the sake of pointing to the growth of privatization, CBD and TRIPS respond to very different interests and even contradict each other in certain aspects. CBD was drafted under the auspices of the United Nations in the context of the Rio Earth Summit and is perceived to take into consideration the interests of resource-rich countries, most of them in the Southern Hemisphere. It was signed and ratified by more than 170 countries. The most notable exception is the United States, whose President signed the Convention in 1993, but whose Congress refused to ratify it. The United States, on the other hand, was the main force behind the TRIPS Agreement, which ultimately serves its technological preponderance. As mentioned above, commercial sanctions in the form of trade retaliations account for the persuasive power of TRIPS.

The CBD explicitly deals with the rights of local people, and it does so in collective terms. Article 8(j) recognizes that each contracting party shall

> subject to its national legislation, respect, preserve and maintain knowledge, innovations and practices of Indigenous and local communities embodying traditional lifestyles relevant for the conservation and sustainable use of biological diversity and promote their wider application with the approval and involvement of the holders of such knowledge, innovations and practices and encourage the equitable sharing of benefits arising from the utilization of such knowledge, innovations and practices.

How are countries to implement the CBD? Several general meetings have already been convened, the fifth held in Nairobi in the spring of 2000, and the issue of Indigenous and local knowledge at these meetings has gained unprecedented importance. Under the sponsorship of Spain, two events to discuss this single issue were organized. While the first one was a seminar, the second, held in Seville about two months before the Nairobi Convention in 2000, brought in official delegations from over one hundred countries and was preceded by an Indigenous Forum.

Thus, the nineties saw a growth in public visibility of the issue of local and Indigenous knowledge. Paradoxically, they also seem to have confined mainstream institutions searching for appropriate approaches to the issue within the narrow boundaries of the decade's generalized push for privatization.

The defense of the expansion of the public domain, important in the UN until the eighties, and which echoes debates advocating public domain for software (see Boyle 1996), lost some ground. Rather, mainstream institutions were arguing for the extension of intellectual property rights to local knowledge with all their associated features and in particular an exclusivity clause.

The problem with applying intellectual property rights to traditional knowledge and enforcing an exclusivity clause is that it changes the basic ways this knowledge is produced. If that knowledge were simply a legacy from the past, there would be no problem at all. But knowledge, as part of culture, is essentially innovative. Local knowledge is based on speculation and experimentation, and it needs to have a proper institutional base. Moreover, traditional knowledge is part of a way of life that has inherent value in itself.

What then is a workable legal logic? Indigenous people have been arguing in several international forums that one cannot separate traditional knowledge from a much larger context, which includes land and sociability. But even if one were to isolate and focus exclusively on traditional knowledge, would the aim be to use it, along with its practices and innovations, for profit in the market, or more inclusively to promote its continued existence? Is it merely present knowledge we would be discussing, or present and future knowledge? That is, are we focusing on available knowledge or rather on the processes that produce knowledge? "What is Traditional in Traditional Knowledge," the final document of the Convention of the Parties in Buenos Aires in 1996, reads, " is not its antiquity but the way it is acquired and used."

It is sometimes argued that there are radical differences between contemporary Western systems of knowledge and traditional knowledge. Whereas there are indeed important differences, lumping together all traditional knowledge systems might underplay precisely what needs to be emphasized: the extreme diversity of these systems. The real conundrum is, as I see it: how is one to organize the interface, not between two very different systems, but rather between one globalized IPR system and a multitude of different local regimes with specific colonial histories?

The issue therefore cannot be discussed in the abstract. Let us take as an example one proposal that is on the table and that has been gaining ground in Ethiopia and in many Latin American and English-speaking African countries, although it originated in Southeast Asia. I am referring to the Community Intellectual Rights as they were originally proposed by the Third World Network (Nijar 1994, 1996). Note that the term property is conspicuously absent in the expression. The basic idea is that traditional knowledge should stay in the public domain for anyone to use, but that originators should share in the benefits when it is used for commercial purposes. Furthermore, these rights should not be subject to time limits. This is in stark contrast to contemporary practice of IPRs, which requires exclusivity and a limited timeframe.

In other words, the expectations of the two systems are reversed: free access and public domain versus monopoly and secrecy; unlimited time frame for intellectual rights versus loss of intellectual rights after a certain time.

It is worth remarking that in the seventies and the eighties, UNESCO and WIPO (World Intellectual Property Organization) devised instruments such as the *domaine public payant* to address similar issues in their dealing with the protection of folklore. *Domaine public payant* is a system by which a user of materials in the public domain is required to pay for a compulsory license. UNESCO and WIPO issued the Tunis Model Law in 1976, which dealt with folklore among other copyright legislation. In 1982, they issued the "Model Provisions for National Laws on the Protection of Expressions of Folklore Against Illicit Exploitation and Other Prejudicial Actions," which was followed by its international instrument counterpart, the "Draft Treaty for the Protection of Expressions of Folklore Against Illicit Exploitation and Other Prejudicial Actions" (Kuruk 1999, 813–16). Although much could be argued in relation to the states being the recipients of the *domaine public payant* fees and there being no necessary provisions for channeling them to the local people, the fact remains that this is an important attempt at dealing with the intangible heritage.

Protection of the Public Domain and the Role of UNESCO

Because of TRIPS, countries have been obliged to respect within their boundaries the intellectual protection granted by other countries. *But the converse is not true: no generalized obligation exists for countries to recognize each other's public domain.* As a result, knowledge that has been in the public domain for generations in one country might be privatized and enjoy IPRs in another country. The original country is not only excluded from benefits but also ironically obliged by the TRIPS Agreement to honor such an intellectual right. What was originally in the public domain in the country could come back, thanks to these regulations, as private property.

This being the situation, it is no wonder that accusations of piracy are being launched against First World countries. Australian breeders are being accused of using material held in trust by the Consultative Group on International Agricultural Research (CGIAR) germplasm banks (in the public domain) and patenting it (RAFI 1997). The United States Patent Office (USPO) granted a patent to a variety of *ayahuasca*, a plant known all over the western Amazon for its hallucinogenic properties. Stabilization of the extract of widely known Indian neem was sufficient for the USPO to grant it a patent, which was subsequently acquired by a giant corporation, W. R. Grace & Co. Indian NGOs are disputing foreign patents on thirteen traditional products, of which the most well known is neem. A notable decision, a first, was achieved in regard to another U.S. patent on turmeric. This patent was revoked by the USPO in 1997, two years after having been granted, after the New Delhi-based Council for Agriculture Research raised objections on the basis of Indian prior traditional knowledge and use of the substance (Shiva 1997).

That a patent on turmeric could have happened in the first place can be partly explained by still another set of double standards in the U.S. patents procedures. Internally, prior art can be proved, as it should be by its very nature, through public use. But for foreign public domain to be recognized in the United States, a written and accessible source is required (Sections 102 a and 102 b of U.S. Patent Law, personal communication by P. Ossorio).

The situation is so unclear and volatile that major germplasm repositories, such as the Kew Gardens, have temporarily suspended providing material on request and the CGIAR banks have called for a moratorium on granting patents on material they hold. Understandably, so has the Coordinating Body for Indigenous Organizations of the Amazon Basin (COICA).

The matters I have been discussing are not merely legal. They have a strong moral component. Legally, any biological resource collected prior to the Convention for Biological Diversity is not bound by its rules. The collector does not have to recognize the source country's sovereignty, nor does the collector have to acknowledge or reward in any way the people who conserved the resource and first experimented with it.

Yet, on moral grounds, important bodies like the aforementioned Kew Gardens and the CGIAR banks feel uneasy with the situation and are struggling to set guidelines. Ethnobotanical databanks, from which many pharmaceutical companies get relevant information, are likely to be involved soon in similar ethical concerns. Similarly, academic researchers have moral qualms about publishing any ethnobotanical data, since this amounts to putting it in an unprotected public domain, free to be appropriated by anyone.

In short, this state of affairs is hindering many kinds of scientific, educational, and cultural activities.

No country on its own can ensure that other countries will respect its internal regulations unless an International Convention is subscribed to. This is where UNESCO and WIPO can have a decisive role. They could develop an international agreement under which countries could make traditional knowledge publicly available, with the provisions that:

- it would not be privatized in other countries
- local and Indigenous communities would share in the benefits of commercial initiatives or products that derive from their knowledge, for example, through an updated version of *domaine public payant*

One might argue that the attempt at enforcing such a model in relation to folklore failed in the eighties for lack of political support. Neither the "Model Provisions" nor the "Draft Treaty" for the Protection of Folklore were adopted anywhere. And yet, one has to consider the unprecedented mobilization of traditional people and some governments around the issue of local and Indigenous knowledge after the Convention for Biological Diversity of 1992. This is a totally new situation that would permit UNESCO to launch a successful initiative.

References

Boyle, James. 1996. *Shamans, Software and Spleens*. Cambridge, MA: Harvard University Press.

Brush, S.B. 1993. Indigenous Knowledge of Biological Resources and Intellectual property rights: The Role of Anthropology. *American Anthropologist* 95: 653–86.

Brush, Stephen, and Doreen Stabinski. 1996. *Valuing Local Knowledge: Indigenous Peoples and Intellectual Property Rights*. Washington, DC: Island Press.

Coombe, Rosemary. 1998. *The Cultural Life of Intellectual Properties: Authorship, Appropriation, and the Law (Post-Contemporary Interventions)*. Durham: Duke University Press.

_____. Intellectual Property, Human Rights and Sovereignty: New Dilemmas in International Law Posed by the Recognition of Indigenous Knowledge and the Conservation of Biodiversity. <htttp://www.law.indiana.edu/glsj/vol6/no1/coom.html>. Indiana Law School Web Team.

Cunningham, A.B. 1993. *Ethics, Ethnobiological Research and Biodiversity*. Gland, Switzerland: World Wildlife Fund for Nature.

Escobar, Arturo. 1994. Biodiversidad, naturaleza y cultura: localidad y lobalidad en las estrategias de conservación. Bogota. Duplicated.

Grain (Genetic Resources Action International). 1997. The International Context of the Sui Generis Rights Debate. Chapter 1 in *Signposts to Sui Generis Rights: Resource Materials from the International Seminar on Sui Generis Rights*. <http://www.grain.org/publications/signposts/chapter1.htm>.

Kuruk, Paul. 1999. Protecting Folklore under Modern Intellectual Property Regimes: A Reappraisal of the Tensions between Individual and Communal Rights in Africa and the United States. *American University Law Review* 48:769–849.

Nijar, Gurdial Singh. 1994. *Towards a Legal Framework for Protecting Biological Diversity and Community Intellectual Rights: A Third World Perspective*. Penang: Third World Network.

_____. 1996. *In Defense of Local Community Knowledge and Biodiversity*. Third World Network Paper 1. Penang: Third World Network.

Posey, Darrell. 1996. *Traditional Resource Rights: International Instruments for Protection and Compensation for Indigenous Peoples and Local Communities*. Gland, Switzerland: IUCN, the World Conservation Union.

RAFI. 1997. Biopiracy Update: The Inequitable Sharing of Benefits. RAFI Communiqué September/October. <http://www.rafi.org/communique/19975.html>.

Shiva, Vandana. 1994. *Biodiversity and Intellectual Property Rights in the Case against Free Trade*. Washington, DC: Island Press.

_____. 1997. The politics of knowledge at the CBD. <http://www.twnside.org.sg/title/cbd-cn.htm>.

UNCTAD/WIPO. 1975. *The Role of the Patent System in the Transfer of Technology to Developing Countries.*
   New York: United Nations.

Safeguarding Traditional Culture and Folklore: Existing International Law and Future Developments

Janet Blake
Visiting Research Fellow
School of Law, University of Glasgow

Introduction

This paper examines existing UNESCO texts[1] and programs relevant to the safeguarding of traditional cultural and folklore heritage ("folklore"),[2] in order to consider the need to elaborate a new Convention; it also examines the viability of these texts and programs as the basis for the new initiative. Recognition of "intangible heritage" as a subject for protection is one of the most significant recent developments of international cultural heritage law,[3] and identifying its character has been a major challenge.[4] Understanding the significance of the transmission of information (e.g., how a carpet is hand-woven) and of the skill of the producer of this heritage is central to its definition. The human (social and economic) context of the production of intangible heritage requires safeguarding as much as the tangible product itself and must be considered in evaluating existing or future protective measures. This perspective addresses the enormous economic and cultural impact of globalization, which is mostly perceived as a threat to the continued existence of this heritage itself,[5] but which also has the potential to aid its preservation.[6] The effects of globalization[7] must be borne in mind when developing any new Convention or other programs for safeguarding folklore. An international standard-setting instrument is a means of countering the economic and cultural effects of globalization,[8] which, while it may reduce the role of states, also increases the importance of local identities in countering global pressures.[9] Giving value to folklore may help states legitimize their role in facing the challenge of globalism by fostering local cultural identities within the framework of the state.[10]

The 1972 UNESCO "World Heritage Convention" and *Recommendation*

The idea of including folklore within the framework of the 1972 World Heritage Convention (WHC) was raised during its drafting.[11] Such heritage may be undervalued by the state,[12] and the WHC would require the state to protect it and the world community to ensure this happens. Central to this Convention is the characterization of its subject as a "universal heritage" deserving of international protection;[13] and its detailed system for international cooperation to support parties in applying this Convention makes it a potential model for raising national and international awareness of folklore.[14] The composition of any World Heritage Committee is crucial, since this Committee formulates the selection criteria and, if it concerned itself with folklore, would need a broad-based membership that reflects the diversity of interest groups.[15] The flexible character of the selection criteria for sites is useful,[16] allowing for re-evaluation in the light of changing world conditions. The provision of finances[17] is important for empowering cultural communities, while educational programs[18] are a valuable means of safeguarding folklore.

It is difficult to see, however, how folklore could be included within the existing definitional terms and provisions of this Convention, which assume that the subject of protection is a physical entity.[19] This presents a major objection to using the WHC as the basis for safeguarding this heritage, since the Convention would require extensive redrafting to be applicable. Certain provisions, however, could usefully be included in a new Convention.[20] In general, the WHC has had the positive effect of encouraging governments to value protected sites, since their inclusion on the World Heritage List lends them an international prestige. [21]

The 1972 *Recommendation*, developed alongside the WHC, creates a two-tiered approach to protection that encourages the preservation of certain internationally outstanding examples of this heritage through the WHC, while also urging Member States to safeguard all components of this heritage on a national level. The latter is an important long-term aim, while the former activity raises government and popular awareness of the existence and importance of this heritage. The Preamble and General Principles of this *Recommendation* contain several ideas highly relevant to folklore and worth considering in drafting a new Convention, in particular, those provisions that reflect the importance of local empowerment and the use of "bottom-up" measures.[22]

The 1989 *Recommendation* — An Evaluation

This *Recommendation* characterizes folklore as part of the "universal heritage of humanity," which raises complex legal issues[23] and seems particularly inappropriate to folklore, given its local rootedness and its centrality to community identity. The local and global can be seen as two sides of one coin,[24] and a universalist approach may be useful in giving value to heritage where the state fails to do so.[25] However, as a legal characterization, it remains problematic. The list of potential threats is open-ended, because of changing social and economic factors such as technological advances.[26] The requirement for governments to take action by applying the principles and measures set out in this *Recommendation* is clear.[27] The definition of "folklore"[28] usefully notes its importance to the cultural and social identity of the community and its dependence on particular methods of transmission. Despite reference to the cultural community, insufficient emphasis is placed on the social context of folklore creation and the know-how and values that underpin it. "Identification"[29] notes that folklore should be safeguarded "by and for the group . . . whose identity it expresses," suggesting a bottom-up approach that recognizes the need to empower the community to safeguard its folklore traditions. This, however, is not followed through in the rest of the text.[30]

A major criticism of this text is that it is heavily weighted towards the needs of scientific researchers and government officials. For example, actions for the "Identification" of folklore and the section on "Conservation"[31] are essentially concerned with collating and documenting what data are available in tangible form.[32] One suspects that researchers will benefit mostly from this, despite reference to the needs of "tradition-bearers."[33] This also implies that the non-utilization and/or evolution of such oral traditions are always a form of degradation rather than integral to the folklore in some cases. Data collection and documentation have their value but are favored over measures that would foster the present and future creation of oral traditions. Another serious failing is the lack of reference to the central role of women in producing and transmitting folklore and to ways of empowering them in this.[34] The equal emphasis placed on folklore and those who transmit it,[35] and on acknowledging the importance of the producer community in preserving folklore in the face of cultural globalization are both positive points.[36] Certain other specific measures are less likely to be of direct benefit to the producers of folklore, such as encouraging regions, municipalities, the media, and associations to create employment for folklorists.[37]

The limitations of using intellectual property rights (IPRs) as a means of safeguarding folklore are noted,[38] which is significant in the light of current consideration of the role of IPRs and copyright in this. Section G appears to place at the forefront practitioners and the development/revitalization of folklore through their exchanges of ideas and experiences, a positive point since the safeguarding of folklore should start from the cultural community itself.[39] However, few of the proposed actions for international cooperation would clearly support, encourage, and inform the creators of folklore themselves, which is a missed opportunity.[40] This *Recommendation* contains provisions which merit consideration for inclusion in a new Convention text (with some amendment or rewording), particularly the Preamble and general introductions to sections. However, the heavy emphasis on the needs of the scientific community is a major weakness, the definition is too narrowly focused, and the *Recommendation* fails to safeguard folklore through the social and economic empowerment of its creators.

Other UNESCO Actions in the Field of Folklore

Living Cultural Properties/Living Human Treasures

This program[41] proposes the establishment of national systems of "living cultural properties," who are exponents of folklore. It reflects concern over the effects of globalization of the economy and culture (especially the communications revolution) on oral and traditional culture and the producer communities.[42] States are invited to submit to UNESCO a list of "living human treasures" in their country for inclusion in a future UNESCO World List.[43] The program focuses on the bearers of this heritage and their ability to transmit the skills, techniques, and knowledge to "apprentices" as the most well-directed response to its increasing vulnerability.[44] This recognizes that the continued existence of folklore is inextricably linked to the social and economic well-being of its creators and that its continued value to them and their way of life must be sustained, even if changed in the modern context.[45] The primary purpose of this system is to preserve the skills and techniques needed for the continuation of this heritage, an element that is missing from international protective measures so far, and that must be included in any future UNESCO instrument. The selection process of exponents of traditional knowledge and techniques for listing them further underlines the crucial role of the practitioners themselves and their apprentices.[46]

Masterpieces of the Oral and Intangible Heritage of Humanity Program (1998)

This aims to develop criteria for the selection of "cultural spaces"[47] and popular/traditional forms of cultural expression to be proclaimed "Masterpieces of Oral and Intangible Cultural Heritage" (henceforth "Masterpieces"), whose survival is essential to the world because of their "universal value."[48] A central aim is to raise awareness amongst governments, NGOs, and the producer communities themselves of the value of this heritage and the urgency of safeguarding and revitalizing it. The description of this heritage as "intangible" as well as "oral" is important, since the identification of the intangible cultural heritage is a major challenge facing cultural heritage law and this program will contribute towards this development.[49] The concept of "cultural spaces" is new and supports recent work on the idea of cultural landscapes.[50] However, the use of the 1989 *Recommendation*'s definition of "folklore" (with a minor addition)[51] limits the development of the concept and perpetuates its weaknesses. Reference to the risk of its disappearance through acculturation[52] points to the desire to safeguard this heritage in response to the effects of cultural and economic globalization. Any instrument designed to safeguard this heritage must balance the right of the communities concerned to take advantage of economic, social, and other developments (which may well have a profound effect on their traditional cultural creations) with the right to preserve the oral and intangible heritage in a living form.[53] The cultural criteria for proclamation include some positive points worth noting,[54] while the organizational criteria are mostly "bottom-up" in approach,[55] which is appropriate to this heritage. This program includes elements that can usefully inform a future Convention text.

UNESCO and WIPO — Intellectual Property Rights and Safeguarding Folklore

The 1989 *Recommendation* calls on Member States to draw the attention of the authorities to the work of UNESCO and WIPO in the area of using intellectual property rights (IPRs)[56] to safeguard folklore. It makes an important proviso, however, that this work relates to only one aspect of folklore protection and stresses the urgent need for separate action in a range of other areas.[57] Clearly, protecting the IPRs of creators and performers of folklore/traditional expressions is imperative to prevent its "improper exploitation" and distortion through commercialization, but this should be seen as a relatively narrow form of protection. Overemphasis on this may distort the way this heritage is viewed and the relationship of the creators to its practice by concentrating on protecting their rights in terms of the product and/or its public performance. This is not to deny the real problem of inappropriate commercialization of folklore and the value of developing legal protection against unauthorized exploitation.[58] It is rather that IPRs do not adequately address the most central concerns for safeguarding folklore — its integrity, its role in expressing the identity of the community for the community, its continued practice in traditional forms, and its valuing by the producer community itself.[59] It is vital to protect legally not only the product (or performance) but also the spontaneous act of creation and the social and cultural context that fostered its production. Furthermore, the definition of the subject of protection in the 1985 Model Provisions[60] excludes many significant aspects of folklore such as beliefs, legends, practical traditions, craft skills, and other know-how.

In considering current moves to develop a new international treaty on the subject,[61] one should bear in mind the limitations of IPRs in relation to folklore. Further examination of the role existing or new IPRs can play in the protection of expressions of folklore is a valuable exercise that may answer a specific need. However, it is potentially damaging to UNESCO's aims in relation to folklore if a new Convention on the IPR issues is drafted independently of one treating this heritage as a whole. If new IPR rules are to be elaborated on folklore, this should be within the framework of a new UNESCO Convention that embraces as broad an understanding as possible of folklore and safeguards not only the product but also the spontaneous act of creation and its social/cultural context.[62] WIPO's exploring innovative ways of using IPRs to protect expressions of folklore in those contexts where this is appropriate would be an important adjunct to UNESCO's work.[63]

Conclusion

In sum, no existing Convention, Recommendation, or other UNESCO text fully addresses the needs of safeguarding folklore, but an effective instrument could be elaborated taking into account the above comments. The 1972 Convention and *Recommendation* contain elements that might usefully be considered for inclusion but cannot by themselves provide the basis for a protective regime. The role of the 1972 WHC in raising international awareness of the value and vulnerability of the cultural heritage should be borne in mind, since such awareness-raising for folklore is needed. The 1989 *Recommendation* has positive points worth keeping, especially some section introductions and the general principles set out in the Preamble, but it has many limitations as it stands. The "Living Human Treasures" and "Masterpieces" programs have much to offer in terms of raising awareness of this heritage, encouraging the development of appropriate national legislation, and developing the conceptual understanding needed in elaborating a new instrument. The UNESCO/WIPO work on applying IPRs to folklore could be very useful if placed within the context of a broad-based Convention on its safeguarding. Essential points are that any new Convention should take a predominantly "bottom-up" approach and seek to empower producer communities; should be broader in focus than the 1989 *Recommendation* definition of folklore; and should aim to foster the social/cultural context and spontaneous act of its creation as well as the product itself.

Notes

1. *Convention Concerning the Protection of the World Cultural and Natural Heritage*, 16 November 1972 ("World Heritage Convention"); *Recommendation Concerning the Protection, at National Level, of the Cultural and Natural Heritage*, 16 November 1972; *Recommendation on the Safeguarding of Traditional Culture and Folklore*, 15 November 1989.

2. The question of terminology is a difficult one. I have chosen to use "folklore" since it is employed in the 1989 *Recommendation*. A more recent UNESCO program in this area refers to "intangible and oral heritage" (see infra n.48), and the argument as to the most appropriate term to employ is open to debate. I suspect lawyers favor the latter since it appears to encompass a broader class of heritage (answering also issues such as the deliberate targeting of cultural or religious monuments during armed conflict and including cultural rights aspects) as well as signaling clearly that it is a new departure from the existing UNESCO instruments, which are limited to "tangible" elements of the cultural heritage.

3. See, for example, Prott 1989, 224–25.

4. Prott 1998, 222–23, 234.

5. See Featherstone and Friedman 1995.

6. Vinson notes that "[t]he broad and integrating anthropological conception of the heritage which has emerged in recent decades should be accentuated by the properties of the networks which favor the integration of related fields such as the performing arts, crafts, oral traditions, into the cultural heritage" (Vinson 1998, 243). She gives the example of a site on Canadian Schoolnet which sets contemporary Inuit artworks in the context of the myths, legends, and traditional way of life of the Arctic Inuit people.

7. For example, globalization threatens the continued practice of traditional arts by turning youth away from traditional (Indigenous) culture towards a "global" culture; it also forces us to redefine

the role of states in the cultural arena and the relationship of private individuals and independent organizations to government.

8.   There exists an apparent contradiction between the universalist nature of the standard-setting instruments of UNESCO (discussed below) and the importance of respecting cultural diversity. UNESCO has also been criticized as expressing a "Western" (even colonialist) view of "global" cultural heritage which does not value other cultural traditions sufficiently. More recently, however, UNESCO programs have increasingly included non-Western views of heritage. Recognition of the importance of intangible/oral heritage is a case in point, given that this heritage has traditionally been undervalued in Western societies and that it may be the predominant form of cultural heritage in some societies. See Lowenthal 1997, 227, 239.

9.   L. Meskell notes "the contradictory tendencies of globalization and localization existing side by side" (Meskell 1998a, 8).

10. In much the same way, cultural heritage in its traditional sense was used to lend legitimacy to the nation-state. Of course, the state may be challenged by cultural groups such as Indigenous peoples and other minorities who seek self-determination, but in general, accepting or increasing the profile of local cultural traditions within a state framework is more positive for the state than not. See "Recasting cultural policy," in UNESCO 1998a, 344.

11. The Bolivian delegation suggested this in the early 1970s.

12. A state may have little motivation to represent the culture of a minority (or class such as women) that has little political or economic power in society.

13. Article 6 states such heritage "constitutes a world heritage for whose protection it is a duty of the international community as a whole to co-operate." See section on the 1989 *Recommendation* for a critique of the "universal heritage of humankind" approach.

14. Articles 8 to 14 deal with establishing the World Heritage Committee ("the Committee"), which selects sites for the World Heritage List and the List of World Heritage in Danger; Articles 15 to 18 establish the World Heritage Fund financed by subventions from parties and from private donations, etc., to provide financial assistance to parties in identifying and preserving listed sites where appropriate; Articles 19 to 26 set out the conditions and arrangements for international assistance in the identification and protection of the world cultural and natural heritage. This is an extremely detailed system, which provides the mechanism for international cooperation and assistance (also called for in Section G of the 1989 *Recommendation*) but which is heavily reliant on state action, and this may render it problematic for the protection of folklore.

15. This point is adequately addressed by the membership of the jury to select "Masterpieces of the Intangible and Oral Heritage," which is likely to produce a balanced group representing the interests of producer communities as well as experts. Notably, the Convention also calls for a sufficient representation of women and youth, who are often under-represented in such fora. Allowing submissions to be made by NGOs (unlike the World Heritage Committee) is also likely to increase their voice.

16. The criteria for selection are contained in the Operational Guidelines (see UNESCO Document WHC-97/WS/1 for the most recent version) prepared by the World Heritage Committee. These can be updated, as they were in 1992 by the inclusion of cultural landscapes in response to the need to list Uluru (a site sacred to Australian Aboriginals) and Tongariro (a site sacred to New Zealand Maoris) that qualify as both cultural and natural world heritage. See Simmonds 1997, 259 and Prott 1998, 234 n.4.

17. Articles 15 to 16; see n.14 above for details.

18. Articles 27 and 28.

19. Article 1 gives a definition of cultural heritage that is broken down into "monuments," "groups of buildings," and "sites"; natural heritage is defined in Article 2. In both sets of definitions, the element concerned must be "of outstanding universal value" from the point of view of history, art, science, ethnology, anthropology, etc.

20. These include the recognition of threats directly relevant to traditional cultures such as technological advances and globalization; the responsibility placed on each state to safeguard those elements of heritage located within their territory. A provision that parties should give mutual support could be extremely valuable where a minority culture in one state comprises the majority culture of another; or where states with advanced legislative systems for safeguarding traditional heritage can advise other parties.

21. Simmonds 1997, 254. The WHC has also been the most successful of UNESCO's Conventions on cultural heritage with 149 state parties.

22. These include provisions that an "active policy" should be developed for conserving this heritage and "giving it a place in community life"[point 13]; that private as well as public-sector financing should be encouraged [point 11]; that responsibility for protection should lie with regional and local bodies as well as national authorities [point 17]; and that voluntary bodies should be set up to encourage local and national authorities to use their powers to safeguard heritage [point 64].

23. The "common heritage of mankind" principle was initially developed in international law in the late 1960s in relation to mineral exploration and exploitation (particularly on the deep seabed) and adapted for use in the 1972 WHC in relation to outstanding elements of cultural heritage. Its use in relation to cultural heritage contains many contradictions, and it is a principle that needs much further elaboration in relation to existing cultural heritage law. Its attraction is that it places a duty on all states to ensure the protection and safeguarding of the heritage concerned; but this often conflicts with local and national claims, thus creating contradictory outcomes. The Parthenon is a good example since it is regarded as a part of the "world heritage" in view of its outstanding character while it remains an essential symbol of Greek cultural identity.

24. See n.9 above.

25. This is the aim of the "Living Human Treasures" program (discussed below). Ironically, the accessibility of much folklore and traditional culture and its ability to speak across cultural borders may actually render it more "universal" than much that is traditionally the subject of cultural heritage instruments, despite its rootedness in a specific community.

26. The danger folklore faces from "multiple factors" is noted (Preamble), and Section D on "Preservation" cites the need to confront serious threats to this heritage from global cultural and economic forces.

27. The Preamble states that Member States are to apply the principles and measures set out in the *Recommendation* "for the safeguarding of folklore" by adopting the legislative measures and other steps necessary to achieve this.

28. Section A, "Definition of Folklore" states, "Folklore (or traditional and popular culture) is the totality of tradition-based creations of a cultural community, expressed by a group or individuals and recognized as reflecting the expectations of a community in so far as they reflect its cultural and social identity; its standards and values are transmitted orally, by imitation or by other means. Its forms are, among others, language, literature, music, dance, games, mythology, rituals, customs, handicrafts, architecture and other arts."

29. Section B, "Identification of Folklore."

30. The specific actions listed in Section B, such as the creation of identification and recording systems and creating a standard typology for folklore, address the needs of researchers and government officials rather than producer communities themselves.

31. Section C on Conservation of Folklore.

32. For section B, see n.30 above. Section C proposes such actions as establishing national archives of folklore material; establishing a national archive function for service purposes; creating museums or folklore sections within existing museums; and training collectors, archivists, and documentarians.

33. Section C (introductory paragraph) states that the object of conservation "in the event of the nonutilization or evolution of folk traditions [is] to give researchers and tradition-bearers access to data enabling them to understand the process through which traditions change."

34. At the time of this writing, a seminar is to be held in Tehran (Iran) on The Role of Women in the Transmission of Oral Cultural Traditions on 26–29 July 1999 within the framework of the 1989 *Recommendation*. This should provide the theoretical basis for developing provisions that would foster and empower women exponents of the intangible/oral heritage. A Draft Resolution to be adopted at this seminar will be presented by the Iranian delegation to the UNESCO General Council in the autumn.

35. Section D (introductory paragraph) on Preservation of Folklore states that "[p]reservation is concerned with protection of folk traditions and those who are the transmitters, having regard to the fact that each people has a right to its own culture."

36. Section D also notes that "adherence to that [traditional] culture is often eroded by the impact of the industrialized culture purveyed by the mass media" and that measures must be taken "to guarantee the status of and economic support for folk traditions both in the communities that produce them and beyond."

37. All but the last of seven proposals in Section E on "Dissemination of Folklore" relate primarily to the interests of folklorists, including: encouraging national, regional, and international events (fes-

tivals, exhibitions, workshops, etc.); encouraging better coverage of folklore material in the national and regional media, including by the employment of folklorists in media organizations; encouraging regions, municipalities, associations, etc. to create employment for folklorists; and facilitating meetings and exchanges between individuals, groups, and institutions concerned with folklore nationally and internationally.

38. Section F on Protection of Tolklore. See n.57 below for details. Other relevant categories of rights already protected by laws that should be enforced nationally are enumerated. Section G on International Co-operation (paragraph c) requires states to cooperate closely so that the "economic, moral and so-called neighboring rights" of interested parties receive international protection. The "other rights" cited in Section F(b) protect the interests (privacy and confidentiality) of the transmitter of tradition, protect the interests of the collector (ensuring that the collection is properly conserved); safeguard collected materials against misuse, and recognize archives' responsibility to monitor the use of materials.

39. Section G, "International Co-operation" (introductory paragraph).

40. The first action requiring cooperation with international and regional associations, institutions, and organizations concerned with folklore could be seen to offer this. The other three actions, however, tend towards serving the interests of the scientific community, by ensuring the protection of specific legal rights associated with various aspects of folklore investigation, production, and performance, and towards general protective measures to avoid damage or other threats to folklore.

41. It was proposed to the Executive Board of UNESCO in 1993 as a means of implementing the 1989 *Recommendation*. See: Decisions Adopted by the Executive Board at its 142nd Session (UNESCO Doc. 142 EX/Decisions, 10 Dec. 1993) and the Guidelines — Human Living Treasures sent to Member States by UNESCO Secretary-General on 16 Sept. 1998.

42. The Guidelines on Living Human Treasures distributed to all Member States describe folklore heritage as an "essential source of identity deeply rooted in the past" now disappearing and being displaced by "a standardized international culture."

43. This is similar in conception to the World Heritage List established by the 1972 WHC.

44. The introduction to the Guidelines states significantly: "One of the most effective ways of safeguarding the intangible heritage is to conserve it by collecting, recording, and archiving. Even more effective would be to ensure that the bearers of that heritage continue to acquire further knowledge and skills and transmit them to future generations." This is fundamental to the whole issue of how to develop an effective protective regime.

45. This contrasts with the 1989 *Recommendation*, which tends to protect the folklore product over its cultural and intellectual context.

46. For example: a serious decline in the number of practitioners and their successors can threaten the existence of folklore, lead to a significant loss of authenticity, or diminish the level of skill or technique of the practitioners and their ability to transmit this to apprentices. A less positive criterion of the program is that selected exponents should be those cultural manifestations that "the State considers have a high historic or artistic value," although this is unsurprising in the context of an intergovernmental organization.

47. Space is to be understood in the anthropological sense as a locus for popular and traditional activities generally characterized by periodicity (cyclical, seasonal, calendrical, etc.).

48. UNESCO Doc.155/EX 15 (1998).

49. Thus far, the UNESCO Conventions and Recommendations protecting the cultural heritage have had physical elements of heritage as their subject of protection. Often, however, the material heritage is the physical evidence of the intangible heritage, while the latter, in turn, is the interface between individuals, groups, and nations and their material culture.

50. See n.17 above.

51. For the "intangible and oral heritage."

52. One criterion for proclaiming a "Masterpiece" is the risk of its disappearance through an accelerated process of transformation, urbanization, or acculturation.

53. Tourism is probably the most difficult of all areas in this regard. It provides economic benefits to folklore producer communities but may, in turn, influence the social fabric out of which the folklore is produced, with a pernicious effect in the long term.

54. These criteria include an item's rootedness in the cultural tradition and history of the community; its role in affirming the cultural identity of the peoples or cultural communities involved; the qual-

ity of know-how and the techniques deployed in its creation; and its value as a unique witness of a living traditional culture.

55. These are set out in Point 6(ii), and include an emphasis on the existence of an adequate local management system with respect to local and national tradition and the desire to sensitize private individuals and members of the community to the value of this heritage and the need for its preservation.

56. In particular, copyright laws.

57. The introductory paragraph of Section F on Protection of Folklore reads: "In so far as folklore constitutes manifestations of intellectual creativity it deserves to be protected in a manner inspired by the protection provided for intellectual productions. Such protection of folklore has become indispensable as a means of promoting further development, maintenance and dissemination of those expressions." However, in relation to the joint work of UNESCO and WIPO, it states [paragraph (a)] that "this work relates to only one aspect of folklore protection and that the need for separate action in a range of areas to safeguard folklore is urgent."

58. The development of "a special (sui generis) type of law for an adequate protection against unauthorized exploitation" as suggested in the Commentary to the Model Provisions for National Laws on the Protection of Expressions of Folklore Against Illicit Exploitation and Other Prejudicial Actions (UNESCO 1985, 6) can provide an important aspect of protection that would be a positive step if taken within the framework of a broader range of measures to safeguard and foster the creation of folklore.

59. It is also questionable whether "rights" is a concept that fits with the view many exponents of folklore and traditional knowledge have of their relationship to knowledge and the natural world.

60. Model Provisions cited in n.58 above. It is difficult to see how traditional crafts such as making *giveh* (handmade slippers) in Iran or traditional cuisines can fall within the definition of "productions consisting of characteristic elements of the traditional artistic heritage."

61. See: UNESCO International Forum on the Protection of Folklore, Phuket (Thailand), 8–10 April 1992; and World Intellectual Property Organization (WIPO) Main Program 11 of the 1998–99 Program and Budget entitled "Global Intellectual Property Issues" WIPO Doc.WO/BC/18/X-WO/PC/8/Y.

62. This includes the empowerment of the producer communities and recognition of the role of gender issues in folklore production, amongst other matters.

63. Any other intergovernmental organization, NGO, or institution working in the area of applying IPRs to the intangible/oral heritage would make a similar contribution.

References

Bhabha, H.K. 1994. *The Locating of Culture*. London: Routledge.

Featherstone, M., ed. 1995. *Global Culture: Nationalism, Globalisation and Modernity*. London: Sage.

Friedman, J. 1995. *Cultural Identity and Global Process*. London: Sage.

ICOMOS. 1994. *Cultural Landscapes*. U.K.: ICOMOS

Joyner, C.C. 1986. Legal Implications of the Concept of the Common Heritage of Mankind. *International and Comparative Law Quarterly* 35:190–99.

Kiss, A.C. 1982 La notion du patrimoine commun de l'humanite. *Receuils de Cours* II:99–256.

Layton, R., ed. 1989. *Conflict in the Archaeology of Living Traditions*. London: Unwin Hyman.

Lowenthal, D. 1997. *The Heritage Crusade and the Spoils of History*. London: Viking.

McGoldrick, D. 1990. Canadian Indians' Cultural Rights. *International and Comparative Law Quarterly* 40:658–69.

Meskell, L. 1998a. Introduction: Archaeology Matters. In *Archaeology Under Fire*. Meskell, L., ed. London: Routledge.

_____, ed. 1998b. *Archaeology Under Fire*. London: Routledge.

Merryman, J. 1986. Two Ways of Thinking about Cultural Property. *American Journal of International Law* 80:831.

Prott, L.V. 1989. Problems of Private International Law for the Protection of the Cultural Heritage. *Receuils de Cours* V:224–317.

_____. 1998. International Standards for Cultural Heritage. In *UNESCO World Culture Report*. Paris: Unesco Publishing, pp. 222–36.

_____ and P.J. O'Keefe. 1992. "Cultural Heritage" or "Cultural Property"? *International Journal of Cultural Property* 1(2):307–20.

Simmonds, J. 1997. UNESCO World Heritage Convention. *Art, Antiquity and Law* 2(3):251–81.

Strati, A. 1990. Deep Seabed Cultural Property and the Common Heritage of Mankind. *International and Comparative Law Quarterly* 40:859–94.

Suter, K.H. 1991.The UNESCO World Heritage Convention. *Environmental and Planning Law Journal* 8(1):4–15.

Sutherland, J. 1997. Emerging New Legal Standards for Comprehensive Rights. *Environmental Policy and Law* 27(1):13–30.

UNESCO. 1998. *UNESCO World Culture Report.* Paris: UNESCO Publishing.

UNESCO. 1998a. Recasting Cultural Policy. In *Commentary to the Model Provisions for National Laws on the Protection of Expressions of Folklore against Illicit Exploitation and Other Prejudicial Actions* (UNESCO 1985). Paris: UNESCO Publishing, pp. 342–46.

Vinson, I. 1998. Heritage and Cyberculture. In *UNESCO World Culture Report.* Paris: UNESCO Publishing, pp. 237–45.

Additional Sources

Crawford, J. 1988. *The Rights of Peoples.* Oxford: Clarendon Press.

Layton, R., ed. 1989. *Who Needs the Past? Indigenous Values and Archaeology.* London: Unwin Hyman.

Prott, L.V., and P.J. O'Keefe. 1984. *Law and the Cultural Heritage, vol. I.* Abingdon: Professional Books.

_____. 1989. *Law and the Cultural Heritage, vol. III.* London: Butterworths.

Thornberry, P. 1991. *International Law and the Rights of Minorities.* Oxford: Clarendon Press.

Cultural Conservation: A Two-way Consultation

Grace Koch
Archives Manager
Australian Institute of Aboriginal and Torres Strait Islander Studies
Canberra, Australia

Audiovisual archives hold unique materials that document the world's intangible cultural heritage. Stories, ceremonies, songs, and, in some cases, languages which have been recorded may no longer be known, but the audiovisual records and their documentation remain. These records are irreplaceable documents of a cultural tradition. In her definition of indigenous heritage, Professor Erica-Irene Daes of UNESCO includes "documentation of indigenous peoples' heritage on film, photographs, videotape and audiotape."[1]

In comparison to print media, photographs, sound recordings, films, and videos provide more immediate access to material documenting oral traditions. The meanings of the contents of such audiovisual material are easily understood by the relevant Aboriginal owners; however, if non-Aboriginal people are to appreciate the importance of these audiovisual documents, there often needs to be supplementary interpretative documentation of a cross-cultural nature. Such documentation allows the knowledge of the "culture community" to be passed on to the scientific/research community, the nation, and the world.

A two-way process needs to be developed between Aboriginal sharers of knowledge and archivists and fieldworkers (who may also be Aboriginal) whereby guidelines are established for collecting and documenting. Various countries have different types of needs.

In Australia, Aboriginal and Torres Strait Islander people are obtaining copies of audiovisual recordings, using them for cultural revitalization in many forms. In order to facilitate this process, the Australian Institute of Aboriginal and Torres Strait Islander Studies (AIATSIS) is actively disseminating copies of its holdings to Indigenous keeping-places and communities. Such repatriation of material meets aspects both of protection and research. For protection, the owners of the materials within the communities can advise on proper access and use for the material. For research, documentation will be enhanced for future consultation.

Dissemination of this audiovisual material and its control in culturally acceptable ways are vital issues for safeguarding intangible cultural heritage. Dissemination is important for enriching Indigenous knowledge, educating the wider community, and promoting research. Within the past decade, several events have raised the public profile of Indigenous cultural materials:

- The Australian Bicentennial celebrations of 1988 and the Indigenous interpretation of the event as a time of mourning publicized aspects of culture as never before. Aboriginal culture has become part of the wider popular culture.
- Government policies require archives and other collecting institutions to move towards self-funding. This means publication and/or access to all information they hold.

- With the advent of the World Wide Web, much cultural material formerly accessible only through in-house catalogues will now be advertised globally through catalogue listings.

It is vital that the traditional owners of this material participate in deciding what can be accessible and how it may be used. It is also crucial that a workable solution be found between collecting institutions and traditional owners for proper care and control within present structures.

Access and handling of audiovisual documents containing Australian Indigenous cultural material has become an issue of concern for the major collecting institutions within Australia. Using examples drawn from my experience as media archivist within the Australian Institute of Aboriginal and Torres Strait Islander Studies, I will discuss:

- the use of audiovisual material for cultural revitalization
- the importance of consultation regarding conditions for conservation of and access to intangible cultural heritage
- considerations for the re-drafting of the UNESCO *Recommendation on the Safeguarding of Traditional Culture and Folklore*

Use of Audiovisual Material for Cultural Revitalization

Reclaiming Rights to Land

The claim to protection of cultural knowledge and rights is deeply connected with the recognition of the interests of Indigenous peoples in their traditional lands. Audiovisual recordings have served as evidence in Aboriginal land claims within existing legislation.

1976 Act

The Aboriginal Land Rights (Northern Territory) Act 1976 gave Aboriginal people in the Northern Territory of Australia a mechanism to claim freehold title to land that had been taken away from them. For them, land title exists in the form of songs, myth, and ritual. Traditionally, people who own the songs own the land and maintain the rights to perform the rituals that nourish the land and its creatures. Evidence has been accepted by the Land Commissioner in the form of knowledge of the songs and the geographical places named in the songs. Recordings of the songs and the ceremonies performed as evidence are held by archives. These have been accepted as exhibits in formal hearings.

Native Title

In 1992, the Meryam people of Murray Island in the Torres Strait questioned the right of the Queensland State Government to control the use of the island without considering their rights. They claimed ownership on the basis of maintaining their customs and laws. Part of their proof consisted of reference to archival materials — wax cylinder recordings, photographs, and films made by the Cambridge Expedition to the Torres Strait in 1898.

As a result of the High Court ruling of 1992 on this case, a new type of land rights known as native title was recognized throughout Australia. Freehold title would not be granted through native title, but recognition of prior ownership and connection with the land would make traditional owners equal partners with developers and others. Sacred sites would be recognized, and any profits from that land would be shared with traditional owners. Native title legislation and procedures are in flux; however, Aboriginal people now have the hope of lodging claims in States where land rights did not exist before. Proof includes recordings of songs, and lawyers and anthropologists work with archivists in locating evidence of cultural continuity.[2]

Stolen Generation

In 1997, a government-funded report, "Bringing Them Home,"[3] was issued showing the hurt and social damage caused by an Australian government policy of removing mixed-race children from their families to orphanages and training colleges. Many of these children did not know the identity of their parents. The poignant testimonies given by the victims of this policy at the hearings were seen to be of such special value that a recommendation was made

> that the Council of Australian Governments ensure the adequate funding of appropriate Indigenous agencies to record, preserve, and administer access to the testimonies of indigenous people affected by the forcible removal policies who wish to provide their histories in audio, audio-visual, or written form.[4]

Language Revival

Before Europeans came to Australia, there were over 250 languages spoken throughout the continent. Now there are only about 25 that are being actively passed on to children.[5] Language, as the primary medium of cultural transmission, is vital to cultural identity. In areas where languages have been lost and populations were most decimated by white contact, Aboriginal people are seeking early recordings to use in language-learning kits. AIATSIS has provided substantial help in supplying these recordings.

Personal Use

Individuals seek copies of photographs and tapes made of their relatives. In some cases, images and tapes preserved in archives are the only ones available of family members. These provide a sense of collective and personal cultural identity and self-esteem.

Importance of Consultation
Regarding Conditions for Conservation of and Access to Intangible Cultural Heritage

Indigenous people are aware that their arts and cultural expression are often being used without their knowledge or permission, sometimes inappropriately or offensively. This also is true for the audiovisual records of this knowledge. Some examples of inappropriate usage of Aboriginal audiovisual material will show why consultation is of the utmost importance.

A film project recorded the language, stories, and history of a particular Aboriginal group. One of the stories was a creation myth applying to one particular tract of land. Unfortunately, the film used the story to describe a different tract of land. The filmmakers did not consider the issue to be important because most viewers would not recognize the difference. The Aborigines, however, feared two outcomes:

- The story, with its proper reference to land, would not be passed on correctly.
- Should the Aborigines want to use the story as evidence for a land claim, the incorrect reference could discredit them.

With the help of the Australian Film Commission, which held a copyright interest in the film, the Aborigines were able to persuade the filmmakers to remove the offending segment, replacing it with something more suitable.

Consultation is vital for the proper care of culturally restricted information. Some objects, songs, and ceremonies should be seen or heard only by initiated men, some others only by women. In Aboriginal tradition, if persons of the wrong gender were to see or hear the information, they could be physically harmed. This harm could come from beliefs about the dangerous nature of the material or from punishments delivered by traditional enforcers of traditional law. A significant amount of motion picture film, photographs, and recorded sound materials collected in Australia did not include reference to the cultural rules of access.

The Internet brings up a host of issues concerning safeguarding traditional cultural materials of an audiovisual nature. A question arises as to how much information should appear and in what form. There is also concern about how Indigenous cultural material is listed in cataloguing records within databases.

For example, earlier in this century when some researchers documented ceremonies, the people recorded did not understand what could happen to the information. Technology did not exist to publicize it far and wide. They did not realize that many people would be able see films and listen to audio recordings of ceremonies, some of which could be dangerous to certain groups of people. Without proper consultation, people developing Web pages for institutions may choose video or audio clips of potentially hazardous material.[6]

These and other questions are examined in detail in the discussion paper, *Our Culture, Our Future: Proposals for Recognition and Protection of Indigenous Cultural and Intellectual Property*. Approximately 3,000 copies of this paper, which describes present copyright protection for Indigenous cultural materials, asks a number of provocative questions, and invites comment, were distributed to Aboriginal and Torres Strait Islander organizations and individuals. Terri Janke, an Aboriginal lawyer specializing in Indigenous copyright issues, wrote up various reform options, including examples from responses to the circulated questions. A final publication should be available this year.

In summary, Indigenous people are aware that their arts and cultural expression are often being used without their knowledge or permission, sometimes inappropriately or offensively. They want to be consulted to ensure that information is used within the proper context. If such information is published, they want to be consulted about its use, to be recognized as the owners of it, and to be paid properly for such use.

Considerations for the Re-Drafting of the 1989 *Recommendation*

First of all, the term folklore is problematic to Aboriginal Australians. Although UNESCO defines the term in a way that includes most aspects of traditional and popular culture, Aboriginal Australians have been using the term "Indigenous cultural property"(ICP). For this section of the paper, I shall use the abbreviation ICP for "folklore."

Identification of ICP

National Inventory of Institutions Concerned with ICP

Any such inventory for Australia needs to have Indigenous people involved in decision-making and policy formation. An Australian Indigenous Cultural Network identifying collections of Indigenous cultural heritage material in institutions is being established by the Australian Foundation for Culture and the Humanities. This "virtual" organization, with the distinguished Aboriginal Elder Patrick Dodson as its director, will concentrate on linking community-based collections, archives, and museums internationally. A coordinated effort also needs to be made with multicultural groups.

But this and other initiatives need proper financial support. UNESCO provides for funding for tangible cultural heritage, such as the restoration of the frieze at Angkor Wat. Intangible cultural heritage needs a similar funding source. Also, there needs to be some sort of wording within the *Recommendation* that specifies government or other continuing support.

Identification and Recording Systems

The International Association of Sound and Audiovisual Archives (IASA), which is a Category B NGO within UNESCO, will have completed its manual on Cataloguing Rules for Audiovisual Materials by September of this year. Issues of cataloguing ICP are dealt with by specialists, including a French ethnomusicologist, Daniele Branger. The rules are designed to be used internationally. This is a major step in standardizing cataloguing conventions.

Conservation of ICP

The opening paragraph lists "researchers and tradition-bearers" being given access to data within archives. Since this section was drafted, there has been worldwide interest via catalogues and Indigenous Web sites in ICP. There needs to be a set of statements referring not only to the preservation of ICP but also to its protection against improper usage. Traditional owners and archivists must work together to set clear guidelines. Within the guidelines, there should be agreed mechanisms for mediation when differences of opinions exist amongst groups of traditional owners.

National Archives Where ICP Can Be Stored and Made Available

Within Australia, a number of national collecting institutions hold different types of ICP with different conditions for access. Emphasis should be put on adequate funding to ensure both proper storage and Indigenous consultation in developing protocols for access and use. As I have mentioned earlier, such protocols have already been established in Australia for ICP, but need to be considered for other cultural material.

Central National Archive Function

Within Australia, the State archives, libraries, and museums are too well established to hand over cataloguing and dissemination to a centralized organization. There is a great need for a national working group made up of information specialists and Indigenous people to set standards for documentation and handling of ICP.

Create Museums or ICP Sections at Existing Museums

Client services for such institutions must take into account the needs of all users. There may be conflicting aims and values between groups of clients, such as the general public and/or researchers versus the traditional owners. With this in mind, a set of Aboriginal and Torres Strait Islander Protocols for Libraries, Archives and Information Services has been compiled for use within Australia.[7] Employment of Indigenous people is one of the recommendations of this document. Other possibilities can include Indigenous membership on steering committees of museums or institutions.

Presenting Traditional and Popular Cultures

Any exhibit or educational program must include Indigenous consultation and approval by the relevant people. "Relevant" is the operative word in that the proper custodians must be involved. For example, an urban Aboriginal man born in Sydney would not be able to speak for a group in the northwest section of the Kimberleys in Western Australia. Mechanisms and firm guidelines need to be established for seeking approval for research and final publication.

Training Conservation and Collecting Staff and Arranging for Copies

Indigenous people should be encouraged and funded to receive such training. Effective mechanisms and policies need to be formulated in consultation with traditional owners according to regional requirements. One such mechanism might mirror that of the national park managements of Uluru (Ayers Rock) and Kakadu, where management plans set employment and training targets for I1ndigenous community members.[8]

It can be difficult to encourage Indigenous people to relocate to where the large collections reside, especially if they are far from home and family. One possible solution would be to persuade large collecting institutions, in conjunction with formal training schemes within universities, to fund and to conduct training and repatriation programs. Indigenous trainees would gain qualifications in their chosen field of conservation, participate in planning for a local keeping-place or working with existing ones, and arrange for archival copies to be sent there. They would have the freedom to relocate back to the community or to stay at the major collecting institution, arranging for further programs. Their qualifications would allow them to be mobile and advance along career paths rather than being stuck at lower levels.

Finally, staff within institutions holding ICP should undergo some cultural awareness training, especially if they deal with Indigenous clientele. The major collecting institutions within Canberra, Australia, have arranged for Indigenous people to present courses to all staff.[9]

Where to Go from Here

These suggestions raise points that could be included within the UNESCO documents either as parts of a new Recommendation or as operational guidelines for the 1989 *Recommendation*. In any case, the issue of consultation with appropriate people and groups should remain a guiding principle for any amendments to the 1989 *Recommendation*.

Notes

1. Professor Erica-Irene Daes, Special Rapporteur of the Sub-Commission, "Principles and Guidelines for the Protection of the Heritage of Indigenous Peoples," para. 11.
2. G. Koch, "This Land is My Land: the Archives Tells Me So; Sound Archives and Response to the Needs of Indigenous Australians," *IASA Journal* 6 (November 1996):14–15.
3. Report of the National Inquiry into the Separation of Aboriginal and Torres Strait Islander Children from Their Families, April 1997.
4. From <http://nativenet.uthscsa.edu/archive/nl/9706/0006.html>.
5. R.M.W. Dixon, "The Endangered Languages of Australia, Indonesia and Oceania." In Robert H. Robins and Eugenius M. Uhlenbeck, eds. *Endangered Languages* (Oxford and New York: Berg Publishers Ltd., 1991), 229.
6. *Our Culture, Our Future: Proposals for Recognition and Protection of Indigenous Cultural and Intellectual Propert*. Australian Institute of Aboriginal and Torres Strait Islander Studies, 1997, p. 32. Written and researched by Terri Janke, Principal Consultant Michael Frankel & Company, Solicitors.
7. See <http://www.llgc.org.uk/iasa/iasa0019.htm> for the IASA cataloguing rules.
8. Australian Library and Information Association. Protocols for libraries, archives and information services. Compiled by Alex Byrne et. al. Deakin: Australian Library and Information Association for the Aboriginal and Torres Strait Islander Library and Information Resource Network, 1995.
9. The author is greatly indebted to Prof. Isobel McBryde for offering suggestions on tangible cultural heritage and for suggesting amendments to this paper.

Indigenous Arts, (Un)Titled

Tressa Berman
Social and Behavioral Sciences Department
Arizona State University West

In a seminal article in *Current Anthropology,* "Can Culture be Copyrighted?" anthropologist Michael Brown raised a cautionary flag in the movement to protect Indigenous knowledge through legal mechanisms of copyright and intellectual property (Brown 1998). The author's concerns for what he construes as "special rights" to "*collective* privacy" warrant attention — if only to allay the fears that IPR "run amok" would result in a cultural apartheid of creative ideas and their execution. The concern for the regulation of *information* and *knowledge* (note the distinction I make) is reminiscent of the retentionist arguments put forth earlier this decade in the United States around repatriation of cultural property when, it was feared, historic and cultural information that had long been in the public trust would be restricted and lost to the greater good of public knowledge. In a larger argument that situates notions of the public trust within liberal democratic ideals, a critical view, and one that I take here, insists on interrogating the assumptions of "public domain" by asking "whose public?" and "by what standards of trust?"

Indigenous artists and scholars share a worldview that privileges cultural knowledge over information and *place* as the primary reference point for meaning and creative work. Lakota legal scholar Vine Deloria, Jr., has remarked that "American Indians hold their land — places — as having the highest possible meaning, and all their [artistic] statements are made with this reference point in mind" (quoted in Basso and Feld 1997). The same could be said of making art. After returning to Santa Clara Pueblo from her years of formal training in urban art centers, ceramic artist Nora Noranjo-Morse reflects how "holding that clay was the first time I ever felt a connection with something greater than myself. . . . I had come home" (quoted in Abbott 1994). Likewise, contemporary Australian Aboriginal painters usually refer to the landmarks of their "country," that is, the Aboriginal territory depicted through the imagery, colors, and materials used in Aboriginal painting (viz. Sutton 1988, 118–120). As Daisy Manybunharrawuy, an Aboriginal bark painter, describes: "I still kept going at bark painting after I married. . . . My father used to tell me a story from the painting. . . . I use white clay from the beach; black from the tree from the bush . . . at Milingimbi. Milingimbi is like home — Milingimbi is like *momu* [grandmother]" (quoted in Caruana and Lendon 1996). And in the public contests over who controls Indigenous land and what gets to count as "Native" art, California Wintu artist Frank La Pena asserts, "Take away Mount Shasta and there is no Wintu Art" (La Pena 1997). It is only when Western law intervenes that place becomes construed in terms of *property*. Reservation boundaries in the United States have already established this fact. Therefore, lifted from their sites of production (that is, place), Indigenous expressions (such as art forms) already enter the realm of property relations, and it is these *relationships* that cultural and intellectual property rights regulate.

Central to a discussion of place and property lies the critical issue of land rights themselves. I take the core point of land rights as a launch point to explore whether cultural and intellectual property rights have a consequence in other realms of legal practice. One way to do this is to consider how such rights shape art and how rights over art are constructed out of the rights to land, emanating from the rights to property. If construed as flowing from land rights, then Indigenous claims to appropriation of artistic designs would insist on a need for *title*. In order to come to terms with how Western law understands appropriation as fashioned from rights to possession (Coombe 1998), it is helpful to understand how art forms move through the discursive contours of the market; because when we are talking about property law in Western terms, we are essentially talking about market relations. In short, I am posing a series of questions: What are the relationships between land, art, and property? More specifically, how does art, and the cultural knowledge required to produce it, become a commodity that can be regulated by property laws? Once understood as "property," how do commodities move through public and private spaces that give them value in both market and cultural terms?

Public Domain

One of the main points of this paper is that Indigenous claims to cultural and intellectual property rest upon claims to Native title that are inextricably related to the historical relations of dispossession. What Brown and others argue in a move *away* from extending IPR to Native ideas and knowledge is a legitimate concern that sees the commodification of knowledge as counter to cultural preservation. These arguments, while instructive, are based on a limited view of property rights as economic rights, which become privileged in the discourse around IPR. What is missing from an economic rights position is attention to the moral rights that Western property regimes also embody (cf. Tsosie 1997). Furthermore, *access* to the law extends beyond the "bundle or rights" inherent in property law to what some theorists have proposed as "bundles of power" (J. Ribot, personal communication).

Access to the law then becomes not only a question of *application*, but one of authorship — again, invoking the question, "Whose public?" At the extreme end of unequal access to the law, it could be argued that Western law itself does not extend to the variety of public constituents (e.g., Indigenous peoples) evenly or equitably. For instance, for American Indians in the United States, the notion of *public* trust resides with a *federal* trust that serves as an overarching regulator and legal artifact of U.S./Indian relations, and one that carries juridical and fiduciary responsibilities. In reading Native claims into the law, the history of legal practice in relation to Indigenous claims to cultural and intellectual property (e.g., iconography) becomes merged with the wider process of colonization as the vantage point from which the history of Native dispossession gets told (cf. Keeshig-Tobias 1997). For instance, appropriation of Indigenous iconography into state and national symbols signifies assimilative practices whereby "Native art" stands in for "Native," and is upheld by Indigenous symbols that are believed to rest in the public domain. Examples range from the Australian boomerang as a marker of Australian national identity to the appropriation of the Zia sun sign as a symbol for the state of New Mexico. In Arizona, Hopi *katsinas* signify "Indianness" from dry cleaners to travel agencies. In Australia, manufacturers of Flash T-shirt designs claimed the Aboriginal designs were in the public domain because they had taken them from books. Following from the Flash T-shirt case, which resulted in an out-of-court settlement for Aboriginal artists, subsequent legal decisions have ruled in favor of Aboriginal plaintiffs claiming violation of copyright. In the now famous *Carpets* case, a judgement was issued against Indofurn Pty Ltd., which was found to have violated the copyright of Aboriginal artists, for whom the High Court found in favor (viz. Johnson 1996). While the decision in the 1993 *Carpets* case recognized the rights of Aboriginal artists under the 1968 *Australian Copyright Act*, Australian law remains premised on *non-recognition of Aboriginal law*.

In Aboriginal customary practices, the complicated proprietary rights bestowed by the Dreaming are further fragmented by collectively sanctioned *use rights*. Australian museums have responded to the need for "privacy rights" by creating men's rooms and women's rooms in storage facilities that house culturally sensitive objects assigned by gender. The argument for a generalized collective privacy becomes a problematic that must then consider rights to production, use rights, and proprietary rights. As I have shown in the context of representation (Berman 1998), the notion of "use rights" presents a conundrum by which tribal sovereignty at the level of government-to-government relations sometimes conflicts with the use rights of objects for which medicine people are caretakers. Extensions of collective privacy rights run counter to U.S. property regimes that are based on notions of possessive individualism and force a unitary voice in tribal claims — such as "the Sioux."

Case law can set precedents for testing the efficacy of intellectual property rights and cultural property laws; however, Indigenous rules governing the production and "ownership" of Indigenous cultural objects often do not follow legal principles. Instead, as in the Australian *Carpets* case, expressions and objects are subject to community-based sanctions. In local community contexts, Indigenous knowledge bears upon cultural property claims by conferring collectively recognized forms of "precedents" and "evidence" — enabling a form of "cultural copyright" (Pinnel and Evans 1994) as a collective right.

Secrecy

The flip side of public domain is privacy. For instance, property law recognizes privacy rights as flowing from rights to exclusion. In cultural property cases, customary practices govern rules for production, display, and (re)distribution. Cultural patrimony — that is, the return of cultural objects to their originating communities — relies on evidence based on the kinds of criteria mentioned directly above (namely, a recognition of collective rights). In distinguishing *information* from *knowledge*, it becomes quite clear that Indigenous knowledge cannot be extracted as an isolate, like a gene cell (viz. Coombe 1998). Rather, it is embedded within shifting matrices of cultural systems that include rights vested through kinship and upheld by community sanction. Extreme forms of privacy lie with "hidden knowledge" — often the very customary practices that sanctify public representatives (such as Aboriginal lawyers or Native American spokespeople) to act on behalf of cultural groups seeking just compensation under IPR in international settings (such as the United Nations International Working Groups on Indigenous Affairs and the World Intellectual Property Organization; see Posey 1998). Forms of cultural knowledge solicited as evidence in cultural property claims may be better preserved *off the record*, as Indigenous peoples increasingly evoke their "right to remain silent," especially in matters of ceremonial disclosure. For instance, as Philip Minthorn,

Washington State Cayuse artist, says in relation to Native claims to museum objects of cultural patrimony:

> Native communities are now required to divulge sacred and esoteric forms of knowledge in order to substantiate their claim or to insure the appropriate disposition of such objects . . .without the guarantee of the protection of that knowledge. (Minthorn 1995, 11)

IPR in such cases offers no protections at the level of community-based group rights. But just as land transforms from place to property, cultural knowledge becomes information when it is taken out of its social and ceremonial contexts and becomes subject to misappropriation and legal protections. Furthermore, intellectual and property rights law requires that Indigenous knowledge stand as a kind of "evidence," subject to the scrutiny of the public record. Examples abound in repatriation cases in the United States, where tribal elders may be asked to testify about the sacred nature of objects in cultural patrimony cases. While the 1990 *Native American Graves Protection and Repatriation Act* states that oral histories and cultural codes of meaning can be used to determine cultural claims to objects, the fact is that ethnohistorical, archaeological, and legal records are privileged in documenting museum collections, and in some cases, American Indian spokespeople report that Native testimony has been expunged from the historical record. In short, it's about whose story gets told, and who has the right to tell it.

The issue of secrecy is related to silence as a way to control the flow of cultural knowledge, and in recent years, as a way to insure that Indigenous knowledge does not become a matter of public record (such as in repatriation cases). On the other hand, silence can be the result of totalizing claims to intellectual property rights and cultural property in the legal debates of who speaks for whom. For example, ways in which some customary practices are silenced lie in the erasure of women's knowledge from museum and legal records — even where women serve as keepers of rights to Indigenous designs and re-distributors of cultural objects (Berman 1997). However, the positioning of objects within social and ceremonial life, and the position of specific individuals to objects themselves, would be impossible to untangle without considering "women's ways of knowing" — from customary rights that govern artistic production to social divisions that allocate the distribution of goods and labor among women who stand at the center of their kin-based networks. Decision-making in repatriation claims takes place at deep community levels, where kinship and ceremonial knowledge — through the input of Native American women — figures prominently. By turning attention to women's contributions, we see that it is not just in the rhetoric of repatriation that women sometimes stand as spokespeople; but repatriated objects are frequently *family* objects, associated with family histories, clans and places of origin, where people and objects converge to create a context for cultural meanings and uses (Jackniss 1996). By comparison, Queensland Murri artists, in referencing artworks that signify their "country," make such claims in relation to homeland as a point of origin and return.

When we consider Aboriginal women's knowledge as producers and (re)distributors of goods, women's "property" takes on new significance and allows us to consider aspects of property law in more culturally relevant terms. While many of the cultural codes that inform the production and circulation of objects fall outside of the regime of U.S. property law, some aspects of common law allow us to shift the discourse of repatriation away from totalizing accounts. An example of Indigenous women's redistributive role is highlighted in the documentary film *Potlatch*, which shows how the return of repatriated objects symbolizes the redistribution of power relations through the transfer of title. In these ways, the redistribution of property rights through repatriation has the potential for redistributing knowledge and power in ways that are symbolized by the act of return itself. For example, *Potlatch* shows the Kramner family's stake in the "continuity and legitimacy of the Kwakiutl potlatch in general and the Kramner family's claim to returned potlatch items from the 1922 confiscation" (Jacknis 1996). The image of the reapportionment of repatriated objects reveals several things: First, the centrality of women is marked by the amassing and redistribution of goods and objects. Second, the social purpose of objects preserved through customary rights becomes re-empowered by a collectively sanctioned locality, in this case the Kwakuitl potlatch at Alert Bay (Harding 1997, 757).

Here we see how cultural appropriation, shown at the extreme end in the confiscation of cultural property, signals how Western law is premised on the abrogation of Native sovereignty. Sovereignty, as both a political and philosophical dimension of cultural rights, is tied to claims of Native title, whether that title is to land, cultural property, or art forms.

Restoration of Sovereign Rights through Title

The above discussion — by exploring some of the dimensions and limitations of IPR for Indigenous knowledge systems — nonetheless suggests that where copyright infringement and IPR can uphold cultural rights to production, distribution, and use, they may also serve to reinforce Native title. Conversely, where IPR and copyright result in the commodified transformation of cultural knowledge to information bytes for public consumption, then new approaches need to be explored. For instance, in my own work with Indigenous artists, cultural rights to production and responsibilities to safeguard artistic motifs and techniques have recently come under scrutiny as the last harbors of Indigenous knowledge, where cultural codes of meaning embedded in art forms and processes of making art seek new forms of protection. Following anthropologist Renato Rosaldo (1989), I take this domain as a new "borderzone" of colonial encounter, where customary and legal practices meet (cf. McMaster 1995).

If we were to take the view that Native title to cultural and intellectual property and their expressions, such as art forms, are inextricable aspects of sovereignty, then a cultural rights argument begins to sound less like "special rights" and more like "human rights" (i.e., toward self-determination). For instance, the Australian *Carpets* case recognized the rights of Aboriginal artists by citing the Vietnam-based manufacturers with an infraction of copyright under the *Australian Copyright Act*, as mentioned earlier. In Australian case law, the *Carpets* case has been compared to the precedent-setting Mabo land claims, in which Aboriginal title was restored to Torres Strait Islanders. A restoration of sovereign rights through title (rather than copyright) might have invoked a broader ruling in the *Carpets* case, by which rights to a particular site entitle artists to the rights over images that flow from that site. From this perspective, a central issue of sovereignty gets raised: Native title (to land) cannot be alienated. The same can be said — and U.S. law now accepts this, as in the Native American Graves Protection and Repatriation Act — of certain cultural objects, which cannot be alienated from their caretakers and their places of origin. One of the better known cases of this involves the Zuni war gods, many of which have been returned by museums and private collectors to the Zuni tribe.

While alienation generally implies privatization, especially of land, inalienability does not conversely (or so it would seem logically) lend itself to the public domain. In the United States, the use of images, generally conceptualized as publicity rights, has been a source of contention between Native communities and commercial exploiters. In the well-documented case of *the Estate of Tasunke Witko a.k.a Crazy Horse v. Vultaggio and Sons, Inc.*, the descendants of Sioux Chief Crazy Horse asserted "defamation, violation of the Estate's right of publicity, and negligent and intentional infliction of emotional distress (in addition to violations of the *Lanham Act* and *American Indian Arts and Crafts Board Act*)" (Newton 1997; Gough 1995). Of relevance here is that the defendants argued that the rights of publicity were in the public domain and did not constitute a violation of privacy. The case itself has yet to be heard on its merits as tribal courts and federal district courts volley for jurisdiction. The Rosebud Sioux tribe has argued that the Rosebud Sioux Tribal Court has inherent and exclusive jurisdiction over personal property rights vested in the case [US Court of Appeals for the Eighth Circuit, 1998 U.S. App.]

Given the jurisdictional problem in the *Crazy Horse* case, and the general trust relationship between the federal government and Indian tribes in the United States, it would seem that the "special rights" argument would be nullified by the unique legal status ascribed to Indigenous peoples, especially in North America and increasingly in Australia. This raises a host of questions that straddle the borderzone between the market and aboriginality. In hammering out legal solutions to the global concern over appropriation without compensation, it would seem that the only way to protect Indigenous creations at the points of their intersection with the market is to treat them like property. The questions unleashed by such an approach demand careful attention to power relations, local knowledge, collective and individual rights, jurisdiction, authorship, and access to the law.

In Australia, I have so far observed that the possibilities to amend copyright laws to better address Aboriginal concerns about appropriation of creative works are moving at a steady if not snowballing rate — despite recent setbacks in land title victories, such as the Wik land settlements that followed on the heels of the Mabo Land Claims victory , and the seemingly slow process of hammering out new policies. Indigenous organizations are at the forefront of these movements — especially as they link land rights to rights over art. While the tome of legal briefs in Australia has nowhere reached U.S. proportions with respect to a body of case law analogous to federal Indian law, I think that the opportunities for including intellectual and cultural property protections into a revised "bundle of rights" in property law may be better positioned in Australia at this time when land rights have merged with cultural rights. In this light, the re-thinking of "property" will force new sets of questions to the fore: Not rhetorically "Can culture be copyrighted?" but more practically, "How will Indigenous peoples write themselves into the law?" Questions of privacy and secrecy as matters of Indigenous knowledge may yet find protections, if public domain is not just a playing field for commodifying Indigenous knowledge, and the rule of law is not just a matter of public opinion.

References

Abbott, Lawrence, ed. 1994. *I Stand at The Center of Good: Interviews with Contemporary Native American Artists*. Lincoln: University of Nebraska Press.

Basso, Keith, and Stephen Feld, eds. 1997. *Senses of Place*. Santa Fe: School of American Research Press.

Berman, Tressa. 1997. Beyond the Museum: The Politics of Representation in Asserting Rights to Cultural Property. *Museum Anthropology* 21(3):19–27.

_____. 1998. The Community as Worksite: American Indian Women's Artistic Production. In *It Takes More than Class: Approaches to The Study of Power in U.S. Workplaces*. Ann Kingsolver, ed. Albany: SUNY Press.

Brown, Michael. 1998. Can Culture Be Copyrighted? *Current Anthropology*. 39(2):193–222.

Caruana, Wally, and Nigel Lendon. 1996. *The Painters of the Wagilag Sisters Story, 1937–1997*. Canberra: National Gallery of Australia.

Coombe, Rosemary. 1998. Comment on Can Culture Be Copyrighted? *Current Anthropology* 39(2).

Ferguson, T.J., Roger Anyon, and Edumund Ladd. 1996. Repatriation at the Pueblo of Zuni: Diverse Solutions to Complex Problems. *American Indian Quarterly* 20(2):251–76.

Gough, Robert. 1995. Malt Liquor Mythos, or "Will the Original Crazy Horse Please Rise?" Cultural Facts and Legal Fictions in the Settlement of Competing Property Rights Claims. Paper presented at the annual American Anthropological Association 93rd Annual Meeting, Atlanta, Georgia.

Harding, Sara. 1997. Justifying Repatriation of Native American Cultural Property. *Indiana Law Journal* 72:723–73.

Jacknis, Ira. 1996. Repatriation as Social Drama: The Kwakuitl Indians of British Columbia, 1922–1980. *American Indian Quarterly* 20(2):277–86.

Johnson, Vivien. 1996. The Case of the Counterfeit Carpets. In *Copyrites: Aboriginal Art in the Age of Reproductive Technologies* (exhibition catalogue). Sydney: National Indigenous Arts Advocacy Association and Macquarie University, p. 39–48.

Keeshig-Tobias, Lenore. 1997. Stop Stealing Native Stories. In *Borrowed Power: Essays on Cultural Appropriation*. Bruce Ziff and Pratima V. Rao, eds. New Brunswick: Rutgers University Press.

La Pena, Frank. 1997. Remarks at California Indigenous artists panel, Native American Art Studies Association meetings, October 1997, Berkeley, California.

McMaster, Gerald. 1995. Borderzones: The "Injun-uity" of Aesthetic Tricks. *Cultural Studies* 9(1):147–63.

Minthorn, Philip. 1995. Medicine Bundles as Aboriginal Curation. Paper presented at American Anthropological Association 93rd Annual Meeting, Atlanta, Georgia.

Newton, Nell. 1997. Memory and Misrepresentation: Representing Crazy Horse in Tribal Court. In *Borrowed Power: Essays on Cultural Appropriation*. Bruce Ziff and Pratima V. Rao, eds. New Brunswick: Rutgers University Press.

Pinnel, Sandra Lee, and Michael J. Evans. 1994. Tribal Sovereignty and the Control of Knowledge. In *Intellectual Property Rights and Indigenous Peoples: A Source Book*. Tom Greaves, ed. Oklahoma City: Society for Applied Anthropology.

Posey, Darryl. 1998. Effecting International Change. *Cultural Survival Quarterly* Summer: 29–35.

Rosaldo, Renato. 1989. *Culture and Truth*. Boston: Beacon Press.

Sutton, Peter, ed. 1988. *Dreamings: The Art of Aboriginal Australia*. New York: George Braziller Publishers and the Asia Society Galleries, pp. 118–20.

Tsosie, Rebecca. 1997. Claims to Cultural Property. *Museum Anthropology* 21(3).

Practical Perspectives: Local Traditions and Methods of Preservation

How to Promote Incentives
for Cultural Heritage Practitioners

Junzo Kawada
Professor of Cultural Anthropology
Faculty of International Studies, Hiroshima City University
Japan

The globalization of communication, accelerating through the rapid flow of human beings and goods as well as information, seems to contribute to the growth of world cultural uniformity. But in fact, the uniformity occurs mainly in technology and in some aspects of lifestyle, that is to say, at the surface levels of culture. In the deeper levels of cultural identity, globalization may create a countercurrent of particular cultural values. This is especially true among minority groups who protest political or economic discrimination by proclaiming their cultural identity. Among majorities too, nostalgic attachment to cultural heritage may arise in response to globalization. In both cases, the cultural heritage tends to be idealized and re-invented. The culture is no longer something to be lived unself-consciously, but has become something to be consciously spoken of and revalued.

In spite of this general tendency towards an awareness of the value of cultural heritage, many of its practices are in danger of disappearing because they are no longer profitable and consequently attract no successors to the present generation. Generally speaking, the real problems are not in globalization per se, but in present-day socio-economic factors that discourage the practitioners of cultural heritage.

The 1989 *Recommendation* stresses "traditional culture and folklore" as important components of cultural heritage. First, the adjective "traditional" implies the aspect of oral and/or bodily transmission of cultural heritage, and the term "folklore" presupposes the common people to be bearers of this heritage, which is rooted in a community and not in particular individuals of elevated social standing. Traditional culture and folklore are intangible cultural heritage in the strict sense — performing arts as well as the physical skills and technical knowledge needed to produce tangible objects like handicrafts. By using both terms, the 1989 *Recommendation* stresses the collective nature of both the practice and the transmission of cultural heritage.

We should know: first, what kinds of cultural heritage are in danger of disappearing and why; and second, why should they be judged worthy of being preserved and even disseminated.

Among the kinds of intangible cultural heritage, we must distinguish between performing arts done for commercial purposes and those that are non-profit by nature. Japanese examples of the first kind of endangered traditions are the puppet theater Bunraku, street performers, strolling players, and the blessing arts done at ceremonial occasions. Bunraku was prosperous until the sixties, and the street performing arts were viable until the Second World War. But nowadays they are in danger of disappearing, and some of them have already disappeared. This is because of changes in their social context, as well as in their inner social organization, particularly the master-apprentice relationship. An intangible cultural heritage of a non-profit nature that is also disappearing is the telling of folk tales.

Very common all over Japan until the sixties and with important local varieties, folk tale-telling declined in the era of high economic growth and subsequent radical changes in everyday life common to industrialized countries. For the conservation of Bunraku, there is a national training school for young players, while for storytelling, many local communities and voluntary associations try to promote performances by aged qualified tellers, and at the same time to train aspirants.

The most delicate sphere is that of remunerated performing arts practiced by individuals. In my personal knowledge, there is an excellent strolling *biwa* lute player and singer, the last one in Kumamoto Prefecture in Japan. This kind of music was traditionally reserved to blind persons. Since strolling performance had become no longer possible, this blind old man lived alone in penury in a remote village. Several researchers of traditional popular music including me recorded his performance, wrote about him in magazines, and organized a concert at which he performed in a small music hall in Tokyo. But he died at a very old age without a successor. Such a popular performing artist and many other strolling players do not qualify for recognition and support as "living national treasures."

I think we can find two kinds of solutions, even if insufficient, to conserve intangible cultural heritage according to its nature. First, for the performing arts like Bunraku that are highly stylized and have fixed content based on written texts, the performing style as a whole must be conserved and transmitted. In such a case, long-term systematic training of novice players is necessary, and consequently a large-scale and financially solid institution is needed. This was the case with the ancient Hue court music of Vietnam. Owing to the efforts of UNESCO and financial support from the Japan Foundation, the National University of Hue began training successors in the tradition of court music.

Second, in traditions like folk tale-telling, what is essential is performance as intimate oral communication between tellers and listeners. In such a case, it is the form and the spirit of the traditional culture that is to be inherited. According to the tradition, even the classic stories are to be told without a fixed text, through the vivid oral composition of each teller. To this end, many Japanese regional, transregional, and library-based associations of storytellers work actively to teach novices the folk tales and their telling and to organize storytelling gatherings for adults and children. Such activities prosper in many countries, especially in Germany and in the United States.

In the case of institutionalized training for classic performing arts like Bunraku and Kabuki, many problems that arise in the modern context were not part of traditional training in the older social context. These theatrical performing arts require team play with roles allotted to each member. But some roles have the spotlight while others labor in obscurity, and there is little possibility to interchange the roles. In the old system established in the feudalistic, status-oriented Tokugawa society and based on the master-apprentice training system, each player would accomplish his own assigned task without overt discontent. But today, young applicants do not want to endure this inequality. Because of this and the decline in performance income due to the decreasing popularity of Bunraku, applicants are fewer in number.

In handicrafts, young people find it difficult to endure a childhood of exacting training in a family or in a master-apprentice relationship if it does not bring sufficient economic compensation. But the case of the traditional fabrication of *akeni* in Kyoto clearly shows that with a sufficient demand and an assured income, even such a highly specialized handicraft can find a young successor. *Akeni* is a trunk for sumo wrestlers, made with thinly sliced and beautifully lacquered bamboo, and it is an important object for sumo wrestlers during seasonal tournaments. For many years only one craftsman, now sixty-four, has made this kind of trunk, and he is fortunate to be succeeded by his thirty-five-year-old son.

Many handicrafts are in crisis, because their use of time and labor makes them unprofitable. In India, I visited handweavers in training centers and in their villages and realized their critical situation. A power loom weaves cloth faster, more cheaply, with better quality than that made by an ordinary handweaver. Specially made high-quality handwoven cloths are destined for their devotees in Western countries. Another problem in the conservation of handicrafts arises from the difficulty in obtaining necessary supporting tools or instruments of good quality, which are themselves made by handicraft, like the special curved nails used by the traditional Japanese shipbuilders. This is similar to the problem in performing arts done by a team, which may be weakened by insufficiently remunerated supporting parts.

In every domain of cultural heritage, it is now necessary to provide incentives for practitioners and their successors in coming generations. Educational activities by UNESCO or by other organizations must be intensified, but at the same time, we have to evaluate properly the role of tourism, a more and more significant and profitable component of globalization. Recently, the character of tourism itself has changed, and many anthropological studies describe its positive effects in the revitalization of cultural heritage and the mutual understanding of cultural diversity. Today, culture is something not only to be spoken about, but also to be presented to other cultures in its own self-image. In this process, we must remain aware that every traditional culture is created and transformed in response to historical contexts. Open-air performances done in Plaza Djamaa al-Fana of Marrakech are not authentic, in the sense that this plaza was originally for the practice of Sufism, but they are authentic in the sense that the performances are self-sustaining and provide a certain satisfaction to both the performers and the spectators, many of whom are tourists. To develop a self-consciousness about traditional cultural heritage is fundamental to human development, a prerequisite for technological and economic development that is based on the revaluation of cultural identity and the recognition of human cultural diversity.

Proposal for a Tripartite Theory (Transformation/ Transcontextualization/ Transposition) and Its Application to the Empowerment of an East Asian Court Music Network, with Emphasis on the Vietnamese Case

Yamaguti Osamu
Professor of Musicology
Graduate School of Letters, Osaka University
Osaka, Japan

Music in Context and in Transcontextualization

The term "text" is understood, as its Latin etymology indicates, as something that is intentionally "woven" by humans. Often used in music to refer only to the words of a song, the term can also be used in a broader sense to imply the whole spectrum of a particular kind of music, i.e., a body of sonic phenomena produced by humans on the basis of a certain way of thinking. The term "context" also originally referred to woven objects. Paired dichotomously with "text," however, the term refers to the situation that surrounds and sustains the existence of the text: for example, the human body, musical instruments, time and place of performance, occasion and function of music, socio-cultural background of performing arts, etc.

As a part of my own newly proposed "applicative musicology," I have based theoretical speculations on a new concept and term: "transcontextualization." I coined this term in 1994 when, for the first time in my life, I became involved in a series of projects dealing with Vietnamese musics. I intended the term to cover a wide range of contextual changes of musical text. These changes may range from the simple repetition of a performance of a musical composition in the same place for the same purpose but at a different time, to complicated transformations of performances done at different times at different places and for different purposes. It is presumed here that music texts change through transmission and diffusion in accordance with the degree of transcontextualization applied to the original.

East Asian Court and Ex-Court Musics As a Network

One of the most ritualistic East Asian court-music traditions is known in Chinese as *yayue* ("elegant music"), though it should be noted that the exact constitution of the term varies from country to country and from one historical period to another. The term and the music were transplanted to Korea as *aak,* to Japan as *gagaku,* and to Vietnam as *nha nhac.* This form of music is one of the commonalties found in the East Asian court traditions that link China, Korea, Japan, and Vietnam in a complex historical network. As noted, usage of the term varies in different countries and in different historical periods, a fact for future study and comparison. It must also be remembered that in each country there are many varieties of music besides "elegant music," and that in China *yayue* is extinct as a tradition.

Transformation of Music in the Context of Its Transmission

The essential parts, if not all, of a piece of music are transformed in direct and indirect performance contexts. For example: (1) cheironomic body movements of a performer often represent basic melodic configurations, dynamic and/or agogic stability, and changes therefrom; (2) "mouth music" or lexically meaningless syllables used as imitative descriptions of melodic or rhythmic phrases often function as mnemonic devices during the teaching/learning process; (3) written notation can be a prescriptive or a descriptive means of recording a particular performance, before or after the performance, respectively (see Seeger 1958); and (4) recording a performance on tape or disc has become increasingly important in the course of the twentieth century. These transformations occur whether they are intended or not and should be fully considered whenever we deal with strategies for safeguarding musical traditions (Yamaguti 1986).

The Case of Vietnam

In March 1994, Tokumaru Yosihiko and I were asked to attend and make concrete proposals to two international conferences sponsored by the Vietnamese government and UNESCO on the subject of safeguarding intangible cultural heritage. We immediately accepted the invitation because we shared memories of our efforts some twenty years before to invite a group of Vietnamese musicians and scholars to Japan. The project, sponsored by the Japan Foundation and called ATPA (Asian Traditional Performing Arts), had ended in failure, at least with respect to Vietnamese participation, and had to deal with various Asian musics for fifteen years without a Vietnamese perspective. We had hoped to better understand Vietnamese court music, the history and current status of which was not as well known as the court musics of Japan or Korea. In the mid-1970s, with the after-effects of the Vietnam War still strongly felt, we had been worried that court music would not survive long enough to be handed down to another generation.

The conferences we attended were held in Hanoi and Hue. In Hanoi, where the main theme was the fifty-three ethnic minority groups of the country, we proposed the "Performing Arts as AV Documentary Training Program." (Incidentally, this project started its feasibility studies in April 1999, five years after our original proposal, and was integrated into a new project called RVMV [Research and Video Documentation Project of Minorities' Intangible Cultural Heritage of Vietnam] in April 2000. As head of this new project, which is to undertake its first stage in bilateral cooperation between Vietnam and Japan, I feel it may take another five years before we can see significant results!)

In Hue we presented a proposal called "the Vietnamese Court Music Revitalization Plan." Our objective was to revitalize the traditions of ex-court musics such as *nha nhac, dai nhac* ("large music"), and *tieu nhac* ("small music"), which had barely managed to survive in Hue. Others who attended the conference, including Tran Van Khe (professor emeritus, University of Paris) and Jose Maceda (professor emeritus, University of the Philippines), voiced their support and pledged their cooperation. The two proposals were immediately approved by UNESCO; details regarding implementation and funding were to be worked out later in Japan.

As it happened, a Vietnamese music and dance troupe had been invited to appear at the Tenth Tokyo Summer Music Festival that year, so while in Hue, Tran arranged to meet with them. The troupe tended to present programs designed for general audiences that featured not only imperial court music and dance but also popular folk songs and musical dramas. Not always regarded as a legitimate court music group, they frequently played court music on non-court-music instruments such as the dan bau (monochord zither). Of course, altering the forms of old music to make it new does not always call for criticism. Nevertheless, in view of the current state of Vietnamese court music, both Tran and I shared the opinion that, even if only for the present, a little criticism was necessary. Tran extended his stay in the country and communicated this opinion to them directly. The members of the troupe took our criticism relatively well: the opportunity to visit Japan was a great incentive, and the fact that foreigners had a strong interest in their ex-court music was useful in raising their own awareness of the need to preserve the tradition.

In addition to this troupe, there were, in fact, other ex-court musicians who gave more authentic performances. In particular, four elderly musicians with their sons and close friends and relatives performed at the opening ceremony of the UNESCO conference. This performance struck me as an appeal: if only they had the opportunity to polish theirs skills, they could return their tradition to its original form.

I suggested a plan that used Korea as a model. In the 1910s, alter the downfall of the Yi dynasty, Korean court music had been on the verge of dying out; today it is preserved as "national music" at the National Center for Korean Traditional Performing Arts (NCKTPA). Court musicians from Hanyang (present-day Seoul) and Tokyo collaborated, and, thanks to the efforts of the musicologist Tanabe Hisao and Korean scholars, Korean court music survived. Even now, the tradition plays a large part in international exchange through both performance and research. It was my feeling that the destiny of Vietnamese court music lay in following a similar path.

We immediately made efforts to implement the Vietnamese Court Music Revitalization Plan. With a research grant from the Toyota Foundation, we were able to start the plan (with Tokumaru as head). We began with basic research projects, such as scholarly documentation of the present state of the tradition, the collection of related documents (many of which were scattered or lost), and historical research.

The research group, consisting of musicologists and specialists in Vietnamese studies, made its first field survey of Vietnam in April 1995 with a grant offered by the Toyota Foundation. Maintaining discreet contact with the Japanese Embassy in Hanoi, we began to plan new ways of developing the project. My idea was to establish a court music course at the College of Arts, Hue University, thus creating a situation similar to that in Seoul. We thought it best to proceed immediately with the education of court musicians at the college level, since the surviving elderly court musicians were getting no younger.

We asked for advice from the Japan Foundation Asia Center and began to help the university apply for financial assistance for the project. After many ups and downs the request was approved in November 1995. It took the Vietnamese Ministry of Education until January 1996 to approve the establishment of a new department. In March, we were told that we would have to wait until September, the beginning of the new academic year. Thinking that it would be a shame to lose the funding we had already received for the first year, I proposed that preparatory activities begin in April, before the official start of the project. At the unofficial inauguration ceremony in April, a performance was given by students who expected to enter the university as court-music majors and who had already begun their training with the elderly musicians.

In the meantime, I noticed that ex-court-music education was taking place below the university level at high schools. High school students and their teachers were invited to

Hyogo Prefecture in Japan, where a series of exchange programs with young Japanese musicians had been instituted.

The official opening ceremony for the new university course took place in early October 1996. By then we were planning two other activities. First, a Korean student of mine, Kim Youngbong, who was familiar with both Korean and Japanese styles of court music, was dispatched to Hue under the sponsorship of the Japan Foundation Asia Center to undertake intensive field research with elderly musicians while they were still active. This idea was initially proposed by Tran Van Khe. After six months of field research, she completed her dissertation (Kim 1998). Prior to this, her Chinese classmate, Zhao Weiping, completed a musico-philological dissertation dealing with the early history of court musics in Japan and Vietnam (Zhao 1997).

The second new activity for the Vietnamese Court Music Revitalization Plan was the planning of an international symposium on East Asian court-music traditions with the involvement of China, Korea, Vietnam, and Japan — the first of its kind in the long history of the East Asian court-music traditions. It was a pleasant surprise that NCKTPA responded to my appeal so quickly that the symposium took place in May 1997 in Seoul (NCKTPA 1997).

(In June 2000, the Nha Nhac Course at the College of Arts, Hue University, produced eleven graduates, who had mastered the basic performance techniques of the Vietnamese court music repertoire as well as acquired scholarly perspective of the music style as placed in the East Asian network. They have already been employed as professional musicians belonging to the Royal Theatre, which is soon to be reconstructed as part of the historical conservation activities in line with an emerging cultural tourism.)

References

Kim, Youngbong. 1998. Transmission and Change in the Music Culture of Central Vietnam: Focussing on Court Music (in Japanese: with summary in English). Dissertation (Doctor of Literature), Osaka University.

NCKTPA. 1997. The 2nd International Council for Asian Music: Aak, Gagaiw, Nha Nhac. Seoul: NCKTPA (National Center for Korean Traditional Performing Arts).

Performing Arts Kenkyûkai, ed. 1996. *Young People Carrying Forward Asian Performing Arts: Vietnam and Japan*. Kobe: Performing Arts Foundation.

Seeger, Charles. 1958. Prescriptive and Descriptive Music Writing. *Musical Quarterly* 44(2):184–95.

Yamaguti, Osamu. 1986. Music and Its Transformations in Direct and Indirect Contexts. In Tokumaru and Yamaguti, pp. 29–37.

Tokumaru, Yosihiko, and Yamaguti, Osamu, eds. 1986. *The Oral and the Literate in Music*. Tokyo: Academia Music Ltd.

Zhao, Weiping. 1997. The Reception and Transculturation of Chinese Music in East Asia: with an Emphasis on the Early Histories of Court Music in Japan and Vietnam (in Japanese: with summary in English) Dissertation (Doctor of Literature), Osaka University.

Tradition-Based Societies:
Local Values for International Cooperation

Mihály Hoppál
Director
European Folklore Institute
(formerly European Centre for Traditional Culture)
Budapest, Hungary

The knowledge that humankind has accumulated, the wonderful technical advances, the marvelous opportunities afforded by the information society of today, have meant for the most part seemingly limitless economic growth, exploitation of the weak, and destruction of the natural environment. We have created an information-based society, but we have not yet achieved a knowledge-based society, in which knowledge is equally distributed and finally leads us towards self-restraint. Perhaps knowledge also leads to moral behavior.

In any event, knowledge leads us to understand the significance of tradition. Over the centuries, local traditions have developed valuable experience, techniques for protecting the environment, and skills for handling social conflict (drama, games, customs, rites, and folk healing skills, to mention but a few), which make up a treasure trove of common knowledge for mankind. It is no accident that exactly ten years have passed since UNESCO accepted the *Recommendation on the Safeguarding of Traditional Culture and Folklore*.

Obviously, cultural traditions and folklore have preserved the elements necessary for expressing the identity of many ethnic groups. Elements consist not only of the stones of ancient buildings and historical ruins or other tangible cultural heritage but also of the intangible. In many cases, these invisible, spiritual traditions — hardly articulated, sometimes only sung or danced — are more meaningful than anything else because people are deeply attached to them. It is precisely the wars and ethnic conflicts of our leaders that suddenly make us realize what imagined, ancient traditions mean for certain nations — the myth for which a history is created or the legend which makes history. Whether they are true or not is of little importance. They can help mobilize crowds, start wars, and build ideological castles in the air. Simply put, local value systems, systems of belief, mythology, prejudice, and differences in customs and religions may provide a basis for conflict. It is not the cultural traditions themselves, however, but ignorance of them, misinformation about them, refusing to recognize their existence, or attempting to eradicate them, which create extreme emotions.

Nor can we make progress without getting to know the cultural traditions of *others*. Events of the last few years clearly show that it is precisely the intangible part of a culture which changes more slowly. The objects of the material world deteriorate, wear out; we throw them away if they are no longer usable; but we like to preserve sayings, proverbs, beliefs, myths, and legends — even if we don't need them every day. And these are the cultural factors that influence emotional decisions, prejudices developed about *others*, our picture of the enemy, and the patterns of national identity and forms of behavior when conflicts occur (e.g., in questions of heroism, honor or revenge, we always act according to the laws of local tradition!). Ethnological research can provide countless examples to prove this statement.

The teachings of Anglo-Saxon social anthropology are not much used in international relations, and unfortunately, the contempt for the cultural identity of certain ethnic groups also conforms to Anglo-Saxon patterns, insofar as it is individual freedoms which are held to be most important. The individual and the present above all else! But we must understand that there are cultures where a respect for the community, for tradition and the past have priority over the individual! In a tradition-based society, it is not the short-term but the long term aims that are important, not fast development (which often goes together with destruction) but the slow process of constructing and maintaining balance.

Therefore, as an anthropologist, I propose the following for international cooperation:

- Educating younger generations to learn to respect the traditions of other nations is the only way to achieve the peaceful coexistence of different ethnic groups.
- Organizing festivals shows the values of local traditions and enables nations to get to know each other's culture. Recognizing the diversity of cultures is part of developing tolerance.
- Documenting local traditions and heritage (a never-ending task) is the only way we can hand something on to the next generation! It is important to carry out this preservation using contemporary means — (e.g., video, film, multimedia) — because this is the only way to reach the masses.

At first glance globalization, with its highly developed communication technology, appears to help international cooperation and conflict prevention. But it is clear by now that globalization is just a new form of colonialism, not only in the Third World but elsewhere too! And this is not only economic neo-colonialism but also a cultural imperialism that brings with it the eradication and annihilation of local cultural traditions! The danger in this is that it denies and disregards the cultural identity of local groups (especially minorities), deprives them of their right to their own cultural heritage, their right to use of their own language, and their right to their own customs, religious precepts, mythology, and moral values. In short, this is the denial of collective cultural rights and freedoms! This is why UNESCO's two new recommendations, Living Human Treasure and Proclamation of the Masterpieces of the Oral and Intangible Heritage of Humanity (supplementing the 1989 Resolution), are particularly important. Though there is a system in Hungary in operation since 1950 that essentially satisfies the requirements of the Living Human Treasure system, and which has awarded prizes to outstanding folk artists every year since its foundation, the work has not been documented. One of the research projects, nearly complete, of the European Folklore Institute (formerly known as the European Centre for Traditional Culture) is a monograph and complete documentation on this subject. Another project that we are supporting records the history of the internationally recognized "Dance House Movement." We have several ongoing projects on the preservation and handing on of traditional folk music (e.g., the publication of the folk music collections of Vikár, Bartók, and Vargyas).

My concrete proposal, therefore, is that the Member States respect the cultures in their own countries and, above all, the cultural heritage of ethnic minorities and pass legislation to ensure that this happens.

Respecting local cultures means, at the same time, upholding cultural identity. The most serious problem for the peaceful coexistence of various national groups, apart from human rights, is in the freedom to declare their collective cultural identity. These are, of course, not new ideas, since one of the Ten Commandments is about precisely this ancient wisdom:

"Honor thy father and thy mother that thou might live long on this earth!" The commandment implies respect for our ancestors, respect for tradition, and the maintenance of the values inherent in local traditions. Allow me to modify the Third Commandment a little, so that I might finish my contribution with it:

Let us honor each other's local traditions, so that we may live long on this earth!

The SADC Databank: The Role of Data Exchange in Empowering Local Institutions

Renato Matusse
Secretary General for Culture, Information and Sport
The Southern African Development Community
Maputo, Mozambique

Introduction

Let me begin by thanking UNESCO and the Smithsonian Institution for having extended this invitation to the Southern African Development Community (SADC) and to me personally to attend this important conference on "Global Assessment of the 1989 *Recommendation on the Safeguarding of Traditional Culture and Folklore*: Local Empowerment and International Cooperation." For us in SADC, this conference comes at a very appropriate time: following the approval by SADC of the Sector for Culture, Information and Sport Regional Policies, Priorities and Strategies, we have embarked on consultations aimed at developing a Regional Protocol on Culture. We are also in the process of preparing a Regional Ministerial Conference on Culture and Development, an event that will bring together government officials drawn from ministries responsible for culture, finance and tourism, education, NGOs, international cooperating partners, and institutions involved in funding culture. This event is scheduled for late November of 1999.

The organizers of this conference have asked me to address the documentation, transmission, and revitalization of culture and the implications of working with grassroots and tradition-bearing communities and with responsible state institutions (archives, regional associations of folklorists, etc.) in the Southern African Development Community. To do this, I will relate the experience we have had in moving towards the establishment of our own regional databank, the Southern African Cultural Information Systems (SACIS), a project aimed at collecting, processing, and disseminating cultural information as a way of enhancing cooperation, interaction, and complementarity.

The Southern African Development Community is an organization of fourteen sovereign states established in 1992 and aimed at promoting regional cooperation and integration. SADC Member States are, by virtue of their membership in the organization, committed to working together towards a common future. SADC Member States are expected to derive benefits on an equal basis.

The creation and strengthening of regional cooperation blocks is part of the Organization of African Unity (OAU) strategy as laid down in the first stage of the 1991 Abuja Treaty. This treaty states that "the [African] Community shall be established gradually in six stages of variable duration over a transitional period not exceeding 34 years." The important role that culture plays in the Regional Integration Agenda has been recognized within SADC as one that can successfully bring grassroots involvement. The SADC Declaration of Heads of State and Government issued in 1992 states that "regional integration will continue to be a pipe dream unless the peoples of the region determine its content, form its direction, and are themselves its active agent." The treaty itself declares that one of the objectives of this regional organization is "to strengthen and consolidate the long standing historical, social and cultural affinities and links among the peoples of the region." Since its inception, SADC has taken the political view that its Regional Integration Agenda must be driven by the people and their will to live together and share in a common destiny. Administratively, SADC has taken a decentralized approach in which each Member State is given a sector to coordinate. Mozambique is responsible for the Sector for Culture, Information and Sport, the sector mandated to strengthen and consolidate the social and historical links among the people of the region. As I have already indicated, this paper concentrates on our own experience, which we hope will empower and involve local participation in arts and culture databanking, exposition, and protection. This experience rotates around SACIS.

The Southern African Information Systems (SACIS)

Rationale, Objectives, and Content

For a country or for a region like SADC to plan ahead, there is a need to know what obtains on the ground and how the available potential and resources can fit in a larger national or regional system. It is often disappointing to learn that local, national, and regional initiatives and infrastructures exist but are not fully exploited by others simply because those capacities do not come to their notice. It is also disappointing at times to observe that each artist, institution, or government attempts to reinvent the wheel with meager resources, skills, and capacities. An inventory of the initiatives, facilities, and infrastructures will get the region to know what obtains where and how such resources or potentialities can be utilized for the benefit of a single country or the entire region. To begin the process of developing such an inventory, SADC launched in 1996 the regional cultural databank known as the Southern African Cultural Information Systems. As indicated above, the idea of establishing a regional databank stems from the fact that the region felt that it would be difficult to launch regional cooperation without first having established an inventory of what obtains in each Member State. Therefore, the main objectives of SACIS are to:

- establish a systematic information base on arts and culture and institutions involved in their development in the region;
- establish a system that will allow accessibility to information by experts and the public in general including art and culture institutions and groups;
- publish information on cultural aspects of the region periodically.

Following from the objectives above, it is clear that SACIS is intended to be an information and management tool for all those concerned with documenting, processing, and disseminating culture, its products, and events. This explains why the initial focus of SACIS will be on the following areas:

- cultural producers and their products. This is the case of cultural enterprises, institutions, and groups, as well as their activities and the products of their activities
- markets for cultural products and events, that is, festivals, fairs, and exhibitions
- cultural policies, conventions, legislation, and copyrights
- languages of SADC

As will be explained later on, the collection of information on these subjects will not be the responsibility of governments alone. The governments will initiate the identification and sensitization of institutions — be these parastatal, private, or non-governmental — to enter into the SACIS network by providing information about them and their activities or by undertaking activities identified in the database.

Beneficiaries, Administration, and Products of SACIS

Right from its launch, SACIS had to identify its beneficiaries. These are intended to be those working in arts and culture both in the development of cultural activities (e.g., artists, arts promoters, researchers, and cultural institutions) and at the level of administration or facilitation of cultural development (e.g., government agenciess, NGOs, and cooperating partners). SACIS will thus contribute to filling in the gap about cultural information in the region, for the region itself and for the rest of the world. Perhaps at this point a question may be asked as to how SACIS will contribute to the work of libraries, archives, local associations, and communities. In my view a number of factors will make those goals realizable. First, SACIS data collection is meant to be participatory, drawing into the network more and more institutions and individuals. SACIS is coordinated by the Sector Coordinating Unit (SCU) in Maputo, Mozambique. In each Member State a national coordinator has been appointed and takes charge of coordinating data collection from the various national institutions that can provide the data relevant to the contents defined regionally. Once processed nationally, the data are then sent to the regional coordinating unit, where they are consolidated and then sent back to each contributing institution through the national coordinator. This means that national and local institutions begin to have a more complete picture of what happens nationally and regionally. They become aware of the potentialities that can be exploited for their own good, be these facilities, events, or opportunities, say, for training. Furthermore, SACIS offers the opportunity for institutions and individuals to experiment with what they learn from others in the SACIS network. Even from the difficulties and mistakes committed by others we learn.

I have been speaking about the participatory nature of SACIS. I now want to bring in the other dimension: that SACIS is also a multi-tiered project catering to both the grassroots and academic levels. Let us consider the thinking being developed for greater grassroots participation and involvement.

A project aimed at the development of telecenters has been drafted by the SCU to serve local communities. Through these telecenters, local communities, cultural associations, and groups could be trained to collect, process, and retrieve data electronically. They would also be trained in basic methods of data collection and database maintenance. This way the region can expand on its capacity to generate and exchange information and contribute to regional cooperation and development.

On an experimental basis, the SCU launched its first catalogue on cultural information of the region last May. This catalogue contains information only from some Member States, but it does give an indication of the wealth of data that would be available to the telecenters. While funding is not available for the development of such telecenters, the SCU is working towards making the information that is being collected available electronically. The other side of the coin is the contribution that SACIS can make to universities, libraries, archives, and professional, hobbyist, and other voluntary associations.

With funding from the Icelandic International Development Agency (ICEIDA) and UNESCO, we have begun to experiment with this. Following the successful staging of the

SADC Theatre Festival in Maputo in June 1997, the SCU approached representatives of each SADC country to write a piece on the status of theater in their home country. Working with the Southern African Broadcasting Association (SABA), the SCU has also begun a process of identifying contributors to another book reviewing the history of use of local languages in the media. The sector is also in the process of establishing links with the Linguistic Association of SADC Universities (LASU) to undertake the production of a SADC Linguistic Atlas. The underlying idea in all these projects is that by bringing those individual contributions together a regional picture is generated. This is important for individual contributors and readers, who begin to realize the potential, the problems, and the opportunities that are available in the region. This is also in line with SACIS' intent to present SADC as a regional cultural unity and to use culture as a central ingredient in regional grassroots participation and involvement with the regional integration agenda.

In our view, the SACIS project will grow to have the ability to link local communities and institutions involved with collection and dissemination of cultural information such as archives, libraries, and cultural associations in the region. Apart from the catalogue mentioned above, we are also commissioning papers that will give readers a regional picture of events. We have just completed editing a book on theater.

Problems, Limitations, and Prospects

The first major problem to be addressed is a lack of information collection and information exchange. We need to drive it home that information is power and a tool for development. We need to enhance the urge for collection and make information available in a timely manner to others who may benefit from it — not keep it to ourselves, sometimes only in our heads.

Trying to encourage the region to collect and exchange more of the available information, the patron of SACIS, Deputy Vice-Chancellor of Eduardo Mondlane University and Informatics Engineer Massingue, wrote in the first catalogue of SACIS, "When we keep our money under the mattress it may fill our hearts with joy that we own it. But at the same time the risks of it being eaten away by mice or devoured by fire are not to be discounted. When the same money is deposited in a bank it earns us interest, but more importantly it is shared by a wider society."

The second problem to be addressed is that of infrastructure. There is a need to provide equipment and appropriate working conditions. Sometimes, the problem may not necessarily be the availability of such facilities but may have its root in the rationalization of what is already available. In order to optimize what is or what is to be available, there may be a need for expert advice, which may be called upon from within other partner sectors.

The third area to be addressed is that of human resources. Already SACIS national coordinators have been appointed. However, if the network is to expand, training will become a necessity. This training, as I have indicated, will include both basic skills in data collection and computer and database use and maintenance. Such training should impress the members of the network on the need to work together for mutual benefit.

The final point to be made relates to international cooperation, which will complement the regional and national efforts. It is critical that SACIS receive the necessary support from the international community. With this in mind, the recent meeting of the Ministers of Culture, Information and Sport took the decision to request the UNESCO Director-General to support this project.

Conclusion

Taking into account the fact that SACIS, working on its own or with other institutions at the regional level, consolidates information emanating from national databanks, individuals, or institutions, we are of the view that those involved will in the end have a clear picture of what is available where, and thus will initiate direct contact with those institutions and organizations. The interest for such contact can be generated by some publications, events, training facilities, or exchange programs. The point is that with availability of information, it is possible for each institution to plan ahead to take advantage of the infrastructure, skills, and possibilities within the country and in the region. SACIS is an example of a regional cooperation mechanism set up by SADC in order to collect and exchange cultural data. Through this mechanism, local communities and organizations as well as governments will be able to develop a regional picture and take advantage of the facilities, skills, and possibilities that obtain in the region. SACIS is also expected to benefit those from other regions including other cultural organizations.

References

Chasle, R., and M. Hudym. 1992. *ACP-EEC Intercultural Dialogue: A Step in Development Cooperation*. Brussels: Foundation for ACP-EEC Cultural Cooperation.

Davis, Shelton H., and Katrinka Ebbe. 1995. *Traditional Knowledge and Sustainable Development*. Washington, DC: International Bank for Reconstruction and Development/The World Bank.

Matusse, R. 1995. The State of Social Sciences in Mozambique: The ARPAC Standpoint. Paper presented at the conference On the State of Humanities in Africa, 29 November–1 December, Nairobi, Kenya.

_____. 1995. Indigenous People and People-Centred Development: Are We Moving South to Meet Ourselves? Paper presented at the Regional Workshop, 23–28 April, Kwazulu Natal, South Africa.

Preserving Bahamian Heritage

Gail Saunders
Director
Department of Archives
The Bahamas

I have been involved with the preservation of Bahamian heritage and culture since the late 1960s, when I began the survey of the records and archives of The Bahamas. Since that time much has happened. The Bahamas established a Public Records Office (National Archives) in 1971. In 1972, the office promulgated rules to regulate searches and inspections of records, the destruction and disposal of public records, and the setting of fees for copying services. Over the next several years, the records and archives were identified, selected, sorted, and listed, staff were trained in various aspects of the work, a repair-bindery and a microfilming program were established, a Research Room became operational, and a Records Management Program was established.

A Guide to the Archives was published in 1973. From a very early time in the Archives' existence, exhibitions were held annually and facsimile booklets printed and distributed to schools and sold to the general public. An Oral History Program was also begun by interviewing and recording on cassette tapes scores of senior citizens. Some transcriptions were completed.

In the absence of a National Museum System, the Department of Archives was designated as the organization in charge of the Bahamas' material heritage — its historic buildings and sites, and its archaeology.

I have worked with a small group of professionals, particularly two enthusiastic and well-qualified history and social studies teachers, Ms. Grace Turner and Ms. Kim Outten from the mid-1980s. Consulting archaeologists Anthony Aarons worked with us between 1988 and 1993 and Dr. Keith Tinker from 1997 to the present. Together, we worked as a team to conserve The Bahamas' material culture. The Department of Archives spearheaded and controlled archaeological projects — the documentation and preservation of historic buildings, the curation of artifacts, and the establishment of a number of museums. The latter included the restoration of Vendue House, a former slave market, and its transformation into the Pompey Museum of Slavery and Emancipation in 1993. Similarly, the Department of Archives also advised and worked with the Central Bank of The Bahamas to restore and refurbish Balcony House, now the Balcony House Museum. The department also set up exhibits in the restored Commissioner's Office and jail in San Salvador, which is now the San Salvador Museum. Preparations are being made to organize museum exhibits at the Long Island Museum.

In cooperation with the Preservation of Historic Buildings Committee of the Bahamas National Trust, the Department of Archives' museum section prepared a Register (list) of Historic Places of New Providence, which was presented to Minister of Education Mr. C.A. Smith in 1993. The Register of Family Islands' historic places is in progress.

In the years leading up to the Quincentennary celebrations, there was feverish activity. The Museum Section advised on and participated in the building of a number of Lucayan *canayes* and also a Lucayan village in San Salvador, which was constructed in 1992. The first Lucayan canaye was developed in May 1992 from plans prepared by Mr. Tony Aarons at the Bahamas National Trust. Included among those constructed were one on the grounds of the Department of Archives, one at the Quincentennial Commission, and one in the Spanish Wells Museum.

Since 1991, the Department of Archives assisted the Ministries of Transport and Finance in the administration of *The Abandoned Wreck Act* (1965) by reviewing salvage permits issued, verifying inventories of artifacts, and giving advice on Government's selection of historic artifacts.

Recently, the Director of Archives and two museologists (curators) have been involved in the National Gallery Committee, which is restoring the nineteenth-century mansion Villa Doyle and converting it into the National Art Gallery.

Not only did the Department of Archives strive to preserve and conserve; it also sought to disseminate historical information which had been largely neglected in the past. It prepared guides, booklets, and a newspaper series, "Aspects of Bahamian History." Additionally, the director was involved with producing a video, *The Bahamas: History and Culture,* which is shown to students and visitors who visit the Archives and the Museum. The director and professional staff also gave numerous talks and lectures to schools, Rotary Clubs, tourism training courses, and various groups.

From early in its history, the Bahamas Archives recognized the importance of creating ties with international and regional bodies. The Archivist assisted in revitalizing the Caribbean Historical Archives Association (CARBICA) and organized an executive meeting in Nassau in 1972. At its conference in Guadeloupe in 1975, I was elected President for four years. The third Caribbean Archives Conference was hosted by the Bahamas Archives in 1979. I also served as secretary and treasurer of CARBICA and Deputy Director. Ms. Elaine Toote is now Treasurer of the organization. CARBICA has served to strengthen and maintain relations between Caribbean archival and archive-related institutions. It has also fostered cooperation and training through the convening of seminars and conferences. The Caribbean Region has been actively engaged in testing the International Records Management Trust Training modules for Archives Administration and Records Management. This has affected the education of archivists and policy formation in the region.

The Department of Archives is also a longstanding member of the International Council on Archives (ICA), the Commonwealth Archivists Association, the American Society of Archivists, the Society of Archivists (Great Britain), and the British Records Association. I served as a member of the executive of the International Council on Archives between 1974 and 1982. The Department of Archives has been mainly involved with the preservation and transmission of tangible cultural heritage. However, it has also contributed significantly to the documentation, preservation, and dissemination of intangible cultural heritage.

I was chosen, as director of The Bahamas Archives, to head the research component, acting as Bahamian curator for the Smithsonian's Folklife Festival in 1994, which featured The Bahamas. Archives staff served as researchers and coordinators for the festival.

Our participation in the Smithsonian's Folklife Festival in 1994 was a significant milestone in the preservation, transmission, and revitalization of intangible culture. The Festival project generated important records including oral history interviews on cassette and video tapes. A wonderful half-hour video was made by the Ministry of Tourism, the coordinating agency for the Festival, showing highlights of Bahamian participation in the planning and staging of the actual Festival. Also produced was a compact disc of folk music by musicians who performed at the Festival, entitled *Islands of Song.*

An educational and cultural kit entitled "Our Bahamian Heritage: A Resource Guide for Teachers" was compiled by the Ministry of Education, the Smithsonian Center for Folklife Programs and Cultural Studies, and the Embassy of the Commonwealth of The Bahamas and produced in 1995. The Resource Guide includes primary level and secondary level sections. The primary level section covers crafts and folk art, music, storytelling, foodways, and celebrations. Included in the secondary level Resource Guide are the same topics, but with additions of an essay on "The Peoples and Cultures of The Bahamas," and a guideline to research entitled "Exploring Your Own Communities." There is also an appendix with additional materials.

The kit also contains two videos, *To Be a Bahamian* and *Island Portraits: Traditional Culture in Andros,* and two audio cassettes with sacred songs and storytelling in The Bahamas. There are also color posters on various aspects of culture such as "Living by Land and Sea," "Making a Basket," "Making Music," "Home Life on a Family Island," "Religious Celebrations," and "Family Names in The Bahamas." The education kit is a wonderful resource for teachers. It is filled with information not usually found in history books and also has suggested questions and activities.

Since 1994 and The Bahamas' participation in the Smithsonian Folklife Festival, there has been a renaissance in the preservation and transmission of the country's cultural heritage. Junkanoo artists have been more active, and many of the artists have become entrepreneurs by creating souvenirs using Junkanoo themes and materials. In 1996, the Junkanoo participants at the 1994 Festival were invited back to perform on the Mall at the Smithsonian Folklife Festival to celebrate Independence Day in the United States. Jackson Burnside, an architect and Junkanoo artist, developed a colorful studio "Doongalik," which features Junkanoo arts, paintings, crafts, and publishing. It also displays traditional elite and folk architecture. Mr. Burnside now hosts a weekly radio show on Junkanoo. Groups also perform at the Ministry of Tourism's "Junkanoo in June" Festival.

Stimulated by the Smithsonian Folklife Festival, The Bahamas' government developed a Heritage Village (or Park) now known as the "Down Home Fish Fry." This village contains vernacular houses, a storytelling porch, a concert stage, and an outdoor oven. It adjoins the conch village developed by the Conch Vendors Association and is the site for various festivals, such as the Sea Food Festival in October and Junkanoo in June which sponsors food and craft vendors and Junkanooers who hold rush-outs every weekend in June.

Additionally, one of the researchers and coordinators of the Bahamian Smithsonian team, Kayla Edwards, now hosts a television program "Mirror, Mirror" which showcases Bahamian history and culture. Former General Manager and Minister of Government Charles Carter hosts a weekly radio program which presents Bahamian folklorists, historians, musicians, and artists.

The Bahamas has also made strides to protect, preserve, and regulate both tangible and intangible heritage. The tangible heritage will be protected by the *Antiquities, Monuments, and Museum Act of 1998,* which comes into operation on 1 July 1999. The Act provides for the declaration and preservation of historical monuments and sites, regulates archaeological excavations, and establishes the National Museum of The Bahamas. It establishes regulations for issuing licenses and permits and provides for preservation, conservation, and restoration. It provides for analysis, documentation, and presentation of antiquities and monuments and for the establishment, operation, and administration of a conservation, archaeological, and paleontological research unit, and of the historical site unit of the National Museum.

The Copyright Act of 1998, enforced from 1 July 1999, makes better provision for the protection of intangible heritage, specifically the rights of performers and others in live performances, such as drama, music, choreography, or recital of a literary work. It also protects authorship of literary, musical, choreographic, audiovisual, and artistic works, motion pictures, and sound recordings.

I feel that I have been fortunate to live at this very exciting and creative time in our history. Much has been achieved in developing new heritage institutions and in preserving the traditional institutions of culture and heritage. It has been an interesting, stimulating, and gratifying experience, and I hope that the current positive trends in preservation, conservation, and transmission of both our tangible and intangible cultural heritage will continue.

Aspects dynamiques des cultures sonores: transformation du métier du griot au Niger sous l'influence du modernisme

Mahaman Garba
Ethnomusicologist
Centre de Formation et de Promotion Musicale
Niamey, Niger

Au Niger, l'exercice des fonctions du griot est dû à une formation spécifique qui lui confère un savoir et un savoir-faire appropriés. De ce fait, dans la société traditionnelle d'antan, le griot ne remplissait des fonctions que dans le domaine qui lui était héréditaire et qu'il maîtrisait parfaitement.

Maître de la parole, fidèle gardien de la tradition orale, conservateur incontesté des moeurs ancestrales, le griot est un personnage qui joue un rôle social très important. Son statut fait de lui le conseiller le plus éclairé et le plus proche du roi, du prince ou du chef de guerre.

Le griot et la société

Le griot joue un rôle prépondérant dans la société. Conteur, poète, moraliste, instructeur, le griot est l'animateur principal de la société dans laquelle il vit. Il est toujours sollicité à prendre part aux grandes cérémonies (mariage, baptême, intronisation, fêtes). Le griot apprend aux jeunes l'histoire de leur société, il leur parle des grands chefs, leurs comportements et leurs règnes. Il leur dit également tous ceux qui ont fait des oeuvres utiles, il leur parle de leurs descendances en leur apprenant les bonnes manières. Dans certaines circonstances le griot est la seule personne habilitée à calmer les tensions sociales. Certains hommes le consultent avant de prendre épouse parce qu'il est mieux placé pour parler de telle ou telle famille, de tel ou tel parent. Le griot joue également le rôle de communicateur et d'informateur. Déclamateur public, il a pour devoir de faire oralement les communiqués en se déplaçant de quartier en quartier, de village en village, de ville en ville.

Quand il y a parfois des divergences de vue entre deux ou plusieurs autorités coutumières, le griot est chargé de recueillir tous les renseignements indispensables lui permettant de lever l'équivoque. En pareilles circonstances il est dépêché pour faire la mise au point à tel ou tel chef coutumier. Personnage très écouté, le griot intervient dans certains foyers pour régler des litiges.

Les ressources du griot

On naît griot, on ne le devient pas. L'art de la parole est un héritage qui se transmet de père en fils, de génération en génération. Le métier qu'exerce le griot lui permet de faire face à ses obligations. C'est un responsable qui a plusieurs bouches à nourrir. Il vit donc du fruit de son travail. Dans la hiérarchie de la cour, ses prérogatives lui donnent droit à un traitement. Il a également certains avantages aux différentes cérémonies qu'il anime.

Il se déplace souvent pour rendre des visites de courtoisie aux chefs coutumiers qu'il connaît. Ce périple lui rapporte de l'argent, des habits, des vivres, des chevaux, des moutons, des chèvres, etc.

Dans certains cas, le griot est invité par les chefs eux-mêmes ou par des personnes riches. Contrairement à ce que beaucoup de gens pensent, le griot n'est pas celui qui indispose et oblige les autres à lui donner. Comme tous ceux qui exercent un métier, le griot vit à la sueur de front.

Le rôle du griot dans la chefferie traditionnelle

Dans l'organigramme de la chefferie coutumière au Niger, le griot occupe une place importante et ses prérogatives sont nombreuses. Il est à la fois le confident, le secrétaire particulier, le conseiller et l'envoyer spécial du chef coutumier. Aucune décision ne peut être prise sans son consentement et son avis est toujours partagé par toute la hiérarchie de la cour.

Dépositaire de la tradition historique et culturelle, le griot est en somme le membre le plus influent de la cour parce que mieux renseigné que quiconque sur les valeurs traditionnelles, la généalogie des familles qui composent l'ethnie ou le groupe ethnique. Héritier de l'art de la parole, sa maîtrise de la langue lui permet de provoquer ou d'apaiser la colère du chef. Il enseigne beaucoup de choses au chef, lui dit le comportement de tel ou tel individu. Il sait tout sur les hommes et leurs biens. Il sert de courroie de transmission entre le chef et ses partenaires. Il est en quelque sorte le trait d'union entre le peuple et son histoire.

Autrefois, le griot était l'intouchable envoyé spécial du guerrier à qui il rapportait fidèlement les messages. Il n'était pas homme à abattre ou à capturer en temps de guerre. Il était utile pour tous ceux qui régnaient.

Le griot dans la société moderne

Avec les transformations qui interviennent dans nos sociétés en mutation, le problème de la fonction du griot se pose avec acuité. De nos jours l'édifice traditionnel n'a plus d'autonomie et de cohérence intrinsèque. Les phénomènes qui se déroulent trouvent leur origine dans ce qu'il est convenu d'appeler *"modernisme."* Aujourd'hui au Niger, la personnalité du griot est victime d'un étrange dédoublement: autrefois détenteur de la tradition orale, les changements sociaux actuels ont fait qu'aujourd'hui peu d'éloges sont dignes de ses mérites. La prolifération de nouveaux griots qui n'ont pas hérité le métier mais en font tout de même un gagne-pain, explique clairement le climat d'hostilité qui caractérise aujourd'hui la condition des vrais griots (hommes de caste).

La modernisation des traditions musicales: cause de la transformation du métier de griot

L'islamisation et la colonisation (le modernisme aidant) ont fait que les fondements culturels et sociaux se sont effrités au Niger. Les structures sociales se sont progressivement vidées de leur finalité et de leur forme originelle. La vie moderne a presque mis fin aux initiatives. L'école occidentale a remplacé le cadre de formation d'antan. Les rapports sociaux sont devenus plus ou moins individualistes. L'ancienne organisation est supplantée par l'Etat national moderne. La vie culturelle est modifiée. Le virus de l'occidentalisation s'est greffé sur nos valeurs traditionnelles. Ces changements d'activités, de problèmes, de rythme de vie ont provoqué une désaffection des pratiques ancestrales. Ce qui du coup a modifié les traditions musicales, entraînant ainsi un changement de comportement du griot de caste. La transformation des traditions musicales a pour base les facteurs suivants: l'Islam, la colonisation, l'européanisation, la modernisation (le développement technologique), les calamités naturelles (famine, sécheresse), l'usage de la musique pour des intérêts politiques et l'indifférence des responsables politiques.

L'Islam

L'islamisation a amené certains griots à abandonner la pratique des musiques rituelles en rapport avec les génies. Le mouvement d'islamisation est à la base de la disparition progressive de certains genres musicaux notamment les musiques de possession. Dans certains lieux, l'impact moralisateur des fanatiques aboutit à l'interdiction de pratiques sociales, ce qui provoque un appauvrissement du répertoire musical. Beaucoup de traditions sont ainsi tombées en désuétude. Des griots, en grand nombre, ont abandonné leur profession pour se consacrer à l'étude du Coran. Ils interdisent à leurs enfants de pratiquer la musique. Ils préfèrent les orienter vers l'école coranique. On voit donc un rejet de la caste sous l'influence de l'Islam.

La colonisation: le griot et le pouvoir traditionnel

Sous la colonisation l'autorité des descendants des rois se réduit quelque part à celle d'une simple chefferie de village. Sur le plan social, les chefs ne sont plus les descendants des rois ou des guerriers, mais des hommes libres, élus sous l'égide de l'administration. L'organisation traditionnelle n'a plus sa rigueur d'antan. De nouveaux hommes dont la puissance relève de celle de l'administration moderne viennent grossir le rang des nobles.

Etant donné que les hommes forts ne sont plus les descendants des héros d'autrefois, le griot se lie désormais aux riches quelle que soit leur descendance. Il les loue pourvu qu'ils soient en mesure de satisfaire ses divers besoins.

L'Européanisation

Le besoin d'acculturation et de déculturation (dans le sens de la modernisation des moeurs) a créé un complexe d'infériorité chez les griots ainsi que certains de leurs enfants. La génération actuelle de parents griots a tendance à mépriser son propre statut et considère le métier comme peu profitable. Ces parents préfèrent orienter leurs fils dans d'autres domaines techniques ou scolaires. Les fils de griots, une fois alphabétisés à l'école occidentale, refusent de pratiquer leur métier de caste. Et pis encore, ils vont jusqu'à cacher leur propre identité et fuient l'appellation de griot. Cependant, certains griots s'efforcent d'assurer la perpétuation de la profession par leurs fils. Mais d'autres jeunes, bien qu'issus de la caste de griots, refusent d'assurer la relève.

La modernisation

Sous l'influence du courant moderniste, de nombreuses danses traditionnelles, des chants récréatifs et éducatifs pour enfants sont abandonnés. Les séances de distraction, les veillées de contes et de devinettes ont été remplacées par des loisirs nouveaux: la télévision, les bals, les surprises-parties, le cinéma, les orchestres modernes, etc.

Les mariages des "intellectuels" ne se déroulent plus comme traditionnellement; ils ne donnent plus lieu aux mêmes types de cérémonies, de rituels, de manifestations de réjouissances, accompagnés de chants et danses animés par les griots. Après les cérémonies religieuses célébrant le mariage, le couple et ses amis se retrouvent chaque soir pour danser au son du tourne-disque pendant une *semaine*. Ce passe-temps communément appelé "semaine" se termine par un bal. Les tambours sont exclus de ces cérémonies de mariage dans les grandes villes et mêmes dans certains villages. Il est aussi regrettable de remarquer que la répercussion des moyens modernes d'information et d'animation (radio, télévision, journaux, chaîne, etc.) tendent reléguer le rôle du griot au second plan et à se passer de ses services.

Si la technologie moderne est en passe de tuer la culture traditionnelle vivante, au moins a-t-elle la possibilité et le mérite de la préserver, à titre documentaire, par des enregistrements, des films, des livres, etc. Cette évocation est un avertissement face au processus de déracinement qui risque de nous laisser ni noirs, ni blancs ni métisses. Car, quoi que nous fassions, nous ne maîtriserions aucune des données culturelles des deux civilisations et de leurs dérivés. Il nous paraît donc nécessaire voire indispensable, pour le maintien d'un certain équilibre psycho-culturel, qu'une symbiose progressive des valeurs traditionnelles et modernes puisse s'effectuer, et non une destruction brutale et forcée d'une civilisation sur l'autre.

Calamités naturelles et difficultés économiques

Il est impossible d'isoler l'aspect économique de l'ensemble des facteurs qui expliquent ou concourent au changement d'attitude du griot. Le chômage rural a entraîné un fort courant d'émigration. Les départs vers les villes continuent pour les paysans paupérisés, exposés aux famines et aux difficultés de la vie. Cette émigration accélère à son tour le développement du chômage dans les villes. Certains jeunes venus de la campagne, préférant le gain facile aux autres métiers, s'adonnent à la pratique musicale sans le savoir héréditaire, sans connaissance aucune des règles de bienséance de caste.

De nos jours, les difficultés économiques et l'incapacité de certains chefs coutumiers à subvenir aux besoins des griots de caste ont provoqué une rupture entre les deux parties. Fort de cette incapacité, le griot se lie aux personnes en mesure de satisfaire ses besoins. Constat du griot traditionnel, il ne reste plus que l'image d'un griot déclamateur de louanges, ambulant et parasite ayant pour source d'inspiration la flatterie. Malgré tout, il existe encore dans les cours des dignitaires traditionnels, des griots professionnels, détenteurs d'un vaste répertoire et d'une technique élaborée.

L'usage de la musique pour les intérêts politiques

Les événements de 1946–1960 ont eu leurs conséquences non seulement sur la vie politique du pays, mais aussi sur la vie culturelle, la musique inclue. C'est ainsi que l'évolution du pays, d'une société traditionnelle féodale pendant la domination coloniale à une république indépendante, justifie la distinction d'une culture musicale avant et après 1960.

La première est dominée par la musique ancestrale: musique de cour des dignitaires, des corps de métiers, des religions du terroir et musique populaire. La seconde est détournée de ses fonctions par le pouvoir politique né des républiques. Cette situation entraîne le dévoiement de quelques instruments et la disparition partielle ou totale de certains genres musicaux authentiques. De cet effritement naîtront la musique néo-traditionnelle et la musique populaire moderne d'impact urbain.

Les musiciens pour leur part étaient amenés, volontairement ou sous des pressions idéologiques, à chanter pour les nouveaux chefs administratifs. L'accès à l'indépendance et la restructuration de l'Etat nigérien ont influencé et influencent encore toute la culture musicale, bouleversant parfois son mode de transmission.

La vie musicale avant 1960

En 1946, le Niger a pris un autre tournant avec les différentes tendances politiques créés à l'époque (le Parti Progressiste Nigérien pour le Rassemblement Africain PPN-RDA, le SAWABA). Aussitôt les griots et musiciens intégrés ont choisi de chanter pour les leaders et membres des partis politiques existants. Ainsi naissait la musique de louanges propagandistes adressées aux personnalités politiques et administratives. Le griot est donc mis au service des riches en quête de popularité aux détriments des chefs coutumiers.

La vie musicale de 1960 à 1987

Depuis l'intronisation de la semaine de la jeunesse, les musiques néo-traditionnelles et folkloriques ont pris le pas sur les formes traditionnelles. Bien entendu, les inconvénients inhérents à cette nouvelle conception de l'art musical sont nombreux. Les musiques sacrées sont banalisées dans leur exécution sur la scène. Les dignitaires quant à eux, détournent la musique de ses fonctions originelles: le répertoire musical est cousu de louanges orientées vers le culte de la personnalité. Les intérêts politiques sont donc la motivation profonde de cette nouvelle orientation qui veut que les musiciens vantent le pouvoir. Mais, en règle générale, les artistes musiciens sont comme des canards sauvages: quand on les met en cage, ils perdent le sens de l'orientation.

Pour reprendre A. Tierou (1983, 117–18), "politiser la musique, ou en faire un moyen de vanter le pouvoir, ou une arme idéologique c 'est tuer à jamais la libération, la spontanéité du génie artistique et l'authenticité."

A partir de 1960, on a donc assisté à la banalisation de certaines musiques séculaires parce qu'elles ont été destinées à des personnes qui n'y avaient pas le droit. Des griots de caste accueillaient parfois des autorités politiques en visite avec leurs ensembles de parade. Ils étaient tenus à chanter leurs louanges. Les connaissances du griot étaient utilisées à des fins politiques. Une majorité de griots déstabilisés par la pression du pouvoir ont abandonné les louanges aux chefs traditionnels pour se lancer dans ce qu'il est convenu d'appeler le culte de la personnalité. Cette situation a duré quinze années au cours desquelles toutes les chansons de l'époque furent créées en l'honneur des autorités gouvernementales, nationales ou locales. Ainsi les préoccupations politiques personnelles passaient avant les motivations culturelles.

Dans un article intitulé "La chanson féminine son ghay-zarma et l'évolution socio-politique au Niger" (1999:3) Boubé Salay Bali abonde dans le même sens: A partir de 1965, la chanson féminine songhay-zarma a été intégrée dans la nouvelle donne. Les cantatrices du *zalay* et du *post-zalay*[1] ont participé activement à la vie politique en ne chantant que pour les hautes personnalités telles que le président de la République, le président de l'Assemblée nationale et les ministres généreux.

De l'autre côté, les jeunes ont été groupés au sein des troupes mixtes. Des festivals sont organisés pour détecter les talents et les voix de rossignols. Deux événements culturels ont marqué la période moderne, la semaine de la jeunesse RDA (1965–1974) et le festival national de la jeunesse sous le régime militaire de Seyni Kountché (1974–1987).

A travers ces deux festivals, la chanson n'est considérée comme un art de divertissement, un art d'épanchement, mais un moyen de propagande politique et idéologique au service des dirigeants. La notion de griot disparaît au profit de troupes, jeunes filles, animateurs de la *Samaria*,[2] etc.

Le culte de la personnalité est cultivé avec un zèle débonnaire. La vie musicale des griots de notre pays a évolué ainsi de 1960 à 1974, année dans laquelle les militaires prenaient les rênes du pouvoir. Quelle ne fut en 1974 la surprise du monde des griots très fieffé à l'ancien pouvoir de se voir interdire de manifestation. Au demeurant la mise en garde était sans ambages. Pas une seule chanson et pour le régime militaire et pour ses chefs. Kountché a été clair à ce niveau. Et connaissant la sévérité du pouvoir et le respect qu'il incarnait aux yeux du peuple, les griots changent le fusil d'épaules. C'est à dire que pendant tout le règne du Conseil Militaire Suprême (C.M.S), les griots ont observé une sorte de pause. Surtout pour les griots qui ne savaient rien faire d'autres que de proférer des louanges.

Cette période va pourtant connaître des changements avec la mort de Kountché en 1987 et l'avènement de la décrispation. Tout pourrait alors reprendre. Tout est libéralisé; l'économie comme la chanson. Ali Saïbou voulait ainsi réaliser le "grand pardon".

Des groupes naissent. Ils sont souvent un mélange de chansons de griots et de création. Dans le même temps la profession du griot est devenue hybride. On ne différencie plus qui est griot, qui est artiste. Seuls les instruments utilisés permettent souvent de se faire une idée du griot ou du genre musical.

Le griot dans un système démocratique

A partir de 1990, avec l'avènement de la démocratie, on assiste à la réhabilitation de la chanson politique. Le seuil des années 1960 est rattrapé et même dépassé. Flash back. Chaque parti a ses artistes ou ses griots, mais fondamentalement dans la confusion et le dénigrement. Cette tendance n'a pas été interrompue ni par la conférence nationale ni par le régime de la transition de la deuxième, troisième ou quatrième république.

L'avènement de la démocratie au Niger a largement contribué à la naissance d'une race de griots propagandistes, à l'image de ceux du temps du RDA qui excellaient dans l'art de la calomnie. Le multipartisme a fait naître des partis politiques tels que le MNSD-NASSARA, le CDS-RAHAMA, le PNDSTARAYA, l'ANDP-ZAMAN LAHIYA pour ne citer que ceux-là. Les adorateurs du gain facile qui prétendent être griots, sans formation ni expérience, se lancent aveuglement dans la pratique musicale.

Attisant la haine entre partis politiques, ces trafiquants de conscience vont jusqu'à tenir des propos désagréables à l'endroit de tel leader pour favoriser tel autre. Mordus par le virus de la délation mais surtout dévorés par la fièvre des sous, ils n'ont d'yeux que pour ceux qui leur mouillent la barbe. Habitués au retournement de la veste, infidèles à leurs engagements, ces nouveaux griots sont craints de tous dans la mesure où tout le monde a compris qu'ils ne visent que leurs propres intérêts. Ils changent de partis comme un caméléon change de couleurs. Le griot de l'ère démocratique est devenu lui-même un politicien qui vend sa voix à qui le veut. Il est arrivé qu'un griot comme Dan Kabo qui ne tarissait pas d'éloges à l'endroit de l'ancien président Mahamane Ousmane quitte le CDS-Raliama. Celui-ci a fini par regagner les rangs du parti de la mouvance présidentielle d'alors le RDP Jama'a. Et comme si le griot n'est pas celui qui cherche des présents, dans un communiqué radiodiffusé Dan Kabo va jusqu'à interdire son parti d'origine (CDS-Rahama) d'utiliser ses chansons composées au nom du dit parti alors qu'en contre-partie, Dan Kabo avait bénéficié d'un traitement à l'époque.

Un griot n'a pas de parti mais il est de toutes les parties. Dans le contexte traditionnel, le griot était fidèlement attaché au chef coutumier; maître de la parole, source intarissable, il était incontournable. Dans le contexte moderne, le griot est devenu celui-là même qui bafoue la tradition.

La démocratie quant à elle, a fait du griot un professionnel de la calomnie, un apôtre de la médisance, un reptile à double langue.

Ce changement d'attitude du griot avait été ressenti en 1981, année dans laquelle un séminaire sur l'assainissement de la fonction du griot avait été organisé. Et pour cause! Plutôt que de jouer son rôle authentique et traditionnel, le griot a choisi la politique propagandiste. Ayant perdu de son honorabilité, il n'est plus le conteur poète, moraliste et confident du chef coutumier. Calomniateur zélé, le griot de la démocratie a pour mission d'empester le climat socio-politique, d'attiser la haine en mettant aux prises des adversaires politiques. Le constat est amer: les griots de cour et de la corporation ont fait place à une race de griots faucons, sans aucune expérience de la pratique musicale et des règles de bienséance liées au métier.

Depuis trente ans, nos griots sont restés dans cet égarement. Ils ne chantent que pour les dirigeants politiques qui les considèrent comme des individus bons à les couvrir d'éloges. Notre musique, nos chants et nos danses traditionnels, qui constituent une fierté nationale, sont en train de disparaître et rien n'indique que les générations à venir sauront un jour les interpréter. Il nous incombe de prendre dès maintenant les mesures qui s'imposent pour les préserver et les vivifier. Pour ce faire, il s'agira de mettre en valeur les hauts faits de notre histoire, les exploits de nos guerriers d'antan contre la domination étrangère, les récits de nos sages, les contes, les légendes, les proverbes, les devinettes et les comptines. Dans ce cas précis il est bon de retenir que *"la richesse et la diversité du patrimoine culturel font la grandeur d'un peuple."*

Les Nigériens dans leur ensemble ont le désir bien légitime de faire de leur pays une nation moderne et, dans cette perspective, les anciens pouvoirs locaux sont en train de perdre de leur notoriété. Cependant, il n'est pas inéluctable que ces modifications administratives *"nécessaires"* entraînent la disparition pure et simple du griot et de certains types de musique dont la fonction peut parfaitement évoluer tout comme les institutions auxquelles elles étaient ou sont encore liées.

A la lumière de ce qui se passe dans la pratique musicale, on constate que les griots se laissent égarer par la politique. D'autres abandonnent le métier pour des considérations religieuses. Le développement de la technologie est en passe de tuer la culture traditionnelle, sous prétexte qu'elle la préserve à titre documentaire. L'observateur attentif, lui, se pose une question: *Que deviendra le griot du deuxième millénaire?*

Notes

1. *Zalay* est un mot de langue Zarma. Zalay en un mot, fut la première révolution qu'a connue la chanson Zarma par sa démarcation de la conception classique de l'art. Le "Zalay", c'est aussi l'ère du mariage des instruments de musique et de la voix féminine. Le phénomène a vu le jour en 1942. Haoua ISSA dite "Hawa Zalay" en réclame la paternité.

   Le "zalay" dans le fond et la forme peut être considéré comme l'équivalent du romantisme, courant littérature et artistique du XIXème siècle en Europe par certains aspects notamment la remise en cause de l'autorité familiale la chanson comme art moderne capable de libérer l'être des contraintes sociales et de son milieu (Boubé Saley Bah, 1994, 31).

2. Organisation de jeunesse.

Bibliographie

Boube, Saley Bah. 1994. La chanson féminine Songhay-Zarrna et l'évolution socio-politique et culturelle au Niger. Conférence présentée dans le cadre des activités de la semaine de la femme, 8 mars.

Borel, François. 1991. Les musiques du quotidien. Rôles de la musique chez les Hawsa du Niger. In *Onde en musique,* Laurent Aubert, éd. Genève: Musée d'ethnographie, p. 39–48.

Camara, Sory. 1976. *Gens de la parole. Essai sur la condition et le rôle des griots dans la société malinké.* Paris la-Haye: Mouton.

Dioulde, L., S. Andres, A. Ousseini et A. Mariko. 1980. Le griot dans la société nigerienne. *Le Sahel* No. 29–30, 31 mars.

Garba, Mahaman. 1992. La Musique des hawsa du Niger. Strasbourg II, USH. Doctorat en ethnomusicologie.

_____ et Jacques Viret. 1992. La Vie musicale au Niger le choc des cultures. *Revue musicale de suisse romande* (3): 119–32 (septembre).

Karimoun, Mahaman. 1972. Rôle du griot dans la société Sonra-Zarma. *Annales de l'Université d'Abidjan. Sériel* 4: 99–102.

Kotchy, Berthélémy. 1971. Fonction sociale de la musique traditionnelle. *Présence Africaine* 93: 80–91.

Labouret, Henri. 1923. A propos du mot griot. *Notes Africaines* 50: 56–57 (avril).

Lichtenhan, Ernst. 1977. Musique sédentaire-musique nomade. In *Musique et société.* Neuchâtel: Musée d'ethnographie, p. 82–94.

Maiga, Ahmadou Djibrilla. 1978. *Le griot en milieu songhay. Mémoire de fin de cycle.* Bamako: Ecole Normale Supérieure.

Mariko, K. A. et A. Tazar. 1980. Griots, artistes et généalogistes en pays de langue hawsa. *Sahel hebdo* (10): 27–30 (du 28-01).

Mikel, Dufrenve. 1974. Art et politique, union générale d'edimois *coil. 10–18.* Paris, 519.

Ministere de la jeunesse des sports et de la culture. 1981. Séminaire national de définition du statut du griot. 16–31 janvier, Niamey.

Monteil, Vincent. 1968. Un cas d'économie ostentatoire: les griots d'Afrique noire. *Cahiers de l'institut des sciences économiques appliquées.* II (4): 773–791 (laboratoire de collège de France associé au CNRS).

Morseck, Boubacar. 1975. Griot et griotisme et la pratique du journalisme en Afrique. *Ethiopiques:* 20–26.

N'ketia, Kwabena. 1972. Les langages musicaux de l'Afrique Sub-Saharienne. Etude comparative. In *Actes de la réunion de Yaoundé* (23–27 Février 1970). La musique africaine. Paris: La revue musicale (288–89): 7-42.

_____. 1976. Le patrimoine musical africain et l'unité africaine. Séminaire culturel de O.U.A. sur la danse, la musique et le folklore africains. Annexe II: 1–17 (16–19 octobre, Addis-Ababa).

Nikiprowetzky, Tolia. 1963. Trois aspects de la musique africaine. In *Mauritanie-Sénégal-Niger*, Nagy, éd. Paris: OCORA.

Ousseini, Abdou. 1976. Essai d'interprétation des aspects ostentatoires et ambivalents dans la problématique du griot. Contribution à l'étude de la pérennité et de la prolifération des griots au Niger. Université II, Mémoire de Maîtrise (sciences sociales et psychologiques).

Sowande, Fela. 1972. Le rôle de la musique dans la société africaine traditionnelle In *Actes de la réunion de Yaoundé* (23–27 février 1970). La musique africaine. Paris: la revue musicale (288–89).

Tierou, Alphonse. 1983. *La danse africaine c'est la vie*. Paris: Maisonnettes et Larose.

Zanetti, Vincent. 1990. Le griot et le pouvoir. Une relation ambiguë. *Cahiers de musiques traditionnelles* (*Dossier:* musique et pouvoir) 3: 161–72.

Zemp, Hugo. 1964. Musiciens autochtones et griots malinkés chez les Dan de Côte d'ivoire. *Cahiers d'études qfricaines,* 15 4(3): 370–82.

_____.1967. Comment on devient musicien quatre exemples de l'ouest-africain. In *La Musique dans la vie,* Tolia Nikiprowetzky, éd. Paris: OCORA, p. 79–103.

Dynamic Aspects of Oral Cultures: Transformation of the Griot's Profession under the Influence of Modernism

Mahaman Garba
Summary by Dawn Elvis

In traditional society in Niger, the griot acquired his function by inheritance and specialized training. Repository of the history and cultural traditions of the society and master of the spoken word, he was poet, moralist, and teacher. As such, he was highly respected for his knowledge and wisdom in all aspects of life, and his counsel was sought by the traditional kings, chiefs, and warriors. Griot was an occupational calling, and its practice was thus the source of the griot's livelihood.

The role and functions of the griot began to change with the passage of the society from feudalism to modernism. The many influences responsible for the change can be listed as Islamization, colonialism, Europeanization, technological change, natural disasters, and the diversion of traditional music to serve political ends. Together these developments led to a progressive politicization of the function of the griot.

As power came to be associated less with the traditional chiefs and warriors and more with the new administrative structures and the political leaders of the era of the republics, the griot pandered to the new power elite, performing songs intended to falsely praise a particular politician or promote certain political groups. This period also witnessed a vulgarization of sacred music, as this music was performed for personages to whom it was not destined by tradition. This trend led to the disappearance of some instruments and some musical genres.

The griots were totally repressed after the military takeover of 1974. When the military ruler Seyni Kountché died in 1987, the general liberalization that followed gave rise to new performing groups who popularized the music. The griot's profession became a sort of hybrid in which it was no longer easy to differentiate the griot from the general artiste.

With the advent of democracy in 1990, a new kind of griot has emerged, the kind that excels in the art of defamation. Their role seems to be to stir up hatred among political adversaries, poisoning the socio-political atmosphere. They operate only in their own interest, willing to change political affiliation for personal gain. Flouting tradition, they evince no experience of the musical norms or of the rules of propriety associated with the griot's calling.

One wonders what will become of the griot in the third millennium. Traditional music, the songs and dances that constitute our national pride, are about to disappear. It is now incumbent upon us to take action to revive and preserve them. This can only be accomplished if we look with pride to our high achievements of the past: the exploits of our ancient warriors against foreign domination, the stories of our sages, and the tales, legends, proverbs, and riddles that make up our history.

Méthodes traditionnelles de transmission de l'oralité: l'exemple du Sosso-Bala

Namankoumba Kouyaté
Counselor for Political, Economic and Cultural Affairs
Embassy of the Republic of Guinea
Bonn, Germany

Introduction

Au coeur des débats sur le rôle et la valeur du patrimoine culturel immatériel, se trouve invariablement posée la problématique de sa conservation et de sa transmission, surtout en ce qui concerne les aspects relevant des traditions orales.

Reconnues depuis déjà plusieurs décennies comme source essentielle de l'identité de nombreuses populations dans le monde, les traditions orales constituent le matériau privilégié de l'histoire du continent africain. En raison de leur extrême fragilité, cette catégorie de sources se révèle comme difficilement manipulables. De surcroît, elle est exposée à des menaces sérieuses de destruction.

Dans un monde en pleine mutation technique et technologique où l'audio-visuel a réalisé des performances sans précédent dans tous les domaines, on est en droit de se demander quel sera l'avenir des cultures traditionnelles et populaires. En effet, face aux agressions culturelles de toutes sortes, il y a un danger réel de voir les traditions orales se désagréger, voire de disparaître de façon irrémédiable. Ce qui porterait un coup fatal aux efforts gigantesques déployés par l'UNESCO depuis un demi siècle pour promouvoir le multi-culturalisme, fondement et garant de la paix dans le monde.

Dès lors, on comprend aisément la nécessité d'une action urgente pour protéger le patrimoine culturel immatériel de l'humanité et surtout d'assurer sa conservation efficace et sa transmission méthodique aux générations montantes.

C'est ici qu'apparaît toute la pertinence de la présente conférence qui voudrait faire une "évaluation globale de la recommandation de 1989 sur la sauvegarde de la culture traditionnelle et populaire: pleine participation locale et coopération internationale". Certes, de gros efforts ont été réalisés dans chacun des Etats membres de l'UNESCO pour la sauvegarde du patrimoine oral national, mais ces efforts n'ont pas toujours abouti aux résultats escomptés pour différentes raisons.

Le manque de moyens matériels et financiers de certains gouvernements et le mauvais choix des cibles à sauvegarder expliquent en partie l'échec des politiques nationales. Bien souvent, on n'a pas compris pue la sauvegarde du patrimoine culturel immatériel nécessite d'abord avant tout la sauvegarde et la transmission des compétences et des techniques que requiert leur création. Ceci ne peut être réalisé qu'en accordant une reconnaissance effective aux personnes qui possèdent au plus haut niveau ces compétences et ces techniques.

Cette idée fondamentale a été comprise très tôt par le gouvernement guinéen qui a procédé à une reconnaissance de fait des personnes possédant au plus haut niveau des compétences et des techniques sur certains vestiges du passé national. C'est ainsi que dès le lendemain de l'Indépendance, la famille des traditionnistes Kouyaté de Niagassola a été reconnue et confirmée dans ses fonctions de gardienne et de gestionnaire du Sosso-Bala, un des témoins matériels les plus anciens et les plus représentatifs de la culture mandingue.

Une étude sommaire du Sosso-Bala et de la pédagogie de transmission dont il constitue le support permettra d'esquisser les grandes lignes d'une politique efficace de sauvegarde et de revitalisation du patrimoine culturel immatériel.

Le royaume du Sosso-Bala: une université de la tradition orale

Le Sosso-Bala est un instrument de musique mythique et un des patrimoines historiques les plus anciens du pays Manding. Il a développé autour de lui durant des siècles un espace culturel vivant qui s'étend au-delà du cadre de son lieu de conservation dans la famille Kouyaté de Niagassola. Niagassola est un village du Manding situé à 135 kms au nord-ouest de la Préfecture de Siguiri.

C'est Niagassola que Charles Monteil désigne dans son ouvrage intitulé "les Empires du Mali",[1] comme le chef-lieu des circonscriptions constituant le Manding septentrional ou Manding primitif. Ses habitants sont pour l'essentiel constitués par les membres du clan Keita qui se réclament de la descendance directe de Soundiata. On y trouve également les Doumbouya, Traoré, Camara, Kanté, Cissé, etc. Tous ces patronymes se réfèrent aux structures sociales du vieux Manding et font de Niagassola un lieu chargé d'histoire.

Origine et histoire du Sosso-Bala

Les origines du Sosso-Bala se confondent avec celle du Royaume de Sosso. Selon la tradition, Soumaoro KANTE, roi de ce petit royaume, avait reçu le balafon d'un esprit supérieur, d'un génie qui pourrait être associé à une sorte de divinité de la musique. Dans tous les cas, le Sosso-Bala occupait une place très importante dans la vie publique et privée de Soumaoro KANTE qui en avait fait un objet de culte personnel. En effet, le balafon sacré tenait lieu d'Oracle au même titre que les Oracles de l'antiquité grecque. La consultation périodique du mystérieux instrument de musique permettait de prévoir les événements heureux ou malheureux touchant la vie du royaume, de même que l'issue des grandes batailles que Soumaoro livrait contre des rivaux.

Source d'inspiration, le Sosso-Bala assurait à Soumaoro de façon permanente, la faveur et le soutien des multiples divinités ou génies qui peuplaient son habitacle sacré. C'était une sorte de grotte spécialement aménagée à cet effet; cela explique que le balafon soit toujours conservé dans la case du conservateur, a l'exclusion de tout autre lieu.

On sait aujourd'hui que le Sosso-Bala a été fabriqué par Soumaoro lui-même. La puissance de création du roi-forgeron dans maints domaines, lui a valu le surnom de "roi sorcier". En effet, Soumaoro a donné la mesure de son génie créateur dans les domaines les plus varies: musique, sciences, techniques, art militaire, médecine (pharmacopée). Toutefois, la date de fabrication de Sosso-Bala reste encore mal connue. On sait seulement que toutes les traditions s'accordent pour dire qu'au moment de la bataille de Kirina en 1235, Soumaoro KANTE possédait déjà le balafon depuis environ 30 ans — ce qui permet d'établir que le balafon a été confectionné 30 ans plus tôt, c'est-à-dire en 1205. L'âge moyen du balafon se déduit alors aisément à partir de cette date et est égal à 794 ans soit près de 8 siècles d'existence.

C'est au cours de l'assemblée historique de Kouroukan-Fouga clairière située au Nord de la ville de Kangaba en République du Mali, que Soundiata KEITA confia la gestion de Sosso-Bala à l'ancêtre éponyme des Diély KOUYATE, Balla Fasséké. Ce sont les descendants de cette famille qui ont le monopole encore aujourd'hui de la conservation de ce précieux patrimoine.

Description sommaire du Sosso-Bala

Long environ de 1,50 cm, le Sosso-Bala est constitué de 20 planchettes soigneusement taillées et de dimension inégale. Sa hauteur au dessus du sol lorsqu'on le place dans la position du jeu est de 0,30 cm environ. Sous chacune des planchettes de bois, il y a une gourde de sonorisation. L'ensemble du balafon a une couleur gris-mât. Aux dires des traditionalistes, le Sosso-Bala a conservé ses dimensions initiales ainsi que l'essentiel des matériaux qui ont servi à sa fabrication.

Pour bien comprendre la corrélation qui existe entre le Sosso-Bala et son espace culturel, il est essentiel de connaître non seulement les méthodes d'entretien, de conservation, mais aussi et surtout les méthodes et les principes qui sous-tendent la pédagogie traditionnelle du Bala-Tigui.[2]

Conservation: entretien et dévolution

Entretien et conservation

L'entretien et la conservation du Sosso-Bala sont régis par un certain nombre de principes intangibles. La responsabilité de cette charge incombe au Bala-Tigui qui doit veiller à maintenir le balafon en bon état et à le protéger contre toute forme d'altération. Il est habilité à le jouer suivant un calendrier rigoureux. Les moments consacrés sont:

- les nuits du lundi et de vendredi (cette prescription de caractère rituel doit être respectée obligatoirement par le Bala-Tigui)
- les célébrations de funérailles d'une grande notabilité du village ou de la province
- les jours de fête

En cas d'empêchement majeur, le Bala-Tigui peut exceptionnellement désigner son cadet pour jouer le balafon. Cette désignation équivaut à une caution morale qui met le remplaçant à l'abri de tout danger.

En cas d'altération d'une partie quelconque du Sosso-Bala (lamelles de bois mal accordées ou gourdes de sonorisation défectueuses), le Bala-Tigui procède lui-même à la réparation. Il peut tout aussi bien recourir à l'assistance d'un de ses frères ou d'un de ses fils suffisamment averti en la matière. Ces différentes opérations se déroulent dans un cadre strictement privé sous la surveillance du Bala-Tigui.

Règles successorales

Le mode de succession à la mort d'un Bala-Tigui obéit à la règle de la primogéniture. Cela signifie que c'est le frère le plus âgé du défunt du clan Kouyaté qui reçoit l'héritage en son lieu de résidence ainsi que tous les biens matériels du défunt: boeufs, mouton, argent. Les épouses du défunt sont elles-mêmes intégrées à cet héritage.

Le successeur peut aussi, à sa seule discrétion, renoncer à son titre de Bala-Tigui s'il estime ne pas être à mesure de remplir toutes les obligations découlant de son nouveau statut. Nulle autre raison ne peut jouer contre son droit, pourvu que sa légitimité, en tant qu'héritier, soit reconnue par tous.

Le Sosso-Bala: support de la pédagogie de l'enseignement du Diély

L'enseignement de Diély est fondé sur un exercice intense de la mémoire et un affinement quasi-spécialisé de l'oreille. Mémoire et fidélité musicales sont ici dans un rapport de nécessaire complémentarité, l'une fixant les récits historiques, l'autre s'attachant à conserver soigneusement la mélodie du chant constituant l'armature de l'histoire. C'est la mémoire auditive qui permet de conserver les morceaux de musique. Il s'agit en effet, d'une reproduction rigoureuse des sons, c'est-à-dire d'une véritable copie. Toute négligence de l'élève dans cette phase d'affinement de l'acoustique est sévèrement punie.

En effet, la musique du balafon transmet toujours un message qui ne peut être compris que par un homme initié. Ce message n'est pas une simple nouvelle, mais il véhicule l'histoire de la famille, du clan, de la province, du royaume ou de l'empire. Seule la pratique instrumentale dont le Sosso-Bala reste la référence principale permet d'accéder à ce message de façon complète.

La relation étroite existant entre la parole, véhicule de la tradition historique et la pratique instrumentale qui en est l'expression constitue le principe majeur de la pédagoqie tradi-tionnelle gui repose sur le trépied fööli-donkili-kuma, c'est-à-dire la musique, le chant et la parole (récit historique). La parole — le langage historique, a en effet un caractère magique, voire un pouvoir de création. Pour en avoir la science, il faut être initié préalablement car un usage abusif et incontrôlé de la parole peut avoir des conséquences catastrophiques pour son auteur.

Ainsi que l'enseigne la tradition, "Kuma ye mökö damuna Mande" (la parole mange l'homme au Manding) . En d'autres termes, si la parole a un pouvoir de création, elle a également un pouvoir de destruction.

L'histoire de la communauté est transmise à tous les membres de la famille du Bala-Tigui dans un contexte de rigueur et de discipline stricte qui met en avant l'engagement et la responsabilité consécutifs à l'usage de la parole. Le texte de l'enseignement du Diély bien que oral, est un texte qui a été transmis sous cette forme depuis des siècles. L'élève devra l'enregistrer méthodiquement sans en changer un mot. C'est là l'origine du caractère spécialisé de la langue historique qui comporte des archaïsmes de langage qu'on ne retrouve plus dans le parler courant.

On comprendra dès lors l'importance de l'initiation dans l'éducation et la formation du jeune Diély. L'enseignement oral sera d'autant plus systématique dans sa forme et dans son contenu que l'élève aura franchi les étapes successives de la vie qui l'intègreront dans la catégorie des "hommes mûrs".

Il apparaît clairement que l'espace culturel crée autour du Sosso-Bala est d'abord et avant tout le cadre familial où se déroulent presque quotidiennement des manifestations culturelles. Car il faut rappeler que dès après l'initiation, (circoncision), un balafon est attribué au jeune Diély. Les séances d'apprentissage constituent des moments d'animation très intense, qui peuvent se transformer en véritables manifestations culturelles familiales.

L'enseignement dispensé est graduel et prend appui sur l'expérience vécue. Les principes majeurs que sont la répétition, la récitation, l'enregistrement par tranche des récits historiques afin de faciliter leur mémorisation, l'affinement de l'acoustique constituent les caractéristiques de l'enseignement traditionnel.

Cette pédagogie traditionnelle reflète un sens très élevé de la conservation et de la transmission du patrimoine, perçu ici comme un attribut essentiel de l'identité du peuple. Elle reflète également un grand souci de transmettre sans altération l'héritage reçu des ancêtres et met en évidence la responsabilité des disciples dans leur fonction future de continuateurs des aînés.

Si les méthodes et principes de transmission ainsi décrits sont encore vivaces pour l'essentiel, il convient de signaler que des menaces objectives de toutes sortes pèsent sur leur devenir. L'identification rapide de ces menaces et leur éradication totale constituent la condition préalable de la survie de l'enseignement traditionnel.

Problèmes et difficultés
d'une bonne conservation du Sosso-Bala et de son site

Depuis quelques années déjà, la précarité des conditions générales de conservation du Sosso-Bala constitue une préoccupation des traditionnistes de Niagassola. Cette préoccupation est d'autant plus justifiée que le Sosso-Bala donne la meilleure illustration de la relation existant entre le patrimoine culturel matériel et le patrimoine culturel immatériel, l'un servant de support à l'autre, l'autre contribuant par sa vitalité au rayonnement de l'un. En somme le Sosso-Bala est l'exemple typique et original de la synthèse harmonieuse du patrimoine culturel matériel et du patrimoine culturel immatériel.

C'est pourquoi la fragilité des infrastructures qui servent d'abri au balafon, la dégradation progressive de l'environnement, les conditions socio-économiques dans lesquelles vivent les Diély, sont entre autres, des facteurs qui, s'ils n'étaient endigués dans l'immédiat, risquent de compromettre la survie du Sosso-Bala et de son espace culturel.

Les infrastructures et l'environnement

Le site naturel du Sosso-Bala est constitué par la concession familiale des traditionnistes Kouyaté évoluant depuis des siècles dans les structures de la grande famille étendue où l'autorité du patriarche Bala-Tigui s'exerce sur l'ensemble des membres de la famille (épouses - frères - cousins - fils - neveux, etc.). Tous vivent dans des cases qui s'ordonnent de façon harmonieuse autour de la case centrale servant de demeure au patriarche. C'est dans cette case centrale que se trouve également le Sosso-Bala dont il ne peut être séparé.

Une telle architecture, ne saurait à l'évidence garantir la sécurité du Sosso-Bala, surtout quand on connaît les conditions particulièrement défavorables de l'environnement physique et la nature des convoitises qui se cristallisent autour des objets d'art dans un monde caractérisé par la piraterie et le trafic.

En effet, la Sous-Préfecture de Niagassola est située dans le Manding septentrional, à 90 kms seulement de la ville malienne de Kita. Cette grande proximité du Sahel en fait une zone fortement marquée par la chaleur et la sécheresse. Aussi, les effets de la désertification sont-ils visibles presque partout à travers des signes comme l'assèchement de nombreux petits cours d'eau et l'appauvrissement extrême de la flore et de la faune. Dès lors, on comprend aisément qu'un tel milieu soit propice aux incendies.

A cet égard, il convient de signaler, que malgré de gros efforts de la population pour améliorer l'habitat, Niagassola a enregistré ces dernières années plusieurs incendies qui ont provoqué la destruction d'importants biens matériels. Il en a résulté au niveau des populations en général et de la famille Kouyaté en particulier, une véritable psychose de l'incendie. Tout dérapage dans ce domaine au niveau de la famille serait fatal à la survie du Sosso-Bala et de son espace culturel, unique en son genre.

A ce danger que représente l'environnement, il faut ajouter les menaces que constituent les pirates et trafiquants d'objets d'art dont l'action déprédatrice a causé et continue de causer de grands préjudices au patrimoine historique culturel du continent.

Les conditions socio-économiques

Dès l'origine, le Diély était considéré comme un des principaux personnages de la cour du roi. Il a toujours vécu au sein des grands dignitaires de la cour royale. Son statut de diplomate et de conseiller des rois lui conférait un grand prestige moral ainsi que des privilèges matériels considérables. Cela lui permettait de couvrir l'ensemble de ses besoins primaires ainsi que ceux de tous les autres membres de sa famille.

Mais, avec la désintégration du "Mansaya" traditionnel (royauté), à la fin du XVIème siècle et au début du XVIIème siècle, et plus tard la destruction des principautés royales issues du démembrement de l'empire du Mali, le Diély a perdu progressivement tous les privilèges matériels. Les descendants des familles royales furent dépouillés de leur pouvoir par la colonisation française. Ils n'étaient donc plus capables de fournir aux historiens officiels les moyens de leur subsistance. C'est ainsi que les Diély ont été contraints de se tourner vers le travail de la terre tout en assumant leur mission historique de gardiens du Sosso-Bala.

On entrevoit aisément la nature des difficultés de toutes sortes auxquelles seront confrontés les traditionnistes de Niagassola, à la suite de cette profonde mutation sociale. Ces difficultés ont été surmontées avec plus ou moins de bonheur, d'abord et avant tout grâce à la forte cohésion des structures sociales dans lesquelles a évolué la famille étendue. C'est cette cohésion qui a permis de regrouper dans un champ unique tous les membres de la famille sous l'autorité du Bala-Tigui, principal gestionnaire de tous les biens. Il faut mentionner que ces efforts des traditionnistes ont été bien souvent confortés par l'action de solidarité de quelques clans de la noblesse (Keita, Kourouma, Traoré, Camara, etc.)

Mais aujourd'hui, les conséquences de la mondialisation de l'économie et les effets pervers des progrès considérables réalisés dans le domaine de l'audio-visuel, ont exercé un impact négatif sur les zones rurales. On assiste ainsi à une désintégration progressive des fondements sociaux de la famille étendue.

Le faible rendement d'une agriculture fondée sur des techniques culturales rudimentaires, accentue de jour en jour la pauvreté des paysans en général et celle du Diély en particulier. En effet, la fascination que la ville et toutes les valeurs culturelles qui s'y développent exercent sur la campagne privent les familles de leurs éléments valides à cause de l'exode rural devenu intense.

Les jeunes Diély en particulier se précipitent vers les centres urbaines soit pour y vendre leur art, soit pour y apprendre un métier en vue d'un emploi rémunéré. Dès lors, on est en droit de s'interroger sur le destin de l'enseignement traditionnel.

En effet, on constate aujourd'hui avec amertume que le nombre de disciples auxquels doit s'adresser l'enseignement du Bala-Tigui est en diminution constante du fait de l'exode rural et de la scolarisation de certains jeunes, amorcée depuis déjà plus d'une trentaine

d'années. Cette fragilité des structures de la famille étendue a provoqué une aggravation de
la pauvreté du Bala-Tigui qui ne peut plus subvenir convenablement à ses propres besoins.
Une telle situation est loin de favoriser les efforts du Bala-Tigui pour un entretien efficace
du Sosso-Bala et le maintien de la vitalité de son espace culturel.

Il y a là un sérieux risque de voir la chaîne de transmission de la tradition orale s'inter-
rompre, ce qui entraînerait du coup la disparition de l'espace culturel original dont le rayonnement fait du Sosso-Bala une université de la tradition orale. D'où la nécessité de
prendre dés à présent les mesures de sauvegarde et de préservation du précieux patrimoine
que constitue le Sosso-Bala.

Politique et stratégie locales et nationales
pour assurer une transmission efficace du patrimoine oral

Depuis son accession à l'indépendance nationale le 02 octobre 1958, la République de
Guinée a engagé un grand combat pour la réhabilitation et la valorisation du patrimoine
culturel, traditionnel et populaire.

Grâce à une identification des personnes-ressources, il a été possible de sensibiliser les
populations à la nécessité de sauvegarder le riche patrimoine traditionnel. La politique mise
en oeuvre à cette époque pour la sauvegarde et la revitalisation du patrimoine oral s'inspi-
rait du principe fondamental du respect des méthodes traditionnelles de transmission. Ces
méthodes sont encore bien vivaces dans de nombreux espaces culturels dont l'importance
cruciale a été mise en évidence au cours de la consultation internationale de l'UNESCO de
Marrakech en juin 1997 sur la préservation de ces espaces. En effet, c'est dans ces espaces
que se déroulent les manifestations culturelles, traditionnelles, et populaires dont la signification historique n'est plus à démontrer. La conservation "in situ" de certains monuments
historiques, comme le Sosso-Bala s'inscrit dans ce cadre. Il s'agit de promouvoir une conception originale du musée qui permet au monument considéré de continuer à jouer
pleinement son rôle dans la société, étant entendu que l'art africain est d'essence utilitaire.

C'est ainsi que tous les vestiges du passé ayant un rôle social défini ont été maintenus dans
leur milieu naturel et confiés aux détenteurs de compétence et de techniques appropriées
pour leur conservation et leur transmission. Cette politique a eu un effet très positif sur le
maintien et le rayonnement de l'espace culturel du Sosso-Bala qui garde encore aujourd'hui
toutes les caractéristiques de l'enseiqnement traditionnel comme indiqué plus haut.

Politique et stratégie locales
de conservation et de transmission du patrimoine oral

Les populations locales de Niagassola, conscientes de leur responsabilité historique dans le
maintien et la préservation du monument que constitue le Sosso-Bala, ont formé des
comités de surveillance pour assurer la sécurité du Balafon sacré. Elles collaborent étroite-
ment avec la famille Dökala dans les efforts que déploie cette dernière pour revitaliser
l'enseignement traditionnel.

En effet, la famille Dökala a mis en place des dispositions pour garantir la continuité de
la chaîne de transmission. Dans ce cadre, le Bala-Tigui et ses frères veillent tout particulièrement à:
- l'entretien périodique des balafons;

- l'apprentissage de la pratique instrumentale par tous les jeunes Diély dès l'âge de 7 ans;
- l'enseignement de l'histoire familiale, locale, régionale, conformément à l'héritage légué par les ancêtres;
- l'assimilation correcte de la fonction sociale et politique du Diély en tant que conseiller, médiateur, diplomate et historien, garant de la mémoire collective du peuple manding;
- l'apprentissage par les jeunes Diély en âge adulte de la technique et de la technologie de fabrication du balafon. A ce niveau, les jeunes Diély doivent apprendre à connaître tous les matériaux entrant dans la confection d'un balafon ainsi que les différentes étapes de cette confection.

Il va sans dire que tout cet enseignement sera dispensé par les aînés après assimilation par les disciples de toutes les connaissances à l'histoire du Sosso-Bala. Il s'agit donc de donner aux jeunes Diély un sens élevé de la responsabilité qui leur incombe dans la conservation et la transmission du patrimoine traditionnel perçu par tout le monde comme un attribut essentiel de l'identité du peuple.

A cet égard, les préparatifs de la cérémonie d'intronisation du Bala-Tigui à Niagassola ont été l'occasion d'un véritable séminaire de formation et de perfectionnement à l'intention de tous les membres de la famille Dökala. C'est ainsi qu'il a été procédé:

- à la réparation et à la mise en bon état de tous les balafons;
- à la confection des nouveaux balafons pour les adultes qui n'en avaient pas encore;
- à l'apprentissage intensif de la pratique instrumentale par les jeunes Diély;
- au contrôle des connaissances de tous ceux qui avaient été désignés pour prendre la parole lors des cérèmonies;
- à une véritable répétition portant sur l'exécution des airs de musique traditionnelle, des chants et des danses ayant un caractère rituel.

La fonction universitaire du Sosso-Bala a été véritablement mise en évidence au cours des préparatifs de cette cérémonie qui a connu une très grande affluence de population de toute la Sous-Région. Dans le cadre de cette politique locale, il a été vivement recommandé à tous les membres de la famille, y compris les fonctionnaires résidant dans les villes, d'améliorer leur pratique instrumentale ainsi que leurs connaissances générales de la tradition. Il leur a été demandé d'initier leurs enfants à la pratique du balafon.

En outre, la famille a décidé la création d'une association dénommée, "Dökala". C'est une association à vocation culturelle chargée d'assurer la sauvegarde et la préservation du Sosso-Bala et de son environnement. Elle a pour but d'apporter des solutions aux différents problèmes de conservation du Sosso-Bala ainsi que les problèmes liés à la transmission correcte du patrimoine oral.

Cette association qui est opérationnelle depuis 1998 vise les objectifs suivants:

- lutter contre tous les facteurs de dégradation et de déperdition de la tradition orale;
- revitaliser le patrimoine oral et assurer sa transmission aux générations futures grâce au respect strict des méthodes de l'enseignement traditionnel ainsi qu'une bonne conservation; protéger l'espace culturel du Sosso-Bala et de son environnement contre les dégradations d'ordre naturel et humain (influence de la poussée du Sahel, incendie et feux de brousse, acte de piratage); valoriser la musique traditionnelle et promouvoir la technologie de fabrication du balafon et la pratique instrumentale, etc.

Cette politique locale vient en appui des efforts que déploie le gouvernement guinéen pour préserver la culture traditionnelle et populaire.

Politique et stratégie nationales

Le gouvernement guinéen a mis en place des plans d'action pour la sauvegarde et la revitalisation du patrimoine oral de Niagassola. Ces plans d'action visent des objectifs à court, moyen et long terme et prennent en compte les principaux aspects suivants:

- collecte systématique, enregistrement sonore et archivage de toutes les traditions orales liées à l'histoire du Sosso-Bala (musique et chants épiques)
- documentation
- transmission

Le Ministère de l'Enseignement Supérieur et de la Recherche Scientifique a mené une véritable campagne de sensibilisation des populations, des intellectuels et des étudiants sur la valeur exceptionnelle du patrimoine traditionnel et populaire ainsi que son rôle dans le renforcement de l'unité et de la cohésion nationale. Il a encouragé ainsi les recherches sur les thèmes consacrés aux aspects multiples de l'évolution de la culture traditionnelle et populaire, en particulier les valeurs culturelles du Sosso-Bala. Aujourd'hui, on compte de nombreuses publications sur le patrimoine oral de Niagassola qui font l'objet d'exploitation par les professeurs de l'université.

Prenant conscience des menaces qui pèsent sur la survie de l'espace culturel de Niagassola, les autorités guinéennes ont pris des mesures pour la création d'infrastructure nouvelles devant abriter le Sosso-Bala et garantir sa sécurité contre les intempéries. Dans le même cadre, il est envisagé l'édification de maisons modernes pour améliorer les conditions d'existence des traditionnistes Kouyaté, ainsi que l'allocation de subventions financières au Bala-Tigui, permettant ainsi de stabiliser les détenteurs de compétences et techniques traditionnelles et leurs disciples.

Pour mener à bien cette politique, le gouvernement a procédé au désenclavement de Niagassola par la restauration de la route carrossable qui le relie à Siguiri, chef-lieu de la Préfecture, située à 135 km. Cette voie est désormais praticable en toute saison et a rendu possible le début d'un mouvement touristique national et international dirigé vers Niagassola.

Il faut signaler à cet égard que quelques chercheurs et hommes des médias venus d'Europe et des Etats-Unis d'Amérique ont déjà visité l'espace culturel de Niagassola. C'est dans ce cadre qu'il est envisagé la construction à une grande échelle d'un campement touristique autour de l'espace culturel du Sosso-Bala.

Pour assurer une transmission efficace et une large diffusion du patrimoine oral, il est prévu l'implantation à Niagassola d'un centre d'études et de recherches sur les traditions orales du pays manding. Ce centre sera géré et animé par les membres de la famille Dökala et dispensera des cours sur le patrimoine culturel traditionnel et populaire aux élèves et étudiants venant de tous les points de la Guinée et des pays de la Sous-Région. Il sera le pôle de référence de toutes les recherches en matière de tradition orale et entretiendra des relations organiques avec les institutions spécialisées de recherches au niveau national (Institut des Recherches des Sciences Sociales - Université et Direction Nationale de la culture à Conakry).

Par ailleurs, le gouvernement guinéen accorde un grand intérêt à la diffusion du patrimoine oral de Niagassola considéré comme support de la conscience historique nationale. Dans ce cadre, des programmes ont été élaborés à la télévision et à la radio pour faire connaître ce riche patrimoine:

- musique traditionnelle, danses rituelles, chansons épiques, etc.
- reportage et interviews des personnalités de la famille Dökala

Il a été procédé à une véritable évaluation de la politique nationale de sauvegarde et de revitalisation du patrimoine oral de Niagassola au cours de l'importante cérémonie d'intronisation du nouveau Bala-Tigui, qui a eu lieu du 10 au 12 avril 1999.

En effet, cette cérémonie qui était placée sous le parrainage du Président de la République a connu la participation du Premier Ministre, accompagné d'une dizaine de ministres et de plusieurs hauts cadres responsables de la Nation. L'engouement suscité par cet événement à l'égard de la culture traditionnelle populaire mandingue exprime avec éloquence la place et le rôle du Sosso-Bala dans l'intégration nationale de la Guinée. En plus de la réaffirmation des grandes lignes de la politique de sauvegarde et de revitalisation du patrimoine oral de Niagassola, il a été souligné l'impérieuse nécessité de renforcer la protection de ce précieux patrimoine et d'assurer avec toute l'efficacité requise la transmission de ses valeurs aux générations montantes. C'est ainsi qu'il a été décidé d'institutionnaliser le Festival du Balafon au royaume du Sosso-Bala.

Ce Festival qui se tiendrait tous les 2 ans à compter de la cérémonie du 11 avril regrouperait, en plus des membres de la famille Dökala, tous les Diély et grands maîtres de la parole de la Guinée et des pays voisins et plus particulièrement les balafonistes.

Parallèlement à ce Festival se tiendrait un colloque consacré à l'histoire et au rôle du balafon dans la société mandingue et dans le monde.

Le Ministère de la Culture et ses services spécialisés ont été chargés de la mise en oeuvre de ces recommandations qui reflètent avec force l'engagement de la Guinée dans le combat pour la sauvegarde et la conservation du patrimoine traditionnel et populaire. Voilà ce qui explique le soutien actif des autorités guinéennes aux recommandations de la consultation internationale de l'UNESCO sur la préservation des espaces culturels et populaires: déclaration du patrimoine oral de l'humanité. Marrakech. 26–28 juin 1997.

Il reste convaincu que par sa richesse et son originalité, l'espace culturel du Sosso-Bala recèle des valeurs culturelles universelles qui méritent de le faire classer comme un chef d'oeuvre du patrimoine oral de l'humanité.

Conclusion

Ainsi qu'on le voit, le Sosso-Bala occupe une place de choix dans les politiques locales et nationales de sauvegarde et de revitalisation des connaissances traditionnelles et des expressions culturelles.

Cette place se justifie par l'extraordinaire richesse de l'espace culturel du Sosso-Bala qui apparaît comme un véritable laboratoire où se perpétue la transmission des valeurs culturelles et traditionnelles selon un rituel devenu séculaire. L'enseignement traditionnel fonctionne sur des principes et des méthodes dont la rigueur est une garantie de l'authenticité des connaissances transmises.

Cependant, cette université de la tradition orale est en butte à de sérieuses et dangereuses agressions résultant de la modernisation socio-économique et de la mondialisation.

Pour éradiquer ces menaces, des mesures urgentes s'imposent et qui passent nécessaire-
ment par la prise en compte de quelques considérations importantes:

- la reconnaissance effective des trésors humains vivants que constituent les membres
  de la famille Dökala, car c'est eux qui possèdent au plus haut niveau les valeurs
  authentiques de civilisation mandingue;
- la stabilisation des membres de la famille Dökala grâce à une allocation de subvention financière significative au patriarche ou Bala-Tigui;
- la restauration des infrastructures servant d'abri au Sosso-Bala pour le protége contre les intempéries;
- le soutien et le renforcement par l'UNESCO et les autres organisations culturelles
  internationales, des politiques locales et nationales élaborees dans ce cadre;
- la création à Niagassola d'un inssitut de la tradition orale où les traditionnistes
  Kouyaté dispenseront leur enseignement conformément aux méthodes traditionnelles de transmission;
- la promotion de la technologie de fabrication du balafon;
- le soutien matériel et financier par les organisations internationales à l'organisation
  du festival bi-annuel du balafon, institutionnalisé par les autorités guinéennes
  depuis le 11 avril 1999, date de l'intronisation de l'actuel Bala-Tigui de Niagassola;
  ce festival visant tout particulièrement la diffusion et la revitalisation des valeurs
  culturelles populaires;
- la construction de campements touristiques susceptibles de générer des recettes au
  bénéfice des traditionnistes grace à un afflux de touristes.

Ces préalables sont indispensables pour créer les meilleures conditions de conservation et
de transmission de l'héritage traditionnel.

L'alphabétisation des membres adultes de la famille Dökala et la scolarisation des Jeunes
Diély peuvent être un facteur de renforcement des méthodes de conservation et de transmission dans le cadre d'une vie culturelle en évolution permanente.

Le gouvernement guinéen a, dépuis des années, déployé des efforts considérables dans
cette voie. Cependant, compte tenu des nombreux défis d'ordre politique, économique et
social auxquels il est confronté, la sauvegarde et la conservation du patrimoine oral de
Niagassola requiert la mise en oeuvre d'une coopération internationale active. Cette conférence doit se pencher sur cette réalité pour inscrire l'espace culturel de Niagassola dans un
programme prioritaire susceptible de sauver les valeurs traditionnelles et populaires en péril.

Notes

1. Monteil, Charles. *Les empires du Mali - étude d'histoire et de sociologie soudanaise* (1929).
2. Bala-Tigui: Patriarche de la famille Dökala.

Customary Methods of Transmitting Oral Tradition: The Case of the Sosso-Bala

Namankoumba Kouyaté
Summary by Dawn Elvis

The adoption of the new concept of a "cultural space" — places where folklife and other presentations of great historical significance can be periodically performed — has brought a new dynamic to the study of the preservation and revitalization of traditional folk heritage. The Sosso-Bala, the "Balafon of Soso," and its cultural space are a fine illustration of such customary methods of transmitting oral tradition.

An instrument whose origin dates back to the thirteenth century, the Sosso-Bala has created a cultural space around itself that is a vibrant, original, and sublime expression of a harmonious synthesis between tangible and intangible cultural heritage. It is still preserved today in Niagassola, in the Siguiri district in Guinea.

The Government of Guinea recognized quite early the need to preserve this instrument in its environment and entrusted its care to the Dökala family, whose descendants, the Kouyaté tradition-keepers, make sure that it is preserved and managed in accordance with time-honored ritual. The family, in turn, has created the "Dökala Association," a non-governmental organization that involves itself with art, music, culture, dance, and education. Local and national preservation policies give pride of place to the sacred Balafon of Sosso because of its unique role in enabling the transmission of the traditional culture of the Mandingo people from generation to generation.

For decades the Government of Guinea has made considerable efforts along these lines. However, these efforts have not achieved the expected results mainly because of a lack of material and financial resources. At the local level, the tradition-keepers are facing serious social and economic difficulties that gravely threaten their cultural transmission functions.

It is therefore important that urgent and effective measures be taken to stabilize the traditions performed in the cultural space of the Sosso-Bala, of which the Dökala family are the sole practitioners, and to stem the rural exodus that is depriving the family of its potential youthful disciples. Such measures, together with financial assistance to the keepers of tradition, are essential prerequisites for adequately maintaining these traditional skills.

International cultural organizations, led by UNESCO, should take urgent steps to support the implementation of local and national policies aimed at safeguarding and revitalizing the cultural space of the Sosso-Bala — the instrument that remains, indisputably, the oldest and the richest traditional heritage of the Mandingo civilization.

Place Jemaa El Fna: Patrimoine oral de l'humanité

Rachid El Houda
Architecte DPLG
Morocco

Problématique

Les habitants de Marrakech et ses visiteurs jouissent, sans le savoir, d'un privilège unique, celui d'être en présence d'un monde épique disparu d'Europe et du reste de l'aire islamique depuis plusieurs siècles.

Juan Goytisolo

C'est ainsi que s'exprimait Juan Goytisolo, écrivain bien connu dans le monde hispanique, francophone et anglophone, dans un article paru dans *El Pais* puis repris dans *Le Monde* et le *Washington Post*.

D'autres personnalités, liées au monde de la culture, écrivains, dramaturges et acteurs ont manifesté un grand interét pour la place et s'en sont inspirés dans leurs créations artistiques. Des urbanistes tentent également de créer des espaces semblables un peu partout dans le monde.

C'est que la place Jemaa El Fna (J.E.F.) offre un spécimen unique de transmission orale de la culture populaire par l'intermédiaire des cercles de la "halqa", sorte de chaire en plein air, où les visiteurs accèdent aux enseignements de la tradition à travers les genres narratifs et les récits des contes des *Mille et Une Nuits*, des épopées de Antar, de Ali, etc.

Aujourd'hui, cette richesse est menacée par l'envahissement d'un modernisme abusif:

* C'est un patrimoine vulnérable vis-à-vis de décisions arbitraires qui pourraient causer sa destruction irréversible car, s'il est aisé de promulguer l'arrêt des manifestations orales sur la place, il est autrement plus difficile de créer un espace d'une telle qualité urbaine, sociale et conviviale par simple décision administrative.
* Un autre aspect rendant cette vulnérabilité plus aigue est la localisation de ces manifestations orales au centre de la cité. Celles-ci se trouvent en compétition inexorable avec les activités plus attrayantes sur le plan économique et seraient condamnées à être délocalisées loin du centre, ce qui signifierait leur disparition certaine dans la mesure où elles seraient éloignées des flux piétons.
* Les conteurs, ces trésors vivants, dépositaires de traditions orales, voient leur nombre diminuer de façon alarmante sans qu'une relève éfficace ne soit assurée; la précarité de leur situation matérielle fragilise davantage le patrimoine de la place.

Programme de Revitalisation

Il a commencé par la création d'une association à but non lucratif dénommée: Association Place Jemaa El Fna, Patrimoine Oral de l'Humanité, dont les objectifs sont:

1. Garantir la perennité de la place J.E.F. comme lieu privilégié d'expression de l'oralité
2. Assurer la continuité de la tradition de la halqa
3. Mettre en oeuvre un programme de recensement, d'enregistrement, d'archivage sur tous supports, de documents et témoignages relatifs à la place et à son histoire
4. Initier et encourager toutes études ayant pour objet l'histoire et le devenir de la place
5. Créer un lieu pour la conservation, l'exposition, la consultation d'archives et de documents se rapportant à la place en particulier et à l'oralité en général
6. Instituer un ou plusieurs prix ayant pour but d'encourager tout effort de création ou de recherche correspondant au but de l'association
7. Coopérer avec toutes personnes ou organisations ayant les mêmes préoccupations, notamment l'UNESCO, les ONG, les fondations et autres
8. Organiser, participer à toutes réunions, séminaires, manifestations nationales et internationales dont le but serait de mieux faire connaître les cultures orales
9. Créer un fond économique ayant pour but de collecter les aides sous toutes formes, de recevoir les subventions et les dons qui serviraient à financer les activités de l'association et le fond d'aide aux vieux acteurs de la place
10. Promouvoir l'édition et la diffusion de toutes publications répondant aux objectifs de l'association
11. De manière générale, entreprendre toute action susceptible de favoriser la réalisation des objectifs de l'association

Cette association a établi un programme d'action réparti sur plusieurs années dont les principaux points sont:

- Recueillir les traditions orales sur differents supports
- Veiller à maintenir les cercles des halqas existantes et rétablir celles qui ont cessé leur activité
- Assurer la formation et la relève des hlaiqis
- Informer et sensibiliser le public aux valeurs du patrimoine
- Sensibiliser les enfants des écoles pour venir écouter et voir le spectacle dans la Place; organiser des tournées nationales dans les écoles pour faire découvrir aux élèves l'art du conteur
- Etablir d'urgence un fond d'aide économique en faveur des hlaiqis âgés qui n'exercent plus leur métier

Aujourd'hui, un an après sa création, l'association est systématiquement solicitée et consultée pour donner son avis sur tout projet de construction ou de rénovation des bâtiments entourant la place.

Jemaa El Fna Square: Humanity's Oral Heritage

Rachid El Houda
Summary by Dawn Elvis

The Jemaa El Fna square is a unique example of the use of the *halqa* (storytelling forum) for the oral transmission of folk culture. The *halqa* is a sort of open-air pulpit where visitors can learn about cultural traditions through various narrative genres. The writer Juan Goytisolo praised the square in a widely published article; persons involved in the arts have found inspiration in the square for their creations; and urban planners across the world are trying to create spaces like it.

Today, this treasure is threatened by a destructive modernism — arbitrary administrative decision-making and economic considerations that would move the facility away from the city center, far from the bustle of pedestrian traffic. It is also threatened by a decline in the numbers of storytellers and their economic viability.

To preserve and revitalize the square, a non-profit association was founded. The association drew up a multiyear plan of action with stated objectives: collecting the various oral traditions; maintaining the *halqas*; training the storytellers; encouraging schoolchildren to come and see the presentation in the square; organizing national contests in schools so the pupils could discover the art of storytelling; and establishing, as a matter of priority, a fund to benefit the older storytellers who no longer are able to practice their trade. A year after its creation, the association is regularly consulted on every construction and renovation project surrounding the square.

Regional Perspectives: Reports of UNESCO Regional Seminars

Report on the Pacific Regional Seminar

Sivia Tora
Director of Culture and Heritage
Ministry of Culture and Heritage
Fiji

Introduction

The Pacific Regional Seminar was held in Noumea, New Caledonia, 11–13 February 1999, jointly organized by UNESCO and the South Pacific Commission (SPC). Of the fourteen countries forwarded the questionnaires, thirteen responded, and twelve countries attended the seminar.

The objectives of the seminar were:

1. To assess the present situation of preserving and safeguarding intangible culture in the region
2. To identify the roles of intangible heritage in the Pacific in relation to current major issues in the Pacific such as assertion of cultural identity, sustainable human development, globalization, peaceful ethnic co-habitation, youth cultures, evolution of new technologies, and environmental deterioration
3. To identify ways and means to reinforce the application of the *Recommendation on the Safeguarding of Traditional Culture and Folklore* in the Pacific
4. To formulate a long-term strategy of cooperation and coordination aimed at the safeguarding, revitalization, legal protection, transmission, and dissemination of Pacific intangible and cultural heritage

Background

Awareness of the 1989 UNESCO *Recommendation* was minimal. Despite this, there are significant current activities in the relevant areas, the result of the Pacific nations' efforts to approach cultural heritage management in a systematic way.

Pacific countries place great importance on the intangible cultural heritage and recognize the value and relevance of systems of traditional knowledge and customary law, which are suitable to their social, cultural, and natural contexts. In the Pacific, the distinction between tangible and intangible cultural heritage is not made. They are considered to be a unified cultural heritage. For the purposes of this paper, this distinction is acknowledged in accordance with the *Recommendation* .

The intangible cultural heritage remains mainly unrecorded because it is oral. The situation is precarious because of the youthful nature of the Pacific population and the pressures of modern social organization and outside influence. In developing countries like the Pacific, where the economies are small and fragile, investment in cultural-sector infrastructure and support remains a low priority compared to that in other sectors such as health, education, and agriculture.

The recent history of the Pacific is one of colonization, in which a colonizing culture was actively promoted to replace the Indigenous cultures. There are, however, examples where Indigenous cultural knowledge and traditional methods of managing the natural resources have gained recognition today as having importance and relevance for sustainable development. In this context, the term "folklore" is not an acceptable term. Our culture is not "folklore" but the sacred norms intertwined with our traditional way of life — the norms that set the legal, moral, and cultural values of our traditional societies. They are our cultural identity.

The Current Situation

Initiatives for the safeguarding and the preservation of traditional culture and folklore and for the protection of the possessors of artistry and skills are subject to several constraints. These include the following:

- Documentation of intangible cultural heritage is constrained through the reluctance to share traditional knowledge. This is because of distrust of outsiders, taboo, and because some knowledge is personal and cannot be divulged to others.
- The need to promote institutional development and capacity building, especially financial and technical support for cultural agencies at local and national levels, continues to be given the highest priorities.
- More effective systems are needed to monitor foreign researchers to ensure that they are responsible and accountable to the communities in which they work.
- The preservation, protection, and further development of intangible cultural heritage require participation of many stakeholders, including non-governmental organizations, local communities, elders, youth, and women.
- The intricacies of the land-tenure and the extended-family systems, which are characterized by communal ownership, suggest very strongly that the legal concept of a singular claimant is grossly inadequate for determining ownership of intellectual cultural property.
- The education system generally places strong emphasis on the three R's. Formal art education is still in its infancy.

Conserving, preserving, and protecting traditional culture and its producers have experienced important developments. These include the following:

- Significant activities are underway in relation to Pacific languages, e.g., revitalizing their usage, compiling dictionaries, and teaching them at all levels in schools. These activities are common throughout the Pacific, but it is still desirable to reinforce the utilization of Pacific languages in all fields. The same degree of effort is not expended for the other aspects of intangible cultural heritage such as music, mythology, rituals, customs, dance, and games, to name a few.
- Symposiums on the relevance of existing intellectual property rights to the Pacific context have been conducted.
- Some efforts have been made to secure the participation of community stakeholders in the identification and documentation of intangible cultural heritage.

The Role of Intangible Cultural Heritage in Today's Major Issues

Pacific peoples are Indigenous, and their multiple group identities and the spiritual unity of each group needs to be fully respected. The importance of integrating cultural factors into development strategies should be drawn to the attention of policy makers. Not only does culture play a supporting role in the tourism industry's potential for employment creation and income generation. More importantly, the preservation of our heritage, which is our identity, is essential for engaging the strength, creativity, and actual cooperation of Indigenous peoples. Moreover, in a Pacific context, cultural identity is inseparable from land ownership. It was also noted that there was an element of contradiction between the assertion of cultural identity and the increasing globalization promoted by specialized institutions.

A "sustainable human development" strategy is not new to the Pacific peoples. It has been practiced through customary laws, taboo, etc., for centuries and needs to be revived and revitalized. Environmental degradation caused by major developmental projects often entails the diminishing or even loss of raw materials necessary to produce traditional material cultural objects. There is increasing recognition that traditional methods in the fields of agriculture and fishery are often effective for environmental sustainability. The effectiveness of traditional methods in conflict resolution was also emphasized.

Legal and Other Protections for Intangible Culture at the National Level

The majority of Pacific countries do not have the legal tools to protect expressions of their Indigenous cultures. Those that have introduced intellectual property rights (IPR) legislation are now questioning its relevance. While the current IPR laws may offer limited protection of community knowledge and innovations, in general they are inappropriate because they seek to privatize ownership; they are designed to be held by individuals and corporations rather than communities; they are expensive to apply for and to maintain; and they give a restrictive interpretation of invention.

The knowledge, use, and modification by local communities of medicinal plants are of critical importance to researchers but have not been given legal recognition and protection, whereas inventions based on this knowledge have. Almost every Pacific island has patent laws, but as far as is known, no patents have been taken out by any Pacific island country, either on bio-chemicals found in plants or on plant genetic material. But there are examples of plant material originating in the South Pacific, taken out of the region for analysis, and refined to isolate bio-chemicals which have either been patented themselves, or which were made into products subsequently patented. The kava is perhaps the best-known example of this.

The following resolutions were endorsed for recommendations to protect intangible cultural heritage:

- Pacific states that have not already done so should establish copyright laws with provisions to protect traditional cultural heritage from being wrongfully misappropriated.
- *Sui generis* IPR and non-legal systems should be developed to protect tangible and intangible cultural heritage that cannot be adequately protected through existing intellectual property laws.

- Governments of Pacific island nations should develop national cultural policies with particular regard to intangible cultural heritage and its customary owners.
- Governments should consider the relevance of traditional socio-political, economic, and environmental protection and take steps for their revitalization.
- In relevant legislation and policies, customary owners should be principal participants in the process of documenting and disseminating their knowledge, including control and sharing of benefits. Appropriate acknowledgement should be made by those who inherit or use traditional knowledge.

Recommendations for Regional and International Cooperation and Coordination

- The Stockholm Action Plan on Cultural Development should be brought to the attention of the South Pacific Forum for discussion, with particular reference to intangible cultural heritage and the 1989 UNESCO *Recommendation on the Safeguarding of Traditional Culture and Folklore*, for possible adoption by the South Pacific Forum Member States.
- Regional Participation Program for the financial year 2000–2001 should include projects and activities related to intangible cultural heritage. National Commissions should be encouraged to actively pursue this.
- At the international level, UNESCO should draw on the expertise of traditional experts to actively support and promote greater awareness of customary systems of ownership, management, and transmission of Indigenous peoples' cultural heritage through undertaking national and regional research and seminars.
- UNESCO should hold a Pacific Regional Meeting in the Year 2000, the UN Year for a Culture of Peace, to revitalize traditional processes of mediation and conflict resolution.
- UNESCO should develop greater coordination with other intergovernmental agencies undertaking similar work such as, *inter alia*, the World Intellectual Property Organization (WIPO), the Secretariat on the Convention of Biological Diversity, and the UN Working Group on Indigenous Populations (WIPG).

Safeguarding Traditional Culture and Folklore in Africa

J. H. Kwabena Nketia
Director
International Centre for African Music and Dance
University of Ghana School of Performing Arts
Accra, Ghana

The African Regional Seminar held at the University of Ghana from 26 to 28 January 1999 followed the format of similar seminars on the UNESCO 1989 *Recommendation on the Safeguarding of Traditional Culture and Folklore*. A synthesis report of twenty-seven completed questionnaires was presented after the formal opening of the seminar. Supplementary country reports and observations were then presented by the participants from the different countries before the issues outlined in the 1989 *Recommendation* were opened for further discussion.

Although references to aspects of Africa's material culture, such as masking traditions, were made, the major concern of the seminar was with Africa's intangible heritage, in particular all forms and expressions of culture cultivated and transmitted by oral tradition and practice, such as music, dance, drama and pageantry, folktales, legends, myths, and other forms of verbal art. These generally occur as events, that is, as something that may be heard or perceived while they last, but which cannot be touched or handled like objects outside their contexts of occurrence or the memory of those who create or perform them.

It was noted that African societies attach a great deal of importance to these traditions because particular forms serve as a medium for the expression of individual and group sentiments and thoughts as well as repositories of history and traditions, while also serving, as in other cultures, simply as creative expressions that may be enjoyed in their own right in recreational, ritual, or ceremonial contexts.

Because such cultural forms and expressions are organized as an integral part of the way of life of African peoples, particular forms may change or disappear when the institutions or lifestyles that support them are modified or abandoned. This process was greatly accelerated in the colonial period wherever new institutions, formal Western education, trade, and industry were established. New values were progressively adopted in such contexts by those who accepted new religions, new economic pursuits, and new lifestyles. In post-colonial Africa this process of change has continued to be aggravated by rural-urban migrations, the impact of the media, and global pressures. Accordingly, while many traditional cultural forms still exist in many communities, especially in the rural areas, there are others in which such traditions have been eroded, weakened, or replaced by new or completely foreign usages.

It was evident from both the synthesis report, the supplementary country reports, and the comments and discussions that followed these observations that awareness of the importance of traditional expressions has increased considerably in Africa itself since the attainment of independence from colonial rule and the intergovernmental Conference on Cultural Policies in Africa held subsequently in Accra in 1975. Hence it was generally recognized that the conservation, preservation, and dissemination of expressions of the intangible heritage must continue to be an important component of the cultural policies of African nations, in view of the fact that this heritage often represents the particular way in which the members of an African community or society express their own cultural identity. But of even more critical importance than this is what it provides as blueprints in terms of knowledge, techniques, and resources for the construction and reconstruction of contemporary African cultures. Accordingly the contemporary relevance of traditional culture and folklore was discussed at some length, since awareness of this might provide additional incentive for the collection, conservation, and dissemination of this heritage on a systematic basis.

It was noted that interest in Africa's intangible cultures has grown outside Africa itself, both on account of their value as sources of aesthetic enjoyment and the challenges they present to the creative imagination. Because of this, audiovisual recordings of expressions of these cultures undertaken at first by a few individual collectors, scholars, and recording companies have become an enterprise from which the culture-bearers themselves derive little or no benefit. It seems, therefore, that contemporary Africa cannot sit back and ignore the need for the legal protection of intangible cultural items from commercial exploitation.

While every African country can create its own legislative instrument, experience shows that this cannot be effective without reference to an international convention, and the preparation of inventories of such material. As existing copyright conventions do not provide for intangible items of cultural heritage transmitted by oral tradition, there is a need for not only a new set of legislative measures for the legal protection of intangible forms of culture but also the transformation of these forms through mechanical means of recording into tangible products.

In light of the foregoing, the safeguarding of traditional culture and folklore was viewed at the regional seminar as a practical issue that must be approached from the realities of the African situation rather than the academic concerns of professional folklorists and archivists that pervade the UNESCO *Recommendation*. It must take into account the need to counteract the aftermath of colonialism and build on Indigenous traditions, including all forms of traditional knowledge and techniques that have survived the impact of colonialism, the rich heritage of languages and oral literature, customary law and practices, traditional institutions, and Indigenous systems of thought, all of which must of course be examined with particular reference to their relevance to specific contemporary contexts of application. There is the need to build bridges between traditional African cultures practiced on the basis of ethnicity and contemporary forms guided by linkages beyond those of ethnicity, bridges between the old and the new, Indigenous and foreign, the literate and the non-literate custodians of culture, always bearing in mind the dynamic nature of the sociocultural situation in Africa and the fact that the present represents the bridge between Africa's past and the future.

To facilitate the safeguarding, conservation, and dissemination of the intangible cultural heritage as well as its legal protection, there is a need to build inventories of traditional culture, using the technical means now available for this purpose.

It became clear at the Regional Seminar that these are issues that need further thought and examination as well as practical measures for dealing with them. They call for far greater attention than many African countries seem to have given them, for the gap between knowledge or awareness of the 1989 *Recommendation* and the urgency which its implementation required became evident in many of the reports that were submitted. Many countries seem to have relied solely on the European concept of festivals for the promotion of consciousness of national identity without also exploring and extending the approaches evident in traditional African festivals. As far as conservation is concerned, many countries do not seem to have gone beyond the random collections and documentation that have emerged out of research projects carried out by individuals and institutions such as regional documentation centers or African Studies Institutes and some social science and humanities departments of local universities, or media houses in need of materials for broadcasting and television, etc. There is a general lack of coordination or concentration on the systematic investigation and collection of the materials of traditional culture and oral traditions as a defined cultural policy at the national level.

It became clear also at the seminar that the institutional models in terms of which some parts of the UNESCO *Recommendation* were formulated substantially do not exist in Africa or are at variance with the realities of the African situation. Many provisions of the 1989 *Recommendation* have not been implemented because of lack of appropriate infrastructure, manpower, and material resources.

As far as methodology is concerned, it was felt that instead of the old "extractive" approach that allowed field collectors to take what they wanted from communities and store it in their archives, a more interactive or community-based approach should be developed and used in Africa for safeguarding traditional culture and expressions of folklore. This process would not only stimulate renewed interest in the community in their own heritage but also ensure that copies of what is recorded and later classified and archived remain in the community for purposes of reference and as a resource for education and other practical purposes. It may give a new boost to oral tradition where it is dead or dying, for in Africa, the oral modes of cultural transmission will continue to have validity wherever group life is sustained. Indeed one can see it at work in contemporary contexts except that it is servicing contemporary popular culture or cultural trends and innovations. We must find ways of bringing it back to the service of traditional cultures through the formation of heritage clubs that establish other lines of cultural transmission through new networks of social relations that go beyond those of households, lineages, and systems of kinship. This will ensure that what is recorded, classified, and archived in national and local repositories will bear a palpable relationship to living traditions and will not eventually become the materials of a dead and forgotten past.

Reporte seminario regional sobre la aplicación de la recomendación sobre la salvaguardia de la cultura tradicional y popular de America Latina y el Caribe

Zulma Yugar
Directora General de Promoción Cultural
Viceministerio de Cultura
República de Bolivia

Desde que en noviembre de 1989, en París, la Conferencia General aprobó la *Recomendación sobre la Salvaguardia de la Cultura Tradicional y Popular*, los Estados y los pueblos comenzaron a valorar al patrimonio cultural intangible como parte vital de la identidad y no sólo como un puente entre el presente y su pasado histórico, sino en tanto forjador de la vida cotidiana que reescribe, en muchos casos, los modos particulares de vida.

La búsqueda de una normativa internacional tan importante como la *Recomendación* referida, que motivaba a los países a proteger su cultura tradicional y popular demandó más de 15 años, pero valió la pena, porque los avances registrados desde finales de los años 80 fueron de real trascendencia.

Primero fue París, luego vinieron muchas otras reuniones sobre el tema. Cito algunas: la realizada en Friburgo, Suiza, en 1990; la de Gorizia, Italia, en 1991; Strá nice, República Checa, en 1995 y la realizada en México en 1997.

El proceso de comprensión y aplicación de la *recomendación* de París fluía, en los países latinoamericanos y caribeños, de forma paralela a los cambios de sus estructuras políticas y sociales, determinados, en muchos casos, por mutaciones de carácter mundial como la transformación de los países socialistas, los avances tecnológicos, las economías globalizadas . . . mutaciones que, por cierto, configuraron una mundialización de la cultura.

Al presente, observamos que los cambios en la esfera internacional han agudizado las diferencias entre ricos y pobres, han hecho más crítica la migración campo-ciudad y han dado lugar al surgimiento de corrientes indigenistas que valorizan la importancia de las características multiculturales y plurilingües de las naciones.

De los 400 millones de habitantes latinoamericanos y caribeños, 60 millones son campesinos. El porcentaje es aún más notorio en mi país, Bolivia, donde casi la mitad de la población es indígena. Se entiende así el énfasis que viene alcanzando la lucha por el empoderamiento — propugnado por la UNESCO — que pasa, inevitablemente, por la defensa de nuestras culturas tradicionales y populares.

Un hecho demostrativo de la participación del pensamiento indígena en el debate internacional y de la importancia que ella le otorga la UNESCO, fue la reunión de representantes gubernamentales de los países de América Latina y el Caribe, realizada en México en 1997, que convocó, también, a representantes indígenas de las diversas regiones, con el objetivo de:

- Realizar un análisis minucioso para identificar las principales tendencias de las culturas tradicionales y populares en la región y en cada país
- Formular líneas de acción para que las distintas poblaciones y grupos étnicos puedan expresar plenamente su creatividad y afirmar su identidad cultural

- Establecer políticas culturales para promover las culturas tradicionales y populares conforme a lo dispuesto en la *Recomendación de la UNESCO Sobre la Salvaguardia de la Cultura Tradicional y Popular*
- Formular recomendaciones sobre la orientación futura y propuestas de proyectos para reforzar la aplicación de la *Recomendación* de la UNESCO, así como una estrategia regional de largo plazo de cooperación entre los países de la región

Es importante señalar que el seminario se desarrolló en base a un cuestionario que respondieron los países participantes sobre el estado de aplicación de la *Recomendación sobre la Salvaguardia de la Cultura Tradicional y Popular*, cuyos resultados definen cuatro problemas que evidencian la marginalidad de aplicación de este tema:

- Se nota la ausencia de las culturas populares dentro de las políticas culturales, la inmediata relación de las Bellas Artes cuando se habla de cultura y el escaso presupuesto destinado.
- Se piensa en Política Cultural al margen del Proyecto Nacional de cada país.
- Se privilegia el rescate sobre el estímulo a la creación.
- En la mayoría de los países la cultura popular no interesa a los medios masivos de difusión.

Estos cuatro puntos que resumen en gran medida la realidad de nuestra región sirvieron de base para la definición de conclusiones, fruto de un trabajo metodológicamente elaborado cuyos resultados pueden resumirse en los siguientes párrafos.

Los procesos democráticos e integradores que vive la región son elementos importante para la búsqueda de consolidación de las culturas tradicionales y populares basados en el respeto y la vivencia pacífica de los pueblos, al mismo tiempo ellos son decisivos, si se fomenta y difunde la diversidad cultural de cada nación.

Los creadores, portadores, transmisores y especialistas de diversas disciplinas que abordan la temática de las culturas populares y tradicionales son componentes esenciales del ámbito de la cultura. Así mismo se considera de alto interés la participación comunitaria que es fomentada por los procesos de descentralización regional, municipal y provincial.

Se valoró la importancia que el Mercosur le confiere a la cultura como elemento integrador, ejemplo de ello es la Carta de Mar del Plata que surge de las Primeras Jornadas del Mercosur.

Se considera de vital importancia la creación en México de un Centro Regional de Culturas Populares de América Latina y el Caribe.

Se valoró positivamente las iniciativas de desarrollo del Foro de Ministros y Responsables de Políticas Culturales de América Latina y el Caribe, la Organización de Estados Americanos (OEA), Organización de Estados Iberoamericanos (OEI), quienes iniciaron tareas en pro de la cultura.

Asimismo surgieron recomendaciones de los países participes del seminario a la UNESCO, las mismas indican lo siguiente:

Se recomienda la conformación del Centro Regional de Culturas Populares y Tradicionales de América Latina y el Caribe, cuya sede se encontraría en México. Asimismo, la creación de tres subsedes, dos en Sudamérica y una en Centroamérica. Las tareas que este centro realizaría son las siguientes:

- Incentivar el registro de las culturas tradicionales utilizando tecnología avanzada.

- Promover el intercambio de información entre diferentes regiones.
- Promover la realización de un inventario de investigadores nacionales y extranjeros.
- Creación de una Red de Información y Documentación de América Latina y el Caribe.
- Convocar a una reunión de autoridades culturales con la finalidad de discutir las conclusiones del Seminario Regional acerca de la Aplicación de la *Recomendación sobre la Salvaguardia de la Cultura Tradicional y Popular* de América Latina y el Caribe. La reunión se efectuará en Oruro, Bolivia, en el segundo semestre de 1999. A la fecha se viene agotando la fase preparatoria, cuyos resultados constan en un primer documento que refleja la posición boliviana frente a la temática que nos ocupa.
- Favorecer la formación y actualización de promotores de cultura popular a través de talleres de capacitación.
- Establecer un premio anual e internacional para creadores (individuales o colectivos) de cultura popular intangible.
- Declarar a las lenguas étnicas, autóctonas y criollas de origen africano, patrimonio cultural intangible de la humanidad.
- Declarar al Carnaval de Oruro en Bolivia, como espacio de patrimonio intangible de la humanidad.
- Convocar a una reunión de expertos en patrimonio cultural con el fin de sustentar la protección jurídica del patrimonio intangible y recomendar que la información y el registro sobre la cultural inmaterial sea igualmente considerado patrimonio documental.
- Que la UNESCO recomiende a los países miembros una asignación presupuestal razonable y suficiente para la realización de proyectos y programas relativos a las culturas tradicionales y populares.
- Mejorar los mecanismos de distribución y difusión de los documentos y recomendaciones elaborados por la UNESCO.
- Difundir y recomendar entre los estado miembros el intercambio de experiencias en materia de leyes y proyectos relativos a las culturas tradicionales y populares así como incluir en sus agendas de trabajo esas temáticas.

Entre las recomendaciones a los Estados Miembros resumimos las siguientes:

- Impulsar los procesos de descentralización; otorgar prioridad a la conservación; incorporar el estudio de la temática en el sistema educativo, a fin de garantizar la conservación de la cultura tradicional y popular intangible.
- Promover y difundir el registro y clasificación de las lenguas nativas.
- Garantizar las condiciones necesarias para crear o mantener espacios para la distintas expresiones de las culturas populares y apoyar la realización de fiestas populares en peligro de extinción.
- Establecer legislaciones que garanticen espacios y horarios para promover la cultura tradicional y popular en los medios de comunicación.
- Destacar la propuesta de UNESCO en relación a los "Tesoros humanos vivos".
- Fomentar un turismo cultural e implementar políticas nacionales y regionales de rescate y conservación.
- Promover leyes de protección e incentivo destinados al apoyo de las culturas tradicionales y populares.
- Propiciar un diálogo permanente con las asociaciones y organizaciones no gubernamentales para incorporar sus experiencias a sus políticas públicas.

Para terminar me cabe informar que estas conclusiones y recomendaciones fueron aplicadas en mi país de tal forma que podemos decir que Bolivia avanzó en este campo. La definición de una Estrategia Nacional basada en la *Recomendación sobre la Salvaguardia de la Cultura Tradicional y Popular* de 1989 permitió la realización de un Seminario Nacional en la ciudad de Oruro, donde estuvieron presentes autoridades departamentales, pueblos indígenas y organismos no gubernamentales que dieron pie a la creación del Consejo Nacional de Culturas Populares de Bolivia, cuyo proceso de consolidación concluye en estos meses.

Asimismo, se dio paso también a considerar esta temática en la agenda política de nuestro país y su incorporación en una nueva "Ley de Propiedad Intelectual" que se promulga en este primer semestre de 1999, de igual manera ya se empieza a trabajar en una "Ley especial de Protección y Fomento a nuestra Cultura Tradicional y Popular" a fin de evitar el plagio de nuestras expresiones folklóricas que hemos venido sufriendo por décadas. Las creaciones y tradiciones bolivianas se las muestra como música andina, sin destacar y respetar el derecho moral, por ejemplo: tradiciones conocidas a nivel mundial como es el caso del Carnaval de Oruro y danzas como el "caporal", "diablada", "morenada" y otros. Al respecto, mi dirección ha elaborado una estrategia sobre la salvaguarda de la Cultura Tradicional y Popular estimando que nuestro gobierno la introduzca como una política de Estado.

El gobierno de Bolivia agradece la disposición de la UNESCO y de instituciones colaboradoras a considerar esta temática tan importante y alentar a que su trabajo se multiplique con proyectos concretos y cuantificables en este nuevo milenio, de los cuales, tengan por seguro Bolivia será parte importante.

Referencias

Documento elaborado sobre documentación referida al Seminario Regional Sobre la Aplicación de la *Recomendación Sobre la Salvaguardia de la Cultura Tradicional y Popular* de América Latina y el Caribe. Documento elaborado por la DGCP y el CNCA. México 1997. Documento "Nuestra Diversidad Creativa". Informe de la Comisión Mundial de Cultura y Desarrollo, presidida por Javier Pérez de Cuellar.

Report of the Latin American and
Caribbean Regional Seminar

Zulma Yugar
Summary by Olivia Cadaval and Peter Seitel

The Latin American and Caribbean Seminar met in a historical context shaped by evolving UNESCO policies on intangible cultural heritage and by political and social change in the countries in the area, and on a global scale, by the transformation of socialist countries, rapid technological development, and a globalizing world economy that has led to globalization of culture. The increasing participation of Indigenous and peasant groups in cultural policy discussions is also an important development.

Based on responses to the questionnaire circulated by UNESCO about the application of the 1989 *Recommendation*, the seminar defined four principal problem areas:

- the absence of folklore in state cultural policies and funding initiatives, the fine arts being the sole form of culture represented in these;
- the marginalization of cultural policy in general in the national projects of countries in the region;
- the privileging of recovery and salvage of traditions over the stimulation of cultural creativity where folklore and traditional culture are attended to at all;
- the indifference of the mass media to traditional culture in most countries.

These areas formed the basis for discussions, which resulted in the following recommendations to UNESCO:

- formation of a Regional Center on Latin American and Caribbean Traditional Culture and Folklore, with a central office in Mexico and three regional offices, two in South America and one in Central America, which would pursue the following work: promote documentation of traditional culture using advanced technology; promote regional interchange of information; create a regional information and documentation network; call a meeting to further the conclusions drawn by the present Seminar; create training workshops for promoters of folklore; create an annual prize for individual or collective creators of traditional culture; declare regional creole languages of African origin part of the intangible cultural heritage of humanity and Bolivia's Oruro carnival an intangible cultural heritage site; call a meeting of experts to support the legal protection of intangible culture;
- urging Member States to allocate a sufficient budget to carry out projects related to traditional culture and folklore;
- improvement of distribution of UNESCO documents and recommendations;
- promotion of the exchange of experiences in developing national laws, projects, and agendas to protect traditional culture.

Recommendations to Member States included the following:

- Stimulate decentralization, giving priority to conservation and promoting it by including traditional culture and folklore in the education system.
- Promote and diffuse documentation and classification of Indigenous languages.
- Guarantee conditions necessary to the creation or maintenance of sites for expression of traditional culture, especially traditional fiestas in danger of extinction.
- Establish legislation to promote traditional culture in the media.
- Give prominence to UNESCO's "Living Human Treasures" project.
- Stimulate cultural tourism and implement national and regional salvage and conservation policies.
- Promote laws to protect and incentives to support traditional culture and folklore.
- Promote a permanent dialogue with NGOs and other organizations to incorporate their experiences into public policy.

In Bolivia work has begun to establish a national folklore council and laws to protect traditional expressions from plagiary and misrepresentation. The author thanks UNESCO and collaborating organizations and looks forward to concrete projects in which she is sure Bolivia will play an important role.

Problems of Traditional Culture and Folklore in Europe

Heikki Kirkinen
Vice-President of the European Academy of Arts, Sciences and Humanities
University of Joensuu
Finland

Introduction

In 1984, UNESCO launched a program on intangible cultural heritage and decided to base it solidly on theoretical studies. In 1989, the General Conference of UNESCO adopted the *Recommendation on the Safeguarding of Traditional Culture and Folklore.* A great number of theoretical studies have been supported by UNESCO, and many international seminars have been organized for studying and discussing this large field of cultural problems. Discussion and action inspired by these studies are under way on all continents.

The European Academy of Arts Sciences and Humanities, in cooperation with UNESCO and the Academy of Finland, organized a seminar on the problems of the protection and development of our common intangible heritage, especially of traditional culture and folklore. The seminar was held in the center of the Finnish Karelia, Joensuu, in the region of the old mythic, Kalevalaic folklore.

The seminar was perepared by President of the European Academy Professor Raymond Daudel and Mrs. Aikawa from UNESCO. Local preparations for the seminar were made by the Karelia Congresses organization in a working group headed by Professor Heikki Kirkinen, Vice-President of the European Academy.

The Intangible Heritage Section had prepared a questionnaire on the application of the *Recommendation on the Safeguarding of Traditional Culture and Folklore* in the countries of Europe. The answers were to be sent directly to the local preparation group of the seminar. Although the allotted time was short, the working group received answers from fifteen European countries, coming from National Commissions for UNESCO or from responsible state offices. Some details were provided in answers prepared by CIOFF.

Main Issues Treated

In cooperation with UNESCO, cultural heritage specialists suggested a general field of study and several main subjects to be discussed. The subjects recommended were:

1. the legal protection of the intangible heritage of minority cultures
2. the protection and promotion of national and local languages
3. the revival of traditional and popular forms of expression (music, art, dance, etc.)
4. the use of new technologies, virtual pictures, the Internet, etc.
5. cultural evolution and its future

The first subject has been addressed in UNESCO programs but less studied by the European Academy. The seminar mostly worked on the subjects 2. to 5. The final theme was adopted to emphasize the importance of long-term perspectives in strategies for safeguarding traditional culture and folklore.

The seminar comprised five sessions in three days: each session was introduced by an individual presentation and continued with general discussion on subjects presented. A special Commission on Recommendations held three meetings preparing recommendations on matters presented and discussed in the sessions. A preliminary list of recommendations was discussed in the last plenary session and adopted after some modifications.

In the opening session, the representatives of the Academy of Finland, the European Academy of Arts, Sciences and Humanities, and UNESCO reported on their organizations' current activities and future directions in the field of culture and cultural policy. The President of the Academy of Finland stressed the idea of "knowledge-based" society and the creation of centers of excellence. The President of the European Academy pointed out the importance of the immaterial cultural heritage created and safeguarded in the practice of the sciences and through their international cooperation. The representative of the Director-General of UNESCO set the work of the seminar in global perspective.

Seminar papers and discussions were divided into four thematic sections. In the first section, *Problems of Culture*, general cultural issues were introduced and discussed from the point of view of traditional culture. The session was opened by Mr. Langlois, eminent architect and writer, who cited a need for respect and protection of the "immaterial patrimony," particularly of the myths which still live and nourish culture in the subconscious of nations and in the collective memory of humankind, for example, the great mythology of ancient Greece.

Cultural tradition can suffer alteration and even distortion, explained Professor Nagy, who warned of dangers brought by rapid change and breaking of continuity in cultural development. Professor Nachev pointed out that the religious tradition can be useful in healing the mental stress that is one of the perils of our busy world. Some participants doubted the relevance of this idea, but its significance in certain cases was admitted.

A special study was made by Professor Schmitt Jensen from Aarhus University of "romanic intercommunicability" as a means of conservation of romanic languages French, Italian, Spanish, and Portuguese. He suggested that the formation of such a linguistic unity would develop bases for broad intercommunicability on different levels. Many Scandinavian people already know how to speak, when needed, a kind of "Scandinavian language." A romanic language would elaborate principles for a new intercommunicability among the Mediterranean peoples and languages. This project could inspire initiatives for regional cooperation among other related languages.

The second section of themes, *Cultural Heritage,* treated some actual problems of traditional culture. Ambassador Kari Bergholm pointed out how important it is to know and appreciate one's own heritage, as expressed in the British proverb, "To be is to be different." This also reveals the necessity of knowing others and opens the mind for contacts and exchanges with people belonging to different cultural traditions. In fact, the International Council of Organizations of Folklore Festivals and Folk Art, presided over by Mr. Bergholm, is an organization functioning as a network of cooperation, promoting the preservation of traditional culture especially in the field of folk music and folk dance.

The problem of cultural identity was central also in the presentation of Professor Anna-Leena Siikala, who analyzed the complicated situation of minority cultures, especially of Finno-Ugrian peoples in Russia in a post-Soviet era beset by rapid changes and economic difficulties. These people provide an example of a quest for cultural identity in our time. The problem of majorities and minorities was viewed at a global level in the comparative study of Professor Sandorfy, who spoke about how majorities may use minorities against each other, e.g., in the Balkan region and in Quebec. His paper challenges readers not only to tolerance, mutual comprehension, and peace but also to a serious discussion of the necessary equilibrium between different majorities and minorities. How large should a minority be as a realistic precondition for autonomy or sovereignty without making peaceful life together impossible in the larger national or cultural community? Majorities shall also have their rights. The speaker noted that emigration is not the only way to avoid conflicts; a minority can also learn to speak the language of the majority. And even in the opposite case, it is possible to learn to love two or even more countries at the same time.

The third section of themes, *New Technologies*, was represented by two specialists in informatics. Counselor Liedes spoke about intellectual property in a time of new information technology. He explained that conceptually, intellectual property is subject matter specified and instituted by law, such as patents, trademarks, industrial designs, and the copyright which "refers to intangible, immaterial objects." Traditionally, copyright refers to artistic creation but today more and more also to intellectual production. It has become one of the most important international fields of law and an object of growing political and commercial interest because of its great commercial and cultural value.

The speaker presented some examples of challenges facing the developers of the copyright system, for example, cyberspace, which is open, fluid, and intangible and has a global location. How can it be possessed by anyone? Global rules are needed as well as harmonization of legislation on matters of copyright and other intellectual properties. The new technology opens effective new ways for cultural creation and diffusion in all the areas of culture and is essential also for future cultural cooperation.

A modern application of new information technology to cultural activities was presented by Dr. Bonacic, who observed that a digital visual language can be used to expand verbal and written communication. Through this "creation of dematerialized contents on the basis of material objects" our immaterial patrimony "can attain a new dimension [of] interactivity . . . [for example via the Internet]." It is possible to create virtual art and to organize virtual exhibitions and communicate between all the areas of humanistic creation. The goal is to obtain a balance between humanity and technology, a goal that can be attained also in the area of traditional culture and folklore.

The fourth section, *Cultural Evolution*, was devoted to a more philosophical theme, to the development of human culture seen in a long-term perspective. It was opened by Professor Sabsay, who expressed his concern for the future of culture in a world dominated by global economic integration, science, and high technology. The global market of capital is also a global market of ideas and values with profound influence even on systems and programs of education.

The basic project for the future is "learning to live together." For the twenty-first century we need education for tolerance and solidarity. We are living in a world in which peace is often interrupted by ethnic, economic, and religious confrontations, creating confusion as to the cultural identities of nations. Social reality propels us towards a technological civilization without frontiers. In this situation, government and public opinion should understand that social and political problems are more important than rapid economic growth.

Professor Eva Kushner regards cultural evolution from another perspective by asking how we ensure that younger generations will be prepared and motivated to transmit their cultural heritage and to benefit from it in their own lives. In a stable society, inherited culture can inspire diffidence or hostility towards the culture, ethnicity, and religion of others. We can see two ways of envisioning cultural identity: one of becoming rooted in a culture without threatening that of others, and one of exploiting cultural difference and inflating the collective ego to squeeze out other collective egos. The first approach is the correct one; culture must be a home and not a prison.

A culture can be regarded as having three levels: the first is the lifestyle (food, clothing, customs, etc.); the second is a common historical memory, language, shared victories and defeats; and the third level is formed of aesthetic, intellectual, religious, and spiritual values. The more open the society, the less the three levels are coercively linked together. In some places and regions, young people willingly appropriate the values transmitted by their elders, but in many others, traditions are more or less forcibly imposed. The abandoning of old traditions in a new multicultural society should be gradual to avoid a vacuum in cultural identity. The speaker concluded: "Thus all the treasures of the intangible heritage are there for the developing subjects to make their own, in a way that may deepen and enhance their relationship to their own culture and open their minds to that of others."

Professor Marcel V. Locquin pointed out how important it is to join science and culture in the study of cultural evolution. The basis of general evolution is physico-chemical life processes. In cultural evolution, the biological paradigm is superseded by psychological, linguistic, and sociological paradigms and finally by rational reflection. This should be taken into consideration in education, study, and research.

The last speaker, Professor Kirkinen, presented a general outline of contemporary theories about cultural evolution by adopting as a starting point the emergence of human culture in biological evolution. He sees germs of cultural behavior already in some species of higher hominids, but man alone has continued to develop his cultural heritage to a higher rational level. Humankind has advanced enormously in technological culture but still has strong atavistic instincts in social and cultural life and a general and awful aggressivity that seems to have roots in genetic heritage. The human being exercises an effect on biological and cultural development but has not yet learned to deeply dominate his forces. The human consciousness of its own place in nature is still obscure and human ethical behavior towards other persons, societies, and cultures that differ is suspicious and repulsive. However, a positive cultural evolution is possible, and we still are able to learn positive values: tolerance, respect, cooperation, and even principles and actions of human solidarity. UNESCO is the best international organization for the coordination and the leadership of the common effort towards the peaceful coexistence and cooperation of all nations and cultures on earth. A practical aim could be a convention for the protection of the diversity of cultures, as we have an agreement by nearly all nations (Rio de Janeiro, 1992) concerning the protection of the diversity of biological species, which is a precondition of biological evolution.

Application of the 1989 *Recommendation*

The questionnaire prepared by UNESCO in partnership with the European Academy of Arts, Sciences and Humanities, and the European answers to this questionnaire formed a background for the discussions of all themes presented at the Joensuu Seminar. Specific themes produced recommendations, and answers to the questionnaire resulted in conclusions. Together they tell about studies and experiences of cultural life at the end of the twentieth century. They also give hints and advice for our work in safeguarding and developing traditional culture and folklore. Therefore, it is useful to present this part of the seminar to the participants of this conference.

We begin with an introductory text of the seminar in Joensuu, the address presented by Mrs. Noriko Aikawa, Director of the Intangible Heritage Section at UNESCO and personal representative of the Director-General of UNESCO, Mr. Federico Mayor.

Excerpts from the Speech of Mrs. Noriko Aikawa

It is symbolic that the present meeting is taking place in Karelia, the "land of the Kalevala," the world-renowned Finnish national epic. Representing UNESCO, I shall describe some aspects of our program on intangible heritage in general and the *Recommendation on the Safeguarding of Traditional Culture and Folklore* in particular.

What is intangible cultural heritage? UNESCO interprets the term culture in its broadest sense, i.e., the set of spiritual, material, intellectual, and emotional features which characterize a society. More often the words "cultural heritage" call to mind monuments and art objects. But there is also an intangible cultural heritage. UNESCO uses the term intangible cultural heritage in the identical manner as the term used for "traditional and popular culture" in the *Recommendation*. Para. A of the *Recommendation* gives the following definition: "Folklore (or traditional and popular culture) is the totality of tradition-based creations of a cultural community, expressed by a group of individuals and recognized as reflecting the expectations of a community in so far as they reflect its cultural and social identity; its standards and values are transmitted orally, by imitation or by other means. Its forms are, among others, language, literature, music, dance, games, mythology, rituals, customs, handicrafts, architecture and other arts."

Confronted with great diversity in forms of cultural expression, UNESCO focuses its program on languages, oral traditions, the performing arts such as music and dance, and handicraft skills.

Nine years have passed since the Organization's General Conference adopted the *Recommendation on the Safeguarding of Traditional Culture and Folklore* in November 1989. During this period after the fall of the Berlin Wall, political upheavals shook many former Communist countries. Today, they are undergoing profound transformations and changes. A number of new countries were born, and many ethnic groups searched for their roots in their rediscovered cultural heritage, which is regarded as a symbol of people's identity. More particularly, many basic aspects of intangible heritage, such as people's traditional philosophies, religions, and knowledge, whose practice had often been prohibited, became important elements of support in the process of nation-building.

In the early nineties, it also became clear that certain economic "development strategies" could not be applied to some communities without taking into account their specific socio-cultural context. Therefore, it was deemed necessary to conduct a thorough study of the history, the traditional ways of thinking, and the functioning of local social systems.

More recently, economic globalization and the rapid progress of communication techniques have accelerated the growing uniformity of cultures around the world. Thus, it has become a matter of urgency to preserve the traditional and popular cultures specific to each community if we want to perpetuate the cultural diversity of the world.

These are the reasons that preserving intangible cultural heritage has become an important issue for UNESCO Member States since the adoption of the *Recommendation* and the appearance of new parameters of humanity's development. When these states started to consider their traditional and popular cultures, they realized that most of them had already been lost or that many of the surviving parts were on the verge of disappearing.

Today's seminar occupies an important place within the framework of UNESCO's activities in the assessment of the present situation of preserving the world's intangible cultural heritage. Soon after the adoption of the *Recommendation* in 1989, the Swiss, Italian, and Spanish national committees of the International Council of Organisations for Folklore Festivals and Folk Art (CIOFF) organized, in cooperation with UNESCO, seminars on the implementation of the *Recommendation*. Those meetings drew the attention of public and private circles in these countries to the need for actively implementing the UNESCO *Recommendation on the Safeguarding of Traditional Culture and Folklore.*

In 1995, UNESCO began regional surveys to observe to what extent the provisions of the *Recommendation* had been applied in each country. The surveys also allow UNESCO to assess the current situation of intangible culture heritage in the Member States. The method used was to first send questionnaires to the countries of the region concerned, then identify the specialized institution capable of analyzing the replies to the questionnaire in order to draft a synthesis report, and, finally, organize a regional seminar in order to examine the synthesis report, assess the situation, identify the problems, and make recommendations for future actions.

UNESCO will carry on the surveys on the application of the *Recommendation* in Tashkent (Republic of Uzbekistan) in October 1998 for Central Asia, in Fiji in December 1998 for the Pacific region, in Accra (Ghana) in January 1999 for the African region, and in Damascus (Syrian Arab Republic [actually held in Beirut, Lebanon, May 1999. Ed.]) in February 1999 for the Arab region. In June 1999, a World Conference will be organized in collaboration with the Smithsonian Institution in Washington, D.C. (U.S.A.). This conference will evaluate the results of all conducted regional surveys, assess the present situation and the role of the intangible cultural heritage in the world today, identify and analyze the major problems encountered in safeguarding and re-dynamizing intangible cultural heritage, and give guidance to a new orientation that UNESCO should follow in its program about intangible cultural heritage.

The present seminar was organized at the kind invitation of the European Academy of Arts, Sciences and Humanities in order to integrate the assessment seminar for the Western European region within the framework of the Academy's seminar on intangible cultural heritage. All the following points put forward in the agenda of the present seminar, i.e., legal protection of minority groups' intangible heritage, the use of a mother tongue, re-dynamizing traditional performing arts, the use of technology for dissemination of intangible heritage and cultural evolution, and its future, are key issues for the future of the intangible cultural heritage.

What does UNESCO expect from the present seminar?

i.   To scrutinize the present situation of the intangible cultural heritage in Western Europe
ii.   To identify its socio-cultural role today with particular reference to its relation to the main issues raised such as globalization, environmental problems, urban problems, youth problems, immigration, unemployment, etc.
iii. To identify the problems specific to the safeguarding and promotion of the intangible heritage in this region. For example, how to maintain cultural specificity in a Europe soon to have a common currency, where globalized culture increasingly prevails: the place given to traditional and popular culture versus that of so-called high culture; the

problem of so-called folklorization; policies necessary to safeguard and protect the traditional and popular culture of minority groups; legal measures to protect against the
illicit use of this genre of culture, and so forth

iv.   To draw up proposals for solutions to these problems through positive utilization of
      new technology and international cooperation

The world will soon enter the third millennium. Cultural evolution is a main part of our
future. In 1947, Albert Einstein stressed: "We are here to counsel each other. We must build
spiritual and scientific bridges linking the nations of the world." Cultural dialogue, a multicultural world, creative diversity, international cultural exchange, all are prerequisites for
a peaceful future. Are existing conditions favorable for such a noble destiny for the entire
world? Guaranteeing the survival of local cultures specific to each tradition and thus maintaining the cultural diversity would be a real challenge for the future of a unified Europe.

Survey Report on the Answers to the Questionnaire

We are studying the place, role, and meaning of our intangible cultural heritage, the essential part of our cultural identity in a contemporary multicultural Europe in the middle of
rapid cultural change. The answers given to the questionnaire prepared by UNESCO came
from fifteen Western European countries. They were prepared by National Commissions for
UNESCO (8) or responsible State officers (7). They came from Andorra, Austria, Denmark,
Finland, Germany, Greece, Hungary, Iceland, Israel, Monaco, Norway, Portugal, Spain,
Sweden, and Switzerland. They represent traditional occidental Europe quite well, including countries from different geographical and cultural areas and countries of different size.

    This report is not a complete scientific analysis of the problems connected to the intan-
gible cultural heritage but an organized synthesis of the attitudes, conceptions, actions, and
plans concerning the safeguarding, use, and future of traditional culture in Western Europe
today as expressed by the answers given by persons who appreciate it and are engaged in
the work of safeguarding and promoting it. The questionnaire and answers were prepared
on the basis of the *Recommendation on the Safeguarding of Traditional Culture and Folklore*
adopted in the General Conference of UNESCO in 1989.

General Application of the Recommendation

The definitions of traditional and popular culture (folklore) seem to be generally adopted.
Only Rheinland (Germany) indicates that "folklore" in Germany does not belong to "popular" culture; Israel remarks that institutions of learning and religious institutions seem not to
have been taken into consideration in the transmission of traditional culture. Ten of fifteen
answers confirm that the bodies and organizations concerned are aware of the
Recommendation, and in seven countries it has been disseminated in the language of the
country. Very few countries have submitted reports to UNESCO. Only two countries have not
answered this question. The general application has been more active than the dissemination.

    Matters concerning traditional culture/folklore are handled mainly on a national level in
most of the countries, on a regional level or as separate policy in some of them. This action
seems to have some effect on the transformation of countries but not very much. It has at
least added interest to the study of the folklore and to the safeguarding and revitalization

of traditional culture in many countries. Some examples — Andorra: services developed in the Ethnological Archives; Denmark: work for folklorists at the universities; Finland: regular action in collection of traditional culture, teaching, and research; Monaco: revitalization of the local language; Spain: network of museums; Sweden: study of present-day phenomena; Switzerland: safeguarding cultural diversity.

Not very much is written about the new measures needed, especially given the rapid changes in European societies. Andorra expects active collection of oral and written materials of traditional culture. Austria and Greece would like new legal measures for the protection of traditional culture, especially by copyrights. Denmark is waiting for more jobs for folklorists in museums and archives, and Finland for a national body of experts to gather knowledge for counseling activities in the work of safeguarding and promoting traditional culture. Iceland expressed a hope that the authorities would be more conscious of the value of the traditional culture of the country. Monaco suggested more cooperation between the cultural organizations and the state institutions; Norway, between the researchers and politicians. Several answers express hope of more cooperation between their own country and UNESCO.

Identification and Preservation of Folklore

Practically all the countries consulted have museums of traditional culture and folklore, and most of them also have ethnological or folklore archives. Most of them have lists or inventories of folklore institutions; only Andorra and Monaco seem not to need them. Most of them are at least partially computerized, and special databanks exist in nearly all countries. These institutions of collection and conservation are generally not nationally coordinated (some of the countries did not answer this question). In Finland, Folklore Archives and the Finnish Literary Society function as leading coordinators on matters of collection and conservation. In Monaco, the central cultural administration has this task, and in Spain regional governments are responsible for it.

The preservation, dissemination, and active use of traditional culture is quite well guaranteed in Western Europe. According to the answers received, traditional culture is taught in school in all countries except Portugal and Sweden. In most countries it is also taught outside of schools in special courses and seminars (especially music and dance), in popular high schools (Nordic countries), and museums (Greece, Iceland). Ethnology or folklore is in university programs in all countries except Andorra and Monaco, which have no university. In Spain university teaching is limited to languages, music, and dance, in Sweden to contemporary ethnology. Traditional culture has quite a strong position at the universities of the Nordic countries.

The great majority of answers assures that research has contributed to the preservation of traditional culture and folklore. Andorra, like some other countries, appreciates documented oral materials collected by researchers from the people, and Norway adds to that the educational materials produced on the basis of research. Finland remarks that it has experience of 150 years in the safeguarding and research of folklore, which has contributed greatly to the success of folklore in Finnish culture. Greece, Hungary, and Israel underline studies and publications produced by research and mention the favorable climate created by this knowledge in the revitalization of traditional culture. Iceland and Monaco thank research for creating new materials for educational and other media.

In general, authorities and amateurs of traditional culture believe that research can enlarge and deepen awareness of the value of traditional culture in the society. However, the National Commissions of Austria, Denmark, and Sweden consider that research has not contributed positively to the preservation of traditional culture in their own countries. In these countries also university teaching and research of traditional culture are not very much developed compared with other countries like Finland, Norway, and Hungary.

All the responding countries have constitutional or legal guarantees of personal rights and liberties for all citizens. These guarantees are interpreted in the democratic spirit of a citizen's free access to his or her own culture. In the Constitution of Portugal, traditional culture is specially mentioned. In Spain, the supervision of legal liberties is delegated to the regional governments. In Sweden, the law gives to Saame peoples and Finns, in their traditional areas of habitation, the right to learn their own language and to use it in limited cases before the state or communal authorities.

In six countries, there is a national council or other organ for coordination and support of the preservation of traditional culture. In Austria it is Forum Volkskultur, in Finland the above-mentioned Folklore Archives and Finnish Literary Society; in Monaco two governmental offices partially direct the preservation of traditional culture; in Norway there is a Council of Folkmusic and Folkdance for this activity; in Portugal the CIOFF organization has partially the same function.

None of these organizations totally directs the preservation of traditional culture; rather they coordinate and give support to the activities of different institutions and organizations working in this field. In all countries financial support comes from state subventions and/or private sources, independent institutions, foundations, and other organizations. The media were mentioned as a source of support and subvention to traditional culture in the answers of Finland, Hungary, Iceland, Monaco, Sweden, and Switzerland (for Romanish language). This area of cooperation could be fruitful in many other countries too.

Dissemination and Protection

The most positive information came from the concrete life of traditional culture and folklore in Europe today. Every country from which we received answers is full of activities in these fields. There are plenty of festivals, courses, seminars, congresses, exhibitions, concerts, dances, open air-theaters, films, audiovisual programs, and other manifestations of traditional culture. Every nation seems to have its own specialties in this great cultural life especially in summertime, but in many cases also in winter or throughout the year.

These events concentrate the results of long fieldwork and preparation made mostly by cultural organizations, communal or regional societies, and private persons. CIOFF is one of the most active international organizations for cooperation in this field. In every country these events receive support and subventions from the state authorities and communal or regional administrations. Many private enterprises, societies, and cultural organizations take part in the subvention of these manifestations.

All this is a new expression of increasing awareness of the importance of traditional culture and folklore for the identity of persons and communities who want to know and manifest their own roots and specific characteristics. Traditional culture forms a basis of their creative capacity in cultural action and strengthens their participation in international exchange. This exchange is one part of a general globalization of knowledge, technology, economy, and culture. Traditional culture and folklore have been drawn into the same process of growing cultural cooperation and exchange in the world. The European cooperation and exchange program has grown towards a more global scope. In traditional culture and folklore we meet cultures very different from ours, and the transformation of cultures continues at a rapid pace. Different cultures must adapt to common life and cooperation and safeguard their creative identity at the same time.

The European organizations of traditional culture have more and more common events with those of other countries. In this process, individuals, organizations, and communities must have a clear consciousness of their own roots and identities. Otherwise they would not be able to contribute in a creative way to the cultural development of our new international community. They might lose their own identity and become assimilated to a passive mass-existence. We need more knowledge and experience in modern international cooperation. It seems that nations have become aware of the necessity to develop cultural cooperation and to support it morally and materially.

The mass media are an important new actor in the field of traditional culture. They can also be a partner and supporter, as we have seen in several answers to the questionnaire mentioned above. Generally speaking there is no coordinated system or infrastructure for promoting folklore materials for media; the main cultural organizations produce materials, and the media take initiatives asking for ideas and materials. Some countries have institutions that prepare and disseminate information through media, like the Folklore Archives in Denmark and Finland and Amt für rheinische Landeskunde in Germany. In many countries universities and cultural organizations prepare educational materials on traditional culture and folklore for schools, for the open market, and today also for the Internet.

In most Western countries, open discussion and public critique are the best methods of assuring that traditional culture and folklore are used in a proper way. Some countries have institutions which try to keep an eye on such approaches, e.g., Ministry of National Cultural Heritage in Hungary and the Council of Folkmusic and Folkdance in Norway. The "intellectual property aspect" also is included in the general legislation on copyrights and other rights of citizens. In general, artists in traditional cultures barely sustain themselves by their earnings. But in some countries like Denmark, Finland, Israel, and Norway, they have regular support from the state or from the private sector.

The protection of the collected materials of traditional culture and folklore is assured in most European countries by general legislation concerning archives and museums and by copyright regulations. In 1985 Spain adopted a special law on the matter; Swedish legislation emphasizes free access to all materials conserved in public archives and museums.

Conclusions

The answers given to the questionnaire prepared by UNESCO may not solve all the problems we studied and discussed at the seminar in Joensuu, September 1998. They do, however, give a general picture of the current life and the role of traditional culture and folklore in Western Europe. We can draw some conclusions that help guide our continued work promoting the life and further development of European and universal intangible heritage:

1. In a rapidly changing world, traditional culture and folklore play an essential role in preserving the identity and diversity of our European cultural heritage.
2. The definition of traditional culture and folklore elaborated by UNESCO has been largely adopted in common use, and we can speak about the same things using the same concepts.

3. Issues regarding traditional culture and folklore are usually handled on the national level, which promotes national cohesiveness and the equal development in different parts of country. The regional and local aspects are taken into consideration.

4. Not very much was written about the problems and measures of future cultural development. This theme could be studied more deeply in another seminar.

5. All countries in Western Europe have good archives and museums of traditional culture and folklore, many of them well organized and computerized. Most countries also have rich private collections. The archives and museums offer free access to their collections with very few, specific, exceptions.

6. The preservation and dissemination of culture is quite well organized. In most countries traditional culture is taught in schools, and in several countries, in special institutions like high schools of folk culture, institutes for music and dance, etc. University teaching and research in traditional culture is organized by nearly all the countries.

7. For the most part, answers recognize that university teaching and research contribute positively to dissemination of knowledge about and awareness of the significance of traditional culture in the life and development of national culture.

8. Legal guarantees of rights and liberties of citizens are included in the Constitutions and other laws of the countries in question. Laws also define the free access of all citizens to their own cultural heritage and the intellectual property of cultural creation.

9. Traditional culture and folklore are subsidized by national, regional, and local authorities and by private funds. The mass media have begun to show interest in traditional culture and folklore and to give subventions for cultural activities.

10. Public programs featuring traditional culture and folklore have attained a great popularity today. Many kinds of festivals, congresses, seminars, concerts, dances, and other manifestations are organized in every country. This is one of the most important features in the general picture of European culture.

11. A growing international cooperation in the field of traditional culture and folklore creates benefits in globalization, a process which opens possibilities for development, challenges cultural identities, and creates the need for cultural safeguards.

12. Several answers expect more cooperation with UNESCO in the study and planning of future development in traditional culture and folklore. That is a challenge for UNESCO.

Recommendations

The seminar on the Protection and Development of Our Intangible Heritage held in Joensuu prepared, discussed, and adopted a list of seventeen recommendations addressed to UNESCO for possible consideration in the preparation of future projects and actions of this great international institution. Several recommendations are directly related to the UNESCO Questionnaire on the Application of the *Recommendation of the Safeguarding of Traditional Culture and Folklore* in countries of Europe, specifically to the answers described in this report.

Report from Yakutiya

Stepanida Borisova
Ministry of Culture
Sakha Republic (Yakutiya)
Russia

My dear fellow conference participants, allow me to thank the organizers of today's conference for the wonderful opportunity to speak about processes in traditional culture in the Republic of Sakha, also known as Yakutiya, one of the largest and most northern regions of Russia.

Traditional society is defined by the ways of knowing and doing of a people. Traditional culture is not only a social environment in which we find ourselves placed and an expression of a people's aspirations but also a way we use to cope with the ever-changing world and a regulator of the social fabric itself.

Why do I place such importance on this? Because Yakutiya is a region of extremes. Because it is one of the most challenging areas in the Russian Federation. There is the challenge of extreme cold for all but three months of the year. The northern part of the Republic is covered in permafrost, making construction very difficult. There is also the challenge of geographical isolation and the consequent socioeconomic hardships. This is why our culture plays such a central role. It provides us with a firm foundation that allows us to gather the strength to move forward.

French anthropologist Claude Lévi-Strauss declared the twentieth century the "century of ethnography." In saying this, he would seem to make clear that this is a time of great urgency for all those who work as scholars and scientists. During this period they have tried to preserve the diversity of cultural heritage, all the while conscious of the encroaching standardization of culture and the blurring of cultural differences across the globe at this historical moment and of the role that revolutionary technologies have played in this.

Since 1917 and the founding of Soviet power in our Republic, dramatic changes have occurred in our lives. Oral traditions were codified for the first time as written documents. But what was once considered 'traditional' then became the detritus of history according to an extensive historical revisionism supported by the ideological and propagandist frameworks of the state. Traditional culture found itself consigned to the trash heap of history, marginalized as archaic and anachronistic, no longer attractive to youth, stripped of its prestige and dignity.

The rich and ancient roots of traditional culture survived in the Republic, however, and once the centralization imposed by Moscow crumbled in 1991, the Republic of Sakha (Yakutiya) set forth on a road to cultural renaissance and national rebirth. The cultural traditions that had been preserved were central to this process.

There was a bright splash of culture:

- The Yakut language, in addition to Russian, became the official language of the state.
- In elementary schools courses like "National Culture" are now required, and in the

Republic's College of Culture and Art, a new department of traditional culture has opened with a newly developed curriculum.

- The holiday of Ee-see-yakh (New Year's day on the Yakutiyan calendar) was declared a national holiday.
- A day of celebration for the national language was introduced.
- Publishers specializing in traditional culture were established.
- Radio and television programs on traditional culture were produced.
- The Ministry of Culture is coordinating a completely new initiative called "The Rebirth of Traditional Culture," which is being accomplished through a series of cultural events and publications.

It is understood that safeguarding traditional culture hinges on concrete displays and outward signs. The Ministry of Culture of the Republic is currently developing a law "On the safeguarding of traditional culture for the peoples of the Republic of Sakha (Yakutiya)." This law will officially formulate founding principles for protective relations between the federal government, private experts, and those who keep traditional culture alive.

I think that by finding support in traditional culture, the people of Yakutiya have proved their ability to survive as an ethnic group with an ethnic identity within both Russian and international communities.

I also think it is impossible to turn back the clock. We cannot expect traditional culture to be the same now as it has been in the past. Now that we have the printed text, audio, and video, the original and authentic appearance of traditional culture is moving away from the past. However, if we look to the future, traditional culture and the authentic personal views that go with it will find new forms of existence, new levels of technological development through text and audio and video recordings.

What do I mean by this? In the area of traditional culture, we have at this moment two tendencies. Firstly, there are those who strongly believe that traditional culture should be portrayed as accurately as possible on the basis of ethnographic reconstruction (e.g. the students' theater "Ai-geh"). Secondly, there are those who, trusting in creativity, seek new forms for this rebirth of traditional culture through things like stage productions, adaptations of works from the literary canon, and explorations of traditional culture through modern music and applied arts.

In 1991, the Republic of Sakha (Yakutiya) formed a local UNESCO working group, which for the past few years has run a series of events of regional, national, and international significance. One event which stands out was the international conference "Shamanism As a Religion: Genesis, Reconstruction, and Tradition" held in 1992. The Republic also held a conference called "Ee-tik Seer" or "The Sacred Places" about sacred, esteemed, and honored places where rituals and sacred acts are performed for the revitalization of traditions and the protection of the environment.

In 1991, following the lead of UNESCO, the celebration of the national holiday Ee-see-yakh was placed on a register of recognized holidays. For the past few years, this holiday, which preserves traditional costumes, rituals, and practices, has taken place Republic-wide, framing the ancient ritual of the veneration of the sun at sunrise. Other rituals associated with this holiday include feeding the spirits of fire and nature, the drinking of fermented mare's milk, and circle dances with singing, all of which are wonderful ways to greet the three-month summer.

We have established a special museum in the Republic, named Khomusa. In the museum collection are hundreds of musical instruments from different countries of the world. The staff of the museum conduct research in the promotion and rebirth of ancient musical instruments.

In the history of the Native peoples of Yakutiya, shamanism was the only form of religious expression. The pressures of the Soviet period resulted in much negative tension between shamanism and the formal social system. This all changed in 1991. Through a renewed freedom for religious expression and a renewed interest in shamanism, we can once more see the way this religion incorporated a worldview of folklore, mythology, and religious beliefs within a distinctly Eastern spiritual tradition.

The heroic epic of Yakut, *Olonkho*, is certainly the finest we have in the native creative tradition and is only the tip of the iceberg. In recent years it has attracted much attention not only from academia but also from leading cultural figures and artists. Theatrical shows have been staged using the tale of *Olonkho*. Librettos have been written, animations have been produced, and the Yakut Dramatic Theater is producing a play in an aesthetic consistent with the epic.

Preserving and rebuilding the traditional culture, folklore, and crafts of Yakutiya are some of the fundamental ways to develop the culture of the people of Sakha. The problems of traditional culture and folklore are being actively and openly discussed now, along with problems of language, literature, social infrastructure, politics, and other crucial issues of the day. As a result, in the northeastern region of Russia, in particular the Republic of Sakha (Yakutiya), a unique process is occurring in the arena of traditional culture. Documentation of this process is extremely useful for the light it throws on issues of cultural unity and on the various ways that cultures develop in the modern world.

On behalf of the Ministry of Culture of the Republic of Sakha (Yakutiya), I would like to extend the hospitality of our Republic in offering to host a future UNESCO seminar on the Safeguarding and Revitalization of Traditional Culture and Folklore in the Republic of Sakha, of the Russian Federation.

Report of the Countries of Central Asia and the Caucasus

Kurshida Mambetova
Head of Culture Department
UNESCO National Commission of the
Republic of Uzbekistan

Introduction

The Regional Seminar on the Application of the UNESCO 1989 *Recommendation* in countries of Central Asia and the Caucasus was jointly organized by UNESCO and the National Commission for UNESCO of the Republic of Uzbekistan.

The Regional Seminar was attended by fourteen participants, representing the Republic of Armenia, the Republic of Azerbaijan, the Republic of Georgia, the Republic of Kazakhstan, the Kyrgyz Republic, the Republic of Uzbekistan, the Republic of Tajikistan, and Turkmenistan. Also in attendance were representatives from the Ministry of Cultural Affairs of the Republic of Uzbekistan, UNESCO Headquarters, the UNESCO Office in Tashkent, Oltin Meros Foundation, the Organizing Committee of the Music Festival Sharq Taronalari, and the National Commission for UNESCO of the Republic of Uzbekistan.

During this seminar, several objectives were achieved:

1. an assessment of the present situation of traditional culture and folklore in the newly independent countries of Central Asia and the Caucasus undergoing a transitional process from the Communist system to democracy and free-market economy. Particular references were made to new societies with new functions, rejection of the politicized past, adapting present state institutions to new realities, etc.;

2. examination of the role intangible cultural heritage (traditional and popular cultures) plays in nation-building. Because it is a symbolic reference to a cultural identity deeply rooted in a people's history, this kind of culture has not been authorized for a long time;

3. an assessment of the socio-cultural role of intangible cultural heritage, particularly in relation to issues such as globalization, the problem of cohabitation among different ethnic groups particularly in urban areas, youth cultures, the rapid evolution of new communication and information technologies, and environmental degradation;

4. formulation of recommendations on future actions and proposals for projects to reinforce the application of UNESCO's *Recommendation*;

5. exploration of possible regional cooperation in safeguarding, legal protection, transmission, revitalization, and dissemination of intangible heritage among countries of the region.

As a result of the above-mentioned seminar, a Resolution was adopted by the participants.

An Overview of Results of the Regional Seminar

The present Report summarizes the following issues that were discussed during the Regional Seminar (Tashkent, 6–8 October 1998):

1. positive and negative aspects of national policies for safeguarding traditional culture in Central Asia and the Caucasus;
2. solutions for common difficulties experienced by the newly independent countries of Central Asia and the Caucasus regarding cultural heritage at the national level;
3. main objectives of further international and regional cooperation on intangible cultural heritage proposed by participants in the Regional Seminar.

The present Report was compiled on the basis of a comprehensive analysis of a) the questionnaires submitted by participating countries, b) a synoptic report prepared on the basis of the questionnaires, c) national reports presented during the seminar, d) results of the round-table discussion, which also was held within the framework of the seminar, and e) resolutions adopted by the participants of the seminar.

First of all, it is very important to note that all participating countries were part of one big country (the former USSR) for a long period of time — more than seventy years. That is why they all have very similar history and common difficulties in the field of safeguarding traditional culture and folklore.

According to the questionnaire results, the 1989 *Recommendation* had not been published and translated into the official languages of the countries of Central Asia and the Caucasus. Taking into account that all participating countries were Republics of the former USSR until 1990, the *Recommendation* was published only in Russian — the official language of the Soviet Union. After 1990, the newly independent states had many economical, political, and social issues, the solving of which was the most immediate task.

In this regard, taking into account the centuries-old traditions of intangible heritage in the countries of Central Asia and the Caucasus, all participants of the seminar noted the great role this heritage plays in the process of nation-building.

That is why safeguarding traditional culture remained a high priority for cultural policy in all states. Many of the participating countries had taken legislative action to guarantee the protection of all forms of cultural heritage.

During the Soviet period, all forms of cultural expression of the countries of Central Asia and the Caucasus (including both of tangible and intangible culture) were under the protection of USSR Law of Culture. Nowadays in all countries of Central Asia and the Caucasus, national legislation provides protection for traditional heritage, including the right of national communities to safeguard their own culture. For example, in Kyrgyzstan the Project of Law on Cultural Heritage is developing; in Tajikistan, protection is provided by the Law on Culture in the State Constitution; in Uzbekistan, by the State Constitution; in Georgia and Azerbaijan, by the Law on Culture. In Kazakhstan national communities have thirty-four national cultural centers.

But participants of the seminar noted that almost all legislation concerning safeguarding of cultural heritage adopted in their countries does not reflect the present needs of traditional culture.

For a long time, material culture was the only recognized folk art in the cultural life of the whole population. But in recent times, there is a tendency toward the privatization and sale of cultural objects, especially in rural places. That is why, in the opinion of the participant from Kyrgyzstan, copyright protection is necessary for the preservation and development of traditional culture and folklore. On this question, representatives of Kazakhstan and Georgia urged that measures be taken to prevent the exchange of folklore for folklorism.

In Resolutions adopted during the seminar, participating countries proposed to organize in cooperation with the World Intellectual Property Organization (WIPO) a Regional Training Seminar on the "Model provisions for national laws on the protection of expressions of folklore against illicit exploitation and other prejudicial actions" for countries of Central Asia and the Caucasus.

Moreover, all participants noted that for more successful preservation of both tangible and intangible heritage, an increase in financial assistance was needed not only from government but also from the private sector. The delegate from Armenia noted that because of a lack of governmental assistance, craftsmen have fewer opportunities for development. Above all, the present political and economic situation does not attract tourists, who are the main consumers of handicrafts.

All participants stressed the importance of developing regional cooperation in the development of cultural tourism, which would stimulate people's creativity and crafts production, raising its economic status in the life of the population and preserving its traditional technologies.

In this regard, the participant from Azerbaijan described one approach to preserving crafts. He spoke about the annual craftsmen's competition, organized by leading companies to promote the national handicrafts, children's creativity, and folklore. The participants from Uzbekistan and Kyrgyzstan described the same type of support for intangible heritage, giving examples of competitions between folk ensembles of different provinces and festivals of folk song in which governmental agencies and private companies award special grants to winners.

Despite the fact that the existing infrastructure for the conservation of folklore documentation corresponds to the needs, almost all countries of Central Asia and the Caucasus do experience problems in preserving and restoring cultural documents. Participants from Azerbaijan, Georgia, Kazakhstan, Kyrgyzstan, Uzbekistan, and Turkmenistan deplored the unsatisfactory conditions in national archives and libraries. They strongly recommended making archiving a high priority in state programs as a potentially very effective means to cultural development. Although the archives of the countries of Central Asia and the Caucasus contain the richest folklore materials, they lack special equipment, especially computers.

Noting the great importance of intangible cultural heritage in relation to the evolution of new technologies in communication and information, participating countries expressed their wish to create a computerized databank of organizations and institutions concerned with traditional culture and folklore in the countries of Central Asia and the Caucasus. It was proposed that UNESCO organize a Regional Training Seminar on the establishment of this computerized inventory and network. The UNESCO HeritageNet Program in the countries of Central Asia could be considered one of the first steps in creating a computerized network between cultural institutions. Meanwhile only three countries — Kazakhstan, Kyrgyzstan, and Uzbekistan — have joined the first stage of implementation of this program.

The need to train professional specialists in the field of cultural management is still great for the countries of Central Asia and the Caucasus, even though this infrastructure exists in Turkmenistan, Kazakhstan, Tajikistan, and Uzbekistan. In other countries such a system either doesn't exist (as in Georgia) or is a special project of the network of departments of traditional culture and folklore (as in Azerbaijan and Kyrgyzstan).

In Georgia, Uzbekistan, Tajikistan, and Kyrgyzstan folklore is taught in folklore clubs and other circles, and in school programs for studying national languages and literature.

Scientific research in all participating countries has made a great contribution to safeguarding traditional culture and folklore. In this regard, Georgia noted in its response to the questionnaire that one stimulus for scholars and scientific institutions to study this problem would also be better financial support. Participants in the seminar also discussed the possible creation of a regular scientific bulletin on traditional culture and folklore.

The establishment of the system for recognizing Living Human Treasures was also discussed during the seminar. Such a system already exists in Uzbekistan, implemented by the Oltin Meros ("Golden Heritage") Foundation and the National Commission for UNESCO of the Republic of Uzbekistan.

The following example illustrates the necessity of establishing ways of preserving folklore and traditional culture in the countries of Central Asia and the Caucasus.

Kyrgyz musical creativity is vividly represented in performers called *akins*, who are often singers, musicians, and composers at the same time. Progressive *akins* improvised songs about the democratic aspirations of the people, their protests against tyranny and the absence of rights, and their dreams about a better life. The creative work of other *akins* was permeated with feudal ideology. They praised the feudal elite and supported their domination. Both musical tendencies developed on the basis of historical conditions. To our regret, there are now no representatives of the first *akins* group, while for the second one favorable conditions exist in Kyrgystan.

In order to preserve the oral traditions of the peoples of the world, UNESCO produces audio-CDs of traditional music in the project series *Traditional Music of the World*. In this collection are several audio-CDs of the oral heritage of Armenia, Azerbaijan, Uzbekistan, Turkmenistan, and Tajikistan. The production of compact discs devoted to traditional music of the countries of Central Asia and the Caucasus should be included within the framework of the UNESCO Collection on Traditional and Folk Music.

Currently, UNESCO is considering the possibility of establishing a UNESCO Prize for Masterpieces of the Oral and Intangible Heritage of Humanity. The oral heritage is exceptionally important for the cultural identities of all the world's peoples, especially in our region, where a very large part of cultural heritage is based on oral heritage.

It was also proposed that there be organized within the Second International Music Festival Sharq Taronalari (Samarkand, 25 August–2 September 1999) a Scientific Conference and exhibition devoted to Eastern traditional music instruments.

Thus, the following items were accepted as priorities for the countries of Central Asia and the Caucasus: the elaboration of legislative acts, development of cultural tourism to preserve and revive intangible heritage, increase of government and private funding for safeguarding of traditional culture and folklore, training of professional specialists in the field of intangible culture, establishment of a Living Human Treasures System, development of communications, and others.

Now, in the world's third millennium, the countries of Central Asia and the Caucasus are striving to revive their traditional and popular cultures, which are part of the heritage of all of mankind. Cultural dialogue, a multicultural world, creative diversity, and international cultural exchange — all are prerequisites for building a peaceful future, which is the noblest mission of UNESCO.

Report on the Regional Seminar for Cultural Personnel in Asia and the Pacific (Held at the Asia-Pacific Cultural Center for UNESCO, Tokyo, February–March 1998)

Florentino H. Hornedo
College of Arts and Sciences, Ateneo de Manila University
Philippines

Background of the Tokyo Seminar

A "Questionnaire on the Application of the *Recommendation on the Safeguarding of Traditional Culture and Folklore* (UNESCO, 1989) in Countries of Asia and the Pacific Region" was sent to twenty countries in the Asia-Pacific Region in 1997. Of these, seventeen responded: Bangladesh, Bhutan, Cambodia, China, India, Indonesia, Iran, Japan, Lao P.D.R., Malaysia, Maldives, Mongolia, Nepal, Pakistan, Papua New Guinea, Philippines, Republic of Korea, Sri Lanka, Thailand, and Vietnam. Questionnaire replies did not arrive from Australia, Myanmar, and New Zealand.

The regional seminar was organized by the Asia-Pacific Cultural Center for UNESCO (ACCU) in cooperation with UNESCO, and was held in Tokyo on 24 February–2 March 1998, with delegates of the seventeen responding countries participating. The seminar aimed to analyze and assess how far the provisions of the 1989 *Recommendation* had been applied in the countries of the Asian region.

Definition of Folklore

The seminar participants were aware of the definition proposed in the 1989 *Recommendation*, and for the purpose of their discussion, they defined "[f]olklore (or traditional and popular culture) [as] the totality of tradition-based creations of a cultural community, expressed by a group or individuals and recognized as reflecting the expectations of a community in so far as they reflect its cultural and social identity; its standards and values are transmitted orally, by imitation or by other means. Its forms are, among others, languages, literature, music, dance, games, mythology, rituals, customs, handicrafts, architecture and other arts" (ACCU 1999, 21).

The Purposes of the Seminar

In her keynote address, Mrs. Noriko Aikawa, Chief, Intangible Cultural Heritage Section, Division of Cultural Heritage, UNESCO, stated that the purposes of the seminar were:

1. to undertake a careful assessment to identify the main tendencies, problems, and difficulties that characterize the evolution of the traditional and popular cultures in this region and in each country;

2. to define strategies in the field of cultural policy to preserve and promote traditional cultures and folklore in line with the provisions of the UNESCO *Recommendation*; and

3. to draw up recommendations for future orientations and project proposals to reinforce application of the UNESCO *Recommendation* with particular reference to regional cooperation (*ibid.*, 15).

The Focus of the Seminar

The seminar focused its attention on two aspects of the application of the *Recommendation*:

1. application of the *Recommendation* as a whole, and
2. application of the principal provisions of the *Recommendation*

Application of the Recommendation As a Whole

Three basic questions concerned institutional awareness of the *Recommendation*, its dissemination in the official languages of the countries, and the submission of reports to UNESCO regarding its application. The mean affirmative response to these points from the seventeen countries is 42.5%. Some 60% had not made the document available in the official country languages and had not sent a report to UNESCO.

From the country responses it appears implicitly that less than half of the participating countries in the Asia-Pacific Region had begun to apply in general the recommendations by 1998.

Application of the Principal Provisions of the Recommendation

This part concerns the (1) identification, (2) conservation, (3) preservation, (4) dissemination, and (5) protection of intangible cultural heritage, and (6) international cooperation (*ibid.*, 24). With regards to the first five items in this list, the statistical indicator for "yes" responses regarding the application of the *Recommendation* is 42%. Its breakdown is as follows:

1. identification of folklore	46.25%
2. conservation	28%
3. preservation	65%
4. dissemination	28.33%
5. protection	42.5%

Only 10% thought the *Recommendation* should be improved eventually. It is noted that in the seventeen countries represented in the Tokyo regional seminar, there has been notable activity and achievement in the preservation and promotion of the intangible cultural heritage of the region, and it is hoped that this will continue at an even more optimal pace. However, both the synthesis of the country answers to the questionnaire (*ibid.*, 21–52) and the "Summary of Participants' Remarks" (53–57) indicate a pervasive sense of continuing inadequacy in the application of the UNESCO *Recommendation* of 1989. And the "Remarks" which close the "Summary" quite clearly indicate the participating countries' "common concerns" (57), expressed as "needs," which are:

1. need for central coordinating agency in many [Asian-Pacific] countries for the preservation and promotion of traditional arts;
2. need to identify and collect/record traditional arts;
3. need for training of professionals to undertake the task of recording, documenting, archiving, and promoting traditional arts;
4. need to protect the rights of traditional artists since they are not covered by the copyright laws;
5. need for more funding to support preservation and promotion as well as training personnel and experts in preservation and promotion;
6. need to make the communities concerned take on the task of preserving their own cultural heritage;
7. need to restore the interest of younger people in the preservation of their community's artistic traditions, and to control the negative effects of foreign culture on the preservation and transmission of [traditional] culture;
8. need for recruitment and training of successors to the aging carriers of traditional culture;
9. need for control of excessive commercialization and negative effects of some forms of tourism.

A tenth recurrent theme in the seminar was a felt need for a continuing assistance of UNESCO at various levels and facets of the application of the 1989 *Recommendation*.

I wish to advert at this point to some significant work which has been and is being done by the ACCU in the field of training cultural personnel in various countries such as Pakistan (1994), Thailand (1994), Vietnam (1996), and Lao P.D.R. (1997). A seminar on the making of a databank for intangible cultural heritage was held in Bangkok, Thailand, in February–March 1999. The Asian/Pacific Music Materials Co-production Program (MCP) has been contributing to preservation and dissemination of the traditional music of the region. The Publicity Program for the Safeguarding of Cultural Heritage in Asia has also made significant contributions to preservation, dissemination, and consciousness-raising regarding traditional cultures. ACCU has been publishing a Directory on Cultural Activities, and has been sponsoring an annual photo contest aimed at highlighting specified aspects of regional culture.

It is to be noted, too, that the country reports (*ibid.*, 63–110) indicate genuine efforts toward the preservation and promotion of intangible cultural heritage despite setbacks, some of which come from the inexorable march of time and change and the negative effects of globalization on individual cultures, especially those handicapped severely by the need to prioritize survival concerns above the arts. The presence in many Asian and Pacific countries of cultural institutions and structures at the highest levels indicates genuine national concern for the preservation and promotion of traditional arts despite limited material and professional resources.

Recommendations of the Asia-Pacific Seminar

As a fitting conclusion to the seminar, the participants formulated declarations and recommendations. In general terms, there has been a consensus: (1) that flexibility is needed, for instance, when policy and/or projects are suggested or determined on whatever levels such as national, regional (as relevant to several adjacent countries), or international (defined here as relevant to the matters of all the Member States of UNESCO; in other words, more or less "global"); (2) that the terms used by the previous, present, and future seminars may be defined and interpreted differently depending on individuals, groups of people, communities, nations, and regions and, therefore, must be carefully dealt with, although much attention has been paid to their appropriate use as judged from the present conditions and connotations, whether overtly or covertly associated with them; (3) that priority should be given to applicability over abstract orientations in formulating general or specific principles and methods of safeguarding the traditional and popular culture of our region; and (4) that our present recommendations are to be read, understood, adopted, criticized, and eventually revised by anybody concerned with the same or related fields of human culture, on the ground that any later evaluations or reconsideration of the present recommendations are to be made known to the UNESCO (Paris) as well as to the ACCU (Tokyo), so the participants of the Regional Seminar can have access to the follow-up actions to these recommendations formulated hereunder.

The declarations and recommendations were addressed (1) to national governments, (2) to UNESCO, and (3) to ACCU, which co-sponsored and hosted the seminar.

Introduction

We, the participants to the 1998 Regional Seminar for Asia and the Pacific held in Tokyo,

1. *Endorsing* in general the provisions of the *Recommendation on the Safeguarding of Traditional Culture and Folklore;*
2. *Recognizing* the need to further strengthen the implementation of the *Recommendation* with the Member States of UNESCO in the context of cultural globalization;
3. *Convinced* of the need to maintain the cultural identity of the world by preserving, as much as possible, local traditional and popular cultures;
4. *Recognizing* the essential role of the possessors of the skills of the intangible heritage and the community they belong to while carrying out various activities to preserve them;
5. *Bearing in mind* the need to pay equal attention both to traditional popular cultures and traditional classical cultures;
6. *Recognizing* that tradition is constantly evolving;
7. *Noting* with concern that traditional cultural expressions are often distorted when they are presented in "festivals" and/or in tourist attractions;
8. *Calling* attention to the importance of raising an awareness of the value of traditional knowledge and skills;
9. *Having* considered the following situations:

   - lack of policy documents, trained personnel in the relevant field, acceptable guidelines for innovation, indexing collections of musical instruments, etc., and appropriate guidelines for tourism;
   - inadequate moral and social supports for the concerned communities;
   - inadequate participation of the private sector and NGOs and also lack of regional and international support and cooperation;
   - insufficient inclusion of cultural studies in the formal and non-formal curricula;
   - that copyright benefits do not go to the originator or possessor; and

10. *Having examined* the provisions of the *Recommendation* (1989) as well as reports of the

regional seminars for Central and Eastern Europe (1995) and for Latin America and the Caribbean (1997),

The members of the present regional seminar (of Asia and the Pacific in 1998) have formulated our own recommendations as follows:

Recommend to our governments to:

1. guarantee the right of access of various cultural communities to their own folklore;
2. introduce into both formal and non-formal curricula the teaching and study of folklore. For this audiovisual materials should be supplied by the government concerned;
3. provide moral and economic supports and social incentives for individuals and institutions cultivating or holding items of folklore. Social incentives and economic support may be in the form of national awards, in cash and kind, and pension to individuals at old age. A portion of tourism earnings should go to the concerned community;
4. identify and recognize living treasures;
5. provide scientific preservation facilities and archives systems;
6. include new innovations and ideas when defining traditional culture;
7. provide provision to set up a national supervisory body to monitor the implementation of the policy. Similarly, bodies may also be formed at local levels to sit periodically to review the progress and make suggestions
8. provide copyright benefit to the communities of the originator or possessors;
9. provide financial support to different communities to perform festivals regularly;
10. utilize both electronic and mass media for broader coverage in popularizing traditional culture and folklore;
11. create an identification and recording system following the UNESCO manual;
12. prepare generally accepted guidelines for tourism where necessary. Activities relating to tourism and festivals should be flexible and decided by the communities;
13. adopt a code of ethics ensuring a proper approach to and respect for traditional culture. The proposed government policy should, however, be flexible, leaving room for communities to meet their own needs and demands;
14. follow the recommendation and guidelines of UNESCO;
15. invest enough funds for the safeguarding and preservation of traditional culture and preservation of traditional and popular cultures;
16. take necessary steps to limit the range of cultural tourists under the national law or local knowledge in order to preserve and protect folklore;
17. emphasize the importance of legislation in achieving effective protection of traditional culture and folklore, where necessary.

Recommend to UNESCO to:

1. strengthen regional cooperation in the preservation and protection of popular traditional culture by:

    *   technology transfer, sharing of views of experts, and exchange of information in relevant fields
    *   holding of seminars and symposia regularly and close coordination among the local bodies
    *   organizing of regional festivals on different aspects of traditional popular culture

2. extend support for the identification, inventory-making, indexing, cataloguing, and recording of traditional heritage and folklore;

3. organize workshops, provide educational facilities including training for the concerned personnel;
4. support programs to identify and recognize international living treasures;
5. call a meeting of experts in legal aspects of the intangible cultural heritage with an aim of giving legal support to the protection of this heritage;
6. assist the Member States to establish their national register.

Recommend to ACCU to:
1. establish a databank center in Asia/Pacific of folk artists, typology, cultural maps, and other folklore materials and encourage all countries to participate;
2. invite experts and organize training courses to train collectors, archivists, documentalists, and other specialists in various levels in the conservation of folklore;
3. continue all the publications of Asian/Pacific folklore — videotapes, CDs, and other programs;
4. hold workshops on different topics to promote regional cooperation.

Recommendation No. 1 to ACCU has already been started. A seminar-workshop was held in Bangkok, Thailand, in February 1999 to inaugurate this project, which is now in progress.

References

ACCU (Asia/Pacific Cultural Center for UNESCO). 1999. *Preservation and Promotion of the Intangible Cultural Heritage: 1998 Regional Seminar for Cultural Personnel in Asia and the Pacific*. Tokyo: Taito Printing Co.

_____ and the Thai National Commission for UNESCO. 1999. *Preservation and Promotion of Traditional/Folk Performing Arts: 1999 Regional Seminar for Cultural Personnel in Asia and the Pacific* (Proceedings of the Seminar held in Bangkok, Thailand 23–26 February 1999).

Cooperation to Save Human Characteristics and Guard Their Survival

Mohsen Shaalan
General Director
Traditional Handcraft Centers
Fine Arts Sector
Ministry of Culture
Arab Republic of Egypt

The time may have come to realize that the traditional and humane features of our world can only be saved through international cooperation among governments and individuals. This could be accomplished by preserving our cultural heritage, lest it be lost beneath the wheel of modern technology embodied in the powerful machines that are replacing our humanity and our generations of inherited traditions and customs.

In May of 1999, I had the honor to be part of a regional study committee in Beirut, on the implementation of the 1989 UNESCO recommendations to preserve traditional and popular culture. I was impressed by the enthusiasm and hard work of the representatives of the participating nations to engage the heritage that is etched on this unique corner of this universe.

The various study groups represented in this committee produced well-balanced proposals on aspects of legality and authenticity, as these relate to the preservation and safeguarding of culture.

With this basis, in the present conference, I am honored to present the following recommendations: UNESCO is urged

- to collect similar proposals from groups representing the different regions, to organize the proposals to preserve folklore in a unified pattern, and to rewrite them in a uniform way emphasizing their essential similarities and their common goals;
- to preserve, protect, and safeguard all aspects of cultural heritage through international legislation that defines and qualifies the various aspects of the folklore of the participating nations;
- to elect a permanent committee or work group to update UNESCO on proposals submitted by the participating nations; this committee would evaluate all the proposals submitted by the various nations and identify the thoughtful and effective ones that warrant further action;
- to secure an international satellite media channel, monitored by UNESCO and funded by world governments and local organizations, which would transmit folklore and highlight messages about the importance of tradition all over the world in objectively researched, informative, and well-produced cultural programs with clear messages;
- to designate an international day for folklore, proclaimed under the umbrella of UNESCO and funded by various governments;
- to inform governments about the significance of introducing folklore to the curriculum at all stages of education, especially in the arts;
- to honor and publicize the achievements of countries that exert special efforts to

preserve and maintain popular culture and folklore. UNESCO should declare special mention of these countries annually;

- to provide intellectual workshops to celebrate, document, and pass on the popular heritage. Towards this end, UNESCO should capitalize on the knowledge of storytellers and experts in authentic handcrafts to publicize popular culture and knowledge. This would preserve the sources of traditional culture;
- to arrange the exchange of traditional and authentic culture and artistic events between nations and to develop proposals for museums that can preserve cultural heritage;
- to facilitate the exchange of curriculums on cultural heritage between nations, especially those who are neighbors or share the same region; this would enable people of different nations to learn about each other;
- to develop plans to collect a variety of heritage materials — parables, customs, poetry, myths, traditional games, and others — to help keep them from extinction;
- to encourage countries to restore local control of folklore and cultural heritage through the just application of copyright law;
- to invite Member Nations to establish legislation to protect culture-bearers' rights;
- to encourage governments to support training centers for folklore and traditional culture;
- to bring together governments and program sponsors at conferences on cultural preservation;
- to designate one country among Arabic-world countries every year to be "Heritage Country," recognizing its efforts in preserving the legacy;
- to produce an Arabic encyclopedia for popular and culture heritage;
- to invite governments to protect traditional and popular heritage within a framework of cultural policy from misuse in tourism;
- to ask governments to include traditional and peoples' heritage (folklore) in educational curriculums at all levels as part of cultural policy;
- to urge governments to give balanced attention to traditional culture in cultural policy;
- to invite governments to explore the interrelationships between popular and folk culture in museum exhibits;
- to assist museums in making use of the Internet to further understanding and preservation of traditional culture;
- to declare an international day for folklore and traditional culture under supervision of UNESCO.

Finally, I hope that representatives can agree on a unified way to preserve and maintain their folklore under the auspices of UNESCO.

Part III

A Call for Action

Final Conference Report

Introduction

1.   The International Conference "A Global Assessment of the 1989 *Recommendation on the Safeguarding of Traditional Culture and Folklore*: Local Empowerment and International Cooperation" was held in Washington, D.C., (U.S.A), on 27–30 June 1999 in collaboration with the Smithsonian Institution.

The purpose of this Conference was to consider the protection of the intangible cultural heritage at the end of the twentieth century and to revisit the *Recommendation on the Safeguarding of Traditional Culture and Folklore* ten years after its adoption in 1989. This Conference is the culmination of eight regional seminars held by UNESCO in order to systematically assess the implementation of the *Recommendation* and the present situation of the safeguarding and revitalization of intangible cultural heritage. The regional seminars were held in: Czech Republic (June 1995) for Central and Eastern Europe; Mexico (September 1997) for Latin America and the Caribbean; Japan (February/March 1998) for Asia; Finland (September 1998) for Western Europe; Republic of Uzbekistan (October 1998) for Central Asia and the Caucasus; Ghana (January 1999) for Africa; New Caledonia (February 1999) for the Pacific; and Lebanon (May 1999) for Arab States. A primary goal of this Conference was to globally assess the present situation and future orientation of the 1989 *Recommendation* [Appendix 1: Agenda, Appendix 2: Annotated Agenda].

Thirty-seven participants from twenty-seven countries (experts, government officials, practitioners of traditional cultures) and forty observers attended the Conference. On arrival, participants received background information documents and working documents. Reports from the eight regional seminars were available throughout the Conference for consultation. Participant papers were also distributed during the Conference and delivered in the relevant working groups [Appendix 3: Participants, Staff, and Fellows and Interns].

2.   The meeting was jointly funded by UNESCO, the Japanese Ministry of Foreign Affairs, the U.S. Department of State, the Rockefeller Foundation, the National Endowment for the Arts, and the Smithsonian Institution Office of International Relations.

Opening Session

3.   The meeting was opened by Dr. Richard Kurin, Director of the Center for Folklife and Cultural Heritage, Smithsonian Institution, who welcomed the participants, observers, and UNESCO representatives and staff to the Conference. He expressed his pleasure that this Conference should be held at the Smithsonian Institution since it complements work

carried out in the Center for Folklife and Cultural Heritage and further forges links between scholars of the Institution and UNESCO.

4.   Mr. Mounir Bouchenaki, Director, Division of Cultural Heritage and World Heritage Center, UNESCO, then addressed the Conference as the representative of the Director-General of UNESCO, Mr. Federico Mayor [this volume, 3–4]. He thanked Dr. Richard Kurin for his kind words of welcome and expressed his gratitude to him and Dr. Anthony Seeger, Director, Smithsonian Folkways Recordings, and their colleagues for their collaboration in hosting the Conference. He also thanked the sponsors for their support for the Conference. He expressed UNESCO's pleasure in being able also to partake in the thirty-fourth annual Smithsonian Folklife Festival, an exhibition of living cultural heritage from the United States and the world.

Referring to the broader definition of "heritage" that countries have come to adopt, he noted that the term now includes elements such as the heritage of ideas, the human genetic heritage, and an ethical heritage, in which diversity is an important and valued feature. This development has occurred alongside the extension of the idea of "tangible heritage" through UNESCO's 1972 Convention concerning the Protection of the World Cultural and Natural Heritage to include cultural monuments, cultural and natural sites, and cultural landscapes. This heritage is vulnerable and risks obliteration in the global trend towards homogenization powered by the global economy, although some technological developments can also provide useful means of preserving and diffusing the world's cultural heritage.

All forms of cultural heritage should be recognized and respected, the speaker continued, including the intangible heritage that supports spiritual values and the symbolic meanings inherent in material heritage. The Conference's subtitle of local empowerment and international cooperation is also consistent with the aims of UNESCO, especially as they address indigenous capacity-building and local participation (especially of the young) in implementing activities. The fact that each human being is unique is the basis for establishing cultural freedom, which is the collective freedom of a group of individuals to develop the life of their choice. To achieve this, it is necessary to promote cultural diversity globally.

In closing, he stated that this Conference can make an enormous contribution to the future direction of safeguarding the world's intangible cultural heritage. He also noted that the recommendations of this Conference will affect the world's tangible heritage as well as the intangible heritage, given the fact that all forms of cultural heritage are intricately intertwined.

5.   Mr. Mounir Bouchenaki conducted the election of Chairperson, Vice-Chairpersons, and Rapporteur:

Chairperson:	Dr. Anthony Seeger, U.S.A.
Vice-Chairpersons:	Dr. Junzo Kawada, Japan
	Ms. Zulma Yugar, Bolivia
Rapporteur:	Dr. Janet Blake, Scotland, United Kingdom

Following this, Dr. Seeger officially took the Chair.

6.   Agenda Item 2: The UNESCO *Recommendation on the Safeguarding of Traditional Culture and Folklore* (1989) — actions undertaken by UNESCO for its implementation (plenary)

Mrs. Noriko Aikawa, Director of the Intangible Heritage Unit of UNESCO, then gave a paper outlining the actions undertaken by UNESCO for the implementation of the 1989 *Recommendation* [this volume, 13–19], noting that, once the instrument was established, Member States showed little interest in its application despite the requirement to apply its provisions and to give effect to the principles and measures it defines. Only six countries submitted reports in response to a request from the Director-General in 1990. An expert report in 1992 gave as a hypothetical reason for this the lacuna of the *Recommendation* to give any specific mandate to UNESCO or to specify any steps for its implementation by Member States. UNESCO's role is limited to promoting it and encouraging states to implement its provisions.

Following the major political changes at the end of the 1980s, in particular the end of the Cold War, as well as the rapid expansion of the market economy and the progress of communications technologies that transformed the world into a more uniform economic and cultural space, many Member States began to take an interest in their traditional cultures and to rediscover their role as a symbolic reference to locally rooted identities. UNESCO sought to reorient its program relating to traditional culture and conducted a scientific evaluation of all activities carried out in that area, modifying its title to "intangible cultural heritage." Several guidelines for this work were created in 1993, following an International Expert Meeting held in Paris, and it was proposed that UNESCO should play an increasingly more catalyzing and instigating role in response to this new understanding.

Mrs. Aikawa then described the "Living Human Treasures" program launched in 1993 enabling Member States to give official recognition to persons possessing exceptional artistry and skills, thus encouraging the progression and transmission of such talent and know-how as a means of safeguarding the traditional cultural heritage. So far, nearly fifty Member States have expressed an interest in establishing such a system.

In 1995, the General Conference decided that a worldwide appraisal of the safeguarding of traditional culture and folklore should be carried out using the *Recommendation* as a frame of reference. Surveys were first carried out through a detailed questionnaire, followed by the convening of the aforementioned eight regional seminars, of which this Conference is a culmination.

In response to the increased interest amongst Member States in the intangible cultural heritage, the General Conference confirmed in 1997 that the program for intangible heritage should be given one of the highest priorities in the cultural field. Shortly thereafter, the General Conference proclaimed cultural spaces and forms of cultural expression as "Masterpieces of the Oral and Intangible Heritage of Humanity." This proclamation served as one of the means to compensate for the fact that the 1972 Convention does not apply to intangible cultural heritage.

Mrs. Aikawa then set out various other activities undertaken by UNESCO to promote the *Recommendation* in the areas of identification, conservation, preservation, dissemination, and protection of folklore. Within the framework of international cooperation, priority action has concentrated on networking and training, while particular problems relating to legal measures in respect of artistic expressions of folklore and traditional knowledge are yet to be identified. The 1989 *Recommendation* remains the principal reference document for all these activities, and it is now timely to reflect upon its role in contemporary and future contexts.

7.   Agenda Item 3: Reports of eight regional and sub-regional seminars (plenary)

The reports from the aforementioned eight regional and sub-regional seminars, held between 1995 and 1999, were delivered to the Conference plenary.

(i) Central and Eastern Europe (Czech Republic seminar)

This was the first regional seminar on the application of the 1989 *Recommendation* and it was held in Strá nice in June 1995 on the basis of completed questionnaires submitted by twelve countries of the Central and Eastern European region. Experts from thirteen countries took part in the seminar.

The responses showed that, in the majority of countries in the region, preservation of traditional culture and folklore is not a priority in cultural policy although most Ministries of Culture support the work of professional institutions and civic associations in this area. Following the transformations in post-Communist states, all-round support for contemporary international mass culture emerged in reaction to the state's previous support for folk cultures. Bodies active in protecting elements of traditional and folk culture face difficulties arising from the weak economies and ensuing lack of technical capacity in most post-Communist countries. In many states in the region, the 1989 *Recommendation* has become a significant instrument for the safeguarding of intangible cultural heritage.

Other issues highlighted in the seminar include the following:

- the importance of traditional and folk culture for safeguarding national identity;
- the overall lack of coordination between central authorities and institutions working towards the safeguarding of traditional culture and folklore, and the lack of coordinated supranational classification and typological systems in all countries;
- the absence of a unique system for folklore education at the primary level;
- the lack of finances to support the promotion, research, and dissemination of folklore;
- the need to develop infrastructures for disseminating folklore in public mass media;
- the lack of specific regulations concerning only and solely the folk artists; and
- the desire to intensify legal obligations for the safeguarding of traditional culture and folklore at the international level.

(ii) Latin America and the Caribbean (Mexico seminar)

The seminar was held in Mexico City in September 1997 with the following objectives, which were based on responses from questionnaires concerning the application of the *Recommendation*, submitted by eleven countries of the Latin American and Caribbean region. Experts from sixteen countries took part in the seminar:

- conducting a detailed analysis of the main aspects of traditional and popular culture in the region;
- setting up lines of action to allow ethnic groups and other communities fully to express their creativity and cultural identity;
- establishing cultural policy to promote traditional and popular culture in line with the *Recommendation*; and
- setting out general orientations and particular projects within a regional strategy of enlarged cooperation amongst states.

The seminar concluded the following:

- the importance of using democratic processes in the region for combining the safeguarding of traditional culture and folklore with the peaceful coexistence of peoples;

- the encouragement of community participation in such programs through processes of regional, municipal, and provincial decentralization; and
- recognition of the fact that the creators, bearers, and transmitters of, and specialists in diverse disciplines related to, these cultures are all essential to success.

The establishment of the Center for Popular Cultures of Latin America and the Caribbean in Mexico was confirmed with two sub-centers in South America and one in Central America. It was proposed that a meeting of the cultural authorities of the region be held in Bolivia in 1999 to discuss the conclusions of this regional seminar and the application of the *Recommendation* in the region.

(iii) Asia (Japan seminar)

Out of twenty countries, seventeen responded to the questionnaire on the *Recommendation*, and a seminar was held in Tokyo in February/March 1998. A total of twenty experts from nineteen Member States in the region participated.

As regards the application of the principal provisions of the *Recommendation*, 48% of responding countries applied the provisions on identification, 28% the provisions on conservation, 28% its provisions for dissemination, and 42% the provisions for protection of folklore. There has been a notable improvement in the regional protection of traditional culture and folklore, although a few states felt that the *Recommendation* should eventually be improved. Recurrent themes in the responses included:

- the need for a central coordinating agency
- the identification and collection of traditional cultural expressions
- the protection of the rights of traditional artists
- the training of professionals and artists
- increased funding
- the encouragement of communities to preserve their own cultural heritage
- revitalization of the interest of youth in traditional culture in the face of the effects of mass media
- the recruitment and training of apprentices
- control of the negative effects of tourism

The country reports indicate genuine efforts towards the safeguarding of this heritage despite setbacks and difficulties. There is also evidence of genuine concern for safeguarding, even if this is not always understood by politicians.

(iv) Western Europe (Finland seminar)

This seminar was organized in Joensuu in September 1998 on the basis of fifteen responses received by the organizing group to a questionnaire on the application of the *Recommendation*. Experts from fourteen countries took part in the seminar. The responses suggested that the main areas to be covered by the seminar should be:

- the legal protection of the intangible heritage of minority cultures;

- the protection and promotion of national and local languages;
- the revival of traditional and popular forms of expression;
- the use of new technologies, visual images, Internet, etc., in relation to this heritage; and
- the evolution of culture and its future.

Outline papers were delivered on four thematic areas: problems of culture, cultural heritage, new technologies, and cultural evolution.

Certain points were raised concerning a general view of life in contemporary Western Europe and the role of traditional culture and folklore within it. These points allowed for certain conclusions to be drawn that will help in the future development of both European and global heritage policies. These conclusions included the following:

- In a rapidly changing world, traditional culture and folklore are becoming essential for the preservation of the identity and diversity of European cultural heritage.
- Issues relating to this heritage are normally handled on the national level with regional and local aspects taken into consideration.
- All the countries of the region have good archives and museums of traditional culture offering free access, and most also have rich private collections.
- The preservation and dissemination of culture is fairly well organized, and traditional culture is taught in schools in most countries.
- Traditional culture and folklore have a great popularity today in terms of festivals, concerts, seminars, etc., and have become one of the most important features of culture today.
- The media are now showing an interest in this aspect of culture.

(v) Central Asia and the Caucasus (Uzbekistan seminar)

A regional seminar was organized in Tashkent in October 1998 on the basis of completed questionnaires submitted by eight countries. A total of fourteen representatives from eight countries attended. Several main objectives of the seminar were achieved, including:

- an analysis of the current status of traditional culture and folklore in the newly independent states of the region, with particular emphasis on the restructuring of societies during the transition from the Communist system to the democratic market economy;
- an examination of the role of traditional and popular cultures in the process of nation-building as symbols of and references to peoples' cultural identity, deeply rooted in their history; an assessment of the socio-cultural role of intangible heritage, particularly in relation to globalism, the cohabitation of different ethnic groups, and the growth of youth culture;
- a formulation of recommendations on future proposals and actions for the reinforcement of the *Recommendation*; and
- an exploration of the possibility of setting up a regional strategy in the field of safeguarding, legal protection, transmission, revitalization, and dissemination of the intangible cultural heritage.

Significant difficulties face the *Recommendation*; it has not yet been translated into the official languages of the region, and the newly independent states face major economic, political, and social problems that need to be addressed as an initial task. All participants noted that intangible cultural heritage plays an important role in nation-building and that it, therefore, remains a priority area in the cultural policy of all these states. Although all states have legislation for safeguarding this heritage, it was felt that it does not fit the needs of traditional culture and that new measures (such as copyright protection) need to be developed. Financial assistance from both public and private sectors needs to be increased and financial support given to craftsmen. The lack of computing infrastructure for archives of folklore materials was noted, as was the desire to create a computerized databank of organizations and institutions related to folklore; a UNESCO training seminar was requested to this end. The need for the training of specialists in the field of cultural management was also identified.

(vi) Africa (Ghana seminar)

The seminar was organized in Accra in January 1999. Participants from seventeen countries took part in the seminar. A questionnaire was sent to forty states, of which twenty-seven sent responses. This provided a good overview of the situation of applying the Recommendation in the region. This was supplemented by further reports from countries.

The seminar reviewed their understanding of the content of traditional culture and folklore. It sought to identify the factors that had sustained it in the past but that are now absent. It was evident that little had been done to implement the Recommendation beyond the steps taken after independence by the newly independent states. Governments were seen to rely on this heritage in strategies for nation-building and encouraging the formation of cultural identity. Reference was made to the role institutions and the media play, but a general lack of coordination, systematic collection, national cultural policies, resources, and manpower, etc., were seen as serious problems. This is unfortunate in light of what oral cultures can bring to the construction and reconstruction of contemporary cultures in Africa under their rubric of: "make the past a part of the present."

In future actions, safeguarding of traditional culture should be understood within the everyday realities of African countries and not from the "academic" perspective embodied in the Recommendation. The need for a manual on folklore to be used as a resource by local teachers was discussed. The use of anthropological techniques for information-gathering by local, literate people was also considered, an action for which there are precedents from early twentieth-century Africa. The need for urgent action in gathering information on traditional cultures was stressed along with the need to revitalize cultures in order to counteract the residue of colonialism.

A major theme of the seminar was reintegrating traditional culture into modern lives and sharing it with members of the world community to show them the cultural context of the African music and dance styles that they have already adopted.

(vii) Pacific (New Caledonia seminar)

The seminar took place in Noumea in February 1999. A total of twelve participants from twelve countries took part in the seminar. Thirteen out of the fourteen countries requested responded to the questionnaire, and, on the basis of these responses, the objectives of the seminar were established: to identify ways and means of reinforcing the application of the *Recommendation* in the region and to formulate a long-term regional strategy aimed at safeguarding, revitalization, legal protection, transmission, and dissemination of Pacific intangible heritage. Short reports were presented by each country. A few countries were unaware of the *Recommendation* due to their status as new Member States of UNESCO.

No distinction is made in the Pacific region between intangible and tangible heritage, although it has been used for the purposes of this study. Furthermore, for many Indigenous people, "folklore" is seen as an inappropriate and pejorative term, "cultural heritage" being much more positive and useful. The intangible heritage of the Pacific is mainly unrecorded and is threatened by the youthful demography of the region as well as by economic problems in the cultural sector. Another significant threat to the intangible heritage is the residue of colonialism and its continuing effects on society. It is recognized strongly that traditional cultures have a relevance today for sustainable development.

The common issues and concerns identified during the seminar included:

- Preservation and future development of the intangible heritage require the involvement of many stakeholders (NGOs, women, youth, elders, and local communities).
- The complexities of the land tenure system and the use of family clan, local, and national shareholding suggest that any system based on a single claimant is grossly inadequate for intellectual cultural property ownership in Pacific societies.
- Current international concerns relating to the exploitation of the environment have given regional states the incentive to revive traditional methods of managing land and sea.

Further points made include the need to:

- encourage communities and stakeholders to take part in documenting this heritage;
- recognize the importance of traditional cultures to development and income generation;
- recognize the threat some major business developments pose to community access to materials used in traditional cultural practices;
- recognize that cultural identity and land ownership are inseparable; and
- devise legal tools (which are now non-existent) and intellectual property laws (which are now inappropriate) to protect community culture.

(vii) Arab States (Lebanon seminar)

This seminar was held in Beirut in May 1999 to consider the question as applied in Arab States. Experts from twelve countries took part in the seminar. Certain main concerns facing Arab States in the field of folklore, outlined in the completed questionnaires submitted by ten countries, were enumerated. These included:

- Budgets reserved for folklore were reduced.
- Traditional industries have become separated from "heritage" and now principally serve tourists.
- Heritage may be lost due to the importance given to everything new, particularly new technologies.

- Heritage could be distorted or stolen by other countries and divided along sectarian lines.
- The institutions concerned with folklore have limited personnel and suffer from the lack of a central body to coordinate work.

The effects of globalization on the cultural heritage were discussed, in the context of the understanding that culture itself is not static. Globalization was seen as a double-edged sword, capable of helping national cultures to revitalize their cultures to face other cultures, but also threatening them with cultural homogeneity. The importance of the preservation of popular and traditional culture for human development was also noted, as was the fact that folklore can be the source of cultural revival while also contributing to economic development. However, one must be careful that the use of folklore for economic ends does not result in damaging the folklore itself. Cultural heritage is threatened by environmental deterioration, but, at the same time, its revitalization can provide the means to creating a better environment as well as forming a part of human identity and dignity.

Participants suggested some measures to solve these folklore-related problems facing Arab States and to lead towards safeguarding and revitalization of cultural heritage. It was suggested that a global development plan be drawn up for popular and traditional heritage and that the necessary legislation be developed to protect this heritage and all persons working in the field. The safeguarding of this heritage is to be understood as a continuous process, and permanent institutions must be created to provide moral and financial support to its practitioners and others. A clear priority also in ensuring the continuity and sustainability of this culture is the introduction of courses related to traditional and popular culture in educational curricula.

8.   Agenda Item 4: Overview of Country Reports and Regional Seminar Reports (plenary)

9.   Dr. Richard Kurin presented a paper on preliminary results from the questionnaire on the application of the 1989 *Recommendation* issued by UNESCO to Member States in 1994 [this volume, 20–35]. This represents the first-ever survey from a global perspective on the application of the *Recommendation*.

The questionnaires were filled out by National Commissions for UNESCO and by other institutions. By and large, respondents were found to be knowledgeable and informed about the situation of folklore in their countries, although several indicated they were not so well informed, and inaccuracies picked up in the questionnaire are in keeping with this. There were some difficulties with the use of terminologies such as "folklore," "preservation," and "conservation," and the degree of elaboration in providing the answers varied greatly.

Dr. Kurin then presented "highlights" from the survey findings, which included the following statistics:

- Although 58% of states were aware of the *Recommendation*, only six countries reported to UNESCO when requested to do so.
- 66% regarded UNESCO cooperation to be important for policy formation.
- Only 30% of respondent states have an infrastructure to meet the needs of folklore preservation.
- In 48% of states, training systems have been set up, and in 18% training is inadequate.
- Only 20% of states use volunteers in gathering documentation on their own culture.
- 68% of states use traditional culture and folklore in educational materials, videos, films, etc., although this is not very coordinated.

- In 50% of states intellectual property rights are protected under national legislation.

The conclusions to be drawn from this survey are, first, that a better survey is needed, since it is extremely hard to measure culture. Second, contrary to what one might expect, there is no correlation between the support for folklore and the level of modernization or development of a State (as would be expected by both "modernist" or "postmodern" perspectives). As a whole, this is an area that is under-institutionalized, under-elaborated, and under-legislated. Although many working in the field of folklore may feel this is how they want it to stay, in the face of economic, sociological, and physical challenges to its continued practice and existence, this may be a dangerous situation.

10.   Dr. Anthony Seeger presented a summary of the eight regional seminars held between 1995 and 1999 to assess the application of the *Recommendation* in Member States [this volume, 36–41]. The meetings tended to follow a similar structure: a history of the *Recommendation* and the issues to be addressed were outlined by a UNESCO representative; a summary of the synoptic reports on its application was made; and short reports were presented by each country delegate.

Many common concerns were voiced at these seminars, but with identifiable regional differences. Latin America and the Caribbean, for example, emphasized the questions of cultural diversity and multiculturalism. The Pacific region raised the difficulty of distinguishing tangible and intangible heritage from their cultural perspective, while Asia noted the need to stress high court cultures as well as other traditional cultures and folklore. The African concept of identity has much changed in the last decade, moving from an emphasis on nation-building to the recognition of multiple identities. While Central and Eastern Europe also analyzed extensively the significance of traditional culture for national identity, they raised important concerns over their financial situation and the problem of transition from the Communist system to a market economy. Western Europe stressed the need to preserve cultural diversity in the face of global intellectual and creative forces; Arab States also referred to the effects of globalization and the challenge it poses for preserving cultural identities. Several regions noted the importance of traditional cultures to the whole of contemporary culture and the under-use of such knowledge at present.

In terms of the 1989 *Recommendation*, the following broad points were made: first, that it is an important instrument and one which requires much wider dissemination. Many identified "folklore" as a problematic term that can be viewed as pejorative. This would need modification in any future new instrument, although no consensus as yet exists over the appropriate term to replace it with. A new instrument should contain certain additional features which include:

- a code of ethics for principles of respect;
- the inclusion of customary owners of traditional culture and folklore as the principal participants in and beneficiaries of the process of documenting and disseminating their knowledge;
- recognition of the collaborative role of the NGOs and other institutions that can assist in preserving this cultural heritage; and
- widening the scope of the *Recommendation* to include the evolving nature of traditional culture and folklore.

11.   Mr. Anthony McCann presented a brief analysis made by a team of experts belonging to the Smithsonian Institution of the 1989 *Recommendation* in today's context

[this volume, 57–61]. He stated that 1999 was a good moment to be carrying out a review of the *Recommendation*, providing new opportunities for communities, non-governmental and intergovernmental organizations amongst others to reassess its roles in contemporary contexts.

A principal point raised regarding the *Recommendation* text is that it is too firmly placed within the institutions of documentation and archiving and reflects the aim of protecting the products rather than the producers of traditional culture and folklore by those means. A balance must be found between the need to document and the need to protect the practices that create and nurture what is later documented. Thus protection needs to move its focus towards the communities themselves. He noted that there is a need also to reassess and critique the language used in the *Recommendation*. The use of "fragility" in relation to traditional (oral) cultures is a misleading metaphor that suggests they are dying cultures rather than living people whose community-based forms of expression are being marginalized by forces that are subject to human will. The use of the term "intangible" needs also to be reviewed as treating ideas as things (rather than as the basis and result of living practices), since the ability/inability to be touched is the quality of a material object.

It is time for an appropriate representation to be given of those whose practices create and nurture this culture. Recognition and respect for the active participation of grassroots practitioners in the production, transmission, and preservation of their cultural expressions and products are essential for meeting the increasing challenges and opportunities in the new global encounter and exchange of cultures. The full and active participation of grassroots cultural representatives with governments and scholars in decisions about the development and implementation of safeguarding folklore and traditional culture is an essential step towards improving the lives of producer communities.

12.   Mr. James Early from the Center for Folklife and Cultural Heritage of the Smithsonian Institution then added some comments concerning agency, collaboration, and relevancy in relation to the 1989 *Recommendation*. He noted that the *Recommendation* fails to talk about the self-motivation of the communities and talked of the need to move towards collaboration with them so that we learn how they document and transmit their culture and what developments they may make in this. On relevancy, he stressed the importance of cultural practices in contemporary as well as historical terms giving the example of South Africa, where a gathering of hundreds of medical tradition-bearers met with doctors trained in "Western" medicine in order to seek ways of collaboration.

13.   Discussion

The Conference was then opened to the floor for questions and comments.

A participant noted the tendency to use research language that separates an item of culture from the consciousness that produced it. He described the disappearance of rowing songs in the Philippines with the introduction of motorized boats as an example of the linkage between practice and a wider consciousness. He also noted the irony of the fact that researchers in the field spoil the truth of their research by the act of asking questions.

Another participant added that we need not only to ask communities what they know but also to understand how they create meaning and apply their knowledge in everyday life. He noted also the impossibility of separating cultural expressions from the economic context, etc.

A participant mentioned that he preferred an understanding of the community and its traditional culture both from inside and outside (and even from a vantage point far from their cultural sphere) — from many perspectives and not just from that of one culture or community.

Another participant added that we certainly recognize the areas of conflict when discussing the concept of culture (such as between Christianity and Islam). He gave an example of a conflict between a tradition in Ghana that no drumming should take place for three weeks before a festival and the wish of the members of a certain church to play drums in church during these banned periods.

Another participant added that cultural preservation concerns all religions, which can be considered the condensed message of tradition passed down to each generation to decode. This does not rule out other traditions such as music or dance. The problem posed today is one of progress and the efforts to be taken against the effects of progress which destroy part of the history and culture of peoples.

A participant who introduced himself as a Native American artist noted that many are still living on tribal lands in New Mexico and are people with a tribal, country, and ethnic affiliation. He continued by saying that there is always a discourse of "we" (experts and administrators) and "they" (community members) rather than the acceptance of all being contributors to a process of problem-solving. Why should not each expert at such a conference next time bring with him or her a true purveyor of tradition?

Another participant agreed that this is a very important point, noting she had attended a meeting in Canada where she had met Native people who were near extinction and felt very isolated. Such cultures under threat seek links to survive by breaking down their isolation.

A participant noted that much has been heard about the protection of intangible culture — but this should not suggest that tangible culture is well protected. For example, there is no protection for the tangible culture of Australian Aboriginals under intellectual property laws. Certainly, intangible culture is more vulnerable, but the tangible elements should not be ignored.

This was responded to with the comment by another participant that when we speak using different languages, it can be very difficult to reach the same idea, to understand what it means and to define the topic. Thus, for example, there is no distinction made between "tangible" and "intangible" culture in the Pacific region. However, it is important that we can reach a consensus.

A participant wished to raise two points: first, that in the last ten years since the *Recommendation* was agreed to, the number of transnational owners of intellectual property has sharply decreased, concentrating ownership in very few entities; second, as far as traditional culture and folklore and intellectual property law are concerned, many important elements are not considered in that law or the language that defines the world in which we operate. This is something later discussions (in working groups) must deal with.

Working Groups

14.   Agenda Item 6: Thematic discussions (working groups)
Following the plenary session of the Conference, the participants (with some observers) divided for one and a half days into three working groups with the following briefs:
Group I: Intangible Cultural Heritage in relation to natural and tangible cultural heritage, and its role in resolving local and national problems related to major contemporary concerns such as cultural identity, gender issues, sustainable human development, globalization, peaceful coexistence of different ethnic groups, conflict prevention, youth cultures, evolution of new technologies in communications and information, environmental deterioration, etc.

Participants: Mr. Ralph Regenvanu, Vanuatu — Chairperson
                    Mr. Russell Collier, Gitxsan, Canada — Rapporteur
                    Ms. Robyne Bancroft, Australia
                    Mr. Mihály Hoppál, Hungary
                    Mr. Miguel Puwainchir, Ecuador
                    Dr. Mahaman Garba, Niger
                    Mr. Rachid El Houda, Morocco
                    Dr. Junzo Kawada, Japan
                    Mrs. Stepanida Borisova, Russia
                    Mr. Andy Abeita, Isleta Pueblo, U.S.A.
                    Mr. Rajeev Sethi, India

Group II: Legal protection of local and national intangible cultural heritage.

Participants: Ms. Manuela da Cunha, Brazil — Chairperson
                    Dr. Tressa Berman, U.S.A — Rapporteur
                    Mrs. Lyndel Prott, UNESCO
                    Dr. Grace Koch, Australia
                    Professor Kamal Puri, Australia
                    Commissioner Preston Thomas, Australia
                    Professor Peter Jaszi, U.S.A
                    Dr. Janet Blake, Scotland, United Kingdom
                    Mr. Brad Simon, U.S.A
                    Ms. Pualani Kanaka'ole Kanahele, U.S.A

Group III: Local, national, regional, and international policies, with particular reference to the transmission, revitalization, and documentation of intangible cultural heritage.

Participants: Professor Kwabena Nketia, Ghana — Chairperson
                    Ms. Sivia Tora, Fiji — Rapporteur
                    Dr. Gail Saunders, The Bahamas
                    Ms. Zulma Yugar, Bolivia
                    Ms. Khurshida Mambetova, Uzbekistan
                    Dr. Florentine Hornedo, Philippines
                    Dr. Osamu Yamaguti, Japan
                    Mr. Renato Matusse, Mozambique
                    Mr. Jean Guibal, France
                    Mrs. Vlasta Ondrusova, Czech Republic
                    Mr. Mohsen Shaalan, Egypt
                    Professor Heikki Kirkinen, Finland
                    Mr. Namankoumba Kouyaté, Guinea
                    Mrs. Juana Nuñez, Cuba

Reports of Working Groups, Proposal of Pilot Projects, and Development of Action Plan

15. Agenda Item 7: Reports from thematic sessions, including group recommendations (plenary)

After working separately throughout the second day, the three working groups returned to the plenary session with their recommendations on the third day of the Conference. The reports took the following forms:

Group I: A Recommendation addressed to governments stating that they should actively support communities in the practices of generation, transmission, authorization, and attribution of traditional knowledge and skills in accordance with the wishes of the communities and in conformity with current international standards of human rights. Three steps that they should consider taking are put forward as well as twelve areas requiring further study by a group of experts [see Appendix 4].

Group II: Considered five broad areas involved with the protection of traditional culture and made recommendations that were incorporated into the final Action Plan of the conference [see Appendix 5].

Group III: Proposed seven recommendations to the governments of Member States and nine recommendations to UNESCO on the basis of discussions within the group and a set of nine points identified at the start of the meeting [see Appendix 6].

Reports and recommendations of the three working groups were presented by the Chairperson and Rapporteur of each group in plenary session. These reports were then discussed and approved by the plenary session.

16.   Agenda Item 8: International cooperation: presentation of pilot projects (plenary)

Mrs. Aikawa presented a proposal for five Pilot Projects of International and Inter-Regional Cooperation drafted by the Secretariat of UNESCO on the basis of recommendations formulated by the majority of regional and sub-regional seminars. These pilot projects will be further developed by the UNESCO Secretariat and will be submitted to funding agencies, foundations, and Member States which are likely to provide UNESCO with voluntary financial contributions. They include the following:

- Regional and International Networking among Institutions Involved with Traditional Culture and Folklore;
- creation of UNESCO Chairs of Traditional Culture and Folklore;
- Feasibility Study for the Elaboration of Legal Protection of Traditional Culture and Folklore in Africa, Latin America, and the Caribbean;
- International Meeting for the Integration of Traditional Culture and Folklore into Cultural Policy;
- Inter-Regional Project on the Revitalization of Traditional Knowledge of Mediation in Conflict Prevention (Africa and the Pacific).

The participants were invited to make further suggestions to UNESCO regarding these pilot projects.

17.   Agenda Item 9: Presentation and approval of the draft Action Plan for safeguarding and revitalization of intangible cultural heritage and final report (plenary)

A Drafting Committee was established in the evening of 29 June to draft an Action Plan. The following participants took part in the Committee:

> Dr. Florentine Hornedo — Chairperson
> Dr. Grace Koch — Rapporteur
> Mr. Andy Abeita
> Dr. Tressa Berman
> Ms. Manuela Carneiro da Cunha
> Mr. Rachid El Houda
> Dr. Junzo Kawada
> Ms. Kurshida Mambetova
> Mr. Ralph Regenvanu
> Mr. Rajeev Sethi

18. The Chairperson and Rapporteur of the Drafting Committee presented the draft Action Plan to the plenary session. The assembly, after having integrated the group recommendations into the draft Action Plan, discussed extensively, modified, and finally approved the Action Plan as modified [see Appendix 7]. The Final Report was read by the Rapporteur, Dr. Janet Blake, and was approved unanimously by the participants.

19. Dr. Richard Kurin and Mr. Mounir Bouchenaki delivered the closing remarks, thanking all of the participants for their fruitful and constructive contributions to the Conference.

Appendix 1: Agenda

I.   Conference opening
II. The UNESCO *Recommendation on the Safeguarding of Traditional Culture and Folklore* (1989) — actions undertaken by UNESCO for its implementation (plenary)
III. Reports of eight regional and sub-regional seminars (plenary)
IV. Overview of country reports and regional seminar reports (plenary)
V.   Analysis of the 1989 *Recommendation* in the context of today — positive and negative aspects (plenary)
VI. Thematic discussions (working groups)
   A. Intangible cultural heritage in relation to natural and tangible cultural heritage, and its role in resolving local and national problems related to today's major issues such as cultural identity, gender issues, sustainable human development, globalization, peaceful coexistence of different ethnic groups, conflict prevention, youth cultures, evolution of new technologies in communication and information, environmental deterioration, etc.
   B. Legal protection of local and national intangible cultural heritage
   C. Local, national, regional, and international policies, with particular reference to the transmission, revitalization, and documentation of intangible cultural heritage
VII. Reports from thematic sessions, including group recommendations (plenary)
VIII. International cooperation: presentation of action plan and pilot projects (plenary)
IX. Presentation and adoption of final Action Plan and final report (plenary)

Appendix 2: Annotated Agenda

I.   Background

The General Conference of UNESCO adopted at its twenty-fifth session (November 1989) the *Recommendation on the Safeguarding of Traditional Culture and Folklore* (this volume, 8–12). This significant act was derived from the consideration that folklore forms part of the heritage of humanity and, as such, it can be a powerful means of bringing together different peoples and social groups and of asserting their cultural identity. In addition, this action underlined the fact that folklore possesses great social, economic, cultural, and political importance in both historical and contemporary cultural contexts. Moreover, folklore, some forms of which are extremely fragile by nature, is an integral part of cultural heritage and living culture. The adoption of the *Recommendation* was meant to encourage various governments to play a decisive role by taking legislative measures, among others, which comply with local constitutional practices, as a means of preserving and safeguarding traditional culture and folklore. With increasing transformations affecting all regions of the world, this task remains urgent in nature.

The *Recommendation* is comprised of seven chapters, including (i) Definition, (ii)

Identification, (iii) Conservation, (iv) Preservation, (v) Dissemination, (vi) Protection, and (vii) International Cooperation. It defines the term "traditional and popular culture" as follows: (para. A) "Folklore (or traditional and popular culture) is the totality of tradition-based creations of a cultural community, expressed by a group or individuals and recognized as reflecting the expectations of a community in so far as they reflect its cultural and social identity; its standards and values are transmitted orally, by imitation or by other means. Its forms are, among others, language, literature, music, dance, games, mythology, rituals, customs, handicrafts, architecture and other arts."

In February 1990, the Director-General of UNESCO distributed a circular letter to Member States inviting them to take all necessary steps towards the implementation of the *Recommendation*. According to the terms outlined in Article IV, paragraph 4, of UNESCO's Constitution, each Member State shall submit recommendations or conventions adopted by UNESCO to competent authorities within a period of one year from the close of the session of the General Conference at which they were adopted. However, by 1991, only six countries had submitted special reports on action undertaken towards the implementation of the *Recommendation*. Moreover, these reports simply affirmed the relevance of existing national legislation and highlighted specific measures taken to familiarize the national authorities concerned with the provisions of the *Recommendation*.

In order to systematically assess the implementation of the *Recommendation* and the present situation of the safeguarding and revitalization of intangible cultural heritage in Member States, UNESCO launched a four-year series of region-by-region surveys, extending from 1995 to 1999. A total of eight regional seminars have been convened: these include (i) Strá nice, Czech Republic (June 1995), for Central and Eastern Europe; (ii) Mexico City, Mexico (September 1997), for Latin America and the Caribbean; (iii) Tokyo, Japan (February/March 1998), for Asia; (iv) Joensuu, Finland (September 1998), for Western Europe; (v) Tashkent, Republic of Uzbekistan (October 1998), for Central Asia and the Caucasus; (vi) Accra, Ghana (January 1999), for Africa; (vii) Noumea, New Caledonia (February 1999), for the Pacific; and (viii) Beirut, Lebanon (May 1999), for Arab States.

The present Conference is the culmination of these regional seminars. Its primary goal is to globally assess the present situation and future orientation of the 1989 *Recommendation on the Safeguarding of Traditional Culture and Folklore*. Intangible cultural heritage is at once rich and diverse, yet for a variety of reasons many producers of traditional and popular culture are abandoning their crafts or ceasing to transmit them to younger generations. There is thus a threat of the disappearance of a great deal of traditional and popular culture all around the world. It is therefore imperative to take urgent steps towards its preservation and revitalization for both current and future generations.

II.   The Objectives of the Conference

The objectives of the Conference are:

A.   To assess the present situation of the safeguarding and revitalization of intangible cultural heritage in the world today

B.   To analyze the relationships between intangible, natural, and tangible cultural heritage, and the role that intangible cultural heritage plays in resolving local and national problems related to major contemporary concerns, such as cultural identity, gender issues, sustainable human development, globalization, peaceful coexistence of different ethnic groups, conflict prevention, youth cultures, evolution of new technologies in communication and information, environmental deterioration, etc.

C.   To examine the legal protection of local and national intangible cultural heritage

D.   To suggest local, national, and international policies, with particular reference to the transmission, revitalization, and documentation of intangible cultural heritage

E.   To examine the future role of the 1989 *Recommendation* within UNESCO Member States

F.   To encourage international cooperation through the development of future strategies and pilot projects

III.   The Organization of the Conference

Following a Conference introduction there will be a survey of actions undertaken by UNESCO for the implementation of the 1989 *Recommendation* (Agenda items 1 and 2, day 1). The Conference will continue with a brief discussion of the results of the regional meetings (Agenda items 3 and 4, day 1), and then break up into three working groups for intensive discussions as per Agenda item 6 (days 1 and 2). Plenary sessions (day 3) will address Agenda items 7–10.

A.   Reports of the Eight Regional Conferences

The procedure of conducting regional surveys operated in the following chronological manner: (i) UNESCO identified a specialized institution-partner in each region; (ii) UNESCO, taking into account regional specificities, drafted a questionnaire pertaining to the application of the *Recommendation*; (iii) UNESCO distributed this questionnaire to the National Commissions of the Member States concerned, requesting them to take necessary steps to ensure that the questionnaire be duly completed; (iv) on the basis of replies to the questionnaire returned, UNESCO and its institution-partner compiled statistics and formulated a comprehensive report which assessed the degree of implementation of the *Recommendation*. These reports proved to be extremely effective in all regional seminars, as they led to fruitful discussions, multiple recommendations, and concrete conclusions.

B.   An Overview of Regional Reports: World Assessment

The regional reports, which focus on local and national tendencies, aspects, difficulties, and queries, illuminate both the contemporary situation and future orientation of intangible cultural heritage. An overview of these reports will thus highlight what has, and what has not, been achieved in UNESCO Member States over the past ten years since the adoption of the *Recommendation*, as well as what needs to be done in the future.

At the request of UNESCO, the Smithsonian Institution has compiled summary and statistical reports based on regional reports on the application of UNESCO's 1989 *Recommendation*, which will be mailed to all conference participants prior to the meeting (this volume, 20–35, 35–41).

C.   Analysis of the 1989 *Recommendation* in the Context of Today: Positive and Negative Aspects

Since the reduction of East-West bipolar tensions 1989, the world has undergone extensive political, economic, and socio-cultural transformations. Moreover, new technologies have emerged that facilitate and also challenge the safeguarding of intangible cultural heritage. Despite such tremendous progress, however, a number of problems have arisen. For such reasons, the time has come to assess the positive and negative aspects of the *Recommendation* in the context of today, particularly through examining its provisions from both a conceptual and legal perspective.

At the request of UNESCO, the Smithsonian Institution is preparing a document on the 1989 *Recommendation* that will be distributed to participants prior to the Conference (this volume, 57–61).

D.   Thematic Discussions (working groups)

Group I. Intangible, natural, and tangible cultural heritage, and the role that intangible cultural heritage plays in resolving local and national problems related to major contemporary concerns such as cultural identity, gender issues, sustainable human development, globalization, peaceful coexistence of different ethnic groups, conflict prevention, youth cultures, evolution of new technologies in communication and information, environmental deterioration, etc.

Among the topics that may be discussed are the following:

Intangible, natural, and tangible cultural heritage. Since the 1970s, UNESCO has been famous for actions it has taken to safeguard great historical monuments, such as the Abu Simbel Temple in Egypt. The "World Heritage List," which has been a UNESCO flagship activity through the 1990s, added "natural heritage" to the existing "tangible cultural heritage — monuments and sites." In November 1998 UNESCO Member States, for whom "cultural heritage" had meant only "tangible cultural heritage," agreed to enlarge the concept of "cultural heritage" by including "intangible cultural heritage" as well.

The UNESCO Executive Board approved at its 155th session (November 1998) a new project, called "Proclamation of Masterpieces of the Oral and Intangible Heritage of Humanity." The approval of this project attests that UNESCO Member States have accepted an enlarged concept of "cultural heritage," one that includes both tangible and intangible heritage. In fact, intangible heritage and tangible heritage have always been closely interconnected: the former has provided meaning to the latter, while the latter has offered physical support to the former. The following examples may illustrate this point: (i) the long frieze of Angkor Wat, which depicts the 1500-year-old legendary epic story of the Ramayana; (ii) the Khmer Court dance, which reflects, even today, the dancing style exhibited by the beautiful *Apsara* ("semi-divine") on the stone reliefs of the temple; and (iii) the symbolism, techniques, and artistry of traditional wall decorations of Mauritanian earth architecture, which have been handed down through centuries from mothers to daughters. Moreover, natural or landscape heritage, such as the Mosi-oa-Tunya (Victoria Falls), of Zambia-Zimbabwe, has given birth to a number of oral traditions, myths, and epics, which endow the natural setting with cultural meaning.

In order to ensure the safeguarding of intangible heritage, an integrated approach is required that would simultaneously consider both tangible and intangible aspects. Moreover, it is essential that local contemporary communities become empowered, and hence participate, towards initiating measures for the safeguarding of their intangible cultural heritage. For this purpose, it is indispensable to provide local populations with appropriate training in heritage management that would emphasize the integration of tangible and intangible heritage.

Group Identity. "Traditional and popular culture" (intangible cultural heritage) can play a significant role in resolving local and national problems related to today's major issues. For instance, for many populations, intangible cultural heritage has continually played a vital role in the assertion and expression of group identity, itself deeply rooted in history. Cosmologies, beliefs, and values conveyed by languages, oral traditions, and diverse cultural manifestations often constitute the foundations of community life. Moreover, in many countries, the assertion of cultural identity based on traditional and popular local cultures has played an integral role in the nation-building process during the postcolonial period.

Gender Issues. In many societies throughout the world, women have always played a vital role in safeguarding and transmitting traditions, rules of conduct, and skills which they regard as indispensable in maintaining familial cohesion and social position. Such forms include, among others, the code of ethics, stories, oral histories, songs, music, languages, shamanism, ritual, and culinary skills. In the production of material culture, where particular symbolism, artistry, and manual skills are expressed in acts of embroidery, weaving, carpet-making, and habitat production, among others, women have been highly successful not only in retaining and transmitting traditional methods and practices but also in adapting them in innovative ways with modern elements, hence yielding novel material and technical forms.

Sustainable Development. The success of sustainable human development requires the adaptation of development strategies to the socio-cultural context of any given society. It is therefore vital to observe and analyze local socio-economic systems as well as modes of thought, behavior, and traditional methods of production, which are transmitted orally. Furthermore, certain expressions of traditional culture and folklore may directly contribute to economic development through the enhancement of cultural industry, specifically in the fields of performing arts and handicraft.

Globalization. The contemporary globalization of economic, political, and social life, accelerated by progress in information and communication technology, has resulted in much cultural penetration and amalgamation. Subsequently, majority cultures have been increasingly absorbing their minority counterparts, thus threatening cultural diversity. For such reasons, it is often argued that globalization has contributed to the growth of cultural uniformity. Revitalization of the intangible cultural heritage specific to each community will thus assist in the preservation of local cultures, whose strengthening is essential to the perpetuation of a worldwide cultural diversity. This diversity, based upon peaceful cohabitation of different ethnic groups, is a prerequisite for the development of a multicultural system, a fundamental element for global peace, the construction of which is the primary task of UNESCO and the United Nations.

Technology. It is true that rapid progress in information and communication technologies may have damaged many traditional and popular local cultures. These technologies, however, are indispensable to preserving and promoting those cultures. Moreover, we should not forget that culture is not static, but continually evolving. New technologies have advanced communication and information processing, and facilitated the emergence of new and various forms of hybridized cultural expressions. Moreover, it is imperative to acknowledge that youths, those most susceptible to technological progress, will continue to produce their own artistic forms; these too will become part of a new heritage, such as ethno-techno music. Hence, we must continually remain attentive to cultural evolution.

Ethnic Conflicts. The number of ethnic conflicts is increasing throughout the world. In order to reduce the number of these conflicts, the representatives of both African and Pacific countries who attended the regional seminars in Accra (January 1999) and Noumea (February 1999), respectively, expressed their strong desire to reconsider traditional wisdom and knowledge as a means of conflict prevention.

Environmental Protection. Environmental deterioration in the world poses serious problems not only for local communities, as it endangers traditional resources, lifestyles, and cultures, but also for the entire planet. Concrete measures to combat such degradation are therefore needed. The revitalization of traditional knowledge, skills, and practices, aiming to regulate natural resources through the implementation, for example, of fishing and hunting taboos, is itself largely constituted in the interrelationship between people and the environment; such revitalization can become beneficial in the struggle against environmental hazards.

Group II. Legal Protection of Local and National Intangible Cultural Heritage

Traditional and popular culture is, by its very nature, multifarious and sometimes threatened with extinction. For this reason, it is imperative to establish legal steps to ensure the safeguarding of intangible cultural heritage throughout the world: i.e., systematic protection on both local and national levels. Such protection must embrace not only intangible cultural heritage in itself but also the practitioners of traditional cultures and folklore.

Traditional and popular culture is also easily subjected to appropriation and commercial exploitation by members of communities other than those that created it. It is imperative to protect intellectual property rights, including both authors' rights and industrial rights of the traditional and popular cultural expression once it is used by a third party or for other purposes. In establishing such a protection system, particular attention should be paid to ensure that benefits be given to the populations who initiated the cultural expression in question.

Group III. Local, National, Regional, and International Policies, with particular reference to the transmission, revitalization, and documentation of intangible cultural heritage

UNESCO's role, as an intergovernmental organization, is to instigate its member governments to take actions in line with UNESCO objectives. It is therefore UNESCO's primary task to raise awareness of member governments and their policy makers on the urgent need to safeguard and revitalize the world's intangible cultural heritage. It is essential to assess — with the aim of elaborating — local, national, and international policies, which would focus particularly on the transmission, revitalization, and documentation of this heritage. The goal is to assist each government to establish appropriate policies in this regard or to promote regional or international cooperation to encourage this effort.

E.   Reports from Group Sessions, including Group Recommendations

The working groups are invited to reunite in plenary in order to discuss and exchange ideas and recommendations derived from individual working sessions.

F.   Future Role of the 1989 *Recommendation* within UNESCO Member States

The *Recommendation* has been in existence for ten years. We are aware of its past and must now consider its future orientation in light of the present situation. It is time to assess the future role of the *Recommendation* within UNESCO Member States in order to ensure the safeguarding and revitalization of the world's intangible cultural heritage. Some UNESCO Member States consider that the time has come for UNESCO to create an International Convention for the safeguarding of intangible cultural heritage after the manner of the World Heritage Convention (November 1972), itself applicable only to tangible and natural heritage, or to modify the existing Convention, if possible, to include intangible heritage. In order to explore a new Convention, the *Recommendation* could be used as a base. In addition, many countries continue to stress the urgent need to establish an international instrument for the protection of intellectual property rights in expressions of traditional culture and folklore. UNESCO and WIPO are today examining this possibility.

G.   International Cooperation: Future Strategies and Pilot Projects

During the Conference, participants are expected to identify problems and challenges for the coming years and to formulate medium-term strategies of international cooperation aiming at the safeguarding and revitalization of intangible cultural heritage throughout the world. Such strategies may define the future orientation of the UNESCO program related to intangible cultural heritage, its priorities, suitable approaches, as well as methods of work to be applied. It is hoped that these strategies will also include concrete measures to improve both the application and effectiveness of the 1989 *Recommendation*.

H.   Presentation of the Final Recommendations

The participants of the Conference are invited to draw up and present various recommendations for the future orientation or reinforcement of the existing 1989 *Recommendation*, addressed to UNESCO, their respective Member States, and specialized institutions such as the Smithsonian Institution.

Appendix 3: Participants, Staff, and Fellows and Interns

Participants

Andy P. Abeita
President
Council for Indigenous Arts and Culture
Peralta, New Mexico
U.S.A.

Noriko Aikawa
Director
Intangible Cultural Heritage Unit
Division of Cultural Heritage
UNESCO

Robyne Bancroft
Australian National University
Canberra
Australia

Tressa Berman
Arizona State University West
Phoenix, Arizona
U.S.A.

Janet Blake
School of Law
University of Glasgow
Glasgow, Scotland
U.K.

Stepanida Borisova
Ministry of Culture
Sakha Republic (Yakutia)
Yakutsk
Russian Federation

Mounir Bouchenaki
Director
Division of Cultural Heritage and World Heritage Centre
UNESCO

Manuela Carneiro da Cunha
Professor of Anthropology
University of Chicago
Chicago, Illinois
U.S.A.

Russell Collier
Strategic Watershed Analysis Team
Gitxsan Nation
Hazelton, British Columbia
Canada

Rachid El Houda
Architecte, DPLG
Marrakech
Morocco

Mahaman Garba
Ethnomusicologue
Centre de Formation et de Promotion Musicale
Niamey
Niger

Jean Guibal
Directeur
Musée Dauphinois
Grenoble
France

Mihály Hoppál
Director
European Centre for Traditional Culture
Budapest
Hungary

Florentino H. Hornedo
College of Arts and Sciences
Ateneo de Manila University
Quezon City, Manila
Philippines

Peter Jaszi
Washington College of Law
Washington, DC
U.S.A.

Pualani Kanaka'ole Kanahele
The Edith Kanaka'ole Foundation
Hilo, Hawai'i
U.S.A.

Junzo Kawada
Professor of Cultural Anthropology
Hiroshima City University

Hiroshima
Japan

Heikki Kirkinen
Vice-President
European Academy of Arts, Sciences and Humanities
University of Joensuu
Joensuu
Finland

Grace Koch
Archives Manager
Australian Institute of Aboriginal and Torres Strait Islander Studies
Canberra
Australia

Namankoumba Kouyaté
Chargé d'Affaires A.I.
Ambassade de la République de Guinée
Bonn
Germany

Kurshida Mambetova
Head of Culture Department
UNESCO National Commission of the Republic of Uzbekistan
Tashkent
Uzbekistan

Renato Matusse
Permanent Secretary and Secretary General
Southern African Development Community (SADC)
Maputo
Mozambique

J.H. Kwabena Nketia
Director
International Centre for African Music and Dance
University of Ghana
Legon, Accra
Ghana

Mamiko Ogawa
Cultural Affairs Department
Ministry of Foreign Affairs
Tokyo
Japan

Vlasta Ondrusova
Deputy Director
Institute of Folk Culture
Strá nice
Czech Republic

Lyndel V. Prott
Chief, International Standards Section
Division of Cultural Heritage
UNESCO

Kamal Puri
Professor of Law
The University of Queensland
Brisbane, Queensland
Australia

Miguel Puwainchir
Alcalde
Municipio de Huamboya
Prov. de Morona Santiago (Amazonia)
Ecuador

Ralph Regenvanu
Curator
Vanuatu Cultural Centre
Port Vila
Vanuatu

Gail Saunders
Director
Department of Archives
Nassau
The Bahamas

Rajeev Sethi
Principal, Rajeev Sethi Scenographers, Pvt. Ltd.
New Delhi
India

Mohsen Shaalan
Ministry of Culture
Cairo
Egypt

Samantha Sherkin
Consultant
Intangible Cultural Heritage Unit

Division of Cultural Heritage
UNESCO

Juana Silvera Nuñez
Presidenta
Comisi\n Nacional Cubana de la UNESCO
La Habana
Cuba

Brad Simon
Director, Legal and Business Affairs
Shockwave.com

Preston Thomas
Commissioner
Aboriginal and Torres Strait Islander Commission
Phillip
Australia

Sivia Tora
Permanent Secretary
Ministry of Women, Culture and Social Welfare
Suva
Fiji

Osamu Yamaguti
Professor of Musicology
Osaka University
Osaka
Japan

Zulma Yugar
Directora General de Promoción Cultural
Viceministerio de Cultura
La Paz
Bolivia

Observers

Mary Jo Arnoldi, Smithsonian Institution
Alberta Arthurs, The Rockefeller Foundation
Barry Bergey, National Endowment for the Arts
Francine Berkowitz, Smithsonian Institution
Gigi Bradford, Center for Arts and Culture, Washington, DC
Rachelle Browne, Smithsonian Institution
Peggy Bulger, American Folklife Center, Library of Congress
Olivia Cadaval, Smithsonian Institution

Shelton Davis, The World Bank
Kreszentia Duer, The World Bank
Alexander P. Durtka, Jr., CIOFF Cultural Commission, International Institute of Wisconsin
William Ferris, National Endowment for the Humanities
Arlene Fleming, The World Bank
Cecile Goli, UNESCO
Charlotte Heth, Smithsonian Institution
Vera Hyatt, Smithsonian Institution
David Hunter, Center for International Environmental Law, Washington DC
Enrique Iglesias, Banco Interamericano de Desarollo, Washington DC
Alan Jabbour, American Folklife Center, Library of Congress
Charles Kleymeyer, Inter-American Foundation
Mary Ellen Lane, Independent Council of American Overseas Research
Brian LeMay, Smithsonian Institution
Ellen McCulloch-Lovell, White House Millennium Commission
William Merrill, Smithsonian Institution
Francis Method, UNESCO
Diana Baird N'Diaye, Smithsonian Institution
Stefan Nitulescu, House of Deputies, Bucharest, Romania
Pennie Ojeda, National Endowment for the Arts
Marc Pachter, Smithsonian Institution
Damien Pwono, The Ford Foundation
Caroline Ramsey, The Crafts Center, Washington, DC
Alison Dundes Renteln, University of Southern California
John Roberts, Ohio State University
Jean Roche, CIOFF (Conseil International des Organisations de Festivals de Folklore et
    d'Arts Traditionnels), Gannat, France
Daniel Salcedo, PEOPLink, Kensington, MD
David Sanjek, BMI Archives, New York, New York
Dan Sheehy, National Endowment for the Arts
Claire Brett Smith, Aid to Artisans Inc., Farmington, CT
Ann Webster Smith, ICOMOS
D.A. Sonneborn, Smithsonian Institution
John Kuo Wei Tchen, New York University
Glenn Wallach, Center for Arts and Culture
Glenn M. Wiser, Center for International Environmental Law
Joe Wilson, The National Council for Traditional Arts
Tomas Ybarra-Frausto, The Rockefeller Foundation

Smithsonian Staff

James Early
John Franklin
Amy Horowitz
Anthony Seeger
Peter Seitel

Fellows and Interns

Maria Elena Cepeda, Ann Arbor, Michigan
Lisa Maiorino, Indianapolis, Indiana
Anthony McCann, Warrenpoint, County Down, Northern Ireland
Jonathan McCollum, Allston, Massachusetts
Chad Redwing, Phoenix, Arizona

Appendix 4: Report of Group I

Monday, 28 June 1999, the first meeting of Group I, 1545–1730

Group I was constituted to discuss the following themes: intangible cultural heritage in relation to natural and tangible cultural heritage and its role in resolving local and national problems related to major issues such as cultural identity, gender issues, sustainable human development, globalization, peaceful coexistence of ethnic groups, conflict prevention, youth cultures, evolution of new technologies in communication and information, environmental deterioration, etc.

The chair, Ralph Regenvanu, asked participants to introduce themselves. After this, Rajeev Sethi began by wondering about the current status of the 1989 *Recommendation*, particularly its conceptualization of the problem it addresses. He questioned whether the terms "folk" and "tradition" overlook the idea and possibility of innovation. He made some suggestions for changes in the wording in the 1989 *Recommendation*, Section A, Definition of Folklore: "Imitation" should become "emulation"; "Games" should become "sports," as the latter encompasses more; "Handicrafts, architecture" — don't we really mean "habitat"? he wondered; "Other arts" seems to be a residual category that is not specific enough.

Regarding Section C, Conservation of Folklore: Mr. Sethi suggested that we first talk about safeguarding people, then archives. Culture is living but dependent on people, whom we need to empower. The language in the 1989 *Recommendation* seems to be condescending.

Pualani Kanahele observed that many peoples base important elements of their cultural identities on their natural environments, thus inextricably linking cultural and natural heritages. What will we do twenty years from now, she wondered, when our environment has become terribly degraded [by commercial development]?

Andy Abeita voiced a concern that practitioners of traditional culture cannot put religion and art in the same category as commodities, but at the same time, we need to come up with similar legal tools for protecting practitioners' ability to continue their creative practices. Rights to ownership of music and prayer come under copyright provisions and thus can be legally enforceable. Without legal protections that the private sector understands, we can engage in endless, and ultimately fruitless, discussions trying to define ourselves.

Rajeev Sethi replied, on the question of handicrafts, that commodification in his experience is based on the needs of the artists. He felt we must help artisans to understand the meaning of new design without abusing their own culture. There is nothing necessarily wrong with innovation.

Pualani Kanahele said she liked Sivia Tora's comment made earlier in the meeting about the impossibility of separating tangible from intangible culture, or dividing cultural heritage from natural heritage of the environment. She clarified what she meant by environmental deterioration, giving an example of large, international hotels being built on the coral polyp, the marine animal that creates coral, the substance of the islands themselves and a central figure in poetic chants about creation.

Rajeev Sethi replied he did not think there is an answer for that kind of problem, not in UNESCO. In India there are a great many tribes displaced in the name of development. There is no answer for this; whom can one turn to?

Miguel Puwainchir responded by quoting a saying that "a person without land is a person without culture." If UNESCO cannot change anything, he charged the group, then we must change UNESCO. Before the Spanish conquest, we had a pure culture, he said. Today, there is much confusion, and culture has become polluted. We need to promote and defend our culture. Otherwise, our culture will die slowly, and we will have accepted that. We should not isolate ourselves, though. We should seek cultural interrelationships. Negative values should be forgotten. For instance, in Bolivia the coca plant has been used for good medicinal purposes. Others have made it an evil drug. What shall we do today? We need to accept the positive values and discard the negative.

He continued: The 1989 *Recommendation* basically describes culture as "things," but culture is also human beings. Why should we separate the two? We need to exchange experiences — this is healthy. Many of the problems being discussed involve alienation. But we must remember that culture is our very nature.

Rachid El Houda observed that he was concerned about some of the discussion. We talk at a formal level, he said, not at the level of substance. Therefore, we need to separate particular legal instruments, etc., from our ways of thinking about culture. There are two ways to consider the issue: We can establish a list of all those things that can be thought of as traditional culture; or we can find out what brings us together through our differences. Differences can bring us together, he asserted. We need ideas that can serve as a basis for us to move forward. Bridges can be built with culture and religion, for example, through the meaning of symbolism that can be explicated in one culture/religion and found to exist in our own culture. We must get past what tries to divide us.

Mahaman Garba wondered whether the connection between religion and preservation was to be regarded as a forbidden topic. The intangible heritage in my country is music, he observed. Some speak about "cultural heritage" and some about "folklore." We should use the former, as it is a more noble term.

We must choose, he continued. Do we want to develop or stay where we are? Evolution has its burdens. People in the Third World like to have television. What was there before that — songs and games? Shall we refuse TV? Education may come from songs and games, but artists can be seen through TV and radio. Otherwise, access to these artists would require travel of thousands of kilometers.

Pualani Kanahele partially summed up the session, saying that we have talked about coexistence and conflict prevention. We must learn how to get along with development also. Yes, she said, we need to know about development, but development must know about us as well. We should consider symbols too and take the positives and negatives of all of this.

Tuesday, 29 June 1999, the second meeting of Group I, 0930–1200

Robyne Bancroft spoke in her presentation (this volume, 70–74) about the necessity of using a holistic approach to understanding Australian Aboriginal culture, which consists of a dense web of relationships between humans and their environment. Their history goes back 60,000 years but is largely ignored. There were over 250 language groups at the time of colonization; only twenty-five active languages exist today. There are now 325,000 Aborigines out of an Australian population of eighteen million. They have survived and have recently emerged onto the international scene. Courts have made important rulings about such vital issues as land rights, and the issue of the "lost generation" (families which were separated by government practices) has begun to be dealt with. Despite some positive laws and rulings, however, there is still a great need to achieve justice.

Aboriginals do not like the terms "folklore" and "mythology," as in Australia these have negative implications. She suggests instead "Indigenous cultural heritage." Current issues of importance to Aboriginal peoples include gender issues, a code of ethics for dealings between Indigenous and non-Indigenous peoples, and the repatriation of human remains from overseas. She presented recommendations: The 1989 *Recommendation* lacks teeth; to remedy this, it should become a UNESCO Convention. The importance of biological diversity needs to be formally recognized; institutions such as UNESCO and the Smithsonian should support Indigenous peoples in their struggle for their rights; and there needs to be more training and career development that is controlled by Indigenous people.

Mihály Hoppál spoke in his presentation (this volume, 182–184) about today's information-based society, in which there is limitless economic growth, but little significant tradition and local knowledge. There is a treasure trove of tradition-based knowledge about the myriad ways that people have learned to live with each other. This includes spiritual traditions. Local value systems can provide a base for conflict resolution. It is not the local systems but a lack of knowledge of the Other that causes conflict. Local value systems, such as prejudices, provide the emotional background for people to engage in conflict with each other. Globalization can be a threat to Indigenous cultures and a guise for a new form of imperialism. It can result in a denial of collective local rights and a threat to minorities. Legislation should be passed to respect and protect the human rights and cultural identity of minorities. Anglo-Saxon-based value systems may not he appropriate for all. He recommended development of: strategies to educate young people to respect the traditions of other nations; festivals that celebrate the diversity of each nation; documentation and preservation of traditions; treatment of the cultural heritages in Member States with respect and passage of laws to enforce respect for these local cultures; honor for each other's traditions so that we may live longer on this earth.

Miguel Puwainchir made a presentation (this volume, 65–66) on what he called "interculturality" — the respect for and knowledge of cultures other than one's own. Today we live with a complex mix of people. By setting up states and nations we have created national cultures and identities that do not recognize local traditions. In Ecuador, Indigenous cultures have united to change the laws and to create a "respected place" for Indigenous peoples, which has enabled them to resist assimilation. In the future we should have nations that have no state cultures, for the latter inevitably make local cultures into "folklore." National curricula should be developed to teach about different cultures, so this is part of general learning, not left to anthropologists and museums. Interculturality will help us avoid globalization of culture, maintain cultural diversity, and defend against the rampant development that is destroying our environment. His recommendations were: states should have no single national culture; local cultures should neither be commodified nor turned into monuments, rather they must be preserved and promoted as living cultures; it is important to learn about other cultures without losing the uniqueness of one's own; UNESCO should promote new ways of thinking about culture, celebrate the diversity of the world, and not allow modern technologies to destroy local cultures.

Mihály Hoppál commented that misunderstanding between cultural groups is based on a lack of knowledge of the history and culture of the Other. In East Europe, he observed, historical myths can be used for modern political ends such as war.

Paulani Kanahele responded to the presentation by saying that globalism is another form of colonialism and is undermining local traditions, particularly among the youth. It is therefore critical to include young people in more rituals and ceremonies, or else these traditions will be lost to globalization. Educating outsiders on cultural matters is a good start, but a difficult task, given the pervasiveness of their prejudices and their resistance to learning about Indigenous cultures. For the reasons Miguel Puwainchir outlines, "myth" and "folklore" are problematic terms that need to be changed.

Russell Collier responded that the terminology used does not make a great deal of difference in the continuous battles now being fought, or those battles yet to be fought, with governments and other forces that threaten Indigenous cultures.

In his presentation (this volume, 194–202), Dr. Mahaman Garba described a case study of a UNESCO project, a center for musical education (Centre de Formation et de Promotion Musicale) in Niger. He began with a brief description of the eight linguistic and ethnic groups in Niger. In that country, there is a caste system which designates the persons who are to pass on the oral tradition and the ones who are to be the musicians. When one such person dies, it is as though a library has burnt down. There has been a great loss of these people without their being replaced, and the traditions and music they carried are also being lost. This problem, along with recommendations for its solution, was brought to UNESCO, which helped begin the center for music training. The work of preserving musical traditions is going forward with the help of UNESCO and other funding sources, especially from Japan. Dr. Garba especially thanked Mrs. Aikawa and Professor Kawada for their efforts on behalf of the center.

Dr. Garba described the three areas of operation of the center — research, training, and promotion. He said that they were also dealing with questions of European ownership of music and musical instruments and of the repatriation of this musical heritage. On the issue of funding, Dr. Garba observed that it is becoming less and less and that the center was not permitted to use the financial assistance to its best advantage as the center's staff wished. He recommended that local experts in cultural development projects be allowed adequate participation in decision-making about the allocation of funds.

Rachid El-Houda made a presentation (this volume, 216–217) about the Jemaa El Fna Square in Marrakech, a World Heritage Site, to explore one kind of connection between tangible and intangible heritage. He gave a brief description of this urban area and its cultural value. Many writers, actors, playwrights have taken professional interest in this square. City planners have tried to emulate its spatial and cultural qualities in other parts of the world. This is a place where many forms of public storytelling have been regularly performed. The square is now under attack from aggressive modernization. This urban space is commercially valuable and therefore a target of commercial development. The value of its rich oral culture does not compute or compete well against this monetary value. It is easy to prohibit and displace the performance traditions for the sake of commercial development, but near impossible to recreate the rich oral culture that thrives in this kind of space. The next difficulty to be faced is loss of these displaced human treasures, which are so difficult to replace. A non-governmental organization has been created to help preserve this area and its traditions. Mrs. Aikawa and UNESCO are greatly to be thanked for their help in this. The goals and objectives of this NGO are: guaranteeing the physical integrity and continuity of the square; recording and documenting its history and the storytelling performed there; preserving the surrounding neighborhoods; establishing cooperation with like-minded groups in Morocco and abroad; raising funds to provide pensions to elderly storytellers and other performers who have lost their livelihood due to age; writing and distributing relevant publications; promoting interest and providing training in traditional crafts and storytelling among youth; combating prejudice and negative stereotypes among local people towards the square and its inhabitants by instilling popular pride in the square and what it represents.

Junzo Kawada gave a presentation (this volume, 175–177) about the social incentives that encourage practitioners in the continuity of their traditions. He began by noting that globalization, along with other economic forces, creates cultural conformity by changing the system of socio-economic rewards so as to discourage the passing along of culture to new generations. Because preserving cultural heritage is not socioeconomically profitable, especially in minority communities, it is difficult to find successors to carry on the traditions. Many handicrafts are in danger because of this. Professor Kawada considered the way in which different kinds of traditions faced this problem and the kinds of assistance relevant for each. Tourism may have a positive effect by preserving the culture and increasing cross-cultural awareness between foreigners and the local population. Money generated from tourism provides incentives to people to practice traditional arts and performances.

Preserving tradition has many social benefits. Making traditional handicrafts helps preserve the environment through the use of natural materials. The revitalization of cultural heritage also empowers the female population, as they have a large role to play in preserving and transmitting culture.

In light of this, Professor Kawada recommended: providing financial incentives for cultural heritage practitioners on a large scale; guarding against the cultural conformity produced by globalization; encouraging cooperation among traditional groups, governments, and NGOs to preserve not-for-profit cultural performances and the training of novices in traditional storytelling; providing training in documenting and recording storytelling.

Stepanida Borisova described in her presentation (this volume, 245–247) the current state of safeguarding traditional culture in the Republic of Sakha (Yakutia) in central Siberia. Until 1991, oral traditions were documented, codified, and revised to fit the state's initiatives. Now there is a resurgence of traditional culture, including the introduction of language and culture in schools and the declaration of culturally significant days. Safeguarding of culture depends on its public display. A UNESCO project is needed to record and help safeguard cultural traditions, including those associated with shamanism and sacred places.

Ralph Regenvanu reported on the state of traditional culture in Vanuatu, an island nation in the Pacific that has experienced colonization, massive depopulation, political independence, and the return of land to its customary owners. After independence, Vanuatu wished to pursue development in other than Western ways, using Indigenous traditions. Now the trend is toward "recolonization," a return to European models. Vanuatu's tradition is totally oral, and programmatic emphasis of the Vanuatu Cultural Centre is therefore on preserving it through documentation and through assistance to communities and training of individuals in methods of recording and documenting traditions and conserving archival materials to protect them against the climate. There is ownership of specific archival materials with controlled access to them, an archival practice that establishes the community trust necessary to record and store a lineage's oral traditions. But the national economic strategy works against the Centre's efforts. The Centre documents traditional events and sites to help protect them and tries to evaluate the efficacy of some traditional practices such as conservation methods for fish and other resources and documenting them for presentation to other groups who wish help in re-establishing their traditions.

Tuesday, 29 June 1999, the third meeting of Group I, 1330–1700

Ralph Regenvanu, after describing a ceremony for the god of the yam harvest and the community issues raised by a women's culture project that documented it, asserted that the greater problem for traditional culture lies at the level of global economic relationships. The problem is that Vanuatu wants, or is being forced, to join the WTO. To do this, Vanuatu will have to open its timber and fishing industries to outside companies and relinquish the right to restrict fisheries and ban the export of logs. Also, to service the national debt, Vanuatu will be forced to export and pay in foreign currency. This is not useful to the local communities. He said the government is powerless and asked UNESCO to help combat this forced modernization brought by the WTO, which does not recognize the importance of local communities and their cultural practices.

Rajeev Sethi responded to this by wondering about the relationship between WTO and UNESCO.

Andy Abeita replied that there is no direct link but rather an overlap in policy and issues. Both are membership organizations, and like bureaucracies, they try to keep everyone happy. We have to have a needs assessment done of our constituency needs. Voices are listened to according to their numbers. We need more statistical information from these local communities.

Noriko Aikawa suggested a recommendation be made that UNESCO work more closely with the WTO.

Ralph Regenvanu confirmed the need for UNESCO to be involved. Vanuatu, for example, needs resources for documentation.

Noriko Aikawa pointed out that it is up to governments of Member States to decide what to do, but we can organize a seminar to discuss these contradictory points.

Ralph Regenvanu said the point is that the government cannot make such a request. It is being forced into seeking foreign exchange.

Russell Collier observed that his people could not depend on the Canadian government to protect their interests. There is no hope that Canada will ever stand up for them.

Andy Abeita then delivered his presentation (this volume, 78–82). The National Indian Arts and Crafts Act deals with products made by non-Indians and illegally sold as being of American Indian origin. It makes this practice illegal at the federal level and implements customs laws to prohibit the practice. Abeita's group, the Indian Arts and Crafts Association, pursues state policies similar to these federal policies, he said. They are now working on copyright laws to be recorded under the UCC to give protection against the possibility of authenticity marks being copied by others. It would help traditional crafts universally if, in the world market, there could be codification for handmade products versus commercially produced ones. The WTO is considering such a law.

Rajeev Sethi wondered what such a law could do if he, as someone from India, wanted to sell a cheaply made bracelet to Italy. And what could be done about design? One could change a design slightly to avoid copyright infringement.

Rachid El Houda observed that when it comes to copyright issues, we can learn from the copyright of software and information technologies. We need to learn what happens in other parts of the world but also find a balance. Ideas are universal though and belong to mankind as a whole, not to an individual, although the initial conception would be an individual's. But ideas that become larger concepts are part of the culture of mankind.

Andy Abeita asserted that only members of the community have the answers. We need to deal with issues on a more personal level rather than a social or purely academic level.

Mahaman Garba said the copyrights are important when everyone is trying to globalize. It reminded him that in certain communities, music is only for the chief. Who then would have the copyright? Tradition gives the right. We have ancestral and then folk/pop music for everybody, but then these can have neotraditional forms, which then also want copyrights.

Russell Collier asserted in his presentation (this volume, 75–77) that his nation in northwest British Columbia has occupied its territory for 10,000 years. Their oral history dates back to the Ice Age — members of his nation have worked with archaeologists on their language about this point. They regard theirs as the "true language" for them, in which an individual can say and think things very differently than one could say them in English. Their identity is also tied to their land, which they occupy from California to Alaska.

Oral histories have become very important in negotiations to settle land claims. This documentation along with complete genealogical data comprised the legal papers that were compiled for land claims, some of which have been filed and refiled for twenty years. The oral histories were confirmed as being valid to uphold and claim titles. Many other Indians are looking at the above decisions to boost their own claims. This idea is spreading. This collection of information is unparalleled — not only folklore but weather patterns, wildlife, fishery patterns. It all starts with documentation.

Robyne Bancroft asked about accessing documentation. She said the Australian government claimed that some information is too sensitive for her own people to know.

Russell Collier responded that they own the material. The government has no real say.

Pualani Kanahele introduced her presentation (this volume, 67–69) by saying she is in awe of the passions demonstrated about tradition. She spoke about Hawaiian traditions and history. Genealogies tell how the ancestors were related to the elements. Names provide this information — what work the ancestors did, their specialized occupations, their relations to chiefs, etc. Nothing is really lost if one looks hard enough, she asserted, but these things are not in history books.

In the latter part of the nineteenth century, history was collected, translated, and eventually put into books. At the turn of the twentieth century there was a loss of culture to the United States. Hawaiian culture came to be considered entertainment. From the 1940s to the 1960s, education was recognized as central to Hawaiian existence. Everyone was to go to college. But some held very stubbornly to traditions.

Sadly, she said, many educated Hawaiians do not know their own culture. Education is power, but soul and passion is culture. Hawaiian culture has been added to the college curriculum. Education has taught them how to fight the battles. Passion has taught them to fight for their hearts. Archaeology helps but does not interpret the culture for them. They are moving ahead by looking to the past. That is why the future is bright, she said.

Appendix 5: Report of Group II
Legal Protection of Local and National Intangible Cultural Heritage

In its first session, the group decided that each person would give a five-minute presentation during the next session based on a submitted paper or one's particular interest in the field of the legal protection of local and national intangible cultural heritage. Two minutes would then be allowed for wrap-up or a brief conversation after each presentation.

The committee decided it would not strictly reassess and critique the 1989 UNESCO document, but produce creative approaches to the preservation of cultural heritage and then consider them in relation to the UNESCO document and to other practices in various regions of the world. This conference would be an opportunity for new, creative, and substantive discourse.

Five broad topics for consideration emerged:

1. *Conceptual Frameworks,* which includes the terminology used to describe traditional culture, the assumptions one makes when discussing traditional culture and its preservation, the relation of political power to cultural preservation and culture, tangible versus intangible, and the question of who are the authors, the creators of culture. Issues such as commodification and the marketability of culture would also be explored;

2. *Legal Provisions and Mechanisms,* which includes discussion of: what is to be protected; how a legal basis for preservation can be sought on the international, national, and local levels; the positive and negative aspects of particular legal mechanisms; and a survey of the current legal situation in relation to traditional culture and its protection;

3. *Extra-Legal Sanctions and Customary Law,* which includes community and non-legalistic solutions for the perpetuation and protection of traditional culture;

4. *Rights-issues,* which includes discussion of authorship, plagiarism and notions of property, copyrights, patents, intellectual property rights, and the feasibility of global legal mechanisms. In general: What rights do people have and how are they to be protected? What are the threats to these rights? What is the appropriate agency to protect traditional cultures?

5. *Public Domain,* which includes consideration of problems with privacy and secrecy and how they play out in the fields of culture and preservation. Special attention was paid to questions of the sacred.

In the second session, based on the revised agenda, participants delivered five-minute summaries of their written papers. These consisted of overviews of legal problems, including synopses of various legal approaches such as the variety of IPR approaches (including trademark, patent, trade secrets, and copyright mechanisms) to address the needs of Indigenous and folk communities. In light of this, two recommendations were made:

- Recognize cultural restrictions as reasonable steps, such as provisions to "silent" contracts, which may find parallels in uniform commercial codes (such as warranties).
- Create a body which could serve a channelling function controlled by tradition-bearers, rather than governments, such as collective rights organizations.

Other summaries raised issues of public domain and secrecy. There were summary statements of regional and national concerns, such as the concerted work of ATSIC in Australia to enforce copyright infringement for Aboriginal artists.

The ensuing discussions flowed from the position paper summaries and moved toward the recommendations stated in the Action Plan. Discussion topics were flagged and addressed to correspond to agenda topics in order to systematically arrive at final recommendations informed by detailed discussions of the topics at hand.

Related issues emerged in relation to living languages and educational programs aimed at the continuation of traditional culture. Levels of protection, such as access to sacred sites, preservation and reparation of sacred objects, raised the overarching question of what do communities want to protect? An objective, therefore, emerged: to match the kind of protection with the kinds of needs communities have.

Issues underpinning this discussion addressed the relationship between legal and nonlegal means, and the problem of consensus regarding threats to traditional knowledge and cultural practices. These were recognized as power relations embedded in the social relations of societies at large. Therefore, the problem of the roles that government should play became a central concern for forging recommendations for protection at the state level.

Discussion in the third session began with Dr. da Cunha remarking that the word "folk-lore" is a problematic term, subject to much debate, especially in anthropological circles. She pointed to Preston Thomas's earlier comment that the term often has pejorative connotations for Indigenous groups and also implies a process of nationalism. Mr. Puri also voiced his objection to the term, stating that often folklore is equated to the public domain and thus is often understood to mean "free for all." He suggested the alternative term "Traditional and Popular Culture." Mr. McCann was quick to point out that "popular culture" can mean mass-produced cultural products such as "Mickey Mouse" and should also be avoided. Consensus decided upon "Traditional Culture" as the least objectionable term.

The conversation then turned to the question "what are we protecting when we talk of traditional culture?" Several had this question in mind. A debate ensued weighing whether it would be wiser first to decide *what* the group wants to protect, or first to discuss the processes of *how* the group wants to protect. In other words, the debate was whether to discuss the legal means of protection or the objects of protection first.

Ms. Prott's list of specific examples of protected cultural phenomena was offered as a good starting point to build a typology. Some dissent was heard, especially from Mr. Puri, who was unsure the wisest path was to begin with specific examples. Mr. Sanjek concurred and suggested that what was truly missing was a conversation on the process-related issues of how one protects local and national cultural heritage.

Mr. Puri interjected that what was really at issue was not what to protect and safeguard, but that the group should be concerned more with the exploitation of existing traditional cultural heritage. He stated that the group should not be talking of the protection to create but rather the protection of the created from exploitation. Mr. Simon said that pastiche, reproduction, authorization, commodification, and the like should also be issues to discuss and address in the final document.

It was then noted that the list of legal issues could be divided into two categories:

- those relating to the maintenance and revitalization of culture
- those relating to the appropriation of knowledge

Mr. Jaszi, opening a new facet of the conversation. then began to ask if intellectual property rights and copyright laws can effectively protect the process of creative development. Mr. McCann pointed out that these rights and laws function on an economic imperative. Another suggested that preemptive patents help the legal protection of creation.

Mr. Puri voiced his opinion that the document created by the working group should have "teeth" and not be watered down. Others suggested this might run the risk of offending the sovereignty of nations. Ms. Prott said that a more diplomatic document, although less dramatic, could cause change along with other documents, helping to reach a collective threshold point for change. For several minutes the debate raged as to the strength or relative diplomacy of the language the group wished to use in the document, many stating that the language should not be alienating, while others decided a bold document would have the best potential effect.

Dr. da Cunha then began discussing the potential good of opening up traditional culture to the public domain, stating the case of pharmaceutical companies (in Peru as an example) that reach private, secretive contracts with Indigenous groups and thus halt the production of knowledge, destroying the very processes one might assume the venture is helping transmit and succeed economically. Her fear was one of privatization and commodification of traditional knowledge, believing that such private business ventures subvert the communities' intellectual property rights. Dr. da Cunha also stated that once traditional knowledge could be put in the public domain, proof of prior art could be established in order to begin the process of protecting community rights.

Mr. Sanjek, Mr. Simon, and Mr. Puri all had comments. Mr. Sanjek warned that public domain becomes a tricky issue on the international stage, and Mr. Simon reminded the group that prior art is only for patent issues and that public domain does not give remuneration or protection to cultural heritages. Mr. Puri stated that for many, including himself, public domain means free use for everyone.

Mr. Sanjek finished by stating that the intellectual property rights system never verifies the veracity of claims of authorship and can be abused, giving the example of the song "Why Do Fools Fall in Love?" being registered to a known crook. His comments hinted at the need for a state or national level of surveillance of intellectual property rights. It was then pointed out by another member that Mr. Sanjek's remarks reflect not the fault of the intellectual property rights system, but a case of fraud inappropriately handled by the legal system.

To end the session, the following was offered as a beginning of the formation of a final document which was presented at the plenary session the following day and became one of the recommendations in the Action Plan:

> In accordance with the obligations of states to protect the right to culture in Article 27 of the International Covenant of Civil and Political Rights, states should take the next step to do the following: communities should be supported to continue their traditional processes of generation, transmission, authorization, and attribution of traditional knowledge and skills in accordance with the wishes of the community in conformity with current international standards of human rights.

Appendix 6: Report of Group III
Local, National, Regional, and International Policies, with Particular Reference to the Transmission, Revitalization, and Documentation of Intangible Cultural Heritage

Prior to commencing the presentation of individual papers, the session opened with a long discussion of different modes of transmission and strategies used to safeguard traditional culture and folklore. Various countries highlighted their own experiences in their respective modes of transmission. The following points were highlighted:

1. The significance of oral traditions is not only their mode of transmission but also, and more importantly, their content, which embodies important historical, cultural, and social knowledge.
2. The possibility of establishing "heritage clubs" in which issues of cultural heritage was discussed as a means of strengthening the transmission of oral traditions.
3. Intangible cultural heritage is often described as endangered just because it is transmitted orally, but there could be something about its cultural content that interrupts the mode of transmission.
4. Suggestions were made about how to strengthen traditional culture and folklore in contemporary contexts.
5. The importance of maintaining community access to materials after they have been officially documented was strongly asserted.
6. Improvisation plays an important role in the transmission of traditional culture and folklore.
7. The role that documentary transcription can play in transmission was discussed.

8. Questions of authenticity should be answered by the traditional communities who create and nurture the forms of expression involved.
9. Transmission necessarily involves interaction between older and younger generations.

The first paper (this volume, 178–181) was presented by Osamu Yamaguti. Its focus was the royal court music of Vietnam. The speaker explored the relationship between Vietnam and surrounding cultures (Korea, Japan, and China), as this affects music; the relationship between the text (music) and context (the royal court itself); and the need to revitalize the traditional court music.

The second paper (this volume, 190–193) was presented by Gail Saunders. The role of archives in the promotion and preservation of intangible cultural heritage in The Bahamas was highlighted. Great mention was made of the participation of The Bahamas in the Smithsonian Folklife Festival in 1994. Following this Festival was a renewed interest in revitalizing traditional culture. Two relevant laws were passed in 1998 and will come into effect on 1 July 1999: a Museum Antiquities Act and a Copyright Act. The latter protects originators' rights. Dr. Saunders asserted that there should be coordination between the agencies who administer tangible and intangible cultural heritage and urged UNESCO to continue the regional meetings for the preservation and dissemination of traditional culture and folklore. Finally, she strongly recommended that the Caribbean should be regarded as a separate region from Latin America.

The third paper (this volume, 159–165) was presented by Grace Koch, who spoke about the role of audiovisual material in the revitalization of local traditions. Today, this material is used by Aboriginal and Torres Strait Islanders as evidence when asserting land claims. Audiovisual documentations of oral history and ritual are particularly important in asserting the claims. The speaker noted that at the beginning of White settlement of Australia, there were 250 Aboriginal languages. Today, only twenty-five are actively spoken. The speaker recommended that active involvement of Indigenous people in archival technique and preservation should be encouraged, as well as cultural awareness training for people working in the conservation and preservation of cultural material.

The fourth paper was presented by Jean Guibal, who stressed that language is the basis of culture, and, as such, deserves special attention. He urged support for linguistic diversity, calling language the essence of culture. He focused on the process of transmission, its diversity, and on the difficulty of transmitting oral tradition in France because the majority of the carriers of this knowledge have disappeared. He also described the role of archives located in museums in the process of transmission. Lastly, the speaker asserted that policies for protecting cultural heritage need to be institutionally based in order to protect forms of intangible cultural heritage. He emphasized that this must be done with the participation of the local communities.

The fifth presentation was made by Heikki Kirkinen (this volume, 234–244), who discussed the revitalization of languages and cultures in Eastern Europe and the Karelian settlement. He noted that, although these communities are now free to develop their own culture, they lack the means to do so. They hope that UNESCO can assist in rehabilitating and re-creating their language and culture. He stressed how important language is to cultural identity.

The sixth paper was presented by Renato Matusse (this volume, 185–189), who envisioned the role of databanks in the SADC countries of southern Africa. He described how a regional unit coordinates national units, which coordinate local units. Information gathered in local databanks is shared with a national unit, is processed, and then goes to the regional unit and to Member States. He spoke of the importance of databanks to regional cooperation.

The seventh presentation was by Namankoumba Kouyaté (this volume, 204–214), who talked about local and national policies on the safeguarding of heritage particularly as regards problems of transmission. The focus was on family traditions and on the musical instrument named the *soso-bala*. The *soso-bala* is a balafon built in its present form for a battle in 1235 A.D. It is today considered the oldest of oral traditions in West Africa. The speaker also mentioned the need to combat the rural-to-urban migration of younger generations in order to ensure the transmission of the rich oral tradition. In addition, he stated that UNESCO should take account of traditional ceremonies held in important cultural spaces.

The eighth presentation was made by Juana Nuñez, who described various activities undertaken by Cuba to protect traditional culture and folklore. These include: an organization of art amateurs; involvement of workers, students, peasants, adolescents, children, and disabled persons in the preservation of intangible cultural heritage; teaching art in schools beginning at the preliminary level; studies of cultural roots and folklore; the extension of national cinematography to rural and mountainous areas; an increase in museums and education; and the elevation of the social positions of writers and artists. She put forward a number of suggestions, including a UNESCO study into the negative effects of mass media in the field of intangible cultural heritage, a revising of UN financial policies, a study of the effects of globalization, the possibility of establishing an international instrument for the protection of intellectual property rights regarding traditional culture and folklore, and the possibility of UNESCO adopting community projects involving different disciplines.

In conjunction with these presentations, various discussions took place. On the basis of these discussions the following recommendations were put forward. It was recommended to the governments of Member States that they:

1. include traditional culture in educational curricula in order to transmit it to the younger generations and encourage their interest in traditional culture and folklore;
2. establish and/or reinforce existing institutional bases for the safeguarding and documentation of traditional culture and folklore;
3. ensure language education and rehabilitation for all ethnic minorities;
4. increase financial assistance for the organization of festivals;
5. ensure free public access to cultural materials;
6. provide cultural awareness training and equipment to people working in the fields of conservation and preservation of cultural material; and
7. encourage the private sector to invest in traditional culture and folklore through incentives such as tax rebates.

It was recommended to UNESCO that it:

1. organize meetings between specialists in the fields of digitized information in order to create regional networks between institutions, and to enable accessibility and dissemination of knowledge;
2. reduce the cultural gap between urban and rural youth by supporting the dissemination of knowledge of traditional cultures through the Internet and the organization of youth camps devoted to the promotion and exchange of traditional cultures;
3. strengthen and promote relations with non-governmental organizations in the field of traditional culture and folklore;

4. provide seminars and technical assistance for training of professional policy makers, managers, and teachers in the field of traditional culture;

5. conduct a feasibility study into the possibility of establishing an international network for the development of cultural tourism;

6. support the publication of a World Folklore Encyclopedia in order to disseminate knowledge, promote diversity, and encourage research in the field of traditional culture and folklore;

7. establish an international World Day for Safeguarding Traditional Culture and Folklore;

8. consider the possibility of establishing a list of endangered communities in order to direct the attention of international society to this problem and to revive them; and

9. encourage further collaboration between intergovernmental agencies such as UNESCO, WIPO (World Intellectual Property Organization), and WIPG (UN Working Group on Indigenous Populations).

Action Plan

A. On the occasion of the Conference "A Global Assessment of the 1989 *Recommendation on the Safeguarding of Traditional Culture and Folklore*: Local Empowerment and International Cooperation," held at the Smithsonian Institution, Washington, D.C., U.S.A., from 27 to 30 June 1999;

1. *Taking into account* the results of the four-year process of evaluating the implementation of the *Recommendation on the Safeguarding of Traditional Culture and Folklore* and the recommendations stemming from the eight Regional and Sub-Regional Seminars [Strá nice (Czech Republic, June 1995, for Central and Eastern European countries); Mexico City (Mexico, September 1997, for Latin American and Caribbean countries); Tokyo (Japan, February/March 1998, for Asian countries); Joensuu (Finland, September 1998, for Western European countries); Tashkent (Republic of Uzbekistan, October 1998, for Central Asia and the Caucasus); Accra (Ghana, January 1999, for the African region); Noumea (New Caledonia, February 1999, for the Pacific Countries); and Beirut (Lebanon, May 1999, for the Arab States)];

2. *Bearing in mind* that the term "folklore" has generally been considered inappropriate, but emphasizing the importance of its definition as it stands in the 1989 *Recommendation on the Safeguarding of Traditional Culture and Folklore,* while recommending a study on a more appropriate terminology, and provisionally continuing to use the term "folklore," along with "oral heritage," "traditional knowledge and skills," "intangible heritage," "forms of knowing, being, and doing," among other terms, all of which, for the purposes of this recommendation, we consider to be equivalent to "traditional culture and folklore" in the definition of the aforementioned 1989 *Recommendation*;

3. *Cognizant* of the impossibility of separating tangible, intangible, and natural heritage in many communities;

4. *Considering* that traditional culture and folklore are primarily based in community activities which express, reinforce, and reflect largely shared values, beliefs, ideas, and practices;

5. *Emphasizing* that the diversity embodied in multiple cultural ways of knowing, being, and doing is an essential characteristic of cultural heritage and is vital in the construction of a peaceful coexistence for all life forms in the future;

6. *Underlining* the specific nature and importance of traditional culture and folklore as an integral part of the heritage of humanity;

7. *Noting* the spiritual, social, economic, cultural, ecological, and political importance of traditional culture and folklore, their role in the histories of peoples, and their place in contemporary society;

8. *Acknowledging* that traditional culture and folklore can be a powerful means of bringing together different peoples and social groups and of asserting their cultural identities in a spirit of understanding and respect for other cultures;

9. *Stressing* the need in all countries for recognition of the role of traditional culture and folklore and the danger that practitioners face from multiple factors;

10. *Concerned* with the fact that the well-being of community members and their practices — whose strength and numbers are threatened daily by powerful forces such as war, forced displacement, intolerant ideologies and philosophies, environmental deterioration, socio-economic marginalization, and global commercialized culture — must be at the center of national and international cultural policy;

11. *Taking into account* that traditional culture and folklore are dynamic and are often adapted through the innovative practices of community life;

12. *Recognizing* that practitioners of traditional culture and folklore must be included to contribute expertise that is crucial to local, national, and international policy-making in such areas as health, environment, education, youth, gender, conflict resolution, the peaceful coexistence of ethnic groups, sustainable human development, and inclusive civic participation as well as fighting chauvinism and intolerance;

13. *Deploring* the exclusion of traditional groups from decision-making concerning the safeguarding of traditional culture and folklore;

14. *Acknowledging* that states are comprised of cultural communities, that these communities and their folklore and beliefs often extend beyond state boundaries, and that individuals may be members of more than one community;

15. *Recognizing* that cultural interaction and exchange leads to the emergence of hybrid genres that reflect these cross-cultural exchanges;

16. *Recognizing* that the preservation of traditional culture and folklore and the right to cultural self-determination in local communities should be consistent with current international standards of human rights;

17. *Observing* the important role that governments and non-governmental organizations can play in collaboration with tradition-bearers in the safeguarding of traditional culture and folklore and that they should act as quickly as possible

B. We, the participants in the Conference "A Global Assessment of the 1989 *Recommendation on the Safeguarding of Traditional Culture and Folklore:* Local Empowerment and International Cooperation," recognize that the following measures need to be taken:

1. develop legal and administrative instruments for protecting traditional communities — who create and nurture traditional culture and folklore — from poverty, exploitation, and marginalization;

2. facilitate collaboration among communities, government and academic institutions, local and non-governmental organizations as well as private-sector organizations in order to address the issues facing traditional groups;

3. ensure meaningful participation of traditional groups in decision-making processes in forums at all levels concerned with issues and policies that affect those groups;

4. develop, in cooperation with communities, adequate education and training, including legal training, for their members and other cultural workers in understanding, preserving, and protecting traditional culture and folklore;

5. develop programs that address the transnational nature of some traditional culture and folklore;

6. give special emphasis to programs that recognize, celebrate, and support women's roles in all aspects of their communities, which have been historically underrepresented, as contributors to traditional cultures and as field workers, scholars, and administrators;

7. provide support for programs of cultural revitalization, particularly for groups displaced by war, famine, or natural disasters and other groups under threat of extinction;

8. undertake measures to assist traditional groups, including legal assistance, in their own efforts to improve their social status and economic well-being, which are essential to their continued cultural practices.

C. Specific Actions: On the basis of the aforementioned principles and needs, we recommend to the Governments of States that they:

1. identify and support programs that encourage public recognition and validation of traditional culture and folklore, continuing to support existing institutions and programs as well as establishing new ones where appropriate;

2. institute and strengthen schemes for the comprehensive welfare of custodians and practitioners of traditional cultures addressing issues such as housing, health care, and occupational hazards;

3. nclude local knowledge in national forums that consider questions such as sustainable human development, globalization, environmental degradation, youth, education, and peaceful coexistence;

4. facilitate and assist communities to develop their traditional material culture and work practices in new contexts as efficient countermeasures to the destruction of the natural environment and the devaluation of the dignity of human labor;

5. provide cultural awareness training to workers in administrative, educational, and other institutions involved with traditional groups;

6. facilitate access for members of traditional groups to relevant educational programs and, where necessary, facilitate the creation — with the community — of multipurpose, community-based centers for education, documentation, and training;

7. provide support to communities to preserve the active, creative use of local languages in areas that include, but are not limited to, education, publishing, and public performance;

8. provide support for the preservation of significant material culture and spaces that are crucial to the transmission of traditional culture and folklore;

9. support local, national, and international symposiums that bring together members of traditional groups, representatives of non-governmental organizations, policy makers, and others to address issues facing traditional groups;

10. identify, understand, encourage, and support traditional educational practices, especially those relating to the very young;

11. create a network of experts to assist local groups, cultural institutions, non-governmental organizations, and commercial organizations in the work of safeguarding traditional culture, especially in areas such as education, tourism, law, and development;

12. consider, if they so desire, the possible submission of a draft resolution to the UNESCO General Conference requesting UNESCO to undertake a study on the feasibility of adopting a new normative instrument on the safeguarding of traditional culture and folklore;

13. act in accordance with the obligations of States to protect the right to culture in Article 27 of the International Covenant of Civil and Political Rights, by actively supporting communities in their practices of generation, transmission, authorization, and attribution of traditional knowledge and skills in accordance with the wishes of the communities, and in conformity with current international standards of human rights and consider taking steps, including, but not limited to, the following:

i. adopting a legal scheme, according to which traditional knowledge can be made available by the community, in compliance with its wishes, for public use with a requirement of remuneration or other benefits in case of commercial use; *and* cooperating to assure mutual recognition by all States of the effects of such schemes;

ii. adopting a *sui generis* legal regime which would ensure protection

- extending for the life of the community;
- vested in the community, or in the individual and the community;
- in accordance with traditional authorization and attribution procedures in the community;
- *and* establishing a body representing the community concerned and the relevant sectors of civil society to balance the competing interests of access and control

iii. in awaiting adoption of a better protective scheme, encouraging modification and use, in accordance with customary laws, of existing intellectual property regimes for the protection of traditional knowledge;

iv. creating task forces to engage in further study of the following issues: content of "prior informed consent"; verification processes (burden of proof, modes of evidence codes); community intellectual rights vis a vis intellectual property rights; relationship to other instruments and Draft Documents (UN Draft Document, WIPO, TRIPS, CBD, Maatatu, SUVA and other Indigenous peoples' declarations); questions of "rights" (authorship. moral, compensation); role of governments; problems of terminology (e.g., definitions and connotations of "folklore," "popular culture," etc.); alternative forms of compensation; promotion of case studies in relation to case law; legal mechanisms/documents specific to handicrafts, music, and other art forms; legal mechanisms applicable to knowledge collected prior to this instrument.

We recommend that UNESCO:

1. promote this Action Plan among its Member States by bringing this meeting to the attention of Member States;

2. establish an international, interdisciplinary network of experts to assist Member States in developing, upon request, concrete programs in conformity with the principles of the present Action Plan;

3. establish an international, interdisciplinary mobile working group of legal experts to work as advisors in collaboration with communities to develop suitable instruments for the protection of traditional culture and folklore;

4. encourage the participation and, wherever necessary, the establishment of international non-governmental organizations with specialist expertise in particular areas of folklore and traditional knowledge to advise UNESCO on the protection of folklore and traditional knowledge;

5. encourage international groups (scholars, cultural professionals, commercial organizations, and legal bodies) to develop and adopt codes of ethics ensuring appropriate, respectful approaches to traditional culture and folklore

6. accelerate the movement for the return of human remains and for repatriation of cultural heritage to assist the revitalization and self-perception of traditional cultures according to their own fundamental values;

7. organize and support the formation of an international forum for the representation of

traditional communities' concerns for safeguarding their own culture as well as regional and international symposiums that bring together members of traditional groups, representatives of non-governmental organizations, policy makers, and others to address issues facing traditional groups, such as women's role in the safeguarding of traditional culture. Symposiums should be held in diverse locations, particularly outside of First World nations — for example, in Yakutia;

8. facilitate the application of new technologies in local, national, and regional documentation centers through networks of collaboration and expertise, including local tradition-bearers;

9. promote traditional culture and folklore on a global scale by such measures as producing regional festivals and declaring a World Day for Safeguarding Traditional Culture and Folklore;

10. continue UNESCO's collaboration with WIPO on issues of common interest;

11. use UNESCO's existing procedures to bring the possible adverse impact of actions on human rights, environment, food, agriculture, livelihood and industry, health and trade on culture to the attention of other UN bodies, such as FAO, WHO, UNICEF, UNIFEM, and others as well as the WTO.

Rapport final

Introduction

1.   La conférence internationale intitulée: Évaluation globale de la Recommandation de 1989 relative à la sauvegarde de la culture traditionnelle et du folklore: Participation locale et coopération internationale s'est tenue à Washington, D.C. (Etats-Unis d'Amérique) du 27 au 30 juin 1999 avec la collaboration de la *Smithsonian Institution*.

L'objectif de la conférence était d'examiner la protection du patrimoine culturel intangible à la fin du vingtième siècle et de réexaminer, dix ans après son adoption en 1989, la Recommandation sur la sauvegarde de la culture et du folklore traditionnels. Cette conférence est l'aboutissement de huit séminaires régionaux organisés par l'UNESCO pour évaluer de façon systématique l'application de la Recommandation et l'état actuel de la protection et de la revitalisation du patrimoine culturel intangible. Les séminaires régionaux se sont tenus dans les pays suivants: République Tchèque (juin 1995) pour les régions Europe centrale et Europe de l'est; Mexique (septembre 1998) pour l'Amérique latine et la Caraïbe; Japon (février/mars 1998) pour l'Asie; République d'Ouzbékistan (octobre 1998) pour l'Asie centrale et le Caucase; Ghana (janvier 1999) pour l'Afrique; Nouvelle-Calédonie (février 1999) pour le Pacifique; le Liban (mai 1999) pour les pays arabes. Un objectif majeur de cette conférence était d'évaluer, à l'échelle mondiale, l'état actuel et les orientations futures de la Recommandation de 1989.

Trente-sept participants représentant vingt-sept pays (spécialistes, fonctionnaires, praticiens de culture traditionnelle) et quarante observateurs ont assisté à la conférence. Les participants ont, à leur arrivée, reçu des documents de fond et de travail. Les rapports des huit séminaires régionaux étaient à la disposition des participants pendant toute la durée de la conférence. En outre, les communications écrites des participants étaient distribuées au cours de la conférence et mises à la disposition des groupes de travail intéressés.

2.   La réunion a été co-financée par l'UNESCO, le Ministère Japonais des Affaires étrangères, le Département d'Etat des Etats-Unis, la Fondation Rockefeller, la National Endowment for the Arts et la Direction des relations internationales de la Smithsonian Institution.

Séance d'ouverture

3.   La réunion a été ouverte par Dr. Richard Kurin, Directeur du *Center for Folklife and Cultural Heritage* de la Smithsonian, qui a souhaité la bienvenue aux participants, observateurs, représentants de l'UNESCO ainsi qu'au personnel de la conférence. Il s'est déclaré heureux que celle-ci se tienne à la Smithsonian puisqu'elle complète les travaux entrepris

par le Center for Folklife and Cultural Heritage et renforce les liens qui existent entre les chercheurs de l'institution et l'UNESCO.

4.   M. Mounir Bouchenaki, Directeur du Centre du patrimoine culturel et du patrimoine mondial à l'UNESCO, s'est ensuite, en sa qualité de représentant du directeur général de l'UNESCO, M. Frederico Mayor, adressé à la conférence (présent volume 3–4). Après avoir remercié Dr. Richard Kurin pour ses gentils mots de bienvenue, il lui exprima, ainsi qu'à Dr. Anthony Seeger, Directeur de *Smithsonian Folkways Recordings* et à leurs collègues, sa gratitude pour leur collaboration dans l'organisation de la conférence. Il remercia ensuite les sponsors pour leur soutien à la conférence. Il exprima le plaisir de l'UNESCO à prendre part au 34ème festival folklorique de la Smithsonian, une exposition du patrimoine culturel vivant des Etats-Unis et du monde.

Faisant référence au sens élargi du mot patrimoine que les pays ont adopté, il a noté que ce terme englobe de nos jours des éléments tels que le patrimoine des idées, le génome humain et un patrimoine éthique dans lesquels la diversité est un aspect qui revêt beaucoup d'importance et de valeur. Cette évolution s'est produite au même moment que le concept de patrimoine tangible a commencé, par l'intermédiaire de la Convention de l'UNESCO de 1972 relative à la protection des patrimoines culturel et naturel du monde, d'inclure les monuments culturels, les sites naturels et culturels ainsi que les paysages culturels. Ce patrimoine est vulnérable et risque d'être oblitéré par les tendances mondiales vers l'homogénéisation qui découlent de la mondialisation de l'économie. En revanche, certaines évolutions technologiques peuvent fournir d'utiles moyens de protection et de diffusion du patrimoine culturel mondial.

Toute forme de patrimoine culturel devrait, toujours selon l'orateur, être reconnue et respectée y compris le patrimoine intangible qui soutient les valeurs spirituelles et les sens symboliques inhérents au patrimoine matériel. Le sous-titre de la conférence (participation locale et coopération internationale) cadre avec les objectifs de l'UNESCO, surtout quand il s'agit de renforcement des capacités indigènes et de participation locale (notamment de la part des jeunes) dans la mise en oeuvre des activités. L'individualité de chaque être humain est à la base de la liberté culturelle qui est la liberté collective dont dispose un groupe d'individus pour choisir son mode de vie. Cet objectif passe par la promotion, à l'échelle mondiale, de la diversité culturelle.

En guise de conclusion, il a déclaré que cette conférence peut énormément contribuer à la direction future des efforts de protection du patrimoine culturel intangible du monde. Il a ajouté que les recommandations de cette conférence vont affecter les patrimoines tangible et intangible dans la mesure où toutes les formes de patrimoine culturel sont intimement liées.

5.   M. Mounir Bouchenaki a présidé à l'élection du président, des vice-présidents et du rapporteur:

       Président: Dr. Anthony Seeger, USA
       Vice-présidents: Dr. Junzo Kawada, Japon
                        Mme Zulma Yugar, Bolivie
                        Rapporteur: Dr. Janet Blake, Ecosse, Royaume-Uni

A la suite de son élection, Dr. Seeger a officiellement assumé la présidence.

6.   Ordre du jour: Rubrique 2: Recommandation de l'UNESCO sur la sauvegarde de la culture traditionnelle et du folklore (1989) — Actions de l'UNESCO pour sa mise en application (Séance plénière)

Mme Noriko Aikawa, Directrice du service Patrimoine intangible de l'UNESCO a, ensuite, présenté dans sa communication l'essentiel des actions menées par l'UNESCO pour la mise en oeuvre de la Recommandation de 1989 (Présent volume, 13–19). Elle a fait valoir que, une fois l'instrument établi, les pays membres se sont peu intéressés à sa mise en application malgré l'exigence de respecter ses dispositions et de rendre effectifs les principes et mesures qu'il définit. Seuls six pays ont présenté un rapport en réponse à la demande lancée par le directeur général en 1990. En 1992, un rapport d'expert a avancé l'hypothèse selon laquelle cette situation serait due à l'absence dans la Recommandation d'un mandat spécifique pour l'UNESCO ou de dispositions précises quant à sa mise en application par les pays-membres. Le rôle de l'UNESCO se limite à celui de promouvoir la Recommandation et d'encourager les Etats à en exécuter les dispositions.

Suite aux bouleversements politiques considérables de la fin des années 80 (notamment la fin de la Guerre froide), à la rapide expansion de l'économie de marché et au progrès des technologies de communication qui ont transformé le monde en un espace économique et culturel plus uniforme, bon nombre de pays membres ont commencé de s'intéresser à leurs cultures traditionnelles et de redécouvrir le rôle qu'elles jouent en tant que référence symbolique à des identités localement enracinées. Dans un souci de recentrer son programme ayant trait à la culture traditionnelle, l'UNESCO a procédé à une évaluation scientifique de toutes les activités dans ce domaine qu'elle a rebaptisé patrimoine culturel intangible. A la suite d'une réunion d'experts internationaux à Paris, plusieurs principes directeurs pour ce genre de travail ont été arrêtés en 1993. Par la même occasion, il a été proposé que l'UNESCO, en réaction à ces nouveaux paramètres, joue un rôle catalyseur et instigateur plus important.

Mme Aikawa a ensuite décrit le projet *Trésors humains vivants* qui a été lancé en 1993 et permet aux pays membres de reconnaître officiellement ces personnes à talents artistiques et aptitudes exceptionnels en vue d'encourager la progression et la dissémination de tels talents ou savoir-faire dans un souci de protéger le patrimoine culturel traditionnel. Une cinquantaine de pays ont déjà exprimé leur désir d'établir un tel système.

La Conférence générale a, en 1995, décidé qu'une évaluation mondiale de la protection de la culture traditionnelle et du folklore devrait être effectuée avec, comme cadre de référence, la Recommandation. Un questionnaire détaillé a d'abord permis de conduire des sondages qui furent suivis par les huit séminaires régionaux sus-cités dont cette conférence est l'aboutissement.

En réaction à l'intérêt accru que les pays membres portent au patrimoine culturel intangible, la Conférence générale a confirmé, en 1997, que le programme pour le patrimoine intangible devrait figurer parmi les grandes priorités culturelles. La Conférence générale a, peu après, proclamé certains espaces culturels et formes d'expression culturelle chefs-d'oeuvre du patrimoine oral et intangible de l'humanité. Cette proclamation fut l'un des moyens de compenser la non-applicabilité de la Convention de 1972 au patrimoine culturel intangible.

Mme Aikawa a ensuite fait état de diverses activités entreprises par l'UNESCO pour promouvoir la Recommandation en matière d'identification, de conservation, de préservation, de diffusion et de protection du folklore. Dans le cadre de la coopération internationale, les actions prioritaires ont porté essentiellement sur la création de réseaux et la formation. Il reste à identifier les problèmes spécifiques aux mesures juridiques liées aux expressions artistiques du folklore et du savoir traditionnels. La Recommandation de 1989 continue d'être le principal document de référence pour toutes ces activités. Le moment est opportun de mener une réflexion sur son rôle dans les contextes contemporain et futur.

7.   Rubrique 3: Rapports des huit séminaires régionaux (Séance plénière)

Les rapports des séminaires régionaux et sous-régionaux qui ont eu lieu entre 1995 et 1999 ont été présentés en séance plénière.

(i) Europe centrale et de l'est (Séminaire de la République Tchèque)

Ce premier séminaire sur l'application de la Recommandation de 1989 fut organisé à Strá nice en juin 1995 sur la base des questionnaires remplis par douze pays de la région Europe centrale/Europe et de l'est. Des experts de treize pays y ont pris part.

Les réponses ont démontré que, dans la majorité des pays de la région, la préservation de la culture et du folklore traditionnels ne représente pas une priorité dans la politique culturelle même si la quasi-totalité des ministères de la culture soutiennent, dans le domaine des activités, des institutions professionnelles et associations civiques. A la suite des transformations dans les Etats post-communistes, un soutien systématique à la culture de masse contemporaine et internationale a fait surface en réaction à celui que l'Etat apportait aux cultures folkloriques. Les organismes actifs dans la protection de la culture traditionnelle et folklorique sont confrontés à des difficultés qui émanent des faibles économies et du manque inhérent de capacité technique dans la plupart des pays post-communistes. Dans beaucoup d'Etats de la région, la Recommandation de 1989 est devenue un instrument important dans la protection du patrimoine culturel intangible.

Parmi les autres questions soulevées au cours du séminaire, il faut noter:

- l'importance de la culture traditionnelle et du folklore dans la sauvegarde de l'identité nationale;
- l'absence totale de coordination entre l'administration centrale et les institutions qui oeuvrent pour la sauvegarde de la culture traditionnelle et du folklore, et le manque, dans tous les pays, de systèmes coordonnés de classification et de typologie au plan supranational;
- l'absence d'un système unifié d'éducation folklorique au niveau primaire;
- le manque de fonds pour soutenir les efforts de promotion, de recherche et de diffusion en matière de folklore;
- la nécessité de mettre au point des infrastructures de diffusion du folklore dans les mass media publics;
- l'absence de réglementations spécifiques à l'intention exclusive des artistes folkloriques; et
- le désir d'accentuer les obligations juridiques pour la sauvegarde de la culture traditionnelle et du folklore au niveau international.

(ii) L'Amérique latine et la Caraïbe (Séminaire du Mexique)

Le séminaire s'est tenu à Mexico en septembre 1997 avec la participation de seize experts. Inspirés des réponses aux questionnaires (remplis par onze pays de la région Amérique latine/Caraïbe) relatifs à l'application de la Recommandation, les objectifs étaient les suivants:

- analyse détaillée des aspects majeurs de la culture traditionnelle et populaire de la région;
- mise en place de mesures pour permettre aux groupes ethniques et autres collectivités d'exprimer complètement leur créativité et leur identité culturelle;

- mise en oeuvre d'une politique culturelle pour promouvoir la culture traditionnelle et populaire conformément à la Recommandation;
- mise en place d'orientations générales et de projets particuliers dans le cadre d'une stratégie régionale de coopération élargie entre les Etats.

Le séminaire a tiré les conclusions suivantes:

- l'importance du recours aux procédés démocratiques dans la région pour conjuguer la sauvegarde de la culture traditionnelle et du folklore et la coexistence pacifique des peuples;
- encourager la participation des collectivités à de tels programmes par l'intermédiaire de mécanismes de décentralisation régionale, municipale et provinciale;
- reconnaître que la réussite passe par les créateurs, dépositaires, émissaires et spécialistes de diverses disciplines ayant trait à ces cultures.

La création au Mexique d'un Centre des cultures populaires de l'Amérique latine et de la Caraïbe a été suivie par l'établissement de deux centres annexes en Amérique du sud et d'un autre en Amérique centrale. Il a été proposé qu'une réunion des autorités culturelles de la région se tienne en Bolivie en 1999 afin de discuter des conclusions de ce séminaire régional et de l'application de la Recommandation dans la région.

(iii) Asie (Séminaire du Japon)

Dix-sept pays sur vingt ont répondu au questionnaire sur la Recommandation et un séminaire fut organisé à Tokyo en février/mars 1998. Vingt experts de dix-neuf Etats membres y ont pris part.

Quant à l'application des principales dispositions de la Recommandation, 48% des pays-répondants ont fait appliquer les dispositions sur l'identification, 28% celles sur la conservation, 28% celles sur la diffusion, et 42% les dispositions sur la protection du folklore. Il y a eu un net progrès dans la protection régionale de la culture traditionnelle et du folklore, même si certains Etats estiment que la Recommandation devrait, à terme, être améliorée. Les thèmes suivants se sont dégagés des réponses:

- nécessité d'un organisme central de coordination;
- identification et collecte d'expressions culturelles traditionnelles;
- protection des droits des artistes traditionnels;
- formation des professionnels et des artistes;
- accroissement des financements;
- mesures d'encouragement aux collectivités pour qu'elles protègent leur propre patrimoine culturel;
- revitalisation, face aux effets des mass media, de l'intérêt de la jeunesse dans la culture traditionnelle;
- recrutement et formation d'apprentis;
- lutte contre les effets négatifs du tourisme.

Les rapports présentés par les divers pays indiquent de véritables efforts de sauvegarde de ce patrimoine malgré les revers et obstacles. Un véritable souci de sauvegarder le patrimoine se manifeste même s'il n'est pas toujours compris des politiques.

(iv) Europe occidentale (Séminaire de la Finlande)

Ce séminaire, organisé à Joensuu en septembre 1998, s'est fondé sur les quinze réponses au questionnaire sur l'application de la Recommandation reçues par le comité d'organisation. Des experts de quatorze pays y ont pris part. Les réponses ont indiqué que le séminaire devrait couvrir les grands thèmes suivants:

- protection juridique du patrimoine intangible des cultures minoritaires;
- protection et promotion des langues nationales et locales;
- renaissance des formes populaires et traditionnelles d'expression;
- utilisation de nouvelles technologies, d'images visuelles, d'Internet etc. dans le domaine du patrimoine;
- évolution de la culture et perspectives d'avenir.

Des communications générales ont été présentées sur les quatre thèmes suivants: problèmes de culture, patrimoine culturel, nouvelles technologies, et évolution culturelle.

Quelques questions ont été soulevées sur la vie en Europe occidentale contemporaine et le rôle qu'y jouent la culture traditionnelle et le folklore. Ces questions ont permis de tirer certaines conclusions qui vont contribuer à l'élaboration future de politiques européenne et mondiale en matière de patrimoine. A noter parmi ces conclusions:

- Dans un monde en rapide évolution, la culture traditionnelle et le folklore deviennent essentiels à la préservation de l'identité et de la diversité du patrimoine culturel européen;
- Les questions relatives à ce patrimoine sont d'ordinaire traitées au niveau national en tenant compte des aspects régionaux et locaux;
- Tous les pays de cette région sont dotés de bonnes archives et de musées à accès libre; la plupart d'entre eux disposent, en outre, de collections privées bien garnies;
- La préservation et la diffusion de la culture sont assez bien organisées et la culture traditionnelle est enseignée dans les écoles de la quasi-totalité de ces pays;
- A l'heure actuelle, la culture traditionnelle et le folklore jouissent d'une grande popularité surtout en matière de festivals, concerts, séminaires, etc. . . . et sont devenus un des aspects les plus importants de la culture;
- Les médias s'intéressent maintenant à cet aspect de la culture.

(v) Asie centrale et Caucase (Séminaire d'Ouzbékistan)

Un séminaire régional s'est organisé à Tashkent en octobre 1998 autour des réponses au questionnaire fournies par huit pays. Quatorze représentants de huit pays y ont participé. Le séminaire a atteint plusieurs de ses objectifs dont les suivants:

- analyse de l'état actuel de la culture traditionnelle et du folklore dans les Etats nouvellement indépendants de la région qui met un accent particulier sur la restructuration des sociétés pendant la période de transition du communisme à l'économie de marché;
- examen du rôle (en tant que symboles et références à l'identité culturelle et profondément historique des peuples) des cultures populaires et traditionnelles dans le processus de renforcement des nations; une évaluation du rôle socio-culturel du patrimoine intangible par rapport, notamment, au mondialisme, à la cohabitation de divers groupes ethniques et au développement de la culture des jeunes;

- formulation de recommandations relatives aux propositions et actions futures pour le renforcement de la Recommandation;
- exploration de la possibilité d'établir une stratégie régionale dans les domaines de sauvegarde, protection juridique, transmission, revitalisation et diffusion du patrimoine culturel intangible.

La Recommandation fait face à des obstacles majeurs; elle n'a pas encore été traduite dans les langues officielles de la région et les Etats nouvellement indépendants sont confrontés à des problèmes économiques, politiques et sociaux auxquels il faudra d'abord trouver une solution. Tous les participants ont fait valoir que le patrimoine culturel intangible joue un rôle important dans la formation des nations et par conséquent, reste prioritaire dans la politique culturelle de tous les Etats. Bien que tous les Etats aient adopté une législation pour protéger ce patrimoine, on a l'impression que celle-ci ne correspond pas aux besoins de la culture traditionnelle et qu'il y a lieu de mettre au point de nouvelles mesures (protection des droits d'auteur, par exemple). Les secteurs public et privé devraient augmenter leur aide financière et les artisans bénéficier d'un soutien financier. Le manque d'équipement informatique pour les archives de matériels folkloriques a été noté ainsi que le désir de création d'une banque de données informatisée des institutions et organismes du secteur folklore. A ce propos, une demande a été introduite pour l'organisation d'un séminaire de formation par l'UNESCO. La nécessité de former des spécialistes en gestion culturelle a, en outre, été identifiée.

(vi) Afrique (Séminaire du Ghana)

Le séminaire a été organisé à Accra en janvier 1999. Des représentants de dix-sept pays y ont pris part. Vingt-sept des quarante pays qui ont reçu le questionnaire ont envoyé des réponses, ce qui a permis d'avoir un bon aperçu de la manière dont la Recommandation a été mise en application dans la région. Les rapports-pays ont ajouté un complément d'informations.

Le séminaire a passé en revue la manière dont le contenu de la culture traditionnelle et du folklore est compris. Celui-ci visait à identifier les facteurs qui avaient soutenu la culture traditionnelle dans le passé et qui ne sont plus. De toute évidence, très peu d'efforts ont été entrepris pour appliquer la Recommandation hormis les mesures prises après l'indépendance par les nouveaux Etats. Le constat était que les gouvernements n'ont eu recours à ce patrimoine que dans le cadre de stratégies de renforcement des nations et de promotion d'une identité culturelle. Le rôle des institutions et des médias a été évoqué. L'absence généralisée de coordination, de collections systématiques, de politiques culturelles nationales, de ressources et d'effectifs était qualifiée de grave. Cette situation est fâcheuse étant donné ce que les cultures orales peuvent apporter à la construction et à la reconstruction des cultures africaines contemporaines conformément au principe de *faire du passé une partie du présent*.

Pour les actions futures, la sauvegarde de la culture traditionnelle devrait être comprise sous l'angle des réalités quotidiennes des pays africains et non l'angle *académique* qu'incarne la Recommandation. La nécessité d'avoir un manuel sur le folklore à l'usage des enseignants locaux a fait l'objet d'une discussion. L'utilisation de techniques anthropologiques pour la collecte d'informations par les populations locales lettrées a aussi été envisagée. Le début du vingtième siècle en Afrique révèle des exemples d'une telle approche. En outre de la nécessité d'une action urgente dans la collecte d'informations sur les cultures traditionnelles, on a aussi mis l'accent sur celle de revitaliser les cultures en vue de contrecarrer les vestiges du colonialisme.

Un thème majeur du séminaire était celui de réintégrer la culture traditionnelle dans la vie moderne et de la partager avec la communauté internationale afin de montrer à celle-ci le contexte culturel de la musique et de la danse africaines déjà adoptées de par le monde.

(vii) Pacifique (Séminaire de la Nouvelle Calédonie)

Le séminaire a eu lieu à Nouméa en février 1999. Douze participants de douze pays y ont pris part. Treize des quatorze pays qui ont reçu le questionnaire y ont répondu. C'est en fonction de ces réponses que les objectifs du séminaire ont été définis: identifier les voies et moyens de renforcer l'application de la Recommandation dans la région; formuler une stratégie régionale à long terme avec comme objectifs la sauvegarde, la revitalisation, la protection juridique, la transmission et la diffusion du patrimoine intangible du Pacifique. Chaque pays a présenté un bref rapport. Les pays qui venaient d'adhérer à l'UNESCO n'étaient pas au courant de la Recommandation.

Dans la région Pacifique, aucune distinction n'est faite entre les patrimoines intangible et tangible, bien que, pour les besoins de cette étude, tel soit le cas. Par ailleurs, une grande partie des peuples indigènes considèrent le mot *folklore* comme déplacé et péjoratif. *Patrimoine culturel* serait plus positif et utile. Le patrimoine intangible du Pacifique est resté essentiellement sans archives et est menacé par le rajeunissement de la population régionale et les problèmes économiques du secteur culturel. Les vestiges du colonialisme et ses effets continus sur la société représentent une autre menace importante sur le patrimoine intangible. On reconnaît fermement que les cultures traditionnelles sont un élément pertinent du développement durable.

Parmi les questions et préoccupations communes du séminaire, il faut noter:

- La préservation et l'évolution du patrimoine intangible exigent la participation d'un grand nombre de parties intéressées (ONG, femmes, jeunes, personnes âgées et collectivités locales);
- Les complexités du régime foncier et le système de copropriété aux niveaux clanique, local et national laissent entendre que tout système reposant sur le concept d'un ayant-droit unique serait grossièrement inadapté au concept de propriété culturelle intellectuelle dans les sociétés du Pacifique;
- Les préoccupations actuelles à l'échelon international en matière d'exploitation de l'environnement ont incité les Etats de la région à ressusciter les méthodes traditionnelles de gestion de la terre et des mers.

On a aussi noté qu'il faudrait:

- encourager les collectivités et autres intéressés à documenter ce patrimoine;
- reconnaître l'importance des cultures traditionnelles dans le développement et la création de revenus;
- reconnaître la menace que l'implantation de grandes entreprises fait peser sur l'accès de la collectivité aux matériaux utilisés dans des pratiques culturelles traditionnelles;
- reconnaître que l'identité culturelle et le régime foncier sont inséparables;

- établir des instruments juridiques (à présent non-existants à l'heure actuelle) et des lois sur la propriété intellectuelle (insuffisantes pour le moment) afin de protéger la culture communautaire.

(viii) Pays arabes (Séminaire du Liban)

Ce séminaire fut organisé à Beyrouth en mai 1999 pour étudier la question telle qu'elle s'applique aux Etats arabes. Des experts de douze pays y ont pris part. Quelques préoccupations des pays arabes dans le domaine du folklore, esquissées dans les questionnaires remplis par dix pays, ont été énumérées. Parmi celles-ci, il faut noter:

- Les budgets alloués au folklore ont été diminués;
- Les industries traditionnelles ont été séparées du secteur *Patrimoine* et servent essentiellement les touristes;
- Le patrimoine risque de disparaître compte tenu de l'importance accordée aux nouveautés, notamment aux nouvelles technologies;
- Le patrimoine peut être l'objet de distorsion (ou même être volé par d'autres pays) et divisé selon des critères sectaires;
- Les institutions qui s'occupent de folklore disposent d'effectifs réduits et souffrent de l'absence d'un organisme central de coordination.

Les effets de la mondialisation ont été discutés en tenant compte de la nature non-statique de la culture. La mondialisation a été perçue comme une arme à double tranchant qui peut aider les pays à revitaliser leurs cultures pour que celles-ci puissent faire face à d'autres cultures mais peut aussi menacer ces pays d'homogénéité culturelle. On a aussi noté l'importance de la préservation des cultures populaires et traditionnelles pour le développement humain et la possibilité que le folklore puisse être source de renaissance culturelle tout en contribuant au développement économique. Il faut cependant veiller à ce que l'utilisation du folklore à des fins économiques ne porte pas préjudice au folklore lui-même. Le patrimoine culturel est sous la menace de la dégradation écologique mais, en même temps, sa revitalisation peut contribuer à la création d'un meilleur environnement et constituer une partie de l'identité et de la dignité humaines.

Les participants ont suggéré des mesures pour résoudre les problèmes auxquels les pays arabes font face en matière de folklore et pour aboutir à une sauvegarde et une revitalisation du patrimoine culturel. Il a été suggéré qu'un plan de développement mondial soit mis au point pour le patrimoine traditionnel et populaire et qu'une législation appropriée soit adoptée pour la protection du patrimoine et des travailleurs du secteur. La sauvegarde de ce patrimoine doit être conçue comme un processus continu et des institutions permanentes doivent être établies pour apporter un soutien moral et financier à ses praticiens et autres intéressés. En outre, une priorité évidente pour assurer la continuité et la viabilité de cette culture serait l'introduction, dans les programmes scolaires, de cours ayant trait à la culture traditionnelle et populaire.

8. Rubrique 4: Vue d'ensemble des rapports-pays et des rapports de séminaires régionaux (Séance plénière)

9. Dr. Richard Kurin a présenté une communication à propos des résultats préliminaires du questionnaire sur l'application de la Recommandation de 1989 que l'UNESCO avait distribué aux pays membres en 1994 (présent volume, 20–35). Ce sondage est le premier de son genre à examiner l'application de la Recommandation dans une perspective mondiale.

Les Commissions nationales pour l'UNESCO et d'autres institutions étaient chargées de remplir les formulaires. En règle générale, ceux qui ont répondu aux questions étaient bien versés dans le domaine du folklore de leur pays. En revanche, plusieurs ont indiqué qu'ils n'étaient pas bien informés, ce qui explique certaines erreurs qu'on retrouve dans le questionnaire. Le sens de quelques mots *comme folklore, préservation, conservation* avait posé problème et le niveau de détail dans les réponses variait considérablement.

Dr. Kurin a ensuite présenté les points saillants des résultats du sondage, y compris les données statistiques suivantes:

- Bien que 58% des Etats soient au courant de la Recommandation, seuls six pays ont répondu à la demande de l'UNESCO;
- 66% estimaient que la coopération avec l'UNESCO était importante pour la mise au point des orientations;
- Seuls 30% des Etats qui ont répondu disposent de l'infrastructure qu'il faut pour la préservation du folklore;
- Dans 48% des pays, des systèmes de formation ont été mis en place et dans 18%, la formation est insuffisante;
- Seuls 20% des Etats ont recours à des bénévoles pour la collecte de documents sur leur propre culture;
- 68% des Etats intègrent la culture traditionnelle et le folklore dans les manuels pédagogiques, les vidéos, les films etc. . . mais ces efforts ne sont pas très bien coordonnés;
- Dans 50% des Etats, une législation nationale protège les droits de propriété intellectuelle.

Les conclusions à tirer de ce sondage sont les suivantes: premièrement, il faut un meilleur sondage puisqu'il est extrêmement difficile de mesurer la culture. Deuxièmement, contrairement à ce que l'on serait tenté de croire, il n'y a aucune corrélation entre le soutien apporté au folklore et le niveau de modernisation ou de développement d'un Etat (comme l'on s'y attendrait selon les perspectives *modernistes* ou *post-modernistes*). En somme, il s'agit là d'un domaine dont le niveau d'institutionnalisation, d'élaboration et de législation reste insuffisant. Bien que beaucoup de professionnels du folklore puissent préférer que la situation reste inchangée, celle-ci risque de poser des dangers compte tenu des défis économiques, sociologiques et matériels auxquels la pratique et l'existence du folklore sont confrontées.

10. Dr. Anthony Seeger a présenté un résumé des huit séminaires régionaux qui se sont tenus entre 1995 et 1999 pour évaluer l'application de la Recommandation dans les pays membres (présent volume, 36–41). Les réunions étaient généralement structurées de la même manière: un représentant de l'UNESCO donnait une vue d'ensemble de l'historique de la Recommandation et des questions à aborder; ensuite suivait un résumé de rapports synoptiques sur l'application de la Recommandation; enfin, le délégué de chaque pays présentait un bref rapport.

Des préoccupations communes ont été évoquées au cours de ces séminaires mais chaque région avait ses particularités. La région Amérique latine/Caraïbe a, par exemple, mis l'accent sur les questions de diversité culturelle et de multiculturalisme. La région Pacifique a évoqué la difficulté qu'il y a à distinguer le patrimoine tangible et l'intangible alors que l'Asie a souligné la nécessité de mettre en relief les cultures de haute cour ainsi que les autres cultures traditionnelles et le folklore. La notion d'identité a beaucoup évolué en

Afrique au cours de la dernière décennie, l'accent étant sur l'acceptation d'une multiplicité d'identités plutôt que sur l'unité nationale. La région Europe de l'est/Europe centrale a aussi procédé à une analyse approfondie de l'importance de la culture traditionnelle dans l'identité nationale et, dans le même temps, a soulevé des questions importantes ayant trait à leur situation financière et au problème de la transition d'un système communiste à une économie de marché. L'Europe occidentale a souligné la nécessité de protéger la diversité culturelle face aux forces intellectuelles et créatives mondiales; les pays arabes ont aussi fait référence aux effets de la mondialisation et au défi qu'elle représente en matière de protection des identités culturelles. Plusieurs régions ont souligné l'importance des cultures traditionnelles pour l'ensemble de la culture contemporaine et l'usage insuffisant qu'on fait de telles connaissances à l'heure actuelle.

Quant à la Recommandation de 1989, les observations générales suivantes ont été faites: premièrement, celle-ci est un instrument important qui demande une plus grande diffusion. Beaucoup considèrent *folklore* comme un terme problématique auquel on peut prêter un sens péjoratif. Tout nouvel instrument devra lui trouver un substitut mais il n'y a pas encore eu de consensus autour du terme qui est censé le remplacer. Un nouvel instrument devrait inclure des aspects supplémentaires dont voici des exemples:

- code d'éthique pour les principes de respect;
- inclusion de propriétaires coutumiers de la culture traditionnelle et du folklore comme acteurs principaux et bénéficiaires dans le processus de documentation et de diffusion de leur savoir;
- reconnaître le rôle de collaborateur que peuvent jouer les ONG et autres institutions susceptibles de contribuer à la préservation du patrimoine culturel;
- élargir la portée de la Recommandation pour inclure la nature évolutive de la culture traditionnelle et du folklore;

11.   M. Anthony McCann a présenté une brève analyse réalisée par une équipe d'experts de la Smithsonian Institution sur l'application de la Recommandation de 1989 dans le contexte actuel (présent volume, 57–61). Il a déclaré que l'année 1999 était bien choisie pour procéder à un examen de la Recommandation et donner aux collectivités, aux organisations non-gouvernementales et intergouvernementales, entre autres, l'occasion de réévaluer le rôle de la Recommandation dans un contexte contemporain.

Un argument important soulevé à propos du texte de la Recommandation est que celui-ci est trop intégré aux institutions de documentation et d'archivage et vise ainsi à protéger les produits plutôt que les producteurs de la culture traditionnelle et du folklore. Il faut établir un équilibre entre la nécessité de documenter et celle de protéger les pratiques qui créent et nourrissent ce qui sera ensuite documenté. Les efforts de protection doivent, de ce fait, se centrer sur les collectivités elles-mêmes. Il a fait valoir qu'il serait nécessaire de procéder à une réévaluation et une critique du langage employé dans la Recommandation. L'emploi du mot *fragilité* par rapport aux cultures traditionnelles (orales) est une métaphore qui prête à confusion car elle laisse entendre qu'il s'agit de cultures moribondes plutôt que d'êtres humains bien vivants dont les formes d'expression émanant de la communauté sont en train d'être marginalisées par des forces qui relèvent de la volonté humaine. L'emploi du terme *intangible* doit aussi être revu puisqu'il donne l'impression qu'on traite les idées comme des objets (plutôt que comme base et résultats de pratiques vivantes) dans la mesure où ce sont les objets matériels qui peuvent être ou ne pas être susceptibles au toucher.

Le moment est venu d'accorder à ceux dont les pratiques créent et nourrissent cette culture la représentation qu'ils méritent. Reconnaître et respecter la participation active de praticiens communautaires à la production, transmission et préservation de leurs expressions et produits culturels est essentiel pour faire face aux défis et opportunités croissants dans les nouvelles rencontres et les nouveaux échanges culturels à l'échelle mondiale. La participation pleine et active des représentants culturels de la base, en collaboration avec les agents de l'Etat et les chercheurs, dans la prise de décisions concernant la mise au point et l'exécution d'actions de sauvegarde du folklore et de la culture traditionnelle est un pas essentiel vers une vie meilleure pour les communautés productrices.

12.   M. James Early du Center for Folklife and Cultural Heritage de la Smithsonian a ensuite fait quelques remarques à propos de collaboration et de pertinence dans le cadre de la Recommandation de 1989. Il a fait remarquer que la Recommandation ne fait pas état de l'auto-motivation des collectivités et a invoqué la nécessité d'une plus grande collaboration avec celles-ci pour nous permettre d'apprendre comment elles documentent et transmettent leur culture et les modifications qu'elles peuvent y apporter. Quant à la notion de pertinence, il a souligné l'importance des pratiques culturelles sur les plans historique et contemporain et a cité l'exemple de l'Afrique du Sud où des centaines de tradi-praticiens ont rencontré des médecins formés en médecine *occidentale* afin d'explorer des possibilités de collaboration.

13.   Débat

On passa ensuite aux débats auxquels l'auditoire prit part.

Un participant a souligné la tendance à employer un langage de recherche qui sépare un élément culturel de la conscience qui l'a produit. Il a décrit la disparition des chants de rameurs aux Philippines avec l'introduction des bateaux à moteur pour illustrer un exemple de lien entre la pratique et une plus grande conscience. Il a, en outre, souligné l'ironie dans le fait que les chercheurs sur le terrain altèrent la vérité de leurs recherches en posant des questions.

Un autre participant a ajouté qu'il nous faut non seulement demander aux communautés ce qu'elles savent mais aussi comprendre comment elles donnent un sens aux choses et appliquent leur savoir au quotidien. Il a ensuite souligné l'impossibilité de séparer les expressions culturelles du contexte économique.

Un participant a fait état de sa préférence pour la connaissance d'une communauté et de sa culture traditionnelle fondée sur une perspective intérieure et extérieure (voire même d'un point très éloigné de sa sphère culturelle), en fait sur plusieurs perspectives et non simplement sur celle d'une seule culture ou communauté.

Un autre participant a ajouté que nous reconnaissons sans doute les domaines de conflit quand nous parlons du concept de culture (Islam et Christianisme, par exemple). Il a cité, comme exemple, un conflit entre une tradition ghanéenne qui interdit tout battement de tam-tam pendant les trois semaines précédant un festival et le désir des membres d'une certaine église de battre le tam-tam à l'église pendant la période d'interdiction.

Un autre participant a ajouté que la préservation culturelle touche toutes les religions qui peuvent être vues comme des messages condensés de traditions qui sont transmises d'une génération à une autre afin d'être décodées. Cela n'exclut pas d'autres traditions telles que la musique ou la danse. Le problème qui se pose de nos jours est celui du progrès et des efforts à entreprendre contre les effets du progrès qui détruit une partie de l'histoire et de la culture des peuples.

Un participant qui s'est présenté comme un artiste amérindien a souligné que beaucoup de gens vivent sur des terres tribales au Nouveau-Mexique avec une affiliation tribale, nationale et ethnique. Il a ensuite ajouté que les discours indiquent toujours une séparation entre *nous* (experts et administrateurs) et *eux* (membres de la communauté) plutôt que de reconnaître que tout le monde contribue à la recherche de solutions. Pourquoi chaque experte ou expert n'emmenerait-il pas à la prochaine réunion un vrai praticien de la tradition?

Un autre participant a convenu qu'il s'agit d'un facteur très important et a souligné que lors d'une réunion au Canada, elle a rencontré des autochtones qui étaient en voie d'extinction et se sentaient très isolés. Ces cultures menacées cherchent à survivre en quittant leur isolement.

Un participant a souligné qu'on a beaucoup entendu parler de la protection des cultures intangibles mais que cela ne devrait pas laisser entendre que la culture tangible est bien protégée. Par exemple, les lois sur la propriété intellectuelle n'apportent aucune protection à la culture tangible des Aborigènes d'Australie. La culture intangible est, certes, plus vulnérable mais les éléments tangibles ne doivent pas être oubliés.

A cela, un autre participant a répondu que, quand nous parlons des langues différentes, nous pouvons avoir beaucoup de mal à arriver à la même idée, à en comprendre la signification et à définir le sujet. Ainsi par exemple, on ne fait pas, dans la région Pacifique, la distinction entre cultures *tangible* et *intangible*. Il importe, cependant, d'arriver à un consensus.

Un participant a soulevé deux questions: premièrement, au cours de la dernière décennie qui a suivi l'adoption de la Recommandation, le nombre de titulaires transnationaux de propriété intellectuelle a considérablement baissé, ce qui concentre les titres de propriété intellectuelle en très peu d'entités; deuxièmement: en ce qui concerne les lois régissant la culture traditionnelle, le folklore et la propriété intellectuelle, il faut noter qu'elles ne tiennent compte ni de plusieurs éléments importants ni du langage qui définit le monde dans lequel nous évoluons. Les débats au niveau des groupes de travail devraient traiter de ces questions.

Groupes de travail

14.   Rubrique 6: Discussions thématiques (Groupes de travail)

A la suite de la séance plénière de la Conférence, les participants et quelques observateurs se sont, pendant une journée et demi, scindés en trois groupes de travail pour se pencher sur les thèmes suivants:

Groupe I: Patrimoine culturel intangible par rapport au patrimoine culturel tangible et naturel et son rôle dans la résolution des problèmes locaux et nationaux liés aux préoccupations contemporaines majeures telles que l'identité culturelle, le genre, le développement humain viable, la mondialisation, la coexistence pacifique de groupes ethniques, la prévention de conflits, les cultures de jeunesse, l'évolution des nouvelles technologies de communication et d'information, la dégradation de l'environnement, etc. . . .

Participants: M. Ralph, Regenvanu, Vanuatu — Président
    M. Russel Collier, Gitxsan, Canada — Rapporteur
    Mme Robyne Bancroft, Australie
    M. Mihály Hoppál, Hongrie
    M. Miguel Puwainchir, Equateur
    Dr. Mahaman Garba, Niger
    M. Rachid El Houda, Maroc
    Dr. Junzo Kawada, Japon

Mme Stepanida Borisova, Russie

M. Andy Abeita, Isleta Pueblo, USA

M. Rajeev Sethi, Inde

Groupe II: Protection juridique du patrimoine culturel intangible aux niveaux national et local

Participants: Mme Manuela da Cunha, Brésil — Présidente

Dr. Tressa Berman, USA — Rapporteur

Mme Lyndel Prott, UNESCO

Dr. Grace Koch, Australie

Prof. Kamal Puri, Australie

Commissaire Preston Thomas, Australie

Prof. Peter Jaszi, USA

Dr. Janet Blake, Ecosse, Royaume-Uni

M. Brad Simon, USA

Mme Pualani Kanaka'ole Kanahele, USA

Groupe III: Politiques locales, nationales, régionales et internationales, notamment en matière de transmission, revitalisation et documentation du patrimoine culturel intangible.

Participants: Prof. Kwabena Nketia, Ghana — Président

Mme Sivia Tora, Fiji — Rapporteur

Dr. Gail Saunders, Bahamas

Mme Zulma Yugar, Bolivie

Mme Khurshida Mambetova, Ouzbékistan

Dr. Florentine Hornedo, Philippines

Dr. Osamu Yamaguti, Japon

M. Renato Matusse, Mozambique

M. Jean Guibal, France

Mme Vlasta Ondrusova, République Tchèque

M. Mohseb Shaalan, Egypte

Prof. Heikki Kirkinen, Finlande

M. Namankoumba Kouyaté, Guinée

Mme Juana Nunez, Cuba

Rapports des groupes de travail, propositions de projets-pilotes et mise au point du plan d'action

15.   Rubrique 7: Rapports des séances thématiques et recommandations de groupes (Plénière)

Après avoir travaillé séparément au cours de la deuxième journée, les trois groupes de travail ont présenté leurs recommandations en séance plénière le troisième jour de la conférence. Les rapports ont pris les formes suivantes:

Groupe I: Une recommandation à l'intention des gouvernements et selon laquelle ceux-ci devraient apporter un soutien actif aux communautés dans la création, la transmission, l'autorisation et l'attribution du savoir et du savoir-faire traditionnels conformément aux désirs des communautés et aux normes internationales en vigueur en matière de droits de l'homme. Trois actions que les gouvernements devraient envisager et douze domaines qui demandent une étude plus approfondie de la part des experts ont été notées [voir appendice 4].

Groupe II: Il a examiné cinq domaines liés à la protection de la culture traditionnelle et fait des recommandations qui ont été incorporées dans le plan d'action final de la conférence [voir appendice 5].

Groupe III: Il a proposé sept recommandations aux gouvernements des pays membres et neuf recommandations à l'UNESCO sur la base des discussions au sein du groupe et d'un ensemble de neuf points qui ont été identifiés au début de la réunion [voir appendice 6].

Les rapports et recommandations des trois groupes de travail ont été présentés en séance plénière par le président et le rapporteur de chaque groupe. Ces rapports y ont ensuite été discutés et approuvés.

16.   Rubrique 8: Coopération internationale: présentation de projets-pilotes (Plénière)

Mme Aikawa a présenté une proposition pour cinq projets-pilotes de coopération internationale et interrégionale. Sur la base des recommandations formulées par la majorité des séminaires régionaux et sous-régionaux, le Secrétariat de l'UNESCO a rédigé l'avant-projet qu'il va ensuite étoffer et présenter aux organismes de financement, fondations et Etats membres susceptibles de fournir des contributions financières volontaires à l'UNESCO. Parmi ces projets, il faut noter:

- Etablissement de réseaux régionaux et internationaux des institutions s'occupant de culture traditionnelle et de folklore;
- Création de chaires UNESCO de culture traditionnelle et folklore;
- Etude de faisabilité pour l'élaboration d'une protection juridique de la culture traditionnelle et du folklore en Afrique, en Amérique latine et dans la Caraïbe;
- Rencontre internationale pour l'intégration de la culture traditionnelle et du folklore dans la politique culturelle;
- Projet inter-régional sur la revitalisation des traditions de médiation pour la prévention de conflit (Afrique et Pacifique).

Les participants ont été invités à faire d'autres suggestions à l'UNESCO à propos de ces projets-pilotes.

17.   Rubrique 9: Présentation et approbation du projet de plan d'action pour la sauvegarde et la revitalisation du patrimoine culturel intangible; rapport final (Plénière) (présent volume, 307–348)

Un comité a été mis sur pied le soir du 29 juin pour rédiger le projet de plan d'action. Il était composé des participants suivants:

Dr. Florentine Hornedo — Présidente

Dr. Grace Koch — Rapporteur

M. Andy Abeita

Dr. Tressa Berman

Mme Manuela Carneiro da Cunha

M. Rachid El Houda

Dr. Junzo Kawada

Mme Kurshida Mambetova

M. Ralph Regenvanu

M. Rajeev Sethi

18.   La présidente et le rapporteur du comité de rédaction ont présenté le projet de plan d'action à la séance plénière. Après avoir intégré les recommandations des groupes de travail dans le projet de plan d'action, l'assemblée l'a longuement débattu, l'a modifié et l'a, finalement, approuvé dans sa version révisée. Le rapport final a été lu par le rapporteur, Dr. Janet Blake, et approuvé à l'unanimité par les participants.

19.   Dr. Richard Kurin et M. Mounir Bouchenaki ont prononcé les allocutions de clôture et remercié tous les participants pour leurs contributions enrichissantes et constructives à la conférence.

Appendice I: Ordre du jour

I.   Ouverture de la conférence

II.   La Recommandation de l'UNESCO sur la sauvegarde de la culture traditionnelle et du folklore (1989): actions de l'UNESCO pour sa mise en application (Séance plénière)

III.   Rapports des huit séminaires régionaux et sous-régionaux (Plénière)

IV.   Vue d'ensemble des rapports/pays et des rapports de séminaires régionaux (Plénière)

V.   Analyse de la Recommandation de 1989 dans le contexte actuel — Aspects positifs et négatifs

VI.   Discussions thématiques (Groupes de travail)

A.   Patrimoine culturel intangible par rapport au patrimoine culturel tangible et naturel et son rôle dans la résolution des problèmes locaux et nationaux liés aux préoccupations contemporaines majeures telles que l'identité culturelle, le genre, le développement humain viable, la mondialisation, la coexistence pacifique de groupes ethniques, la prévention de conflits, les cultures de jeunesse, l'évolution des nouvelles technologies de communication et d'information, la dégradation de l'environnement etc. . . .

B.   Protection juridique du patrimoine culturel intangible aux niveaux national et local

C.   Politiques locales, nationales, régionales et internationales, notamment en matière de transmission, revitalisation et documentation du patrimoine culturel intangible.

VII.   Rapports des séances thématiques y compris les recommandations de groupes (Plénière)

VIII. Coopération internationale: présentation du plan d'action et des projets-pilotes

IX.   Présentation du plan d'action et du rapport finals (Plénière)

Appendice 2: Ordre du jour annoté

I.   Historique

La Conférence générale de l'UNESCO a adopté, à sa 25e session (novembre 1989), la Recommandation sur la sauvegarde de la culture traditionnelle et populaire (texte intégral ci-joint). Cet important instrument est issu du principe que la culture traditionnelle et populaire fait partie du patrimoine universel de l'humanité, et qu'à ce titre elle peut être un puissant moyen de rapprochement des différents peuples et groupes sociaux et d'affirmation de leur identité culturelle. Ils ont souligné son importance sociale, économique, culturelle et politique dans le contexte culturel passé et présent. En outre, la culture traditionnelle et populaire, dont certaines formes sont par définition très fragiles, fait partie intégrante du patrimoine culturel et de la culture vivante. L'adoption de la recommandation visait à encourager divers gouvernements à jouer un rôle décisif en adoptant des mesures notamment législatives, conformément aux pratiques constitutionnelles de chacun d'entre eux, afin d'assurer la préservation et la sauvegarde de la culture traditionnelle et populaire. Compte tenu des bouleversements qui n'épargnent aucune région du monde, cette tâche reste plus que jamais d'actualité.

La Recommandation comprend sept chapitres: (i) définition, (ii) identification, (iii) conservation, (iv) préservation, (v) diffusion, (vi) protection et (vii) coopération internationale. La "culture traditionnelle et populaire" est "l'ensemble des créations émanant d'une communauté culturelle fondées sur la tradition, exprimées par un groupe ou par des individus et reconnues comme répondant aux attentes de la communauté en tant qu'expression de l'identité culturelle et sociale de celle-ci, les normes et les valeurs se transmettant oralement, par imitation ou par d'autres manières. Ses formes comprennent, entre autres, les langues, la littérature, la musique, la danse, les jeux, la mythologie, les rites, les coutumes, l'artisanat, l'architecture et d'autres arts".

En février 1990, le Directeur général de l'UNESCO a adressé aux Etats membres une lettre circulaire les invitant à prendre toutes les mesures nécessaires pour assurer la mise en oeuvre de la Recommandation. Aux termes de l'article IV, paragraphe 4, de l'Acte constitutif de l'UNESCO, chaque Etat membre soumettra les recommandations ou conventions adoptées par l'Organisation aux autorités nationales compétentes, dans le délai d'un an à compter de la clôture de la session de la Conférence générale au cours de laquelle elles auront été adoptées. En 1991, cependant, seuls six pays avaient soumis des rapports spéciaux sur les mesures prises pour mettre en oeuvre la Recommandation. En outre, ces rapports se limitaient à affirmer la pertinence de la législation nationale en vigueur et à signaler des mesures particulières destinées à familiariser les autorités nationales compétentes avec les dispositions de la Recommandation.

Afin de procéder à une évaluation systématique de l'application de la Recommandation, ainsi que des activités de sauvegarde et de revitalisation du patrimoine culturel immatériel dans les Etats membres, l'UNESCO a lancé, entre 1995 et 1999, une série d'enquêtes région par région. Au total, huit séminaires régionaux ont été organisés, comme suit: (i) Strá nice, République tchèque (juin 1995), pour l'Europe centrale et orientale; (ii) Mexico, Mexique (septembre 1997), pour l'Amérique latine et la Caraïbe; (iii) Tokyo, Japon (février-mars 1998), pour l'Asie; (iv) Joensuu, Finlande (septembre 1998), pour l'Europe occidentale; (v) Tashkent, République d'Ouzbékistan (octobre 1998), pour l'Asie centrale et le Caucase; (vi) Accra, Ghana (janvier 1999), pour l'Afrique; (vii) Nouméa, Nouvelle-Calédonie (février 1999), pour le Pacifique; et (viii) Beyrouth, Liban (mai 1999), pour les Etats arabes.

La présente Conférence est le point culminant de ces séminaires régionaux. Son principal objectif est d'évaluer la situation dans le monde et de dégager les perspectives d'avenir en ce qui concerne la Recommandation de 1989 sur la sauvegarde de la culture traditionnelle et populaire. Le patrimoine culturel immatériel est à la fois riche et varié; pourtant, pour diverses raisons, de nombreux producteurs de culture traditionnelle et populaire abandonnent leurs arts ou cessent de les transmettre aux jeunes générations. A cause de cela, il y a une grande menace de disparition de nombreux aspects de la culture traditionnelle et populaire dans le monde. D'où la nécessité de prendre d'urgence des mesures pour en assurer la préservation et la revitalisation tant pour les générations actuelles que pour celles à venir.

II.   Objectifs de la Conférence

Les objectifs de la Conférence sont issus des résultats des séminaires régionaux qui proposent de:

A.   Faire le point de la situation actuelle en matière de sauvegarde et de revitalisation du patrimoine culturel immatériel dans le monde aujourd'hui;

B.   Analyser les relations entre le patrimoine culturel immatériel, le patrimoine culturel matériel (physique) et le patrimoine naturel, ainsi que le rôle que le premier joue dans la résolution des problèmes locaux et nationaux touchant à d'importantes préoccupations de notre époque, telles que l'identité culturelle, les questions liées aux femmes, le développement humain durable, la mondialisation, la coexistence pacifique de différents groupes ethniques, la prévention des conflits, les cultures des jeunes, l'évolution des nouvelles technologies de la communication et de l'information, la dégradation de l'environnement, etc.;

    C.   Examiner la protection juridique du patrimoine culturel immatériel à l'échelle locale et nationale;

    D.   Suggérer des politiques locales, nationales et internationales, concernant en particulier la transmission, la revitalisation et la documentation dans le domaine du patrimoine culturel immateriel;

    E.   Discuter les mesures futures d'application de la Recommandation de 1989;

    F.   Encourager la coopération internationale par le biais de l'élaboration de stratégies futures et de projets pilotes.

III.   Organisation de la Conférence

Après une introduction à la Conférence, un aperçu des mesures prises par l'UNESCO pour assurer la mise en oeuvre de la Recommandation de 1989 (points 1 et 2 de l'ordre du jour; 1er jour) sera présenté aux participants. La Conférence continuera avec une brève discussion sur les conclusions des réunions régionales (points 3 et 4 de l'ordre du jour; 1er jour), avant de se scinder en trois groupes de travail pour un examen approfondi des thèmes définis au point 6 de l'ordre du jour (1er et 2e jours). Les points 7 à 10 seront abordés en plénière (3e jour).

    A.   Rapports des huit conférences régionales

Les étapes de la procédure suivie pour mener les enquêtes régionales ont été les suivantes: (i) l'UNESCO a identifié comme partenaire dans chaque région une institution spécialisée; (ii) en tenant compte des spécificités régionales, l'UNESCO a établi un questionnaire concernant l'application de la Recommandation; (iii) l'UNESCO a distribué ce questionnaire aux Commissions nationales des Etats membres concernés, en leur demandant de prendre les mesures nécessaires pour faire que ce questionnaire soit dûment rempli; (iv) sur la base des réponses reçues, l'UNESCO et l'institution partenaire ont établi des statistiques et élaboré un rapport global évaluant le degré de mise en oeuvre de la Recommandation. Ces rapports se sont révélés très utiles dans tous les séminaires régionaux, donnant lieu à des débats fructueux, à de nombreuses recommandations et à des conclusions concrètes.

    B.   Aperçu des rapports régionaux: Evaluation mondiale

Les rapports régionaux, qui se concentrent sur les tendances, aspects, difficultés et interrogations aux niveaux local et national, illustrent tant la situation actuelle que les perspectives d'avenir du patrimoine culturel immatériel. Un aperçu d'ensemble de ces rapports permettra, par conséquent, de savoir ce qui a été fait ou non dans les Etats membres de l'UNESCO au cours des dix années qui ont suivi l'adoption de la Recommandation, ainsi que de définir ce qui doit être entrepris dans l'avenir.

A la demande de l'UNESCO, la Smithsonian Institution a établi, à partir des rapports régionaux sur l'application de la Recommandation de 1989 de l'UNESCO, un rapport de synthèse mondial, ainsi que des statistiques, qui seront envoyés par courrier à tous les participants avant la tenue de la Conférence.

    C.   Analyse de la Recommandation de 1989 dans le contexte d'aujourd'hui: aspects positifs et négatifs

Depuis que se sont atténuées les tensions bipolaires entre l'Est et l'Ouest en 1989, le monde a subi d'importantes transformations politiques, économiques et socio-culturelles. En outre, les nouvelles technologies apparues facilitent la sauvegarde du patrimoine culturel immatériel, tout en posant un défi dans ce domaine. Toutefois, malgré ces immenses progrès, un certain nombre de problèmes ont surgi. Ainsi, le moment est-il venu d'évaluer les aspects positifs et négatifs de la Recommandation dans le contexte d'aujourd'hui.

La Smithsonian Institution a entrepris d'élaborer un document sur la Recommandation de 1989 qui sera distribué aux participants avant la Conférence.

D.   Discussions thématiques (Groupes de travail)

Groupe I. Le patrimoine culturel immatériel et physique, le patrimoine naturel et le rôle que le patrimoine immatériel peut jouer dans la résolution des problèmes locaux et nationaux touchant aux grandes préoccupations de notre époque, telles que l'identité culturelle, les questions liées aux femmes, le développement humain durable, la mondialisation, la coexistence pacifique de différents groupes ethniques, la prévention des conflits, les cultures des jeunes, l'évolution de nouvelles technologies de communication et d'information, la dégradation de l'environnement, etc.

Voici quelques thèmes susceptibles d'être abordés:

Patrimoine culturel matériel et immatériel et patrimoine naturel. L'UNESCO s'est rendue célèbre par ses actions prises en vue de sauvegarder de grands monuments historiques, tels que les temples d'Abou Simbel en Egypte. La "Liste du patrimoine mondial", activité phare de l'UNESCO pendant les années 90, réunit dans une convention unique le "patrimoine naturel" et le "patrimoine culturel matériel" (monuments et sites). En novembre 1998, les Etats membres de l'UNESCO, pour qui le "patrimoine culturel" s'était jusque-là borné au "patrimoine culturel matériel", sont convenus d'étendre cette notion au "patrimoine culturel immatériel".

A sa 155e session (novembre 1998), le Conseil exécutif de l'UNESCO a approuvé un nouveau projet relatif à la proclamation des "chefs-d'oeuvre du patrimoine oral et immatériel de l'humanité". L'approbation de ce projet témoigne du fait que nombreux Etats membres de l'UNESCO, pour lesquels "patrimoine culturel" signifiait surtout "patrimoine culturel matériel (physique)," ont accepté un sens plus large, incluant le patrimoine à la fois matériel et immatériel. De fait, patrimoine matériel et patrimoine immatériel ont toujours été intimement liés, le premier donnant un sens au second et le second un support matériel au premier. Les exemples suivants illustreront ce point: (i) la longue frise d'Angkor Vat, qui dépeint l'histoire de la légendaire épopée du Ramayana vieille de 1.500 ans; (ii) la danse de la Cour khmère, qui reflète, aujourd'hui encore, le style de danse déployé par les belles *Apsaras* ("demi-divinités") sur les bas-reliefs en pierre du temple; et (iii) la symbolique, les techniques et la qualité artistique des ornementations murales traditionnelles de l'architecture mauritanienne en terre, qui ont été transmis de mère en fille à travers les siècles. En outre, le patrimoine naturel ou paysager, tel que les chutes Victoria (Mosi-oa-Tunya) en Zambie et au Zimbabwe, a donné naissance à un certain nombre de traditions orales, de mythes et d'épopées, qui lui confèrent une dimension culturelle.

Une approche intégrée, qui prenne en compte les aspects à la fois matériels et immatériels, est donc nécessaire pour assurer la sauvegarde du patrimoine immatériel. En outre, il est indispensable aujourd'hui de doter les populations locales de moyens qui leur permettront de participer à l'adoption de mesures visant à sauvegarder leur patrimoine culturel immatériel. Il faut, pour cela, leur dispenser une formation appropriée en matière de gestion du patrimoine, qui souligne l'intégration des patrimoines matériel et immatériel.

Identité collective. "La culture traditionnelle et populaire" (patrimoine culturel immatériel) peut jouer un rôle important dans la résolution des problèmes locaux et nationaux touchant aux grandes préoccupations de notre époque. Ainsi, pour de nombreuses populations, le patrimoine culturel immatériel n'a cessé de jouer un rôle vital dans l'affirmation et l'expression de l'identité collective, elle-même profondément ancrée dans l'histoire. Les cosmologies, croyances et valeurs, véhiculées par les langues, les traditions orales et diverses manifestations culturelles, constituent souvent les fondements de la vie de la communauté. En outre, dans beaucoup de pays, l'affirmation de l'identité culturelle, fondée sur la culture traditionnelle et populaire locale, a joué un rôle à part entière dans le processus d'édification de la nation au lendemain de la période coloniale.

Questions liées aux femmes. Dans beaucoup de sociétés de par le monde, les femmes ont toujours joué un rôle vital dans la sauvegarde et la transmission des traditions, des règles de conduite et des savoir-faire, qu'elles considèrent comme indispensables au maintien de la cohésion familiale et de la position sociale. Entrent dans cette catégorie le code moral, les contes, les histoires orales, les chansons, la musique, les langues, le chamanisme, les pratiques rituelles et les savoir-faire culinaires. Dans la production de culture matérielle, où un certain symbolisme, une qualité artistique et une dextérité manuelle particuliers s'expriment notamment dans la broderie, le tissage, la confection de tapis et la construction d'habitats, les femmes ont su non seulement conserver et transmettre les méthodes et les pratiques traditionnelles, mais aussi les adapter de façon novatrice en y intégrant des éléments modernes, en créant des matériaux et des formules techniques nouvelles.

Développement durable. Le succès du développement humain durable implique l'adaptation des stratégies de développement au contexte socio-culturel d'une société donnée. Il est donc vital d'observer et d'analyser les systèmes socio-économiques locaux ainsi que les modes de pensée et de comportement et les méthodes de production traditionnelles, tels que ceux transmis oralement. En outre, certaines expressions de la culture traditionnelle et populaire peuvent contribuer au développement économique en mettant en valeur l'industrie culturelle, notamment dans les domaines des arts d'interprétation et de l'artisanat.

Mondialisation. La mondialisation actuelle de la vie économique, politique et sociale, accélérée par le progrès des technologies de l'information et de la communication, a produit une interpénétration et un amalgame culturels. Par conséquent, les cultures majoritaires ont, de plus en plus, absorbé leurs compléments minoritaires, menaçant ainsi la diversité culturelle. C'est pourquoi l'on affirme souvent que la mondialisation a contribué à accroître l'uniformité culturelle. La revitalisation du patrimoine culturel immatériel, propre à chaque communauté, aidera donc à préserver les cultures locales, dont le renforcement est indispensable à la perpétuation de la diversité culturelle dans le monde. Cette diversité, fondée sur la coexistence pacifique des différents groupes ethniques, est une condition préalable à l'avènement d'un système multiculturel, élément fondamental de la paix mondiale, dont la construction est une tâche primordiale de l'UNESCO et des Nations Unies.

Technologie. Certes, le progrès rapide des technologies de l'information et de la communication a peut-être causé du tort à de nombreuses cultures traditionnelles et populaires locales. Mais ces technologies sont indispensables à la préservation et à la mise en valeur de ce patrimoine. En outre, il ne faut pas oublier que la culture n'est pas statique, mais en constante évolution. Les nouvelles technologies ont fait progresser la communication et l'information, favorisant l'émergence de formes nouvelles et variées d'expressions culturelles métissées. Enfin, il est impératif de reconnaître que les jeunes, qui sont les plus sensibles au progrès technologique, possèdent et continueront de produire leurs propres formes artistiques qui, à leur tour, viendront à faire partie d'un nouveau patrimoine; tel est le cas, par exemple, de la musique ethno-techno. Nous devons donc rester constamment attentifs à l'évolution culturelle.

Conflits ethniques. Le nombre de conflits ethniques ne cesse de croître dans le monde. Pour lutter contre cette tendance, les représentants de pays d'Afrique et du Pacifique, qui ont participé aux séminaires régionaux d'Accra (janvier 1999) et, respectivement, de Nouméa (février 1999), ont manifesté un vif désir de revenir à la sagesse et au savoir traditionnels comme moyens de prévention des conflits.

Protection de l'environnement. La dégradation de l'environnement dans le monde pose de sérieux problèmes non seulement aux communautés locales, dont elle menace les ressources, la culture et le mode de vie traditionnels, mais aussi à la planète tout entière. Des mesures concrètes sont donc nécessaires pour lutter contre cette dégradation. Cependant, la revitalisation des savoirs, des savoir-faire et des pratiques traditionnels, qui visent à réguler l'exploitation des ressources naturelles par l'institution, par exemple, de tabous en matière de pêche et de chasse, dépend dans une large mesure de la relation entre la population et l'environnement; elle peut, à son tour, être utile dans la lutte contre les risques liés à l'environnement.

Groupe II. Protection juridique du patrimoine culturel immatériel à l'échelle locale et nationale

La culture traditionnelle et populaire est, de par sa nature même, très variée et parfois menacée d'extinction. Les mesures législatives peuvent assurer la sauvegarde du patrimoine culturel immatériel dans le monde entier, accordant une protection systématique aux niveaux à la fois local et national. Cette protection doit embrasser non seulement le patrimoine culturel immatériel lui-même, mais aussi les hommes qui sont porteurs de ces cultures traditionnelles et populaires.

La culture traditionnelle et populaire peut aussi faire facilement l'objet d'une appropriation et d'une exploitation commerciale par les membres de communautés autres que celles qui l'ont créée. Il est impératif de protéger les droits *sui generis* de l'expression traditionnelle et populaire lorsqu'elle est utilisée par des tiers ou à d'autres fins. Lors de l'établissement d'un tel système de protection, il convient de veiller en particulier à ce que des avantages matériels soient accordés aux populations qui ont donné naissance à l'expression culturelle en question.

Groupe III. Politiques locales, nationales, régionales et internationales concernant en particulier la transmission, la revitalisation et la documentation dans le domaine du patrimoine culturel immatériel

Le rôle de l'UNESCO, en tant qu'organisation intergouvernementale, est d'inciter les gouvernements membres à prendre des mesures en conformité avec les décisions de sa Conférence générale. L'UNESCO a donc pour tâche primordiale de sensibiliser les décideurs au sein des gouvernements membres et leurs stratèges au fait qu'il est urgent de sauvegarder et de revitaliser le patrimoine culturel immatériel du monde. Une évaluation est nécessaire afin d'élaborer des politiques locales, nationales et internationales, qui mettent l'accent en particulier sur la transmission, la revitalisation et la documentation de ce patrimoine. L'objectif est d'aider chaque gouvernement à établir des politiques appropriées à cet égard ou de promouvoir la coopération régionale ou internationale pour encourager cet effort.

E.   Rapport des groupes de travail, incluant leurs recommandations

Les groupes de travail sont invités à se réunir en plénière afin d'examiner et de confronter les idées et les recommandations issues des différentes séances de travail.

F.   Rôle futur de la Recommandation de 1989 au sein des Etats membres de l'UNESCO

La Recommandation existe depuis dix ans. Nous sommes conscients de la situation passée et présente et devons maintenant envisager les perspectives d'avenir. Plus précisément, il est temps d'évaluer le rôle futur de la Recommandation au sein des Etats membres de l'UNESCO afin d'assurer la sauvegarde et la revitalisation du patrimoine culturel immatériel mondial. Tandis que certains Etats membres de l'UNESCO considèrent que le moment est venu pour l'UNESCO de réviser la Recommandation de 1989, ou d'en créer une nouvelle, d'autres proposent d'élaborer une convention internationale pour la sauvegarde du patrimoine culturel immatériel sur le modèle de la Convention du patrimoine mondial (1972), qui s'applique actuellement uniquement au patrimoine matériel (culturel et naturel). De toute manière, il est prématuré de décider quelle forme devrait prendre une telle convention: il est plutôt nécessaire de développer un régime *sui generis* différent applicable aux aspects spécifiques de cette forme particulière de patrimoine. Une autre suggestion est d'amender la Convention du patrimoine mondial, mais l'amendement de la Convention a été pour le moment rejeté (étude à l'occasion du 20e anniversaire de la Convention) et, pour les raisons mentionnées, ne semble pas être une bonne solution. D'autres analogies ont été suggérées telles que le régime de la propriété intellectuelle: l'OMPI et l'UNESCO ont étudié les perspectives d'une protection *sui generis*.

G.   Coopération internationale: Stratégies futures et projets pilotes

Pendant la Conférence, les participants sont censés identifier les problèmes et les défis pour les années à venir et formuler des stratégies à moyen terme de coopération internationale visant à la sauvegarde et à la revitalisation du patrimoine culturel immatériel dans le monde entier. Ces stratégies pourraient aider à définir l'orientation future du programme de l'UNESCO concernant le patrimoine culturel immatériel, ses priorités, les approches et les méthodes de travail appropriées. Il est à espérer que ces stratégies incluront des mesures concrètes pour améliorer à la fois l'application et l'efficacité de la Recommandation de 1989.

H.   Présentation des recommandations finales

Les participants à la Conférence sont invités à élaborer et à présenter diverses recommandations concernant l'orientation future ou le renforcement de la Recommandation de 1989, à l'intention de l'UNESCO, de ses Etats membres et des institutions spécialisées telles que la Smithsonian Institution.

Appendice 3: Participants, personnel, chercheurs-boursiers et stagiaires

Participants

Andy P. Abeita
Président
Council for Indigenous Arts and Culture
Peralta, Nouveau-Mexique
Etats-Unis

Noriko Aikawa
Directeur
Section Patrimoine culturel intangible
Direction Patrimoine culturel
UNESCO

Robyne Bancroft
Australian National University
Canberra
Australie

Tressa Berman
Arizona State University West
Phoenix, Arizona
Etats-Unis

Janet Blake
Faculté de droit
University of Glasgow
Glasgow, Ecosse
Royaume-Uni

Stepanida Borisova
Ministère de la culture
République de Sakha (Iakoutie)
Iakoutsk
Fédération Russe

Mounir Bouchenaki
Directeur
Centre du patrimoine mondial et du patrimoine culturel
UNESCO

Manuela Carneiro da Cunha
Professeur d'anthropologie
University of Chicago
Chicago, Illinois
Etats-Unis

Russell Collier
Strategic Watershed Analysis Team
(Equipe d'analyse stratégique du bassin-versant)
Nation Gitxsan
Hazelton, Colombie Britannique
Canada

Rachid El Houda
Architecte, DPLG
Marrakech
Maroc

Mahaman Garba
Ethnomusicologue
Centre de formation et de promotion musicale

Niamey
Niger

Jean Guibal
Directeur
Musée Dauphinois
Grenoble
France

Mihály Hoppál
Directeur
Centre européen de culture traditionnelle
Budapest
Hongrie

Florentino H. Hornedo
Faculté des Arts and Sciences
Ateneo de Manila University
Quezon City, Manila
Philippines

Peter Jaszi
Washington College of Law
Washington, DC
Etats-Unis

Pualani Kanaka'ole Kanahele
La Fondation Edith Kanaka'ole
Hilo, Hawai'i
Etats-Unis

Junzo Kawada
Professeur d'anthropologie culturelle
Hiroshima City University
Hiroshima
Japon

Heikki Kirkinen
Vice-président
European Academy of Arts, Sciences and Humanities
University of Joensuu
Joensuu
Finlande

Grace Koch
Administrateur des archives
Australian Institute of Aboriginal and Torres Strait Islander Studies
Canberra
Australie

Namankoumba Kouyaté
Chargé d'Affaires A.I.
Ambassade de la République de Guinée
Bonn
Allemagne

Kurshida Mambetova
Chef de la direction Culture
Commission nationale de l'UNESCO de la République d'Ouzbékistan
Tashkent
Ouzbékistan

Renato Matusse
Secrétaire permanent et Secrétaire général
Southern African Development Community (SADC)
Maputo
Mozambique

J.H. Kwabena Nketia
Directeur
International Centre for African Music and Dance (Centre international de musique et danse africaines)
University of Ghana
Legon, Accra
Ghana

Mamiko Ogawa
Service des affaires culturelles
Ministère des affaires étrangères
Tokyo
Japon

Vlasta Ondrusova
Directeur-adjoint
Institute of Folk Culture (Institut du folklore)
Strá nice
République Tchèque

Lyndel Prott
Directeur, Service des normes internationales
Direction du patrimoine culturel
UNESCO

Kamal Puri
Professeur de droit
The University of Queensland
Brisbane, Queensland
Australie

Miguel Puwainchir
Alcalde
Municipio de Humboya
Prov. De Moronal Santiago (Amazonie)
Equateur

Ralph Regenvanu
Commissaire
Centre culturel de Vanuatu
Port Vila
Vanuatu

Gail Saunders
Directrice
Section Archives
Nassau
Bahamas

Rajeev Sethi
Directeur, Rajeev Sethi Scenographers, Pvt. Ltd.
New Delhi
Inde

Mohsen Shaalan
Ministère de la culture
Caire
Egypte

Samantha Sherkin
Consultant
Section Patrimoine culturel intangible
Direction Patrimoine culturel
UNESCO

Juana Silvera Nuñez
Présidente
Comisision Nacional Cubana de la UNESCO
La Havane
Cuba

Brad Simon
Directeur des affaires juridiques et économiques
Shockwave.com

Preston Thomas
Commissaire
Aboriginal and Torres Strait Islander Commission
Phillip
Australie

Sivia Tora
Secrétaire permanent
Ministère des femmes, de la culture et des affaires sociales
Suva
Fiji

Osamu Yamaguti
Professeur de musicologie
Osaka University
Osaka
Japon

Zulma Yugar
Directora General de Promocion Cultural
Viceministerio de Cultura
La Paz
Bolivie

Observateurs

Mary Jo Arnoldi, Smithsonian Institution
Alberta Arthurs, The Rockefeller Foundation
Barry Bergey, National Endowment for the Arts (Fonds national des arts)
Francine Berkowitz, Smithsonian Institution
Gigi Bradford, Center for Arts and Culture, Washington, DC
Rachelle Browne, Smithsonian Institution
Peggy Bulger, American Folklife Center, Bibliothèque du Congrès
Olivia Cadaval, Smithsonian Institution
Shelton Davis, Banque mondiale
Kreszentia Duer, Banque mondiale
Alexander P. Durtka, Jr., CIOFF Cultural Commission, International Institute of Wisconsin
William Ferris, National Endowment for the Humanities (Fonds national des sciences humaines)
Arlene Fleming, Banque mondiale
Cecile Goli, UNESCO
Charlotte Heth, Smithsonian Institution
Vera Hyatt, Smithsonian Institution
David Hunter, Center for International Environmental Law, Washington, DC
Enrique Iglesias, Banco Interamericano de Desarollo, Washington, DC
Alan Jabbour, American Folklife Center, Bibliothèque du Congrès
Charles Kleymeyer, Inter-American Foundation
Mary Ellen Lane, Independent Council of American Overseas Research
Brian LeMay, Smithsonian Institution
Ellen McCulloch-Lovell, White House Millennium Commission
William Merrill, Smithsonian Institution
Francis Method, UNESCO
Diana Baird N'Diaye, Smithsonian Institution

Virgil Stefan Nitulescu, Chambre des députés, Bucarest, Roumanie
Pennie Ojeda, National Endowment for the Arts
Marc Pachter, Smithsonian Institution
Damien Pwono, The Ford Foundation
Caroline Ramsey, The Crafts Center, Washington, DC
Alison Dundes Renteln, University of Southern California
John Roberts, Ohio State University
Jean Roche, Delégué permanent du CIOFF (Conseil International des Organisations de
　　Festivals de Folklore et d'Arts Traditionnels), Gannat, France
Daniel Salcedo, PEOPLink, Kensington, MD
David Sanjek, BMI Archives, New York, New York
Dan Sheehy, National Endowment for the Arts
Claire Brett Smith, ICOMOS
D.A. Sonneborn, Smithsonian Institution
John Kuo Wei Tchen, New York University
Glenn Wallach, Center for Arts and Culture
Glenn M. Wiser, Center for International Environmental Law
Joe Wilson, The National Council for Traditional Arts
Toma Ybarra-Frausto, The Rockefeller Foundation

Personnel de la Smithsonian

James Early
John Franklin
Amy Horowitz
Anthony Seeger
Peter Seitel

Chercheurs-boursiers et stagiaires

Maria Elana Cepeda, Ann Arbor, MI
Lisa Maiorino, Indianapolis, IN
Anthony McCann, Warrenpoint, County Down, Irlande du nord
Jonathan McCollum, Allston, MA
Chad Redwing, Phoenix, AZ

Appendice 4: Rapport du groupe I

Lundi 28 juin 1999: Première réunion du groupe I, 15h45–17h30
　　Le groupe I devait discuter des thèmes suivants: Patrimoine culturel intangible par rapport
au patrimoine culturel tangible et naturel et son rôle dans la résolution des problèmes locaux
et nationaux liés aux préoccupations contemporaines majeures telles que l'identité culturelle,
le genre, le développement humain viable, la mondialisation, la coexistence pacifique de
groupes ethniques, la prévention de conflits, les cultures de jeunesse, l'évolution des nouvelles
technologies de communication et d'information, la dégradation de l'environnement etc.

Le président, Ralph Regenvanu, a demandé aux participants de se présenter. Après les présentations, Rajeev Sethi a commencé par se poser des questions sur l'état actuel de la Recommandation de 1989, notamment sa conceptualisation du problème en question. Il s'est demandé si des termes tels que *folk* (gens) et *tradition* ne passent pas sous silence l'idée et la possibilité d'innovation. Il a suggéré des modifications à la terminologie de la section A de la Recommandation qui a trait à la définition du folklore: *imitation* devrait être remplacé par *émulation*; *jeux* par *sports* puisque ce dernier terme est plus large. Quant à *artisanat* et *architecture*, n'entend-on pas par là *habitat*? s'est-il demandé. *Autres arts* semble être une catégorie résiduelle, pas suffisamment spécifique.

A propos de la section C qui porte sur la conservation du folklore, M. Sethi a suggéré que l'on parle d'abord de la sauvegarde des peuples avant celle des archives. La culture est vivante mais dépend des peuples à qui nous devons accorder plus de pouvoir. Le langage de la Recommandation de 1989 semble condescendant.

Pualani Kanahele a fait remarquer que beaucoup de peuples fondent d'importants éléments de leur identité culturelle sur l'environnement naturel et établissent ainsi des liens inextricables entre les patrimoines culturel et naturel. Que ferons-nous dans vingt ans, s'est-elle demandé, quand notre environnement sera gravement dégradé [par le développement économique]?

Andy Abeita a exprimé son inquiétude du fait que les praticiens de la culture traditionnelle ne peuvent pas classer l'art et la religion dans la même catégorie que les marchandises. Mais, il nous faut, en même temps, trouver des instruments juridiques semblables pour protéger ces praticiens dans leurs activités créatrices. Les dispositions sur les droits d'auteur couvrent les droits de propriété de la musique et de la prière et peuvent donc être invoquées pour protéger ceux-ci. A défaut de protections juridiques qui puissent être comprises du secteur privé, nous pouvons entrer dans d'éternels débats (à terme, stériles) pour essayer de nous définir.

Rajeev Sethi a répondu, à la question sur l'artisanat, que la commercialisation repose, d'après son expérience, sur les besoins de l'artisan. Son sentiment était qu'il nous faut aider les artisans à comprendre le sens de nouveaux concepts sans porter préjudice à leur culture. L'innovation n'est pas forcément mauvaise.

Pualani Kanahele a déclaré qu'elle appréciait l'observation faite par Sivia Tora au début de la réunion à propos de l'impossibilité de séparer la culture tangible de la culture intangible ou le patrimoine culturel du patrimoine naturel. Elle a précisé sa réflexion sur la dégradation de l'environnement en citant l'exemple de l'aménagement de grands hôtels internationaux sur le polype corallien, l'animal marin à l'origine du corail, l'essence même des îles et l'objet de chants poétiques sur la création.

Rajeev Sethi a répondu qu'il ne pensait pas qu'il y avait une solution à un tel problème, du moins pas au niveau de l'UNESCO. En Inde, un grand nombre de tribus ont été déplacées au nom du développement. Il n'y a pas de solution à cette situation. A quel saint se vouer?

Miguel Puwainchir a répondu en citant l'adage selon lequel *une personne sans terre est une personne sans culture*. Si l'UNESCO ne peut rien changer, il nous incombe de changer l'UNESCO, a-t-il lancé au groupe. Avant la conquête espagnole, dit-il, nous avions une culture pure. Aujourd'hui, la confusion règne et la culture est devenue polluée. Il nous faut promouvoir et défendre notre culture. Sinon, elle va mourir à petit feu et nous aurons accepté cette fin. En revanche, nous ne devons pas nous isoler. Il nous faudrait rechercher les relations interculturelles. Les valeurs négatives doivent être oubliées. En Bolivie, par exemple, la coca a été utilisée comme une plante médicinale. D'autres l'ont utilisée comme une drogue nocive. Que faire aujourd'hui? Accepter les valeurs positives et rejeter les négatives.

La Recommandation de 1989, continua-t-il, décrit les cultures essentiellement comme des *objets* mais la culture, c'est aussi l'être humain. Pourquoi séparer les deux? Il nous faut échanger des expériences — C'est sain comme activité. Beaucoup de problèmes dont nous discutons portent sur l'aliénation mais il faut se rappeler que la culture est notre nature même.

Rachid El Houda a exprimé son inquiétude à propos de quelques éléments de la discussion. Nous parlons en termes officiels, a-t-il déclaré, et nous n'abordons pas le fond des choses. Nous devons donc séparer certains instruments juridiques de nos modes de pensée sur la culture. Il y a deux façons d'aborder la question: nous pouvons dresser une liste de tout ce qu'on peut considérer comme culture traditionnelle; ou nous pouvons trouver ce qui nous unit par l'intermédiaire de nos différences. Les différences peuvent nous unir, a-t-il déclaré. Il nous faut des idées qui puissent nous servir à avancer. Des ponts peuvent être construits avec la culture et la religion. Par exemple, un symbolisme qui peut être expliqué dans une culture/religion peut aussi exister dans la nôtre. Nous devons faire abstraction de ce qui tend à nous diviser.

Mahaman Garba s'est demandé si le lien entre religion et préservation devrait être considéré comme sujet tabou. La musique est, selon lui, le patrimoine intangible de son pays. Certains disent *patrimoine culturel*, d'autres *folklore*. Nous devrions employer le premier terme parce qu'il est plus noble.

Il nous faut choisir, a-t-il encore déclaré. Voulons nous nous développer ou rester sur place? L'évolution a ses inconvénients. Les gens du tiers-monde veulent avoir la télévision. Qu'y avait-il auparavant? Des chants et des jeux? Doit-on refuser la télévision? Les jeux et les chants peuvent bien être éducatifs mais on peut voir les artistes à la télé ou les entendre à la radio. A défaut de ces médias, il faudrait parcourir des milliers de kilomètres pour avoir accès à ces artistes.

Pualani Kanahele a résumé en partie la séance en disant que nous avons parlé de co-existence et de prévention de conflit. Nous devons aussi apprendre à composer avec le développement. Oui, a-t-elle déclaré, nous devons connaître le développement mais le développement doit également nous connaître. Nous devons tenir compte des symboles aussi, des aspects positifs aussi bien que négatifs de tout cela.

Mardi, 29 juin 1999: Deuxième réunion du groupe I, 9h30–12h

Robyne Bancroft a, dans son exposé (présent volume, 70–74), parlé de la nécessité d'une approche holistique pour comprendre la culture aborigène d'Australie qui consiste en un dense réseau de relations entre les êtres humains et leur environnement. Leur histoire, généralement méconnue, remonte à plus de 60 000 ans. Il existait plus de 250 groupes linguistiques à l'époque de la colonisation; il n'en reste plus que 25 langues actives. Il y a maintenant 325 000 Aborigènes parmi les 18 millions d'habitants que compte l'Australie. Ils ont survécu et sont récemment apparus sur la scène internationale. La justice a rendu d'importants arrêts sur des questions vitales telles que le régime foncier. On commence à faire face à la situation de la " génération perdue " (des familles séparées à cause de certaines pratiques de l'Etat). Malgré les arrêts et lois favorables, il y a toujours un besoin pressant de justice.

Les termes *folklore* et *mythologies* ne plaisent pas aux Aborigènes parce qu'ils ont une connotation négative en Australie. Elle propose l'emploi du terme *patrimoine culturel indigène*. Parmi les questions auxquelles les peuples aborigènes accordent de l'importance, il faut noter: problématique hommes-femmes; un code d'éthique pour régir les relations entre les populations indigènes et les non-indigènes; et le rapatriement de dépouilles mortelles. Elle a présenté des recommandations: La Recommandation de 1989 manque de force. Pour remédier à cela, il faudrait en faire une convention de l'UNESCO; l'importance de la biodiversité doit être officiellement reconnue; des institutions telles que l'UNESCO et la Smithsonian devraient soutenir les peuples indigènes dans leur lutte pour leurs droits; il faut davantage de programmes de formation et de valorisation professionnelle qui soient gérés par les peuples indigènes.

Mihály Hoppál a parlé dans son exposé (présent volume: 182–184) de la société contemporaine, axée sur l'information, à croissance économique illimitée mais qui manque de savoir et de tradition locaux proprement dits. Il existe une mine de savoir empreint de tradition sur les divers moyens par lesquels les gens ont appris à cohabiter. Les traditions spirituelles figurent parmi ceux-ci. Les systèmes locaux de valeur peuvent servir de base à la résolution des conflits. Ce ne sont pas les systèmes locaux mais la méconnaissance de l'Autre qui cause les conflits. Les systèmes locaux de valeur, tels que les préjugés, représentent le soubassement émotionnel des conflits. La mondialisation peut représenter une menace aux cultures indigènes et le masque d'une nouvelle forme d'impérialisme. Elle peut avoir comme conséquence celle de nier les droits collectifs locaux et de faire peser une menace sur les groupes minoritaires. Des lois devraient être votées pour assurer le respect et la protection des droits humains et l'identité culturelle des minorités. Les systèmes de valeur anglo-saxons ne sont pas pour tout le monde. Il a recommandé la mise au point de stratégies pour sensibiliser les jeunes et leur faire respecter les traditions d'autres nations; l'organisation de festivals qui célèbrent la diversité de chaque nation; la documentation et la préservation des traditions; le traitement respectueux des patrimoines culturels dans les pays membres et l'adoption de lois pour veiller au respect de ces cultures locales; un traitement honorable de toutes nos traditions pour que l'on puisse vivre longtemps sur cette terre.

Miguel Puwainchir a consacré son exposé (présent volume, 65–66) à ce qu'il a appelé *interculturalité* — le respect et la connaissance de cultures autres que la nôtre. Nous vivons de nos jours dans une complexe diversité démographique. En fondant des Etats et des nations, nous avons créé des cultures et identités nationales qui ne reconnaissent pas les traditions locales. En Equateur, les indigènes se sont unis pour faire modifier les lois et créer un *espace de respect* pour eux en vue de résister à l'assimilation. Dans l'avenir, il nous faudrait des nations dénuées de cultures étatiques car celles-ci finissent toujours par transformer les cultures locales en *folklore*. Il faudrait mettre au point, à l'intention du grand public, des programmes éducatifs nationaux sur les différentes cultures pour éviter que les anthropologues et musées soient seuls à détenir ce savoir. L'interculturalité nous aidera à éviter la mondialisation de la culture, à maintenir la diversité culturelle et à nous défendre contre le développement démesuré qui détruit notre environnement. Ses recommandations sont les suivantes: les Etats ne devraient pas avoir une culture nationale unique; les cultures locales ne devraient être transformées ni en marchandises ni en monuments mais, au contraire, doivent être préservées et promues en tant que cultures vivantes; il importe de s'informer sur les autres cultures sans pour autant perdre la particularité de sa propre culture; l'UNESCO devrait promouvoir de nouveaux modèles de réflexion sur les cultures, célébrer la diversité mondiale et veiller à ce que les technologies modernes ne détruisent pas les cultures locales;.

Mihály Hopál a fait valoir que le malentendu entre groupes culturels a pour origine l'ignorance de l'histoire et de la culture de l'Autre. En Europe de l'est, a-t-il déclaré, les mythes historiques peuvent être, dans les temps modernes, utilisées à des fins politiques telles que la guerre.

Paulani Kanahele a répondu à l'exposé en disant que le mondialisme est une autre forme de colonialisme qui mine les traditions locales, notamment chez les jeunes. Il importe, par conséquent, d'inclure davantage les jeunes dans les rituels et cérémonies, pour éviter que ces traditions ne disparaissent dans la globalisation. Sensibiliser les étrangers sur les questions culturelles représente un bon départ mais n'est pas chose facile compte tenu de la ténacité de leurs préjugés et leur refus de s'informer sur les cultures indigènes. Pour les raisons soulignées par Miguel Puwainchir, *mythe* et *folklore* sont des termes problématiques qu'il faut remplacer.

Russell Collier a répondu que la terminologie employée importe peu dans les batailles actuelles ou à venir contre les gouvernements et autres forces qui menacent les cultures indigènes.

Dans son exposé (présent volume, 194–202), Dr. Mahaman Garba a présenté une étude de cas d'un projet de l'UNESCO relatif à un centre de formation musicale (Centre de formation et de promotion musicale) au Niger. Il a tout d'abord décrit brièvement les huit groupes linguistiques et ethniques du Niger. Dans ce pays, il existe un système de castes qui désigne les personnes censées transmettre la tradition orale et celles qui doivent devenir musiciens. Quand une telle personne meurt, c'est comme si toute une bibliothèque avait brûlé. Un grand nombre de ces personnes ont disparues sans être remplacées. La tradition et la musique dont elles étaient les dépositaires disparaissent également. Ce problème ainsi que des propositions en vue de sa résolution ont été présentés à l'UNESCO qui a contribué au lancement du centre de formation musicale. La préservation des traditions musicales progresse grâce au soutien de l'UNESCO et d'autres bailleurs de fonds, notamment japonais. Dr. Garba a particulièrement remercié Mme Aikawa et Prof. Kawada pour leurs efforts à l'endroit du centre.

Dr. Garba a décrit les trois champs d'action du center — recherche, formation, promotion. Il a aussi déclaré qu'ils s'occupaient de questions portant sur les droits de propriété des Européens en matière de musique et d'instruments de musique et sur le rapatriement de ce patrimoine musical. Quant au financement, Dr. Garba a souligné que les fonds ne cessent de diminuer et que le centre n'avait pas le droit d'utiliser l'aide financière de façon optimale conformément au souhait du personnel. Il a recommandé qu'on permette aux experts locaux en matière de projet de développement culturel de participer plus activement aux prises de décision concernant l'allocation des fonds.

Rachid El-Houda a fait un exposé (présent volume, 216–217) sur la Place Jemaa El Fna de Marrakech (un site Patrimoine mondial) pour explorer un des rapports entre les patrimoines tangible et intangible. Il a procédé à une brève description de cette zone urbaine et de son importance culturelle. Un grand nombre d'écrivains, d'acteurs, de dramaturges ont porté un intérêt professionnel à ce square. Des urbanistes ont essayé de reproduire ses qualités spatiales et culturelles dans d'autres régions du monde. Des conteurs de tout genre ont régulièrement fait des représentations publiques sur cette place. Celle-ci subit les agressions de la modernisation. Fort de sa valeur commerciale, cet espace urbain est devenu la cible des promoteurs économiques. La valeur de sa riche culture orale ne pèse pas lourd devant sa valeur monétaire. Il est facile d'interdire et de déplacer les spectacles traditionnels pour les besoins du commerce mais quasiment impossible de recréer la riche culture orale qui s'épanouit dans ce genre d'espace. Un autre problème est celui de la perte de ces trésors humains déplacés qui sont si difficiles à remplacer. Une organisation non-gouvernementale a été fondée pour préserver cette place et ses traditions. Mme Aikawa et l'UNESCO doivent être vivement remerciés pour leur aide dans cette entreprise. La dite ONG a comme mission: garantir l'intégrité et la continuité matérielles de la place; archiver et documenter son histoire et les contes qui y font l'objet de représentations; protéger les quartiers environnants; coopérer avec des groupes marocains et étrangers animés du même esprit; lever des fonds pour assurer une pension aux conteurs et autres artistes qui ne peuvent plus gagner leur vie à cause de leur âge avancé; rédiger et distribuer des publications pertinentes; intéresser les jeunes et les former dans le domaine de l'artisanat et des contes traditionnels; combattre les préjugés et images négatives des populations locales à l'endroit de la place et de ses habitants en créant un sentiment de fierté populaire envers le square et ce qu'il représente.

Junzo Kawada a fait un exposé (présent volume, 175–177) à propos des incitations sociales qui encouragent les praticiens à assurer la continuité de leur tradition. Il a commencé par souligner que la mondialisation, conjuguée à d'autres forces économiques, crée une conformité culturelle en transformant le système de récompenses socio-économiques et, ainsi, décourage la transmission de la culture aux nouvelles générations. La préservation du patrimoine culturel n'étant pas rentable au plan socio-économique, notamment chez les groupes minoritaires, il est difficile de trouver dans les nouvelles générations des porteurs du flambeau de la tradition. Bon nombre d'activités artisanales sont en péril à cause de ce phénomène. Le professeur Kawada a examiné la manière par laquelle diverses traditions ont fait face à ce problème et l'aide qui convient à chacune d'entre elles. Le tourisme peut avoir un effet positif en préservant la culture et en rehaussant la conscience interculturelle qui existe entre les étrangers et les populations locales. Les recettes touristiques stimulent la pratique des arts traditionnels.

La préservation des traditions revêt plusieurs avantages sociaux. La fabrication d'objets d'art traditionnel permet de protéger l'environnement grâce à l'utilisation de matériaux naturels. En outre, la revitalisation du patrimoine culturel accorde plus d'influence aux femmes qui ont un rôle plus important à jouer dans la préservation et la transmission de la culture.

Compte tenu de ce qui précède, Prof. Kawada a présenté les recommandations suivantes: fournir des incitations financières à grande échelle aux praticiens du patrimoine culturel; se prémunir contre la conformité culturelle qui découle de la mondialisation; encourager la coopération entre groupes traditionnels, gouvernements et ONG en vue de préserver les représentations culturelles à but non lucratif et assurer la formation de novices dans l'art du conte traditionnel; établir des programmes de formation en matière de documentation et d'enregistrement des contes.

Stepanida Borisova a décrit dans son exposé (présent volume, 245–247) l'état actuel de la sauvegarde de la culture traditionnelle dans la république de Sakha en Sibérie centrale. Les traditions orales étaient, jusqu'en 1991, documentées, codifiées et révisées en fonction des initiatives de l'Etat. Il y a, de nos jours, une résurgence de la culture traditionnelle y compris l'enseignement de la langue et de la culture dans les écoles et la proclamation de journées ayant une signification culturelle. La sauvegarde de la culture dépend de sa présentation publique. Un projet de l'UNESCO est nécessaire pour documenter et contribuer à la sauvegarde des traditions culturelles y compris celles qui ont trait au chamanisme et aux lieux sacrés.

Ralph Regenvanu a fait un compte-rendu sur la culture traditionnelle à Vanuatu, une île-nation du Pacifique qui a connu la colonisation, un dépeuplement massif, l'indépendance et la rétrocession des terres à ses propriétaires coutumiers. Après l'indépendance, Vanuatu a voulu poursuivre une voie de développement inspirée, non des valeurs occidentales, mais des traditions indigènes. A l'heure actuelle, la tendance est à la *recolonisation*, au retour aux modèles européens. La tradition de Vanuatu est exclusivement orale. Le Centre culturel de Vanuatu a donc axé ses programmes sur les efforts de préservation de la tradition par la documentation et l'aide aux collectivités ainsi que la formation des particuliers en matière d'archivage, de documentation des traditions et de techniques de conservation des archives pour les protéger contre le climat. Certains matériels d'archive appartiennent au centre et leur accès est limité. Cette pratique garantit la confiance de la communauté, confiance sans laquelle les traditions orales d'une lignée ne peuvent être archivées et stockées. La stratégie économique nationale va, cependant, à contre-courant des efforts du centre. Le centre documente des événements et sites traditionnels en vue de les protéger. Il tente, en outre, d'évaluer l'efficacité de certaines pratiques traditionnelles telles que les méthodes de conservation du poisson et d'autres ressources; de les documenter et de les présenter à d'autres groupes qui veulent être aidés dans leurs efforts de rétablir leurs traditions.

Mardi 29 juin 1999: Troisième réunion du groupe I, 13h30–17h

Après avoir décrit une cérémonie dédiée au dieu de la moisson de l'igname et les questions soulevées au sein de la communauté par le projet culturel des femmes qui l'a documentée, Ralph Regenvanu a fait valoir que le plus grand problème de la culture traditionnelle se situe au niveau des relations économiques mondiales. Le problème est que Vanuatu est désireux ou forcé à adhérer à l'OMC. Pour ce faire, Vanuatu devra ouvrir ses secteurs du bois et de la pêche à des compagnies étrangères et renoncer à son droit d'imposer des restrictions sur la pêche et d'interdire l'exportation des grumes. Pour assurer le service de sa dette, Vanuatu sera, en outre, forcé d'exporter et de payer en devise étrangère. Les communautés locales ne voient aucune utilité dans cette situation. Il a déclaré que le gouvernement, impuissant, a demandé à l'UNESCO de l'aider à lutter contre cette modernisation imposée par l'OMC qui ne reconnaît pas l'importance des communautés locales et leurs pratiques culturelles.

Rajeev Sethi a répondu en se demandant ce qu'était la relation entre l'OMC et l'UNESCO.

Andy Abeita a répondu qu'il n'y a pas de lien direct mais plutôt un chevauchement sur certaines questions et orientations. Elles sont toutes deux des organisations qui regroupent des pays membres et, comme toute bureaucratie, veulent satisfaire tout le monde. Nous devons procéder à une évaluation des besoins de notre base. Plus on est nombreux, plus on est écoutés. Il nous faut davantage de données statistiques sur ces communautés locales.

Noriko Aikawa a suggéré une recommandation qui demanderait à l'UNESCO de travailler en plus étroite collaboration avec l'OMC.

Ralph Regenvanu a confirmé la nécessité d'une plus grande participation de l'UNESCO. Vanuatu a, par exemple, besoin de ressources pour la documentation.

Noriko Aikawa a souligné qu'il incombe aux pays membres de décider de leurs actions mais qu'un séminaire peut être organisé pour discuter de ces contradictions.

Ralph Regenvanu a déclaré que, en fait, l'Etat ne peut présenter une telle requête. On le force à chercher des devises étrangères.

Russell Collier a fait valoir que son peuple ne peut compter sur le gouvernement canadien pour la défense de ses intérêts. Il n'y a aucun espoir que le Canada devienne le champion de leur cause.

Andy Abeita fit ensuite son exposé présent volume, 78–82). La loi intitulée *Indian Arts and Crafts Act* porte sur les produits fabriqués par des non-indiens et vendus de façon illicite comme s'ils étaient d'origine amérindienne. La dite législation interdit, au niveau fédéral, de telles pratiques et prévoit des réglementations douanières à cette fin. Abeita a ajouté que son association, *The Indian Arts and Crafts Association,* préconise des politiques semblables au niveau des Etats fédérés. Des efforts sont actuellement entrepris pour que les lois de copyright soient enregistrées au niveau de l'UCC afin de se prémunir contre la possibilité de copies illicites des labels d'authenticité. L'adoption dans le marché mondial de codifications séparées pour les produits artisanaux et les produits industriels serait bénéfique aux artisans traditionnels du monde entier. L'OMC envisage une telle loi.

Rajeev Sethi s'est posé la question de savoir quel serait l'effet d'une telle loi si, en tant que ressortissant de l'Inde, il voulait vendre un bracelet de qualité médiocre en Italie. Et qu'en serait-il du design? On pourrait légèrement modifier un design pour contourner la loi sur les droits d'auteur.

Rachid El Houda a souligné que, en matière de droits d'auteur, on pourrait s'inspirer des règles de copyright de logiciel et de technologies de l'information. Nous devons nous informer sur ce qui se passe dans le reste du monde mais aussi trouver un équilibre. Les idées sont, après tout, universelles et appartiennent à toute l'humanité bien que la conception initiale provienne d'un individu. Mais les idées qui deviennent de grands concepts font partie du patrimoine humain.

Andy Abeita a fait valoir que seuls les membres de la communauté détiennent les réponses. Il nous faut aborder les questions à un niveau plus personnel et non au niveau social ou purement académique.

Mahaman Garba a déclaré que le copyright est important quand tout le monde tente de mondialiser. Cela lui a rappelé que chez certains groupes, la musique est réservée exclusivement au chef. Qui, dans ces cas, va détenir les droits d'auteur? C'est la tradition qui octroie le droit d'auteur. Il y a, d'une part, la musique ancestrale et, d'autre part, la musique Pop ou Folk pour tout le monde. Mais celle-ci peut avoir des formes néo-traditionnelles et exiger le copyright.

Russel Collier a déclaré dans son exposé (présent volume, 75–77) que sa nation en Colombie britannique du nord-ouest occupe son territoire depuis 10 000 ans. Leur histoire orale remonte à la Glaciation — des membres de sa nation ont collaboré avec des archéologues qui étudiaient leur langue. Ils considèrent cette langue comme la *vraie langue* car elle permet à une personne d'exprimer et de penser des concepts tout à fait différents de ce que l'anglais lui permettrait. Leur identité est liée à la terre qu'ils occupent de la Californie à l'Alaska.

L'histoire orale est devenue très importante dans les négociations au sujet de revendications territoriales. Cette documentation et les données généalogiques ont constitué les dossiers juridiques présentés dans les affaires de revendications territoriales dont certaines ont été introduites à plusieurs reprises dans un intervalle de vingt ans. L'histoire orale a été reconnue comme valable pour confirmer et réclamer des titres. Un grand nombre d'Indiens ont recours à ces décisions pour raffermir leurs revendications. Cette idée fait école. Cette collection d'informations qui comprend non seulement des données folkloriques mais aussi des renseignements sur le climat, la faune et la flore, la pêche, est sans précédent. Tout commence par la documentation.

Robyne Bancroft a posé une question sur l'accès à la documentation. Elle a déclaré que le gouvernement australien prétend que certains dossiers sont trop sensibles pour qu'on y donne accès au peuple Aborigène.

Russel Collier a répondu que les documents leur appartiennent et que l'Etat n'a vraiment rien à dire là-dessus.

Pualani Kanahele a introduit son exposé (présent volume, 67–69) en exprimant son émerveillement devant la passion qu'engendre la tradition. Elle a parlé des traditions et de l'histoire hawaiiennes. La généalogie illustre les rapports qui existaient entre les ancêtres et les éléments. Les noms des gens révèlent l'occupation des ancêtres, leur domaine de spécialisation, leurs rapports avec les chefs etc. . . . Rien n'est vraiment perdu, il suffit de bien chercher, a-t-elle affirmé. Mais ces données ne se trouvent pas dans les livres d'histoire.

Vers la fin du dix-neuvième siècle, l'histoire fut recueillie, traduite et, ensuite, écrite dans les livres. Au début du vingtième siècle, il y a eu une perte de culture au contact des Etats-Unis. La culture hawaiienne vint à être considérée comme divertissement. Des années 40 jusqu'aux années 60, l'éducation s'avéra être un élément central de l'existence hawaiienne. Tout le monde devait faire des études universitaires. Mais certains se sont très fermement accrochés aux traditions.

Il est triste, a-t-elle déclaré, que beaucoup de Hawaiiens instruits ne connaissent pas leur culture. La culture hawaiienne a été ajoutée au programme universitaire. L'éducation leur a appris à lutter. La passion leur a appris à se battre pour leur coeur. L'archéologie est utile mais n'interprète pas la culture pour eux. Ils progressent en s'inspirant du passé. C'est la raison pour laquelle, a-t-elle déclaré, l'avenir est radieux.

Appendice 5: Rapport du groupe II
Protection juridique du patrimoine culturel intangible
aux niveaux local et national

Durant la première séance, le groupe a décidé que chacun ferait, à la séance suivante, un exposé de cinq minutes inspiré d'une communication écrite ou portant sur un intérêt particulier de l'orateur dans le domaine de la protection juridique du patrimoine culturel intangible local ou national. Deux minutes seraient ensuite consacrées à la conclusion ou à une brève conversation après l'exposé.

Le comité prit la décision de ne pas procéder strictement à une réévaluation et une critique du document de l'UNESCO de 1989 mais de produire des approches imaginatives à la préservation du patrimoine culturel pour ensuite les examiner à la lumière du document de l'UNESCO et des pratiques dans diverses régions du monde. Cette conférence-ci serait l'occasion d'un débat de fond, nouveau et créatif.

Cinq grands sujets à examiner se dégagèrent:

1. *Cadres conceptuels:* terminologie employée pour décrire la culture traditionnelle, les a priori dans la discussion sur la culture traditionnelle et sa préservation, les rapports entre le pouvoir politique, la préservation culturelle et la culture, les contrastes entre tangible et intangible, la question de l'identité des auteurs, des créateurs de la culture. Des questions telles que la transformation en marchandise et les possibilités de commercialisation de la culture seraient aussi à l'étude.

2. *Dispositions et mécanismes juridiques:* domaines à protéger; comment trouver une base juridique à la préservation aux niveaux international, national et local; aspects positifs et négatifs de certains mécanismes juridiques; vue d'ensemble de l'état actuel du droit en matière de culture traditionnelle et de protection etc. . . .

3. *Sanctions extra-juridiques et droit coutumier:* solutions communautaires et non-légalistes pour la perpétuation et la protection de la culture traditionnelle etc. . . .

4. *Droits:* Auteurs; plagiat et notions de propriété, copyright, brevets, droits de propriété intellectuelle et la faisabilité de mécanismes juridiques internationaux. Questions générales: De quels droits le public dispose-t-il et comment doit-on les protéger? Quelles sont les menaces qui pèsent sur ces droits? Quel est l'organisme le mieux habilité à protéger les cultures traditionnelles?

5. *Domaine public:* Questions relatives à la vie privée et à la confidentialité; comment ces facteurs se manifestent-ils sur la culture et sa préservation? Une attention particulière a été portée au sacré.

Au cours de la deuxième séance selon l'ordre du jour révisé, les participants ont présenté des résumés de cinq minutes de leurs communications écrites. Il s'agissait de récapitulations de problèmes juridiques, y compris des résumés de diverses approches juridiques telles que la variété d'approches IPR (marque déposée, brevet , secret industriel, mécanisme de copyright etc.) pour répondre aux besoins des populations indigènes et des praticiens du folklore. Deux recommandations ont été proposées:

- Reconnaître les restrictions culturelles comme étant des mesures raisonnables du même genre que les dispositions de contrats *muets* dont les équivalents peuvent exister dans les codes de commerce uniformes (par exemple, les garanties).
- Créer un organe (du genre organisation de droits collectifs) qui puisse canaliser les activités et qui serait administré par les représentants de la tradition et non ceux de l'Etat.

D'autres résumés ont soulevé des questions relatives au domaine public et à la confidentialité. Il y avait des déclarations sommaires sur des préoccupations régionales ou nationales telles que les efforts entrepris par l'ATSIC en Australie pour faire appliquer les lois de copyright au nom des artistes aborigènes.

Les discussions qui ont suivies ont d'abord porté sur les résumés de communications avant de continuer sur les recommandations du plan d'action. Les sujets de discussion étaient organisés et centrés sur les thèmes de l'ordre du jour afin d'aboutir systématiquement à des recommandations finales qui soient le fruit de discussions détaillées des sujets en question.

Des questions connexes ont été soulevées par rapport aux langues vivantes et aux programmes éducatifs pour la continuation de la culture traditionnelle. Le débat sur les niveaux de protection tels que l'accès aux sites sacrés, la préservation et la réparation des objets sacrés, a soulevé la question fondamentale de savoir ce que les communautés veulent protéger. Un objectif s'est donc dégagé: faire correspondre la protection aux besoins des communautés.

Les questions sous-jacentes à cette discussion étaient centrées sur les relations entre voies juridiques et non-juridiques et le problème du consensus relatif aux menaces sur le savoir traditionnel et les pratiques culturelles. Celles-ci étaient perçues sous l'angle des rapports de force ancrés dans les relations sociales. La question du rôle que l'Etat devrait jouer est, par conséquent, devenue une préoccupation majeure dans l'élaboration de recommandations pour la protection au niveau étatique.

Dr. da Cunha a lancé la discussion de la troisième séance en soulignant que le mot *folklore* est problématique, qu'il fait l'objet de multiples débats surtout parmi les anthropologues. Elle a fait référence à l'observation antérieure de Preston Thomas selon laquelle le terme a une connotation péjorative pour les groupes indigènes et laisse entendre un processus de nationalisme. M. Puri a aussi émis son objection à propos du mot en déclarant que le folklore est souvent assimilé au domaine public et signifie pour beaucoup que " tout est permis ". Il a suggéré au lieu de *folklore*, *culture populaire* et *traditionnelle*. M. McCann s'empressa de souligner que *culture populaire,* pouvant signifier produits culturels de masse du genre Mickey Mouse, devrait être évité. Le consensus se fit autour de *culture traditionnelle,* terme considéré comme étant moins problématique.

La conversation porta ensuite sur la question de savoir ce que nous protégeons quand nous parlons de culture traditionnelle. Beaucoup avaient cette question en tête. Le débat qui suivit visait à déterminer s'il serait plus sage de définir tout d'abord *la nature* de ce que le groupe veut protéger ou, au contraire, discuter de *la méthode* de protection. Autrement dit, le débat était de savoir s'il fallait, en premier lieu, discuter des moyens juridiques de protection ou bien de l'objet de la protection.

La liste d'exemples spécifiques de phénomènes culturels protégés présentée par Mme Prott a été considérée comme un bon point de départ pour constituer une typologie. Il y a eu des voix discordantes, notamment celle de M. Puri qui n'était pas sûr que la voie la plus sage était de commencer par des exemples spécifiques. M. Sanjek qui partageait son opinion a fait valoir que ce qui manquait vraiment c'était une conversation sur les questions relatives aux procédés de protection du patrimoine culturel local et national.

M. Puri a ajouté que la vraie question n'était pas celle de savoir ce qu'il fallait protéger et sauvegarder. Le groupe devrait, à son avis, se préoccuper davantage de l'exploitation du patrimoine culturel traditionnel existant. Il a déclaré que le groupe ne devrait pas parler de la protection de la création mais plutôt de la protection contre l'exploitation du " créé ". M. Simon a ajouté que les pastiches, la reproduction, l'autorisation, la commercialisation et autres sujets devraient faire l'objet de débat et figurer dans le document final.

Il a été ensuite indiqué que les questions juridiques pourraient se diviser en deux catégories:

- maintien et revitalisation de la culture
- appropriation du savoir

M. Jaszi, ouvrant un nouveau chapitre dans la conversation, a posé la question de savoir si les droits de propriété intellectuelle et de droits d'auteur peuvent assurer une protection effective du processus de développement créatif. M. McCann a souligné que ces droits et ces lois fonctionnent sur un impératif économique. Un autre a laissé entendre que des brevets anticipatoires aident la protection juridique de la création.

M. Puri a exprimé l'opinion selon laquelle le document créé par le groupe de travail devrait avoir plus de poids et non pas être édulcoré. D'autres ont laissé entendre qu'une telle approche pourrait risquer d'offusquer la souveraineté des nations. Mme Prott a déclaré qu'un document plus diplomatique, certes moins spectaculaire, pourrait, ajouté à d'autres documents, apporter des changements, contribuer à faire atteindre un seuil collectif de changement. Pendant plusieurs minutes, le débat fit rage à propos du langage (diplomatique ou fort) que le groupe comptait employer dans le document, beaucoup faisant valoir que le langage ne doit pas aliéner alors que d'autres décidèrent qu'un document hardi aurait le meilleur effet potentiel.

Dr. da Cunha commença ensuite à discuter de l'avantage potentiel d'ouvrir la culture traditionnelle au domaine public et à citer le cas de sociétés pharmaceutiques, au Pérou par exemple, qui passent des contrats privés et secrets avec des groupes indigènes et ainsi mettent fin à la production du savoir et détruisent les processus qu'elles étaient censées aider à se perpétuer et à réussir sur le plan économique. Elle craint la privatisation et la commercialisation du savoir traditionnel car, pense-t-elle, de telles opérations privées subvertissent les droits de propriété intellectuelle des communautés. Dr. da Cunha a aussi déclaré que, une fois le savoir traditionnel placé dans le domaine public, les preuves d'un art antérieur peuvent être établies en vue d'entamer le processus de protection des droits communautaires.

MM Sanjek, Simon et Puri avaient tous des commentaires à faire. M. Sanjek a lancé la mise en garde selon laquelle le concept de domaine public devient imprévisible au plan international. M. Simon a rappelé au groupe que la notion d'art antérieur ne s'applique qu'aux questions de brevet et que le domaine public n'assure pas la rémunération ou la protection des patrimoines culturels. M. Puri a déclaré que beaucoup dont lui-même pensent que quand on dit domaine public cela signifie accès illimité pour tout le monde.

M. Sanjek a conclu en disant que le système de droits de propriété intellectuelle ne peut pas déterminer l'auteur d'une oeuvre et peut faire l'objet d'abus. Il a cité l'exemple de la chanson *Why do fools fall in love?* qui a été inscrite au nom d'un escroc bien connu. Ses observations faisaient allusion à la nécessité d'un organisme étatique ou national de surveillance des droits de propriété intellectuelle. Un autre participant a ensuite souligné que les propos de M. Sajek n'illustrent pas un manquement du système mais un cas de fraude mal gérée par la justice.

En guise de conclusion, le texte suivant a été proposé comme contribution initiale au document final. Il a été présenté le lendemain à la séance plénière et est devenu une des recommandations du plan d'action:

> En accord avec les obligations des états de protéger le droit à la culture qui figure dans l'Article 27 de la Convention internationale sur les droits civiques et politiques, les états doivent faire le premier pas pour parvenir à ce qui suit: les communautés doivent être soutenues pour continuer leur processus traditionnel de création, transmission, autorisation et attribution du savoir et des compétences traditionnels en accord avec les vœux de la communauté et en conformité avec les normes actuelles internationales sur les droits de l'homme.

Appendice 6: Rapport du Groupe III
Politiques nationales, régionales et internationales, avec une référence particulière à la transmission, la renaissance et la documentation du patrimoine culturel intangible

Avant de commencer la présentaions des exposés individuels, la séance s'est ouverte par une longue discussion des différents modes de transmission et les stratégies utilisées pour sauvegarder la culture traditionnelle et le folklore. Différents pays ont souligné leur propre expérience dans leurs modes de transmission respectifs. Les points suivants ont été soulignés:

1. L'importance des traditions orales n'est pas seulement fonction de leur mode de transmission mais surtout de leur contenu qui incarne un important savoir historique, culturel et social;
2. La possibilité d'établir des *clubs Patrimoine* pour discuter des questions de patrimoine culturel en vue d'un renforcement de la transmission des traditions orales;
3. Le patrimoine culturel intangible est souvent décrit comme un phénomène en danger pour la simple raison qu'il est transmis oralement alors que l'interruption du mode de transmission pourrait provenir du contenu culturel même;
4. Des moyens de renforcer la culture traditionnelle et le folklore dans des contextes contemporains ont été proposés;
5. L'importance de maintenir l'accès de la communauté aux matériels une fois ceux-ci officiellement documentés a été vigoureusement soulignée;
6. L'improvisation joue un rôle important dans la transmission de la culture traditionnelle et du folklore;
7. Le rôle que la transcription de documents peut jouer dans la transmission a été discuté;
8. Les réponses aux questions d'authenticité doivent être apportées par les communautés traditionnelles qui créent et nourrissent les formes d'expression dont il s'agit;

9. La transmission exige une interaction entre les vieilles et les jeunes générations.

La première communication (présent volume, 178–181) a été présentée par Osamu Yamaguti. Elle portait sur la musique de cour royale au Viêt-Nam. L'orateur a exploré les relations musicales entre le Viêt-Nam et les cultures environnantes (Corée, Japon et Chine); le lien entre le texte (la musique) et le contexte (la cour royale) et enfin la nécessité de revitaliser la musique de cour traditionnelle.

La deuxième communication (présent volume) a été présentée par Gail Saunders. Elle a mis en exergue le rôle des archives dans la promotion et la préservation du patrimoine culturel intangible aux Bahamas et a souvent fait mention de la participation des Bahamas au festival folklorique de la Smithsonian en 1994. A la suite de ce festival, un regain d'intérêt pour la revitalisation de la culture traditionnelle s'est manifesté. Deux lois pertinentes (Museum Antiquities Act et Copyright Act) ont été votées en 1998 et vont entrer en vigueur le 1er juillet 1999. La loi sur le copyright va protéger les droits des créateurs. Dr. Saunders a fait valoir qu'il devrait y avoir une coordination entre organismes chargés d'administrer le patrimoine culturel tangible et intangible. Elle a ensuite exhorté l'UNESCO à continuer d'organiser les réunions régionales sur la préservation et la diffusion de la culture traditionnelle et du folklore. En dernier lieu, elle a vivement recommandé que la Caraïbe soit considérée comme une région séparée de l'Amérique latine.

La troisième communication (présent volume, 159–165) a été présentée par Grace Koch qui a parlé du rôle de l'audio-visuel dans la revitalisation des traditions locales. De nos jours, les Aborigènes et habitants des îles Torres Strait ont recours au matériel audio-visuel pour appuyer leurs revendications territoriales. La documentation audio-visuelle de l'histoire orale et des rituels est particulièrement importante pour faire valoir ces revendications. L'oratrice a souligné qu'à l'arrivée des blancs en Australie, il y avait 250 langues aborigènes. A l'heure actuelle, seules 25 langues sont activement parlées. L'oratrice a recommandé que l'on encourage une participation active des peuples indigènes dans l'archivage et la préservation, ainsi qu'une sensibilisation culturelle pour ceux qui travaillent dans le domaine de la conservation et de la préservation du matériel culturel.

La quatrième communication a été présentée par Jean Guibal qui a souligné que la langue est le fondement de la culture et, de ce fait, mérite une attention particulière. Il a encouragé le soutien à la diversité linguistique, la langue étant, selon lui, l'essence de la culture. Il a mis l'accent sur le processus de transmission, sa diversité et la difficulté qu'il y a en France de transmettre la tradition orale puisque la quasi-totalité des détenteurs de ce savoir ont disparu. Il a, en outre, décrit le rôle des archives de musée dans la transmission. En dernier lieu, l'orateur a fait valoir que les politiques de protection du patrimoine culturel doivent être institutionnalisées afin de protéger diverses formes de patrimoine culturel intangible. Il a insisté que cette action soit menée de concert avec les communautés locales.

La cinquième communication a été présentée par Heikki Kirkinen (présent volume, 234–244) qui a parlé de la revitalisation des langues et cultures de l'Europe de l'est et de l'implantation Carélienne. Il a laissé entendre que même si, de nos jours, ces communautés sont libres de développer leur propre culture, elles n'en ont pas les moyens. Elles ont l'espoir que l'UNESCO peut les aider à réhabiliter et à recréer leur langue et culture. Il a mis l'accent sur l'importance de la langue à l'identité culturelle.

La sixième communication a été présentée par Renato Matusse (présent volume, 185–189) qui a exploré le rôle de banques de données dans les pays de la SADC en Afrique australe. Il a décrit la manière par laquelle une structure régionale coordonne les activités des structures nationales qui, à leur tour, coordonnent celles des instances locales. Les informations recueillies dans des banques de données locales sont partagées avec la structure nationale, traitées et ensuite acheminées vers l'instance régionale et les pays membres. Il a parlé de l'importance des banques de données à la coopération régionale.

La septième communication a été présentée par Namankoumba Kouyaté (présent volume, 204–214] qui a parlé de politiques nationales et locales sur la sauvegarde du patrimoine notamment en matière de transmission. L'exposé a essentiellement porté sur les traditions familiales et un instrument de musique appelé *sosobala*. Le sosobala est un balafon conçu dans sa présente forme pour une bataille qui a eu lieu en 1235. Il est considéré comme la plus ancienne des traditions orales en Afrique de l'ouest. L'orateur a aussi fait état de la nécessité de combattre l'exode rural chez les jeunes générations pour garantir la transmission de la riche tradition orale. Il a, en outre, déclaré que l'UNESCO devrait tenir compte des cérémonies traditionnelles qui se tiennent dans des espaces culturels importants.

La huitième communication a été présentée par Juana Nuñez qui a décrit les diverses initiatives entreprises par Cuba pour protéger la culture traditionnelle et le folklore. Parmi celles-ci, il faut noter: une organisation des amateurs de l'art; la participation des ouvriers, étudiants, paysans, adolescents, enfants et personnes handicapées à la préservation du patrimoine culturel intangible; enseignement de l'art dès l'école primaire; études des racines culturelles et du folklore; vulgarisation de la cinématographie nationale dans les zones rurales et montagneuses; augmentation du nombre de musées et de programmes éducatifs; et une élévation de la position sociale des écrivains et des artistes. Elle a avancé un certain nombre de recommandations dont: une étude par l'UNESCO des effets négatifs des mass media sur le patrimoine culturel intangible; une révision des politiques financières de l'ONU; une étude sur les effets de la mondialisation; la possibilité d'établir un instrument international pour la protection des droits de propriété intellectuelle dans le cadre de la culture traditionnelle et du folklore; la possibilité d'adoption par l'UNESCO de projets communautaires pluridisciplinaires.

En outre de ces communications, plusieurs discussions eurent lieu et furent à l'origine des recommandations suivantes. Il a été recommandé que les gouvernements des pays membres:

1. incorporent la culture traditionnelle dans les programmes éducatifs en vue de la transmettre aux jeunes générations et d'encourager celles-ci à porter un intérêt à la culture traditionnelle et au folklore;
2. établissent et/ou renforcent les capacités institutionnelles existantes pour la sauvegarde et la documentation de la culture traditionnelle et du folklore;
3. assurent l'enseignement et la réhabilitation des langues pour toutes les minorités ethniques;
4. accroissent l'aide financière à l'organisation des festivals;
5. garantissent l'accès du public au matériel culturel;
6. fournissent des programmes de sensibilisation culturelle et l'équipement nécessaire à ceux qui travaillent dans le domaine de la conservation et de la préservation du matériel culturel;
7. encouragent le secteur privé, par l'intermédiaire d'incitations telles que les abattements fiscaux, à investir dans la culture traditionnelle et le folklore.

Il a été recommandé que l'UNESCO:

1. organise des réunions de spécialistes dans les domaines de l'information numérisée

en vue de créer des réseaux régionaux d'institutions et de faciliter l'accessibilité et la diffusion du savoir;

2. rétrécisse le fossé culturel entre les jeunesses urbaine et rurale en appuyant la diffusion, par Internet, des connaissances relatives aux cultures traditionnelles et l'organisation de colonies de jeunes consacrées à la promotion et à l'échange de cultures traditionnelles;

3. renforce et encourage les relations avec les organisations non-gouvernementales dans le domaine de la culture traditionnelle et du folklore;

4. organise des séminaires et fournisse une assistance technique pour la formation des décideurs, chefs de service et enseignants du secteur de la culture traditionnelle;

5. effectue une étude de faisabilité sur l'éventualité d'un réseau international pour le développement du tourisme culturel;

6. soutienne la publication d'une Encyclopédie du folklore mondial afin de diffuser le savoir, de promouvoir la diversité et d'encourager la recherche en matière deculture traditionnelle et de folklore;

7. établisse une journée mondiale pour la sauvegarde de la culture traditionnelle et du folklore;

8. envisage la possibilité d'établir une liste des collectivités en voie d'extinction afin d'attirer sur celles-ci l'attention de la communauté internationale et de les faire revivre;

9. encourage une plus grande collaboration entre les organismes intergouvernementaux tels que l'UNESCO, l'OMPI (Organisation mondiale de la propriété intellectuelle) et le WGIP (Groupe de travail des Nations-Unies sur les populations indigènes).

Plan d'action

Appendice 7 du rapport final

A. A l'occasion de la conférence intitulée: Evaluation globale de la Recommandation de 1989 relative à la sauvegarde de la culture traditionnelle et du folklore: Participation locale et coopération internationale qui s'est tenue à la Smithsonian Institution à Washington, D.C. (Etats-Unis d'Amérique) du 27 au 30 juin 1999;

1. *Compte tenu* des résultats du processus de quatre ans pour l'évaluation de l'application de la Recommandation relative à la sauvegarde de la culture traditionnelle et du folklore et des recommandations découlant des huit séminaires régionaux et sous-régionaux [Strá nice, République Tchèque (juin 1995) pour les régions Europe centrale et Europe de l'est; Mexico, Mexique (septembre 1998) pour l'Amérique latine et la Caraïbe; Tokyo, Japon (février/mars 1998) pour l'Asie; Tachkent, République d'Ouzbékistan (octobre 1998) pour l'Asie centrale et le Caucase; Accra, Ghana (Janvier 1999) pour l'Afrique; Nouméa, Nouvelle-Calédonie (février 1999) pour le Pacifique; Beyrouth, Liban (mai 1999) pour les pays arabes;

2. *Compte tenu du fait* que le terme "folklore" est généralement considéré comme ne convenant pas, tout en insistant sur l'importance de sa définition telle qu'elle figure dans la Recommandation de 1989 relative à la sauvegarde de la culture traditionnelle et du folklore, tout en recommandant que l'on fasse une étude pour trouver une terminologie qui convienne mieux, et en continuant à utiliser provisoirement le terme "folklore", ainsi que les expressions "patrimoine oral", "savoir et compétences traditionnels", "patrimoine intangible", "formes de savoir, d'être et de faire", parmi d'autres expressions, que nous considérons toutes comme étant équivalentes à "culture traditionnelle et folklore" selon la définition qui figure dans la Recommandation de 1989 susmentionnée;

3. *Sachant* qu'il est impossible dans de nombreuses sociétés de séparer le patrimoine tangible, intangible et naturel;

4. *Considérant* que la culture traditionnelle et le folklore sont surtout basés sur les activités communautaires qui expriment, renforcent et reflètent des valeurs, croyances et pratiques très partagées;

5. *Soulignant* que la diversité qui est incarnée dans de nombreuses pratiques culturelles de savoir, d'être et de faire est une caractéristique essentielle du patrimoine culturel et qu'elle est essentielle pour l'élaboration d'une coexistence pacifique de toutes les formes de vie dans l'avenir;

6. *Soulignant* la nature spécifique et l'importance de la culture traditionnelle et du folklore comme faisant partie intégrante du patrimoine de l'humanité;

7. *Notant* la nature spécifique et l'importance de la culture traditionnelle et du folklore, leur rôle dans l'histoire, et leur place dans la société contemporaine;

8. *Reconnaissant le fait* que la culture traditionnelle et le folklore peuvent représenter un

349

moyen puissant de rassembler des peuples et des groupes sociaux différents et d'affirmer leur identité culturelle dans un esprit de bonne compréhension et de respect des autres cultures;

9. *Insistant* sur le besoin de tous les pays de reconnaître le rôle de la culture traditionnelle et du folklore et le danger auquel tous les praticiens sont confrontés;

10. *Concerné par* le fait que le bien-être des membres de la communauté et ses pratiques — dont la force et les nombres sont menacés tous les jours par des forces puissantes telles que les guerres, les déplacements forcés, les idéologies et les philosophies intolérantes, la dégradation de l'environnement, la marginalisation socio-économique, et la culture mondiale de commercialisation — doivent être au centre de la politique culturelle nationale et internationale;

11. *Tenant compte du fait* que la culture traditionnelle et le folklore sont dynamiques et sont souvent adaptés grâce à des pratiques novatrices de la vie communautaire;

12. *Reconnaissant* qu'il faut inclure les praticiens de la culture traditionnelle et du folklore pour qu'ils apportent leur expertise qui a une importance capitale quant aux décisions prises au niveau local, national et international dans des domaines tels que la santé, l'environnement, l'éducation, la jeunesse, le genre, la résolution des conflits, la coexistence pacifique des groupes ethniques, le développement humain durable, la participation civique sans exclusion, ainsi que la lutte contre le chauvinisme et l'intolérance;

13. *Déplorant* l'exclusion des groupes traditionnels des prises de décisions qui concernent la sauvegarde de la culture traditionnelle et du folklore;

14. *Reconnaissant* que les Etats sont faits de communautés culturelles, que ces communautés, leurs folklores et leurs croyances s'étendent souvent au-delà des frontières des Etats et que des personnes peuvent être membres de plusieurs communautés;

15. *Reconnaissant* que l'interaction et les échanges culturels conduisent à l'émergence de genres hybrides qui reflètent ces échanges entre les cultures;

16. *Reconnaissant* que la sauvegarde de la culture traditionnelle et du folklore et le droit à l'autodétermination culturelle dans les communautés locales doivent être en conformité avec les normes internationales sur les droits de l'homme;

17. *Observant* le rôle important que les gouvernements et les organisations non-gouvernementales peuvent jouer en collaborant avec les porte-drapeau de la tradition pour sauvegarder la culture traditionnelle et le folklore et le fait qu'ils doivent agir le plus rapidement possible;

B. Nous, participants à la conférence intitulée: Evaluation globale de la Recommandation de 1989 relative à la sauvegarde de la culture traditionnelle et du folklore: Participation locale et coopération internationale, reconnaissons qu'il faut prendre les mesures suivantes:

1. Créer des instruments juridiques et administratifs pour mettre les communautés traditionnelles qui créent la culture traditionnelle et le folklore et qui veillent à leur développement à l'abri de la pauvreté, l'exploitation et la marginalisation.

2. Faciliter la collaboration entre les communautés, les institutions gouvernementales et non-gouvernementales, les organismes gouvernementaux et non-gouvernementaux ainsi que les organismes du secteur privé afin de s'occuper des problèmes auxquels les groupes traditionnels sont confrontés;

3. S'assurer que, lors de forums, les groupes traditionnels participent de manière constructive au processus de prise de décision à tous les niveaux qui traitent des questions et des politiques qui touchent ces groupes;

4. Créer en coopération avec les communautés des programmes d'éducation et de formation, y compris de formation juridique, pour leurs membres et autres travailleurs de

la culture, afin de permettre à leurs membres de comprendre, sauvegarder et protéger la culture traditionnelle et le folklore;

5. Créer des programmes qui s'occupent de la nature transnationale de certaines cultures traditionnelles et de certains folklores;

6. Accorder une importance spéciale aux programmes qui reconnaissent, célèbrent et soutiennent le rôle des femmes dans tous les domaines de leur communauté, en particulier ceux où elles sont traditionnellement sous-représentées, pour leur contribution aux cultures traditionnelles et en tant qu'agricultrices, érudites et administratrices;

7. Soutenir les programmes de renaissance culturelle, en particulier pour les groupes qui ont été déplacés à cause de la guerre, de la famine, ou de désastres naturels, ou encore pour les groupes menacés d'extinction;

8. Entreprendre des mesures — notamment pour l'aide juridique — qui aident les groupes traditionnels qui ont entrepris de prendre les choses en main pour améliorer leur niveau social et leur bien-être économique, ce qui est essentiel à la continuation de leurs pratiques culturelles.

C. Actions spécifiques:

Basé sur les principes et les besoins susmentionnés, nous recommandons aux gouvernements des Etats:

1. D'identifier et de consolider les programmes qui encouragent la reconnaissance publique et la validation de la culture traditionnelle et du folklore, de continuer à soutenir des organismes et des programmes existants, et d'en créer de nouveaux le cas échéant;

2. De mettre en place et de renforcer des programmes qui ont pour but de veiller au bien-être des détenteurs et des praticiens des cultures traditionnelles en ce qui concerne le logement, les services médicaux et les risques professionnels.;

3. D'inclure des connaissances locales à des forums nationaux qui traitent de questions telles le développement humain durable, la mondialisation, la détérioration de l'environnement, la jeunesse, l'éducation, et la coexistence pacifique;

4. De faciliter et aider les communautés à développer leur culture matérielle traditionnelle et leurs façons de travailler dans de nouveaux contextes pour contrer efficacement la destruction de leur milieu naturel et la dévaluation de la dignité du travail humain;

5. De faire une campagne de sensibilisation culturelle pour les employés des secteurs administratifs, éducatifs et autres qui ont affaire aux groupes traditionnels;

6. De faciliter l'accès des membres des groupes traditionnels à des programmes éducatifs pertinents et, si nécessaire, faciliter la création — avec la communauté — de centres communautaires polyvalents pour l'éducation. la documentation et la formation;

7. De donner de l'aide aux communautés pour sauvegarder l'usage actif et créateur des langues locales dans des domaines tels que l'éducation, l'édition, les représentations publiques, etc.

8. D'aider à sauvegarder les espaces et la culture matérielle importants qui jouent un rôle essentiel dans la transmission de la culture traditionnelle et le folklore;

9. De soutenir les symposiums locaux, nationaux et internationaux qui réunissent des membres de groupes traditionnels, des représentants d'organisations non-gouvernementales, des décideurs et autres pour aborder les problèmes auxquels les groupes traditionnels sont confrontés;

10. D'identifier, comprendre, encourager, et soutenir les pratiques éducatives traditionnelles, en particulier celles qui sont destinées aux très jeunes;

11. De créer un réseau d'experts qui aident les groupes locaux, les institutions culturelles, les organismes non-gouvernementaux à sauvegarder la culture traditionnelle en particulier dans le domaine de l'éducation, du tourisme, du droit et du développement;

12. De considérer — s'ils le désirent — l'éventuelle soumission d'une ébauche de résolution pour la Conférence générale de l'UNESCO qui demanderait à l'UNESCO d'entreprendre une étude de faisabilité pour l'adoption d'un nouvel instrument normatif portant sur la sauvegarde de la culture traditionnelle et du folklore;

13. D'agir en accord avec les obligations des Etats pour protéger les droits à la culture qui figurent dans l'article 27 de la Convention internationale sur les droits civiques et politiques en soutenant activement les communautés dans leurs pratiques de création, transmission, autorisation et attribution de la connaissance et des compétences traditionnelles en accord avec les vœux des communautés et en conformité avec les normes internationales actuelles pour les droits de l'homme et
De considérer prendre des mesures, y compris ce qui suit, mais sans y être limité:

   i. Adopter un système juridique selon lequel la communauté — selon ses vœux — peut rendre les connaissances traditionnelles accessibles au public sous réserve de rémunération ou autres avantages s'il y a usage commercial; et coopérer pour assurer la reconnaissance mutuelle par tous les Etats des effets de telles mesures.

   ii. Adopter un régime juridique *sui generis* qui assurerait protection

   - aussi longtemps que la communauté existe;
   - acquis à la communauté, ou à une personne et à la communauté;
   - en accord avec les procédures traditionnelles d'autorisation et d'attribution de la communauté;
   - *et* en établissant un organisme qui représente la communauté concernée et les secteurs correspondants de la société civile pour contrebalancer les intérêts rivaux de l'accès et du contrôle;

   iii. Dans l'attente de l'adoption d'un meilleur système de protection, encourager la modification et l'usage, en accord avec le droit coutumier, de régimes existants de la propriété intellectuelle pour la protection du savoir traditionnel.

   iv. Créer des groupes de travail pour qu'ils se livrent à de plus amples études sur les sujets suivants:
   contenu du "consentement préalable informé"; processus de vérification (charge de preuve, modalité de codes de preuves); droit intellectuel communautaire par rapport au droit sur la propriété industrielle; relations avec tout autre instrument et ébauches de Documents (ébauche de document de l'ONU, WIPO, TRIPS, CBD, déclaration de Maatatu, SUVA et autres déclarations de peuples indigènes); questions de "droits" (de paternité, moraux, de compensation); rôle des gouvernements; problème de terminologie (par exemple, les définitions et connotations de "folklore", "culture populaire", etc.); autres formes de compensation; promotion d'études de cas en rapport avec le droit jurisprudentiel; procédures/documents juridiques s'appliquant à l'artisanat, la musique ou autre forme artistique; procédures juridiques s'appliquant au savoir rassemblé avant la rédaction de cet instrument.

Nous recommandons que l'UNESCO:

1. Fasse la promotion de ce Plan d'action parmi ses Etats membres en soumettant cette réunion à l'attention des Etats membres;

2. Etablisse un réseau international interdisciplinaire d'experts afin d'aider les Etats membres à créer, à la demande, des programmes concrets qui soient conformes aux principes de ce Plan d'action;

3. Etablisse un groupe de travail mobile international et interdisciplinaire qui soit composé d'experts juridiques qui travaillent comme conseillers en collaboration avec les communautés pour créer des instruments adéquats pour la protection de la culture traditionnelle et du folklore;

4. Encourage la participation et, partout où cela est nécessaire, l'établissement d'organisations internationales non-gouvernementales qui disposent d'expertise spécialisée dans des domaines particuliers du folklore et du savoir traditionnel afin de conseiller l'UNESCO sur la protection du folklore et du savoir traditionnel;

5. Encourage des groupements internationaux (chercheurs, professionnels de la culture, organismes commerciaux, et entités juridiques) à créer et à adopter des codes déontologiques qui assurent que des démarches appropriées et respectueuses sont suivies vis-à-vis de la culture traditionnelle et du folklore;

6. Accélère le mouvement pour le retour des restes humains et pour le rapatriement du patrimoine culturel afin de contribuer à la renaissance des cultures traditionnelles et à la perception qu'elles ont d'elles-mêmes selon leurs propres valeurs fondamentales;

7. Organise et soutienne la formation d'un forum international qui aurait pour but de présenter les préoccupations des communautés traditionnelles quant à la sauvegarde de leur propre culture mais aussi de symposiums régionaux et internationaux qui rassemblent des membres de groupes traditionnels, des représentants d'organisations gouvernementales, des décideurs et autres personnes qui traitent des questions auxquelles sont confrontés les groupes traditionnels, telles que le rôle des femmes dans la sauvegarde de la culture traditionnelle. Il faudrait que les symposiums se tiennent dans des endroits variés, en particulier dans des nations qui ne sont pas des pays industrialisés, par exemple à Yakutia;

8. Facilite l'application des nouvelles technologies dans des centres de documentation locaux, nationaux et régionaux par l'intermédiaire de réseaux de collaboration et d'expertise, qui font également intervenir les porte-drapeau locaux de la tradition;

9. Encourage la culture traditionnelle et le folklore sur une échelle mondiale par l'intermédiaire de mesures comme l'organisation de festivals régionaux et la déclaration d'une Journée mondiale de la sauvegarde de la culture traditionnelle et du folklore;

10. Continue la collaboration de l'UNESCO avec le WIPO sur des questions d'intérêt commun;

11. Utilise les procédures existantes de l'UNESCO pour signaler à la FAO, l'OMS, l'UNICEF, l'UNIFEM, et d'autres organisations telles que l'OMC quel est l'effet négatif possible d'actions sur les droits de l'homme, l'environnement, la nourriture, l'agriculture, les moyens d'existence et l'industrie, la santé et le commerce et les répercussions sur la culture.

Informe final de la conferencia

Introducción

1.   Del 27 al 30 de junio de 1999 se realizó en Washington, D.C. (EEUU) la Conferencia Internacional con el título "Evaluación global de la Recomendación sobre la protección del folclor y la cultura tradicional de 1989: potestación local y cooperación internacional", en colaboración con la Institución Smithsoniana.

La conferencia tuvo como fin considerar la protección del patrimonio cultural intangible a fines del siglo XX, y repasar la Recomendación sobre la Protección del folclor y la cultura tradicional a diez años de su adopción en 1989. Con esta conferencia culminaron ocho seminarios regionales realizados por la UNESCO para evaluar sistemáticamente el cumplimiento de esa Recomendación y la situación actual en materia de protección y revitalización del patrimonio cultural intangible. Los seminarios regionales se realizaron en: República Checa (junio de 1995) para Europa Central y Oriental; México (septiembre de 1997) para América Latina y el Caribe; Japón (febrero–marzo de 1998) para Asia; Finlandia (septiembre de 1998) para Europa Occidental; República de Uzbekistán (octubre de 1998) para Asia Central y el Cáucaso; Ghana (enero de 1999) para Africa; Nueva Caledonia (febrero de 1999) para el Pacífico; y Líbano (mayo de 1999) para los Estados Árabes. Un objetivo central de la conferencia fue evaluar globalmente la situación actual y futura orientación de la Recomendación de 1989 [Apéndice 1: Temario, Apéndice 2: Temario Acotado].

Asistieron a la conferencia 37 participantes de 27 países (expertos, funcionarios oficiales, practicantes de culturas tradicionales) y 40 observadores. A su llegada los participantes recibieron documentos informativos preliminares y de trabajo. Durante la conferencia se contó con los informes de los ocho seminarios regionales, para efectos de consulta. También se distribuyeron las ponencias de los participantes, presentadas a los grupos de trabajo correspondientes [Apéndice 3: Participantes, personal, miembros y residentes].

2.   La reunión fue financiada conjuntamente por la UNESCO, el Ministerio de Relaciones Exteriores del Japón, el Departamento de Estado de los EEUU, la Fundación Rockefeller, el Fondo Nacional de las Artes y la Oficina de Relaciones Internacionales de la Institución Smithsoniana.

Sesión de apertura

3.   Abrió la reunión el doctor Richard Kurin, director del Centro de Folclor y Patrimonio Cultural de la Institución Smithsoniana, quien dio la bienvenida a los partici-

pantes, observadores, representantes y personal de la UNESCO. Manifestó su beneplácito porque la conferencia se realizara en la Institución Smithsoniana, como complemento al trabajo del Centro de Folclor y Patrimonio Cultural de fortalecer los vínculos entre académicos de la institución y la UNESCO.

4. El señor Mounir Bouchenaki, director de la División de Patrimonio Cultural y el Centro de Patrimonio Mundial de la UNESCO, se dirigió a la conferencia en representación del señor Frederico Mayor [este volumen, 3–4]. Agradeció al doctor Kurin por su amable bienvenida y expresó su agradecimiento a éste, al doctor Anthony Seeger — director de Grabaciones Smithsonian Folkways — y a los colegas de ambos, por su colaboración para auspiciar la conferencia. También agradeció a los patrocinadores su apoyo a la misma, y expresó satisfacción por parte de la UNESCO por poder participar al mismo tiempo en el 34° Festival Folclórico Smithsoniano, una exhibición de tradiciones culturales vivas de los Estados Unidos y del mundo.

Refiriéndose a la definición más amplia de "patrimonio" que han adoptando los países, comentó que en la actualidad ese término abarca elementos tales como el patrimonio de ideas, el patrimonio genético humano y un patrimonio ético, en que la diversidad es un rasgo importante y apreciado. Ello ha ocurrido a la par que se ha ampliado la idea de "patrimonio tangible" con la Convención de la UNESCO de 1972 sobre la Protección del Patrimonio Cultural Mundial, para abarcar monumentos culturales, hitos culturales y naturales, y parajes culturales. Este patrimonio es vulnerable y corre riesgo de extinción bajo la tendencoa mundial hacia una homogenización impulsada por la globalización económica, aunque ciertos adelantos tecnológicos también pueden ser medios útiles para conservar y difundir el patrimonio cultural del mundo.

Agregó que deben reconocerse y respetarse todas las formas de patrimonio cultural, incluyendo el patrimonio intangible que sustenta los valores espirituales y significados simbólicos inherentes al patrimonio material. El subtítulo de la conferencia, sobre potenciación local y cooperación internacional, también es congruente con las metas de la UNESCO, especialmente en lo que atañe al fortalecimiento de capacidades autóctonas y la participación (de los jóvenes, especialmente) en las actividades de cumplimiento. El hecho de que cada ser humano es único constituye la base para establecer la libertad cultural, que es la libertad colectiva de un grupo de individuos para desarrollar la vida que elijan. Para conseguirlo es necesario fomentar la diversidad a escala mundial.

Para concluir, dijo que esta conferencia puede brindar un gran aporte al rumbo futuro de la protección del patrimonio cultural intangible del mundo. También señaló que las recomendaciones de la conferencia afectarían tanto el patrimonio intangible como el patrimonio tangible a nivel global, ya que todas las formas de patrimonio cultural están íntimamente entrelazadas.

5. El señor Mounir Bouchenaki ofició la elección de presidente, vicepresidentes y relatora:

Presidente:	Dr. Anthony Seeger, EEUU
Vicepresidentes:	Dr. Junzo Kawada, Japón
	Sta. Zulma Yugar, Bolivia
Relatora:	Dra. Janet Blake, Escocia, Reino Unido

Acto seguido, el doctor Seeger asumió oficialmente la presidencia.

6. Punto 2 del temario: Recomendación de la UNESCO sobre Protección del Folclor y la Cultura Tradicional (1989); acciones emprendidas por la UNESCO en cumplimiento de la misma (sesión plenaria).

La señora Noriko Aikawa, directora de la Unidad de Patrimonio Intangible de la UNESCO, dió una ponencia en la que esbozó las acciones emprendidas por la UNESCO en cumplimiento de la Recomendación de 1989 [este volumen, 13–19] y señaló que, una vez establecido el instrumento, los Estados miembros mostraron poco interés en su aplicación, no obstante el requisito de aplicar sus disposiciones y hacer efectivos los principios y medidas que ahí se definen. Sólo seis países presentaron informes en respuesta a la solicitud del director general en 1990. Como posible razón de lo anterior, un estudio, de 1992, identifica la carencia de un mandato específico de la UNESCO en ese informe, o la especificación de pasos a seguir en su cumplimiento, para los estados miembros. El papel de la UNESCO se limita a promover y a alentar a los estados a aplicar sus disposiciones.

Tras los grandes cambios políticos de fines de los años ochenta, especialmente el fin de la Guerra Fría, así como la rápida expansión de la economía de mercado y el progreso en tecnología de comunicaciones, que transformaron el mundo en un espacio económico y cultural más integrado, muchos estados miembros comenzaron a interesarse en sus culturas tradicionales y a redescubrir el papel de éstas como referencia simbólica a las identidades de raigambre local. La UNESCO procuró dar un nuevo rumbo a su programa relativo a la cultura tradicional, y llevó a cabo una evaluación científica de todas las actividades realizadas en ese ámbito, modificándole el título a "patrimonio cultural intangible". En 1993 se crearon varias pautas para estas labores, tras celebrarse en París una reunión internacional de expertos, y se propuso que la UNESCO jugase un papel más catalítico e instigador en respuesta a este nuevo acuerdo.

La señora Aikawa pasó entonces a describir el programa "Tesoros Humanos Vivientes" lanzado en 1993, que faculta a los estados miembros para otorgar reconocimiento oficial a personas poseedoras de excepcionales destrezas y dotes artísticas, contribuyendo así a la progresión y transmisión de tales talentos y conocimientos, como manera de salvaguardar el patrimonio cultural tradicional. Casi cincuenta Estados miembros han manifestado interés en establecer un sistema tal hasta el momento.

En 1995 la Conferencia General decidió que debía llevarse a cabo una evaluación a nivel mundial, empleando la Recomendación como marco de referencia, de la protección del folclor y la cultura tradicional. Como primera medida se condujeron encuestas empleando un cuestionario detallado, seguidas por la realización de los ocho seminarios regionales ya mencionados, culminando en la presente conferencia.

En respuesta al renovado interés de los estados miembros en el patrimonio cultural intangible, en 1997 la Conferencia General confirmó que el programa de patrimonio intangible recibiría una de las máximas prioridades en el área cultural. Poco después la Conferencia General proclamó los espacios y formas de expresión culturales "Obras Maestras del Patrimonio

Oral e Intangible de la Humanidad". Esa proclama se constituyó en una de las maneras de compensar por el hecho de que la Convención de 1972 no se aplica al patrimonio cultural intangible.

La señora Aikawa trazó señaló luego algunas otras actividades emprendidas por la UNESCO para impulsar la Recomendación en las áreas de identificación, conservación, defensa, diseminación y protección del folclor. En el marco de la cooperación internacional se ha dado especial prioridad a las actividades de capacitación y establecimiento de redes, mientras que aún quedan por definirse los problemas particulares concernientes a la acción jurídica en relación con las expresiones artísticas del folclor y los conocimientos tradicionales. La Recomendación de 1989 sigue siendo el principal documento de referencia para todas estas actividades y resulta oportuno reflexionar ahora sobre el papel de la misma en los contextos contemporáneo y a futuro.

7.   Punto 3 del temario: Informes de los ocho seminarios regionales y subregionales (sesión plenaria).

Se presentaron en sesión plenaria de la conferencia los informes de los ocho seminarios regionales y subregionales ya mencionados realizados entre 1995 y 1999.

(i) Europa Central y Oriental (seminario de la República Checa)

Este fue el primer seminario regional sobre la aplicación de la Recomendación de 1989, realizado en Strá nice en junio de 1995, en base a los cuestionarios presentados por doce países de la región de Europa Central y Oriental. En el seminario participaron expertos de trece países.

Las respuestas indicaron que la mayoría de los países de la región no dan prioridad en su política cultural a la defensa del folclor y la cultura tradicional, aunque la mayoría de los Ministerios de Cultura apoyan la labor de instituciones profesionales y asociaciones cívicas en este campo. Tras las transformaciones acaecidas en los estados post-comunistas, surgió un apoyo generalizado a la cultura de masas contemporánea e internacional, como reacción al anterior apoyo del estado a las culturas populares. Los organismos activos en la defensa de ciertos elementos de la cultura tradicional y popular enfrentan dificultades resultado de las débiles economías y la consecuente falta de capacidad técnica en la mayoría de los países post-comunistas. En muchos Estados de la región la Recomendación de 1989 se ha convertido en importante instrumento para proteger los patrimonios culturales intangibles.

Entre otros asuntos que se trataron en ese seminario figuran los siguientes:

- la importancia de la cultura tradicional y popular en la conservación de la identidad nacional;
- una falta generalizada de coordinación entre las autoridades centrales y las instituciones que laboran en defensa del folclor y la cultura tradicional; una ausencia de sistemas tipológicos y de clasificación supranacional coordinada en todos los países;
- la ausencia de un sistema único de educación folclórica a nivel elemental;
- falta de medios económicos para sustentar el fomento, las investigaciones y la diseminación del folclor;
- la necesidad de desarrollar infraestructuras para diseminar el folclor en los medios públicos de difusión;
- la falta de reglamentos específicos relativos única y exclusivamente a los artistas folclóricos; y
- el deseo de intensificar las obligaciones legales para proteger el folclor y la cultura tradicional en el ámbito internacional.

(ii) América Latina y el Caribe (seminario de México)

El seminario se realizó en la ciudad de México en septiembre de 1997, con objetivos basados en los cuestionarios sobre la aplicación de la Recomendación, presentados por once países de la región latinoamericana y caribeña. Participaron en el seminario expertos de dieciséis países. Ellos:

- realizaron un detallado análisis de los principales aspectos de la cultura tradicional y popular en la región;
- trazaron pautas de acción para permitirle a los grupos étnicos y otras comunidades expresar plenamente su creatividad e identidad cultural;
- establecieron la política cultural de fomentar la cultura tradicional y popular siguiendo los lineamientos de la Recomendación; y
- definieron orientaciones generales y proyectos particulares como parte de una estrategia regional de cooperación ampliada entre los estados.

El seminario concluyó en lo siguiente:

- la importancia de usar los procesos democráticos de la región para combinar la protección de la cultura tradicional y popular con la coexistencia pacífica de las poblaciones;
- alentar la participación comunitaria en tales programas mediante procesos de descentralización regional, municipal y provincial; y
- reconocer el hecho de que los creadores, portadores y transmisores de estas culturas, así como los especialistas en diversas disciplinas relativas a ellas, todos son esenciales para el éxito.

Se confirmó el establecimiento del Centro de Culturas Populares de América Latina y el Caribe, en México, con dos sub-centros en Sudamérica y uno en América Central. Se propuso la celebración, en Bolivia 1999, de una reunión de las autoridades culturales de la región, en 1999, para tratar las conclusiones de este seminario regional, así como la aplicación de la Recomendación en esta región.

(iii) Asia (seminario del Japón)

De veinte países, diecisiete respondieron al cuestionario sobre la Recomendación, y en febrero/marzo de 1998 se realizó un seminario en Tokio. Participaron un total de veinte expertos de diecinueve Estados Miembros de la región.

En cuanto a la aplicación de las principales disposiciones de la Recomendación, el 48 por ciento de los países que respondieron aplicaron las disposiciones sobre identificación, 28 por ciento las disposiciones sobre conservación, 28 por ciento las disposiciones sobre diseminación, y 42 por ciento las disposiciones sobre protección del folclor. Ha habido una palpable mejora en la protección del folclor y la cultura tradicional en la región, aunque algunos estados consideraron que la Recomendación debería mejorarse en algún momento. Entre los temas más reiterados en las respuestas estuvieron:

- la necesidad de una agencia coordinadora central;
- la identificación y compilación de las expresiones de cultura tradicional;
- la protección de los derechos de los artistas tradicionales;
- la capacitación de profesionales y artistas;
- aumentar el financiamiento;
- alentar a las comunidades a conservar su propio patrimonio cultural;
- reavivar el interés de los jóvenes en la cultura tradicional ante los efectos de los grandes medios de comunicación;
- reclutar y capacitar aprendices; y
- moderar los efectos negativos del turismo.

Los informes por país indican auténticos esfuerzos por salvaguardar este patrimonio, no obstante los reveses y dificultades. También hubo indicios de auténtico interés de los políticos en la conservación, aunque a veces no la entiendan.

(iv) Europa Occidental (seminario de Finlandia)

Este seminario se organizó en Joensuu en septiembre de 1988, en base a quince respuestas al cuestionario sobre la aplicación de la Recomendación. Participaron en el seminario expertos de catorce países. Las respuestas indicaron que los principales temas a cubrirse en seminario debían ser:

- la protección jurídica del patrimonio cultural de la culturas minoritarias;
- la protección y fomento de los lenguajes nacionales y locales;
- la revitalización de formas de expresión tradicionales y populares;
- el uso de nueva tecnología, imágenes visuales, la internet, etc., en relación con este patrimonio; y
- la evolución y futuro de la cultura.

Se presentaron ponencias informativas sobre cuatro áreas temáticas: problemas de la cultura, patrimonio cultural, tecnología nueva y evolución cultural.

Se plantearon ciertos puntos relativos a la visión general de la vida en la Europa Occidental moderna y, dentro de ello, el papel del folclor y la cultura tradicional. Estos puntos permitieron obtener ciertas conclusiones para la formulación de la política de patrimonio tanto a nivel europeo como mundial. Entre esas conclusiones figuraron las siguientes:

- En un mundo que cambia rápidamente, el folclor y la cultura tradicional se están haciendo esenciales para la conservación de la identidad y diversidad del patrimonio cultural europeo;
- Normalmente los temas relativos a este patrimonio se manejan a nivel nacional tomando en cuenta los aspectos regionales y locales;
- Todos los países de la región tienen buenos archivos y museos de cultura tradicional de libre acceso, y muchos tienen también ricas colecciones privadas;
- La conservación y diseminación de la cultura están bastante bien organizadas, y la cultura tradicional se enseña en las escuelas de la mayoría de estos países;
- El folclor y la cultura tradicional gozan actualmente de gran popularidad en el sentido de festivales, conciertos, seminarios, etc., y se han convertido en uno de los rasgos más importantes de la cultura en la actualidad; y
- Ahora los medios informativos muestran interés en este aspecto de la cultura.

(v) Asia Central y el Caúcaso (seminario de Uzbekistán)

En octubre de 1998 se organizó en Tashkent un seminario basado en los cuestionarios presentados por ocho países. En total asistieron catorce representantes de ocho países. Se realizaron varios de los objetivos principales del seminario como:

- un análisis de la condición actual del folclor y la cultura tradicional de los estados recién independizados de la región. Esto se hizo con especial énfasis en la reestructuración de las sociedades durante la transición del sistema comunista al del libre mercado democrático;

- un examen del papel de las culturas tradicionales y populares en el proceso de construcción nacional, en tanto símbolos y referencias a la identidad cultural de las poblaciones, profundamente arraigados en su historia;
- una evaluación del papel sociocultural del patrimonio intangible, particularmente en relación con la globalización, la convivencia de distintos grupos étnicos y el auge de la cultura juvenil;
- formulación de recomendaciones sobre futuras propuestas y acciones para fortalecer la Recomendación; y
- una exploración de la posibilidad de organizar una estrategia regional en el campo de proteger, amparar legalmente, transmitir, revitalizar y diseminar el patrimonio cultural intangible.

La Recomendación enfrenta todavía importantes dificultades. Aún no se ha traducido a los idiomas oficiales de la región y los estados recién independizados enfrentan grandes problemas económicos, políticos y sociales que deben abordarse como primera medida. Todos los participantes coincidieron en que el patrimonio cultural intangible juega un papel importante en la construcción nacional, y por consiguiente no deja de ser un área prioritaria de la política cultural de esos estados. Aunque todos los estados tienen legislación para proteger dicho patrimonio, se consideró que esta no se ajusta a las necesidades de la cultura tradicional y que se tienen que desarrollar nuevas medidas (tales como protección de derechos de autor). Se debe aumentar la ayuda financiera de los sectores tanto público como privado y brindarle apoyo financiero a los artesanos. Se registró una carencia de infraestructura de computación en los archivos de materiales folclóricos y se expresó el deseo de crear una base de datos computarizada conteniendo organizaciones e instituciones relativas al folclor; al final se solicitó un seminario de capacitación de la UNESCO. También se identificó la necesidad de capacitar especialistas en el campo de la administración cultural.

(vi) Africa (seminario de Ghana)

Este seminario se organizó en Accra en enero de 1999, con participantes de diecisiete países. Se envió un cuestionario a cuarenta Estados, de los cuales veintisiete enviaron respuestas. Ello ofreció una buena perspectiva de la situación en cuanto a la aplicación de la Recomendación en la región. A ello se sumaron informes complementarios de los países.

El seminario pasó revista a su concepto del contenido del folclor y la cultura tradicional, procurando identificar los factores que la han sustentado en el pasado pero que ahora están ausentes. Se vio que se había hecho poco por poner en práctica la Recomendación, fuera de los pasos emprendidos después de su independencia por algunos estados recién independizados. Se consideró que los gobiernos han recurrido a este patrimonio en sus estrategias de construcción nacional y para alentar la formación de una identidad nacional. Se hizo referencia al papel que juegan las instituciones y los medios de difusión, pero se consideró que existen graves deficiencias en materia de coordinación, acopio sistemático, política cultural nacional, recursos, personal, etc. Ello resulta desafortunado a la luz de lo que pueden aportar las culturas orales en la construcción y reconstrucción de las culturas contemporáneas en África, bajo su consigna de "hacer del pasado parte del presente".

En cualquier acción futura la protección de la cultura tradicional debe entenderse en el marco de las realidades cotidianas de los países africanos y no desde la perspectiva "académica" que encarna la Recomendación. Se habló de la necesidad de un manual de folclor para uso de los maestros locales como recurso de enseñanza. También se pensó en emplear técnicas antropológicas para la recopilación de información por parte de personal local educado, acción que cuenta con antecedentes en el África de principios del siglo XX. Se recalcó la necesidad de emprender una acción urgente para recabar información sobre las culturas tradicionales y de revitalizar estas culturas, a fin de contrarrestar los rezagos del colonialismo.

Un tema importante de este seminario fue la reintegración de la cultura tradicional a la vida moderna, compartiéndola con los integrantes de la comunidad internacional para mostrarles el contexto cultural de la música y los estilos de baile africanos que ya se han adoptado.

(vii) El Pacífico (seminario de Nueva Caledonia)

El seminario se realizó en Noumea en febrero de 1999. En él participaron doce representantes de otros tantos países. De los catorce países a los que se pidió responder al cuestionario trece presentaron sus respuestas. En base a estas se establecieron los objetivos del seminario: identificar medios y formas de fortalecer la aplicación de la Recomendación en la región; y formular una estrategia regional de largo plazo con miras a proteger, revitalizar, amparar legalmente, transmitir y diseminar el patrimonio intangible del Pacífico. Cada país hizo una breve presentación. Algunos países desconocían la Recomendación, dada su reciente incorporación como estados miembros de UNESCO.

En la región pacífica no se hizo distinción entre patrimonio tangible e intangible, aunque sí se hizo tal distinción para efectos de este estudio. Para mayor gravedad, para muchas poblaciones indígenas el término "folclor" se considera impropio y peyorativo. El término "patrimonio cultural" es mucho más útil y positivo. El patrimonio intangible del Pacífico permanece indocumentado, en gran medida, y corre riesgo por la juventud demográfica de la región, así como las dificultades económicas del sector cultural. Otra amenaza importante al patrimonio intangible son los rezagos de colonialismo y sus efectos endémicos en la sociedad. Se reconoce vivamente que las culturas tradicionales son de gran relevancia y actualidad para el desarrollo sostenible.

Los siguientes son algunos de los temas y preocupaciones comunes identificados durante el seminario:

- La conservación y futuro desarrollo del patrimonio intangible requieren involucrar a todas las partes interesadas (ONG, mujeres, jóvenes, tercera edad y comunidades locales);
- Las complejidades del régimen agrario y el empleo de sistemas de propiedad locales, nacionales y de clan familiar dictan que cualquier sistema basado en beneficiarios individuales es completamente inadecuado para la propiedad de cultura intelectual en las sociedades del Pacífico; y
- La actual atención internacional al tema de la explotación del medio ambiente ha incentivado a los estados de la región a revivir los métodos tradicionales de manejo de mar y tierra.

Se señalaron entre otras necesidades las de:

- alentar a las comunidades y a las partes interesadas a involucrarse en la documentación de este patrimonio;

- reconocer la importancia de las culturas tradicionales en el desarrollo y la generación de ingreso;
- reconocer la amenaza que algunas empresas comerciales representan para el acceso de la comunidad a los materiales empleaos en las prácticas culturales tradicionales;
- reconocer que la identidad cultural y la propiedad de la tierra son inseparables; y
- formular instrumentos jurídicos (que por ahora no existen) y leyes de propiedad intelectual (por ahora inadecuadas) para proteger la cultura de las comunidades.

(vii) Estados Árabes (seminario del Líbano)

Este seminario se realizó en Beirut en mayo de 1999 para considerar la cuestión en su aplicación a los Estados Árabes. Participaron en el seminario expertos de doce países. Se enumeraron ciertas preocupaciones centrales que enfrentan estos estados en el ámbito cultural, esbozadas en los cuestionarios presentados por diez países. Entre ellas figuran:

- Se han reducido las partidas presupuestarias para el folclor;
- Las industrias tradicionales se han desvinculado del "patrimonio" y ahora sirven principalmente a los turistas;
- El patrimonio puede perderse por la importancia que se da a todo lo novedoso, especialmente la tecnología nueva;
- Las instituciones que se ocupan del folclor tienen poco personal y carecen de un organismo central que coordine su trabajo.

Se trataron los efectos de la globalización en el patrimonio cultural, partiendo del entendido que la cultura misma no es estática. La globalización se vio como una espada de doble filo, capaz de ayudar a las culturas nacionales a revitalizar sus culturas para hacer frente a otras culturas, pero amenazándolas, también, de homogeneización cultural. También quedó asentada la importancia de conservar la cultura popular y tradicional para el desarrollo humano, así como el hecho de que el folclor puede ser fuente de revitalización cultural a la vez que contribuye al desarrollo económico. Sin embargo, hay que cuidarse de que el uso del folclor con fines económicos no acabe por perjudicar el folclor mismo. El patrimonio cultural es amenazado por el deterioro del medio ambiente, pero al mismo tiempo su revitalización puede brindar los medios para crear un medio ambiente mejor, así como formar parte de la identidad y dignidad humanas.

Los participantes propusieron algunas medidas para resolver estos problemas, de índole folclórica, que enfrentan los Estados Árabes, y para encaminarlos hacia la protección y revitalización del patrimonio cultural. Se recomendó formular un plan general de desarrollo del patrimonio popular y tradicional; y que se formulen las leyes necesarias para proteger este patrimonio y todas las personas que laboran en este campo. La protección del patrimonio debe entenderse como un proceso continuo. Deben crearse instituciones permanentes que brinden apoyo moral y económico a los practicantes y demás involucrados. Otra prioridad evidente para garantizar la continuidad y sostenimiento culturales es la introducción de cursos relativos a la cultura tradicional y popular en los programas educativos.

8.   Punto 4 del temario: Consideración general de los informes por país y de los seminarios regionales (sesión plenaria).

9.   El doctor Richard Kurin presentó una ponencia sobre los resultados preliminares del cuestionario sobre la aplicación de la Recomendación de 1989 enviado por la UNESCO a los estados miembros en 1994 [este volumen, 20–35]. Este cuestionario es la primera

encuesta que se haya realizado desde una perspectiva global sobre la aplicación de dicha Recomendación.

Los cuestionarios fueron completados por las Comisiones Nacionales de la UNESCO y otras instituciones. Se encontró que, en general, los encuestados estaban bien versados y eran conocedores de la situación del folclor en sus países, aunque varios indicaron no estar tan bien informados, como lo corroboran algunas imprecisiones captadas en los cuestionarios. Hubo algunas dificultades con el empleo de términos tales como "folclor", "preservación" y "conservación", y gran variedad en el grado de elaboración con que se dieron las respuestas.

Luego el doctor Kurin presentó algunos rasgos sobresalientes de los hallazgos de la encuesta. Entre ellos están los siguientes datos estadísticos:

- Aunque el 58 por ciento de los estados estaban al tanto de la Recomendación, sólo seis países presentaron informes a la UNESCO cuando se les solicitó hacerlo;
- El 66 por ciento consideraban que la cooperación de la UNESCO es importante para la formulación de políticas;
- Sólo 30 por ciento de los estados que respondieron tienen infraestructura para suplir las necesidades de la conservación del folclor;
- Se han establecido sistemas de capacitación en 48 por ciento de los estados, la capacidad es inadecuada en otro 18 por ciento;
- Sólo 20 por ciento de los Estados usan voluntarios para la documentación sobre su propia cultura;
- El 68 por ciento usan el folclor y la cultura tradicional en materiales educativos, videos, películas, etc., aunque eso no está muy bien coordinado; y
- En el 50 por ciento de los estados los derechos de propiedad intelectual están protegidos por las leyes nacionales.

Las conclusiones derivadas de esta encuesta fueron: primero, que se necesita una encuesta mejor, ya que es sumamente difícil medir la cultura. Segundo, contra lo esperado, no hay correlación entre el apoyo al folclor y el grado de modernización o desarrollo de un estado (como se esperaría tanto de la perspectiva "modernista" como de la "post-modernista"). Contando todo esto, este es un campo que no se ha institucionalizado, elaborado ni legislado lo suficiente. Aunque muchas personas que trabajan en folclor podrían pensar que así es como quieren que permanezca la situación, ello podría ser una condición peligrosa, a la luz de los obstáculos económicos, sociológicos y físicos que enfrenta la existencia y práctica del folclor.

10. El doctor Anthony Seeger hizo un recuento de los ocho seminarios regionales celebrados de 1995 a 1999 para evaluar la aplicación de la Recomendación en los estados miembros [este volumen, 35–41]. Las reuniones tendieron a seguir una estructura similar: un representante de la UNESCO daba una historia de la Recomendación y de los temas a tratar; se hacía un resumen de los informes sinópticos sobre su aplicación; y los delegados de cada país presentaban breves informes.

En estos seminarios se expresaron muchas preocupaciones comunes, pero con diferencias regionales identificables. América Latina y el Caribe, por ejemplo, hicieron hincapié en temas de diversidad cultural y multiculturalismo. La región del Pacífico habló de las dificultades de distinguir entre patrimonio tangible e intangible desde su propia perspectiva cultural, mientras que el Asia recalcó la necesidad de hacer énfasis en las culturas cortesanas, así como otras culturas tradicionales y el folclor. El concepto africano de identidad ha cambiado mucho en la década pasada, trasladando el énfasis de la construcción nacional al reconocimiento de identidades múltiples. Aunque en Europa central y oriental también se analizó extensamente la importancia de la cultura tradicional en la identidad nacional, se manifestaron importantes preocupaciones sobre la situación financiera y la transición del sistema comunista a una economía de mercado. Europa Occidental destacó la necesidad de conservar la diversidad cultural frente a fuerzas intelectuales y creativas de alcance global; los estados árabes también hablaron de los efectos de la globalización y el reto que ésta supone para la conservación de las identidades culturales. Varias regiones observaron la importancia de las culturas tradicionales en el conjunto de la cultura contemporánea y la sub-utilización que actualmente se hace de ellas.

En términos de la Recomendación de 1989, se hicieron los siguientes señalamientos generales: primero, que se trata de un instrumento importante, que requiere mucha mayor diseminación. Muchos hablaron del "folclor" en tanto término problemático que puede verse como peyorativo. Ello requeriría modificación en cualquier instrumento utilizado en el futuro, aunque no existe aún consenso en cuanto al término correcto con que podría reemplazarse. El nuevo instrumento debe contener, entre otros rasgos adicionales, los siguientes:

- un código de ética con principios de respeto;
- la inclusión de los practicantes del folclor y la cultura tradicional como principales partícipes y beneficiarios del proceso de documentación y diseminación de sus conocimientos;
- un reconocimiento del papel de colaboración de las ONG y otras instituciones que puedan ayudar a conservar este patrimonio cultural; y
- ampliar el alcance de la Recomendación a fin de abarcar la naturaleza cambiante del folclor y la cultura tradicional.

11.   El señor Anthony McCann presentó un breve análisis de la Recomendación de 1989 en el contexto actual, realizado por un equipo de expertos afiliados a la Institución Smithsoniana [este volumen, 57–61]. Dijo que el año 1999 era un buen momento para llevar a cabo la revisión de la Recomendación y ofrecer nuevas oportunidades a las comunidades y organizaciones no gubernamentales e intergubernamentales, entre otras, de revaluar su papel en el contexto contemporáneo.

Una de las principales observaciones, relativas al texto de la Recomendación, fue que se ubica demasiado firmemente del lado de las instituciones que documentan y archivan, como reflejo de la finalidad de proteger, con esos medios, el producto en vez de los productores del folclor y la cultura tradicional. Debe buscarse un equilibrio entre el afán de documentar y la necesidad de proteger las prácticas que crean y nutren lo que luego se documentará. La protección debe, pues, cambiar de enfoque hacia las comunidades mismas. Observó que existe también la necesidad de hacer una nueva evaluación crítica del lenguaje usado en la Recomendación. Hablar de "fragilidad" en referencia a las culturas tradicionales (orales) es una metáfora desconcertante que da la impresión de que son culturas moribundas en vez de gente viva cuyas formas de expresión, derivadas de la comunidad, son marginadas por fuerzas sujetas a la voluntad humana.

También hay que reconsiderar el uso de la expresión "intangible" por cuanto se refiere a las ideas como si fuesen cosas (en vez de la base y resultado de prácticas vivas), ya que la posibilidad o imposibilidad de ser tocado (tangible) es propiedad de los objetos materiales.

Agregó que es hora de dar representación adecuada a aquellos cuyas prácticas crean y nutren esta cultura. El reconocimiento y respeto a la participación activa de los practicantes de base en la producción, transmisión y conservación de sus expresiones y productos culturales son esenciales para enfrentar los crecientes retos y oportunidades que ofrece el nuevo encuentro e intercambio global de culturas. La participación plena y activa de los representantes culturales de base con los gobiernos y académicos en las decisiones sobre el desarrollo y aplicación de medidas para proteger el folclor y la cultura tradicional es un paso esencial hacia una mejor vida para las comunidades practicantes.

12. A continuación el señor James Early, del Centro de Folclor y Patrimonio Cultural de la Institución Smithsoniana, hizo algunos comentarios adicionales sobre la agencia, su colaboración y relevancia en relación con la Recomendación de 1989. Señaló que la Recomendación no habla de la motivación propia de las comunidades, se refirió a la necesidad de pasar a la colaboración con dichas comunidades para aprender cómo documentan y transmiten su cultura; y qué progreso pueden realizar en ello. En cuanto a relevancia, recalcó la importancia de las prácticas culturales en términos tanto históricos como contemporáneos, dando el ejemplo de Sudáfrica, donde una colectividad de centenares de practicantes de medicina tradicional se reunieron con médicos educados en la medicina "occidental" para hallar formas de colaboración.

13. Discusión.

Luego quedó abierta la discusión para preguntas y comentarios de todos los participantes.

Un participante identificó la tendencia a usar un lenguaje de investigación que separa un objeto cultural de la conciencia que lo produjo. Describió la desaparición de las canciones de los remeros filipinos, con el advenimiento de las lanchas motorizadas, como ejemplo de vínculo entre la práctica y una conciencia más general. También señaló la ironía de hecho de que los investigadores de campo vician la verdad de sus investigaciones con el simple hecho de hacer preguntas.

Otro participante agregó que no sólo hay que preguntarle a las comunidades lo que saben sino entender también cómo crean significados y aplican sus conocimientos en la vida cotidiana. Observó también la imposibilidad de separar las expresiones culturales del contexto económico, etc.

Un participante mencionó que él prefería comprender la comunidad y su cultura tradicional tanto desde adentro como desde afuera (y aun desde un punto de vista muy distante de su ámbito cultural), desde muchas perspectivas y no sólo de la de una cultura o comunidad.

Otro participante agregó que cuando se habla del concepto de cultura ciertamente se reconocen las áreas de conflicto (tales como entre el cristianismo y el islam). Dio el ejemplo de un conflicto entre una tradición en Ghana, de que no se deben tocar tambores por tres semanas antes de un festival, y el deseo de los miembros de cierta iglesia, que querían tocar tambores en su iglesia durante esos períodos vedados.

Otro participante agregó que la conservación de la cultura compete a todas las religiones, que pueden considerarse el mensaje condensado de tradiciones que se van transmitiendo para que cada generaciones lo descifre. Ello no excluye otras tradiciones tales como la música o la danza. El problema que se presenta hoy es el del progreso y los esfuerzos a emprenderse para contrarrestar el efecto del progreso de destruir parte de la historia y la cultura de los pueblos.

Un participante, que se identificó como artista nativo americano, observó que en Nuevo México todavía viven en tierras comunales muchas personas de filiación tribal, nacional y étnica. Siempre se habla — continuó — de "nosotros" (expertos y administradores) y "ellos" (miembros de la comunidad), en vez de aceptar que todos contribuyen a un proceso de solución de problemas. ¿Por qué no cada experto trae a conferencias próximas a un verdadero portador de la tradición?

Otra participante coincidió en que este es un punto muy importante, y observó que ella había asistido en Canadá a una reunión en que conoció nativos que estaban al borde de la extinción y se sentían muy aislados. Tales culturas amenazadas buscan vínculos para sobrevivir y así rompen su aislamiento.

Un participante observó que se había oído mucho sobre la protección de la cultura intangible, pero que ello no debe dar pie a pensar que la cultura tangible está bien protegida. Las leyes de propiedad intelectual no ofrecen ninguna protección, por ejemplo, a la cultura tangible de los aborígenes australianos. Indudablemente que la cultura intangible es más vulnerable, pero tampoco deben descuidarse los elementos tangibles.

A ello respondió otro participante con el comentario de que, cuando hablamos usando diferentes idiomas, puede ser muy difícil llegar a un entendimiento de lo que significa y a definir el tema. Así, por ejemplo, en la región del Pacífico no se hace ninguna distinción entre cultura "tangible" e "intangible". No obstante, es importante llegar a un consenso.

Un participante quiso puntualizar dos cosas: primero, que en los diez años desde que se acordó la Recomendación, el número de propietarios transnacionales de propiedad intelectual ha disminuido marcadamente, concentrando esa propiedad en manos de unas pocas entidades; segundo, que en lo que concierne al folclor y la cultura tradicional, y las leyes de propiedad intelectual, muchos elementos importantes son omitidos en la ley o en el lenguaje con que se define el mundo en que operamos. Esto es algo que deberá abordarse luego en las discusiones (de los grupos de trabajo).

Grupos de trabajo

14.   Punto 6 del temario: Discusiones por temas (grupos de trabajo).Concluida la sesión plenaria de la conferencia, los participantes (y algunos observadores) se dividieron por día y medio en tres grupos de trabajo con los siguientes temas:
Grupo I: Patrimonio cultural intangible, en lo relativo al patrimonio cultural natural y tangible, y su papel en la solución de problemas locales y nacionales relativos a los grandes temas contemporáneos, tales como identidad cultura, cuestiones de género, desarrollo humano sustentable, globalización, coexistencia pacífica de diversos grupos étnicos, prevención de conflictos, culturas juveniles evolución de la nueva tecnología de comunicación e información, deterioro del medio ambiente, etc.

Participantes: Sr. Ralph Regenvanu, Vanuatu — presidente
Sr. Russell Collier, Gitxsan, Canadá — relator
Sta. Robyne Bancroft, Australia
Sr. Mihály Hoppál, Hungría
Sr. Miguel Puwainchir, Ecuador
Dr. Mahaman Garba, Níger
Sr. Rachid El Houda, Marruecos
Dr. Junzo Kawada, Japón
Sra. Stepanida Borisova, Rusia
Sr. Andy Abeita, Pueblo Isleta, Estados Unidos
Sr. Rajeev Sethi, India

Grupo II: Protección jurídica del patrimonio intangible local y nacional.
Participantes: Sta. Manuela da Cunha, Brasil — presidenta
Dra. Tressa Berman, Estados Unidos — relatora
Sra. Lyndel Prott, UNESCO

Dra. Grace Koch, Australia

Profesor Kamal Puri, Australia

Comisionado Preston Thomas, Australia

Profesor Peter Jaszi, Estados Unidos

Dra. Janet Blake, Escocia, Reino Unido

Sr. Brad Simon, Estados Unidos

Sta. Pualani Kanaka'ole Kanahele, Estados Unidos

Grupo III: Política local, nacional, regional e internacional, con referencia especial a la transmisión, revitalización y documentación del patrimonio cultural intangible.

Participantes: Profesor Kwabena Nketia, Ghana — presidente

Sta. Sivia Tora, Fiji — relatora

Dra. Gail Saunders, Bahamas

Sta. Zulma Yugar, Bolivia

Sta. Khurshida Mambetova, Uzbekistán

Dra. Florentine Hornedo, Filipinas

Dr. Osamu Yamaguti, Japón

Sr. Renato Matusse, Mozambique

Sr. Jean Guibal, Francia

Sra. Vlasta Ondrusova, República Checa

Sr. Mohsen Shaalan, Egipto

Profesor Heikki Kirkinen, Finlandia

Sr. Namankoumba Kouyaté, Guinea

Sra. Juana Núñez, Cuba

Informes de los grupos de trabajo, propuestas de proyectos piloto, y desarrollo del plan de acción

15.   Punto 7 del temario: Informes de las sesiones por tema, incluidas las recomendaciones de grupo (sesión plenaria).

Después de trabajar por separado durante todo el segundo día, los tres grupos de trabajo regresaron, el tercer día de la conferencia, a la sesión plenaria, con sus recomendaciones. Los informes se dieron de la siguiente forma:

Grupo I: Se dirigió una recomendación a los gobiernos en la que se afirma que éstos deben apoyar activamente a las comunidades en sus actividades de generación, transmisión, autorización y atribución del conocimiento y habilidades tradicionales, de conformidad con las normas internacionales vigentes en materia de derechos humanos. Se plantearon tres pasos que deben considerar los estados, así como doce áreas en que se requiere más estudio por parte de un grupo de expertos [ver Apéndice 4].

Grupo II: Se trataron cinco áreas generales relativas a la protección de la cultura tradicional, y se hicieron recomendaciones que se incorporaron al Plan de Acción final de la conferencia [ver Apéndice 5].

Grupo III: Se propusieron siete recomendaciones a los gobiernos de los estados miembros y nueve recomendaciones a la UNESCO, en base a las discusiones del grupo y en una serie de nueve puntos definida desde el comienzo de la reunión [ver Apéndice 6].

Los informes y recomendaciones de los tres grupos de trabajo fueron presentados en sesión plenaria por los presidentes y relatores de cada grupo. Luego los informes fueron considerados y aprobados en sesión plenaria.

16.   Punto 8 del temario: Cooperación internacional: presentación de proyectos piloto (sesión plenaria)

La señora Aikawa presentó una propuesta de cinco Proyectos Piloto de Cooperación Internacional e Inter-regional, redactados por la Secretaría de la UNESCO con base en las recomendaciones formuladas por la mayoría de los seminarios regionales y sub-regionales. Estos proyectos piloto serán elaborados, en mayor detalle, por la Secretaría de la UNESCO, que los presentará, a los fondos y entidades donantes así como a los estados miembros que potencialmente hagan aportes económicos voluntarios a la UNESCO. Entre ellos figuran:

- El establecimiento de redes regionales e internacionales entre instituciones que se ocupan del folclor y la cultura tradicional;
- La creación de cátedras de folclor y cultura tradicional de la UNE SCO;
- Un estudio de factibilidad para la elaboración de salvaguardas jurídicos del folclor y la cultura tradicional en África, América Latina y el Caribe;
- Una reunión internacional para incorporar el folclor y la cultura tradicional a la política cultural;
- Un proyecto interregional sobre la revitalización del conocimiento tradicional en la mediación y prevención de conflictos (África y el Pacífico).

Se invitó a los participantes a hacer más sugerencias a la UNESCO sobre estos proyectos piloto.

17.   Punto 9 del temario: Presentación y aprobación del borrador de plan de acción para salvaguardar y revitalizar el patrimonio cultural intangible, e informe final (sesión plena-ria) [este volumen, 354–399].

En la noche del 29 de junio se estableció un Comité de Redacción para elaborar un plan de acción. Formaron parte del mismo los siguientes participantes:

    Dra. Florentine Hornedo — presidenta
    Dra. Grace Koch — relatora
    Sr. Andy Abeita
    Dra. Tressa Berman
    Sta. Manuelo Carneiro da Cunha
    Sr. Rachid El Houda
    Dr. Junzo Kawada
    Sta. Khurshida Mambetova
    Sr. Ralph Regenvanu
    Sr. Rajeev Sethi

18.   La presidenta y la relatora del Comité de Redacción presentaron el borrador del plan de acción en sesión plenaria. Tras incorporar las recomendaciones de los grupos al borrador del plan de acción, el pleno discutió en detalle, modificó y finalmente aprobó el plan de acción con las alteraciones acordadas. El informe final fue leído por la doctora Janet Blake, relatora, y aprobado unánimemente por los participantes.

19.   El doctor Richard Kurin y el señor Mounir Bouchenaki pronunciaron los discursos de clausura, agradeciendo a todos los participantes sus fructíferos y constructivos aportes a la conferencia.

Apéndice 1: Temario

I.   Apertura de la conferencia

II.   Recomendación de la UNESCO sobre Protección del Folclor y la Cultura Tradicional (1989); acciones emprendidas por la UNESCO en cumplimiento de la misma (sesión plenaria)

III.   Informe de los ocho seminarios regionales y subregionales (sesión plenaria)

IV.   Consideración general de los informes por país y de los seminarios regionales (sesión plenaria)

V.   Análisis de la Recomendación de 1989 en el contexto contemporáneo: aspectos positivos y negativos (sesión plenaria)

VI.   Discusión por temas (grupos de trabajo)

    A. Patrimonio cultural intangible en lo relativo al patrimonio cultural natural y tangible.Su papel en la solución de problemas locales y nacionales relativos a los grandes temas contemporáneos, tales como identidad cultural, cuestiones de género, desarrollo humano sostenible, globalización, coexistencia pacífica de diversos grupos étnicos, prevención de conflictos, culturas juveniles, evolución de la nueva tecnología de comunicación e información, deterioro del medio ambiente, etc.

    B. Protección jurídica del patrimonio intangible a nivel local y nacional

    C. Política local, nacional, regional e internacional con referencia especial a la transmisión, revitalización y documentación del patrimonio cultural intangible

VI.   Informe de las sesiones por tema, incluyendo las recomendaciones de grupo (sesión plenaria)

VII. Cooperación internacional: presentación de proyectos piloto (sesión plenaria)

VIII. Presentación y aprobación del borrador del plan de acción e informe final (sesión plenaria)

Apéndice 2: Acotaciones al temario

I.   Antecedentes

En su vigésima quinta Conferencia General (noviembre de 1989), la UNESCO adoptó la Recomendación sobre Protección del Folclor y la Cultura Tradicional [este volumen, 8–12]. Esta importantísima acción surgió de la preocupación de que el folclor forma parte del patrimonio de la humanidad y como tal puede ser un medio potente para aglutinar diferentes pueblos y grupos sociales y afianzar, así, su identidad cultural. Además la acción recalcó el hecho de que el folclor posee gran importancia social, económica, cultural y política tanto en el contexto cultural histórico como en el actual. Aún más, el folclor, cuyas manifestaciones son algunas veces muy frágiles por su propia naturaleza, es parte integral del patrimonio cultural y de la cultura viva. La Recomendación se adoptó con miras a alentar a los gobiernos a jugar un papel decisivo, tomando medidas legislativas, entre otras, para conservar y proteger el folclor y la cultura tradicional. Con el creciente número de transformaciones que afectan a todas las regiones del mundo, la tarea propuesta retiene toda su vigencia.

La Recomendación se compone de siete capítulos, a saber: (i) Definición, (ii) Identificación, (iii) Conservación, (iv) Preservación, (v) Diseminación, (vi) Protección y (vii) Cooperación Internacional. El término "folclor y cultura tradicional" queda definido como sigue (párrafo A): "Folclor (o cultura tradicional y popular) es la totalidad de las creaciones de una comunidad cultural basadas en la tradición, expresadas por un grupo de individuos y reconocida como reflejo de las expectativas de una comunidad en tanto reflejo de su identidad social y cultural; sus normas y valores se transmiten oralmente, por imitación o de otras maneras. Sus formas son, entre otras, el lenguaje, la literatura, la música, la danza, los juegos, la mitología, los rituales, las costumbres, las artesanías, la arquitectura y otras artes".

En febrero de 1990 el director general de la UNESCO difundió una circular a los estados miembros, en la que los invitaba a tomar todas las medidas necesarias para hacer valer la Recomendación. Según los términos expuestos en el artículo IV, párrafo 4, de la Constitución de la UNESCO, cada estado debe presentar las recomendaciones o convenios adoptados por la UNESCO a las autoridades competentes dentro de un plazo de un año desde el cierre de la sesión de la Conferencia General en que se hayan adoptado. Para 1991, sin embargo, sólo seis países habían presentado informes especiales sobre acciones emprendidas para hacer efectiva la Recomendación. Lo que es más, dichos informes se limitaban a corroborar la existencia y relevancia de la legislación nacional existente, y exponían medidas específicas que se habían tomado para familiarizar a las autoridades nacionales competentes con lo dispuesto en la Recomendación.

Para evaluar sistemáticamente la aplicación de la Recomendación y la situación actual de los Estados miembros en materia de salvaguardia y revitalización del patrimonio cultural intangible, la UNESCO realizó una serie de encuestas, región por región, por cuatro años, de 1995 a 1999. Se hanrealizado un total de ocho seminarios regionales: (i) Strá nice, República Checa (junio de 1995), para Europa central y oriental; (ii) México, DF, México (septiembre de 1997), para América Latina y el Caribe; (iii) Tokio, Japón (febrero–marzo de 1998), para el Asia; (iv) Joensuu, Finlandia (septiembre de 1998), para Europa occidental; (v) Tashkent, República de Uzbekistán (octubre de 1998), para el Asia central y el Cáucaso; (vi) Accra, Ghana (enero de 1999), para el África; (vii) Noumea, Nueva Caledonia (febrero de 1999), para el Pacífico; y (viii) Beirut, Líbano (mayo de 1999) para los estados árabes.

La actual conferencia es la culminación de estos seminarios regionales. Su propósito principal es evaluar globalmente la situación actual y orientación futura de la Recomendación de 1989 para Proteger el Folclor y la Cultura Tradicional. El patrimonio intangible es, a la vez, rico y diverso, mas por una serie de motivos muchos productores de cultura tradicional y popular están abandonando sus artes o dejando de transmitirlas a las generaciones jóvenes. Consecuentemente existe la amenaza de que desaparezca gran parte de la cultura tradicional y popular en muchas partes del mundo. Por lo tanto es imperativo tomar medidas urgentes hacia su conservación y revitalización tanto para las generaciones actuales como las futuras.

II.   Objetivos de la conferencia

Los objetivos de la conferencia fueron:

A.   Evaluar la situación actual en materia de salvaguardar y revitalización del patrimonio cultural intangible en el mundo contemporáneo;

B.   Analizar las relaciones entre patrimonio cultural intangible, natural y tangible para observar el papel que juega el patrimonio cultural intangible en la solución de problemas locales y nacionales relativos a los grandes temas contemporáneos, tales como la identidad cultural, los temas de género, el desarrollo humano sostenible, la globalización, la coexistencia pacífica de diferentes grupos étnicos, la prevención de conflictos, las culturas juveniles, la evolución de nueva tecnología de comunicaciones e información, el deterioro del medio ambiente, etc.;

C.   Estudiar la protección jurídica del patrimonio cultural intangible local y nacional;

D.   Recomendar medidas locales, nacionales e internacionales, particularmente en lo referente a la transmisión, revitalización y documentación del patrimonio cultural intangible;

E.   Estudiar el papel futuro de la Recomendación de 1989 en los estados miembros de la UNESCO;

F.   Fomentar la cooperación internacional a través del desarrollo de futuras estrategias y proyectos piloto

III.   Organización de la conferencia

Tras la introducción a la conferencia se llevará a cabo una encuesta de acciones emprendidas por la UNESCO para la aplicación de la Recomendación de 1989 (puntos 1 y 2 del temario, día 1). La conferencia continuará con una breve discusión de los resultados de las reuniones regionales (puntos 3 y 4 del temario, día 1), luego se dividirán en tres grupos de trabajo para las discusiones en profundidad que especifica el punto 6 del temario (días 1 y 2). Los puntos del 7 al 10 del temario se abordarán en sesión plenaria (día 3).

A.   Informes de las ocho conferencias regionales

El procedimiento para la realización de encuestas regionales operó en forma cronológica: (i) en cada región la UNESCO identificó una institución especializada que fungiese como compañera de trabajo; (ii) tomando en cuenta las especificidades de cada lugar, la UNESCO elaboró un cuestionario sobre la aplicación de la Recomendación; (iii) la UNESCO repartió el cuestionario entre las Comisiones Nacionales de los Estados miembros correspondientes y les solicitó tomar las medidas necesarias para que el cuestionario se completara debidamente; (iv) con base en las respuestas al cuestionario recibidas por la UNESCO, y sus socios de trabajo en cada región, se compilaron datos estadísticos y se prepararon informes amplios para evaluar el grado de aplicación de la Recomendación. Dichos informes demostraron ser muy efectivos en todos los seminarios regionales ya que ocasionaron discusiones provechosas, múltiples recomendaciones, y conclusiones concretas.

B.   Repaso general de los informes regionales: evaluación mundial

Los informes regionales, que prestan atención a pautas, aspectos, dificultades e interrogantes de corte local y nacional, arrojan luz tanto sobre la situación contemporánea como la orientación futura del patrimonio cultural intangible. El repaso de dichos informes, por consiguiente, revela que y que no se ha logrado en los estados miembros de UNESCO en los diez años desde que se adoptó la Recomendación, así como lo que se tiene que hacer en el futuro.

A solicitud de la UNESCO la Institución Smithsoniana ha compilado informes sumarios y estadísticos, basados en los informes regionales sobre la aplicación de la Recomendación de 1989, de la UNESCO, que serán enviados a todos los participantes de la conferencia antes de realizarse la reunión [este volumen, 20–35, 36–41].

C.   Análisis de la Recomendación de 1989 en el contexto actual: aspectos positivos y negativos

Desde que las tensiones entre Oriente y Occidente se redujeron en 1989, el mundo ha experimentado grandes transformaciones políticas, económicas y socioculturales. Más aún, ha aparecido tecnología nueva que facilita, pero también complica, salvaguardar el patrimonio cultural intangible. A pesar de tan grandes avances ha surgido una cantidad de dificultades. Por tales motivos ha llegado la hora de evaluar los aspectos positivos y negativos de la Recomendación en el contexto actual, con particular atención a sus disposiciones desde la perspectiva tanto conceptual como jurídica. La Institución Smithsoniana está preparando, a solicitud de la UNESCO, un documento sobre la Recomendación de 1989, el cual se distribuirá a los participantes antes de la conferencia [este volumen, 57–61].

D.   Discusiones por tema (grupos de trabajo)

Grupo I. Patrimonio intangible, natural y tangible. Discusión sobre el papel que juega el patrimonio cultural intangible en la solución de problemas locales y nacionales relativos a los grandes temas contemporáneos tales como la identidad cultural, asuntos de género, desarrollo humano sustentable, globalización, coexistencia pacífica de diversos grupos étnicos, prevención de conflictos, culturas juveniles, evolución de nueva tecnología de comunicaciones e información, deterioro de medio ambiente, etc.

Entre los temas que podrían tratarse figuran los siguientes:

Patrimonio cultural intangible, natural y tangible. Desde los años setenta, la UNESCO se ha dado a conocer por las acciones que ha emprendido para proteger los grandes monumentos históricos, tales como el Templo de Abu Simbel, en Egipto. La "Lista de Patrimonio Mundial", que fue una iniciativa abanderada por la UNESCO, durante los años noventa, agregó el "patrimonio natural" a la fórmula "patrimonio cultural tangible . . . monumentos y sitios históricos", ya existente. En noviembre de 1998 los estados miembros de la UNESCO, para los cuales "patrimonio cultural" sólo había significado "patrimonio cultural tangible", acordaron ampliar el concepto de "patrimonio cultural" incluyendo en él también el "patrimonio cultural intangible".

La Junta Ejecutiva de la UNESCO, en su 155ª sesión (noviembre de 1998), aprobó un nuevo proyecto llamado "Proclamación de las Obras Maestras del Patrimonio Oral e Intangible de la Humanidad". La aprobación de dicho proyecto da fe de que los estados miembros de la UNESCO han aceptado un concepto ampliado de "patrimonio cultural". Este incluye tanto el patrimonio tangible como el intangible. De hecho, los patrimonios intangible y tangible siempre han estado íntimamente entrelazados: el primero da significado al segundo, mientras que este último brinda apoyo físico al primero. Los siguientes ejemplos podrían ilustrar el caso: (i) el largo friso de Angkor Wat que describe los 1.500 años de la legendaria épica del Ramayana; (ii) la danza de la corte de Khmer que hasta la fecha aún refleja el estilo de baile de las hermosas Apsara ("semideidades") de los litorelieves del templo; y (iii) el simbolismo, las técnicas y la artesanía de las decoraciones murales tradicionales de la arquitectura en tierra de Mauritania, transmitidas por siglos de madres a hijas. Más aún, el patrimonio natural, o paisajístico, como por ejemplo las Mosi-oa-Tunya (cataratas de Victoria), de Zambia y Zimbabwe, ha dado nacimiento a una variedad de tradiciones orales, mitos y epopeyas que dan significado cultural al entorno natural.

Para salvaguardar el patrimonio intangible, se requiere un enfoque integrado que tenga en cuenta, al mismo tiempo, tanto los aspectos tangibles como los intangibles. Aún más, es esencial que las comunidades locales contemporáneas tengan la facultad de participar en la iniciación de medidas de protección de su patrimonio cultural intangible. Para tal efecto es indispensable brindar a estas poblaciones una adecuada capacitación en administración del patrimonio con énfasis en la integración de los patrimonios tangible e intangible.

Identidad de grupo. La "cultura tradicional y popular" (patrimonio cultural intangible) puede jugar un importante papel en la solución de problemas locales y nacionales relativos a los grandes temas de la actualidad. En muchas poblaciones, por ejemplo, el patrimonio cultural intangible ha jugado un papel vital en la afirmación y expresión de la identidad de grupo que, a su vez, tiene una profunda raigambre histórica. Cosmologías, creencias y va-lores transmitidos por los idiomas tradiciones orales, y diversas manifestaciones culturales, a menudo constituyen los cimientos de la vida en comunidad. Es más, en muchos países la reiteración de la identidad cultural, basada en las culturas locales tradicionales y populares, ha jugado un papel integral en el proceso de construcción nacional de período post-colonial.

Asuntos de género. En muchas sociedades del mundo la mujer siempre ha jugado un papel vital en salvaguardar y transmitir tradiciones, reglas de conducta y habilidades que se consideran indispensables para mantener la cohesión de la familia y su posición en sociedad. Entre estas manifestaciones se cuentan los códigos de ética, los cuentos e historias orales, canciones, música, idiomas, shamanismo, ritos y artes culinarias. En la producción de cultura material, donde un cierto simbolismo, artesanía y destrezas manuales se expresan en obras de bordado, tejido y producción de hábitat, entre otros, las mujeres han tenido gran éxito no sólo reteniendo y transmitiendo los métodos y prácticas tradicionales, sino también adaptándolos en formas innovadoras con elementos modernos, creando así nuevos materiales y modalidades técnicas.

Desarrollo sostenible. El desarrollo humano requiere, para su éxito, la adaptación de las estrategias de desarrollo al contexto sociocultural de una sociedad dada. Por consiguiente es vital observar y analizar tanto los sistemas socioeconómicos, modalidades de pensamiento y conducta asi como los métodos tradicionales de producción que se transmiten por la vía oral. Más aún, ciertas expresiones de folclor y cultura tradicional pueden contribuir directamente al desarrollo económico al introducir mejoras a la industria cultural, específicamente en los campos de las artes representativas y artesanías.

Globalización. La globalización contemporánea de la vida económica, política y social, acelerada por los avances en tecnología de comunicaciones e información, ha redundado en una gran penetración y amalgamación de las culturas. Consecuentemente las culturas mayoritarias vienen absorbiendo cada vez más a sus contrapartes minoritarias, lo que representa una amenaza a la diversidad cultural. Por tales motivos suele argumentarse que la globalización ha contribuido al crecimiento de una uniformidad cultural. Es así como la revitalización del patrimonio cultural, específico a cada comunidad, ayudará a conservar las culturas locales, cuyo fortalecimiento es esencial para la perpetuación de la diversidad cultural, a escala mundial. Tal diversidad, basada en la coexistencia pacífica de diferentes grupos étnicos, es requisito indispensable para el desarrollo de un sistema multicultural, elemento fundamental de la paz mundial, cuya construcción es tarea primordial de la UNESCO y las Naciones Unidas.

Tecnología. Si bien es cierto que el progreso acelerado de la tecnología de comunicaciones e información puede haber perjudicado las culturas tradicionales y populares locales, al mismo tiempo dicha tecnología es indispensable para conservar y fomentar esas culturas. Además, no debemos olvidar que la cultura no es algo estático, sino en permanente evolución. La nueva tecnología ha permitido avances en el procesamiento de la información y las comunicaciones y ha facilitado el surgimiento de nuevas y diversas formas de expresiones culturales híbridas. Es imperativo reconocer también que los jóvenes, los más susceptibles al progreso tecnológico, seguirán produciendo sus propias formas artísticas. Estas formarán parte de un nuevo patrimonio, como por ejemplo la música etnotécnica. Por consiguiente hay que seguir permanentemente atentos a la evolución cultural.

Conflictos étnicos. Por todo el mundo va en aumento el número de conflictos étnicos. Para reducir el número de tales conflictos los representantes de los países africanos y de la cuenca del pacífico, que asistieron a los seminarios regionales de Accra (enero de 1999) y Noumea (febrero de 1999), respectivamente, expresaron con ahínco su deseo de reconsiderar la sabiduría y los conocimientos tradicionales en tanto un medio de prevención de conflictos.

Protección del medio ambiente. El deterioro del medio ambiente mundial plantea graves problemas no sólo a las comunidades locales — ya que amenaza los recursos, estilos de vida y culturas tradicionales — sino a todo el planeta. Por lo tanto es menester crear medidas concretas para combatir ese deterioro. La revitalización del conocimiento, las habilidades y prácticas tradicionales, que apuntan a regular los recursos naturales mediante la aplicación de tabúes en materia de caza y pesca, por ejemplo, en sí mismos constituyen una interrelación entre los pueblos y el medio ambiente; tal revitalización puede ser beneficiosa en la lucha contra los peligros ambientales.

Grupo II. Protección jurídica del patrimonio intangible local y nacional

La cultura tradicional y popular es muy variada por naturaleza y está amenazada, a veces, por la extinción. Por este motivo es imperativo establecer pasos legales para garantizar el cuido del patrimonio cultural intangible en todo el mundo. Esto significa su protección sistemática a nivel tanto local como nacional. Tal protección debe acoger no solamente el patrimonio cultural intangible en sí mismo sino los propios practicantes del folclor y las culturas tradicionales.

La cultura tradicional y popular fácilmente puede estar sujeta a apropiación y explotación comercial por miembros de comunidades distintas a las que la crearon. Urge proteger los derechos de propiedad intelectual, sin faltar los derechos tanto de autor como industriales de la expresión cultural tradicional y popular, una vez utilizada por terceros o con otros fines. Al establecer dicho sistema, debe prestarse especial atención a garantizar que los beneficios lleguen a las poblaciones que iniciaron la expresión cultural en cuestión.

Grupo III. Política local, nacional, regional e internacional en referencia a la transmisión, revitalización y documentación del patrimonio cultural intangible

El papel de la UNESCO, en tanto organización intergubernamental, es instar a los gobiernos integrantes a emprender acciones acordes con los objetivos de la UNESCO. La primera tarea de la UNESCO es, por consiguiente, hacer conciencia entre esos gobiernos y sus estamentos dirigentes, de la urgente necesidad de salvaguardar y revitalizar el patrimonio cultural intangible del mundo. Es esencial evaluar — con fines de elaboración — toda política local, nacional o internacional con particular enfoque en la transmisión, revitalización y documentación de este patrimonio. El objetivo es el de ayudar a todos los gobiernos a establecer la política más atinada, en este sentido, y/o promover la cooperación regional o internacional para fomentar el esfuerzo.

E.　　Informes de las sesiones de grupo, con las recomendaciones de grupo

Se invita a los grupos a reunirse en sesión plenaria para intercambiar ideas y recomendaciones derivadas de las sesiones de trabajo individuales.

F.　　Papel futuro de la Recomendación de 1989 entre los estados miembros de UNESCO

La Recomendación lleva diez años de existencia. Somos conscientes de su pasado y ahora debemos atender a su orientación futura, a la luz de la situación actual. Es hora de evaluar el papel futuro de la Recomendación, entre los Estados miembros de la UNESCO, para garantizar la protección y revitalización del patrimonio cultural intangible del mundo. Algunos estados miembros de UNESCO consideran que ha llegado el momento para que la UNESCO cree una convención internacional para salvaguardar el patrimonio cultural intangible, a la manera de la Convención Mundial sobre Patrimonio (noviembre de 1972) — de aplicación exclusiva al patrimonio tangible y natural — o modificar la convención existente, de ser posible, a fin de incluir en ella el patrimonio intangible. La Recomendación se usaría como base para explorar esa nueva convención. Adicionalmente, muchos países siguen recalcando la urgente necesidad de establecer un instrumento internacional para la protección de los derechos de propiedad intelectual en las expresiones de folclor y cultura tradicional. La UNESCO y la Organización Mundial de la Propiedad Intelectual (OMPI) examinan actualmente esta posibilidad.

G.   Cooperación internacional: futuras estrategias y proyectos piloto

Se espera que en el curso de la conferencia los participantes identifiquen los problemas y desafíos para los años venideros y formulen estrategias, de mediano plazo, para la cooperación internacional con miras a salvaguardar y revitalizar el patrimonio cultural intangible por todo el mundo. Tales estrategias podrían definir la futura orientación del programa de UNESCO relativo al patrimonio cultural intangible, sus prioridades, enfoques y métodos de trabajo a aplicarse. Se espera también que estas estrategias abarquen medidas concretas para mejorar tanto la aplicación como la efectividad de la Recomendación de 1989.

H.   Presentación de las recomendaciones finales

Se invita a los participantes de la conferencia a redactar y presentar varias recomendaciones, dirigidas a la UNESCO, para la futura orientación o fortalecimiento de la actual Recomendación de 1989, sus respectivos estados miembros y entidades especializadas tales, como la Institución Smithsoniana.

Apéndice 3: Participantes, personal, y asociados e internos

Participantes

Andy P. Abeita
presidente
Consejo de Artes y Cultura Indígenas
Peralta, Nuevo México
Estados Unidos

Noriko Aikawa
directora
Unidad de Patrimonio Cultural Intangible
División de Patrimonio Cultural
UNESCO

Robyne Bancroft
Universidad Nacional Australiana
Canberra
Australia

Tressa Berman
Universidad Occidental del Estado de Arizona
Phoenix, Arizona
Estados Unidos

Janet Blake
Facultad de Derecho
Universidad de Glasgow
Glasgow, Escocia
Reino Unido

Stepanida Borisova
Ministerio de Cultura
República de Sakha (Yakutia)
Yakutsk
Federación Rusa

Mounir Bouchenaki
director
División de Patrimonio Cultural y Centro de Patrimonio Mundial
UNESCO

Manuela Carneiro da Cunha
Profesora de Antropología
Universidad de Chicago
Chicago, Illinois
Estados Unidos

Russell Collier
Equipo de Análisis de Parte aguas Estratégicos
Nación Gitxsan
Hazelton, Columbia Británica
Canadá

Rachid El Houda
arquitecto, DPLG
Marrakech
Marruecos

Mahaman Garba
etnomusicólogo
Centro de Formación y Fomento Musical
Niamey
Níger

Jean Guibal
director
Musée Dauphinois
Grenoble
Francia

Mihály Hoppál
director
Centro Europeo para la Cultura Tradicional
Budapest
Hungría

Florentino H. Hornedo
Facultad de Artes y Ciencias

Universidad Ateneo de Manila
Ciudad Quezón, Manila
Filipinas

Peter Jaszi
Colegio de Derecho de Washington
Washington, DC
Estados Unidos

Pualani Kanaka'ole Kanahele
Fundación Edith Kanaka'ole
Hilo, Hawai
Estados Unidos

Junzo Kawada
profesor de antropología cultural
Universidad de la Ciudad de Hiroshima
Hiroshima
Japón

Heikki Kirkinen
vicepresidente
Academia Europea de Artes, Ciencias y Humanidades
Universidad de Joensuu
Joensuu
Finlandia

Grace Koch
administradora de archivos
Instituto Australiano de Estudios Aborígenes y de los Isleños del Estrecho de Torres
Canberra
Australia

Namankoumba Kouyaté
Chargé d'Affaires A.I.
Embajada de la República de Guinea
Bonn
Alemania

Kurshida Mambetova
jefe del Departamento de Cultura
Comisión Nacional de la República de Uzbekistán, UNESCO
Tashkent
Uzbekistán

Renato Matusse
secretario permanente y secretario general

Comunidad Sudafricana de Desarrollo (SADC)
Maputo
Mozambique

J.H. Kwabena Nketia
director
Centro Internacinoal de Música y Danza Africana
Universidad de Ghana
Legon, Accra
Ghana

Mamiko Ogawa
Departamento de Asuntos Culturales
Ministerio de Relaciones Exteriores
Tokio
Japón

Vlasta Ondrusova
vicedirectora
Instituto de Cultura Popular
Strá nice
República Checa

Lyndel Prott
jefe, Sección de Normas Internacionales
División de Patrimonio Cultural
UNESCO

Kamal Puri
profesor de derecho
Universidad de Queensland
Brisbane, Queensland
Australia

Miguel Puwainchir
alcalde
Municipio de Huamboya
Provinicia de Morona Santiago (Amazonía)
Ecuador

Ralph Regenvanu
curador
Centro Cultural de Vanuatu
Puerto Vila
Vanuatu

Gail Saunders
directora

Departamento de Archivos
Nassau
Bahamas

Rajeev Sethi
socio principal, Rajeev Sethi Scenographers, Pvt. Ltd.
Nueva Delhi
India

Mohsen Shaalan
El Cairo
Egipto

Samanta Sherkin
consultora
Unidad de Patrimonio Cultural Intangible
División de Patrimonio Cultural
UNESCO

Juana Silvera Núñez
presidenta
Comisión Nacional Cubana de la UNESCO
La Habana
Cuba

Brad Simon
director de Asuntos Jurídicos y Comerciales
Shockwave.com

Preston Thomas
comisionado
Comisión de Aborígenes e Isleños del Estrecho de Torres
Phillip
Australia

Sivia Tora
secretaria permanente
Ministerio de la Mujer, Cultura y Bienestar Social
Suva
Fiji

Asamu Yamaguti
profesor de musicología
Universidad de Osaka
Osaka
Japón

Zulma Yugar
Directora General de Promoción Cultural
Viceministerio de Cultura
La Paz
Bolivia

Observadores

Mary Jo Arnoldi, Institución Smithsoniana
Alberta Arthurs, Fundación Rockefeller
Barry Bergey, Fondo Nacional de Bellas Artes
Francine Berkowitz, Institución Smithsoniana
Gigi Bradford, Centro de las Artes y la Cultura, Washington, DC
Rachelle Browne, Institución Smithsoniana
Peggy Bulger, Centro de Vida Folclórica Americana, Biblioteca del Congreso
Olivia Cadaval, Institución Smithsoniana
Shelton Davis, Banco Mundial
Kreszentia Duer, Banco Mundial
Alexander P. Durtka, Jr., Comisión Cultural CIOFF, Instituto Internacional de Wisconsin
William Ferris, Fondo Nacional de las Humanidades
Arlene Fleming, Banco Mundial
Cecile Goli, UNESCO
Charlotte Heth, Institución Smithsoniana
Vera Hayatt, Institución Smithsoniana
David Hunter, Centro para el Derecho Ambiental Internacional, Washington, DC
Enrique Iglesias, Banco Interamericano de Desarrollo, Washington, DC
Alan Jabbour, Centro de Vida Folclórica Americana, Biblioteca del Congreso
Charles Kleymeyer, Fundación Interamericana
Mary Ellen Lane, Consejo Independiente de Investigación Americana en el Exterior
Brian LeMay, Institución Smithsoniana
Ellen McCulloch-Lovell, Comisión del Milenio de la Casa Blanca
William Merrill, Institución Smithsoniana
Francis Method, UNESCO
Diana Baird N'Diaye, Institución Smithsoniana
Virgil Stefan Nitulescu, Cámara de Diputados, Bucarest, Rumania
Pennie Ojeda, Fondo Nacional de Bellas Artes
Marc Pachter, Institución Smithsoniana
Damien Pwono, Fundación Ford
Caroline Ramsey, The Crafts Center, Washington, DC
Alison Dundes Rentein, Universidad del Sur de California
John Roberts, Universidad del Estado de Ohio
Jean Roche, Delegada Permanente del Consejo Internacionales de Organizaciones de Festivales Folclóricos y de las Artes Tradicionales (CIOFF), Gannat, Francia
Daniel Salcedo, PEOPLink, Kensington, Maryland
David Sanjek, Arhivos BMI, Nueva York, Nueva York
Dan Sheehy, Fondo Nacional de Bellas Artes
Claire Brett Smith, Aid to Artisans, Inc., Farmington, Connecticut
Ann Webster Smith, ICOMOS

D.A. Sonneborn, Institución Smithsoniana
John Kuo Wei Tchen, Universidad de Nueva York
Glenn Wallach, Centro de las Artes y la Cultura
Glenn M. Wiser, Centro para el Derecho Ambiental Internacional
Joe Wilson, Consejo Nacional de las Artes Tradicionales
Tomas Ybarra-Frausto, Fundación Rockefeller

Personal de la Institución Smithsoniana

James Early
John Franklin
Amy Horowitz
Anthony Seeger
Peter Seitel

Asociados e Internos

María Elena Cepeda, Ann Arbor, Michigan
Lisa Maiorino, Indianápolis, Indiana
Anthony McCann, Warrenpoint, Condado de Down, Irlanda del Norte
Jonathan McCollum, Allston, Massachusetts
Chad Redwing, Phoenix, Arizona

Apéndice 4: Informe del Grupo I

El lunes 28 de junio de 1999, de las 1545 a las 1730, se integró la primera reunión del Grupo 1, para tratar los siguientes temas: el patrimonio cultural intangible en relación con el patrimonio cultural natural y tangible, y su papel en la solución de problemas locales y nacionales relativos a los grandes temas de la actualidad, tales como identidad cultural, asuntos de género, desarrollo humano sustentable, globalización, coexistencia pacífica de grupos étnicos, prevención de conflictos, culturas juveniles, evolución de tecnología nueva en comunicaciones e información, deterioro del medio ambiente, etc.

El presidente, Ralph Regenvanu, pidió que se presentaran los participantes, después de esto Rajeev Sethi hizo averiguaciones sobre el estado actual de la Recomendación de 1989, particularmente en su conceptualización de la problemática que aborda. Cuestionó si los términos "folclor" y "tradición" quizá no pasan por alto la idea y la posibilidad de innovación. Presentó algunas sugerencias para cambiar la redacción de la Recomendación de 1989, en su sección A, definición de folclor: "Imitación" debería cambiarse por "emulación"; "juegos" debería cambiarse por "deporte", que abarca más; "artesanías", "arquitectura", realmente no queremos decir "hábitat"? preguntó; "otras artes" daba la impresión de categoría residual, no lo suficientemente específica.

En cuanto a la sección C, conservación del folclor, el señor Sethi sugirió que deberíamos hablar primero de proteger a las personas, y luego los archivos. La cultura es viva, pero depende de las personas, a las que debemos potenciar. El lenguaje de la Recomendación de 1989 parece condescendiente.

Pualani Kanahele observó que muchas poblaciones basan importantes elementos de sus identidades culturales en sus ambientes naturales, ligando así, inextricablemente, los patrimonios cultural y natural. ¿Qué haremos dentro de veinte años — preguntó — cuando nuestro medio ambiente esté terriblemente degradado [por el desarrollo comercial]?

Andy Abeita expresó la preocupación de que los practicantes de la cultura tradicional no pueden colocar la religión y el arte en la misma categoría que las mercancías; al mismo tiempo, sin embargo, se tienen que formular instrumentos jurídicos parecidos para proteger la posibilidad de que los practicantes sigan dedicados a sus prácticas creativas. Los derechos de propiedad de la música y las oraciones están amparados por las leyes de derechos de autor y, por tanto, se pueden hacer cumplir. A menos que se cuente con protección jurídica inteligible para el sector privado, podríamos perdernos en discusiones interminables e infructíferas tratando de llegar a un acuerdo``.

En materia de artesanías, respondió Rajeev Sethi, la experiencia enseña que la comercialización siempre responde a las necesidades de los artistas. Consideró que debemos ayudarle a los artesanos a entender el significado de un nuevo diseño, sin menosprecio de su propia cultura. En sí misma, la innovación no es necesariamente mala.

Pualani Kanahele expresó su agrado por un comentario anterior de Sivia Tora, en la misma reunión, sobre la imposibilidad de separar la cultura tangible de la intangible, o de distinguir entre patrimonio cultural y patrimonio natural del medio ambiente. Aclaró lo que quería decir con deterioro ambiental, dando el ejemplo de los grandes hoteles internacionales que se construyen sobre el coral, material creado por el pólipo marino del mismo nombre, esencia misma de las islas y figura central de sus cánticos poéticos sobre la creación.

Rajeev Sethi respondió que no creía que exista respuesta para esa clase de problema, al menos en la UNESCO. En la India hay una gran cantidad de tribus desplazadas en aras del desarrollo. Esto no tiene respuesta; ¿a quién acudir?

Miguel Puwainchir respondió citando el dicho de que "una persona sin tierra es una persona sin cultura". Si la UNESCO no puede cambiar nada, declaró al grupo, entonces debemos cambiar la UNESCO. Antes de la conquista española, dijo, teníamos una cultura pura. Ahora hay mucha confusión, y la cultura se ha contaminado. Debemos promover y defender nuestra cultura, sino nuestra cultura se irá muriendo y lo habremos aceptado. Pero no debemos aislarnos. En Bolivia, por ejemplo, la planta de la coca se ha usado con fines medicinales benignos. Otros, sin embargo, la han convertido en una droga maligna. ¿Qué hacer ahora? Debemos aceptar los valores positivos y descartar los negativos.

La Recomendación de 1989 describe la cultura, en esencia, como "cosas" — continuó — pero la cultura también son los seres humanos. ¿Por qué separar las dos cosas? Necesitamos intercambiar experiencias; eso es saludable. Muchos de los problemas tratados tienen que ver con el enajenamiento. Pero debemos recordar que la cultura es nuestra naturaleza misma.

Mahaman Garba se preguntó si la interrelación entre religión y conservación debería considerarse un tema prohibido. En su país, observó, el patrimonio intangible es la música. Algunos hablan de "patrimonio cultural, otros, de "folclor". Debemos usar la expresión anterior, que es un término más noble.

Tenemos que escoger, prosiguió. ¿Vamos a desarrollarnos, o quedarnos donde estamos? La evolución trae sus taras. A los pueblos del Tercer Mundo les gusta la televisión. ¿Qué había antes de eso? ¿Canciones, juegos? ¿Debemos rechazar la televisión? Las canciones y los juegos pueden dar educación, pero los artistas también se pueden expresar por radio y televisión. Sino el acceso a esos artistas requeriría viajar miles de kilómetros.

Pualani Kanahele resumió, en parte, la sesión diciendo que se había hablado de coexistencia y prevención de conflictos. También debemos aprender a llevarnos bien con el desarrollo. Sí, dijo, debemos reconocer el desarrollo, pero el desarrollo también debe reconocernos a nosotros. Debemos considerar también los símbolos y entresacar de todo esto lo positivo y lo negativo.

Martes, 29 de junio de 1999, segunda reunión del Grupo 1, de 0930 a 1200

Robyne Bancroft habló en su ponencia [este volumen, 70–74] sobre la necesidad de aplicar un enfoque integrado a la comprensión de la cultura aborigen australiana, que consiste en una densa red de relaciones entre seres humanos y su medio ambiente. Su historia tiene 60,000 años de antigüedad, pero pasa desapercibida en gran medida. En tiempos de la colonización había más de 250 grupos lingüísticos; en la actualidad sólo quedan 25 idiomas activos. Existen actualmente 325,000 aborígenes australianos, de una población total de 18 millones. Han sobrevivido y en tiempos recientes se han proyectado a la palestra internacional. Los tribunales han vertido dictámenes importantes sobre cuestiones tan vitales como el derecho a la tierra y se ha comenzado a tratar el tema de la "generación perdida" (familias separadas por medidas del gobierno). A pesar de algunas leyes y dictámenes positivos aún hay una gran necesidad de lograr justicia.

Los aborígenes no favorecen términos como "folclor" y "mitología", ya que éstos tienen connotaciones negativas en Australia. Bancroft sugiere en cambio "patrimonio cultural indígena". Entre los temas de actualidad e importancia para los pueblos aborígenes están los de género, un código de ética para el trato entre pueblos indígenas y no indígenas, y la repatriación de restos humanos en el exterior. Hizo algunas recomendaciones: La Recomendación de 1989 carece de eficacia. Para remediarlo debería convertirse en una convención de la UNESCO. Se debe reconocer formalmente la importancia de la diversidad biológica; instituciones tales como UNESCO y la Institución Smithsoniana debieran apoyar a las poblaciones indígenas en la lucha por sus derechos; debiera haber más capacitación y fomento vocacional controlados por poblaciones indígenas.

Mihály Hoppál habló en su ponencia [este volumen, 182–184] sobre la actual sociedad informática, en la que existe un crecimiento económico sin límites, pero muy poca tradición o conocimiento local de importancia. Hay una abundancia de conocimientos tradicionales sobre las incontables formas en que la gente ha aprendido a vivir en sociedad. Ello incluye tradiciones espirituales. Los sistemas de valores locales pueden servir de base para la solución de conflictos. La causa de tales conflictos no son los sistemas mismos, sino la falta de conocimiento sobre los ajenos. Los sistemas de valores locales, tales como los prejuicios, forman el trasfondo emocional en que las poblaciones traban conflictos entre sí. La globalización puede ser una amenaza a las culturas indígenas y disfrazar nuevas formas de imperialismo. Esto puede redundar en la negación de los derechos colectivos locales y amenazar a las minorías. Debe adoptarse una legislación que garantice el respeto y la protección de los derechos humanos y la identidad cultural de las minorías. Los sistemas de valores del molde anglosajón podrían no ser los indicados para toda la gente. Hoppál recomendó elaborar estrategias para enseñarle a los jóvenes a respetar las tradiciones de otras naciones; festivales que celebren la diversidad de cada nación; documentación y preservación de tradiciones; trato respetuoso de los patrimonios culturales en los estados miembros, en el sentido de adoptar leyes que obliguen al respeto de dichas culturas locales; honrar cada quien las tradiciones de los demás para que podamos vivir más largo tiempo en esta tierra.

Miguel Puwainchir presentó una ponencia [este volumen, 65–66] sobre lo que él llamó "interculturalidad", es decir, el respeto y conocimiento de culturas ajenas a la propia.

Vivimos con una mezcla compleja de gentes. El establecimiento de Estados y Naciones creó culturas e identidades nacionales que desconocen las tradiciones locales. En Ecuador las culturas indígenas se han unido para cambiar las leyes y crear un "lugar de respeto" a los pueblos indígenas, que les ha permitido resistirse a la asimilación. En el futuro debe haber naciones sin culturas de estado, ya que éstas inevitablemente convierten las culturas locales en "folclor". Deben desarrollarse programas nacionales de educación que enseñen sobre diferentes culturas, para que eso haga parte de la enseñanza en general, y no sólo para antropólogos y museos. La interculturalidad nos ayudará también a evitar la globalización de la cultura, a mantener la diversidad cultural y a defendernos del desarrollo sin control que destruye nuestro ambiente. Puwainchir recomendó los estados que no tengan una cultura única; las culturas locales no se deben ni comercializar ni erigir en monumentos sino conservarse y promoverse como culturas vivas; es importante conocer de otras culturas sin perder la autenticidad de la propia; la UNESCO debe promover nuevas formas de ver la cultura, celebrar la diversidad del mundo y no dejar que la tecnología moderna destruya las culturas locales.

Mihály Hoppál comentó que la falta de comprensión entre grupos culturales nace del desconocimiento de la historia y cultura de la otra parte. En Europa oriental, observó, los mitos históricos suelen usarse con fines políticos modernos, tales como la guerra.

Pualani Kanahele respondió a la ponencia diciendo que el globalización es otra forma de colonialismo que socava las tradiciones locales, especialmente entre los jóvenes. Por ello es vital incluir a los jóvenes en más rituales y ceremonias, o sino esas tradiciones sucumbirán ante la globalización. Educar culturalmente a los extranjeros sería un buen punto de partida, aunque difícil, dado el arraigo de sus prejuicios y su resistencia al aprendizaje de las culturas indígenas. Los términos "mito" y "folclor" son problemáticos, por las razones que da Miguel Puwainchir, y deben cambiarse.

Russell Collier respondió que la terminología que se emplee realmente no importa tanto en la continuidad de las luchas que se libran o están por librarse contra los gobiernos u otras fuerzas que amenazan las culturas indígenas.

El doctor Mahaman Garba describió en su ponencia [este volumen, 194–202] el caso experimental de un proyecto de la UNESCO, un centro de educación musical (Centre de Formation et de Promotion Musicale) en Níger. Comenzó con una breve descripción de los ocho grupos lingüísticos y étnicos de Níger. En ese país existe un sistema de castas que nombra a los que han de transmitir la tradición oral y los que van a ser músicos. Cuando muere una de estas personas, es como si se hubiera incendiado una biblioteca. Ha habido muchas pérdidas humanas irreemplazables y también se están perdiendo las tradiciones y la música que encarnaban. Este problema, con su correspondiente solución, se llevó a la UNESCO, que ayudó a iniciar el centro de educación musical. La labor de conservación de las tradiciones musicales avanza ahora con la ayuda de UNESCO y otras fuentes de financiamiento, especialmente del Japón. El doctor Garba agradeció específicamente a la señora Aikawa y al profesor Kawada por sus esfuerzos en pro del centro.

El doctor Garba describió los tres ámbitos de operaciones del centro: investigación, capacitación y fomento. También están dirimiendo la cuestión de la propiedad europea de la música y los instrumentos musicales, dijo, con miras a repatriar este patrimonio musical. Las fuentes de financiamiento, observó Garba, se están haciendo cada vez menos y no se ha permitido al centro aplicar la ayuda económica para su máximo provecho, como lo deseaba el personal del centro. En las decisiones de asignación de recursos, recomendó, debe darse participación adecuada a los expertos locales en proyectos de desarrollo cultural.

Rachid El-Houda presentó una ponencia [este volumen, 216–217] sobre la plaza Jemaa

El Fna en Marrakech, un hito de patrimonio mundial, para explorar un tipo de puente entre cultura tangible e intangible. Dio un breve esbozo de esta zona urbana y su valor cultural. Muchos escritores, actores y dramaturgos se han interesado profesionalmente en esta plaza. Los urbanistas han tratado de imitar sus cualidades espaciales y culturales en otras partes del mundo. Se trata de un lugar en el que se realizan cotidianamente muchas formas de narración pública de cuentos. Ahora la plaza está asediada por el desarrollo comercial agresivo. Su espacio urbano es de gran valor comercial y por tanto es blanco de desarrollo comercial. El valor de su rica cultura oral no da cuenta ni compite bien contra su valor monetario. Es fácil desterrar y desplazar las tradiciones representativas en aras del desarrollo comercial, pero sería prácticamente imposible recrear la rica cultura oral que medra en espacios como este. La siguiente dificultad que se enfrentaría sería la pérdida de tan rico tesoro humano, tan difícil de reemplazar una vez desplazado. Fue creada una organización no gubernamental para ayudar a conservar la zona, con sus tradiciones. Hay que agradecer inmensamente a la señora Aikawa y a la UNESCO por su ayuda en esto. Las metas y objetivos de esta ONG son: garantizar la integridad física y la continuidad de la plaza; consignar y documentar su historia y la narrativa que aquí se practica; proteger los vecindarios aledaños; establecer lazos con grupos de persuasión similar en Marruecos y en el exterior; recabar fondos para dar pensiones a cuentistas ancianos y otros representantes que han abandonado su arte por la edad; redactar y divulgar las publicaciones correspondientes; fomentar interés y ofrecer capacitación en las artesanías tradicionales y la narración de cuentos entre los jóvenes; combatir los prejuicios y estereotipos negativos de la población local contra la plaza y sus habitantes, inspirando orgullo popular en la plaza y lo que ella representa.

Junzo Kawada hizo una presentación [este volumen, 175–177] sobre los incentivos sociales que animan a los practicantes a seguir en sus tradiciones. Comenzó observando que la globalización, junto con otras fuerzas económicas, da pie a la conformidad cultural cuando, alterando el sistema de recompensas socioeconómicas, desalienta la transmisión de cultura a las nuevas generaciones. Ya que la conservación de patrimonio cultural no arroja ganancias en el sentido socioeconómico, especialmente en las comunidades minoritarias, es difícil hallar sucesores que perpetúen las tradiciones, por lo cual están en peligro muchas artesanías. El profesor Kawada consideró las formas en que las diferentes tradiciones enfrentan este problema, y los tipos de ayuda más adecuados a cada una. El turismo puede tener un efecto positivo al conservar la cultura y fomentar una mayor conciencia multicultural entre extranjeros y pobladores locales. Los ingresos derivados del turismo motivan a los residentes a seguir practicando y representando las artes tradicionales.

El conservar la tradición arroja muchos beneficios sociales. La fabricación de artesanías tradicionales ayuda a conservar el medio ambiente mediante el uso de materiales naturales. La revitalización del patrimonio cultural también potencia a la población femenina, ya que la mujer tiene un papel importante qué jugar en la conservación y transmisión de la cultura.

A la luz de todo ello el profesor Kawada recomendó: dar incentivos económicos a los practicantes del patrimonio cultural en gran escala; cuidarse del conformismo cultural causado por la globalización; alentar la cooperación entre grupos tradicionales, gobiernos y ONG para mantener las representaciones culturales sin fines de lucro y la capacitación de aprendices en la narrativa tradicional; y ofrecer capacitación en la documentación y el registro de dicha narrativa.

Stepanida Borisova describió en su ponencia [este volumen, 245–247] la condición vigente en la protección de la cultura tradicional en la República de Sakha (Yakutia) en

Siberia central. Hasta 1991 las tradiciones orales se documentaban, codificaban y revisaban según conviniera a las iniciativas del estado. Ahora hay un resurgimiento de la cultura tradicional, que abarca la introducción del idioma y la cultura en las escuelas, y la proclamación de días feriados en fechas de importancia cultural. La protección de la cultura depende de que se la exhiba públicamente. Se requiere un proyecto de la UNESCO para registrar y ayudar a salvaguardar las tradiciones culturales, incluidas las que tienen que ver con el shamanismo y los lugares sagrados.

Ralph Regenvanu dio un informe sobre la condición de la cultura tradicional en Vanuatu, nación isleña del Pacífico, que ha experimentado la colonización, una gran despoblación, la independencia política y el retorno de la tierra a sus propietarios originales. Tras su independencia, Vanuatu quería buscar el desarrollo en modalidades no occidentales, basándose en tradiciones indígenas. Ahora hay una tendencia a la "recolonización", un regreso al molde europeo. La tradición de Vanuatu es totalmente oral y, por consiguiente, el énfasis programático del Centro Cultural de Vanuatu es conservarla mediante la documentación, la ayuda a las comunidades y la capacitación de individuos en los métodos de registro y documentación de tradiciones y la conservación de materiales de archivo para protegerlos del clima. Se tiene propiedad de ciertos materiales de archivo con acceso limitado, práctica que establece la fe pública necesaria para consignar y almacenar las tradiciones orales de un linaje. Sin embargo, la estrategia económica nacional milita en contra de los esfuerzos del Centro Cultural. El centro documenta los hechos y sitios tradicionales para protegerlos y trata de evaluar la eficacia de ciertas prácticas tradicionales, tales como los métodos de conservación de peces y otros recursos, documentándolos para presentarlos a otros grupos que deseen ayuda para restablecer sus tradiciones.

Martes, 29 de junio, tercera reunión del Grupo 1, de 1330 a 1700

Ralph Regenvanu, tras describir una ceremonia al dios de la cosecha de ñame y los temas de la comunidad suscitados por un proyecto de cultura femenina que lo documentó, afirmó que el problema principal de la cultura tradicional se ubica en el plano de las relaciones económicas globales. El problema es que Vanuatu aspira — o lo están forzando — a integrarse a la OMC (Organización Mundial del Comercio). Para hacerlo, Vanuatu tendría que abrir sus industrias pesquera y maderera a compañías extranjeras y renunciar al derecho de restringir la pesca o controlar la exportación de madera. Además, para pagar la deuda nacional, Vanuatu se verá forzado a exportar y pagar en divisas extranjeras. Eso no conviene a las comunidades locales. Dijo que el gobierno se siente impotente y pidió a la UNESCO ayudar a combatir esta modernización forzada causada por la OMC, que no reconoce la importancia de las comunidades locales y sus prácticas culturales.

Rajeev Sethi respondió reflexionando sobre la relación entre UNESCO y la OMC.

Andy Abeita respondió que no existen lazos directos, sino más bien un intercambio en temas y pautas. Ambas son organizaciones de afiliados y, al igual que cualquier burocracia, tratan de complacer a todas las partes. Tenemos que realizar una evaluación de las necesidades de nuestros representados, dijo. Las voces son escuchadas en proporción a su cuantía. Se requiere

más información estadística de estas comunidades locales.

Noriko Aikawa sugirió recomendar que la UNESCO colabore más estrechamente con la OMC.

Ralph Regenvanu reiteró la necesidad de involucrar a la UNESCO. Vanuatu, por ejemplo, requiere recursos para la documentación.

Noriko Aikawa señaló que compete a los gobiernos de los estados miembros decidir qué hacer, pero se puede organizar un seminario para considerar estas contradicciones.

Ralph Regenvanu respondió que el problema es justamente que el gobierno no puede hacer tal solicitud; le están forzando a conseguir divisas extranjeras.

Russell Collier observó que su pueblo no puede depender de que el gobierno canadiense le proteja sus intereses. No hay esperanza de que el Canadá jamás los defienda.

Luego presentó su ponencia Andy Abeita [este volumen, 75–82]. La Ley Nacional de Artes y Artesanías Indígenas contempla el problema de productos hechos por personas que no son indígenas, que se venden ilegalmente como bienes de origen indígena americano. La ley tipifica esta práctica como delito federal y da leyes de aduana para combatirlo. El grupo de Abeita, la Asociación de Artes y Artesanías Indígenas, impulsa la adopción de medidas estatales similares a la política federal, explicó. También están elaborando ahora leyes de derechos de autor para registrarlas con la UCC, para proteger contra la posibilidad de que otros copien las marcas de autenticidad. Sería de gran ayuda para las artesanías tradicionales de todo el mundo si hubiese una codificación en el mercado mundial, que separe los bienes hechos a mano de los producidos comercialmente. La OMC tiene bajo consideración una ley semejante.

Rajeev Sethi se preguntaba qué podría hacer tal ley si él, como natural de la India, quisiera vender una pulsera de fabricación barata en Italia. ¿Y qué sería del diseño? Cualquiera puede cambiar ligeramente un diseño para evadir las leyes de propiedad intelectual.

En lo que atañe al tema de los derechos de autor, comentó Rachid El Houda, puede aprenderse mucho de los derechos de autor en programática y tecnología de información. Tenemos que averiguar lo que ocurre en otras partes del mundo, pero al mismo tiempo mantener un equilibrio. Las ideas, sin embargo, son universales, y pertenecen a la humanidad entera, no a un solo individuo, aunque el concepto inicial nazca de un individuo. Las ideas que se convierten en conceptos mayores, sin embargo, pasan a formar parte de la cultura de la humanidad.

Andy Abeita afirmó que sólo los miembros de las comunidades tienen las respuestas. Tenemos que tratar las cosas en un plano más personal, menos social o puramente académico.

Mahaman Garba dijo en su ponencia [este volumen, 194–202] que su nación del noroeste de la Columbia Británica ha ocupado ese territorio por 10,000 años. Su historia oral se remonta a la anterior glaciación; miembros de su nación han trabajado con arqueólogos sobre este tema lingüístico. Ellos consideran que su propio idioma es el "verdadero idioma", en el que el individuo puede pensar y decir las cosas de modo muy distinto a como se dirían en inglés. Su identidad, además, está ligada a su tierra, que ocupan desde California hasta Alaska.

Las historias orales han sido muy importantes en las negociaciones para dirimir pleitos por tierras. Esta documentación, más los datos genealógicos completos, constituían toda la documentación legal compilada para los reclamos de títulos de bienes raíces, algunos de los cuales se han presentado repetidamente por veinte años. Las historias orales se confirman como bases válidas para defender y reclamar títulos sobre la tierra. Muchos otros indígenas están contemplando estas decisiones para robustecer sus propios reclamos. La idea se está difundiendo. Esta colección de información no tiene parangón: no sólo en materia de folclor, sino de pautas meteorológicas, de vida silvestre, de pesca. Todo parte de la documentación.

Robyne Bancroft preguntó sobre el acceso a la documentación. Dijo que el gobierno australiano cataloga cierta información como demasiado delicada para conocerla su gente.

Russell Collier respondió que el material es de ellos; el gobierno no tiene nada qué ver.

Pualani Kanahele introdujo su ponencia [este volumen, 67–69] diciendo que la tenía asombrada tal apasionamiento por la tradición. Habló de las tradiciones y la historia de Hawai. Las genealogías narran la relación de sus antepasados con los elementos. Los nombres mismos dan toda la información: qué labores fungían los ancestros, sus especialidades, sus parentescos con los jefes, etc. Realmente no se ha perdido nada si uno busca con suficiente ahínco, dijo, pero estas cosas no se encuentran en los libros de historia.

En la última parte del siglo XIX la historia se compiló, se tradujo, y por fin se consignó en los libros. A la vuelta del siglo XX la cultura sucumbió ante los Estados Unidos. La cultura hawaiana pasó a ser considerada entretenimiento. De los años cuarenta a los sesenta, de este siglo, se reconoció la educación como elemento central de la existencia en Hawai. Todo el mundo tenía que ir a la universidad. Pero algunos se apegaron tercamente a las tradiciones.

Tristemente, dijo, muchos hawaianos educados no conocen su propia cultura. La educación es poder, pero la cultura es alma, pasión. Ahora la cultura hawaiana se ha agregado a los pénsum universitarios. La educación les ha enseñado a librar sus batallas. La pasión les ha enseñado a luchar por sus corazones. La arqueología les ayuda, pero no les interpreta la cultura. Para avanzar, han vuelto la vista al pasado. Por eso, dijo, el futuro es halagüeño.

Apéndice 5: Informe del Grupo II
Protección legal del patrimonio cultural intangible local y nacional

En la primera sesión el grupo decidió que en la siguiente cada persona hiciera una presentación de cinco minutos, basada en una de las ponencias presentadas o en su área específica de interés en el campo de la protección legal del patrimonio cultural intangible local y nacional. Después de cada exposición se permitirían dos minutos de recapitulación o breve conversación.

El comité decidió no hacer una revaluación crítica exhaustiva del documento de UNESCO de 1989, sino producir enfoques creativos para la conservación del patrimonio cultural, para luego considerarlos en relación con el documento de la UNESCO y con otras prácticas en distintos lugares del mundo. La conferencia sería una oportunidad para un nuevo discurso creativo y sustantivo.

Se suscitaron cinco temas amplios para su consideración:

1. *Marcos conceptuales,* que incluye la terminología empleada para describir la cultura tradicional, los supuestos que se hacen cuando se habla de cultura tradicional y su conservación, la relación entre poder político y conservación de la cultura, cultura tangible versus intangible, y el tema de quiénes son los autores, los creadores de la cultura. También se examinarían temas como el de la comercialización y objetivación de la cultura;

2. *Disposiciones y mecanismos legales,* que incluye la discusión de: qué es lo que se debe proteger; cómo se puede procurar un fundamento jurídico para la conservación en los planos internacional, nacional y local; aspectos positivos y negativos de ciertos mecanismos jurídicos; y un repaso de la situación legal actual en lo relativo a cultura tradicional y la protección de la misma;

3. *Sanciones extrajudiciales y derecho consuetudinario,* que incluye soluciones de comunidad, no jurídicas, para perpetuar y proteger la cultura tradicional;

4. *Cuestiones de derechos,* que incluye la discusión de autoría, plagio y conceptos de propiedad, derechos de autor, patentes, derechos de propiedad intelectual y la factibilidad de mecanismos legales de alcance global. En general: ¿Qué derechos tiene la gente, y cómo

se van a defender? ¿Cuáles son las amenazas a estos derechos? ¿Qué instancias son idóneas para proteger las culturas tradicionales?

5. *Dominio público,* que considera cuestiones de confidencialidad y secreto y cómo se resuelven en los ámbitos de la cultura y la conservación. Se prestó atención especial al tema de lo sagrado.

En la segunda sesión, basada en el temario modificado, los participantes hicieron resúmenes de cinco minutos de sus ponencias escritas. Estos consistieron de repasos a problemas legales, incluidas sinopsis de diversos enfoques jurídicos, tales como la variedad de enfoques de derechos de propiedad intelectual (marcas registradas, patentes, secreto comercial y mecanismos de derechos de autor) para suplir las necesidades de los pueblos y comunidades indígenas y su folclor. A la luz de lo anterior se hicieron dos recomendaciones:

- Reconocer, como medidas razonables, restricciones culturales tales como disposiciones de contratos "silenciosos", que pueden tener paralelo en los códigos comerciales uniformes (ley de garantías, por ejemplo)
- Crear un organismo que tenga una función canalizadora, no en poder de los gobiernos, sino de los portadores de la tradición, como por ejemplo las organizaciones de derechos colectivos

En otros resúmenes aparecieron temas como secreto de dominio público. Hubo declaraciones sumarias de preocupaciones regionales y nacionales, tales como las labores de la ATSIC, en Australia, por combatir la violación de derechos de autores de artistas aborígenes.

Las siguientes discusiones emanaron de los resúmenes presentados y contribuyeron a las recomendaciones expresadas en el Plan de Acción. Se identificaron temas de discusión que corresponden a puntos del temario, para poder concluir sistemáticamente con recomendaciones informadas por las discusiones detalladas de los temas bajo consideración.

Surgieron temas afines relativos a los idiomas vivos y los programas educativos encaminados a mantener vigente la cultura tradicional. Los niveles de protección, tales como el acceso a los santuarios religiosos y la conservación y reparación de objetos sagrados, condujeron a una inquietud más amplia: ¿qué es lo que las comunidades buscan proteger? Surgió así el siguiente objetivo: adecuar la clase de protección a las necesidades que tienen las comunidades.

Temas subyacentes a la discusión tenían que ver con la relación entre medios legales, o jurídicos, y medios no jurídicos, y el problema del consenso ante las amenazas al conocimiento tradicional y las prácticas culturales. Estas se reconocieron como relaciones de poder insertadas en las relaciones sociales de la sociedad en general. Por tanto, el problema del papel que debe jugar el gobierno se presentó como una preocupación central en la formulación de recomendaciones de protección a nivel del estado.

Las discusiones de la tercera sesión comenzaron con los comentarios de la doctora da Cunha, en el sentido de que el término "folclor" resulta problemático, sujeto a mucho debate, especialmente en medios antropológicos. Se remitió al anterior comentario de Preston Thomas, de que el término tiene connotaciones peyorativas para con los grupos indígenas y, además, conlleva un proceso de nacionalismo. El señor Puri también registró su oposición al término, explicando que a menudo se equipara el folclor con el dominio público y, por tanto, se entiende que quiere decir "de libre acceso al público". Sugirió usar en cambio el término "cultura tradicional y popular". El señor McCann señaló en el acto que "cultura popular" también puede referirse a productos culturales producidos en masa, tales como "Mickey Mouse", y también debiera evitarse. Se decidió por consenso que el término menos objetable es "cultura tradicional".

Las pláticas pasaron luego al asunto de "¿qué es lo que estamos protegiendo cuando hablamos de cultura tradicional?" Varios tenían en mente la misma pregunta. Comenzó así un diálogo para ponderar si fuera más prudente decidir primero qué es lo que el grupo desea proteger, o debatir primero cómo quiere protegerlo. En otras palabras, se debatió si debía considerarse primero los medios o los objetos de la protección jurídica.

La señorita Prott ofreció una lista de ejemplos específicos de fenómenos culturales protegidos como punto de partida para fijar la tipología. Hubo disensión, especialmente por parte del señor Puri, quien dudaba que los ejemplos específicos fuesen el mejor camino a seguir. Coincidió en ello el señor Sanjek , quien indicó que lo que de veras faltaba era conversar sobre temas del proceso de cómo se protege el patrimonio cultural local y nacional.

El señor Puri intervino para decir que lo que realmente está en juego no es qué proteger y guardar, sino que el grupo debía ocuparse más bien de la explotación del patrimonio cultural tradicional existente. Dijo que el grupo no debía hablar de protección para crear, sino proteger lo ya creado de la explotación. El señor Simon dijo que el pastiche, la reproducción, la autorización, la comercialización, etc., son temas que también debía abordar el documento final.

Se señaló entonces que la lista de temas legales podía dividirse en dos categorías:

- lo relativo al mantenimiento y revitalización de la cultura;
- lo relativo a la apropiación de conocimientos.

El señor Jaszi dio otro giro a la conversación preguntando si los derechos de propiedad intelectual y las leyes de derechos de autor pueden, en efecto, proteger el proceso de desarrollo creativo. El señor McCann indicó que esas leyes y esos derechos obedecen a imperativos económicos. Otro participante señaló que las patentes preventivas ayudan a proteger jurídicamente el proceso creativo.

El señor Puri expresó su opinión de que el documento creado por el grupo de trabajo debía tener fuerza y no diluirse. Otros respondieron que corrían el riesgo de ofender la soberanía de las naciones. La señorita Prott dijo que un documento más diplomático, aunque menos dramático, podría coadyuvar al cambio, en combinación con otros documentos, y ayudar a vencer el umbral colectivo para el cambio. Por varios minutos cundió un debate sobre el lenguaje fuerte o relativamente diplomático que debiera usar el grupo; muchos decían que el documento no debía ser ofensivo, pero otros insistían en que un documento audaz tendría el máximo efecto en potencia.

Luego la doctora da Cunha entró en la discusión del beneficio en potencia de abrir la cultura tradicional al dominio público, dando el caso de casas farmacéuticas (en Perú, por ejemplo), que celebran contratos privados, secretos, con grupos indígenas, deteniendo así la producción de conocimientos, destruyendo los mismísimos procesos que se supondría que esta acción ayuda a transmitir y alcanzar éxito económico. La doctora da Cunha dijo que una vez que el conocimiento tradicional se coloca en el ámbito público, puede establecerse prueba del arte anterior a ello, para poder iniciar el proceso de proteger los derechos comunitarios.

Los señores Sanjek, Simon y Puri, hicieron todos comentarios. El señor Sanjek advirtió que el dominio público se vuelve un tema escabroso en el ámbito internacional, y el señor Simon recordó al grupo que el arte anterior sólo se aplica a asuntos de patentes, y el dominio público no ofrece remuneración ni protección a los patrimonios culturales. El señor Puri expresó que para muchos, como él mismo, inclusive, dominio publico quiere decir libre uso para todos.

El señor Sanjek concluyó diciendo que el sistema de derechos de propiedad intelectual nunca verifica la veracidad de las declaraciones de autoría, y dio el ejemplo de la canción "¿Por qué se enamoran los tontos?", que está registrada a nombre de un reconocido plagiador. Sus comentarios apuntaron a la necesidad de un nivel estatal o nacional de vigilancia de los derechos de propiedad intelectual. Luego otro participante señaló que los comentarios de Sanjek no reflejan deficiencia alguna del régimen de derechos de propiedad inte-lectual, sino un caso de fraude que no manejó bien el sistema judicial.

Para concluir la sesión, se propuso el siguiente texto como inicio de la formación de un documento final que se presentó en la plenaria del día siguiente, y que se convirtió en una de las recomendaciones del Plan de Acción:

De conformidad con las obligaciones de los estados de proteger el derecho a la cultura en el Artículo 27 del Convenio Internacional de Derechos Civiles y Políticos, los estados deben dar un paso más y hacer lo siguiente: debe apoyarse a las comunidades para que sigan en sus procesos tradicionales de generación, transmisión, autorización y atribución de conocimientos y destrezas tradicionales, según los deseos de la comunidad y en acato de las actuales normas internacionales de derechos humanos.

Apéndice 6: Informe del Grupo III
Política local, nacional, regional e internacional, con referencia especial a la transmisión, revitalización y documentación del patrimonio cultural intangible

Antes de dar comienzo a la presentación de las respectivas ponencias, la sesión se dedicó a una extensa discusión de los diferentes modos de transmisión y estrategias para salvaguardar el folclor y la cultura tradicional. Varios países pusieron de relieve experiencias en sus respectivos modos de transmisión. Se destacaron los siguientes puntos:

1. La importancia de las tradiciones orales no radica sólo en su modo de transmisión sino, lo que es más importante, en su contenido, que encarna importantes conocimientos históricos, culturales y sociales;

2. La posibilidad de establecer "clubes patrimoniales", en que se traten temas de patrimonio cultural, en tanto una manera de fortalecer la transmisión de las tradiciones orales;

3. El patrimonio cultural intangible se describe, muchas veces, como en peligro sólo porque se transmite oralmente, pero podría haber algo en su contenido cultural que interrumpe el modo de transmisión;

4. Se hicieron sugerencias sobre cómo fortalecer el folclor y la cultura tradicional en los diferentes contextos contemporáneos;

5. Se sostuvo, de forma vehemente, la importancia de mantener acceso comunitario a los materiales después de que se hayan documentado oficialmente;

6. La improvisación juega un papel importante en la transmisión del folclor y la cultura tradicional;

7. Se habló del papel que puede jugar la transcripción documental en la transmisión;

8. Las cuestiones de autenticidad deben responderlas las comunidades tradicionales que crean y nutren las respectivas formas de expresión;

9. La transmisión necesariamente conlleva una interacción entre generaciones mayores y menores.

La primera ponencia [este volumen, 178–181] fue presentada por Osamu Yamaguti, sobre la música de la corte real de Vietnam. El orador exploró la relación entre Vietnam y las culturas circundantes (Corea, Japón y China) en cuanto afectan la música; la relación entre texto (música) y contexto (la propia corte real) y la necesidad de revitalizar la música tradicional de la corte.

La segunda ponencia [este volumen, 190–193] fue presentada por Gail Saunders. Ella destacó el papel de los archivos en el fomento y conservación del patrimonio cultural intangible en las Bahamas. Se hizo amplia mención de la participación de las Bahamas en el Festival Folclórico Smithsoniano de 1994. Después de ese festival se revivió el interés por revitalizar la cultura tradicional. En 1998 se aprobaron dos leyes para este fin, que entrarán en vigor el 1º de julio de 1999: una Ley de Antigüedades de Museo y una Ley de Derechos de Autor. Esta última protege los derechos de los originarios. La doctora Saunders afirmó que debe haber coordinación entre las entidades que administran los patrimonios culturales tangible e intangible, e instó a la UNESCO a seguir realizando reuniones regionales para la conservación y diseminación del folclor y las culturas tradicionales. Por último, recomendó, enfáticamente, que se considere al Caribe como una región aparte de América Latina.

La tercera ponencia [este volumen, 159–165] fue presentada por Grace Koch, quien habló sobre el papel de los materiales audiovisuales en la revitalización de las tradiciones locales. Tales materiales son utilizados, actualmente, por los aborígenes australianos y los isleños del Estrecho de Torres como evidencia en sus reclamos de tierras. Los rituales y la documentación audiovisual de la historia oral son particularmente importantes para presentar tales reclamos. La oradora señaló que al comienzo de la colonización blanca de Australia había 250 lenguas aborígenes. En la actualidad sólo se hablan activamente 25. La oradora recomendó una participación activa de las poblaciones indígenas en las técnicas de archivo y conservación, lo mismo que una capacitación en conciencia cultural para los que trabajan que cuidan y conservan el material cultural.

La cuarta ponencia fue presentada por Jean Guibal, quien reiteró que el lenguaje es la base de la cultura y, como tal, amerita atención especial. Guibal instó a apoyar la diversidad lingüística, y llamó al lenguaje la esencia de la cultura. Se concentró en el proceso de transmisión, en su diversidad y en lo difícil de transmitir la tradición oral en Francia debido a qe ya han desaparecido la mayoría de sus exponentes. También describió el papel de los archivos, ubicados en museos, en el proceso de transmisión. Por último, el orador afirmó que las medidas de protección del patrimonio cultural tienen que partir de bases institucionales para proteger las formas del patrimonio cultural intangible. Destacó que ello debe hacerse con la participación de las comunidades locales.

La quinta presentación correspondió a Heikki Kirkinen [este volumen, 234–244], quien habló sobre la revitalización de los idiomas y las culturas de Europa oriental y el asentamiento kareliano. Señaló que aunque estas comunidades ahora están en libertad de desarrollar su propia cultura, carecen de los medios de hacerlo. Esperan que la UNESCO pueda ayudar a rehabilitar y recrear su idioma y su cultura. Destacó lo importante que es el idioma para la identidad cultural.

La sexta ponencia fue presentada por Renato Matusse [este volumen, 185–189], quien hizo un vaticinio del papel de los bancos de datos en los países del sur de África, que pertenecen a la SADC. Explicó cómo las unidades regionales coordinan las unidades nacionales, que a su vez coordinan las locales. La información recabada en estas últimas se comparte con la unidad nacional se procesa, y luego pasa a la unidad regional y de ahí a los estados miembros. Expuso la importancia de los bancos de datos para la cooperación regional.

La séptima presentación fue la de Namankoumba Kouyaté (este volumen, 204–214), quien habló sobre la política local y nacional en cuanto a protección del patrimonio, particularmente en lo relativo a problemas de transmisión. Su enfoque fueron las relaciones fami-liares y el instrumento musical conocido como la sosobala. Este instrumento es un balafón construido en su forma original como para una batalla del año 1235 d.C. Hoy se considera la más antigua de todas las tradiciones del África occidental. El orador también hizo refe-rencia a la necesidad de combatir la migración de las generaciones jóvenes, del campo a la ciudad, para poder garantizar que se siga transmitiendo esa rica tradición oral. Dijo, además, que la UNESCO debe tener en cuenta las ceremonias tradicionales que se celebran en ciertos espacios culturales importantes.

La octava ponencia corrió por parte de Juana Núñez, quien describió varias actividades emprendidas por Cuba para proteger el folclor y la cultura tradicional. Entre ellas figuran: una organización de artistas aficionados; la participación de trabajadores, estudiantes, campesinos, adolescentes, niños y personas incapacitadas en la conservación del patrimonio cultural intangible; la enseñanza del arte desde el nivel preliminar en las escuelas; estudios de las raíces culturales y el folclor; la extensión de la cinematografía nacional a las zonas rurales y montañosas; el aumento de los museos y la educación; y la elevación de la posición social de artistas y escritores. Propuso una serie de sugerencias, entre ellas un estudio de UNESCO sobre los efectos negativos de los medios de comunicación de masas en el patrimonio cultural intangible; una revaluación de la política fiscal de la ONU; un estudio sobre los efectos de la globalización, la posibilidad de establecer un instrumento internacional para la protección de los derechos de propiedad intelectual en materia de folclor y cultura tradicional; y la posibilidad de que la UNESCO adopte proyectos comunitarios en diferentes disciplinas.

Aparte de las anteriores presentaciones tuvieron lugar varias discusiones. Sobre la base de esas discusiones se formularon las siguientes recomendaciones. Se recomendó a los estados miembros que:

1. incluyan la cultura tradicional en los programas educativos para poder transmitirla a las generaciones más jóvenes y alentar su interés en el folclor y la cultura tradicional;
2. establezcan y/o fortalezcan sus bases institucionales actuales para salvaguardar y documentar el folclor y la cultura tradicional;
3. garanticen a todas las minorías étnicas educación o rehabilitación de sus idiomas;
4. aumenten la asistencia económica a la organización de festivales;
5. garanticen libre acceso público a los materiales culturales;
6. ofrezcan equipo y capacitación, en conciencia cultural, a las personas que trabajan en los campos de la conservación y protección del material cultural; y
7. Alienten al sector privado a invertir en folclor y cultura tradicional mediante incentivos tales como exenciones tributarias.

Se recomendó a la UNESCO que:

1. organice reuniones de especialistas en el campo de la información digitalizada para crear redes inter-institucionales regionales y ofrecer accesibilidad y divulgación del conocimiento;

2. reduzca la brecha cultural entre juventudes urbanas y rurales apoyando la disemi-
    nación del conocimiento de las culturas tradicionales por internet y organizando
    campamentos juveniles dedicados al fomento e intercambio de culturas tradicionales;

3. fortalezca y fomente las relaciones con organizaciones no gubernamentales en el
    campo del folclor y la cultura tradicional;

4. ofrezca seminarios y asistencia técnica para la capacitación de los gestores de políti-
    ca profesionales, gerentes y maestros del área de la cultura tradicional;

5. realice un estudio de factibilidad sobre la posibilidad de establecer una red interna-
    cional para el desarrollo del turismo cultural;

6. apoye la publicación de una Enciclopedia Folclórica Mundial para diseminar
    conocimientos, promover la diversidad y alentar las investigaciones en el campo del
    folclor y la cultura tradicional;

7. establezca un Día Mundial de Protección del Folclor y la Cultura Tradicional;

8. considere la posibilidad de establecer una lista de comunidades en riesgo, para enfo-
    car la atención de la sociedad internacional en este problema y revivirlas; y

9. alentar mayor cooperación entre entidades intergubernamentales tales como
    UNESCO, OMPI (Organización Mundial de la Propiedad Intelectual) y el WIPG
    (Grupo de Trabajo sobre Poblaciones Indígenas, de la ONU).

Plan de Acción

Apéndice 7 del informe final

A. Con ocasión de la Conferencia "Evaluación Global de la Recomendación de 1989 sobre la Protección del Folclor y la Cultura Tradicional: Potenciación Local y Cooperación Internacional", realizada en el Instituto Smithsoniano en Washington, D.C., Estados Unidos, del 27 al 30 de junio de 1999;

1. *Tomando en cuenta* los resultados del proceso de evaluación, por cuatro años, de la aplicación de la Recomendación, sobre la Protección del Folclor y la Cultura Tradicional y las recomendaciones emanadas de los ocho seminarios regionales y subregionales [Strá nice (República Checa, junio de 1995, para los países de Europa central y oriental; México, D.F. (México, septiembre de 1997, para los países latinoamericanos y del Caribe); Tokio (Japón, febrero–marzo de 1998, para los países asiáticos); Joensuu (Finlandia, septiembre de 1998, para los países de Europa Occidental); Tashkent (República de Uzbekistán, octubre de 1998, para el Caúcaso y Asia central); Noumea (Nueva Caledonia, febrero de 1999, para los países del Pacífico); y Beirut (Líbano, mayo de 1999, para los Estados Árabes];

2. *Teniendo en cuenta* que el término "folclor" generalmente se ha considerado inapropiado, pero destacando la importancia de su definición en la Recomendación de 1989 sobre la Protección del Folclor y la Cultura Tradicional, a la vez que se recomienda el estudio de terminología más apropiada, y se sigue usando provisionalmente el termino "folclor", junto con "patrimonio oral", "conocimientos y destrezas tradicionales", "patrimonio intangible", "formas de saber, ser y hacer", entre otros términos, todos los cuales, para efectos de esta recomendación, son considerados equivalentes a "folclor y cultura tradicional" en la definición de la antedicha Recomendación de 1989;

3. *Conocedores* de la imposibilidad de separar patrimonio tangible, intangible y natural en muchas comunidades;

4. *Considerando* que el folclor y la cultura tradicional se basan principalmente en actividades de comunidad que expresan, refuerzan y en gran medida reflejan valores, creencias, ideas y prácticas compartidas;

5. *Destacando* que la diversidad que se expresa en las múltiples formas culturales de saber, ser y hacer es una característica esencial del patrimonio cultural y es vital en la construcción de la futura coexistencia pacífica entre todas las formas de vida;

6. *Subrayando* la naturaleza específica y la importancia del folclor y la cultura tradicional como parte integral del patrimonio de la humanidad;

7. *Tomando nota* de la importancia espiritual, social, económica, cultural, ecológica y política del folclor y la cultura tradicional, su papel en la historia de los pueblos y su lugar en la sociedad contemporánea;

8. *Reconociendo* que el folclor y la cultura tradicional pueden ser un potente medio para

reunir a diferentes pueblos y grupos sociales y de reiterar sus identidades culturales con ánimo de comprensión y respeto hacia otras culturas;

9. *Haciendo hincapié* en la necesidad de todos los países de que se reconozca el papel del folclor y la cultura tradicional, y el peligro de múltiples factores que enfrentan los practicantes;

10. *Preocupados* por el hecho de que el bienestar de los miembros de la comunidad, y sus prácticas, — cuya fuerza y número son amenazados a diario por poderosas fuerzas tales como la guerra, los desplazamientos forzados, las ideologías y filosofías intolerantes, el deterioro del medio ambiente, la marginación socioeconómica y la cultura comercializada global — deben ser el centro de la política cultural nacional e internacional;

11. *Tomando en cuenta* que el folclor y la cultura tradicional son dinámicos y se adaptan, muchas veces, mediante las prácticas innovadoras de la vida en comunidad;

12. *Reconociendo* que los practicantes del folclor y la cultura tradicional deben incluirse para que aporten experiencias cruciales a la gestión política local, nacional e internacional en áreas tales como salud, medio ambiente, educación, juventud, género, resolución de conflictos, coexistencia pacífica de los grupos étnicos, desarrollo humano sostenible y la participación cívica sin exclusiones, así como la lucha contra el chauvinismo y la intolerancia;

13. *Deplorando* la exclusión de los grupos tradicionales de la toma de decisiones relativa a la protección del folclor y la cultura tradicional;

14. *Reconociendo* que los estados se componen de comunidades culturales, que estas comunidades y su folclor y sus creencias a menudo se extienden allende los confines del estado, y que los individuos pueden ser miembros de más de una comunidad;

15. *Reconociendo* que la interacción y el intercambio culturales conducen al surgimiento de géneros híbridos que reflejan esos intercambios entre culturas;

16. *Reconociendo* que la conservación del folclor y la cultura tradicional y el derecho a la autodeterminación cultural de las comunidades locales debe ser congruente con las actuales normas internacionales de derechos humanos;

17. *Observando* el importante papel que pueden jugar los gobiernos y las organizaciones no gubernamentales, en colaboración con los portadores de las tradiciones, en la protección del folclor y la cultura tradicional y que deben actuar a la mayor brevedad;

B. Nosotros, los participantes de la conferencia "Evaluación Global de la Recomendación de 1989 sobre la Protección del Folclor y la Cultura Tradicional: Potenciación Local y Cooperación Internacional", reconocemos que deben tomarse las siguientes medidas:

1. Elaborar instrumentos jurídicos y administrativos para proteger a las comunidades tradicionales — las que crean y nutren el folclor y la cultura tradicional — de la pobreza, la explotación y la marginación;

2. Facilitar la colaboración entre comunidades, gobiernos e instituciones académicas, organizaciones locales y no gubernamentales, así como las organizaciones del sector privado, para abordar los temas que afectan a los grupos tradicionales;

3. Garantizar la participación sensible de los grupos tradicionales en los procesos de toma de decisiones en todos los foros que se ocupan de los temas y medidas que afectan a dichos grupos;

4. Elaborar, en cooperación con las comunidades, planes de educación y capacitación adecuados, sin faltar la capacitación jurídica, para sus miembros y demás trabajadores culturales con el objetivo de que entiendan, conserven y protejan el folclor y la cultura tradicional;

5. Desarrollar programas que aborden la naturaleza transnacional de algunos elementos de folclor y cultura tradicional;

6. Dar especial énfasis a programas que reconozcan, celebren y apoyen en las comunidades el papel de la mujer en todos sus aspectos, históricamente mal representado, como contribuyentes a las culturas tradicionales y como pioneras, académicas y administradoras;

7. Brindar apoyo a los programas de revitalización cultural, especialmente a grupos desplazados por guerras, hambrunas o desastres naturales, y otros grupos en peligro de extinción;

8. Emprender medidas, incluyendo la asistencia legal, para ayudar a los grupos tradicionales en sus propios esfuerzos por mejorar su condición social y bienestar económico, que son esenciales para seguir practicando sus culturas.

C. Acciones específicas: Con base en los anteriores principios y necesidades, recomendamos a los gobiernos de los estados que:

1. Identifiquen y apoyen programas que alienten el reconocimiento público y la validación del folclor y la cultura tradicional, manteniendo su apoyo a las instituciones y programas existentes, así como estableciendo otros nuevos cuando corresponda;

2. Instituir y fortalecer esquemas para el bienestar general de los custodios y practicantes de las culturas tradicionales, abordando temas tales como vivienda, salud y riesgos de oficio;

3. Incluir el conocimiento local en los foros nacionales en los que se consideran asuntos tales como el desarrollo humano sostenible, la globalización, el deterioro del medio ambiente, la juventud, la educación y la coexistencia pacífica;

4. Facilitar y ayudar a las comunidades en el desarrollo de su cultura material tradicional y sus prácticas laborales en nuevos contextos, para contrarrestas la destrucción del medio ambiente natural y la degradación de la dignidad del trabajo humano;

5. Ofrecer capacitación en conciencia cultural a los trabajadores de las instituciones administrativas, educativas, etc., que se relacionen con los grupos tradicionales;

6. Facilitar el acceso de los miembros de los grupos tradicionales a los programas educativos correspondientes y, donde haga falta, facilitar la creación —con la comunidad— de centros multifuncionales, arraigados en la comunidad, para la educación, la documentación y la capacitación;

7. Dar apoyo a las comunidades para conservar el uso activo, creativo de los idiomas locales en áreas que incluyen, sin exclusión, la educación, la publicación y las representaciones públicas;

8. Dar apoyo a la conservación de la cultura material y los espacios significativos y cruciales para la transmisión del folclor y la cultura tradicional;

9. Apoyar los simposios locales, nacionales e internacionales, que reúnan a los miembros de grupos tradicionales, representantes de organizaciones no gubernamentales, gestores políticos y demás para tratar la problemática que enfrentan los grupos tradicionales;

10. Identificar, entender, alentar y apoyar las prácticas educativas tradicionales, especialmente las referidas a los más jóvenes;

11. Crear una red de expertos para ayudarle a los grupos locales, instituciones cultu-rales, organizaciones no gubernamentales y entidades comerciales en la labor de salvaguardar la cultura tradicional, especialmente en campos tales como la educación, el turismo, el derecho y el desarrollo;

12. Considerar, si así lo desean, la posible presentación de un borrador de resolución a la Conferencia General de la UNESCO, solicitando a UNESCO que emprenda un estudio sobre la factibilidad de adoptar un nuevo instrumento normativo sobre la protección del folclor y la cultura tradicional;

13. Obrar de conformidad con las obligaciones de los estados de proteger el derecho a la cultura, del Artículo 27 del Convenio Internacional de Derechos Civiles y Políticos, apoyando activamente a las comunidades en sus prácticas de generación, transmisión, autorización y atribución de conocimientos y destrezas tradicionales conforme a los deseos de las comunidades, y conforme a las actuales normas internacionales de derechos humanos, y

Considerar tomar medidas incluyendo las siguientes:

(i) Adoptar un esquema jurídico mediante el cual se ponga a disposición de la comunidad el conocimiento tradicional, de acuerdo a sus deseos, para uso público con el requisito de remuneración u otros beneficios, en caso de uso comercial, y cooperar para asegurar el reconocimiento mutuo de todos los estados según lo disponga dicho esquema;

(ii) Adoptar un régimen legal sui géneris que garantice protección

- que se extienda por toda la vida de la comunidad;
- que resida en la comunidad, o en el individuo y la comunidad;
- que concuerde con los procedimientos de autorización y atribución tradicionales en cada comunidad;
- y establecer un organismo representativo de la comunidad, y los sectores correspondientes de la sociedad civil, para equilibrar los intereses encontrados de acceso y control;

(iii) Mientras se adopta un mejor esquema de protección, alentar la modificación y el uso de los regímenes existentes de propiedad intelectual, de acuerdo con las leyes vigentes, para la protección del conocimiento tradicional;

(iv) Crear grupos de trabajo encargados de estudiar más a fondo los siguientes temas:

contenido de "consentimiento de información anterior"; procesos de verificación (a carga de la prueba, modalidades de código de evidencia); derechos intelectuales de la comunidad vis á vis derechos de propiedad intelectual; relación con otros instrumentos y borradores (Documento Borrador de la ONU, OMPI, TRIPS, CBD, Maatatu, SUVA y otras declaraciones de grupos indígenas); cuestiones de "derechos" (autoría, moral, compensación); papel de los gobiernos; problemas de terminología (e.g. definiciones y connotaciones de "folclor", "cultura popular", etc.); formas alternas de compensación; promoción de casos ejemplares en relación con la jurisprudencia legal; mecanismos/documentos jurídicos específicos para las artesanías, la música y otras expresiones artísticas; mecanismos aplicables a conocimientos adquiridos antes de este instrumento.

Recomendamos que la UNESCO:

1. Impulse este Plan de Acción entre los estados miembros, poniendo a dichos estados en conocimiento de esta reunión;

2. Establezca una red interdisciplinaria internacional de expertos para ayudar a los estados miembros a desarrollar, cuando así lo soliciten, programas concretos congruentes con los principios de este Plan de Acción;

3. Establezca un grupo móvil interdisciplinario internacional de expertos jurídicos que

sirvan de asesores, en colaboración con las comunidades, en la elaboración de instrumentos adecuados para proteger el folclor y la cultura tradicional;

4. Aliente la participación y, donde haga falta, el establecimiento de organizaciones no gubernamentales con experiencia especializada en ámbitos particulares del folclor y el conocimiento tradicional, para que asesoren a la UNESCO en la protección del folclor y los conocimientos tradicionales;

5. Aliente a los grupos internacionales (académicos, profesionales de la cultura, organizaciones comerciales y entidades jurídicas) a elaborar y adoptar códigos de ética que garanticen un trato correcto y respetuoso al folclor y la cultura tradicional;

6. Acelere el movimiento por el retorno de los restos humanos y la repatriación del patrimonio cultural para ayudar a revitalizar el concepto propio de las culturas tradicionales, de acuerdo a sus propios valores fundamentales;

7. Organice y apoye la formación de un foro internacional que represente las preocupaciones de las comunidades tradicionales por salvaguardar su propia cultura, así como simposios regionales e internacionales que reúnan a los miembros de los grupos tradicionales, representantes de organizaciones no gubernamentales, gestores políticos, y otros para abordar los temas que enfrentan los grupos tradicionales. Por ejemplo el papel de la mujer en la protección de la cultura tradicional. Los simposios deben realizarse en diferentes lugares, especialmente fuera del Primer Mundo; en Yakutia, por ejemplo.

8. Facilite la aplicación de nueva tecnología en centros de documentación locales, nacionales y regionales, mediante redes de colaboración y experiencia, que incluyan a los portadores de la tradición local;

9. Promueva el folclor y la cultura tradicional, a escala mundial, mediante medidas tales como la organización de festivales regionales y declarando un Día Mundial de Protección del Folclor y la Cultura Tradicional;

10. Mantenga la actual colaboración entre UNESCO y OMPI en asuntos de interés común;

11. Aproveche los procedimientos existentes de la UNESCO para poner al corriente a otros organismos de la ONU, tales como la FAO, OMS, UNICEF, UNIFEM y otros, así como a la OMC, del impacto potencialmente adverso a la cultura de acciones en derechos humanos, medio ambiente, alimentos, agricultura, sustento e industria, salud y comercio.